Foundations of Sport and Exercise Psychology

Second Edition

Robert S. Weinberg, PhD
Miami University

Daniel Gould, PhD
University of North Carolina at Greensboro

Human Kinetics

Library of Congress Cataloging-in-Publication Data

Weinberg, Robert S. (Robert Stephen)
    Foundations of sport and exercise psychology / Robert S. Weinberg,
Daniel Gould. -- 2nd ed.
      p.   cm.
    Includes bibliographical references and index.
    ISBN 0-88011-824-5
    1. Sports--Psychological aspects. 2. Exercise--Psychological
aspects. I. Gould, Daniel, 1952- . II. Title.
    GV706.4.W38   1999
    796´.01--dc21   98-52438
                                                     CIP

ISBN: 0-88011-824-5

Developmental Editors: Marni Basic and Rebecca Crist; **Assistant Editor:** Henry V. Woolsey; **Permissions Manager:** Terri Hamer; **Copyeditor:** Anne Heiles; **Proofreader:** Erin Cler; **Indexer:** Nancy Ball; **Production Manager:** Kris Ding; **Graphic Designer:** Robert Reuther; **Graphic Artist:** Angela K. Snyder; **Photo Editors:** Kristin King and Boyd LaFoon; **Cover Designer:** Jack Davis; **Photographer (front cover):** Tim DeFrisco/ DeFrisco Photography; **Photographer (back cover):** Tony Demin/International Stock; **Illustrator:** Mic Greenberg; **Printer:** Edwards

Printed in the United States of America

10 9 8 7 6 5 4 3 2 1

Human Kinetics
Web site: http://www.humankinetics.com/

United States: Human Kinetics
P.O. Box 5076
Champaign, IL 61825-5076
1-800-747-4457
e-mail: humank@hkusa.com

Canada: Human Kinetics
475 Devonshire Road Unit 100
Windsor, ON N8Y 2L5
1-800-465-7301 (in Canada only)
e-mail: humank@hkcanada.com

Europe: Human Kinetics
P.O. Box IW14
Leeds LS16 6TR, United Kingdom
+44 (0)113-278 1708
e-mail: humank@hkeurope.com

Australia: Human Kinetics
57A Price Avenue
Lower Mitcham, South Australia 5062
(08) 82771555
e-mail: humank@hkaustralia.com

New Zealand: Human Kinetics
P.O. Box 105-231, Auckland 1
09-523-3462
e-mail: humank@hknewz.com

Dedication

To Mom—who raised me, guided me, and believed in me no matter what. I could not have asked for a better teacher and mentor!

Dan

To my family—the most important part of my life.

Bob

Brief Contents

v

Contents

Contents

Contents

Part VII Facilitating Psychological Growth and Development 453

Preface

The study of human behavior is at once complex and important, and thus it has intrigued people for many years. This book focuses on human behavior in certain types of situations—namely, sport and exercise settings. In essence, it examines what motivates people, what angers them, and what scares them; how their emotions affect their performances; how they regulate their thoughts, feelings, and emotions; and how their behaviors can become more effective.

Perhaps you want to be a physical educator, coach, fitness instructor, athletic trainer, or even a sport psychologist. Or maybe you are simply curious about how people behave in sport and exercise settings and why they behave in these ways. In any case, *Foundations of Sport and Exercise Psychology* has been designed to meet your need for information. It will, we hope, provide you with an overview of sport and exercise psychology, bridge the gap between research and practice, convey fundamental principles of professional practice, and capture some of the excitement of the world of sport and exercise.

From our own perspectives, sport psychology has significantly changed our lives and the lives of many athletes, coaches, and other sport and exercise professionals we have worked with and trained over the years. We have felt enriched by our studies in this field, and we want to give something back to it through writing this comprehensive, introductory text on sport and exercise psychology. In the first edition our goal was to create a book for introductory sport and exercise psychology classes that bridged up-to-date research and practice, capturing the best of what we had learned from coaches, scholars, exercisers, sports medicine personnel, and athletes.

Since that first edition we have received a great deal of feedback from teachers and students indicat-ing that we have been successful in reaching our goal. We have been pleased that our book has helped fill a void in the teaching of sport and exercise psychology. But as with any academic text, there is always room for improvement and updating; hence our decision to write a second edition. In this edition, we have held to the basic goals and objectives of our first edition and have tried to also incorporate the insightful comments and suggestions we have received to make this second edition an even better text.

We have updated every chapter with the latest research and practice in sport and exercise psychology. In some cases these changes were extensive, as the research and subsequent implications for best practice have developed significantly. In other chapters the changes are less dramatic because those particular areas have not grown or altered significantly in the past several years. In addition, we have eliminated and condensed some chapters to provide a greater focus to the book. We also have presented even more practical examples, case studies, and anecdotes to help students understand different theories, concepts, and research. More in-depth questions are provided after each chapter as opportunities for students to think more critically about applying the material, leading you from research to practice.

When you finish the course, we would like to hear from you regarding your thoughts on the book. We wrote this textbook for you, and you are in the best position to give feedback to help better meet the needs of students in the future (earlier feedback helped us immensely in revising the first edition). We hope you will enjoy learning about sport and exercise psychology as much as we continue to do.

Acknowledgments

This book would not have been possible if not for the tireless work of countless dedicated sport and exercise psychologists throughout the world. It is because of their research, writing, and consulting that the field has advanced so far in recent years. And it is for this reason we acknowledge all their efforts.

We would also like to recognize the teachers, coaches, and athletes with whom we have had the opportunity to consult. Indeed, they have taught us a great deal about sport and exercise psychology.

We would like to thank the staff at Human Kinetics for helping make this book possible. In particular, special thanks to developmental editors Marni Basic and Rebecca Crist for their careful attention to detail and all the changes necessary in such a large revision.

Finally, we would like to acknowledge our families. In particular, Dan would like to thank his wife Deb and children Kevin and Brian. Bob would like to thank his mom and dad, brother Randy, and children Josh and Kira. They all deserve a great deal of thanks for their patience in allowing us the time and space needed to write a book of this magnitude. Their unconditional social support was always there just when we needed it. So thanks, everybody.

Credits

Fig 2.1
Adapted, by permission, from R. Martens, 1975, *Social psychology and physical activity* (New York: Harper & Row), 146. Copyright 1975 by Rainer Martens. Adapted by permission of the author.

Fig 2.2a
Adapted, by permission, from W. Morgan, 1979, *Coach, athlete and the sport psychologist* (Toronto: University of Toronto School of Physical and Health Education), 185.

Fig 2.2b
Adapted, by permission, from W. Morgan, 1979, *Coach, athlete and the sport psychologist* (Toronto: University of Toronto School of Physical and Health Education), 183.

Table 2.1
Adapted, by permission, from T. Orlick, 1986, *Coaches training manual to psyching for sport* (Champaign, IL: Human Kinetics), 30.

Fig 3.7
Adapted, by permission, from M. Weiss and N. Chaumeton, 1992, Motivational orientations in sport. In *Advances in sport psychology*, edited by T. Horn (Champaign, IL: Human Kinetics), 90.

Fig 5.1
Adapted, by permission, from R. Martens, 1975, *Social psychology and physical activity* (New York: Harper & Row), 69.

Reward Preferences Questionnaire (p. 118)
Adapted, by permission, from F. Martin and J. Lumsden, 1987, *Coaching: An effective behavioral approach* (St. Louis: Mosby Yearbook).

Fig 6.3
Adapted, by permission, from J. Kimiecik and G. Stein, 1992, "Examining flow experiences in sport contexts: Conceptual issues and methodological concerns," *Journal of Applied Sport Psychology* 4 (2): 147.

Fig 8.1
Adapted, by permission, from A. Carron, 1982, "Cohesiveness in sports groups: Interpretations and considerations," *Journal of Sports Psychology* 4 (2): 131.

Group Environment Questionnaire (p. 171)
Adapted, by permission, from A. Carron, L. Brawley, and W. Widmeyer, 1985, "The development of an instrument to assess cohesion in sport teams: The group environment questionnaire," *Journal of Sport Psychology* 7: 244-267.

Fig 8.2
Adapted, by permission, from A. Carron, W. Widmeyer, and L. Brawley, 1985, "The development of an instrument to assess cohesion in sports teams: The environment questionnaire," *Journal of Sports Psychology* 7 (3): 248.

Fig 8.4
Adapted, by permission, from B. Cratty, 1983, *Psychology in contemporary sport: Guidelines for coaches and athletes* (Needham Heights, MA: Allyn & Bacon), 285.

Fig 8.5
Adapted, by permission, from A. Carron and J. Ball, 1977, "Cause-effect characteristics of cohesiveness and participation motivation in intercollegiate hockey," *International Review of Sport Sociology* 12: 49-60.

Table 8.1
Adapted, by permission, from A. Carron and H. Spink, 1993, "Team building in an exercise setting," *The Sport Psychologist* 7 (1): 13.

Table 8.2
Adapted from H. Prapavessis, A. Carron, and K. Spin, 1997, "Team building in sport groups," *International Journal of Sport Psychology* 28 (4).

Table 9.1
Adapted, by permission, from F. Smoll and R. Smith, 1980, Psychologically-oriented coach training programs: Design, implementation and assessment. In *Psychology of motor behavior and sport* 1979, edited by C. Nadeau et al. (Champaign, IL: Human Kinetics), 115.

Fig 9.1
Adapted, by permission, from P. Chelladurai, 1980, "Leadership in sport organization," *Canadian Journal of Applied Sport Sciences* 5: 226.

Fig 9.2
Reprinted, by permission, from R. Martens, 1987, *Coaches guide to sport psychology* (Champaign, IL: Human Kinetics), 35.

Fig 10.1
Reprinted, by permission, from R. Martens, 1987, *Coaches guide to sport psychology* (Champaign, IL: Human Kinetics), 48.

Listening Skills Test (p. 211)
Reprinted, by permission, from R. Martens, 1987, *Coaches guide to sport psychology* (Champaign, IL: Human Kinetics), 56.

Fig 11.2
Adapted, by permission, from R. Butler and L. Hardy, 1992, "The performance profile: Theory and application," *The Sport Psychologist* 6 (3): 257.

Table 11.2
Adapted, by permission, from J. Taylor, 1995, "A conceptual model for integrating athletes' needs and sport demands in the development of competitive mental preparation strategies," *The Sport Psychologist* 9 (3): 342.

Table 11.3
Adapted, by permission, from R. Vealey, 1988, "Future directions in psychological skills training," *The Sport Psychologist* 2: 326.

Table 11.4
Adapted, by permission, from D. Gould, 1983, Developing psychological skills in young athletes. In *Coaching science update*, edited by N. Wood (Ottawa: Coaching Association of Canada), 4-10.

The Sport Psychology Consultant Evaluation Form (p. 241)
Adapted, by permission, from J. Partington and T. Orlick, 1987, "The sport psychology consultant evaluation form," *The Sport Psychologist* 1 (4): 312.

Fig 12.1
Reprinted, by permission, from L. Hardy, G. Jones, and D. Gould, 1996, *Understanding psychological preparation for sport: Theory and practice for elite performers* (Chichester, England: John Wiley & Sons), 14.

Fig 12.2
Adapted, by permission, from R. Smith, 1980, A cognitive-affective approach to stress management training for athletes. In *Psychology of motor behavior and sport–1979*, edited by C. Nadeau et al. (Champaign, IL: Human Kinetics), 56.

Fig 13.2
Adapted, by permission, from A. Pavio, 1985, "Cognitive and motivational functions of imagery in human permformance," *Canadian Journal of Applied Sport Sciences* 10: 222-28.

Sport Imagery Questionnaire (p. 278)
Adapted, by permission, from R. Martens, 1982, *Imagery in Sport*. Unpublished paper presented at the Medical and Scientific Aspects of Elitism in Sport Conference.

Fig 14.2
Adapted, by permission, from D. Feltz, 1984, Self-efficacy as a cognitive mediator of athletic performance. In *Cognitive sport psychology*, edited by W. Straub and J. Williams (Lansing, NY: Sport Science Associates), 192.

Sport Confidence Inventory (p. 298)
Adapted, by permission, from ACEP, 1989, *ACEP sport psychology* (Champaign, IL: Human Kinetics), 251.

Short- and Long-Term Goals (p. 314)
Reprinted, by permission, from T. Orlick, 1986, *Coaches training manual to psyching for sport* (Champaign, IL: Human Kinetics), 15.

Fig 16.2
Adapted, by permission, from R. Nideffer, 1993, Concentration and attention control training. In *Applied sport psychology: Personal growth to peak performance* (Mountain View, CA: Mayfield), 248.

Fig 17.1
Adapted, by permission, from B. Long, 1984, "Aerobic conditioning and stress innoculation: A comparison of stress-management interventions," *Cognitive Therapy and Research* 8 (5): 529.

Table 17.1
Adapted, by permission, from C. Taylor, J. Sallis, and R. Needle, 1985, "The relation of physical activity and exercise to mental health," *Public Health Reports* 100: 195-202.

Table 18.1
Data from Canadian Fitness and Lifestyle Research Institute, 1992.

Table 18.2
Adapted, by permission, from B. Marcus et al., 1992, "The stages and processes of exercise adoption and maintenance in a worksite sample," *Health Psychology* 11: 389.

Fig 19.1
Adapted, by permission, from M. Anderson and J. Williams, 1988, "A model of stress and athletic injury: Prediction and prevention," *Journal of Sport and Exercise Psychology* 10 (3): 297.

Tables 20.1 and 20.2
Adapted, by permission, from D. Garner and L. Rosen, 1991, "Eating disorders among athletes: Research and recommendations," *Journal of Applied Sport Science Research* 5 (2): 100-107.

Tables 20.3, 20.4, and 20.5
Adapted, by permission, from L. Bump, 1988, Drugs and sport performance. In *Successful coaching*, edited by R. Martens (Champaign, IL: Human Kinetics), 135-147.

Fig 21.2
Adapted, by permission, from R. Smith, 1986, "Toward a cognitive-affective model of athletic burnout," *Journal of Sport Psychology* 8 (1): 40.

Table 21.1
Adapted, by permission, from D. Gould et al., 1996, "Burnout in competitive junior tennis players: A quantitative psychological assessment," *The Sport Psychologist* 10 (4): 341-366.

Table 21.2
Adapted, by permission, from A. Hackney, S. Perlman, and J. Nowacki, 1990, "Physiological profiles of overtrained and stale athletes," *Journal of Applied Sport Psychology* 2 (1): 21-33.

Table 22.1
Adapted, by permission, from M. Ewing and V. Seefeldt, 1989, "Participation and attrition patterns in American agency-sponsored and interscholastic sports: An executive summary," *Final Report Sporting Goods Manufacturer's Association* (North Palm Beach, FL: Sporting Goods Manufacturer's Association).

Fig 22.1
Adapted, by permission, from D. Gould and L. Petlichkoff, 1988, Participation motivation and attrition in young athletes. In *Children in Sport*, edited by F. Smoll, R. Magill, and M. Ash (Champaign, IL: Human Kinetics), 161-178.

Fig 24.2
Adapted, by permission, from V. Seefeldt, 1987, *Handbook for youth sports coaches* (Reston, VA: National Association for Sport and Physical Education), 139-151.

Table 24.1
Reprinted, by permission, from S. Miller, B. Bredemeier, and D. Shields, 1997, "Sociomoral education through physical education with at-risk children," *Quest* 49 (1): 119.

Table 24.2
Adapted, by permission, from D. Gould, 1981, Sportsmanship: Build character or characters. In *A winning philosophy for youth sports programs*, edited by Youth Sports Institute (Lansing, MI: Institute For The Study of Youth Sports).

Table 24.3
Reprinted, by permission, from D. Shields and B. Bredemeier, 1995, *Character development and physical activity* (Champaign, IL: Human Kinetics), 208.

Introduction

Your Road Map to Understanding Sport and Exercise Psychology

Most of you do not get into a car to begin a long trip without a destination in mind and a plan to get there. You pick a specific place and use a road map to find the best, most enjoyable route.

Ironically, though, some students read textbooks with no plan and no educational destination (other than getting the next day's assignment completed on time). Failing to set a goal and plan of study with your textbooks is much like driving without a destination and road map: You spend a lot of time driving aimlessly.

Your understanding of sport and exercise psychology will come easier if you set a plan and keep a goal in mind while reading this text. You can use this introduction as a road map or a model to achieve two goals: (a) a better understanding of sport and exercise psychology and (b) knowledge of how to apply sport psychology and exercise settings. This book has seven parts:

1. Getting Started

2. Understanding Participants

3. Understanding Sport and Exercise Environments

4. Understanding Group Processes

5. Enhancing Performance

Your Road Map to Understanding Sport and Exercise Psychology

Part I

Getting Started

Part II

Understanding Participants

Part V

Enhancing Performance

Part IV

Understanding Group Processes

Part III

Understanding Sport and Exercise Environments

Part VI

Enhancing Health and Well-Being

Part VII

Facilitating Psychological Growth and Development

Finish

6. Enhancing Health and Well-Being
7. Facilitating Psychological Growth and Development

Although these parts and their chapters work well when read in order, your instructor may elect to change the order to fit your particular class. That's okay, as we have designed each chapter to stand alone, without depending on knowledge from the previous chapters.

The practical road map we have included will help you move through the text in whatever order your professor assigns. The model (see p. xx) will help you tie together the specifics into a coherent whole. In it you'll see eight stops—points of interest—on your journey to understanding sport and exercise psychology. Part I, Getting Started, is where you prepare for the journey. In chapter 1 you will be introduced to the field of sport and exercise psychology, its history, and its contemporary directions and likely paths for the future. You will also learn how closely research and practice are linked and how you can make that connection even stronger.

The next stop on your journey is part II, Understanding Participants. Effective teaching, coaching, and training rests on understanding the psychological makeup of the people you work with—what makes them tick! Hence, the three chapters in this part focus on individuals, whether they are exercisers, athletes, rehabilitation clients, or physical education students. It is important to understand people in terms of their personalities, motivational orientations, achievement motivation, competitiveness, and anxiety levels.

You must also consider the situations or environments in which people function. For this reason part III, Understanding Sport and Exercise Environments, examines major environmental influences affecting sport and exercise participants. You will learn about competition and cooperation and how feedback and reinforcement influence people.

The fourth stop on your journey is part IV, Understanding Group Processes, which focuses on the workings of groups. Most teachers, coaches, and exercise leaders work with groups, so it is critical to understand team dynamics, group cohesion, leadership, and communication.

Enhancing individual performance is a mainstay of sport and exercise psychology. For this reason part V, Enhancing Performance, is one of the longest stops on our journey, consisting of six chapters. Here you will learn how to develop a psychological skills training program to regulate arousal, use imagery to improve performance, enhance self-confidence, set effective goals, and strengthen concentration.

Part VI, Enhancing Health and Well-Being, introduces you to the joint roles of psychological and physical development in motivating people to exercise, enjoying the benefits of exercise, treating athletic injuries, and aiding rehabilitation. You will find critical information here about combatting substance abuse, eating disorders, and overtraining

One of the most important functions that sport and exercise professionals have is helping people with their psychological growth and character development. Part VII, Facilitating Psychological Growth and Development, concludes the text with discussions of three special issues: children in sport, aggression, and character development.

The book ends with a short section we have aptly called Finish. Here, we reinforce the research-to-practice orientation of the text. After studying the seven parts of the book you will have not only an excellent idea of what sport and exercise psychology involves but also specific knowledge of how to use the information effectively.

A road map does little good sitting in the car's glove compartment. This is also true of the model we have employed. So, before you read a chapter, see where it fits into the model. And as you read each chapter, ask yourself these questions:

1. What can I do as a professional to use this information effectively?

2. What personal and situational considerations will influence how I will use and modify this information?

3. Will my primary goal in using this information be to help participants enhance performance, develop and grow personally, or a combination of these objectives?

4. How can I integrate this information and derive efficient, effective strategies for practice?

We have tried to make this book user-friendly in several ways. Specifically, key points in the margins of each chapter summarize information that is crucial to remember. Boxes highlight new research, case studies, and research-to-practice examples. In an accompanying student workbook you can find exercises to complete to aid your understanding of material. Finally, review the summary and review questions at the end of each chapter to know that you have a thorough grasp of the chapter's content. Along these lines, we have also included critical thinking questions at the end of each chapter to give you an opportunity for in-depth analysis of important topics.

Part I

Getting Started

In this part we'll focus on getting you, the future sport and exercise science practitioner, started on your journey to understanding sport and exercise psychology. First, to inform you of the nature of sport and exercise psychology we'll describe what this ever-growing field involves. Chapter 1 introduces you to the field, details some of its history, and defines its current status. Here we'll describe what sport and exercise psychologists do, discuss orientations to studying the field, and present the field's future directions and opportunities. Since bridging science and practice is an important concept, the chapter also introduces the main ways knowledge is gained in sport psychology, emphasizing the importance of teaming scientific and practical knowledge to allow you to better assist students, athletes, and exercisers psychologically.

© Human Kinetics

Welcome to Sport and Exercise Psychology

After reading this chapter you should be able to

1 describe what sport and exercise psychology is,

2 understand what sport and exercise psychology specialists do,

3 know what training is required to be a sport and exercise psychologist,

4 understand major developments in the history of sport and exercise psychology,

5 distinguish between scientific and professional practice knowledge,

6 integrate experiential and scientific knowledge,

7 compare and contrast orientations to the field, and

8 describe career opportunities and future directions in the field.

Jeff, the point guard on the high school basketball team, becomes overly nervous in competition. The more critical the situation, the more nervous he becomes and the worse he plays. Your biggest coaching challenge this season will be helping Jeff learn to manage stress.

Beth, fitness director for the St. Peter's Hospital Cardiac Rehabilitation Center, runs an aerobic fitness program for recovering patients. She is concerned, however, because some clients don't stick with their exercise programs after they start feeling better.

Mario had wanted to be a physical educator ever since he can remember. He feels frustrated now, however, because his high school students have so little interest in learning lifelong fitness skills. Mario's goal is to get the sedentary students motivated to engage in fitness activities.

Patty is the head athletic trainer at Campbell State College. The school's star running back, Tyler Peete, has achieved a 99% physical recovery from knee surgery. The coaches notice, however, that in practices he still favors his formerly injured knee and is hesitant when making cutbacks. Patty knows that Tyler is physically recovered but needs to regain his confidence.

Tom, a sport psychologist and longtime baseball fan, just heard about his dream position, a consulting job. The owners of the Chicago Cubs, fed up with the team's lack of cohesion, have asked him to quickly design a training program in psychological skills. If Tom can construct a strong program in the next week, he will be hired as the team's sport psychology consultant.

If you become a coach, an exercise leader, a physical educator, an athletic trainer, or even a sport psychologist, you also will encounter the kinds of situations Jeff, Beth, Mario, Patty, and Tom faced. The field of sport and exercise psychology offers a resource for solving such problems and many other practical concerns. In this chapter you will be introduced to this exciting area of study and learn how sport and exercise psychology can help you solve practical problems.

What Is Sport and Exercise Psychology?

Simply stated, sport and exercise psychology is the scientific study of people and their behaviors in sport and exercise contexts and the practical applications of that knowledge (Gill 1979). Sport and exercise psy-

Sport and exercise psychology is the scientific study of people and their behaviors in sport and exercise activities and the practical application of that knowledge.

chologists identify principles and guidelines that professionals can use to help adults and children participate in and benefit from sport and exercise activities.

Most people study sport and exercise psychology with two objectives in mind: (a) to understand how psychological factors affect an individual's physical performance and (b) to understand how participation in sport and exercise affects a person's psychological development, health, and well-being. They pursue this study by asking the following kinds of questions:

Objective a: Understand the effects of psychological factors on physical or motor performance.

How does anxiety affect a basketball player's accuracy in free-throw shooting?

Does lacking self-confidence influence a child's ability to learn to swim?

How does a coach's reinforcement and punishment influence a team's cohesion?

Does imagery training facilitate the recovery process in injured athletes and exercisers?

Objective b: Understand the effects of participating in physical activity on psychological development, health, and well-being.

Does running reduce anxiety and depression?

Do young athletes learn to be overly aggressive from participating in youth sports?

Does participation in daily physical education classes improve a child's self-esteem?

Does participation in college athletics enhance personality development?

Sport psychology applies to a broad population base. Although some professionals use it to help elite athletes achieve peak performance, many others are concerned more with children, the physically and mentally disabled, seniors, and average participants. Recently, more and more sport psychologists have focused on the psychological factors involved in exercise, developing strategies to encourage sedentary people to exercise or assessing the effectiveness of exercise as a treatment for depression. To reflect

> *Sport and exercise psychologists seek to understand and help elite athletes, children, the physically and mentally disabled, seniors, and average participants achieve peak performance, personal satisfaction, and development through participation.*

this broadening of interests, the field is now called sport and exercise psychology, and some individuals are starting to focus only on the exercise aspects of the field.

What Sport and Exercise Psychology Specialists Do

Contemporary sport psychologists pursue varied careers. They serve three primary roles in their professional activities: conducting research, teaching, and consulting (see Figure 1.1). We'll discuss each of these briefly.

The Research Role

A primary function of participants in any scholarly field is to advance the knowledge within the field. They do this by conducting research. Most sport and exercise psychologists in a university conduct research. They might, for example, study what moti-

vates children to be involved in youth sport, how imagery influences proficiency in golf putting, how running for 20 minutes four times a week affects an exerciser's anxiety levels, or what the relationship is between movement education and self-concept among elementary physical education students. Sport psychologists then share their findings with colleagues and participants in the field. This sharing produces advances, discussion, and healthy debate at professional meetings and in journals (see the box on p. 6).

The Teaching Role

Many sport and exercise psychology specialists teach university students courses such as exercise psychology, applied sport psychology, and the social psychology of sport. They may also teach such courses as personality psychology or developmental psychology if they work in a psychology department or courses such as motor learning and control or sport sociology if they work in a sport science program.

The Consulting Role

A third important role is consulting with individual athletes or athletic teams to develop psychological skills for enhancing competitive performance and training. In fact, the U.S. Olympic Committee and some major universities employ full-time sport psychology consultants, and hundreds of other teams and athletes use consultants on a part-time basis for psychological skills training. Many sport

Teaching

Research

Consulting

Figure 1.1   *The roles of sport and exercise psychologists.*

American Sport and Exercise Psychology Organizations and Journals

Organizations

- *Association for the Advancement of Applied Sport Psychology (AAASP)*

  This organization is solely designed to promote research and practice in applied sport and exercise psychology. Three subareas focus on health psychology, intervention-performance enhancement, and social psychology.

- *American Psychological Association (APA) Division 47—Sport and Exercise Psychology*

  Among the newest of almost 50 divisions in the APA (the largest professional psychology organization in the United States), this organization emphasizes both research and practice in sport psychology.

- *North American Society for the Psychology of Sport and Physical Activity (NASPSPA)*

  This is the oldest organization focusing on the psychological aspects of sport and physical activity. The organization focuses on research in the subareas of motor development, motor learning and control, and social psychology and physical activity.

Journals

- *Journal of Applied Sport Psychology*

  Begun in 1989 this is the official journal of AAASP and publishes applied sport psychology research and professional practice articles.

- *Journal of Sport and Exercise Psychology*

  This journal publishes basic and applied sport and exercise psychology research studies. Begun in 1979, it is the oldest and most respected research journal in the field.

- *The Sport Psychologist*

  This journal, which began in 1987, publishes both applied research and professional practice articles designed to facilitate the delivery of psychological services to coaches and athletes.

---

psychology consultants work with coaches through clinics and workshops.

Some sport and exercise psychologists now work in the fitness industry, designing exercise programs that maximize participation and promote psychological and physical well-being. Some consultants work as adjuncts to support a sports medicine or physical therapy clinic, providing psychological services to injured athletes.

Sport Psychology Specialties

A significant distinction in contemporary sport psychology exists between two types of specialties: *clini-* *cal* sport psychology and *educational* sport psychology. The distinction between these two specialties and the training needed for each are important to know.

Clinical Sport Psychology

Clinical sport psychologists have extensive training in psychology to learn to detect and treat individuals with emotional disorders (e.g., severe depression, suicidal tendencies). Licensed by state boards to treat individuals with emotional disorders, clinical sport psychologists have received additional training in sport and exercise psychology and the sport sciences. Clinical sport psychologists are

Coming Off the Bench: A Sport Psychology Consulting Case Study

Jerry Reynolds was referred to Ron Hoffman, Southeastern University sport psychology consultant, at the end of his freshman year of varsity basketball. Jerry had had a successful high school career, lettering in three sports and starting every basketball game. On a full scholarship at Southeastern, Jerry worked harder than anyone else on the team and improved his skills. Still, he did not make the starting five. In the second half of the season's first contest, Coach Johnson put Jerry into the game. As he moved to the scorer's table and awaited the substitution whistle, Jerry found that he was much more nervous than ever before. His heart was pounding, and he could not shut off the chatter in his mind. He entered the game and had a disastrous performance. He threw the ball away several times, picked up two silly fouls, and failed to take an open shot. Coach Johnson took Jerry out. After the game, Jerry's coaches and teammates told him it was just nerves and to relax. But Jerry could not relax, and a pattern of high anxiety and deteriorating performance ensued. After a few more disasters Jerry rode the pine for the remainder of the season.

Jerry hesitated to see a sport psychologist. He did not think he was mentally ill, and he was kind of embarrassed about the idea of going to see a shrink." Much to Jerry's surprise, Dr. Hoffman was a regular guy who talked a lot like a coach. So Jerry agreed to meet with him every couple of weeks.

Working with Dr. Hoffman, Jerry learned it was common to experience anxiety when making the transition from high school to college ball. After all, 90% of the players he had defeated in high school were no longer competing. Hoffman also pointed out to Jerry that after starting for 3 years in high school, it was no surprise if he had a hard time adjusting to coming off the bench and entering a game cold. He was experiencing a new kind of pressure, and his response to the pressure—his nervousness—was to be expected.

Dr. Hoffman taught Jerry how to relax by using a breathing technique called centering. He taught him to control negative thoughts and worries by stopping them with an image and replacing them with more positive affirmations. Jerry developed a mental preparation routine for coming off the bench, including stretches to keep loose and a procedure to help him focus as he waited at the scorer's table.

Jerry practiced these psychological techniques extensively in the off-season and refined them during early season practices and scrimmages. After he was able to come off the bench without falling apart, he worked on taking open shots and quickly playing to his full potential.

That season Jerry accomplished his goal of coming off the bench and helping the team with a solid performance. He did not quite break into the starting lineup, but Coach Johnson expressed his confidence in him by using him in tight situations. Jerry felt happy to be contributing to the team.

Clinical sport and exercise psychologists treat those athletes and exercisers who have severe emotional disorders.

needed because, just as in the normal population, some athletes and exercisers develop severe emotional disorders and require special treatment (Brewer & Petrie, 1996). Eating disorders and substance abuse are two areas in sport and exercise where the specialized skills of a clinical sport psychologist can often help sport and exercise participants.

Educational Sport Psychology

Educational sport psychology specialists have extensive training in sport and exercise science, physical education, and kinesiology, and they understand the psychology of human movement, particularly as it relates to sport and exercise contexts. These specialists often have taken advanced graduate training in psychology and counseling. They, however, are not trained to treat individuals with emotional disorders, nor are they licensed psychologists.

A good way to think of an educational sport psychology specialist is as a mental coach" who,

Educational sport psychology specialists are "mental coaches" who educate athletes and exercisers about psychological skills and their development. They are not trained to work with individuals who have severe emotional disorders.

through group and individual sessions, educates athletes and exercisers about psychological skills and their development. Anxiety management, confidence development, and improved communication are some of the areas that educational sport psychology specialists address. When an educational sport psychology consultant encounters an athlete with an emotional disorder, he or she refers the athlete to either a licensed clinical psychologist or, preferably, a clinical sport psychologist for treatment.

Both clinical and educational sport and exercise psychology specialists must have a thorough knowledge of both psychology and exercise and sport science (see Figure 1.2). In 1991 the Association for the Advancement of Applied Sport Psychology (AAASP) began a certified consultant program. To qualify for certification as sport and exercise consultants, people must have advanced training in both psychology and the sport sciences. This is designed to protect the public from unqualified individuals professing to be or calling themselves sport and exercise psychologists.

The History of Sport and Exercise Psychology

Today, sport and exercise psychology is more popular than ever before. It is a mistake, however, to think it has only recently developed. Sport psychology dates back to the turn of the 20th century (Wiggins, 1984). Its history falls into five periods, which are highlighted here along with some specific individuals and events from each period. These various periods have distinct characteristics and yet are interrelated. Together they contributed to the field's development and growing stature.

Period 1—The Early Years (1895–1920)

In North America, sport psychology began in the 1890s. Norman Triplett, a psychologist from Indiana University and a bicycle-racing enthusiast, wanted to understand why cyclists sometimes rode faster when they raced in groups or pairs than when they rode alone (Triplett, 1898). First, he verified that his initial observations were correct by studying cycling racing records. To test his hunch further, he also conducted an experiment in which young children were to reel in fishing line as fast as they could. Triplett found that children reeled in more line when they worked in the presence of another child. This experiment allowed him to predict more reliably when bicycle racers would have better performances.

In Triplett's day psychologists and physical educators were only beginning to explore psychological

Sport and Exercise Psychology

Sport science knowledge domain	Psychology knowledge domain
Biomechanics	Abnormal psychology
Exercise physiology	Clinical psychology
Motor development	Counseling psychology
Motor learning and control	Developmental psychology
Sports medicine	Experimental psychology
Sport pedagogy	Personality psychology
Sport sociology	Physiological psychology

Figure 1.2   The relationship of knowledge in the sport science and psychology domains to the field of sport and exercise psychology.

Norman Triplett

aspects of sport and motor skill learning. They measured athletes' reaction times, studied how people learn sport skills, and discussed the role of sport in personality and character development, but they did little to apply these studies. Moreover, people dabbled in the area of sport psychology, but no one specialized in the field.

Highlights

- 1897 Norman Triplett conducts first social psychology and sport psychology experiment studying the effects of others on cyclists' performance.
- 1899 E.W. Scripture of Yale describes personality traits that he felt could be fostered via sport participation.
- 1903 G.T.W. Patrick discussed the psychology of play.
- 1914 R. Cummins assesses motor reactions, attention, and abilities as they pertain to sport.
- 1918 As a student, Coleman Griffith conducts informal studies of football and basketball players at the University of Illinois.

Period 2—The Griffith Era (1921–1938)

Coleman Griffith was the first North American to donate a significant portion of his career to sport psychology and today is credited with being the father of American sport psychology (Kroll & Lewis, 1970). A University of Illinois psychologist who also worked in the Department of Physical Welfare (Physical Education and Athletics), Griffith devel-

Coleman Griffith

oped the first laboratory in sport psychology, helped initiate one of the first coaching schools in America, and wrote two classic books, *Psychology of Coaching* and *Psychology of Athletics*. He also conducted a series of studies on the Chicago Cubs baseball team and developed psychological profiles of such legendary players as Dizzy Dean. He corresponded with Notre Dame football coach Knute Rockne about how best to psych teams up and questioned hall-of-famer Red Grange about his thoughts while running the football. Ahead of his time, Griffith worked in relative isolation, but his high-quality research and deep commitment to improving practices remain an excellent model for sport and exercise psychologists.

Highlights

- 1921–1931 Griffith publishes 25 research articles about sport psychology.
- 1925 University of Illinois research-in-athletics laboratory established. Griffith appointed director.
- 1926 Griffith writes *Psychology of Coaching*.
- 1928 Griffith writes *Psychology of Athletics*.

Period 3—Preparation for the Future (1938–1965)

Franklin Henry at the University of California, Berkeley, was largely responsible for the field's scientific development. He devoted his career to the scholarly study of the psychological aspects of sport and motor skill acquisition. Most important, Henry trained many other energetic physical educators who later became university professors and initiated systematic research programs. Some of his students

9

Franklin Henry

became administrators who reshaped curriculums and developed sport and exercise science as we know it today.

Other investigators in the 1938–1965 period, such as Warren Johnson and Arthur Slatter-Hammel, helped lay the groundwork for future study of sport psychology. They helped create the academic discipline of exercise and sport science; however, applied work in sport psychology was still limited.

Highlights

- 1938 Franklin Henry assumes position in Department of Physical Education at the University of California, Berkeley, and establishes psychology of physical activity graduate program.
- 1949 Warren Johnson assesses precompetitive emotions of athletes.
- 1951 John Lawther writes *Psychology of Coaching.*
- 1965 First World Congress of sport psychology held in Rome.

Period 4—The Establishment of Academic Sport Psychology (1966–1977)

By the mid-1960s physical education had become an academic discipline, and sport psychology had become a separate component within this discipline, distinct from motor learning. Motor learning specialists focused on how people acquire motor skills (not necessarily sport skills) and on conditions of practice, feedback, and timing. In contrast, sport psychologists studied how psychological factors—anxiety, self-esteem, and personality—influence sport and

Bruce Ogilvie

motor skill performance and how participation in sport and physical education influences psychological development (e.g., personality, aggression).

Applied sport psychology consultants also began working with athletes and teams. Bruce Ogilvie of San Jose State University was one of the first to do so, and he is often called the father of North American applied sport psychology. Concurrently with the increased interest in the field, the first sport psychology societies were established in North America.

Highlights

- 1966 Clinical psychologist Bruce Ogilvie and Thomas Tutko write *Problem Athletes and How to Handle Them* and begin to consult with athletes and teams.
- 1967 B. Cratty of UCLA writes *Psychology of Physical Activity.*
- 1967 First annual North American Society for the Psychology of Sport and Physical Activity conference (NASPSPA) held.
- 1974 Proceedings of NASPSPA conference published for the first time.

Period 5—Contemporary Sport and Exercise Psychology (1978–Present)

Since the mid-1970s we have witnessed tremendous growth in sport and exercise psychology, especially in the applied area. Later in this chapter you will learn about contemporary sport and exercise psychology in detail, but some of the key developments are highlighted here.

Highlights

- *Journal of Sport Psychology* (now called *Sport and Exercise Psychology)* is established.
- 1980 U.S. Olympic Committee develops Sport Psychology Advisory Board.
- 1984 American television coverage of Olympic Games emphasizes sport psychology.
- 1985 U.S. Olympic Committee hires first full-time sport psychologist.
- 1986 The first applied scholarly journal, *The Sport Psychologist*, is established.
- 1986 The Association for the Advancement of Applied Sport Psychology is established.
- 1987 American Psychological Association Division 47 (Sport Psychology) is developed.
- 1988 U.S. Olympic team is accompanied by officially recognized sport psychologist for the first time.
- 1989 *Journal of Applied Sport Psychology* begins.
- 1991 AAASP establishes "certified consultant" designation.

Ferruccio Antonelli

gist Ferruccio Antonelli, who was both the first president of the ISSP and the first editor of IJSP. Sport and exercise psychology is now well recognized throughout the world as both an academic area of concentration and a profession. The prospect of continued growth remains bright.

Sport and Exercise Psychology Around the World

Sport and exercise psychology thrives worldwide. Salmela (1992), for instance, has estimated that 2,700 sport and exercise psychologists now work in more than 61 different countries. Most of these specialists live in North America and Europe, and major increases in activity have also occurred in Latin America, Asia, and Africa in the last decade.

Sport psychologists in Russia and Germany began working at about the time that Coleman Griffith began his work at the University of Illinois. The International Society of Sport Psychology (ISSP) was established in 1965 to promote and disseminate information about sport psychology throughout the world. ISSP has sponsored eight World Congresses of Sport Psychology—focusing on such topics as human performance, personality, motor learning, wellness and exercise, and coaching psychology—that have been instrumental in promoting awareness and interest in the field. Since 1970 ISSP has also sponsored the *International Journal of Sport Psychology (IJSP).*

Credit for much of the international development of sport psychology goes to Italian sport psycholo-

Bridging Science and Practice

Reading a sport and exercise psychology textbook and actually working professionally with exercisers and athletes are very different activities. To understand the relationship between the two, you must be able to integrate scientific textbook knowledge (scientifically derived knowledge) with practical experience (professional practice knowledge). We will help you develop the skills to do this so you can better use sport and exercise psychology knowledge in the field.

Scientifically Derived Knowledge

Sport and exercise psychology is above all a science. Hence, it is important that you understand how scientifically derived knowledge comes about and works; that is, you need to understand the scientific method. Science is dynamic—something that scientists do (Kerlinger, 1973). Science is not simply an accumulation of facts discovered through detailed observations but rather a process, or method, of learning about the world through the systematic, controlled, empirical, and critical filtering of knowledge acquired through experience. In applying science to psychology, the goals are to describe, explain, predict, and allow control of behavior.

Let's take an example. Dr. Jennifer Jones, a sport psychology researcher, wants to study how movement education affects children's self-esteem. Dr. Jones first defines self-esteem and movement education and determines what age groups and particular children she wants to study. She then explains why she expects movement education and self-esteem to be related (e.g., the children would get recognition and praise for learning new skills). Dr. Jones's research is really after prediction and control: She wants to show that using movement education in similar conditions will consistently affect children's self-esteem in the same way. To test such things, science has evolved some general guidelines for research:

1. The scientific method dictates a systematic approach to studying a question. It involves standardizing the conditions; for example, one might assess the children's self-esteem under identical conditions with a carefully designed measure.

2. The scientific method involves control of conditions. Key variables, or elements in the research (e.g., movement education or changes in self-esteem), are the focus of study, with other variables controlled (e.g., the person doing the teaching) so as not to influence the primary relationship.

3. The scientific method is empirical, which means it is based on observation. Objective evidence must support beliefs, and this evidence must be open to outside evaluation and observation.

4. The scientific method is critical, meaning that it involves rigorous evaluation by the researcher and other scientists. Critical analysis of ideas and work helps ensure conclusions are reliable.

Theory

A scientist's ultimate goal is a theory, or a set of interrelated facts that presents a systematic view of some phenomenon in order to describe, explain, and predict its future occurrences. Theory allows scientists to organize and explain large numbers of facts in a pattern that helps others understand them. Theory then turns to practice.

One example is the social facilitation theory (Zajonc, 1965). Since Norman Triplett's first reel-

A theory is a set of interrelated facts presenting a systematic view of some phenomenon in order to describe, explain, and predict its future occurrences.

winding experiment on children (see section titled "The History of Sport and Exercise Psychology"), psychologists had studied how the presence of an audience affects performance, but their results were inconsistent. Sometimes people performed better in front of an audience, and other times they performed worse. Zajonc saw a pattern in the seemingly random results and formulated a theory. He noticed that when people performed simple tasks or jobs they knew well, having an audience influenced their performance positively. However, when people performed unfamiliar or complex tasks, having an audience harmed performance. In his social facilitation theory, Zajonc contended that an audience creates arousal in the performer, which hurts performance on difficult tasks that had not been learned (or learned well) and helps performance on well-learned tasks.

Zajonc's theory increased our understanding of how audiences influence performance at many levels (students and professionals) and in many situations (sports, exercise, etc.). It consolidated many seemingly random instances into a theory basic enough for performers, coaches, and teachers to remember and to apply in a variety of circumstances. As the saying goes, nothing is more practical than a good theory!

Of course, not all theories are equally useful. Some are in early stages of development, and others have already passed the test of time. Some theories have a limited scope, and others a broad range of application. Some study few variables, and others a complex matrix of variables and behaviors.

Studies Versus Experiments

An important way scientists build, support, or refute theory is by conducting studies and experiments. A study involves an investigator observing or assessing factors without changing the environment in any way. For example, a study comparing the effectiveness of goal setting, imagery, and self-talk in improving athletic performance might have a written questionnaire given to a sample of high school cross-country runners just before a race. The researchers could compare what techniques the fastest 20 runners used compared with the slowest 20 runners. They would not be changing or manipulating any factors, but simply observing whether faster runners

Determining causal relationships is the main advantage that conducting experiments has over conducting studies.

reported using particular mental skills (e.g., imagery). But they would not know whether the goal setting, imagery, and self-talk caused some runners to go faster or whether running faster stirred the runners to set more goals and so forth. Studies have limited ability to identify what scientists call *causal* (cause and effect) relations between factors.

An experiment differs from a study in that the investigator manipulates the variables along with observing them, then examines how changes in one variable affect changes in others. Runners might be divided into two equal groups. One, called the experimental group, would receive training in how to set goals and use imagery and positive self-talk. The other, called the control group, would not receive any psychological skills training. Then, if the experimental group outperformed the control group (with other factors that might affect the relation being controlled), the reason, or cause, for this would be known. A causal relation would be demonstrated.

Strengths and Limitations of Scientifically Derived Knowledge

Each method of obtaining knowledge has strengths and limitations. The scientific method is no different in this regard (see Table 1.1). The major strength of scientifically derived knowledge is that it is reliable; that is, scientific findings are consistent or repeatable. Not only is the methodology systematic and controlled, but the scientists also are trained to be as objective as possible. One of their goals is to collect unbiased data, where the data or facts speak for themselves without being influenced by the scientist's personal interpretation.

On the negative side, the scientific method is slow and conservative because reliability must be judged by others. It also takes time to be systematic and controlled—more time than most practitioners have. A breakthrough in science usually comes after years of research. For this reason it's

not always practical to insist that science guide all elements of practice.

Sometimes scientific knowledge is reductionistic. That is, because it is too complex to study all the variables of a situation simultaneously, isolated variables may be selected that are of the most critical interest. By reducing a problem to smaller, manageable parts, however, the whole picture may be compromised or diminished.

Another limitation of science is its overemphasis on internal validity. That is, science favors the extent to which results of an investigation can be attributed to the treatment utilized, usually judging it by how well scientists conform to the rules of scientific methodology and how systematic and controlled they were in conducting their study. Too much emphasis on internal validity can cause scientists to overlook external validity, or whether the issue has true significance or utility in the real world. If a theory has no external validity, its internal validity doesn't count for much. Finally, scientific knowledge tends to be conservative.

Professional Practice Knowledge

Professional practice knowledge refers to knowledge gained through experience. Perhaps, for example, you spend a lot of time helping exercisers, athletes, and physical education students enhance their performance and well-being, and in the process you pick up a good deal of practical understanding or information. Professional practice knowledge comes from many sources and ways of knowing, including these:

Scientific method

Systematic observation

Single case study

Shared public experience

Introspection (examining your thoughts or feelings)

Table 1.1

Strengths and Limitations of Scientifically Derived Knowledge

Strengths	Limitations
Highly reliable	Reductionistic/Conservative—often slow to evolve
Systematic & controlled	Lack of focus on external validity (practicality)
Objective & unbiased	

Intuition (immediate apprehension of knowledge in the absence of a conscious, rational process)

Although exercise leaders, coaches, and athletic trainers ordinarily do not use the scientific method, they do use theoretically derived sport and exercise principles to guide their practice.

For example, volleyball coach Theresa Hebert works with the high school team. She develops her coaching skills in a variety of ways. Before the season begins, she reflects (uses introspection) on how she wants to coach this year. During team tryouts she makes a practice of systematic observation of the new players as they serve, hit, and scrimmage. Last season, she remembers, the team captain—a star setter—struggled, so Coach Hebert wants to learn as much about her as possible to help her more this year. To do this, she talks with other players, teachers, and the setter's parents. In essence, she conducts a case study. When she and her assistant coaches compare notes on their scouting the next opponent, shared public experience occurs. Coach Hebert often uses intuition also—for example, she decides to start Sarah over Rhonda today, the two players having similar ability, because it feels right to her. Of course, these methods are not equally reliable; however, in combination they lead to effective coaching. Like her players, Coach Hebert will sometimes make mistakes. But these errors or miscalculations also become sources of information to her.

Professional practice knowledge is guided trial-and-error learning. Whether you become a physical therapist, coach, teacher, exercise leader, or athletic trainer, you will use your knowledge to develop strategies and then to evaluate their effectiveness. With experience, an exercise and sport science professional becomes more proficient and more knowledgeable in practical ways.

Strengths and Limitations of Professional Practice Knowledge

Table 1.2 lists the major strengths and limitations of professional practice knowledge. This practical knowledge is usually more holistic than scientifically derived knowledge, reflecting the complex interplay of many factors—psychological, physical, technical, strategic, and social. And unlike science, professional practice knowledge tends to absorb novel or innovative practices. Coaches, teachers, exercise leaders, and trainers enjoy using new techniques. Another plus is that practical theories do not have to wait to be scientifically verified, so they can be used immediately.

On the down side, professional practice can produce fewer and less precise explanations than science can. It is more affected by bias than is science, and thus less objective. Practical knowledge tends to be less reliable and definitive than scientifically based knowledge. Often a teacher knows a method works, but does not know why. This can be a problem if he wants to use the method in a new situation or revise it to help a particular student.

Integrating Scientific and Professional Practice Knowledge

The gap you may sense between reading a textbook and pursuing professional activities is part of a larger division between scientific and professional practice knowledge. Yet bridging this gap is paramount, for the combination of the two kinds of knowledge is what makes for effective applied practice.

There are several causes for this gap (Gowan, Botterill, & Blimkie, 1979). Until recently, few opportunities existed to transfer results of research to professionals working in the field: physical educators, coaches, exercise leaders, athletes, exercisers, and trainers. Second, some sport and exercise psychologists were overly optimistic about using research to revolutionize the practice of teaching sport and physical activity skills. Although basic laboratory research was being conducted in the 1960s and 1970s, little connection was then made to actual field situations (external validity). The gap must close, however, and practitioners and researchers must communicate to integrate their worlds.

Table 1.2
Strengths and Limitations of Professional Practice Knowledge

Strengths	Limitations
Holistic	Less reliable
Innovative	Lack of explanations
Immediate	Greater susceptibility to bias

Taking an Active Approach to Sport and Exercise Psychology

To effectively use sport and exercise psychology in the field requires actively developing knowledge. The practitioner must blend the scientific knowledge of sport and exercise psychology with professional practice knowledge. Reading a book like this, taking a course in sport and exercise psychology, or working as a teacher, coach, or exercise leader is simply not enough. You must actively integrate scientific knowledge with your professional experiences and temper these with your own insights and intuition.

To take an active approach means applying the scientific principles identified in subsequent chapters of this book to your practice environments. Relate these principles to your own experiences as an athlete, exerciser, and physical education student. In essence, use the gym, the pool, or the athletic field as a mini-experimental situation where you test your sport and exercise psychology thoughts and understanding of principles. Evaluate how effective these ideas are and in what situations they seem to work the best. Modify and update them when needed by keeping current regarding the latest sport and exercise psychology scientific findings.

In using this active approach, however, it is imperative that you have realistic expectations of sport and exercise psychology research findings. Most research findings are judged to be significant based on probability. Hence, these findings probably won't hold true 100% of the time. They should work or accurately explain behavior the *majority* of the time. When they do not seem to predict or explain behavior adequately, analyze the situation relative to the explanation for why the principle works. See if you need to consider overriding personal or situational factors at work in your practice environment.

Sport and Exercise Psychology as an Art

It is especially important to recognize the individuality of students, exercisers, and athletes. Psychology is a social science. It is different from physics: Whereas inanimate objects do not change much over time, human beings do. Humans involved in sport and exercise also think and manipulate their environment, which makes behavior more difficult (but not impossible) to predict. Coach "Doc" Counsilman (Kimiecik & Gould, 1987), legendary Olympic swim coach and key proponent of a scientific approach to coaching, best summed up the need to consider individuality when he indicated that coaches coach by using general principles, the science of coaching. The *art of coaching* enters as they recognize when and in what situations to individualize these general principles. This same science-to-practice guiding principle holds true in sport and exercise psychology.

Sport and Exercise Psychology Orientations

Some coaches believe teams win games through outstanding defense, other coaches believe teams win through a wide-open offensive system, and still others believe wins come through a structured and controlled game plan. Like coaches, sport psychologists differ in how they view successful interventions. Contemporary sport and exercise psychologists may choose from many different orientations to the field, three of the most prevalent being psychophysiological, social-psychological, and cognitive-behavioral approaches.

Psychophysiological Orientation

Sport and exercise psychologists with a psychophysiological orientation believe the best way to study behavior during sport and exercise is to examine the physiological processes of the brain and their influences on the physical activity. They typically assess heart rate, brain wave activity, and muscle action potentials, determining relationships between these psychophysiological measures and sport and exercise behavior. An example is using biofeedback techniques to train elite marksmen to fire between heartbeats in order to improve accuracy (Landers, 1985).

> *The science of coaching focuses on the use of general principles. The art of coaching is recognizing when and how to individualize these general principles.*

> *Psychophysiological sport and exercise psychologists study behavior through its underlying psychophysiological processes occurring in the brain.*

People with a social-psychological orientation focus on how behavior is determined by a complex interaction of the environment and one's personal make-up.

Social-Psychological Orientation

Social-psychologically oriented sport and exercise psychologists assume that behavior is determined by a complex interaction of the environment (especially the social environment) and personal makeup of the athlete or exerciser. Those taking the social-psychological approach often examine how an individual's social environment influences his or her behavior and how the behavior influences the social-psychological environment. For example, social-psychologically oriented sport psychologists might examine how a leader's style and strategies foster group cohesion and influence participation in an exercise program (Carron & Spink, 1993).

Cognitive-Behavioral Orientation

Those psychologists adopting a cognitive-behavioral orientation emphasize the athlete's or exerciser's cognitions or thoughts and behaviors, believing thought to be central in determining behavior. Cognitive-behavioral sport psychologists might, for instance, develop self-report measures to assess self-confidence, anxiety, goal orientations, imagery, and intrinsic motivation. Then they would see how these assessments are linked to changes in an athlete's or an exerciser's behavior. For example, groups of junior tennis players who were either burned out or not burned out were surveyed regarding a battery of psychological assessments. Burned out, as compared with non–burned out tennis players, were found to have less motivation. They also reported being more withdrawn, had more perfectionist personality tendencies, and used different coping strategies for stress. (Gould, Tuffey, Udry, & Loehr, 1996a). Thus, links between the athletes'

A cognitive-behavioral orientation to sport and exercise psychology assumes that behavior is determined by both the environment and cognition with thoughts and interpretation playing an especially important role.

thoughts and behaviors and the athletes' burnout status were examined.

The Present and Future of Sport and Exercise Psychology

Now that you have learned about the field of sport psychology, including its history, scientific base, and orientations, it is important to understand the significant current and future trends in the area. Eight trends will be briefly discussed.

1. More people are interested in acquiring training in psychological skills and applied work. Consulting and service opportunities are more plentiful than ever, and more sport psychologists are helping athletes and coaches achieve their goals. Exercise psychology has opened new service opportunities for helping people enjoy the benefits of exercise. For these reasons applied sport and exercise psychology will continue to grow into the next century (Cox, Qui, & Liu, 1993; Murphy, 1995).

2. There is greater emphasis on counseling and clinical training for sport psychologists. Accompanying the increased emphasis on consulting is a need for more training in counseling and clinical psychology (McCullagh & Noble, 1996). Those individuals who want to assume a role in sport and exercise consulting will have to understand not only sport and exercise science but counseling and clinical psychology as well. Graduate programs are being developed in counseling and clinical psychology, with an emphasis in sport and exercise psychology.

3. Ethics and competence issues are receiving greater emphasis. Some problems have accompanied the tremendous growth in sport and exercise consulting (Murphy, 1995). For example, unqualified people might call themselves sport psychologists and unethical individuals might promise more to coaches, athletes, and exercise professionals than they can deliver. That is, someone might claim to be a sport psychologist (who has no training in the area) and promise that buying his or her imagery tape will make an 80% free-throw shooter out of a 20% shooter. This is why the AAASP organization has begun a certification program for sport and exercise psychology consultants. Ethical standards for sport psychology specialists have also been developed (see the box on p. 17). Physical education, sport, and exercise leaders should become informed consumers who can discriminate between legitimate, useful information and fads or gimmicks. They must also be familiar with ethical standards in the area.

■ MORE INFORMATION ■

Ethical Standards for Sport and Exercise Psychologists

Sport psychology is a young profession, and only recently have its organizations—such as the Association for the Advancement of Applied Sport Psychology (AAASP) and the Canadian Society for Psychomotor Learning and Sport Psychology—developed ethical guidelines. Those guidelines are based on the more general American Psychological Association's Ethical Standards (1992), and at their core is the general philosophy that sport psychology consultants should respect the dignity and worth of individuals and honor the preservation and protection of fundamental human rights. The essence of this philosophy is that the athlete's or exerciser's welfare must be foremost in mind.

There are six areas (general principles) outlined in the AAASP ethical guidelines:

1. *Competence.* Sport psychologists strive to maintain the highest standards of competence in their work and recognize their limits of expertise. If a sport psychologist has little knowledge of team building and group dynamics, for example, it would be unethical to lead others to believe that he or she does or to work with a team.

2. *Integrity.* Sport and exercise psychologists demonstrate high integrity in science, teaching, and consulting. They do not falsely advertise, and they clarify their roles (e.g., inform athletes they will be involved in team selection) with teams and organizations.

3. *Professional and scientific responsibility.* Sport and exercise psychologists always place the best interests of their clients first. For instance, it would be unethical to study aggression in sport by purposefully instructing one group of subjects to start fights with the opposing team (even if much could be learned from doing so). Those conducting research are also responsible for safeguarding the public from unethical professionals. If a sport psychologist witnesses someone making false claims (e.g., that someone can eat all he wants and burn off all the extra fat via imagery), he or she is ethically bound to point out the misinformation and to confront or report the offender to a professional organization.

4. *Respect for people's rights and dignity.* Sport psychologists respect the fundamental rights (e.g., privacy and confidentiality) of the people with whom they work. They do not publicly state with whom they consult unless they have permission to do so. No bias is shown on the basis of such factors as race, gender, and socioeconomic status.

5. *Concern for welfare of others.* Sport psychologists seek to contribute to the welfare of those with whom they work. Hence, an athlete's psychological and physical well-being always come before winning.

6. *Social responsibility.* Sport and exercise psychologists contribute to knowledge and human welfare while always protecting participants' interests. An exercise psychologist, for instance, would not offer an exercise program designed to reduce depression to one group of experimental participants without making the same program available to control group subjects at the end of the experiment. Offering the treatment only to the experimental group would not be socially responsible, and indeed it would be unethical.

4. Specializations and new subspecialties are developing. In the past 25 years knowledge in sport psychology has exploded. Sport psychologists now, unlike their forerunners, cannot be experts in every area that you will read about in this text. They instead specialize in particular areas of interest (Rejeski & Brawley, 1988). These sport and exercise specializations appear especially in North America and Great Britain; else-where in the world, sport psychology encompasses both sport psychology as defined here and motor learning or motor control (the acquisition and control of skilled movements as a result of practice). In North America and England, however, sport psychology and motor learning are seen as separate subspecialties. We expect this trend toward specialization to continue.

5. Tension continues to exist between practitioners of academic and applied sport psychology. This textbook is based on the philosophy that sport psychology will best develop with an equal emphasis on research and professional practice; however, not all sport psychologists hold this view. Some tension has developed between academic (research) and applied sport psychology consultants, each group feeling that the other's activities are less crucial to the development of the field. While such tension is certainly undesirable in our view, it is not unique. Similar disagreement, for example, exists in the broader field of psychology. Sport psychologists must continue working to overcome this destructive thinking.

6. Qualitative research methods are receiving more attention. The 1990s have seen a change in the way sport and exercise psychologists conduct research. While traditional quantitative research is still being conducted, many investigators are broadening the way they conduct research by employing qualitative (nonnumeric) methods. Such methods collect data via observation or interviews; instead of analyzing numbers or ratings statistically, researchers analyze the respondents' words and stories or narration for trends and patterns. This has been a healthy development for the field, and it will gain even greater importance as more qualitative research is amassed.

7. Applied sport psychologists have more work opportunities than ever, but only limited chances at full-time positions. A dilemma exists for applied sport psychologists. On the one hand, they have more opportunities than ever before to work with teams and consult with athletes. Many consultants now work part-time with elite amateur athletes through various national sport governing bodies (NGBs), such as the U.S. Tennis Association and U.S. Ski and Snowboard Association. Some NGBs, the U.S. Olympic Committee, and several universities have full-time sport psychology consultants to serve varsity athletes, and many professional teams employ a sport psychologist. Despite today's opportunities to consult with high-level, elite athletes, however, few full-time consulting positions exist. Furthermore, advanced graduate training is

■ MORE INFORMATION ■

Learn More About Sport and Exercise Psychology

Learn more about sport and exercise psychology by surfing the Net and connecting to these Web sites.

Sport Psychology Organizations

American Alliance for Health, Physical Education, Recreation and Dance
http://www.aahperd.org/
Association for the Advancement of Applied Sport Psychology
http://spot.colorado.edu/~aaasp/
Division 47 of the American Psychological Association
http://www.psyc.unt.edu/apadiv47/
North American Society for Psychology of Sport and Physical Activity
http://grove.ufl.edu/~naspspa/

Other Organizations, Associations, and Sites

American Sport Education Program
http://www.asep.com/
Coaching Association of Canada
http://www.coach.ca/
Internet Information on Sport Psychology
http://www.gettysburg.edu/response/ref/sportpsy.html/
Sport Psychology Information
http://spot.colorado.edu/~collinsj/
University of Washington's Husky Sport Psychology Services
http://weber.u.washington.edu/~hsps/

needed to become a qualified sport psychology specialist. Hence, people should not expect to quickly obtain full-time consulting positions with high-profile teams and athletes simply on the basis of a degree in sport psychology.

8. Sport psychology is gaining increased acceptance and recognition of its usefulness. Many universities now offer sport and exercise psychology courses, and some graduate programs include up to five or six different courses. Research and professional resources are increasingly available to students. Sport and exercise psychology has become a recognized sport science of considerable utility. However, we believe the greatest gains are still to come. Tremendous help becomes available to sport and exercise participants from information about sport and exercise psychology supplied to physical education teachers, coaches, fitness instructors, and athletic trainers. With this up-to-date information, physical activity professionals make great strides toward achieving their various goals. In short, the field of sport and exercise psychology has much to offer you, the future physical education teachers, coaches, fitness specialists, and athletic trainers.

SUMMARY

1 *Describe what sport and exercise psychology is.*

Sport and exercise psychology is the scientific study of the behavior of people engaged in sport and exercise activities and the application of the knowledge gained. Researchers in the field have two major objectives: (a) to understand how psychological factors affect a person's motor performance and (b) to understand how participating in physical activity affects a person's psychological development. Despite enormous growth in recent years, sport psychology dates back to the early 1900s and is best understood within the framework of its five distinct historical periods.

2 *Understand what sport and exercise psychology specialists do.*

Contemporary sport and exercise psychologists engage in different roles, including conducting research, teaching, and consulting with athletes and exercisers.

3 *Know what training is required to be a sport and exercise psychologist.*

Not all sport and exercise psychology specialists are trained in the same way. Clinical sport and exercise psychologists are trained specifically in psychology to treat athletes and exercisers with severe emotional disorders, such as substance abuse or anorexia. Educational sport psychology specialists receive training in exercise and sport science and related fields and serve as mental coaches, educating athletes and exercisers about psychological skills and their development. They are not trained to assist people with severe emotional disorders.

4 *Understand major developments in the history of sport and exercise psychology.*

Sport and exercise psychology has a long and rich history dating back 100 years. Its history falls into five periods. The first period, the early years (1895–1920), was characterized by isolated studies. During the Griffith era (1921–1938), Coleman Griffith became the first American to specialize in the area. The third period, preparation for the future (1939–1965), was characterized by the field's scientific development due to the educational efforts of Franklin Henry. During the establishment of the academic discipline (1966–1977), sport and exercise psychology became a valued component of the academic discipline of physical education. The period of contemporary sport and exercise psychology (1978–present) has been distinguished by tremendous growth, considerable research, and interest in application and consulting.

5 *Distinguish between scientific and professional practice knowledge.*

The field of sport and exercise psychology is above all a science. For this reason it is imperative to understand the basic scientific process and how scientific knowledge is developed. Scientific knowledge alone, however, is not enough to guide professional practice. You must also understand how professional practice knowledge develops.

6 *Integrate experiential and scientific knowledge.*

It is imperative that scientific knowledge be integrated with the knowledge gained from professional practice. This active process of integrating scientific and professional practice knowledge will greatly benefit you in using psychological skills as you work in applied sport and exercise settings.

7 *Compare and contrast orientations to the field.*

Several approaches can be taken to sport and exercise psychology, including social-psychological, psychophysiological, and cognitive-behavioral orientations. Social-psychological sport psychologists focus on how complex interactions between the social environment and personal makeup of the athlete or exerciser influence behavior. Psychophysiological sport psychologists study physiological processes of the brain and their influence on physical activity, whereas cognitive-behavioral sport psychologists examine how an individual's thoughts determine behavior.

8 *Describe career opportunities and future directions in the field.*

Although there are more career opportunities than ever before, only limited numbers of full-time consulting positions are now available. Indeed, sport and exercise psychology is flourishing and has much to offer those interested in working in sport and physical activity settings. Trends point to such future directions as an increased interest in psychological skills training and applied work; more counseling and clinical training for sport psychologists; increased emphasis on ethics and competence; increased specialization; some continuing tension between academic and applied sport psychologists; and more qualitative research.

KEY TERMS

sport and exercise psychology
clinical sport psychologists
educational sport psychology specialists
scientific method
systematic approach
control
empirical
critical
theory
social facilitation theory
study
experiment
experimental group
control group

unbiased data
reductionistic
internal validity
external validity
professional practice knowledge
introspection
systematic observation
case study
shared public experience
intuition
psychophysiological orientation
social-psychologically oriented
cognitive-behavioral orientation

REVIEW QUESTIONS

1. What is sport and exercise psychology and what are its two general objectives?

2. Describe the major accomplishments of the five periods in the history of sport and exercise psychology. What contributions did Coleman Griffith and Franklin Henry make to sport and exercise psychology?

3. Describe three roles of sport and exercise psychology specialists.

4. Distinguish between clinical and educational sport psychology. Why is this distinction important?

5. Define science and explain four of its major goals.

6. What is a theory and why are theories important in sport and exercise psychology?

7. Distinguish between a research study and an experiment.

8. Identify the strengths and limitations of scientifically derived and professional practice knowledge. How does each develop?

9. Describe the gap between research and practice, why it exists, and how it can be bridged.

10. Briefly describe the social-psychological, psychophysiological, and cognitive-behavioral orientations to the study of sport and exercise psychology.

11. Why is there a need for certification in contemporary sport and exercise psychology?

12. Identify and briefly describe the six major ethical principles in sport and exercise psychology.

13. What career opportunities are there in sport and exercise psychology?

CRITICAL THINKING QUESTIONS

1. Describe the active approach to using sport and exercise psychology.

2. You are interested in investigating how self-confidence is related to athletic injury recovery. Design both a "study" and an "experiment" to do so.

3. Think of the career you would like to pursue (e.g., sport and exercise psychologist, coach, athletic trainer, sports journalist). Describe how knowledge and the practice of sport psychology can affect you in that career.

Part II

Understanding Participants

Are successful athletes distinguished by certain key personality characteristics? What motivates people to participate in physical activity? Why are some people so motivated to achieve competitive success, whereas others dread the mere thought of competition? How does one psych up for optimal performance without psyching out?

These are some of the important questions addressed at the first stop on our journey to understanding sport and exercise psychology. This part focuses on personal factors—personality characteristics, individual orientations, and emotions—that affect performance and psychological development in sport, physical education, and exercise settings.

Personality, discussed in chapter 2, is important to understand because to work effectively with students, athletes, and exercisers you need to know what makes them tick as individuals. The information in this chapter will help you better understand the psychological makeup of those you will work with.

Chapter 3 focuses on the various theories and underpinnings of motivation. A person-by-person situation interaction model of motivation is presented and used to help you understand motivation in a variety of physical activity contexts. Achievement motivation, competitiveness, and attributions (three explanations used to account for behavior) are also discussed. The information in this chapter will help you understand why some people are go-getters, whereas others seem to lack motivation. You'll learn how situational factors influence participant motivation. Most importantly, you will be presented with effective strategies for enhancing a person's level of motivation.

Chapter 4 examines arousal and anxiety. Here you'll learn why students and athletes become uptight and how anxiety and arousal influence performance—why do athletes sometimes psych up for a big game and sometimes become psyched out? You'll also learn to identify major sources of stress that affect participants in sport and exercise.

Chapter 2

© Human Kinetics

Personality and Sport

After reading this chapter you should be able to

1 describe what makes up personality and why it is important,

2 discuss major approaches to understanding personality,

3 identify how personality can be measured,

4 assess personality tests and research for practicality and validity,

5 comprehend the relationship between personality and behavior in sport and exercise,

6 describe how cognitive strategies are related to athletic success, and

7 apply what you know of personality in sport and exercise settings to better understand people's personalities.

25

By 1992 more than a thousand articles had been published on aspects of sport personality (Ruffer, 1976a, 1976b; Vealey, 1989, 1992), most of them written during the 1960s and 1970s. This voluminous research demonstrates how important researchers and practitioners consider the role of personality to be in sport and exercise settings. Researchers have asked, for example, what causes some students to be excited about physical education classes, whereas others don't even bother to "dress out." They have questioned why some exercisers stay with their fitness program whereas others lose motivation and drop out, whether personality tests should be used to select athletes for teams; and whether athletic success can be predicted by an athlete's personality type.

What Is Personality?

Have you ever tried to describe your own personality? If you have, you probably found yourself listing adjectives like funny, outgoing, happy, stable, and so on. Maybe you remembered how you reacted in various situations. Is there more to personality than these kinds of attributes? Many theorists have attempted to define personality, and they agree on one description: uniqueness. In essence, personality refers to the characteristics—or blend of characteristics—that make a person unique.

Personality is the sum of those characteristics that make a person unique. The study of personality helps us work better with students, athletes, and exercisers.

One of the best ways to understand personality is through its structure. Think of personality as divided into three separate but related levels (see Figure 2.1): a psychological core, typical responses, and role-related behavior (Hollander, 1967; Martens, 1975).

Psychological Core

The most basic level of your personality is called the psychological core. The deepest component, it includes your attitudes and values, interests and motives, and beliefs about yourself and your self-worth. In essence, the psychological core represents the centerpiece of your personality and is "the real you," not who you want others to think you are. For example, your basic values might revolve around the importance of family, friends, and religion in your life.

Typical Responses

Typical responses are the ways we each learn to adjust to the environment or how we usually respond to the world around us. For example, you might be happy-go-lucky, shy, and even-tempered. Often your typical responses are good indicators of your psychological core. That is, if you consistently respond to social situations by being quiet and shy, you are likely to be introverted, not extroverted. However, if someone observed your being quiet at a party and from that evidence alone concluded you were introverted, that person could well be mistaken—it may have been this particular party situation that caused you to be quiet. Your quietness may not have been a typical response.

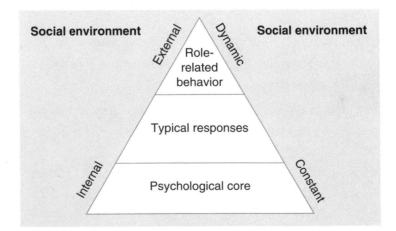

Figure 2.1 *A schematic view of personality structure.*
Adapted from Martens, 1975b.

Role-Related Behavior

How you act based on what you perceive your social situation to be is called role-related behavior. This behavior is the most changeable aspect of personality: Your behavior will change as your perceptions of the environment change. Different situations require playing different roles. You might, on the same day, play the roles of student at a university, coach of a Little League team, employee, and friend. Likely you'll behave differently in each of these situations; for example, you'll probably exert more leadership as a coach than as a student or employee. Roles can conflict with each other. For example, a parent who is coaching her child's soccer team might feel a conflict between her coaching and parenting roles.

Why Study Personality Structure?

As you saw in Figure 2.1, the three levels of personality encompass a continuum from internally driven to externally driven behaviors. To simplify it, compare your levels of personality to a chocolate-covered cherry. Everyone sees the outside wrapper (role-related behavior), those who go to the trouble to take off the wrapper see the chocolate layer (typical responses), and only the people interested or motivated enough to bite into the candy see the cherry center (psychological core).

The psychological core is not only the most internal of the three levels and the hardest to get to know, it is also the most stable part of your personality. It remains fairly constant over time. On the other end of the continuum are the most external, role-related behaviors, which are subject to the greatest influence from the external social environment. For example, you might always tell the truth because being truthful is one of your core values. But your behavior might vary in some areas, such as being aloof in your role as a fitness director and affectionate in your role as a parent. Usually your responses lie somewhere in between, however, because they result from the interaction of your psychological core and role-related behaviors.

Both stability and change are desirable in personality. The core, or stable, aspect of personality provides the structure we need to function effectively in society, whereas the dynamic, or changing, aspect allows for learning.

As coaches, physical educators, trainers, and exercise leaders we can be more effective when we understand the different levels of personality structure that lie beyond the role-related behaviors particular to a situation. Getting to know the real person (i.e., the psychological core) and his or her typical modes of response produces insight into the individual's motivations, actions, and behavior. In essence, we need to know what makes people tick to choose the best way to help them. Especially when working long-term with people, such as over a season or more, it's helpful to understand more about their individual core values (i.e., psychological core).

Approaches to Personality

Psychologists have looked at personality from several viewpoints. Four of their major ways of studying personality in sport and exercise have been called the psychodynamic, trait, situation, and interactional approaches.

The Psychodynamic Approach

Popularized by Sigmund Freud and neo-Freudians, such as Carl Jung and Eric Erickson, the psychodynamic approach to personality is characterized by two themes (Cox, 1998). First, emphasis is placed on unconscious determinants of behavior, such as what Freud called the *id,* or instinctive drives, and how these conflict with the more conscious aspects of personality, such as the *superego* (one's moral conscience) or the *ego* (the conscious personality). Second, this approach focuses on understanding the person as a whole, rather than identifying isolated traits or dispositions.

The psychodynamic approach is complex; it views personality as a dynamic set of processes that are constantly changing and often in conflict with one another (Vealey, 1992). For example, those taking a psychodynamic approach to the study of personality might discuss how unconscious aggressive instincts conflict with other aspects of personality, such as one's superego, to determine behavior. Special emphasis is placed on how adult personality is shaped by the resolutions of conflicts between unconscious forces and the values and conscience of the superego in childhood.

Although the psychodynamic approach has had a major impact on the field of psychology, especially on clinical approaches to psychology, it has had little impact in sport psychology. Swedish sport psychologist Erwin Apitzsch (1995) has urged North Americans to give more attention to this approach, however, pointing out the support that it receives in non-English studies of its value to sport. Apitzsch has measured defense mechanisms in athletes and used this information to help performers better cope with stress and anxiety. Specifically, he contends that athletes often feel threatened and react with anxiety. As a defense against their anxiety, athletes display various unconscious defense mechanisms, such as maladaptive repression (the athletes freeze or become paralyzed during play) or denial of the problem. When inappropriate defense mechanisms are employed, the athletes' performance and satisfaction are affected. Through psychotherapy, however, athletes can learn to effectively deal with these problems.

A weakness of the psychodynamic approach is that it focuses almost entirely on internal determinants of behavior, giving little attention to the social environment. For this reason many contemporary sport psychology specialists do not adopt it. Moreover, it is unlikely that most sport psychology specialists, especially those trained in educational sport psychology, will become qualified to use a psychodynamic approach.

You should recognize, however, that not all the behavior of an exerciser or athlete is under conscious control, and at times it may be appropriate to focus on unconscious determinants of behavior. For example, a world-class aerial skier experienced a particularly bad crash, and when he recovered, he could not explain his inability to execute the complex skill he was injured on. He described that in the middle of executing the skill he would freeze up, "like a deer caught in headlights." Moreover, extensive cognitive-behavioral psychological strategies (described later in this chapter), which have been successfully used with other skiers, were not effective in helping him. The athlete eventually was referred to a clinical psychologist who took a more psychodynamic approach to the problem and had more success with that method.

The Trait Approach

The trait approach assumes that the fundamental units of personality—its traits—are relatively stable. That is, personality traits are enduring and consistent across a variety of situations. Taking the trait approach, psychologists consider that the causes of behavior generally reside within the person. They minimize the role of situational or environmental factors. Traits are considered to predispose a person to act a certain way, regardless of the situation or circumstances. If an athlete is competitive, for example, he or she will be predisposed to playing hard

> *The trait approach, which dominated the early study of personality, did not take into consideration the particular situations that might also influence an individual's behavior.*

and giving all, regardless of the situation or score. A predisposition, however, does not mean that the athlete will always act this way; it simply means that the athlete is *likely* to be competitive in sport situations.

The most noted of the trait proponents in the 1960s and 1970s included Gordon Allport, Raymond Cattell, and Hans Eysenck. Cattell developed a personality inventory with 16 independent personality factors (16 PF) that he believed describe a person (1965). Eysenck and Eysenck (1968) viewed traits as relative, the two most significant traits ranging on continuums from introversion to extroversion and from stability to emotionality. They argued that personality could best be understood by considering traits that are relatively enduring and stable over time.

However, simply knowing an individual's personality traits will not always help us predict how he or she will behave in a particular situation. For example, some people anger easily during sport activity, whereas others seldom get angry. Yet the individuals who tend to get angry in sport may not necessarily become angry in other situations. So simply knowing an individual's personality traits does not necessarily predict (or tell you) whether he or she will act on them. The predisposition toward anger does not tell you what specific situations will provoke that response. This observation led some researchers to study personality by focusing on the situation or environment that might trigger behaviors, rather than personality traits.

The Situation Approach

The situation approach argues that behavior is determined largely by the situation or environment. It draws from social learning theory (Bandura, 1977a), which explains behavior in terms of observational learning (*modeling*) and social reinforcement (*feedback*). Simply stated, this approach holds that environmental influences and reinforcements shape the way you behave. You might act confident, for instance, in one situation but tentative in another, regardless of your particular personality traits. Furthermore, if the influence of the environment is strong enough, the effect of personality traits will be minimal. For example, if you are introverted and shy, you still might act assertively or even aggressively if you see someone getting mugged. Many football players are gentle and shy off the field, but the game (the situation) requires them to act aggressively. Thus, the situation would be a more important determinant of their behavior than would be their particular personality traits.

Although the situation approach is not as widely embraced by sport psychologists as the trait approach is, Martin and Lumsden (1987) contend that you can influence behavior in sport and physical education by changing the reinforcements in the environment. Still, the situation approach, like the trait approach, cannot truly predict behavior. A situation can certainly influence someone's behavior, but other people will not be swayed by the same situation.

The Interactional Approach

The **interactional approach** considers the situation and person as codeterminants of behavior—that is, as variables that together determine behavior. In other words, knowing both an individual's psychological

> *Situations alone are not enough to predict behavior accurately—an individual's personality traits must also be considered.*

traits and particular situation are helpful to understand behavior. Not only do personal traits and situational factors independently determine behavior, but at times they interact or mix with each other in unique ways to influence behavior. For example, a person with a high hostility trait won't necessarily be violent in all situations (e.g., as a frustrated spectator at a football game in the presence of his mother). However, when the hostile person is placed in the right potentially violent situation (e.g., as a frustrated spectator at a football game with his roughneck friends), his violent nature might be triggered. In that particular situation violence might result (e.g., he hits a spectator from the other team who boos his or her favorite player).

Researchers using an interactional approach ask these kinds of questions:

© Photo: Action Images

■ Will extroverts perform better in a team situation and introverts in an individual (i.e., nonteam) situation?

■ Will highly motivated people adhere to a formal exercise program longer than exercisers with low self-motivation?

■ Will self-confident children prefer competitive sport and youngsters with low self-confidence prefer noncompetitive sport situations?

Most sport and exercise psychologists favor the interactional approach to studying behavior. Bowers found that the interaction between persons and situations could explain twice as many behaviors as traits or situations alone (1973). The interactional approach requires investigating how people react individually in particular sport and physical activity settings.

For example, Fisher and Zwart (1982) studied the anxiety that athletes showed in different basketball situations—before, during, and after the game. Here are a few of the game situations:

■ With 2 seconds left and the score tied 70–70, you have just been fouled and your free throw might win the game.

■ The crowd is very loud and is directing most of its comments toward you.

■ You have just made a bad play and your coach is criticizing you.

■ You are in the locker room after losing a game you really expected to win.

Given these situations, the athletes were asked to report to what degree they would react in these ways (worded as in the study):

a. Get an uneasy feeling.
b. React overemotionally.
c. Want to avoid the situation.
d. Get a "choking" feeling.
e. Enjoy the challenge.

The athletes' reactions to each basketball situation are colored by their particular mental and emotional makeup. Jeff, who is usually anxious and uptight, may "choke" before shooting free throws with a tied score, whereas Pat, who is laid back and less anxious, might enjoy the challenge. How would you react?

Measuring Personality

When research is conducted appropriately, it can shed considerable light on how personality impacts behavior in sport and exercise settings. Psychologists have developed ways to measure personality that can help us understand personality traits and states. Many psychologists distinguish between an individual's typical style of behaving (*traits*) and the situation's effects on behavior (*states*). This distinction between psychological traits and states has been critical in the development of personality research in sport. However, even though a given psychological trait predisposes someone to behave in a certain way, the behavior doesn't necessarily occur in all situations. Therefore, you should consider both traits and states as you attempt to understand and predict behavior.

> *Both situations and psychological traits should be considered to understand and predict behavior.*

■ CASE STUDY ■

The Interactional Approach

Two women enroll in an exercise class. Maureen has high self-esteem, and Cher has low self-esteem. The class is structured so that each participant takes a turn leading the exercises. Because she is confident in social situations and about how she looks, Maureen really looks forward to leading the class. She really likes being in front of the group, and after leading the class several times has even given thought to becoming an instructor. Cher, on the other hand, is not confident getting up in front of people and feels embarrassed by how she looks. Unlike Maureen, Cher found leading class to be anxiety provoking. All she could think about were the negative comments the class must be making while watching her. Although she really likes to exercise, there is no way she wants to be put in the situation of having to get up in front of class again. Not surprisingly, Cher loses interest in the class and drops out.

Trait and State Measures

Look at these sample questions from trait and state measures of confidence (Vealey, 1986). They highlight the differences between trait and state measures of confidence in a sport context. The Trait Sport Confidence Inventory asks you to indicate how you "generally" or typically feel, whereas the State Sport Confidence Inventory asks you to indicate how you feel "right now," at a particular moment in time in a particular situation.

Situation-Specific Measures

Although general scales provide some useful information about personality traits and states,

---

Trait Sport Confidence Inventory

Think about how self-confident you are when you compete in sport. Answer the 3 questions below based on how confident you *generally* feel when you compete in your sport. Compare your self-confidence to the most self-confident athlete you know. Please answer as you really feel, not how you would like to feel (circle number).

		Low				Medium				High
1. Compare your confidence in your ability to execute the skills necessary to be successful to the most confident athlete you know.		1	2	3	4	5	6	7	8	9
2. Compare your confidence in your ability to perform under pressure with that of the most confident athlete you know.		1	2	3	4	5	6	7	8	9
3. Compare your confidence in your ability to concentrate well enough to be successful with that of the most confident athlete you know.		1	2	3	4	5	6	7	8	9

State Sport Confidence Inventory

		Low				Medium				High
1. Compare the confidence you feel right now in your ability to execute the skills necessary to be successful with that of the most confident athlete you know.		1	2	3	4	5	6	7	8	9
2. Compare the confidence you feel right now in your ability to perform under pressure with that of the most confident athlete you know.		1	2	3	4	5	6	7	8	9
3. Compare the confidence you feel right now in your ability to concentrate well enough to be successful with that of the most confident athlete you know.		1	2	3	4	5	6	7	8	9

> *We can predict behavior better when we have more knowledge of the specific situation and how individuals respond to particular types of situations.*

situation-specific measures will predict behavior more reliably for given situations because they consider both the personality of the participant and the specific situation (interactional approach). For example, a researcher named Sarason in 1975 observed that some students did poorly on tests when they became overly anxious. These students were not particularly anxious in other situations, but taking exams made them freeze up.

Sarason devised a situationally specific scale to measure how anxious a person usually feels before taking exams (i.e., test anxiety). This situation-specific test could predict anxiety right before exams (state anxiety) better than a general test of trait anxiety could.

Sport-Specific Measures

Now look at some of the questions and response formats from the Test of Attentional and Interpersonal Style (Nideffer, 1976), and the Profile of Mood States (POMS; McNair, Lorr, & Droppleman, 1971). Notice that the questions do not directly relate to sport or physical activity. Rather, they are general and more about overall attentional styles and mood.

Test of Attentional and Interpersonal Style

Using the following scale please check the answer that most nearly fits the way you see yourself.

0 = Never
1 = Rarely
2 = Sometimes
3 = Frequently
4 = Always

_____ I get caught up in my thoughts and become oblivious to what is going on around me.

_____ I have difficulty clearing my mind of a single thought or idea.

_____ It is easy for me to direct my attention and focus narrowly on something.

_____ At stores, I am faced with so many choices that I can't make up my mind.

_____ I am good at rapidly scanning crowds and picking out a particular person or face.

Profile of Mood States

Below is a list of words that describe feelings people have. Indicate how you have been feeling this past week, including today.

_____ Energetic

_____ Tense

_____ Fatigued

_____ Confused

_____ Full of pep

_____ Annoyed

Scoring

0 = Not at all
1 = A little
2 = Moderately
3 = Quite a bit
4 = Extremely

Sport-specific measures of personality predict behavior in sport settings better than do general personality tests.

Until recently, almost all of the trait and state measures of personality in sport psychology came from general psychological inventories, without specific reference to sport or physical activity. Sport-specific tests provide more reliable and valid measures of personality traits and states in sport and exercise contexts. For example, rather than test how anxious you are before giving a speech or going out on a date, a coach might test how anxious you are before a competition (especially if excess anxiety proves detrimental to your performance). A sport-specific test of anxiety assesses precompetitive anxiety better than a general anxiety test does. Psychological inventories developed specifically for use in sport and physical activity settings include

- the Sport Competition Anxiety Test to measure competitive trait anxiety (Martens, 1977),
- the Competitive State Anxiety Inventory-2 to measure precompetitive state anxiety (Martens, Burton, Vealey, Bump, & Smith, 1982), and
- the Trait-State Confidence Inventory to measure sport confidence (Vealey, 1986).

Some tests have been developed even for particular sports: These inventories can help identify a person's areas of psychological strength and weakness in that sport or physical activity. After gathering the results a coach can advise players on how to build the strengths and reduce or eliminate the weaknesses. An example of a sport-specific test includes the Tennis Test of Attentional and Interpersonal Style (Van Schoyck & Grasha, 1981).

Fluctuations Before and During Competition

Feelings change before and during a competition. Usually states are assessed shortly before (within 30 minutes of) the onset of a competition or physical activity. Although a measurement can indicate how someone is feeling at that moment, these feelings might change during the competition. For example, Matthew's competitive state anxiety 30 minutes before playing a championship football game might be very high. But once he "takes a few good hits" and gets into the flow of the game, his anxiety might drop to a moderate level. In the fourth quarter, Matt's anxiety might increase again when the score is tied. Such fluctuations should be considered in evaluating personality and reactions to competitive settings.

Sample Items From the Tennis Test of Attentional and Interpersonal Style

Please check the answer that most nearly fits the way you see yourself. Use the following scale:

0 = Never
1 = Rarely
2 = Sometimes
3 = Frequently
4 = Always

_____ When playing tennis, I find myself distracted by the sights and sounds around me.

_____ When playing doubles, I am aware of the movements and positions of all the players on the court.

_____ I am good at quickly analyzing a tennis opponent and assessing strengths and weaknesses.

_____ When playing tennis, I get anxious and block out everything.

■ APPLICATION ■

Consider Traits and States to Understand Behavior

Terry is a confident person in general; he usually responds to situations with higher confidence than Tim, who is low trait-confident. As a coach you are interested in how confidence relates to performance, and you want to know how Tim and Terry are feeling immediately before a swimming race. Although Tim is not confident in general, he swam on his high school swim team and is confident of his swimming abilities. Consequently, his state of confidence right before the race is high. Conversely, although Terry is highly confident in general, he has had little swimming experience and is not even sure he can finish the race. Thus, his state confidence is low right before the race. If you measured only Tim's and Terry's trait confidence, you would be unable to predict how confident they feel before swimming. On the other hand, if you observed Tim's and Terry's state confidence in a different sport—baseball, for example—their results might be different.

This example demonstrates the need to consider both trait and state measures to investigate personality. State and trait levels alone are less significant than the difference between a person's current state level and trait level. This difference score represents the impact of situation factors on behavior. Terry's and Tim's state anxiety levels differed because of experience in swimming (a situation factor).

Using Psychological Measures

The knowledge of personality is critical to success as a coach, teacher, or exercise leader. You may be tempted to use psychological tests to gather information about the people whom you want to help professionally. Bear in mind, however, that psychological inventories alone cannot actually predict athletic success. And they have sometimes been used unethically—or at least inappropriately—and administered poorly. Indeed, it isn't always clear how psychological inventories should be used! Yet it is essential that professionals understand the limitations and the uses and abuses of testing to know what to do and what not to do.

You want to be able to make an informed decision—that is, to be an informed consumer—on how (or whether) to use personality tests. These are some important questions to consider about psychological testing:

■ Should psychological tests be used to help select athletes for a team?

■ What qualifies someone to administer psychological tests?

■ Should coaches give psychological tests to their athletes?

■ What types of psychological tests should be used with athletes?

■ How should psychological tests be administered to athletes?

In 1985 the American Psychological Association (APA) provided the following seven helpful guidelines on the use of psychological tests.

> *All psychological tests contain a degree of measurement error; use caution in interpreting their results.*

Know the Principles of Testing and Measurement Error

Before you administer and interpret psychological inventories, you should understand testing principles, be able to recognize measurement errors, and have well-designed and validated measures. Not all psychological tests have been systematically developed and made reliable. Making predictions or inferences about an athlete's or exerciser's behavior and personality structure on the basis of these tests would be misleading and unethical. Test results are not absolute or irrefutable.

Even valid tests that have been reliably developed may have measurement errors. Suppose you wish to measure self-esteem in 13- to 15-year-old physical education students. You choose a good test developed for adults, inasmuch as there are no tests specifically for youngsters. If the students do not fully understand the questions, however, the results would not be reliable. Similarly, if you give a test developed on a predominantly white population to African-American and Hispanic athletes, the results might be less reliable due to cultural differences. In these situations, a researcher should conduct pilot testing with that specific population to establish the reliability and validity of the test instrument.

People usually want to present themselves in a favorable light. Sometimes they answer questions in what they think is a "socially desirable" way, a response style known as "faking good." For example, an athlete may fear letting her coach know how nervous she gets before competition, so she skews her answers in a precompetitive anxiety test, trying to appear calm, cool, and collected.

Know Your Limitations

The American Psychological Association recommends that people administering tests be aware of the limitations of their training and preparation. However, some people do not recognize the limits of their knowledge, or they use and interpret test results unethically, which can be damaging to the athletes. For instance, it is inappropriate to use personality inventories developed to measure psychopathology (abnormality, such as schizophrenia or manic depression) to measure a more normal increase in anxiety.

> *Individuals need special training (e.g., certification, course work) in psychological assessment to be qualified to interpret results from personality tests.*

> *Using personality inventories to select athletes for a team or to cut them from a team is an abuse of testing that should not be tolerated.*

Furthermore, it is inappropriate to give physical education students a clinical personality test.

Do Not Use Psychological Tests for Team Selection

Using only psychological tests to select players for a team is an abuse because the tests are not yet accurate enough to be predictive. For example, determining if an athlete has the "right" psychological profile to be a middle linebacker in football or point guard in basketball on the basis of psychological tests alone is unfair. Some psychological tests may have a limited use, but they must be considered in conjunction with physical performance measures, coach evaluations, and the actual levels of play.

Include Explanation and Feedback

Athletes, students, and exercisers should be told the purpose of the tests, what they measure, and how the test is going to be used—before they actually complete the tests. They should receive specific feedback about the results to allow them to gain insight into themselves from the testing process.

Assure Confidentiality

It is essential to assure people that their answers will remain confidential in whatever tests they take (and to ensure that this confidentiality is maintained!). With this assurance test takers are more likely to answer truthfully. When they fear exposure, they may fake or falsify their answers, which can distort the true findings of the test and make interpretation virtually useless. Students in a physical education class might wonder if a test will affect their grades, and in these circumstances they will be more likely to exaggerate their strengths and minimize their weaknesses. If you do not explain the reasons for testing, test takers typically become suspicious and wonder

© Mary Langenfeld/Langenfeld Photos

if the coach will use the test to help select starters or weed out players.

Take an Intraindividual Approach

It is often a mistake to compare an athlete's psychological test results with the norms, even though in some specific cases such a comparison might be useful. Athletes or exercisers might seem to score high or low in anxiety, self-confidence, or motivation in relation to other people, but the more critical point is to determine how they are feeling relative to how they usually feel (an intraindividual approach). Use this psychological information to help them perform better and enjoy the experience more, but relative to their own standards—not the scores of others.

Take the example of assessing an exerciser's motivation. It isn't as important to know if the individual's motivation to exercise is high or low compared with other exercisers so much as how it compares with competing motivations the exerciser has (e.g., being with his family or carrying out her job responsibilities).

Understand and Assess Specific Personality Components

A clear understanding of the components of personality provides you with some perspective for using

and interpreting psychological tests. For example, to measure someone's personality, you would certainly be interested in her psychological core. You would select specific types of tests to gain an accurate understanding of the various aspects of her personality. To measure more unconscious and deeper aspects of personality you could use a projective test, for example. Projective tests usually include pictures or written situations, and the test takers are asked to project their feelings and thoughts about these materials. Hence, someone might be shown a photo of an exhausted runner crossing a finish line at the end of a highly contested track race and then be asked to write about what is happening. A high-achieving, confident person might emphasize how the runner made an all-out effort to achieve his goal, whereas a low-achiever might project feelings of sorrow for losing the race in a close finish.

Projective tests are interesting, but they are often difficult to score and interpret. Consequently, sport psychologists usually assess personality in sport by looking at typical responses invoked by the actual situation they are interested in. For instance, a coach wants to know more than whether an athlete is generally anxious—he or she also wants to know how the athlete deals with competitive anxiety. So a test that measures anxiety in sport would be more useful

■ APPLICATION ■

Dos and Don'ts in Personality Testing

Dos

- Inform participants about the purpose of the personality test and exactly how it will be used.
- Allow only qualified individuals who have an understanding of testing principles and measurement error to give personality tests.
- Integrate personality test results with other information obtained about the participant.
- Use sport- and exercise-specific tests whenever possible, giving them in consultation with a sport psychologist.
- Use both state and trait measures of personality.
- Provide participants with specific feedback concerning the result of the test.
- Compare individuals against their own baseline levels rather than against normative information.

Don'ts

- Do not use clinical personality tests that focus on abnormality to study an average population of sport and exercise participants.
- Do not use personality tests to decide who makes a team or program and who doesn't.
- Do not give or interpret personality tests unless you are qualified to do so by the APA or another certifying organization.
- Do not use personality tests to predict behavior in sport and exercise settings without considering other sources of information, such as observational data and performance assessments.

to a coach or sport psychologist than would a test that measures anxiety in general. Likewise, a test that measures motivation for exercise would be more useful to an exercise leader than a general motivation test would be.

Personality Research in Sport and Exercise

The research from the 1960s and 1970s yielded few useful conclusions about the relationship of personality to sport performance. In part these meager results stemmed from methodological, statistical, and interpretive problems, which we will discuss later. Researchers were divided into two camps. Morgan (1980) described one group as taking a credulous viewpoint; that is, these researchers believed that personality is closely related to athletic success. The other group, he said, had a skeptical viewpoint, arguing that personality is not related to athletic success.

Neither the credulous nor the skeptical viewpoint appears to have proved to be correct. Rather, some relationship exists between personality and sport performance, but it is far from perfect. That is, although personality traits and states can help predict sport behavior and success, they are not precise. For example, the fact that some Olympic long-distance runners exhibit introverted personalities does not mean that a long-distance runner needs to be introverted to be successful. Similarly, although many successful middle linebackers in football have aggressive personalities, other successful middle linebackers do not.

We'll now turn our focus to the research on personality, sport performance, and sport preference. But remember that personality alone doesn't account for behavior in sport and exercise. Some caution is needed in interpreting the findings of personality research because an attribution or assumption of cause-and-effect relationships between personality and performance was a problem in many of the early studies.

Athletes and Nonathletes

Try to define an athlete. It isn't easy. Is an athlete someone who plays on a varsity or interscholastic team? Who demonstrates a certain level of skill? Who jogs daily to lose weight? Who plays professional sports? Who plays intramural sports? Keep this ambiguity in mind as you read about studies that have compared personality traits of athletes and nonathletes. Such ambiguity in definitions has weakened this research and clouded its interpretation.

One large comparative study of athletes and nonathletes tested almost 2,000 college males using Cattell's 16 PF, which measures 16 personality factors or traits (Schurr, Ashley, & Joy, 1977). No single personality profile was found that distinguished athletes (defined for the study's purposes as a member of a university intercollegiate team) from nonathletes. However, when the athletes were categorized by sport, several differences did emerge. For example, compared with nonathletes, athletes who played *team* sports exhibited less abstract reasoning, more extroversion, more dependency, and less ego strength. Further, compared with nonathletes, athletes who played *individual* sports displayed higher levels of objectivity, more dependency, less anxiety, and less abstract thinking.

Hence, some personality differences appear to distinguish athletes and nonathletes, but these specific differences cannot yet be considered definitive. Schurr et al. (1977) found that team-sport athletes were more dependent, extroverted, and anxious but less imaginative than individual-sport athletes. Of course, it's possible that certain personality types are drawn to a particular sport, rather than that participation in a sport somehow changes one's personality. The reasons for these differences remain unclear.

Female Athletes

As more women compete in sport, it is important to understand the personality profile of female athletes. In 1980 Williams found that successful female athletes differed markedly from the "normative" female in terms of personality profile. Compared with female nonathletes, women athletes were found to be more achievement-oriented, independent, aggressive, emotionally stable, and assertive. Most of these traits are desirable for sports. Apparently, outstanding athletes have similar personality characteristics, regardless of being male or female.

Positive Mental Health and the Iceberg Profile

After comparing personality traits of more successful with less successful athletes using a measure called the Profile of Mood States (POMS), Morgan developed a mental health model that he reported as being effective in predicting athletic success (Morgan, 1979b, 1980; Morgan, Brown, Raglin, O'Connor, & Ellickson, 1987). Basically, the model suggests that positive mental health as assessed by a certain pattern of POMS scores is directly related to athletic success and high levels of performance.

Morgan's model predicts that an athlete who scores above the norm on the POMS subscales of neuroticism, depression, fatigue, confusion, and anger and below the norm on vigor will tend to pale in comparison with an athlete who scores below the norm on all of these traits except vigor, on which he scores above the norm. Successful elite athletes in a variety of sports (e.g., swimmers, wrestlers, oarsmen, and runners) are characterized by what Morgan called the iceberg profile that reflects positive mental health. The iceberg profile of a successful elite athlete is formed by vigor being above the mean of the population whereas tension, depression, anger, fatigue, and confusion are below the mean of the population (see Figure 2.2a). Notice that the profile looks like an iceberg, with all negative traits below the surface (population norms) and the one positive trait (vigor) above the surface. In contrast, less successful elite athletes have a flat profile, scoring at or below the 50th percentile on all psychological factors (see Figure 2.2b). According to Morgan this reflects negative mental health.

Few personality differences are evident between male and female athletes, particularly at the elite level.

Morgan's mental health model proposes that successful athletes exhibit greater positive mental health than less successful (or unsuccessful) athletes exhibit.

No specific personality profile has been found that consistently distinguishes athletes from nonathletes.

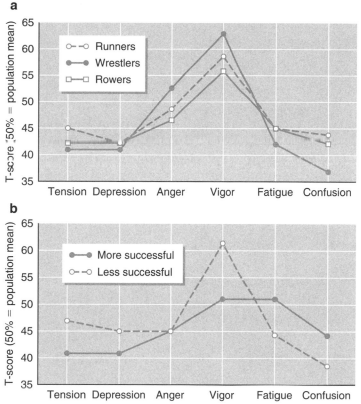

Figure 2.2 *(a) Iceberg profiles for elite wrestlers, distance runners, and rowers; (b) psychological profiles of more and less successful elite athletes.*
Adapted from Morgan, 1979.

Predicting Performance

Morgan (1979b) psychologically evaluated 16 candidates for the 1974 United States Heavyweight Rowing Team using the POMS, correctly predicting 10 of the 16 finalists. This success and similar studies led him to conclude that more successful athletes exhibit the iceberg profile and more positive mental health. You might think that these impressive statistics mean you should use psychological tests for selecting athletes to a team. However, as you will later read, most sport psychologists vehemently oppose using psychological tests for team selection. Personality testing is far from perfect (only 10 of 16 rowers were correctly predicted), and athletes might be unfairly and erroneously selected or cut from a team.

Morgan's mental health (iceberg profile) model has received some criticism in recent years (Renger,

Tests can help identify an athlete's psychological strengths and weaknesses, and this information can be used to develop appropriate training in psychological skills.

1993; Rowley, Landers, Kyllo & Etnier, 1995; Terry, 1995). Renger (1993), for instance, felt that results had been misinterpreted. He noted there was insufficient evidence to conclude that the profile differentiates athletes of varying levels of ability, only athletes from nonathletes. Similarly, Rowley et al. (1995) conducted a statistical review (called a meta analysis) of all the iceberg profile research and found that the profile did indeed differentiate successful from less successful athletes, but accounted for a very small percentage of their performance variation (less than 1%). Rowley and his coauthors warn that the evidence does not justify using the instrument as a basis of team selection and that users must be careful to protect against social desirability effects (participants "faking good" to impress their coaches). Terry (1995) also warns that the POMS is not a test for "identifying champions," as Morgan had originally proposed in his iceberg profile model of mental health. At the same time, he argues that this does not imply that the test is useless. He indicates that optimal mood profiles are most likely sport-dependent; therefore it is critical that mood changes in athletes be compared with their own previous mood levels and not with large group norms. Based on research and his experience in consulting with athletes, Terry recommends that the POMS test be used in the following ways:

- As a general monitor of the athlete's mind-set
- As a catalyst for discussion during one-on-one sessions
- As an intervention in its own right (to improve one's mood over time)
- For early problem identification
- As a monitor of the mood of team officials and support staff
- As a monitor of training load (see chapter 21 for more details)
- As a monitor during the acclimatization process
- For identification of overtrained athletes (also see chapter 21)
- As a monitor during rehabilitation from overtraining (also see chapter 21)
- As a monitor of emotional responses to injury (see chapter 19 for more details)
- For performance prediction (but not athlete selection)
- As a contributor to the individualization of mental training

Thus, iceberg profile research clearly has implications for professional practice. However, the recent criticisms of this research have shown that it is not possible on the simple basis of giving a personality measure to realistically select teams or accurately predict major variations in athletic performance. This type of personality data, however, has some useful purpose. It can help sport psychologists discover the kinds of psychological traits and states associated with successful athletes—and once these psychological factors are understood, athletes can work with sport psychologists and coaches to develop psychological skills for improving performance. For example, psychological skills training (see chapters 11 to 16) can help exercisers and athletes cope more effectively with anger and anxiety.

In summary, personality tests are useful tools that help us better understand, monitor, and work with athletes and exercisers. They are not magical instruments that allow us to make sweeping generalizations about individuals' behaviors and their performances.

Exercise and Personality

Sport psychologists have investigated the relation between exercise and personality. We will briefly review the relation between exercise and two personality dispositions: Type A behavior and self-concept.

Type A Behavior

The Type A behavior pattern is characterized by a strong sense of urgency, an excess of competitive drive, and an easily aroused hostility. The antithesis of the Type A behavior pattern is called Type B. Initially, a link was found between Type A behavior and increased incidence of cardiovascular disease. More recently, it has been suspected that the anger-hostility component of the Type A construct is the most significant disease-related characteristic. Although the causes of Type A behavior have not been conclusively determined, considerable evidence points to the sociocultural environment, such as parental expectations of high standards in performance, as the likely origin (Girdano, Everly, & Dusek, 1990).

Early efforts to modify Type A behavior through exercise interventions have had mixed results. One positive study showed that a 12-week aerobics program was not only associated with reductions in Type A behavior but also helped participants significantly reduce cardiovascular reactivity to mental stress (Blumenthal et al., 1988). Thus, changing Type A behavior patterns through exercise could result in positive health benefits.

Self-Concept

Exercise appears to have a positive relationship also with self-concept (Biddle, 1995; Marsh & Redmayne, 1994; Sonstroem, 1984; Sonstroem, Harlow, & Josephs, 1994). Sonstroem (1984) suggested that these changes in self-concept might be associated with the *perception* of improved fitness, rather than with actual changes in physical fitness. Although

> *Type A behavioral patterns apparently can be altered through exercise, which can lead to reducing the risk of cardiovascular disease.*

> *Exercise and increased levels of fitness appear to be associated with increases in self-esteem, especially among individuals initially low in self-esteem.*

studies so far have not proved that changes in physical fitness produce changes in self-concept, exercise programs seem to lead to significant increases in self-esteem, especially with subjects who initially show low self-esteem.

Parallel to the sport personality research, the exercise and self-concept research has shown that it is best to think of self-concept or self-esteem not only as a general trait (global self-esteem) but also as including numerous content-specific dimensions, such as social self-concept, academic self-concept, and physical self-concept. As you might expect, research shows that exercise participation has the greatest effect on the physical dimension of self-concept (Fox, 1997; Marsh & Sonstroem, 1995). This relationship will be discussed more in chapter 17.

Cognitive Strategies and Success

Although some differences are evident among the personality traits and dispositions of athletes and exercisers, researchers have not been satisfied with the utility of their information thus far. More recently researchers have turned from studying traditional traits to examining those mental strategies, skills, and behaviors athletes use for competition and how they relate to performance success (Auweele, Cuyper, Van Mele, & Rzewnicki, 1993). Although these factors are not personality traits in the traditional sense, researchers consider them to reflect behavioral aspects of personality and to interact with personality characteristics.

One of the first studies to take this approach was when Mahoney and Avener (1977) investigated gymnasts competing for berths on the U.S. Men's Gymnastics Team. They found that the gymnasts who made the team coped better with anxiety, used more internal imagery, and had more positive self-talk than those who didn't make the team.

More recently, Smith, Schutz, Smoll, and Ptacek (1995) developed and validated a new measure of sport-specific psychological skills, the Athletic Coping Skills Inventory-28 (ACSI). The ACSI not only yields an overall score of an athlete's psychological skills but also gives seven subscale scores, which include the following:

Olympic medalists, unlike nonmedalists, internalize their strategies to the extent that they react automatically to adversity.

- Coping with adversity
- Peaking under pressure
- Goal setting and mental preparation
- Concentration
- Freedom from worry
- Confidence and achievement motivation
- Coachability

They examined the relationship between the overall scale and subscale scores and athletic performance in two studies. In the first study, 762 high school male and female athletes representing a variety of sports completed the ACSI. They were classified as being "underachievers" (those who had a coach's talent rating that exceeded their actual performance ratings), "normal achievers" (those who had ratings equal to their actual performance), and "overachievers" (those who were rated by their coaches as performing above their talent level). The study showed that the overachieving athletes had significantly higher scores on several subscales (coachability, concentration, coping with adversity) as well as higher total scale scores. These results show that psychological skills can assist athletes in getting the most out of their physical talent.

The second study (Smith & Christensen, 1995) sampled quite a different group of athletes: 104 minor league professional baseball players. ACSI scores were related to such performance measures as batting averages for hitters and earned run averages for pitchers. Interestingly, as with the high school athletes from the first study, expert ratings of *physical* skills did not relate to ACSI scores. Moreover, psychological skills accounted for a significant portion of performance variations in batting and pitching, and these skills contributed even more than physical ability (remember that these were all highly skilled and talented athletes, so this does not mean physical talent is unimportant). Finally, higher psychological skill scores were associated with player survival or continued involvement in professional baseball 2 and 3 years later. Thus, performance in elite sport appeared clearly related to mental skills.

A third study using the ACSI was recently conducted with Greek athletes (basketball, polo, and volleyball) at both the elite and non-elite levels (Kioumourtzoglou, Tzetzis, Derri, & Mihalopoulou, 1997). It revealed a number of differences, most notably that the elite athletes all showed superior ability, compared with the non-elite controls, to cope with adversity. The elite athletes were also better at goal setting and mental preparation.

Although Smith and his colleagues (1995) acknowledge that the ACSI is a useful measurement tool for research and educational purposes, they warn that it should not be used for team selection. They argue that if athletes think the ACSI is being used for selection purposes, they are likely to knowingly give answers that will make themselves look good to coaches or to unwittingly indicate certain responses in hopes that they will become true.

In-Depth Interview Techniques

Researchers recently have attempted to investigate the differences between successful and less successful athletes by taking a **qualitative approach** (a growing methodological trend in the field, as mentioned in chapter 1). In-depth interviews are conducted to probe the coping strategies that athletes employ before and during competition. The interview approach provides coaches, athletes, and sport psychologists with much more in-depth personality profiles of an athlete than do paper and pencil tests. For example, all 20 members of the 1988 U.S. Olympic freestyle and Greco-Roman wrestling teams were interviewed. Compared with non-

medalist wrestlers, Olympic medal winners used more positive self-talk, had a narrower and more immediate focus of attention, were better prepared mentally for unforeseen negative circumstances, and had more extensive mental practice (Gould, Eklund, & Jackson, 1993).

One wrestler described his ability to react automatically to adversity:

> *Something I've always practiced is to never let anything interfere with what I'm trying to accomplish at a particular tournament. So, what I try to do is if something is [maybe going] to bother me . . . completely empty my mind and concentrate on the event coming up. . . . My coping strategy is just to completely eliminate it from my mind, and I guess I'm blessed to be able to do that. (Gould et al., 1993)*

Medalists seemed able to maintain a relatively stable and positive emotional level because their coping strategies became automatic, whereas nonmedalists experienced more fluctuating emotions as a consequence of not coping well mentally. Take the following example of a nonmedalist Olympic wrestler:

© Human Kinetics

I had a relaxation tape that seemed to give me moments of relief. . . . It got to the point where what you would try to do was not think about wrestling and get your mind on other things. But inevitably . . . you would bind up and get tight, [your] pulse would pick-up, and your palms and legs and hands or feet [would be] sweating. You go through that trying to sleep, and I would resort to my relaxation tape. I don't think I coped very well with it really. (Gould et al., 1993)

Mental Plans

Mental planning is a large part of cognitive strategies. Some additional quotes from Olympic athletes may help to further explain the benefits and workings of the mental strategies that the wrestlers mentioned (Orlick & Partington, 1988):

The plan or program was already in my head. For the race I was on automatic, like turning the program on cruise control and letting it run. I was aware of the effort I was putting in and also of my opponent's position in relation to me, but I always focused on what I had to do next.

Before I start, I focus on relaxing, on breathing calmly. I feel activated but in control since I'd been thinking about what I was going to do in the race all through the warm-up. I used the period just before the start to clear my mind, so when I did actually start the race all my thoughts about what I would be doing in the race could be uncluttered.

I usually try to work with my visualization on what is likely I'm going to use. Different wrestlers have different moves, you know. They always like to throw a right arm spin or something, and I'll visualize myself blocking that and things like that.

Canadian Olympic athletes learn a systematic series of mental strategies to use before the competition and during it, including refocusing plans. Thus, they come prepared mentally not only to perform but also to handle distractions and unforeseen events, before and during the competition (Orlick & Partington, 1988). These mental plans especially help athletes whose sense of control (a personality trait) is low; the plans allow them to feel more in control, regardless of situational influences. Table 2.1 provides an example of a detailed refocusing plan for a Canadian Olympic Alpine skier.

This skier's refocusing plan to meet the demands of the situation shows how important it is to study not only an athlete's personality profile but also an in-depth description of his or her cognitive strategies and plans. In this way, coaches can continually structure practices and training environments to meet the situation and maximize performance and personal growth.

Your Role in Understanding Personality

Now that you have learned something about the study of personality in sport and exercise settings, how can

■ APPLICATION ■

Mental Strategies Used by Successful Athletes

- To enhance confidence they practice specific plans to deal with adversity during competition.
- They practice routines to deal with unusual circumstances and distractions before and during a competition.
- They concentrate wholly on the upcoming performance, blocking out irrelevant events and thoughts.
- They use several mental rehearsals prior to competition.
- They don't worry about other competitors before a competition, focusing instead on what is controllable.
- They develop detailed competition plans.
- They learn to regulate arousal and anxiety.

Table 2.1

Refocusing Plan for an Olympic Alpine Skier

Action	Strategy
Prevent hassle	Use adrenaline and anger as positives instead of their bringing me down.
	Let coaches or other personnel rectify the problem.
Delay in start	Relax, think of anything and everything that makes me happy.
Loss of ideal focus in race run	Think of the course in "sections" and deal with a mistake as a mistake in the previous "section"; entering the "new section," a refocusing occurs.
	Think and deal with the remainder of the course as previously rehearsed.
Mistake in race run	Deal with the mistake as I would a loss of focus.
	Go for the future, not the past.
Poor performance—first run	Think of second run with a "nothing-to-lose" attitude.
Poor performance—final run	Determine what went wrong and why. Learn from the mistake, train, and see the mistake dissolve mentally and physically.
	Make the poor performance a challenge to defeat.

Adapted from Orlick, 1986.

you use the information to better understand the individuals in your classes and on your teams? Many later chapters will explore the practical aspects of changing behaviors and developing psychological skills. In the meantime, use these guidelines to help you better understand the people with whom you work now and to consolidate what you have learned about personality structure.

1. Consider both personality traits and situations. To understand someone's behavior, consider both the person and his or her situation. Along with understanding personality, always consider the particular situation in which you are teaching or coaching.

2. Be an informed consumer. To know how and when to use personality tests, understand the ethics and guidelines for personality testing. This chapter has provided some guidelines, and as a professional it will be your responsibility to understand the dos and don'ts of personality testing.

3. Be a good communicator. Although formal personality testing can disclose a great deal about people, so can sincere and open communication. Asking questions and being a good listener can go a long way toward establishing rapport and finding out about a person's personality and preferences. A more detailed discussion of communication is presented in chapter 10.

4. Be a good observer. Another good way to gain valuable information about people's personalities is to observe their behavior in different situations. If you combine your observation of an individual's behavior with open communication, you'll likely get a well-rounded view and understanding of his or her personality.

5. Be knowledgeable about mental strategies. A constellation of mental strategies facilitates the learning and performance of physical skills. Be aware of and implement these strategies appropriately in your programs, selecting them to benefit an individual's personality.

SUMMARY

1 *Describe what makes up personality and why it is important.*

Personality refers to the characteristics or blend of characteristics that make individuals unique. It comprises three separate but related levels: a psychological core, the most basic and stable level of personality; typical responses, or the ways each person learns to adjust to the environment; and role-related behaviors, or how a person acts based on what he or she perceives the situation to be. Role-related behavior is the most changeable aspect of personality. It is important to understand personality to improve teaching and coaching effectiveness for those with whom we interact.

2 *Discuss major approaches to understanding personality.*

Four major routes to studying personality in sport and exercise are the psychodynamic, trait, situation, and interactional approaches. The psychodynamic approach emphasizes the importance of unconscious determinants of behavior and of understanding the person as a whole by identifying isolated traits. It has had little impact in sport psychology. The trait approach assumes that personality is enduring and consistent across situations and that psychological traits predispose individuals to behave in consistent ways, regardless of the situation. In contrast, the situational approach argues that behavior is determined largely by the environment or situation. Neither the trait nor the situational approach has received widespread support in the sport psychology literature. Most researchers take an interactional approach to the study of sport personality, which considers personal and situational factors as equal determinants of behavior.

3 *Identify how personality can be measured.*

To measure personality, psychological traits (an individual's typical style of behaving) and states (the situation's effects on behaviors) should both be assessed in an interactional approach. Although general personality scales provide some useful information about personality states and traits, situation-specific measures (e.g., sport-specific measures) will predict behavior more reliably.

4 *Assess personality tests and research for practicality and validity.*

While useful, psychological tests alone have not proved to be accurate predictors of athletic success. And when they are used, it must be in ethical fashion. Personality test users must know the principles of testing and measurement error; know their own limitations relative to test administration and interpretation; not use tests alone for team selection; always give athletes test explanations and feedback; assure confidentiality; and, take an intraindividual approach to testing.

5 *Comprehend the relationship between personality and behavior in sport and exercise.*

Exercise has been found to enhance self-concept, especially the physical component of one's self. Type A behavior has been shown to be an important personality factor influencing wellness. Although some personality differences have been found by comparing athletes with nonathletes and comparing athletes from different sports, the most interesting and consistent findings come from comparing less successful athletes with more successful athletes exhibiting more positive mental health. These results, however, have limited application.

6 *Describe how cognitive strategies are related to athletic success.*

In recent years researchers have turned their attention away from measuring traditional traits and more to the examination of cognitive or mental strategies, skills, and behaviors that athletes use. Successful athletes, compared with their less successful counterparts, possess a variety of psychological skills. These include arousal regulation and management, high self-confidence, better concentration and focus, feelings of being in control and not forcing things, positive imagery and thoughts, commitment and determination, goal setting, well-developed mental plans, and well-developed coping strategies.

7 *Apply what you know of personality in sport and exercise settings to better understand people's personalities.*

As a professional in sport and exercise, you need to gather information about the personalities of people with whom you work. Specifically, consider both personality traits and situations, be an informed consumer, be a good communicator, be a good observer, and be knowledgeable about mental strategies.

KEY TERMS

psychological core
typical responses
role-related behavior
psychodynamic approach
trait approach
situation approach
interactional approach

situation-specific measures
intraindividual approach
projective tests
mental health model
iceberg profile
meta analysis
qualitative approach

REVIEW QUESTIONS

1. Discuss the three levels of personality, including the stability of the different levels.
2. What is the psychodynamic approach to personality and why is it important?
3. Compare and contrast the situation, trait, and interactional approaches to personality. Which approach is most common among sport psychologists today? Why?
4. Discuss three problems in early personality research in sport and exercise settings.
5. Compare and contrast state and trait measures of personality. Why are both needed for a better understanding of personality in sport?
6. Why are sport-specific personality inventories more desirable than general psychological inventories for measuring personality in sport and exercise? Name examples of both sport-specific and general personality measures.
7. Discuss four important guidelines for administering psychological tests and providing feedback from the results of these tests.
8. Discuss the research comparing the personalities of athletes and nonathletes. Do athletes have a unique personality profile?
9. Do male and female athletes have different personality profiles? Are the differences between male and female athletes as great as those between athletes compared with nonathletes? Do individual and team-sport athletes have different personality profiles?
10. Discuss Morgan's mental health model and the "iceberg profile" as they relate to predicting athletic success. Can athletic success be predicted from psychological tests? Explain.
11. What personality factors are related to exercise behavior?
12. Compare and contrast the cognitive strategies of successful athletes compared with less successful ones.

CRITICAL THINKING QUESTIONS

1. Should psychological tests be used for team selection? Explain your answer.
2. What is your role in understanding personality? When might you consider using personality tests? Discuss other ways to assess participants' personalities.

Chapter 3

© Human Kinetics

Motivation

After reading this chapter you should be able to

1 define motivation and its components,
2 describe typical views of motivation and whether they are useful,
3 detail useful guidelines for building motivation,
4 define achievement motivation and competitiveness and indicate why they are important,
5 compare and contrast theories of achievement motivation,
6 explain how achievement motivation develops, and
7 use fundamentals of achievement motivation to guide practice.

Dan is a co-captain and center on his high school football team. His team does not have outstanding talent, but if everyone gives maximum effort and plays together, the team should have a successful season. When the team's record slips below .500, however, Dan becomes frustrated with some of his teammates who don't seem to try as hard as he does. Despite being more talented than he, these players don't seek out challenges, are not as motivated, and in the presence of adversity often give up. Dan wonders what he can do to motivate some of his teammates.

Like Dan, teachers, coaches, and exercise leaders often wonder why some individuals are highly motivated and constantly strive for success, while others seem to lack motivation and avoid evaluation and competition. In fact, coaches frequently try to motivate athletes with inspirational slogans: "Winners never quit!" "Go hard or go home!" "Give 110 percent!"

Physical educators also want to motivate inactive children—who often seem more interested in playing video games than volleyball. And exercise leaders and physical therapists routinely face the challenge of motivating clients to stay with an exercise or rehabilitation program.

Although motivation is critical to the success of all these professionals, many do not understand the subject well. To have success as a teacher, coach, or exercise leader requires a thorough understanding of motivation, including the factors affecting it and the methods of enhancing it in individuals and groups. Often the ability to motivate people, rather than the technical knowledge of a sport or physical activity, is what separates the very good instructors from the average ones.

In this chapter, we will introduce you to the topic of motivation.

What Is Motivation?

Motivation can be defined simply as the direction and intensity of one's effort (Sage, 1977). Sport and exercise psychologists can view motivation from several specific vantages, including achievement motivation, motivation in the form of competitive stress (see chapter 4), and intrinsic and extrinsic motivation (see chapter 6). These varied forms of motivation are all parts of the more general definition of motivation. Hence, we understand the specifics of motivation through this broader, holistic

Motivation is the direction and intensity of effort.

context, much as a football coach views specific plays from the perspective of a larger game plan or offensive or defensive philosophy. But what exactly do these components of motivation, direction and intensity of effort, involve?

Direction of Effort

The direction of effort refers to whether an individual seeks out, approaches, or is attracted to certain situations. For example, a high school student may be motivated to go out for the tennis team, a coach to attend a coaching clinic, a businesswoman to join an aerobics class, or an injured athlete to seek medical treatment.

Intensity of Effort

Intensity of effort refers to how much effort a person puts forth in a particular situation. For instance, a student may attend physical education class (approach a situation) but not put forth much effort during class. On the other hand, a golfer may want to make a winning putt so badly that he becomes overly motivated, tightens up, and performs poorly. Finally, a weightlifter may work out 4 days a week like her friends, yet differ from them in terms of the tremendous effort or intensity she puts into each workout.

The Relationship Between Direction and Intensity

While for discussion purposes it is convenient to separate the direction from the intensity of effort, for most people direction and intensity of effort are closely related. For instance, students or athletes who seldom miss class or practice and always arrive early typically expend great effort during participation. Conversely, those who are consistently tardy and miss many classes or practices often exhibit low effort when in attendance.

Problems With Vaguely Defining Motivation

Although we have defined motivation using Sage's terms of intensity and direction, the term *motivation* is used in more varied ways in daily life. It is often vaguely defined or not defined at all. Motivation is discussed loosely in any of the following ways:

- As an internal personality characteristic (e.g., she's a highly motivated individual—a real go-getter)
- As an external influence (e.g., I need something to motivate me—to get me going on my running program)

© Human Kinetics

■ As a consequence or explanation for our behavior (e.g., I just wanted it too much and was overly motivated)

Vague definitions of motivation and using the term in so many different ways have two disadvantages. First, if coaches and teachers tell students or athletes that they need more motivation without telling them what they specifically mean by the term, the student or athlete will have to infer the meaning. This can easily lead to misunderstandings and conflict. An exercise leader, for example, might tell her students that they need to be "more motivated" if they want to achieve their desired levels of fitness, meaning that the students need to set goals and work harder toward achieving those goals. A student with low self-esteem, however, might mistakenly interpret the instructor's remarks as a description of his personal-

ity (e.g., I am lazy and do not care), which can negatively affect the student's involvement.

Second, as practitioners we develop specific strategies or techniques for motivating individuals, but we may not recognize how these various strategies interact. In chapter 6 you'll learn how extrinsic rewards, such as trophies and money, can sometimes have powerful positive effects in motivating individuals, but these strategies can often backfire and actually produce negative effects on motivation, depending on how the external rewards are used.

Views of Motivation

Each of us develops a personal view of how motivation works, a theory on what motivates people. We are likely to do this by learning what motivates ourselves and observing how other people are motivated. For instance, if someone has a physical education teacher she likes and feels is successful, she will probably try to use or emulate many of the same motivational strategies that the teacher uses.

Moreover, people often act out their personal views of motivation, both consciously and subconsciously. A coach, for example, might make a conscious effort to motivate students by giving them positive feedback and encouragement. Another coach, believing that people are primarily responsible for their own behaviors, might spend little time creating situations to enhance motivation.

Although there are thousands of individual views, most people fit motivation into one of three general orientations that parallel the approaches to personality discussed in chapter 2. These include the trait-centered orientation to motivation, the situation-centered orientation, and the interactional orientation.

The Trait-Centered View

The trait-centered view (also called the participant-centered view) contends that motivated behavior is primarily a function of individual characteristics. That is, the personality, needs, and goals of a student, athlete, or exerciser are the primary determinants of motivated behavior. Thus, coaches often describe an athlete as a "real winner," implying that this individual has a personal makeup that allows him to excel in sport. Similarly, another athlete may be described as a "loser" who has no get-up-and-go.

Some people have personal attributes that seem to predispose them to success and high levels of motivation, whereas others seem to lack motivation, personal goals, and desire. However, most of us would agree that we are in part affected by the situations in which we are placed. For example, if a teacher does not create a motivating learning environment, student motivation will consequently decline. Conversely, an excellent leader who creates a positive environment will greatly increase motivation. Thus, ignoring environmental influences on motivation is unrealistic and is one reason sport and exercise psychologists have not endorsed the trait-centered view for guiding professional practice.

The Situation-Centered View

In direct contrast to the trait-centered view, the situation-centered orientation contends that motivation level is determined primarily by situation. For example, Brittany might be really motivated in her aerobic exercise class but unmotivated in a competitive sport situation.

Probably you would agree that situation influences motivation, but can you also recall situations in which you remained motivated despite a negative environment? For example, maybe you played for a coach you didn't like who constantly yelled at and criticized you, but still you did not quit the team or lose any of your motivation. In such a case the situation was clearly not the primary factor influencing your motivation level. For this reason, sport and exercise psychology specialists do not recommend the situation-centered view of motivation as the most effective for guiding practice.

The Interactional View

The view of motivation most widely endorsed by sport and exercise psychologists today is the participant-by-situation interactional view. "Inter-actionists" contend that motivation results neither solely from participant factors, such as personality, needs, interests, and goals, nor solely from situational factors, such as a coach's or teacher's style or the win-loss record of a team. Rather, the best way to understand motivation is to examine how these two sets of factors interact (see Figure 3.1).

Interactional View of Motivation: A Research Example

Sorrentino and Sheppard (1978) studied 44 male and 33 female swimmers in three Canadian universities, testing them twice as they swam a 200-yard, freestyle time trial individually and then as part of a relay team. The situational factor they assessed was whether each swimmer had a faster split time when swimming alone or when swimming as part of a relay team. The researchers also assessed a personality characteristic in the swimmers, namely, their affiliation motivation, or the degree to which one sees the group involvement as an opportunity for social approval versus social rejection. The objective of the study was to see whether each swimmer was oriented more toward social approval (that is, viewing competing with others as a positive state) or toward rejection (that is, feeling threatened by an affiliation-oriented activity, such as a relay, where he or she might let others down).

As the investigators predicted, the approval-oriented swimmers demonstrated faster times swimming in the relay than when swimming alone (see Figure 3.2). After all, they had a positive orientation toward

> *The best way to understand motivation is to consider both the person and the situation and how they interact.*

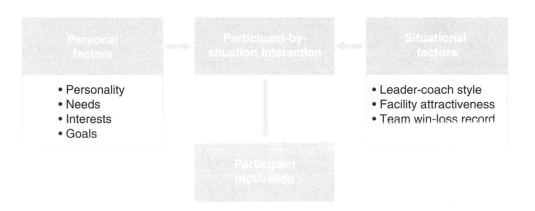

Figure 3.1 *Participant-by-situation interactional model of motivation.*

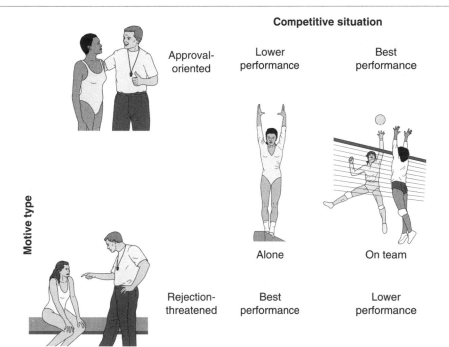

Figure 3.2 *The interaction of a coach's motivational style and competitive situation on performance.*

seeking approval from others—their teammates. In contrast, the rejection-threatened swimmers, who were overly concerned with letting their teammates down, swam faster alone than they swam in the relay.

From a coaching perspective, these findings show that the four fastest individual swimmers would not necessarily make the best relay team. Depending on the athletes' personalities, some would perform best in a relay and others would perform best individually. Many experienced team sport coaches agree that starting the most highly skilled athletes does not guarantee having the best team in the game.

The swimming study's results clearly demonstrate the importance of the interactional model of motivation. Knowing only a swimmer's personal characteristics (motivational orientation) was not the best way to predict behavior (the individual's split time) because performance depended on the situation (performing individually or in a relay). Similarly, it would be a mistake to look only at the situation as the primary source of motivation, because the best speed depended on whether a swimmer was more approval-oriented or rejection-threatened. The key, then, was to understand the interaction between the athlete's personal makeup and the situation.

Five Guidelines for Building Motivation

The interactional model of motivation has important implications for teachers, coaches, trainers, exercise

51

To enhance motivation you must analyze and respond not only to a player's personality but also to the interaction of personal and situational characteristics. Because motivations may change over time, you should continue to monitor people's motives for participation even months after they've begun.

leaders, and program administrators. In fact, some fundamental guidelines can be derived from this model for professional practice.

Guideline 1: Both Situations and Traits Motivate People

When attempting to enhance motivation, consider both situational and personal factors. Often when teachers, trainers, coaches, or exercise leaders work with students, athletes, or clients who seem to lack motivation, they immediately attribute this lack to the participant's personal characteristics. "These students don't care about learning," "This team doesn't want it enough," or "Exercise is just not a priority in these folks' lives"—such phrases ascribe personal attributes to people and, in effect, serve to dismiss the poor motivation or avoid the responsibility for helping the participants develop motivation. At other times, instructors fail to consider the personal attributes of their students or clients and instead put all the blame on the situation (e.g., "This material must be boring." "What is it about my instructional style that inhibits the participant's level of motivation?").

In reality, low participant motivation usually results from a combination of personal and situational factors. Personal factors do cause people to lack motivation, but so do the environments in which people participate. And often it may be easier for an instructor to change the situation than to change the needs and personalities of the participants. The key, however, is not to focus attention only on the personal attributes of the participants or only on the situation at hand but to consider the interaction of these factors.

Guideline 2: People Have Multiple Motives for Involvement

Consistent effort is necessary to identify and understand participants' motives for being involved in sport, exercise, or educational environments. There are several ways to accomplish this.

Understand Why People Participate in Physical Activity

Researchers know why most people participate in sport and exercise. In a study by Gould and Petlichkoff (1988), the major motives that the youths cited for sport participation were improving their skills, having fun, being with friends, experiencing thrills and excitement, achieving success, and developing fitness. Wankel (1980) found that adults cited different motives for joining an exercise program, including health factors, weight loss, fitness, self-challenge, and feeling better. Their motives for continuing in the exercise program included enjoyment, the organization's leadership (e.g., the instructor), the activity type (e.g., running, aerobics), and social factors. What motivates you to participate in sport and physical activity?

People Participate for More Than One Reason

Most people have multiple motives for participation. For example, you may lift weights because you want to tone your body. Yet, lifting weights also makes you feel good, plus you enjoy the camaraderie of your lifting partners. Thus, you do not lift for only one reason.

People Have Competing Motives for Involvement

At times people have competing motives. For instance, a person may want to exercise at the club after work and also to be with her family. As a coach, teacher, or exercise leader, you'll want to be aware of such conflicting interests because they can affect participation.

People Have Both Shared and Unique Motives

Although it is possible to identify why people usually participate in sport and exercise, we need to remember that motives for participation vary greatly and can be unique to each individual. For example, many of us would cite physical fitness, fun, and friendship as major motives for sport participation. However, some of us might have motives that are more individual, such as parental pressure or needing something to do. Still others might have highly idiosyncratic motives, such as the need to physically dominate others or because they actually experience a sense of calmness from competition. Hence, people have both shared and unique motives for participation.

Because people have such a diverse range of motives for sport and exercise participation, you need to be aware of your students', athletes', or exercisers' motives for involvement. Following these guidelines should improve your awareness:

1. Observe the participants and see what they like and do not like about the activity.

2. Informally talk to others (e.g., teachers, friends, and family members) who know the student, athlete, or exerciser, and solicit information about the person's motives for participation.

3. Periodically ask the participants to write out or tell you their reasons for participation.

Motives Change Over Time

Continue to monitor motives for participation: Research has shown that motives change over time. For instance, the reasons some individuals cited for beginning an exercise program (e.g., health and fitness benefits) were not necessarily the same motives they cited for staying involved (e.g., social atmosphere of the program; Wankel, 1980). Consequently, continuing to emphasize fitness benefits and ignore the social aspect after people have begun the exercise program is probably *not* the most effective motivational strategy.

Guideline 3: Change the Environment to Enhance Motivation

Knowing why people become involved in sport and exercise is important, but this information alone is insufficient to enhance motivation. You need to use what you learn about your participants to structure the sport and exercise environment to meet their needs.

Provide Both Competition and Recreation

Not all participants will have the same desire for competition and recreation. Opportunities need to be provided for both. For example, many park district directors have learned that although some adult athletes prefer competition, others do not. Thus, the directors divide the traditional competitive softball leagues into "competitive" and "recreational" divisions. This choice enhances participation rates by giving people what they want.

Provide Multiple Opportunities

Meeting participant needs isn't always simple. Structuring a situation to enhance motivation may mean constructing an environment to meet multiple needs. For example, elite performers demand rigorous training and work at a very intense level. Some coaches mistakenly think that world-class athletes need only rigorous physical training, but the truth is these elite athletes often also want to have fun and enjoy the companionship of their fellow athletes. When coaches pay more attention to the motives of fun and fellowship, along with optimal physical training, they enhance motivation and improve their athletes' performance.

Adjust to Individuals Within Groups

The most difficult but important component of structuring sport and exercise is individualizing coaching and teaching. That is, each exerciser, athlete, and student has his or her unique motives for participation, and effective instructors must provide an environment to meet these diverse needs. Experienced coaches have known this for years. Legendary football coach Vince Lombardi (whom the Super Bowl trophy is named after), for example, structured his coaching environment to meet the needs of individual athletes (Kramer & Shaap, 1968). Lombardi had a reputation as a fiery, no-nonsense coach who was constantly on his players' backs. All-pro guard Jerry Kramer, for instance, has said that Lombardi always yelled at him. (But Coach Lombardi was also clever: Just when Kramer was discouraged enough to quit because of the criticism, Lombardi would provide some much-needed positive reinforcement.) In contrast to the more thick-skinned Kramer, his teammate all-pro quarterback Bart Starr was extremely self-critical. The coach recognized this and treated Starr in a much more positive way than he treated Kramer. Lombardi understood that these two players had different personalities and needs, which required a coaching environment flexible enough for them both.

Individualizing is not always easy to accomplish. Physical educators might be teaching six different classes of 35 students each, and aerobics instructors might have classes with as many as 100 students in them. Without assistants it is impossible to structure the instructional environment in the way Lombardi did. This means today's physical educators must be both imaginative and realistic in individualizing their environments.

> *To enhance motivation, structure teaching and coaching environments to meet the needs of all participants.*

Of course, a junior high school physical educator cannot get to know her students nearly as well as a personal trainer with one client or a basketball coach with 15 players on his team. However, the physical educator could, for example, have students identify on index cards their motives for involvement ("What do you like about physical education class? Why did you take the class?"), assess the frequency that various motives are mentioned, and structure the class environment to meet the most frequently mentioned motives. If more students indicated they preferred noncompetitive activities to traditional competitive class activities, the instructor could choose to structure class accordingly. You might offer options within the same class and have half the students play competitive volleyball on one court and the other half play noncompetitive volleyball on a second court.

Guideline 4: Leaders Influence Motivation

As an exercise leader, physical educator, or coach you have a critical role in influencing participant motivation. At times your influence may be indirect and you won't even recognize the importance of your actions. For example, a physical educator who is energetic and bubbly will, on personality alone, give considerable positive reinforcement in class. Over the school year her students come to expect her upbeat behavior. However, she may have a bad day and, although she does not act negatively in class, not be up to her usual cheeriness. Because her students know nothing about her circumstances, they perceive that they did something wrong and consequently become discouraged. Unbeknownst to the teacher, her students are influenced by her mood (see Figure 3.3).

You too will have bad days as a professional and will need to struggle through them, doing the best job you can. The key thing to remember is to be aware that your actions (and inaction) on such days can influence the motivational environment. Sometimes you may need to act more upbeat than you feel. If that's not possible, inform your students that you're not quite yourself, so they don't misinterpret your behavior.

Figure 3.3 *"She was pretty upset with us tonight. I wonder what we did wrong."*

Guideline 5: Use Behavior Modification to Change Undesirable Participant Motives

We have emphasized the need for structuring the environment to facilitate participant motivation because the exercise leader, trainer, coach, or teacher usually has more direct control over the environment than over the motives of individuals. This does not imply, however, that it is inappropriate to attempt to change a participant's motives for involvement.

A young football player, for example, may be involved in his sport primarily to inflict injury on others. This player's coach will certainly want to use behavior modification techniques (see chapter 6) to change this undesirable motivation. That is, the coach will reinforce good clean play, punish aggressive play designed to inflict injury, and simultaneously discuss appropriate behavior with the player. Similarly, a cardiac rehabilitation patient beginning exercise at a doctor's orders may need behavior modification from her exercise leader to gain intrinsic motivation to exercise. Behavior modification techniques to modify undesirable participant motives are certainly appropriate in some settings.

Developing a Realistic View of Motivation

Motivation is a key variable in both learning and performance in sport and exercise contexts. People

As a leader, recognize that you are critical to the motivational environment and that you influence motivation both directly and indirectly.

sometimes forget, however, that motivation is not the only variable influencing behavior. Sportswriters, for instance, typically ascribe a team's performance to motivational attributes—the extraordinary efforts of the players; laziness; the lack of incentives that follow from million-dollar, no-cut professional contracts; or a player's ability (or inability) to play in clutch situations. A team's performance, however, often hinges on nonmotivational factors, such as injury, playing a better team, being overtrained, or failing to learn new skills. Besides the motivational factors of primary concern to us here, biomechanical, physiological, sociological, medical, and technical-tactical factors are also significant to sport and exercise, and they warrant consideration in any analysis of performance.

Some motivational factors are more easily influenced than others. It is easier for an exercise leader to change her reinforcement pattern, for instance, than it is for her to change the attractiveness of the building. (This is not to imply that cleaning up a facility is too time-consuming to be worth the trouble. Consider, for example, how important facility attractiveness is in the health club business.) Professionals need to consider what motivational factors they can influence and how much time (and money) it will take to change them. As you read the case study later in this chapter, think about how to realistically develop effective strategies for enhancing participant motivation.

Achievement Motivation and Competitiveness

Throughout the first part of the chapter we have emphasized the importance of individual differences

■ CASE STUDY ■

Breathing Life Into the Gym: A Physical Educator's Plan for Enhancing Student Motivation

Kim is a second-year physical education teacher at Kennedy Junior High School, the oldest building in the district. The school, which is pretty run down, is scheduled to be closed in the next 5 years, so the district doesn't want to invest any money in fixing it up. During the first several weeks of class, Kim notices that her students are not very motivated to participate.

To determine how to motivate her students, Kim narrowly examines her own program. She realizes she is using a fairly standard program based on the required curriculum, and begins to think of ways to modernize the routine. First, she notices the gym itself is serviceable, but dingy with use and age.

Kim realizes that student motivation would likely improve if the facility was revamped, but she also knows that renovation is unlikely. So, she decides to take it into her own hands to improve things. First, she cleans up the gym and gets permission to take the old curtains down. Next, she brightens the gym by backing all the bulletin boards with color and hanging physical fitness posters on the walls. She also talks to the custodian, thanking him for helping get rid of those old curtains and asking about changing his cleaning schedule so the gym gets swept up right after lunch.

Of course Kim realizes that improving the physical environment is not enough to motivate her students to participate in class. She herself must also play an important role. She reminds herself to make positive, encouraging remarks during class and to be upbeat and optimistic. Perhaps the most important thing Kim does to enhance her students' motivation is to ask them what they like and dislike about gym class. Students tell her that fitness testing and exercising at the start of class are not much fun. However, these are mandated in the district curriculum and must be done. (Besides, many of her students are couch potatoes and badly need the exercise!)

Kim works to make the fitness testing a fun part of a goal-setting program, where each class earns points for improvement. She tallies the results on a bulletin board for students to see. The "student of the week" award also focuses on the one youngster who makes the greatest effort and shows the most progress toward her or his fitness goal. Exercising to rap music is also popular with students.

Through talking to her students, Kim is surprised to learn of their interest in sports other than the "old standards," volleyball and basketball. They say they'd like to play tennis, swim, and golf. Unfortunately, swimming and golfing are not possible because of the lack of facilities, but Kim is able to introduce tennis into the curriculum by obtaining racquets and balls through a U.S. Tennis Association program in which recreational players donate their used equipment to the public schools.

At the end of the year, looking back, Kim is generally pleased with the changes in her students' motivation. Sure, some kids are still not interested, but most seem genuinely excited about what they are learning. In addition, the students' fitness scores have improved over those of previous years. Finally, her student-of-the-week program is a big hit—especially for those hard-working students with average skills who are singled out for their personal improvement and effort.

> *Use behavior modification techniques to change undesirable motives and strengthen weak motivation.*

in motivation. In essence, individuals not only participate in sport and physical activity for different reasons, they also are motivated by different methods and situations. Therefore, it is important to understand why some people seem so highly motivated to achieve their goals (like Dan in the football example at the beginning of the chapter) and others seem to go along for the ride. We will start by discussing two related motives for affecting performance and participation in sport: achievement motivation and competitiveness.

What Is Achievement Motivation?

Achievement motivation refers to a person's efforts to master a task, achieve excellence, overcome obstacles, perform better than others, and take pride in exercising talent (Murray, 1938). It is a person's orientation to strive for task success, persist in the face of failure, and experience pride in accomplishments (Gill, 1986).

Not surprisingly, coaches, exercise leaders, and teachers have an interest in achievement motivation: These are the precise characteristics that allow athletes to achieve excellence, exercisers to gain high levels of fitness, and students to maximize learning.

Like the general views of motivation and personality, views of achievement motivation in particular have progressed from a trait-oriented view of a person's "need" for achievement to an interactional view that emphasizes more changeable achievement goals and how these affect and are affected by the situation. Achievement motivation in sport is popularly called competitiveness.

What Is Competitiveness?

Competitiveness is defined as "a disposition to strive for satisfaction when making comparisons with some standard of excellence in the presence of evaluative others" (Martens, 1976, p. 3). Basically, Martens views competitiveness as achievement behavior in a competitive context, with social evaluation as a key component. It is important to look at a situation-specific achievement orientation: Some people who are highly oriented toward achievement in one setting (e.g., competitive sports) are not in other settings (e.g., math class).

Martens's definition of competitiveness is limited to those situations where one is evaluated by or has the potential to be evaluated by knowledgeable others. Yet many people compete with themselves (e.g., trying to exceed your own running time from the previous day), even when no one else evaluates the performance. The level of achievement motivation would bring out this self-competition, whereas the level of competitiveness would influence behavior in socially evaluated situations. For this reason, we discuss achievement motivation and competitiveness together in this chapter.

Effects of Motivation

Achievement motivation and competitiveness deal not just with the final outcome or the pursuit of excellence—they deal also with the psychological journey of getting there. If we understand why motivation differences occur in people, we can intervene positively. Thus, we are interested in how a person's competitiveness and achievement motivation influence a wide variety of behaviors, thoughts, and feelings, including the following:

- Choice of activity (e.g., seeking out opponents of equal ability to compete against or looking for players of greater or lesser ability to play with)
- Effort to pursue goals (e.g., how often you practice)
- Intensity of effort in the pursuit of goals (e.g., how consistently hard you try during a workout)
- Persistence in the face of failure and adversity (e.g., when the going gets tough, do you work harder or take it easier?)

Theories of Achievement Motivation

Four theories have evolved over the years to explain what motivates people to act. They are need achievement theory, attribution theory, achievement goal theory, and competence motivation theory. We will consider each of these in turn.

Need Achievement Theory

Need achievement theory (Atkinson, 1974; McClelland, 1961) is an interactional view that considers both personal and situational factors as important predictors of behavior. Five components make up this theory, including personality factors or motives, situational factors, resultant tendencies, emotional reactions, and achievement-related behaviors (see Figure 3.4).

Personality Factors

According to the need achievement view, each of us has two underlying achievement motives: to achieve success and to avoid failure (see Figure 3.4). The motive to achieve success is defined as "the capacity to experience pride or satisfaction in accomplishments," whereas the motive to avoid failure is "the capacity to experience shame or humiliation as a consequence of failure" (Gill, 1986, p. 60). The theory contends that behavior will be influenced by balance of these motives. In particular, high achievers demonstrate high motivation to achieve success and low motivation to avoid failure. They enjoy evaluating their abilities and are not preoccupied with thoughts of failure. In contrast, low achievers demonstrate low motivation to achieve success and high motivation to avoid failure. They worry and are preoccupied with thoughts of failure. The theory makes no clear predictions for those with moderate or other levels of each motive (Gill, 1986).

Situational Factors

As you learned in chapter 2, information about traits alone is not enough to accurately predict behavior. Situations must also be considered. There are two primary considerations you should recognize in need achievement theory: the probability of success in the situation or task and the incentive value of success. Basically, the probability of success depends on whom you compete against and the difficulty of the task. That is, your chance of winning a tennis match would be lower against Martina Hingis than against a novice. The value you place on success, however, would be greater, as it is more satisfying to beat a skilled opponent than it is to beat a beginner. Settings that offer a 50-50 chance of succeeding (e.g., a difficult but attainable challenge) provide high achievers the most incentive for engaging in achievement behavior. However, low achievers do not see it this way, because to them losing to an evenly matched opponent might maximize their feeling shame.

Resultant Tendencies

The third component in Figure 3.4 is the resultant or behavioral tendency, derived by considering an individual's achievement motive levels in relation to situational factors (e.g., probability of success or incentive value of success). The theory is best at predicting situations where there is a 50-50 chance of success. That is, high achievers seek out challenges in this situation because they enjoy competing against others of equal ability or performing tasks that are not too easy or too difficult.

Low achievers, on the other hand, avoid such challenges, instead opting either for easy tasks where success is guaranteed or for unrealistically hard tasks where failure is almost certain. Low achievers sometimes prefer very difficult tasks because no one expects them to win. For example, losing to Michael

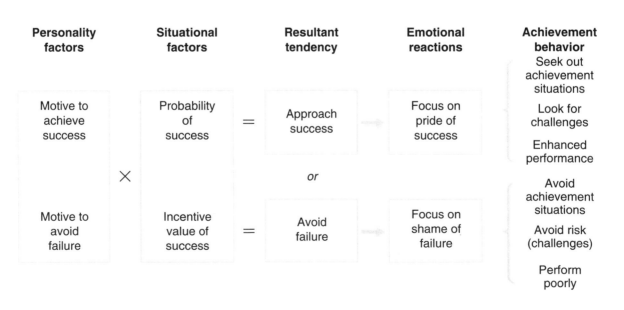

Figure 3.4 *Need achievement theory.*

Jordan one-on-one in basketball certainly would not cause shame or embarrassment. Low achievers do not fear failure—they fear the negative evaluation associated with failure. A 50-50 chance of success causes maximum uncertainty and worry, and thus it increases the possibility of demonstrating low ability or competence. If low achievers cannot avoid such a situation, they become preoccupied and distraught because of their high need to avoid failure.

Emotional Reactions

The fourth component of the need achievement theory is the individual's emotional reactions, specifically how much pride and shame he or she experiences. Both high and low achievers want to experience pride and minimize shame, but their personality characteristics interact differently with the situation to cause them to focus more on either pride or shame. High achievers focus more on pride, whereas low achievers focus more on shame and worry.

Achievement Behavior

The fifth component of the need achievement theory indicates how the four previous components interact to influence behavior. High achievers select more challenging tasks, prefer intermediate risks, and perform better in evaluative situations. Low achievers avoid intermediate risk, perform worse in evaluative situations, and avoid challenging tasks—by selecting tasks so difficult they are certain to fail or tasks so easy they are guaranteed success.

Achievement motivation is the tendency to strive for success, persist in the face of failure, and experience pride in accomplishments. Achievement motivation in sport and exercise settings focuses on self-competition, whereas competitiveness influences behavior in socially evaluative situations.

High achievers select challenging tasks, prefer intermediate risks, and perform better when evaluated. Low achievers avoid challenging tasks, avoid intermediate risks, and perform worse when evaluated.

The Significance of Need Achievement Theory

These performance predictions of the need achievement theory serve as the framework for all contemporary achievement motivation explanations. That is, even though more recent theories offer different explanations for the thought processes underlying achievement differences, the behavioral predictions between high and low achievers are basically the same. The most important contribution of need achievement theory is its task preference and performance predictions.

Attribution Theory

Attribution theory focuses on how people *explain* their successes and failures. This view, originated by Heider (1958) and extended and popularized by Weiner (1985, 1986), holds that literally thousands of possible explanations for success and failure can be classified into a few categories (see Figure 3.5). These most basic attribution categories are **stability** (being either fairly permanent or unstable), **locus of causality** (whether the cause of one's behavior is external or internal to him- or herself), and **locus of control** (a factor that is or is not under our control.

Attributions as Causes of Success and Failure

A performer's success or failure can be attributed to a variety of possible explanations (attributions). For example, you may win a swimming race and attribute your success to

- a stable factor (e.g., your talent or good ability) or an unstable factor (e.g., good luck),
- an internal cause (e.g., your tremendous effort in the last 50 meters) or an external cause (e.g., an easy field of competitors), and
- a factor you can control (e.g., your race plan) or a factor out of your control (e.g., your opponents' physical conditioning).

Or you may drop out of an exercise program and attribute your failure to

- a stable factor (e.g., your lack of talent) or an unstable factor (e.g., the terrible instructor),

Attribution theory focuses on how individuals explain their successes and failures.

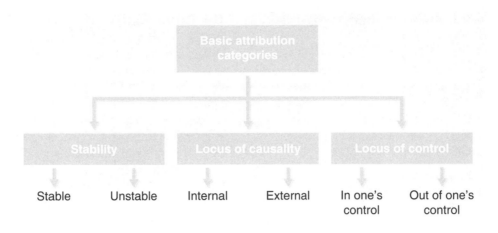

Figure 3.5 *Weiner's basic attribution categories.*

■ an internal cause (e.g., your bad back) or an external cause (e.g., the exercise facility's being too far from your home), and

■ a factor you can control (e.g., your lack of effort) or a factor out of your control (e.g., the cost of the program).

Why Attributions Are Important

Attributions affect expectations of future success or failure and emotional reactions (Biddle, 1993; McAuley, 1993b). Attributing performance to certain types of stable factors has been linked to expectations of future success. For example, if Susie, an elementary physical education student, ascribes her gymnastics performance success to a stable cause (e.g., her high ability), she will expect the outcome to occur again in the future and will be more motivated and confident. She may even ask her parents if she can sign up for after-school gymnastics. In contrast, if Zachary attributes his performance success in tumbling to an unstable cause (e.g., luck), he won't expect it to occur regularly and his motivation and confidence will not be enhanced. He probably wouldn't pursue after-school gymnastics. Of course, a failure also can be ascribed to a stable cause, such as low ability, which would lessen confidence and motivation, or to an unstable cause (e.g., luck), which would not.

> *How performers explain or attribute their performance affects their expectations and emotional reactions, which in turn influence future achievement motivation.*

Attributions to internal factors and to factors in our control (e.g., ability, effort) rather than to external factors or factors outside our control (e.g., luck, task difficulty) often result in emotional reactions like pride and shame. For example, a lacrosse player will experience more pride (if successful) or shame (if unsuccessful) if she attributes performance to internal factors than she would if she attributes it to luck or an opponent's skill (see Table 3.1).

Achievement Goal Theory

Recently both psychologists and sport exercise psychologists have focused on achievement goals as a way of understanding differences in achievement (Duda, 1993; Dweck, 1986; Maehr & Nicholls, 1980; Nicholls, 1984; Roberts, 1993). According to the **achievement goal theory**, three factors interact to determine a person's motivation: achievement goals, perceived ability, and achievement behavior (see Figure 3.6). To understand someone's motivation, we must understand what success and failure mean to that person. And the best way to do that is to examine a person's achievement goals and how they interact with his or her perceptions, or perceived ability, of competence (self-worth).

Outcome and Task Orientations

Holly may compete in bodybuilding because she wants to win trophies and have the best physique of anybody in the area. She has adopted an **outcome goal orientation** (also called a **competitive goal orientation**), where the focus is on comparing herself with and defeating others. Holly feels good about herself (has high perceived ability) when she wins, but not so good about herself (has low perceived ability) when she loses.

Table 3.1

Attributions and Achievement Motivation

Attributions	Psychological result
STABILITY FACTORS	**EXPECTANCY OF FUTURE SUCCESS**
Stable	Increased expectation of success
Unstable	Decreased expectation of success
CAUSALITY FACTORS	**EMOTIONAL INFLUENCES**
Internal cause	Increased pride or shame
External cause	Decreased pride or shame
CONTROL FACTORS	**EMOTIONAL INFLUENCES**
In one's control	Increased motivation
Out of one's control	Decreased motivation

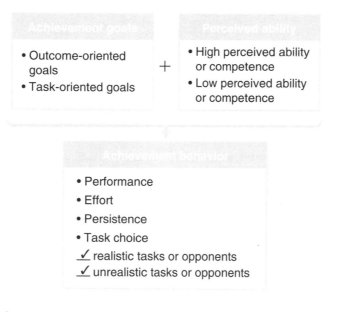

Figure 3.6 *Three key factors in the achievement goal approach.*

Sarah also likes to win contests, but she primarily takes part in bodybuilding to see how much she can improve her strength and physique. She has adopted a task goal orientation (also called a mastery goal orientation), where the focus is on improving relative to her own past performances. Her perceived ability is not based on a comparison with others.

For a particular situation, some people can be both task and outcome oriented. For example, a person might want to win the local turkey trot but also to set a personal best time for the race. However, according to researchers in achievement goal orientation, most people tend to be higher on either task or outcome orientation.

The Value of a Task Orientation

Sport psychologists argue that a task orientation more often than an outcome orientation will lead to a strong work ethic, persistence in the face of failure, and optimal performance. This orientation can protect a person from disappointment, frustration, and a lack of motivation when others exceed his or her performance (which often cannot be controlled). Because focusing on personal performance provides greater control, individuals

61

> *An outcome goal orientation focuses on comparing performance with and defeating others, whereas a task goal orientation focuses on comparing performance with personal standards and personal improvement. It is best to adopt a task orientation, which emphasizes comparisons with your own performance standards rather than with the performances of others.*

become more motivated, therefore, and persist longer in the face of failure.

Task-oriented people also select moderately difficult or realistic tasks and opponents. They do not fear failure. And because their perception of ability is based on their own standards of reference, it is easier for them to feel good about themselves and to demonstrate high perceived competence than it is for outcome-oriented individuals.

Problems With Outcome Orientation

In contrast to task-oriented individuals, outcome-oriented people will have more difficulty maintaining high perceived competence. They judge success by how they compare to others, but they cannot necessarily control how others perform. After all, at least half of the competitors must lose, which can lower a fragile perceived competence. People who are outcome oriented and have low perceived competence

demonstrate a low or maladaptive achievement behavioral pattern (Duda, 1993). That is, they are likely to reduce their efforts, cease trying, or make excuses. To protect their self-worth they are more likely to select tasks where they are guaranteed success or where they are so outmatched no one would expect them to do well. They tend to perform less well in evaluative situations (see the case study below).

Importance of Motivational Climate

In recent years sport psychologists have not only studied how goal orientations and perceived ability work together to influence motivation of physical activity participants but also how the social climate influences one's goal orientations and motivation level (Ntoumanis & Biddle, 1997). Some psychologists now contend, for example, that the social climates of achievement settings can vary significantly in several dimensions. These include such things as the tasks that learners are asked to perform, student-teacher authority patterns, recognition systems, student ability groupings, evaluation procedures, and times allotted for activities to be performed (Ames, 1992).

Research has revealed that in a motivational climate of mastery or task goal orientation there are more adaptive motivational patterns, such as positive attitudes, increased effort, and effective learning strategies. In contrast, a motivational climate of outcome orientation has been linked with less adaptive motivational patterns, such as low persistence, low effort, and attributing failures to [low] ability (Ntoumanis & Biddle, 1997).

■ CASE STUDY ■

Problems Associated With an Outcome Goal Orientation

After years of hard work, Dave became a member of the U.S. Ski Team. He had always set outcome goals for himself: becoming the fastest skier in his local club, winning regional races, beating arch rivals, and placing at nationals. Unfortunately, he got off to a rocky start on the World Cup circuit. He wanted to be the fastest American downhiller and to place in the top three at each World Cup race, but with so many good racers it became impossible to beat them consistently. To make matters worse, because of his lowered world ranking Dave skis well back in the pack (after the course has been chopped up by the previous competitors), which makes it virtually impossible to place in the top three.

As Dave becomes more frustrated by his failures, his motivation declines. He no longer looks forward to competitions; he either skis out of control, focused entirely on finishing first, or skis such a safe line through the course that he finishes well back in the field. Dave blames his poor finishes on the wrong ski wax and equipment. He does not realize that his outcome goal orientation, which served him well at the lower levels of competition where he could more easily win, is now leading as well to lower confidence, self-doubts, and less motivation.

Most importantly, researchers think that motivational climates influence the types of achievement goals participants adopt, with task-oriented climates being associated with task goals and outcome-oriented climates with outcome goals. This certainly suggests that coaches, teachers, and exercise leaders play an important role in facilitating motivation through the psychological climates they create.

Competence Motivation Theory

A final theory that has been used to explain differences in achievement behavior, especially in children, is competence motivation theory (Weiss & Chaumeton, 1992). Based on the work of developmental psychologist Susan Harter (1988), this theory holds that people are motivated to feel worthy or competent and, moreover, such feelings are the primary determinants of motivation (see Figure 3.7). The competence motivation theory also contends that athletes' perceptions of control (feeling control over whether they can learn and perform skills) work along with self-worth and competence evaluations to influence their motivation. However, these feelings do not influence motivation directly. Rather, they influence affective or emotional states (such as enjoyment, anxiety, pride, and shame) that in turn influence motivation.

If a young soccer player, for example, has high self-esteem, feels competent, and perceives that he or she has control over the learning and performance of soccer skills, then efforts to learn the game will increase his or her enjoyment, pride, and happiness. These positive affective states will in turn lead to increased motivation. In contrast, if an exerciser has low self-esteem, feels incompetent and that personal actions have little bearing on increasing fitness, negative affective responses will result, such as anxiety, shame, and sadness. These feelings will lead to a decline in motivation.

Considerable research has demonstrated the link between competence and motivation (Weiss, 1993). The left side of the model (see Figure 3.7) also shows that feedback and reinforcement from others and various motivational orientations (such as goal orientations and trait anxiety) influence feelings of self-esteem, competence, and control. Wong and Bridges (1995) tested this model using 108 youth soccer players and their coaches. They measured perceived competence, perceived control, trait anxiety, and motivation, as well as various coaching behaviors. As you might expect, they found that trait anxiety and coaching behaviors predicted perceived competence and control, which in turn were related to the player's motivation levels. Hence, the perceptions of competence and control that young athletes have are critical determinants of whether they will strive toward achievement. This tells you that enhancing perceived competence and control should be primary goals of professionals in exercise and sport science.

What Theories of Achievement Motivation Tell Us

To compare how these four theories explain achievement motivation, Table 3.2 summarizes major predictions from each of them, showing how high and

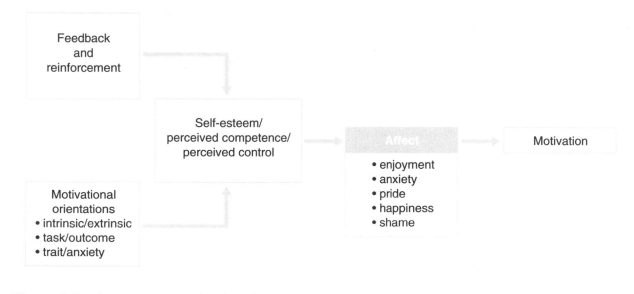

Figure 3.7 *Competence motivation theory.*
Adapted from Weiss and Chaumeton, 1992.

■ APPLICATION ■

Guiding Achievement Orientation and Competitiveness

- Consider the interaction of personal and situational factors in influencing achievement behavior.
- Emphasize task or mastery goals and downplay outcome goals.
- Monitor and alter your attributional feedback.
- Assess and correct inappropriate participant attributions.
- Help participants determine when to compete and when to focus on individual improvement.
- Enhance perceptions of competence and control.

Table 3.2

What Theories of Achievement Motivation Tell Us

	High achiever	Low achiever
Motivational orientation	High motivation to achieve success	Low motivation to achieve success
	Low motivation to achieve failure	High motivation to achieve failure
	Focuses on the pride of success	Focuses on shame and worry that may result from failure
Attributions	Ascribes success to stable and internal factors within one's control	Ascribes success to unstable and external factors outside one's control
	Ascribes failure to unstable and external factors outside one's control	Ascribes failure to stable and internal factors within one's control
Goals adopted	Usually adopts task goals	Usually adopts outcome goals
Perceived competence/ control	Has high perceived competence and feels that achievement is within his or her control	Has low perceived competence and feels that achievement is outside his or her control
Task choice	Seeks out challenges and able competitors/tasks	Avoids challenges; seeks out very difficult or very easy tasks/competitors
Performance	Performs well in evaluative conditions	Performs poorly in evaluative conditions

low achievers differ in terms of their motivational orientation and attributions, the goals they adopt, their task choices, perceived competence and control, and their performance. We next discuss how a person's achievement motivation and competitiveness develop.

Developing Achievement Motivation and Competitiveness

Do you learn achievement motivation? At what age do children develop achievement tendencies? Can sport and exercise professionals influence and motivate children toward certain kinds of achievement?

Achievement motivation and competitiveness are believed to develop in three stages (Scanlan, 1988; Veroff, 1969). These stages are sequential—that is, you must move through one stage before progressing to the next (see Figure 3.8). Not everyone makes it to the final stage, and the age at which each stage is reached varies considerably. These are the three stages:

1. Autonomous competence stage. In this stage, which is thought to occur before the age of 4 years, a

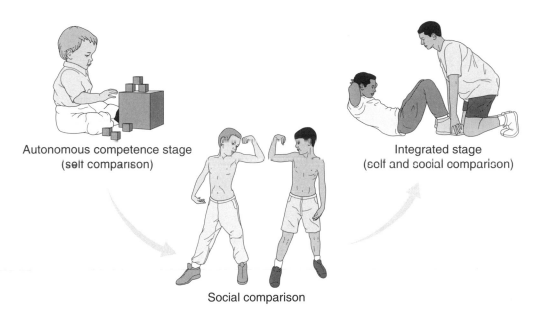

Autonomous competence stage
(self comparison)

Social comparison

Integrated stage
(self and social comparison)

Figure 3.8 *Three stages in the development of achievement motivation.*

child focuses on mastering his or her environment and on self-testing. For example, Brandon is a preschooler who is highly motivated to learn to ride his tricycle, and he couldn't care less that his sister Eileen can ride better than he can. He rarely compares himself to others.

2. Social comparison stage. In the social comparison stage, which begins at about the age of 5 years, a child focuses on directly comparing his or her performance to others, unlike the autonomous stage with its self-referenced standards. This is the "Who is faster, bigger, smarter, and stronger stage?" as children seem preoccupied with comparing themselves to others.

3. Integrated stage. The integrated stage involves both social comparison and autonomous achievement strategies. The person who fully masters this integration knows when it is appropriate to compete and compare him- or herself to others and when it is appropriate to adopt self-referenced standards. This stage, which integrates components from the previous two stages, is the most desirable. There is no typical age for entering this stage.

The Importance of Distinguishing Between Stages

Recognizing the developmental stages of achievement motivation and competitiveness helps us to understand better the behavior of people we work with, especially children. Thus, we will not be surprised when a preschooler is disinterested in competition or when

fourth and fifth graders seem preoccupied with it. An integrated achievement orientation, however, must ultimately be developed, and it is important to teach children when it is appropriate or inappropriate to compete and compare themselves socially.

Influencing Stages of Achievement Motivation

The social environment in which a person functions has important implications for achievement motivation and competitiveness. Significant others can play an important role in creating a positive or negative climate.

Parents, teachers, and coaches all play especially important roles. Teachers and coaches directly and indirectly create motivational climates. They define tasks and games as competitive or cooperative, group children in certain ways (e.g., picking teams through a public draft where social comparison openly occurs), and differentially emphasize task or outcome goals (Ames, 1987; Roberts, 1993).

As professionals we can play significant roles in creating climates that enhance participant achievement motivation. For example, Treasure and Roberts (1995) created both task and outcome motivational climates in a youth soccer physical education class study. They found that after 10 sessions of having players participate in each climate, players who performed in the mastery climate focused more on effort, were more satisfied, and preferred more challenging tasks than outcome-climate participants. Hence, motivational climate influenced the students' achievement motivation.

Using Achievement Motivation in Professional Practice

Now that you have a better understanding of what achievement motivation and competitiveness involve and how they develop and influence psychological states, you can draw implications for professional practice. To help you consolidate your understanding, we will now discuss some methods you can use to help people you work with.

Recognize Interactional Factors in Achievement Motivation

You know now that the interaction of personal and situational factors influences the motivation particular students, athletes, and exercisers have to achieve. What should you watch for to guide your practice? In essence you assess the participants'

- stage of achievement motivation,
- goal orientations,
- attributions they typically make about their performances, and
- situations they tend to approach or avoid.

Let's take two examples. Jose performs well in competition, seeks out challenges, sets mastery goals, and attributes success to stable internal factors such as his ability. These are desirable behaviors, and he is most likely a high achiever. You see, however, that Felix avoids competitors of equal ability, gravitates toward extreme competitive situations—where either success or failure is almost certain—focuses on outcome goals, becomes tense in competitions, and attributes failure to his low ability (or success to external, unstable factors, such as luck). He demonstrates maladaptive achievement behavior, and he will need your help and guidance.

Felix may even suffer from **learned helplessness**, an acquired condition in which a person perceives that his or her actions have no effect on the desired outcome of a task or skill (Dweck, 1980). In other words, the person feels doomed to failure and that

■ CASE STUDY ■

Helpless and Hopeless Johnny

Johnny is a fifth grader in Ms. Roalston's second-period physical education class. He is not a very gifted student, but he can improve with consistent effort. However, after observing and getting to know Johnny, Ms. Roalston has become increasingly concerned. He demonstrates many of the characteristics of learned helplessness that she learned about in her university sport psychology and sport pedagogy classes.

- Johnny seldom tries new skills, usually opting instead to go to the back of the line.
- When Johnny does try a new skill and fails in his first attempt, he asks why he should even try since he's no good at sports.
- His reaction to initial failure is embarrassment and decreased effort.
- He feels so bad about his physical competence that he just wants to get out of the gym as quickly as possible.

Johnny has all the characteristics of learned helplessness. Ms. Roalston remembers that learned helplessness is not a personality flaw or Johnny's fault. Rather, it results from an outcome goal orientation, maladaptive achievement tendencies, previous negative experiences with physical activity, and attributing performance to uncontrollable, stable factors, especially low ability. Equally important, learned helplessness can vary from being specific to a particular activity (e.g., learning to catch a baseball) to being more general (e.g., learning any sport skill). Ms. Roalston knows that learned helplessness can be overcome by giving Johnny some individual attention, repeatedly emphasizing mastery goals, and downplaying outcome goals. Attributional retraining or getting Johnny to change his low-ability attributions for failure will also help him. It will take some time and hard work, but she intends to make helping get Johnny out of his helpless hole a major goal for the year.

nothing can be done about it. He or she probably makes unhelpful attributions for failure and feels generally incompetent (see the box on p. 66).

Emphasize Task Goals

There are several ways to help prevent maladaptive achievement tendencies or rectify learned helpless states. One of the most important strategies is to help people set task goals and downplay outcome goals. Society emphasizes athletic outcomes and student grades so much that downplaying outcome goals is not always easy to do. Luckily, however, sport and exercise psychologists have learned a great deal about goal setting (see more in chapter 15).

Monitor and Alter Attributional Feedback

In addition to downplaying outcome goals and emphasizing task or individual-specific mastery goals, it is crucial that you be conscious of the attributions you make while giving feedback. It is not unusual for teachers, coaches, or exercise leaders to unknowingly convey subtle but powerful messages through the attributions that accompany their feedback. Adults influence a child's interpretations of performance success—and future motivation— by how they give feedback (Horn, 1987). For example, notice how this physical educator provides feedback to a child in a volleyball instructional setting:

> *You did not bump the ball correctly. Bend your knees more and contact the ball with your forearms. Try harder—you'll get it with practice.*

The coach not only conveys instructional information to the young athlete but also informs the child that he can accomplish the task. The instructor also includes the message that persistence and effort pay off.

In contrast, consider the effects of telling that same child the following:

> *You did not bump the ball correctly! Your knees were not bent and you did not use your forearms. Don't worry, though—I know baseball is your game, not volleyball.*

Although well-meaning, this message informs the young athlete that he will not be good at volleyball, so don't bother trying. Of course you should not make unrealistic attributions (e.g., telling an exerciser that

with continued work and effort she will look like a model when in fact her body type makes this unlikely). Rather, the key is to emphasize mastery goals by focusing on individual improvement and then link attributions to those individual goals (e.g., "I'll be honest. You'll never have a body like Cindy Crawford, but with hard work you can look and feel a lot better than you do now").

When you work with children, attributing performance failure to their low effort may be effective only if they believe they have the skills they need to ultimately achieve the task (Horn, 1987). If Jimmy feels that he is totally inept at basketball, telling him that he didn't learn to dribble because he did not try will not increase his achievement motivation—it may only reinforce his low perception of ability. Do not make low-effort attributions with children under the age of 9 unless you also reassure them that they have the skills to accomplish the task. Most importantly, the child must believe he has the skills to perform the task.

Assess and Correct Inappropriate Attributions

It is important to monitor and correct inappropriate or maladaptive attributions that participants make of themselves. Many performers who fail (especially those with learned helplessness) attribute their failure to low ability, saying things like "I stink" or "Why even try? I just don't have it." Teaching children in classroom situations to replace their lack-of-ability attributions with lack-of-effort attributions helped them alleviate performance decrements after failure—it was more effective even than actual success (Dweck, 1975)! If you hear students or clients make incorrect attributions for successful performances, such as "That was a lucky shot," correct them and indicate that it was hard work and practice that made the shot successful, not luck. You have an important responsibility to ensure that participants use attributions that will facilitate achievement motivation and efforts.

> *Teaching children in classroom situations to replace lack-of-ability attributions with lack-of-effort attributions helped alleviate performance decrements following failure.*

Table 3.3

Attributional Guidelines for Providing Instructor Feedback

	Dos	Don'ts
Student/client failure	Emphasize the need to try harder and exert effort. However, link such attributions to individual goals and capabilities.	Make low ability attributions that signify that a lack of personal improvement isn't possible.
Student/client success	Attribute success to ability. Attribute success to high effort.	Attribute success to luck. Attribute success to task ease.
General		Make insincere or false attributions of any kind.

Make consistent and repeated use of achievement motivation strategies.

Determine When Competitive Goals Are Appropriate

You are also responsible for helping participants determine when it is appropriate to compete and when it is appropriate to focus on individual improvement. Competing is sometimes a necessity in society (for example, to make an athletic team or to gain admission to a selective college). At times, however, competing against others is counterproductive. You wouldn't encourage a basketball player to not pass off to teammates who have better shots or a cardiac rehabilitation patient to exceed the safe training zone to be the fastest jogger in the group.

The key, then, is developing judgment. Through discussion you can help students, athletes, and exercisers make good decisions in this area. Society emphasizes social evaluation and competitive outcomes so much that you will need to counterbalance by stressing a task (as compared to an outcome) orientation (see chapter 5 for additional guidelines). Talking to someone once or twice about this issue is not enough: Consistent, repeated efforts are necessary to promote good judgment about appropriate competition.

Enhance Feelings of Competence and Control

Enhancing perceived competence and feelings of control are critical ways to foster achievement motivation in physical activity participants, especially children (Weiss, 1993). You can do so by keeping practices and competitions fun as well as achievement-focused and by matching participant skills and abilities. Instructors can enhance competence by using appropriate feedback and reinforcement and by helping create individualized challenges and goals for participants (see chapters 6 and 15, respectively). Maximizing the *involvement* of all participants is critical for enhancing competence. You can find additional means of enhancing competence in chapter 14.

SUMMARY

1 *Define motivation and its components.*

Motivation can be defined as the direction and intensity of effort. The direction of effort refers to whether an individual seeks out, approaches, or is attracted to certain situations. The intensity of effort refers to how much effort a person puts forth in a particular situation.

2 *Describe typical views of motivation and whether they are useful.*

Three views of motivation include the trait-centered view, the situation-centered view, and the interactional view. Among these models of motivation, the participant-by-situation, interactional view is the most useful for guiding professional practice.

3 *Detail useful guidelines for building motivation.*

Five fundamental observations, derived from the interactional view of motivation, make good guidelines for practice. First, participants are motivated both by their internal traits and by situations, and, second, it is important to understand their motives for involvement. Third, structure situations to meet the needs of participants. Fourth, recognize that as a teacher, coach, or exercise leader you play a critical role in the motivational environment, and, fifth, use behavior modification to change undesirable participant motives. Furthermore, you must also develop a realistic view of motivation. Recognize that other, nonmotivational factors influence sport performance and behavior and learn to assess whether motivational factors may be readily changed.

4 *Define achievement motivation and competitiveness and indicate why they are important.*

Achievement motivation refers to a person's efforts to master a task, achieve excellence, overcome obstacles, perform better than others, and take pride in exercising talent. Competitiveness is a disposition to strive for satisfaction when making comparisons with some standard of excellence in the presence of evaluative others. These notions are important because they help us understand why some people seem so motivated to achieve and others seem simply to "go along for the ride."

5 *Compare and contrast theories of achievement motivation.*

Theories of achievement motivation include the (a) need achievement theory, (b) attribution theory, (c) achievement goal theory, and (d) competence motivation theory. Together these theories suggest that high and low achievers can be distinguished by their motives, the tasks they select to be evaluated on, the effort they exert during competition, their persistence, and their performance. High achievers usually adopt mastery (task) goals and have high perceptions of their ability and control. They attribute successes to stable and internal factors like high ability; they attribute failure to unstable, controllable factors like low effort. Low achievers, on the other hand, usually have low perceived ability and control, judge themselves more on outcome goals, and attribute successes to luck or ease of the task (external, uncontrollable factors); they attribute failure to low ability (an internal, stable attribute).

6 *Explain how achievement motivation develops.*

Achievement motivation and its sport-specific counterpart, competitiveness, develop through stages that include (a) an autonomous stage when the individual focuses on mastery of her environment, (b) a social comparison stage when the individual compares herself with others, and (c) an integrated stage when the individual both focuses on self-improvement and uses social comparison. The goal is for the individual to reach an autonomous, integrated stage and to know when it is appropriate to compete and compare socially and when to instead adopt a self-referenced focus of comparison.

7 *Use fundamentals of achievement motivation to guide practice.*

Parents, teachers, and coaches significantly influence the achievement motivation of children. They can create climates that enhance achievement and counteract learned helplessness. They can best do this by (a) recognizing interactional influences on achievement motivation, (b) emphasizing individual task goals and downplaying outcome goals, (c) monitoring and providing appropriate attributional feedback, (d) teaching participants to make appropriate attributions, (e) discussing with participants when it is appropriate to compete and compare themselves socially and when it is appropriate to adopt a self-referenced focus, and (f) facilitating perceptions of competence and control.

KEY TERMS

motivation
direction of effort
intensity of effort
trait-centered view
   (participant-centered view)
situation-centered orientation
interactional view
achievement motivation
competitiveness
need achievement theory
probability of success
incentive value of success

resultant tendency (behavioral tendency)
attribution theory
stability
locus of causality
locus of control
achievement goal theory
outcome goal orientation
   (competitive goal orientation)
task goal orientation
   (mastery goal orientation)
competence motivation theory
learned helplessness

REVIEW QUESTIONS

1. Explain the direction and intensity aspects of motivation.
2. Identify three general views of motivation. Which should be used to guide practice?
3. How does the swimming-relay study (by Sorrentino and Sheppard) support the interactional model of motivation?
4. Describe five fundamental guidelines of motivation for professional practice.
5. What are the primary motives people have for participating in sport? What are their primary motives for participating in exercise activities?
6. When is it appropriate to use behavior modification techniques to alter motivation for sport and exercise involvement?
7. What major factors besides motivation should you consider to understand performance and behavior in exercise and sport settings?
8. Give examples of motivational factors that are readily influenced.
9. What is the difference between achievement motivation and competitiveness?
10. In what ways does achievement motivation influence participant behavior?
11. Explain and distinguish four theories to explain achievement motivation.
12. How do high and low achievers differ in the types of challenges and tasks they select?
13. What are attributions? Why are they important in helping understand achievement motivation in sport and exercise settings?
14. Distinguish between an outcome (competitive) versus a task (mastery) goal orientation. Which should be most emphasized in sport, physical education, and exercise settings? Why?
15. Identify the three stages of achievement motivation and competitiveness. Why are these important?
16. Discuss how a teacher's or coach's attributional feedback influences participant achievement?
17. What is learned helplessness? Why is it important?

CRITICAL THINKING QUESTIONS

1. List at least three ways to better understand someone's motives for sport and physical activity involvement.
2. Design a program to eliminate learned helplessness in performers. Be sure to indicate how you will foster an appropriate motivational climate.

© Human Kinetics

Arousal, Stress, and Anxiety

After reading this chapter you should be able to

1 discuss the nature of stress and anxiety (what it is and how it is measured),

2 identify the major sources of anxiety and stress,

3 explain how and why arousal and anxiety-related emotions affect performance, and

4 compare and contrast ways to regulate arousal, stress, and anxiety.

Jason comes to bat in the bottom of the final inning with two outs and two men on base. With a hit his team will win the district championship; with an out his team will lose the biggest game of the season. Jason steps into the batter's box, his heart pounding and butterflies in his stomach, and has trouble maintaining concentration. He thinks of what a win will mean for his team and of what people might think of him if he does not deliver. Planting his cleats in the dirt, Jason squeezes the bat, says a little prayer, and awaits the first pitch.

If you're involved in athletics, you have probably faced the elevated arousal and anxiety of situations such as Jason's. Sport and exercise psychologists have long studied the causes and effects of arousal, stress, and anxiety in the competitive athletic environment and other areas of physical activity. Many health care professionals are interested in both the physiological and psychological benefits of regular exercise. Does regular exercise lower stress levels? Will patients with severe anxiety disorders benefit from intensive aerobic training and need less medication? Consider how stress-provoking learning to swim can be for people who have had a bad experience in water. How can teachers reduce this anxiety?

Defining Arousal, Stress, and Anxiety

Although many people use the terms arousal, stress, and anxiety interchangeably, sport and exercise psychologists find it important to distinguish among them. They use precise definitions for the phenomena they study to have a common language, reduce confusion, and diminish the need for long explanations.

Arousal

Arousal is a blend of physiological and psychological activity in a person, and it refers to the intensity dimen-

> *Arousal is a general physiological and psychological activation, varying on a continuum from deep sleep to intense excitement.*

sions of motivation at a particular moment. The intensity of arousal falls along a continuum (see Figure 4.1) ranging from not at all aroused (i.e., comatose) to completely aroused (i.e., frenzied; see Gould, Greenleaf, & Krane, in press). Highly aroused individuals are mentally and physically activated; they experience increased heart rates, respiration, and sweating. Arousal is not automatically associated with either pleasant or unpleasant events. You might be highly aroused by learning you have won $10 million. You might be equally aroused by learning of the death of a loved one.

Anxiety

Anxiety is a negative emotional state characterized by nervousness, worry, and apprehension and associated with activation or arousal of the body. Thus, anxiety has a thought component (e.g., worry and apprehension) called **cognitive anxiety.** It also has a **somatic anxiety** component, which is the degree of physical activation perceived. In addition to the distinction between cognitive and somatic anxiety, another important distinction to make is between state and trait anxiety.

State Anxiety

At times we refer to anxiety in discussing a *stable* personality component; other times we use the term

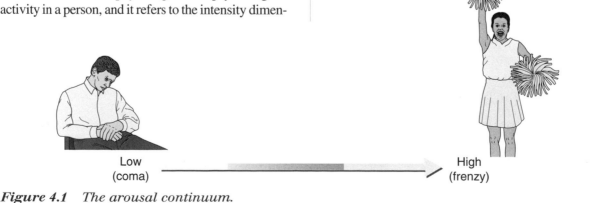

Figure 4.1   *The arousal continuum.*

Low
(coma)

High
(frenzy)

> *Anxiety is a negative emotional state with feelings of nervousness, worry, and apprehension associated with activation or arousal of the body.*

> *State anxiety is a temporary, ever-changing emotional state of subjective, consciously perceived feelings of apprehension and tension, associated with activation of the autonomic nervous system.*

> *Trait anxiety is a behavioral disposition to perceive as threatening circumstances that are objectively not dangerous and to then respond with disproportionate state anxiety. Highly trait-anxious people usually have more state anxiety in highly competitive, evaluative situations than do people with lower trait anxiety.*

to describe a *changing* mood state. **State anxiety** refers to the ever-changing mood component. It is defined more formally as an emotional state "characterized by subjective, consciously perceived feelings of apprehension and tension, accompanied by or associated with activation or arousal of the autonomic nervous system" (Spielberger, 1966, p. 17). For example, a player's level of state anxiety would change from moment to moment during a basketball game. She might have a slightly elevated level of state anxiety (feeling somewhat nervous and noticing her heart pumping) prior to tip-off, a lower level once she settles into the pace of the game, and then an extremely high level (feeling very nervous, with her heart racing) in the closing minutes of a tight contest.

Cognitive state anxiety concerns the degree to which one worries or has negative thoughts, whereas **somatic state anxiety** concerns the moment-to-moment changes in perceived physiological activation. Somatic state anxiety is not necessarily a change in one's physical activation, but one's perception of such a change.

Trait Anxiety

Unlike state anxiety, **trait anxiety** is part of the personality—an acquired behavioral tendency or disposition that influences behavior. In particular, trait anxiety predisposes an individual to perceive as threatening a wide range of circumstances that objectively are not actually dangerous physically or psychologically. The person then responds to these circumstances with state anxiety reactions or levels that are disproportionate in intensity and magnitude to the objective danger (Spielberger, 1966, p. 17).

For instance, two field-goal kickers having equal physical skills may be placed under identical pressure

(e.g., to kick the winning field goal at the end of the game), yet have entirely different state anxiety reactions because of their personalities (that is, their levels of trait anxiety). Rick is more laid-back (low trait-anxious) and does not perceive kicking the game-winning field goal as overly threatening. Thus, he does not experience more state anxiety than would be expected in such a situation. Ted, however, is high trait-anxious and consequently perceives the chance to kick (or, in his view, to miss) the winning field goal as very threatening. He experiences tremendous state anxiety—much more than we would expect in such a situation. (For a summary of the interrelationships among arousal, trait anxiety, and state anxiety, see Figure 4.2.)

Measuring Arousal and Anxiety

Sport and exercise psychologists measure arousal, state anxiety, and trait anxiety in various physiological ways and through psychological measures. To measure arousal they look at changes in these physiological signs: heart rate, respiration, skin conductance (recorded on a voltage meter), and biochemistry (they can assess changes in substances such as catecholamines). They look also at how people rate their arousal level with a series of statements (such as "my heart is pumping," "I feel peppy"), using numerical scales ranging from low to high. These self-perceptions that people report are called **self-reporting measures** or **self-report scales.**

To measure state anxiety psychologists use both global and multidimensional self-report measures. In the global measures people rate how nervous they feel, using self-report scales from low to high. A total score is calculated by summing the scores of individual items. The multidimensional self-report measures are used in about the same way, but people rate how worried (cognitive state anxiety) and how physiologically activated they feel, again using

73

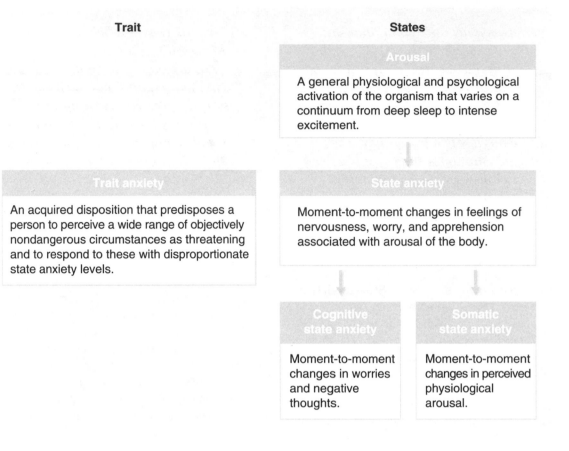

Trait

States

Arousal

A general physiological and psychological activation of the organism that varies on a continuum from deep sleep to intense excitement.

Trait anxiety

An acquired disposition that predisposes a person to perceive a wide range of objectively nondangerous circumstances as threatening and to respond to these with disproportionate state anxiety levels.

State anxiety

Moment-to-moment changes in feelings of nervousness, worry, and apprehension associated with arousal of the body.

Cognitive state anxiety

Moment-to-moment changes in worries and negative thoughts.

Somatic state anxiety

Moment-to-moment changes in perceived physiological arousal.

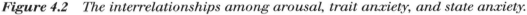

Figure 4.2 *The interrelationships among arousal, trait anxiety, and state anxiety.*

self-report scales ranging from low to high. Subscale scores for cognitive and somatic anxiety are obtained by summing scores for items representing each type of state anxiety.

Psychologists also use global and multidimensional self-reports to measure trait anxiety. The formats for these measures are similar to state anxiety assessments, but instead of people rating how anxious they feel right at that moment, they are asked how they "typically" feel.

To better understand the differences among cognitive state anxiety, somatic state anxiety, and trait anxiety, complete the sample questions from some self-report scales on p. 76.

Relationship Between Trait and State Anxiety

A direct relationship exists between a person's levels of trait anxiety and state anxiety. Research has consistently shown that those who score high on trait anxiety measures also experience more state anxiety in highly competitive, evaluative situations. This re-

lationship is not perfect, however. A highly trait-anxious athlete might have a tremendous amount of experience in a particular situation and for that reason she might not perceive a threat and the corresponding high state anxiety. Similarly, some highly trait-anxious people learn coping skills to reduce the state anxiety they experience in evaluative situations. Still, generally speaking, knowing a person's level of trait anxiety is usually helpful in predicting how he or she will react to competition, evaluation, and threatening conditions.

Stress and the Stress Process

Stress is defined as "a substantial imbalance between demand [physical and/or psychological] and response capability, under conditions where failure to meet that demand has important consequences" (McGrath, 1970, p. 20). It is a process, a sequence of events that will lead to a particular end. According to a simple model that McGrath proposed, stress consists of four interrelated stages, which are depicted

© Tim DeFrisco/DeFrisco Photography

Stress occurs when there is a substantial imbalance between the physical and psychological demands placed on an individual and his or her response capability–and under conditions where failure to meet the demand has important consequences.

in Figure 4.3: environmental demand, perception of demand, stress response, and behavioral consequences. We will briefly describe the individual stages here.

Stage 1: Environmental Demand

In the first stage of the stress process some type of demand is placed on an individual. The demand might be physical or psychological, such as a physical education student having to execute a newly learned volleyball skill in front of her class or parents pressuring a young athlete to win the race.

Stage 2: Perception of Demand

The second stage of the stress process is the individual's perception of the physical or psychological demand. People do not perceive demands in exactly the same way. For instance, two eighth graders may view having to demonstrate a newly learned volleyball skill in front of class quite differently. Maya may enjoy the attention of being in front of the class, whereas Issaha may feel threatened. That is, Issaha perceives an imbalance between the demands placed on him (having to demonstrate in front of the class) and his ability to meet those demands. Maya perceives no such imbalance, or perceives it only to a nonthreatening degree.

A person's level of trait anxiety greatly influences how he or she perceives the world. Highly trait-anxious people tend to perceive more situations (especially evaluative and competitive ones) as threatening than lower trait-anxious people do. For this reason trait anxiety is an important influence in Stage 2 of the stress process.

75

Competitive State Anxiety Inventory-2 (CSAI-2)

Below are several statements that athletes have used to describe their feelings before a competition. Read each statement and then circle the appropriate number to the right of the statement to indicate how you *feel at this moment*. There are no right or wrong answers. Don't spend too much time on any one statement, but choose the answer that best describes your feelings.

	Not at all	Somewhat	Moderately so	Very much so
1. I am concerned about this competition.	1	2	3	4
2. I feel nervous.	1	2	3	4
3. I feel at ease.	1	2	3	4
4. I have self-doubts.	1	2	3	4
5. I feel jittery.	1	2	3	4
6. I feel comfortable.	1	2	3	4
7. I am concerned that I may not do as well in this competition as I could.	1	2	3	4
8. My body feels tense.	1	2	3	4
9. I feel self-confident.	1	2	3	4

Sport Competition Trait Anxiety Test (SCAT)

Below are some statements about how persons feel when they compete in sports and games. Read each statement and decide if you hardly ever, sometimes, or often feel this way when you compete in sports and games. For each question, circle the number that corresponds to your choice. There are no right or wrong answers. Do not spend too much time on any one question. Remember to choose the word that describes how you usually feel when competing in sports and games.

	Hardly ever	Sometimes	Often
1. Before I compete I feel uneasy.	1	2	3
2. Before I compete I worry about my not performing well.	1	2	3
3. When I compete I worry about making mistakes.	1	2	3
4. Before I compete I am calm.	1	2	3
5. Before I compete I get a queasy feeling.	1	2	3
6. Just before competing I notice my heart beats faster than usual.	1	2	3

Stage 3: Stress Response

The third stage of the stress process is the individual's physical and psychological response to a perception of the situation. If someone's perception of an imbalance between demands and response capability causes her to feel threatened, increased state anxiety results, bringing with it increased worries (cognitive state anxiety), heightened physiological activation (somatic state anxiety), or both. Other reactions, too, such as changes in concentration and increased muscle tension, accompany increased state anxiety.

Stage 4: Behavioral Consequences

The fourth stage is the actual behavior of the individual under stress. If a volleyball student perceives an imbalance between capability and demands and feels increased state anxiety, does his performance deteriorate? Or does the increased state anxiety increase intensity, thereby improving performance?

The final stage of the stress process feeds back into the first. If a student becomes overly threatened and performs poorly in front of the class, the other children may laugh; this negative social evaluation would become an additional demand on the child (Stage 1). The stress process, then, becomes a continuing cycle (see Figure 4.3).

Implications for Practice

The stress process has a number of implications for practice. If a corporate fitness specialist is asked by her company's personnel director to help develop a stress-management program for the company's employees, for example, Stage 1 of the model suggests that she determine what demands are placed on the employees (e.g., increased workloads, unrealistic scheduling demands, hectic travel schedules). An analysis of Stage 2 might lead her to question who is experiencing or perceiving the most stress (e.g., individuals in certain divisions or with certain jobs or those with certain personality dispositions). Stage 3 would call for studying the reactions the employees are having to the increased stress—somatic state anxiety, cognitive state anxiety, attention-concentration problems, and so on. Stage 4 analysis would focus on the subsequent behavior of employees feeling increased stress, such as greater absenteeism, reduced productivity, or decreased job satisfaction. By understanding this stress cycle the fitness director can target her efforts to reduce stress. She might suggest physical activity (most likely in Stage 3) or other means of stress management (e.g., time-management seminars, restructured work schedules). She has a better grasp of the specific causes and consequences of stress, which allows her to design more effective stress-management activities.

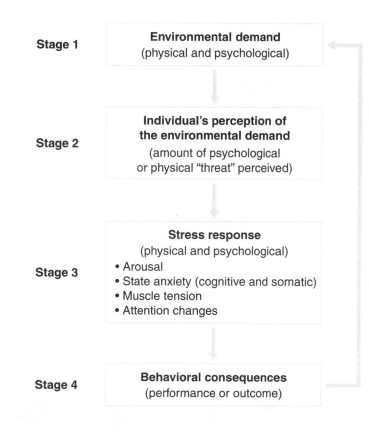

Figure 4.3   *The four-stage stress process.*

Sources of Stress and Anxiety

There are literally thousands of specific sources of stress. Exercise psychologists have also shown that major life events, such as a job change or a death in the family, as well as daily hassles, such as an auto breakdown or a problem with a co-worker, cause stress and affect physical and mental health (Willis & Campbell, 1992). In athletes, stressors include worry about performing up to capabilities, financial costs and time needed for training, self-doubts about talent, and relationships or traumatic experiences outside of sport, such as the death of a family member (Scanlan, Stein, & Ravizza, 1991). Gould, Udry, Bridges, and Beck (1997a) recently found that injured elite athletes experienced psychological (e.g., fear, shattered hopes and dreams), physical, medical or rehab-related, financial, and career stress sources, along with missed opportunities outside the sport (e.g., unable to visit another country with the team). These thousands of specific stress sources fall into some general categories determined by both situation and personality.

Situational Sources of Stress

There are two common sources of situational stress. These general areas are (a) the importance placed on an event or contest and (b) the uncertainty that surrounds the outcome of that event (Martens, 1987).

Event Importance

In general, the more important the event, the more stress-provoking it is. Thus, a championship contest is more stressful than a regular season game, just as taking college boards is more stressful than taking a practice exam. Little League baseball players, for example, were observed each time they came to bat over an entire baseball season (Lowe, 1971). The batters' heart rates were recorded while they were at bat, as were their nervous mannerisms on deck. How critical the situation at bat was in the game (e.g., bases loaded, two outs, last inning, close score) and how important the game was in the season standings were both rated. The more critical

> *The more important an event, the more stress-provoking it will be.*

> *The greater the degree of uncertainty an individual feels about an outcome or others' feelings and evaluations, the greater the state anxiety and stress.*

> *High trait anxiety and low self-esteem are related to heightened state anxiety reactions in athletes.*

the situation, the more stress and nervousness the young athletes exhibited.

The importance placed on an event is not always obvious, however. An event that may seem insignificant to most people may be very important for one particular person. For instance, a regular-season soccer game may not seem particularly important to most players on a team that has locked up a championship. Yet, it may be of major importance to a particular player who is being observed by a college scout. You must continually assess the importance participants attach to activities.

Uncertainty

Uncertainty is a second major situational source of stress—and the greater the uncertainty, the greater the stress. Often we cannot do anything about uncertainty. For example, when two evenly matched teams are scheduled to compete, there is maximum uncertainty, but little can or should be done about it. After all, the essence of sport is to match up evenly matched athletes and teams. However, at times teachers, coaches, and sports medicine professionals create unnecessary uncertainty by not informing participants of such things as the starting lineups, how to avoid injury in learning high-risk physical skills (e.g., vaulting in gymnastics), or what to expect while recovering from a serious athletic injury. Trainers, teachers, and coaches should be aware of how they might unknowingly create uncertainty in participants.

Personal Sources of Stress

Some people will characterize situations as important and uncertain, viewing them with greater anxiety than other people will. Two personality dispositions that consistently relate to heightened state anxiety reactions are high trait anxiety and low self-esteem (Scanlan, 1986). A third important anxiety disposition for those interested in exercise is social physique anxiety.

Trait Anxiety

As previously discussed, trait anxiety is a personality factor that predisposes a person to view competition and social evaluation as more or less threatening. A highly trait-anxious person perceives com-

petition as more threatening and anxiety provoking than a lower trait-anxious person does.

Self-Esteem

Self-esteem is also related to perceptions of threat and corresponding changes in state anxiety. Low self-esteem athletes, for example, have less confidence and experience and more state anxiety than do athletes with high self-esteem. Strategies for enhancing self-confidence are important means of reducing the amount of state anxiety that individuals experience.

Social Physique Anxiety

Social physique anxiety is a personality disposition defined as " the degree to which people become anxious when others observe their physiques" (Hart, Leary, & Rejeski, 1989). It reflects a person's tendency to become nervous or apprehensive when having their body evaluated (Eklund, Kelley, & Wilson, 1997). People with high social physique anxiety report more stress during fitness evaluations and experiencing more negative thoughts about their bodies. These individuals are likely to avoid fitness settings because they fear how others will evaluate their physiques. If you can reduce their social physique anxiety by having them exercise in less revealing shorts and T-shirts, instead of tight-fitting clothes, you can increase their participation in physical activity (Crawford & Eklund, 1994).

How Arousal and Anxiety Affect Performance

One of the most compelling relationships that sport and exercise psychologists study is how arousal and anxiety affect performance positively and negatively. Most of us recognize readily enough when our nerves make us feel vulnerable and out of control. But how exactly do physiological and psychological arousal function to the advantage of one person and the detriment of another? How does it happen that even in our own performance on a single afternoon, we can notice fluctuations in anxiety levels and their effects?

Sport and exercise psychologists have studied the relation of anxiety and performance for decades. They haven't reached definitive conclusions, but they have illuminated aspects of the process that have several implications for helping people psych up and perform better—rather than psyching out and performing poorly. Some 50 years ago researchers concentrated on drive theory, which was later used in the 1960s and 1970s to explain social facilitation. In the past quarter century psychologists have found the inverted-U theory more convincing, and still more recently they have proposed some variations and newer hypotheses, including the concepts of zones of optimal functioning, the catastrophe phenomenon, and the reversal theory. We will discuss each of these briefly.

Drive Theory

Psychologists first saw the relationship between arousal and performance as a direct, linear one (Spence & Spence, 1966). In their view, called **drive theory,** as an individual's arousal or state anxiety increases, so too does his or her performance: The more psyched up an athlete becomes, for example, the better she or he performs. Most athletes, of course, can remember that they also sometimes became overly aroused or overly anxious and then performed more poorly. So little scholarly support now exists for the drive theory (Martens, Vealey, & Burton, 1990).

You may recall the social facilitation theory (the example of a theory we used in chapter 1). Zajonc had observed a pattern in the seemingly random way in which people sometimes performed better in front of an audience and at other times performed worse. His observation was that when people performed tasks they knew well or that were simple, having an audience was a positive effect, whereas when they performed less familiar or more complex tasks, their performance suffered. So Zajonc's social facilitation theory contended that an audience creates arousal in the performer, which hurts performance on difficult tasks that are not yet learned but helps performance on well-learned tasks.

An audience need not be present for social facilitation to occur. The theory refers more broadly to the effects of the presence of others on performance,

Social facilitation theory predicts that the presence of others helps performance on well-learned or simple skills and inhibits or lessens performance on unlearned or complex tasks.

including coaction (two people performing simultaneously), or performing a task simultaneously with others. Zajonc (1965) used drive theory to show that the presence of others increases arousal in the performer, and this increased arousal (drive) increases or brings out the performer's dominant response (the most likely way to perform the skill). When people perform well-learned or simple skills (e.g., sit-ups), the dominant response is correct (positive performance) and the increased arousal facilitates performance. When they perform complex or unlearned skills (e.g., a novice golfer's learning to drive a golf ball), the presence of others increases arousal and causes their dominant response more often to be incorrect (poorer performance). Thus, social facilitation theory predicts that an audience (that is, "coaction," or others being present) inhibits performance on tasks that are complex or have not been learned thoroughly and enhances performance on tasks that are simple or have been learned well.

The implications are that you would want to eliminate audiences and evaluation as much as possible in learning situations. For example, if you were teaching a gymnastic routine, you would not want to expose youngsters to an audience too soon. It is critical that instructors eliminate or lessen audience and coaction effects in learning environments to make them as arousal-free as possible. However, when participants are performing well-learned or simple tasks, you might want to encourage people to come watch.

While the drive and social facilitation theories explain how an audience can hurt performance when one is learning new skills, it does not explain so well how an audience affects a person's performing well-learned skills. It predicts that as arousal increases, performance increases in a straight line. If this were true, we would expect highly skilled athletes to consistently excel in all high-pressure situations. Yet nervousness and choking in the clutch occur even at the elite level. For this reason, we can only conclude that on well-learned skills an audience may sometimes enhance performance and at other times inhibit it. The views presented next will give you a better understanding of how increased arousal or anxiety influences performance on well-learned tasks.

The Inverted-U Hypothesis

Dissatisfied with the drive theory, most sport psychologists turned to the **inverted-U hypothesis** to explain the relationship between arousal states and performance (Landers & Boutcher, 1998). This view holds that at low arousal levels performance will be

below par (see Figure 4.4); the exerciser or athlete is not psyched up. As arousal increases, so too does performance—up to an optimal point where best performance results. Further increases in arousal, however, cause performance to decline. So this view is represented by an inverted-U that reflects high performance with the optimal level of arousal and lesser performance, with either low or very high arousal.

Most athletes and coaches accept the general notions of the inverted-U hypothesis. After all, most people have experienced underarousal, optimal arousal, and overarousal. But despite the acceptance of the hypothesis in general, it has come under criticism recently (Gould & Udry, 1994a; Hardy, 1990). Critics rightly question the shape of the arousal curve, whether optimal arousal always occurs at the mid point of the arousal continuum, and the nature of the arousal itself. In essence, the inverted-U has taken us as far as it can, but we need more explicit explanations now. Hence, sport psychologists have begun to explore other views, hoping to more specifically understand the arousal-performance relationship.

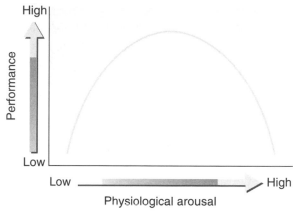

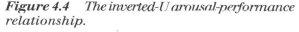

Figure 4.4 *The inverted-U arousal-performance relationship.*

Individualized Zones of Optimal Functioning

Yuri Hanin, a noted Russian sport psychologist, presented an alternative view that he calls **individualized zones of optimal functioning** (IZOF) model.

He found that top athletes each have a zone of optimal state anxiety in which their best performance occurs (1980, 1986, 1997). Outside this zone, poor performance occurs.

Hanin's IZOF view differs from the inverted-U hypothesis in two important ways. First, the optimal level of state anxiety does not always occur at the midpoint of the continuum but rather varies from individual to individual. That is, some athletes have a zone of optimal functioning at the lower end of the continuum, some in the midrange, and others at the upper end (see Figure 4.5), Second, the optimal level of state anxiety is not a single point but a bandwidth. Thus, coaches and teachers should help participants identify and reach their own, specific optimal zone of state anxiety.

The IZOF model has good support in the research literature (Gould & Tuffey, 1996). In addition, Hanin (1997) has expanded the IZOF notion beyond anxiety to show how zones of optimal functioning use a variety of emotions, such as determination, pleasantness, and laziness. He concludes that for best performance to occur, athletes need individualized optimal levels not only of state anxiety but of a variety of other emotions as well. A major coaching implication of the IZOF model, then, is that coaches must help their athletes achieve the ideal recipe of emotions they each need for best performance.

> *A person's zone of optimal functioning may be at the lower, middle, or upper end of the state anxiety continuum.*

Multidimensional Anxiety Theory

Hanin's IZOF hypothesis did not examine whether the components of state anxiety—somatic and cognitive anxiety—affect performance the same way. These state anxiety components are generally thought to influence performance differentially: That is, physiological (somatic state anxiety) arousal and worry (cognitive state anxiety) affect performers differently. Your heart racing or pounding and your mind reiterating negative predictions, for instance, can affect you differently.

Multidimensional anxiety theory predicts that cognitive state anxiety (worry) is negatively related to performance. That is, increases in cognitive state anxiety lead to decreases in performance. But it predicts that somatic state anxiety (which is physiologically manifested) is related to performance in an inverted-U, with increases in the anxiety facilitating performance up to an optimal level, after which performance declines with additional anxiety. Although studies have shown that these two anxiety components differentially predict performance, the precise predictions of multidimensional anxiety theory have not been consistently supported (Gould, Greenleaf, & Krane, in press; Hardy, Jones, & Gould, 1996). As a result, multidimensional anxiety theory has little support for its performance predictions and is of little use in guiding practice.

Catastrophe Model

Hardy's catastrophe view addresses another piece of the puzzle. According to his model, performance depends on the complex interaction of arousal and cognitive anxiety (1990; 1996). The **catastrophe model** predicts that physiological arousal is related

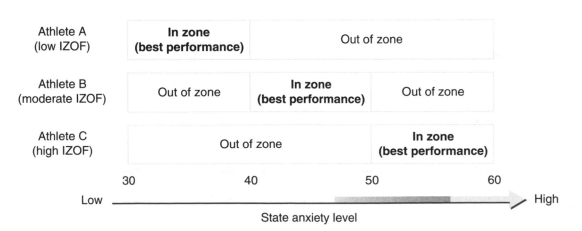

Figure 4.5 *Individualized zones of optimal functioning (IZOF).*

■ RESEARCH ■

Home-Court Advantage: Myth or Reality?

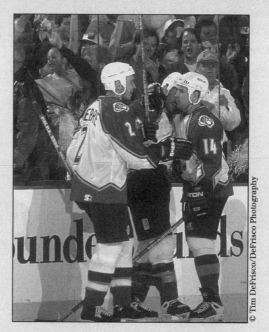

One way spectators influence performance is by providing support and encouragement for the home team. In fact, in many sports, teams battle throughout the season for the best record so that they can have the home-court advantage during the playoffs. Do teams really win more at home than on the road?

Research has found that teams actually do win more at home, with the advantage being fairly small in football and baseball but quite large in basketball and hockey. Since the latter two sports are played in intimate indoor sites, compared with the more open outdoor stadiums of baseball and football, it may be that the proximity of the fans to the action and the noise level they generate in enclosed facilities enhance players' performance. The continual flow of activity in hockey and basketball might also make it easier for a crowd to get emotionally involved and thus play a part in motivating and arousing the players. The increased level of involvement is reflected in elevated noise levels and emotional outbursts, such as sustained booing of referees or opposing coaches.

Despite the evidence supporting the home-court advantage during the regular season, recent findings have indicated that this advantage might be lost in the playoffs and championship games. In fact, the home court might even become a disadvantage. For example, Baumeister and Steinhilber (1984) found in baseball World Series played from 1924 to 1982 that in series that went at least five games, the home team won 60% of the first two games but only 40% of the last two games. And in the 26 series that have gone to a final and deciding seventh game, the home team won only 38% of the time. To test the generalizability of these results, a similar analysis was conducted on professional basketball. Home teams won 70% of the first four games. However, during the fifth and sixth games, the home team's winning percentage was 46%, dropping to a dismal 38% for the deciding seventh game.

Thus, the home-court "advantage" turned to a disadvantage as games became more critical and the pressure mounted. Game statistics were gathered to determine how and why this occurred. In both baseball and basketball the visiting team's performance remained fairly constant throughout the series. However, the home teams had a significant decrease in performance as games became more critical, producing more errors in baseball and lower foul shooting in basketball. In essence, home teams were choking under pressure instead of getting a lift from their fans. Researchers argue that supportive spectators can create expectations for success, which in turn can increase self-consciousness in athletes, causing them to think too much instead of simply playing and performing automatically, which is characteristic of highly skilled athletes.

However, there appears to be a shift in the success of home teams in basketball over the past 10 years. Specifically, from 1984 to 1994 the home team won 18 consecutive seventh-and-deciding games during the National Basketball Association playoffs. It's possible that coaches and athletes have become more knowledgable about putting too much pressure on themselves in critical games, thus reducing self-consciousness and letting the emotion of hometown fans carry them to victory.

The catastrophe model predicts that with low worry, increases in arousal or somatic anxiety are related to performance in an inverted-U manner. With great worry, the increases in arousal improve performance to an optimal threshold beyond which additional arousal causes a rapid and dramatic decline in performance.

to performance in an inverted-U fashion, but only when an athlete is not worried or has low cognitive state anxiety (see Figure 4.6a). If cognitive anxiety is high (i.e., the athlete is worrying), however, the increases in arousal at some point reach a kind of threshold, just past the point of optimal arousal level, and afterward a rapid decline in performance— the "catastrophe"—occurs (see Figure 4.6b). So physiological arousal (i.e., somatic anxiety) can have markedly different effects on performance, depending on the amount of cognitive anxiety one is experiencing. Moreover, amid high worry, once overarousal and the catastrophe occurs, performance deteriorates *dramatically*. This is different than the steady decline predicted by the inverted-U hypothesis, and recovery takes longer.

If you inspect Figure 4.6b more closely, you can see that under conditions of high cognitive anxiety as physiological arousal increases, performance also increases until an optimal arousal level is reached (marked as *part a* on the curve). After that point, however, a catastrophic drop in performance occurs; the performer drops down to a low level of perfor-

mance (marked as *b* on the curve). Once the athlete is at that part of the curve, the individual would need to greatly decrease his or her physiological arousal before being able to regain previous performance levels. The catastrophe model predicts, then, that after a catastrophic drop in performance, the athlete must (a) completely relax physically, (b) cognitively restructure by controlling or eliminating worries and regaining confidence and control, and (c) reactivate or arouse him- or herself in a controlled manner to again reach the optimal level of functioning. Doing so is no easy task, so it is understandably very difficult to quickly recover from a catastrophic drop in performance.

Finally, as you look at the two graphs in Figure 4.6 you can see that an athlete's absolute performance level is actually higher under conditions of high cognitive anxiety than under conditions of low cognitive anxiety. This shows that cognitive anxiety or worry is not necessarily bad or detrimental to performance. In fact, this model predicts that you will perform better with some worry, provided that your physiological arousal level does not go *too* high (i.e., a little bit of tension heightens an athlete's effort and narrows attention, giving the individual an edge over other performers). Performance deteriorates only under the combined conditions of high worry plus high physiological arousal.

Although there is some scientific support for the catastrophe model, it is difficult to test (Hardy, 1996; Hardy, Jones, and Gould, 1996). Still, you can derive from it an important message for practice, namely, that for optimal performance an ideal physiological arousal level isn't enough: It is also necessary to manage or control cognitive state anxiety (worrying).

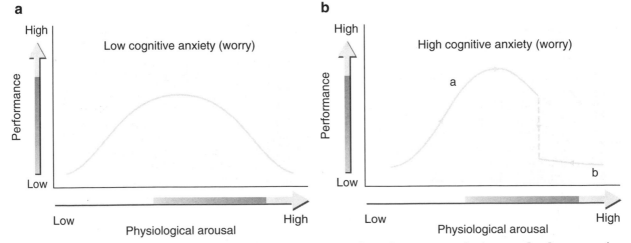

Figure 4.6 *Catastrophe theory predictions: (a) arousal-performance relation under low cognitive state anxiety; (b) arousal-performance relation under high cognitive state anxiety.*

How a performer interprets arousal may influence performance.

Reversal Theory

Kerr's application of reversal theory (1985, 1997) contends that how arousal affects performance depends basically on an individual's interpretation of his or her arousal level. Joe might interpret high arousal as a pleasant excitement, whereas Jan might interpret it as an unpleasant anxiety. She might see low arousal as relaxation, whereas Joe sees it as boring. Athletes are thought to make quick shifts—reversals—in their interpretations of arousal. So an athlete may perceive arousal as positive one minute and then reverse the interpretation to negative the next minute. Reversal theory predicts that for best performance, however, athletes must interpret their arousal as *pleasant excitement*, rather than as unpleasant anxiety.

Reversal theory's key contributions to our understanding of the arousal-performance relationship are twofold: First it emphasizes that one's interpretation of arousal, not just the amount of arousal one feels, is significant, and second that performers can shift or reverse their positive or negative interpretations of arousal from moment to moment. Hence, it offers an interesting alternative to previous views of the arousal-performance relationship. Yet few tests of its predictions have been made to date, so it is too early to draw any firm conclusions about the merit of its scientific predictions.

Anxiety Direction and Intensity

Most researchers had assumed that anxiety has only negative effects on performance. English sport psychologist Graham Jones and his colleagues (Jones, 1995; Jones, Hanton, & Swain, 1994), however, have recently shown that an individual's interpretation of anxiety symptoms is important for understanding the anxiety-performance relationship. People can view anxiety symptoms either as positive and helpful to performance (facilitating) or as negative and harmful to performance (debilitating). In fact, to fully understand the anxiety-performance relationship you must examine both the intensity of a person's anxiety (how much anxiety she feels) and its direction (her interpretation of that anxiety as being facilitating or debilitating to performance). Jones et al. basically contend that viewing anxiety as facilitative leads

to superior performance whereas viewing it as debilitating leads to poor performance.

Sport psychologists have already found some support for this association between how anxiety is perceived and performance level. For example, good balance beam performances have been associated with gymnasts' interpreting cognitive anxiety as facilitating (Jones, Swain, & Hardy, 1993). Similarly, elite swimmers have reported both cognitive and somatic anxiety as more facilitative and less debilitating than have non-elite swimmers (Jones & Swain, 1992). Hence, how an athlete interprets the direction of anxiety (as facilitative or debilitating) has significant effect on the anxiety-performance relationship. It follows that coaches should try to help athletes view increased arousal and anxiety as conditions of excitement instead of fear.

Significance of Arousal-Performance Views

There is certainly no shortage of arousal-performance views—so many that it is easy to get confused. So let's summarize what these recent views tell us for practice. The zones of optimal functioning, multidimensional anxiety, catastrophe, reversal and direction and intensity views offer several guidelines (Gould & Udry, 1994a; Hardy, Jones & Gould, 1996):

1. Arousal is a multifaceted phenomenon consisting of both physiological activation and an athlete's interpretation of that activation (e.g., state anxiety, confidence, facilitative anxiety). We must help performers find the optimal mix of these emotions for best performance. Moreover, these optimal mixes of arousal-related emotions are highly individual and task-specific. Two athletes participating in the same event may not have the same optimal arousal level, and a person's optimal arousal level for performing a balance beam routine would be quite different from the optimal arousal level for a maximum bench press in power weightlifting.

2. Arousal and state anxiety do not necessarily have a negative effect on performance. The effects can be positive and facilitating or negative and debilitating, depending largely on how the performer interprets changes. In addition, self-confidence is critical to facilitating heightened arousal as positive (psyching up) as opposed to negative (psyching out).

3. Some optimal level of arousal leads to peak performance, but the optimal levels of physiological activation and arousal-related thoughts (worry) are not necessarily the same!

4. Both the catastrophe and reversal theories suggest that interaction between levels of physiological activation and arousal-related thoughts appear more important than absolute levels of each. Some people perform best with relatively low optimal arousal and state anxiety, whereas others perform their best with higher levels.

5. An optimal level of arousal is thought to be related to peak performance, but it is doubtful that this level occurs at the midpoint of the arousal continuum. Excessive arousal likely does not cause slow, gradual declines in performance but "catastrophes" that are difficult to reverse.

Why Arousal Influences Performance

Understanding why arousal affects performance can help you to regulate arousal, both in yourself and others. For instance, if heightened arousal and state anxiety lead to increased muscle tension in Nicole, a golfer, then progressive muscle relaxation techniques may reduce her state anxiety and improve performance. Thought control strategies, however, may work better for Shane, another golfer, who needs to control excessive cognitive state anxiety.

There are at least two explanations for how increased arousal influences athletic performance: (a) increased muscle tension and coordination difficulties and (b) changes in attention or concentration levels.

Muscle Tension and Coordination Difficulties

Many people who experience great stress report muscle soreness, aches, and pains. Athletes who experience high levels of state anxiety might say, "I don't feel right," "My body doesn't seem to follow directions," or "I tensed up" in critical situations. Comments like these are natural: Increases in arousal and state anxiety cause increases in muscle tension and can also interfere with coordination.

For example, some highly trait-anxious and lower trait-anxious college students were watched closely as they threw tennis balls at a target. As you might expect, the higher trait-anxious students experienced considerably more state anxiety than the lower trait-anxious subjects (Weinberg & Hunt, 1976). Moreover, electroencephalograms (EEGs) monitoring

electrical activity in the students' muscles showed that increased state anxiety caused the highly anxious individuals to use more muscular energy before, during, and after their throws. Thus, increased muscle tension and coordination difficulties contributed to the students' inferior performance.

Attention and Concentration Changes

Increased arousal and state anxiety also influence athletic performance through changes in attention and concentration (Nideffer, 1976). First, increased arousal causes a narrowing of a performer's attentional field (Landers, Wang, & Courtet, 1985). For example, Joe is a goalie in ice hockey and needs to maintain a broad but optimal focus of attention as three opponents break into his end of the ice. If he becomes preoccupied with Tim, who has the puck, and does not attend to the other players on the periphery, Tim will simply pass off to a teammate on the wing for an easy score. Under normal conditions, Joe can maintain his optimal attentional focus (see Figure 4.7a), but if he is underaroused (see Figure 4.7b), his attention focus may be too broad, focusing on both task-relevant (e.g., the opposing players) and irrelevant cues (e.g., the crowd). When he experiences excessive levels of arousal and state anxiety, however, his attention focus narrows too much and he is unable to survey the entire playing surface (see Figure 4.7c). One athlete who experienced severe anxiety problems put it this way: "When the pressure is on, it's like I'm looking through the tube in a roll of toilet paper." In psychological terms, increased arousal causes a narrowing of the attentional field, which negatively influences performance on tasks requiring a broad external focus.

When arousal is increased, performers also tend to scan the playing environment less often. For example, Tony is a wrestler who experiences high levels of arousal and state anxiety. He becomes preoccupied with executing one move on an opponent so does not visually or kinetically scan the opponent's total body position for other potential opportunities. Thus, Tony's performance deteriorates as he scans less often, and potential scoring opportunities consequently go undetected.

Increased arousal and state anxiety cause increased muscle tension and can interfere with coordination.

Arousal and state anxiety narrow one's attentional field, decrease environmental scanning, and cause a shift to the dominant attentional style and to inappropriate cues.

a. Optimal attentional field —
moderate (optimal) arousal

b. Attentional field too broad —
low arousal

c. Attentional field too narrow —
high arousal

Figure 4.7 *Attentional narrowing under conditions of high arousal.*

Arousal and state anxiety also cause changes in attention and concentration levels by affecting attention style (Nideffer, 1976). Athletes must learn to shift their attention to appropriate task cues (see chapter 16). For example, a quarterback in football needs to shift from a broad external span when surveying the field for open receivers to a narrow external focus when delivering a pass. Each individual has a dominant attention style. Increased arousal can cause performers to shift to a dominant attention style that may be inappropriate for the skill at hand.

Increased arousal and state anxiety also cause athletes to attend to inappropriate cues. For instance, most athletes perform well-learned skills best when they fully concentrate on the task. Unaware of their levels of concentration, they perform on automatic pilot or in a "flow zone" (see chapter 16). Unfortunately, excessive cognitive state anxiety sometimes causes performers to focus on inappropriate task cues by "worrying about worrying" and becoming overly self-evaluative. This, in turn, affects optimal concentration.

Implications for Practice

You can integrate your knowledge of arousal, stress, and anxiety by considering its implications for professional practice. Five of the most important guidelines are to

1. identify the optimal combination of arousal-related emotions needed for best performance;
2. recognize how personal and situational factors interact to influence arousal, anxiety, and performance;
3. recognize the signs of increased arousal and anxiety in sport and exercise participants;
4. tailor coaching and instructional practices to individuals; and
5. develop confidence in performers to help them cope with increased stress and anxiety.

Identify Optimal Arousal-Related Emotions

One of the most effective ways to help people achieve peak performance is to increase their awareness of how arousal-related emotions can lead to peak performances (see chapter 12 for specific techniques). Once this is accomplished, teaching athletes various psychological strategies (e.g., imagery and developing preperformance routines) can help them regulate arousal.

Think of arousal as an emotional temperature, and arousal-regulation skills as a thermostat. The athlete's goals are to identify the optimal emotional temperature for his best performance and then to learn how to "set" his thermostat to this temperature—either by raising (psyching up) or lowering (chilling out) his emotional temperature.

Recognize the Interaction of Personal and Situational Factors

As with other behaviors, you can best understand and predict stress and anxiety by considering the interaction of personal and situational factors (see Figure 4.8). For instance, many people mistakenly assume that the low trait-anxious athlete will always be the best performer because she will achieve an optimal level of state anxiety and arousal needed for competition. In contrast, the highly trait-anxious athlete is assumed to consistently choke. But this is not the case.

Where the importance placed on performance is not excessive and some certainty exists about the

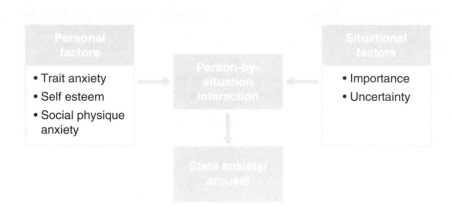

Figure 4.8 *Interactional model of anxiety.*

outcome, you might expect a highly trait-anxious swimmer to experience some elevated arousal and state anxiety because she is predisposed to perceive most competitive situations as somewhat threatening. It seems likely that she would move close to her optimal level of arousal and state anxiety. In contrast, a competitor with low trait anxiety may not perceive the situation as very important because he does not feel threatened. Hence, his level of arousal and his state anxiety remain low, and he has trouble achieving an optimal performance.

In a high-pressure situation, where the meet has considerable importance and the outcome is highly uncertain, these same swimmers react quite differently. The higher trait-anxious swimmer perceives this situation as even more important than it is and responds with very high levels of arousal and state anxiety: She overshoots her optimal level of state anxiety and arousal. The less trait-anxious swimmer also experiences increased state anxiety, but because he tends to perceive competition and social evaluation as less threatening, his state anxiety and arousal will likely be in an optimal range.

Looking at the interaction of personal factors (such as self-esteem, social physique anxiety, and trait anxiety) and situational factors (such as event importance and uncertainty) is a better predictor of arousal, state anxiety, and performance than looking at either set of these factors alone.

Recognize Arousal and State Anxiety Signs

The interactional approach has several implications for helping exercise and sport participants manage stress. Chief among them is the need to identify people who are experiencing heightened stress and

> *To accurately detect an individual's anxiety level you must know the various signs and symptoms of increased stress and anxiety.*

anxiety. This is not easy to do. Coaches, for example, have been found to be inaccurate predictors of their athletes' anxiety levels. Hanson and Gould found that only one of four college cross-country coaches accurately read their athletes' state and trait anxiety levels (1988). Coaches who could accurately read the anxiety levels did not think it was an easy task; rather, they worked hard to learn about their athletes.

You can more accurately detect a person's anxiety levels if you are familiar with the signs and symptoms of increased stress and anxiety:

- Cold, clammy hands
- Need to urinate frequently
- Profuse sweating
- Negative self-talk
- Dazed look in the eyes
- Increased muscle tension
- Butterflies in stomach
- Feeling ill
- Headache
- Cotton (dry) mouth
- Constantly sick
- Difficulty sleeping
- Inability to concentrate
- Consistently performs better in noncompetitive situations

88

Although no specific number or pattern of symptoms characterize a high level of stress, those people who experience high levels of state anxiety often exhibit several of these signs. The key is to notice changes in these variables between stressful and unstressful environments (e.g., when a normally positive athlete becomes negative).

One of the best (though often overlooked) ways to understand what people are feeling is to ask them! Encourage your participants to talk freely about their feelings with you. Be empathic by trying to see things from their perspectives (i.e., how you would feel in their situation at their level of experience). This allows you to associate specific behavioral patterns with varying levels of stress and anxiety and to better read their anxiety levels. In addition, coaches can create a mutually supportive environment where athletes feel comfortable talking about their experiences and feelings.

Tailor Coaching Strategies to Individuals

It is important to individualize teaching, exercise, and coaching practices. At times arousal and state anxiety levels will need to be reduced, at other times maintained, and at still other times facilitated (see chapter 12 for specific strategies). The teacher or coach should recognize when and with whom arousal and state anxiety need to be enhanced, reduced, or maintained.

For example, if a student or athlete with high trait anxiety and low self-esteem must perform in a highly evaluative environment, the teacher or coach would best de-emphasize the importance of the situation and instead emphasize the performer's preparation to execute. A pep talk stressing the importance of the situation and performing well would only add stress and increase arousal and state anxiety beyond an optimal level. Someone with moderate levels of trait anxiety and self-esteem may be best left alone in the same highly evaluative situation. This individual's arousal and state anxiety would probably be elevated but not excessive. However, an athlete with very low trait anxiety and high self-esteem may need a pep talk before performing in a nonthreatening environment—to *increase* arousal.

> *Sometimes arousal and state anxiety will need to be reduced, other times maintained, and still other times facilitated.*

Instructors who have students or clients with high social physique anxiety should encourage these exercisers to wear clothes that cover their bodies, and they can minimize social evaluation of physiques by creating settings that eliminate observation by passersby. The keys, then, are to know a person's personal characteristics, read the current level of state anxiety, and treat the individual appropriately.

Develop Performers' Confidence

One of the most effective methods of helping people control their stress and anxiety is to assist them in developing their confidence. Highly confident people who believe in their abilities experience less state anxiety. Moreover, when they do experience anxiety they tend to interpret their increased anxiety as facilitative versus debilitating. Two important strategies for enhancing confidence are to foster a positive environment and to instill a positive orientation to mistakes and losing (see chapter 14 for some other excellent strategies).

One major source of stress is uncertainty, which often results when athletes or students participate in negative practice environments. For instance, some coaches harp on mistakes that players make, yelling and screaming all through practice. Then on game day these same coaches say how confident they are in their athletes' abilities. But after hearing so much negative feedback in practice, the athletes may not believe what the coach says on game day.

A productive approach for facilitating confidence is to create a positive practice environment. Give frequent and sincere encouragement. That way, when athletes encounter stressful environments, they will have confidence in their abilities to meet the demands of their situations.

Foster a positive, productive orientation to mistakes—and even to losing. When individuals make mistakes, they typically become frustrated and often overly aroused and anxious. This leads to unproductive attention changes and increased muscle tension, which further deteriorate performance.

It is useful to teach people to view mistakes in a more productive light. Just as legendary UCLA basketball coach John Wooden did with his players, good sport psychologists teach performers not to view mistakes as bad or evil, but as building blocks to success (Smoll & Smith, 1979). No performer is happy to make mistakes, but getting upset only makes a mistake a complete mistake. Instead, try to gain at least a partial success by staying cool and learning from the mistake: Use it as a building block to success. Mastering this strategy reduces anxiety, making for a more productive learning and performance environment.

Still another effective way to build confidence is through simulation training (Hardy et al., 1996). Simulation training involves having athletes practice under pressure and learn how to respond effectively when they feel nervous. Legendary North Carolina basketball coach Dean Smith ended every practice with a game situation. For example, he might say, "Your team has the ball and is down by 2 points with 30 seconds left in the game" or "Your team is up by 1 point with only 5 seconds of play left, and the other team has the ball." Thus, he not only taught his players the best strategies to use in these pressure situations but also allowed them to gain confidence in their playing under pressure. Similarly, most football teams practice variations of the "2-minute drill" to familiarize themselves with pressure situations and develop confidence in their executing plays and strategies appropriate for each specific situation.

SUMMARY

1 *Discuss the nature of stress and anxiety (what it is and how it is measured).*

Stress, arousal, and anxiety each have distinct meanings. Stress is a process. It occurs when people perceive an imbalance between the physical and psychological demands on them and their ability to respond. Arousal is the blend of physiological and psychological activity in a person that varies on a continuum from deep sleep to intense excitement. Anxiety is a negative emotional state with feelings of nervousness, worry, and apprehension associated with activation or arousal of the body. It also has cognitive and somatic and trait and state components.

2 *Identify the major sources of anxiety and stress.*

Some situations produce more state anxiety and arousal than others (e.g., events that are important and where the outcome is uncertain). Stress is also influenced by personality dispositions (e.g., trait anxiety and self-esteem). Individuals with high trait anxiety, low self-esteem, and high social physique anxiety experience more state anxiety.

3 *Explain how and why arousal and anxiety-related emotions affect performance.*

Arousal-related emotions, such as cognitive and somatic state anxiety, are related to performance. Arousal and anxiety influence performance by inducing changes in attention and concentration and by increasing muscle tension. Hanin's individualized zones of optimal functioning, Hardy's catastrophe model, Kerr's interpretation of reversal theory, and Jones's distinction between the direction and intensity of anxiety should guide practice. An optimal recipe of emotions is related to peak performance, and when performers are outside this optimal range, poor performance results. This optimal combination of emotions needed for peak performance does not necessarily occur at the midpoint of the arousal–state anxiety continuum, and the relationship between arousal and performance depends on the level of cognitive state anxiety (worry) a performer exhibits.

4 *Compare and contrast ways to regulate arousal, stress, and anxiety.*

An interactional model of motivation should guide teachers and coaches in their efforts to help students and athletes manage arousal and state anxiety. Creating a positive environment and a productive orientation to mistakes and losing is an effective way to manage stress. Additionally, the following five guidelines for managing stress should be followed: (a) identify the optimal combination of arousal-related emotions needed for best performance; (b) recognize how personal and situational factors interact to influence arousal, anxiety, and performance; (c) recognize the signs of increased arousal and anxiety in sport and exercise participants; (d) tailor coaching and instructional practices to individuals; and (e) develop confidence in performers to help them cope with increased stress and anxiety.

KEY TERMS

arousal
anxiety
cognitive anxiety
somatic anxiety
state anxiety
cognitive state anxiety
somatic state anxiety
trait anxiety
self-reporting measures (or self-report scales)

stress
social physique anxiety
drive theory
inverted-U hypothesis
individualized zones of optimal functioning
multidimensional anxiety theory
catastrophe model
reversal theory

REVIEW QUESTIONS

1. Distinguish between the terms *arousal, state anxiety, trait anxiety, cognitive state anxiety,* and *somatic state anxiety.*
2. How can you measure arousal and anxiety?
3. Define stress and identify the four stages of the stress process. Why are these stages important? How can they guide practice?
4. What are the major sources of situational stress?
5. Identify three personal sources of stress.
6. What is social facilitation theory? What implications does this theory have for practice?
7. Discuss the major differences in how arousal relates to performance according to the following theories:

   - Drive theory
   - Inverted-U hypothesis
   - Multidimensional anxiety theory
   - Individualized zone of optimal functioning
   - Catastrophe model
   - Reversal theory
   - Anxiety direction and intensity view

8. Describe the major signs of increased state anxiety in athletes.

CRITICAL THINKING QUESTIONS

1. How might you tailor coaching strategies to individuals trying to deal with stress and anxiety? (Give an example.)
2. Discuss three implications for professional practice that you derived from the theories and scientific data in this chapter.
3. The chapter began with the story of Jason coming to bat in a pressure situation. Given what you have learned, what can Jason do to manage his anxiety and play well?

Understanding Sport and Exercise Environments

In part II you learned how a person's psychological makeup influences her or his behavior in physical education, sport, and exercise contexts. People do not exist in vacuums, however, and as you learned, a person-by-situation interactional model is the best way to understand behavior psychologically.

In part III, we'll focus on two major classes of situational factors that influence behavior. Chapter 5 examines the important environmental impact that competition and cooperation have on a person's behavior. Virtually everything we do as professionals in sport, teaching, and exercise settings involves competition or cooperation to some degree. In this chapter you'll read that competition and cooperation are learned behaviors, how they influence performance, the positive and negative effects of competitive and cooperative settings, and ways to balance competition and cooperation so that healthy development is maximized.

Chapter 6 focuses on feedback and reinforcement. You'll learn how these factors affect learning and performance. We offer guidelines for giving feedback and reinforcement to people in sport and exercise settings. The chapter closes with an examination of how rewards can both enhance and undermine the natural, intrinsic motivation of participants. This intrinsic motivation, in turn, can help lead performers to achieving peak performance states.

© Human Kinetics

Competition and Cooperation

After reading this chapter you should be able to

1 understand the difference between competition and cooperation,
2 describe the process of competition,
3 detail the psychological studies of competition and cooperation,
4 discuss the social factors influencing competition and cooperation,
5 explain why competition can be both good and bad, and
6 better understand how to balance competitive and cooperative efforts.

From the anecdotes former athletes tell, it is evident that competitive sport can affect participants very differently in terms of personal growth and development. For example, Hall-of-Famer quarterback Roger Staubach states, "Because of athletics and my experiences in sport, I learned to handle things in business and life." In contrast, Tom House, former major league baseball pitcher, says, "The longer the exposure to the professional sport environment, the further athletes drift from an ability to understand and cope with the demands of the real world." Many competitive sport participants argue that competitive sport not only can bring out cooperative efforts among teammates pursuing a common goal but also help prepare a person for life. Others, however, argue that competitive sport can produce self-centered athletes who avoid dealing with real-life issues.

Who is right? The answer is that people on both sides of this argument may be right because virtually all sport and physical activity involves both competition and cooperation. Players cooperate with their teammates while they compete against their opponents. Sometimes there is even competition *within* a team, as players battle for playing time and starting positions. Therefore, the interactions of these competitive and cooperative forces and their effects on participants are complex. Let us start by trying to define what we mean by competition and cooperation.

Defining Competition and Cooperation

The term competition is popularly used to refer to a variety of different situations. For example, we compete against others, against ourselves, against the clock or record book, and against objects and the elements (rock climbing, white-water rafting). But in defining competition, most researchers have focused on situations in which people compete against others in organized physical activities. For example, Coakley (1994) defines competition as "a social process that occurs when rewards are given to people on the basis of how their performances compare with the performances of others doing the same task or participating on the same event" (p. 78). According to this definition, rewards in competition are limited to those who outperform others. Thus, besides competition's being a process, it has a reward structure in competition, which fosters the notion that the success of one participant or team automatically causes the failure of others. In essence, competition always involves a direct comparison of participants.

Another process in which success can be measured and performance rewarded is cooperation. Cooperation has been defined as "a social process through which performance is evaluated and rewarded in terms of the collective achievements of a group of people working together to reach a particular goal" (Coakley, 1994, p. 79). This definition implies that a cooperative reward structure is characterized by the mutual involvement of more than one participant. Rewards are therefore shared equally by everyone in the group, and group success depends on the collective achievement of all the participants. A team winning a championship shares in the victory, even though some of its players might have actually contributed more than other members in terms of performance.

It is important to understand that successful achievement-oriented, hard-working people are not necessarily competitive. They may simply combine strong achievement orientations with cooperative or individualistic orientations. In fact, cooperative people are just as likely to be successful as are competitive people. Research has indicated that competitive reward structures, although useful in relatively simple physical tasks of short duration, are less effective than cooperative reward structures for tasks that are complex and that involve coming up with solutions for difficult problems (Kohn, 1986).

Although research concerning competition now dates back more than a century (Triplett, 1898), the first concerted effort to study competition was initiated by Morton Deutsch (1949) who noted that few everyday situations are purely cooperative or competitive. He argued that most social interactions involve some kind of goal-directed behavior that rewards the person (or persons) for achieving the goal while also requiring some type of cooperative effort from everyone involved. Basketball is a good example: Each player on a team must cooperate to win the game, but players might also be vying against each other for playing time and a starting position in the lineup.

Although there were isolated early studies regarding competition and cooperation in the 1950s and 1960s, there was no conceptual framework to help guide the research in this area. Fortunately Rainer Martens (1975a) developed a specific model that gave a framework to further studies of competition in sport and exercise environments. His model takes into account the many social influences that impact competitive behaviors in sport. Furthermore, Martens's definition then was similar to the one later developed by Coakley; both regarded competition as a process. However, Martens's definition and approach to competition also focused on *social evaluation*. He argued that in order to maximize the participants' personal development it is critical to understand the social influences that help structure the activity environment. Thus, Martens's social evaluation approach not only defines competition but also helps us to understand the competitive process in sport.

Competition Is a Process

According to Martens, competition is more than a single event; rather it involves a process that encompasses four distinct events or stages, which are illustrated in Figure 5.1. You should note that this process somewhat resembles the model of stress presented in chapter 4, which provides a good way to view the competitive process. Notice in the figure that though these stages are distinct, they also are linked to one another.

The competitive process will be experienced differently by individuals. Therefore, the person is at the focal point of the process and can influence the relationship among the different stages. Personal attributes such as previous experience, ability, motivation, and attitudes are just some of the factors that might influence a person's responses in competition. As with any social process, each stage is influenced by the other stages, as well as by such external environmental factors as feedback and external rewards.

Stage 1—The Objective Competitive Situation

Martens proposes a definition of the **objective competitive situation,** stemming from social evaluation theory (Festinger, 1954), that includes a standard for comparison and at least one other person. The comparison standard can be an individual's past performance level (e.g., 4:10 in the mile run), an idealized performance level (e.g., a 4-minute mile), or another individual's performance (e.g., your main rival has run a 4:05 mile). The primary thing that distinguishes a competitive situation from other comparison situations is that the criteria for comparison are known

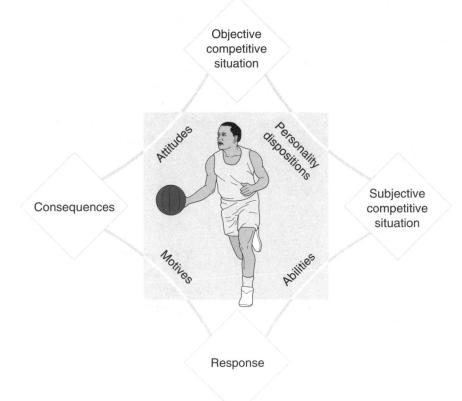

Figure 5.1 The competitive process.
Adapted from Martens, 1975.

> *The four stages of competition are (a) the objective competitive situation, (b) the subjective competitive situation, (c) the response, and (d) the consequences of the response. In an objective competitive situation "an individual's performance is compared with some standard of excellence, in the presence of at least one other person who is aware of the criterion for comparison." (Martens, 1975).*

by at least one person in a position to evaluate the performance.

Consider these examples with Martens's definition in mind. You go out alone for a 3-mile jog, setting a goal for yourself to run this distance in 21 minutes (your previous best was 22 minutes). This would not be considered competition because only you are aware of the standard of excellence you are striving to beat. However, if you ran with a friend and told her about your goal to run 3 miles in 21 minutes, it would be competition because your friend is aware of the criteria for evaluation and can evaluate your performance.

Some people argue that the first example is also competition inasmuch as you are competing against yourself. Martens would not necessarily disagree with this point of view, but he argues that to study competition scientifically, we must delimit its scope. Without another person involved to evaluate the comparison process, almost anything might be called competition. How would one know if you were trying to run 3 miles in 21, 20, or 19 minutes? By having another person there, the exact parameters of competition can be well defined. Martens states that most activities commonly thought to be competitive are indeed covered by his definition, so we really don't lose much by limiting the definition to include another person.

Stage 2—The Subjective Competitive Situation

Regardless of whether people are in an objective competitive situation because they seek it or because circumstances place them in it, they must evaluate the situation in some way. This brings into play the next stage, the subjective competitive situation, which involves how the person perceives, accepts, and appraises the objective competitive situation. Here the individual's unique background and at-

> *Competitiveness is the personality characteristic that best predicts how people appraise the objective competitive situation.*

tributes become important. Such factors as perceived ability, motivation, the importance of the competitive situation, and the opponent may well influence the subjective appraisal of the competitive setting.

For example, one gymnast may look forward to competing in a championship meet as a means of gaining experience, whereas another gymnast facing the same objective situation may dread the upcoming meet. Similarly, one runner in an adult fitness class may want to turn every jog into a race, whereas another seeks to avoid comparisons with other runners in his class.

Highly competitive people tend to seek out competitive situations and be more motivated to achieve in them than people are who have lower levels of competitiveness. Trait competitiveness alone, however, will not adequately predict how a person will respond to a particular competitive situation; other situational variables (e.g., type of sport, coach, parents, teammates) also exert strong influences on behavior.

Since competitiveness is such an important personal factor in the competitive process, let's take a closer look at it. Gill and Deeter attempted to more clearly define the term, first developing the Sport Orientation Questionnaire (SOQ) to provide a reliable and valid measure of competitiveness (1988). Sample questions from the questionnaire follow.

Using the SOQ, Gill and Deeter found three types of competitive orientations, all of which represent different subjective outcomes of a competitive situation.

- **Competitiveness** is an enjoyment of competition and desire to strive for success in competitive sport settings. A competitive person simply loves to compete and actively seeks competitive situations.

- **Win orientation** is a focus on interpersonal comparison and winning in competition. It is more important to beat other competitors than to improve on personal standards.

- **Goal orientation** is a focus on personal performance standards. The goal is to improve one's own performance, not to win the competition.

■ MORE INFORMATION ■

Objective and Subjective Outcomes of Competition

Deutsch defined competition as a situation in which rewards are distributed unequally among participants based on their performances. Martens views this definition as inadequate to study competition in sport because it does not factor in the subjective as well as objective rewards inherent in sport competition. Say you have a chance to play Michael Jordan in a one-on-one basketball game, with the first player to score 21 points winning the game. You obviously do not expect to beat the best player in the world, so you set a goal for yourself to score 5 points. If you lose the competition 21–6 (objective outcome) but are happy to have scored more than 5 points (subjective outcome), then you would consider yourself successful, even though you lost on the scoreboard. On the other hand, Michael Jordan might be disappointed that you scored even 1 point off him. As you can see, it is quite possible for the goals one strives for and the rewards sought to be entirely different for each competitor. Deutsch's reward definition is not sensitive to these differential outcomes and goals in sport competition; thus, the competition model proposed by Martens is more useful for studying competitive behavior in sport and physical activity.

Sport Orientation Questionnaire

The following statements describe reactions to sport situations. We want to know how you usually feel about sports and competition. Read each statement and circle the letter that indicates how much you agree or disagree with each statement on the scale. There are no right or wrong answers; simply answer as you honestly feel. Do not spend too much time on any one statement. Remember—choose the letter that describes how you *usually* feel.

	Strongly agree	Slightly agree	Neither agree nor disagree	Slightly disagree	Strongly disagree
1. I am a determined competitor.	A	B	C	D	E
2. Winning is important.	A	B	C	D	E
3. I am a competitive person.	A	B	C	D	E
4. I set goals for myself when I compete.	A	B	C	D	E

A person's competitive orientation affects how he or she perceives the competitive situation. For example, Gill found that males scored higher on the competitive and win orientations, and females higher on the goal orientation (1988). Athletes vary greatly in their competitive orientations, but Gill's study suggests that more of them are oriented toward improving their own performances (goal orientation) than on winning. The various orientations athletes have to the competitive situation impact how they subjectively perceive the objective competitive situation. It is important to note that individuals can be high on more than one orientation. For example, research with elite athletes has revealed that they are high on both win and goal orientations (Hardy, Jones, & Gould, 1996). Anyone structuring a sport program should consider these different competitive orientations.

99

Stage 3—Response

According to Martens's competitive process model, after a person appraises a situation, she decides to either approach or avoid it. The chosen **response** initiates the third stage of the model. If the decision is not to compete, then the response stops there. However, a response to compete can occur at the behavioral, physiological, psychological, or all three levels. For example, at the behavioral level, you might decide what type of opponent you prefer to play: someone better than you, so you might improve; someone worse than you, so you can make sure you win; or someone equal to you, so you have a challenging competition. On a physiological level, your response might be that your heart starts to beat faster and your hands become cold and clammy. Several psychological factors, both internal and external, can also affect a person's response. Motivation, confidence, and perceived ability level are just a few of the internal factors affecting the response. Facilities, weather, time, and opponent ability are some external influences.

Stage 4—Consequences

The final stage of the competitive process results from comparing the athlete's response with the standard of comparison. **Consequences** are usually seen as being either positive or negative, and many people equate positive consequences to success and negative consequences to failure. However, as we discussed earlier, the athlete's perception of the consequences is more important than the objective outcome. For example, although you might have lost the game, you might still perceive the outcome as positive if you played well and met your own standard of excellence.

These feelings of success and failure do not occur in isolation: They feed back into the process and affect subsequent competitive events. A Little League baseball player who strikes out three times with runners in scoring position but who feels encouraged and is instructed in proper batting technique may yet improve his batting average. This should contribute to his having a more positive outlook in future games and change the way the player approaches the next objective competitive situation. Another player who is criticized for striking out

© Human Kinetics

■ CASE STUDY ■

Demonstrating the Model of Competition

Mr. Davis is a physical education teacher at a junior high school. He has been teaching volleyball skills the past few weeks and recently the class has started to play some competitive games. Mark, who is outgoing and athletic, looks forward to the competition; he enjoys the challenge and the chance to show his classmates his skills. John, on the other hand, is shy and not very athletic. He is nervous and apprehensive about the competition because he is unsure of his skills and afraid of embarrassing himself.

Mr. Davis is aware that Mark views competition positively, whereas John would like to avoid competition at all costs (subjective competitive situation). Mark likes to compete against people as good as or better than himself because he sees this as a challenge, whereas if John has to compete, he likes to play against a weaker opponent so that he doesn't look too bad (response).

In a competition, Mark handles winning and losing very well because his self-esteem is not threatened if he should play poorly or his team should lose. He has succeeded often in sport, receiving supportive feedback from coaches and parents in the past. In contrast, John has experienced a lot of failure, often receiving criticism and even ridicule for his athletic endeavors. Naturally he feels threatened and apprehensive about losing or performing poorly (consequences).

Because Mr. Davis understands this process of competition and how students are different, he structures his physical education class to meet the needs of both John and Mark. Of course, he tries always to be positive and encouraging to his students. He also sets up different types of learning situations and lets students choose among them. For example, on one court he sets up teams and a competition for those who seek out a challenge and enjoy the excitement of competition. On another court, the emphasis is on learning and improving skills, not on competing. On this court students who are still unsure of themselves can learn without the pressure of competition. Davis attempts to structure his physical education class so that students enjoy themselves, acquire skill, and develop a positive feeling toward sport and physical activity.

three times might develop a more apprehensive and negative approach to future games. Modifying the rules (e.g., not keeping score, allowing a player to stay at bat until he or she hits the ball into fair territory) or the facilities and equipment (e.g., lowering the rim in basketball, using smaller balls for basketball, volleyball, or football) can influence perceptions of success and failure. The case study in the box above gives some useful and appropriate modifications for young participants: It shows how a junior high physical education teacher might apply Martens's model.

Using Martens's Model

Martens's model helps demonstrate how competition can be enhanced or decreased during its different stages. In the objective competitive situation, for example, a person competes against some standard of excellence. Making the standard of comparison simply beating an opponent might accentuate competition, whereas making the standard one's past

performance might reduce it. Thus, a runner's goal might be to improve her 10K time by 5 seconds instead of to finish in a certain position.

In a subjective competitive situation, a coach might manipulate the situation by emphasizing to the gymnast the importance of the competition and settling for nothing less than first place. Having parents and friends at the meet might also accentuate the importance of performing well, which would probably increase the pressure and anxiety the athlete feels. Conversely, the coach could focus on team cooperation and encourage players to give each other emotional support. The coach could tell the gymnasts, "Go out and do your best—enjoy yourselves." This orientation would influence the gymnasts' subjective perception of the competitive situation.

It is important that administrators, coaches, and parents know how to help performers feel more successful about sport experiences. Taking a participant-centered approach by modifying rules, facilities, and equipment to provide more action, more scoring,

101

> *Competition is inherently neither good nor bad. It is neither a productive nor a destructive strategy—it is simply a process.*

closer games, and more personal involvement can create positive experiences for all participants.

In essence, competition is a "learned" social process (rather than being innate) that is influenced by the social environment (including coaches, parents, friends, sport psychologists, etc.). Competition is inherently neither good nor bad. It is simply a process, and the quality of leadership largely determines whether it will be a positive or negative experience for the participant. Thus, you should consider the many factors that can influence the relationship between the objective competitive situation, subjective competitive situation, response, and consequences of the competitive process.

Psychological Studies of Competition and Cooperation

People have been competing in sports for hundreds of years, but only recently have sport psychologists systematically studied competitive and cooperative behaviors in sport. It might be useful to review some of the classic and pioneer psychological investigations into the processes of competition and cooperation.

Triplett's Cyclists

The first experiment that investigated the effects of competition on performance was documented in 1898 by Norman Triplett (whose influence we discussed briefly in Chapter 1). Triplett noted that racers showed varying performances (as measured in time) when they raced alone, with a pacer, or in competition with another racer. By consulting the records of the Racing Board of the League of American Wheelmen, he found that cyclists were faster when racing against or with another cyclist than when racing alone against the clock. Thus, for the first time, face-to-face competition against fellow competitors was shown to potentially enhance performance.

Deutsch's Puzzles

In Morton Deutsch's classic study (1949) college students were required to solve puzzle problems dur-

ing a 5-week span, using both competitive and cooperative instructions. Students in the competitive condition were told that a reward (a grade in the class) would be given to the person within the group with the best average number of puzzles solved. Students in the cooperative condition were told that they would be evaluated by their group's ranking in relation to four other groups who were also solving puzzles and would receive a reward as a team. In essence, the students' appraisal of the objective competitive situation was manipulated to affect their subjective appraisal and evaluation of the competitive situation (to be either more competitive or cooperative). Results revealed that students in the competitive group were self-centered, directed their efforts at beating others, had closed communication, and exhibited group conflict and mistrust. Students in the cooperative group, however, communicated openly, shared information, developed friendships, and actually solved more puzzles than their competitive counterparts.

One implication from Deutsch's study is that teams work together better when they have a common goal and when reaching that goal produces similar rewards for all participants. For example, if one basketball team member is most interested in the scoring title and the others are interested in winning their division, a counterproductive conflict of interests potentially exists. Consequently, it is important for coaches to make sure that all players understand their roles and strive toward common goals. This can be accomplished by emphasizing the unique role and contribution of each team member. To Deutsch, the potential negative effects of competition were so destructive that in 1982 he called for a planned reduction of competitive situations in society, since these often led to conflict. He had concluded from decades of research that competitive conflicts can be resolved by communication, coordination, shared goals, and control of threat.

Competition and Aggression

It's not news that a primary focus on winning and beating an opponent can produce hostility and aggression among teams. Fighting has often erupted in professional and college sports that encourages contact and collision between players, such as football, hockey, and basketball. It is not the competition per se that produces the aggressive behavior and hostility. Rather, the feelings and behavior stem from the focus on doing whatever it takes to win, even when this means unfair play or injuring an opponent. In his book *They Call Me Assassin* (1980), former pro football player Jack Tatum describes the premeditated, deliberate attempts at injuring opposing players to take them out of commission. More recently, in 1996, an NFL coach was said to have offered a "bounty" for any defensive player who could knock the opposing quarterback out of the game.

You can see in the next two examples how the focus on winning and on one's own glory can be a catalyst producing negative behaviors in competition. First, two teammates competing for a starting position might develop hostility and try to undermine each other's play. Second, as suggested by figure skater Tonya Harding's involvement in the attack on Nancy Kerrigan, competition for the same spot might lead to one competitor's deliberately injuring another. In fact, as bizarre as it might seem, a mother planned to murder a young girl competing to be a high school cheerleader so that her daughter could make the cheerleading team.

But certainly not all sport competition results in the type of aggressive behavior just noted. In fact, competitive sport can also help athletes learn to work together to strive for mutual goals and reduce the overemphasis and pressure on winning. This not only can create a positive social environment, but it can also improve performance (Sherif & Sherif, 1969).

For example, teammates might cooperate, trying to help each other be the best player possible— because in the long run this will help the team as a whole. To help their teams veteran NFL quarterbacks typically mentor their younger quarterback teammates, even though the younger players may eventually take their jobs. Two rivals, however, might focus solely on beating each other, without concern about how they play, as long as they win. Or they might view each other as allies, in the sense that each plays better because of the high performance level of the other. A great performance by one spurs the other to even greater heights. Thus, the way performers view competition determines whether its impact is positive or negative.

How Competition and Cooperation Score

We can see the potential negative effects of competition when we look at the relation between competition and performance. Johnson and Johnson (1985) thoroughly analyzed 122 studies conducted between 1924 and 1981 for the effects of competitive and cooperative attitudes on performance. In 65 studies cooperation was seen to produce higher achievement and performance than competition, with only

■ RESEARCH ■

Reducing Competition Through Cooperation

Sherif and Sherif conducted three field experiments with 11- and 12-year-old boys in isolated camps (1969). First, two groups were formed and each was provided the opportunity to develop a strong group identity. Sports and games were a large part of the groups' activities, and teamwork and group identity were emphasized. In the next phase of the study, Sherif and Sherif deliberately induced intergroup conflict, much of it through sport competitions that emphasized a winner and a loser. In addition, they had refreshments put on a camp table for a party, and one group was invited up first. The first group ate almost all the food, leaving little for the second group, which naturally felt resentful.

The third phase attempted to reduce or eliminate the hostility that the experimenters had helped to build, but the boys maintained their dislike and ill will toward each other. Finally, situations were contrived, such as repairing a leak in the camp's water pipe and fixing a damaged food supply truck, that forced the two groups to cooperate for what the experimenters termed "superordinate goals." These situations were set up so that neither group could achieve a highly desired outcome without the help of the other group. These cooperative efforts resulted in both reducing hostility and conflict between the groups and developing friendships and communication between them. Thus, the studies underscore the critical roles that the social context and the emphasis placed on competition play in determining whether competition is beneficial and productive. Inherently, competition is neither good nor bad.

8 studies showing the opposite. Furthermore, in 108 studies cooperation promoted higher achievement than independent or individualistic work, whereas the opposite occurred in only 6 studies. The superiority of cooperation held across a variety of tasks involving memory and the quality, accuracy, and speed of performance. It certainly appears that we should promote cooperation over competition in physical education and sport. In fact, Johnson and Johnson concluded from their review that there is no type of task for which cooperative efforts are less effective than are competitive or individualistic efforts. Rather, on most tasks, cooperative efforts are more effective in promoting achievement.

However, the nature of the experimental tasks in many of these studies called for a cooperative strategy over a competitive strategy. That is, if subjects had chosen to compete, their performances would be poorer than when they cooperated. As noted earlier, it's not that competition itself produces negative consequences: It is the overemphasis on winning that is counterproductive.

In fact, competitive orientations often lead to high levels of achievement in individual as well as team sports. For example, although Michael Jordan needed to cooperate with his teammates to form the unit that helped the Chicago Bulls dominate the NBA in the 1990s, it is generally recognized that his extremely competitive nature was what really drove him to reach the highest level of success and excellence. In essence, many situations in the world of sport and physical activity call for a blend of cooperative and competitive strategies and orientations. Finding the right mix for the specific situation is the real challenge.

Experimental Games: Prisoner's Dilemma

Psychologists have also studied competition and cooperation through the use of experimental games. The "prisoner's dilemma," based on the not-uncommon strategy of questioning more than one prisoner suspected of the same crime, is the most popular of these games. The prisoners are usually separated, and each is told that the coconspirator has confessed to obtain an advantage in the final proceedings. Each prisoner is then urged separately to "make a deal," confess, and obtain a lighter sentence (or possibly be set free) by testifying against the other.

The most advantageous thing for both prisoners to do is to maintain their innocence. However, each prisoner has to guess the behavior of the other to decide whether to cooperate with the police or to cooperate with each other. For example, if both prisoners choose not to confess, they will both spend only a short time in jail on minor charges. However, if one prisoner chooses to confess and implicate the partner, he will get off scot-free while the partner gets the jail term.

In a sport setting, for example, two highly sought college athletes might have been recruited by means that violated NCAA regulations. One athlete has second thoughts and is told by an NCAA investigator that if he goes public with these irregularities, his penalty will be significantly reduced but the others involved will be severely punished. If he doesn't go public now, the NCAA can still pursue and prove some minor violations. Therefore, the athlete must decide whether to cooperate with his teammate in keeping their secret or with the investigator by "ratting" on his teammate.

Competitors Drawing in Cooperators

In an interesting study, Kelley and Stahelski (1970) used the prisoner's dilemma to investigate how effective competitive responses were compared with cooperative ones. In their study, competitive players were paired with cooperative players. Over a series of games, the competitive players were able to draw their cooperative partners into competition. In essence, cooperators began by cooperating but were forced into competitive responses by their opponents. The cooperators knew they were being forced to change their style of play and compete, whereas the competitors perceived only the conflict of the game and were oblivious to the cooperative overtures being offered. It appears, then, that competitive-oriented individuals can control the nature of a competition and draw cooperative-oriented performers into competition. Kelley and Stahelski (1970) conclude that "it is simply that the competitor's experience has been severely biased or limited by his or her tendencies to be aggressive, egotistic, exploitive, and rivalistic in interpersonal relationships."

Let's take a look at a real-life example of this principle. Imagine you are playing in a pickup basketball game, and you're simply interested in getting some exercise and having some fun (i.e., you're a cooperator). As you drive to the basket, another player pushes you in the back onto the floor. You're really angry and confront the player, but all he says is, "That's how we play here. If you don't like it, leave." (i.e., he's a competitor). Now you have to decide if you want to leave or stay. If you stay, you would most likely have to adopt the competitive style

© Human Kinetics

of the people playing the game. If you leave, you don't get the exercise you were hoping to get. But in any case, the competitor has dictated the kind of action and behavior required by the cooperator.

Overcoming the Dilemma

Usually a physical education teacher has both competitive- and cooperative-oriented students in class, and one solution is to group students according to their degree of competitiveness. In this way both competitive- and cooperative-oriented students have a chance to explore and derive satisfaction from their class experience. Another solution is to structure some activities that are best performed competitively and others that are oriented toward cooperation. Later in the chapter we will discuss ways to enhance cooperation in sporting situations.

Cross-Cultural Studies of Competition and Cooperation

One way to understand how competitive and cooperative orientations are learned is to study their development in different cultures. For example, in one study (Madsen & Shapira, 1970) Anglo-American children, particularly those in urban areas, showed higher degrees of competitiveness than Mexican children. Children raised in a cooperative and sometimes communal environment, such as the kibbutz in Israel, exhibit the highest level of cooperation (Madsen & Shapira, 1977). Some studies demonstrate that the way parents reward or punish success and failure affects the development of competitive or cooperative orientations. For instance, American mothers typically reward their children after success, whereas Mexican mothers typically reward their children after both success and failure.

The findings indicate that cultures differ in fostering competitive or cooperative attitudes. In fact, there are certain cultures where there is little or no sign of competition in the games that children play (Kohn, 1986). For example, among some native American peoples, orientations are so strong that tribal members either avoid competition or redefine competitive situations to emphasize cooperative relationships. A high school football coach in Arizona recently complained, "Students at Hopi High School aren't used to our win-at-all costs, beat-the-other-man mentality. Their understanding of

105

■ RESEARCH ■

Does Sport Competition Transfer to Life Skills and Achievement

A persistent question that has been asked over the years is "To what extent does competitive sport participation help individuals prepare for life?" This is a summary of the results from studies investigating different aspects of this question (Coakley, 1997):

- *Sport participation and academic achievement.* Studies have found in general that varsity athletes have higher GPAs and higher educational aspirations than those who do not participate on varsity teams. This positive relationship is most likely to occur when sport participation somehow alters important relationships in a young person's life. Specifically, when participation leads parents, friends, coaches, counselors, or teachers to take young people more seriously as humans and students and to give them more academic support and encouragement, participation will be associated with positive academic outcomes. However, when participation occurs outside of school-sponsored sports, relationships do not seem to change in academically relevant ways. This is true also when athletes participate in "minor sports" or are low-status substitutes in "major sports," are African-American, and are in schools where academics are heavily emphasized and rewarded over and above performance.

- *Sport participation and social or occupational mobility.* Research has found that former athletes, as a group, have no more and no less career success than others from comparable backgrounds. In addition, former athletes do not appear to have any systematic mobility advantage over their peers in similar jobs: That is, former athletes have a wide range of career successes and failures. Individual motivational or personality differences rather than sport experience itself seems to be a better predictor of occupational success.

- *Sport participation and deviant behavior.* The question of whether participation in competitive sport may "keep young people off the street" and out of trouble has been hotly debated in recent years. Correlational analyses have not found higher rates of deviance among athletes than among nonathletes, and this finding has been replicated across sports, societies, gender, and socioeconomic status (Hanrahan & Gallois, 1993). However, research has also not consistently found that competitive sport participation actually reduces the prevalence of deviant behavior. The nature of the specific sport experience, differences among individuals, and the competitive environment all interact to determine the impact of sport participation on deviance.

Coakley (1997) argues that sport participation will have a positive effect on reducing athletes' deviant behavior *if* they play sports in connection with a clearly expressed emphasis on the following: (a) philosophy of nonviolence, (b) respect for self and others, (c) the importance of fitness and the control of self, (d) confidence in physical skills, and (e) a sense of responsibility. In essence, simply getting kids off the streets to play sport is not enough to reduce deviance. If we emphasize hostility toward others—using aggression as a strategy and bodies as tools, dominating others, and winning at all costs—then we cannot expect rates of deviance to decrease.

what it means to be a good Hopi goes against what it takes to be a good football player" (Coakley, 1994, p. 91).

Therefore, it is not enough to say that we are competitive by nature; rather the kinds of reinforcements we receive and our environment apparently can be critical determinants of our attitudes. This idea is consistent with Sherif and Sherif's (1969) classic studies of summer camps described earlier, where the social environment

and evaluations the boys received were critical in shaping their competitive or cooperative behaviors.

Is Competition Good or Bad?

As things now stand, the competitive ethic is a driving force in sports. You hear people say, "Competition brings out the best in us," "Without competi-

© Claus Andersen

tion, even minimal productivity would disappear," and "To compete is to strive for goals and reach for success." Many Americans equate success with victory, doing well with beating somebody: They subscribe to an attitude attributed to former Green Bay Packer coach Vince Lombardi that winning isn't everything, it's the only thing. Thus, whether they call it the competitive urge, competitive spirit, or competitive ethic, many people consider this type of thinking synonymous with the American way of life. For example, middle distance runner and one-time holder of numerous world records, Mary Decker Slaney described her orientation toward competition:

> *From the time I started running, I won. . . . To me, that was the only place to finish. I wasn't like some kids who would finish second and say, "I ran a good time." Good time, heck. I want to win. I'll do anything I have to win.*

Likewise, a successful high school basketball coach had this to say about competition and winning:

> *Through the years I've developed my own philosophy about high school basketball. Winning*

isn't all that matters. I don't care how many games you win. It's how many championships you win that counts.

This overemphasis on winning is seen in the scoring procedure in NFL games. Specifically, although a regular-season game in the National Football League can end in a tie (after one quarter of overtime), the Super Bowl is played out until some team finally wins. The assumption is that nobody would be satisfied with a Super Bowl that ended in a tie. We want a clear winner. Similarly, a coach's win-loss record is often the overriding criterion for his or her success. College presidents may claim that education is more important than athletics, but a coach who graduates all his players but doesn't achieve a winning record is seldom retained, much less rewarded. At the home level, some parents hold their children back a grade in school so with that extra year they can be bigger and stronger and thus more likely to achieve success in football.

The preoccupation with winning sometimes leads to cheating. One winner of the All-American Soap Box Derby was disqualified for cheating and forfeited his $7,500 scholarship when officials discovered that

107

■ MORE INFORMATION ■

Competition:
Is It Different for Boys and Girls?

With the increased participation of girls in competitive sport (both organized and un-organized), researchers have recently focused on the experiences of boys and girls in competitive sport. Coakley (1997) has indicated that boys and girls often have these very different experiences while playing competitive sports and games:

© Human Kinetics

- Boys play competitive games more frequently than girls.
- Girls play in predominantly male groups more often than boys play games in predominantly female groups.
- When boys are with friends, they play in larger groups than girls do.
- Girls' games are more spontaneous, im-aginative, and freer of structure than boys' games.
- Boys see themselves as more physically skilled than girls see themselves, even though gender differences in actual skill levels are small or nonexistent.
- Boys' games are more aggressive, involve taking greater risks, and reward individual achievement to a greater extent than do girls' games.
- Boys play games that are more complex than games girls play; they have more rules, a greater number of different positions (roles), and more interdependence (teamwork).

an electromagnet gave his car an unfair starting advantage. The abuse of steroids to improve performance is also a form of cheating. Although many Olympic athletes probably have found ways to get around the standardized drug testing performed on elite and professional athletes, numerous others have been disqualified (such as Ben Johnson's disqualification from winning the 1988 Olympic gold medal in the 100-meter dash).

Many elementary school physical education teachers complain about their students being overly competitive. Some adult exercisers have trouble working at their own pace because they want to keep up with their fitness-crazy friend. Some exercisers get caught up trying to do more than the "other guy." More and more experts who note the overemphasis on winning have become proponents of cooperative sport and working together. In fact, new games have been developed that emphasize cooperation over competition (Coakley, 1986). The late tennis great

Arthur Ashe says this about cultivating a cooperative frame of mind:

I associate the killer instinct with a heightened emotional state, and I would not want to be known as somebody who had it. . . . I like harmony in everything. To me, there should be harmony among the crowd, court officials, and even the ball boys. (1981, p. 176)

The potential negative effects of competition do not mean, however, that competition or competitive sport is necessarily bad or that it causes these negative consequences. There are also many instances where competition has produced positive, healthy outcomes. For example, author James Michener states:

I am always on the side of healthy competition. I love it. I seek it out. I prosper under its lash. I have always lived in a fiercely competitive

108

■ MORE INFORMATION ■

Unstructured Sport: An Opportunity for Enhanced Cooperation and Growth

Most of today's sport for youth is structured and organized; there are coaches, officials, defined teams, schedules, strict rules, and parental involvement. But youngsters also play another type of sport or games, which has been termed unorganized, unstructured, or informal. Observational studies (including interviews of young athletes) have revealed tremendous differences in the philosophy and implementation of these two approaches to sport competition. Specifically, when youth get together and play on their own, they are predominantly interested in four things (Coakley, 1997):

1. *Action, especially leading to scoring.* Action is enhanced in numerous ways, including (a) fewer players playing the game, which usually leads to more opportunities to get involved (e.g., more at-bats in baseball and more chances to handle the ball in team sports), (b) eliminating free throws in basketball, and (c) eliminating halftimes or time-outs.

2. *Personal involvement in the action.* Youngsters typically maximize involvement through clever rule modifications and handicap systems that keep highly skilled players from dominating the action or give advantages to less-skilled players. These are some examples: (a) no strikeouts in baseball—the batter is up until she hits a fair ball, (b) everyone has a chance to be a receiver and catch the ball in football, (c) use of "do over" or "interference" calls to compensate for mistakes, (d) having a good hitter hit only to a certain part of the field, and (e) decision making in the form of rules interpretation (since there are no official umpires).

3. *Closely matched teams.* Each team should have a good chance to win. Typically, teams are chosen by captains who each get one choice at a time. But deals are also arranged. For example, if there is a particularly good player, the other captain may get two or three picks to offset the one pick of this particularly talented athlete. Even during the game, trades are often made and teams rearranged to help equalize the teams and keep the competition close and equal.

4. *Opportunities to reaffirm friendships during the game.* There is time for players to talk informally with friends and "fool around" during small breaks in the action. Baseball teams that are at-bat offer ample opportunities for informal interactions and discussions having nothing to do with the game (e.g., what they will be doing that evening).

In summary, these informal and unorganized games are generally action-centered, whereas organized sport is rule-centered. The experience in unorganized sport revolves around the maintenance of action, with the action maintained through decision making and managing relationships among players. The experience in organized sport revolves around learning and following the rules, as well as obeying the adults who make and enforce the rules. This is not to say that unorganized sport is more valuable than organized sport. Rather, unorganized sport does provide valuable opportunities for cooperation, decision making, creativity, and action that are not always readily available in organized sport. In essence, unorganized sport participation can complement the benefits provided by organized sport. However, many parents are concerned with the safety about their children's playing unsupervised and hesitate to let them play in an unsupervised environment. Therefore, another way to achieve the positive outcomes of unstructured sport is for coaches and parents to make organized sport more child-centered, focusing on skill development, fun, and personal growth.

world and have never shied away. I live in such a world now and I would find life quite dull without the challenge. (1976)

Similarly, in his retirement speech, Magic Johnson told how much his rivalry with Larry Bird had meant to him. Magic felt he had to raise the level of his game to stay competitive with Bird. Their competition served these superstars as positive motivation to continually improve and refine their skills.

Especially with youth sport, the quality of adult leadership by parents, coaches, and others becomes crucial in determining whether competition affects young athletes positively or negatively. Any of you who have competed in sport know that competition can be fun, exciting, challenging, and positive. Coaches and teachers should teach youngsters when it is appropriate to compete and when it is appropriate to cooperate. In fact, in most team sports, competition and cooperation occur simultaneously. Therefore, an integrated approach offers the greatest opportunities for personal development and satisfaction.

Enhancing Cooperation

The positive outcomes produced by cooperative efforts are familiar to those in business, educational, and organizational settings. Yet most sports and game settings retain a competitive focus, and most sport psychology texts emphasize the various psychological factors that enhance performance in these competitive settings. Certainly, competitive sports offer positive benefits, including character development, discipline, and teamwork. With so much evidence from diverse fields attesting to the positive effects of *cooperation*, however, it's worthwhile to look at how cooperative games can complement traditional competitive sport and physical education.

Component Structure of Games

Canadian sport psychologist Terry Orlick (1978) argues that the design of a game will largely influence what the predominant behavioral response is, be it competitive, individualistic, cooperative, or some combination of these. Competition and cooperation are complementary relationships giving people scope to realize their unique potential in sport and physical activity. They have different potential interactions—ranging from purely cooperative to purely competitive—that a coach or exercise leader must understand to structure a good mix

of physical activities and games. Most activities can be classified into these categories, as defined by Orlick:

Competitive Means–Competitive Ends
The goal is to beat someone else or everyone else from the outset to the end. You might expect this goal, for example, in a 100-yard race or the game King of the Mountain.

Cooperative Means–Competitive Ends
Participants cooperate within their group but compete outside their group, as you might find in soccer, basketball, football, and hockey, when team members work together and try to coordinate their movements to defeat an opponent. However, not all team members are necessarily assured cooperation (cooperative independent means) within teams: A basketball player, for example, can hog the ball and not pass to teammates. To ensure cooperative independent means with younger athletes, a rule can be introduced, such as requiring everyone to receive a pass before a shot could be taken at the basket.

Individual Means–Individual Ends
One or more players pursue an individual goal without cooperative or competitive interaction. Some sport examples might include cross-country skiing, calisthenics, and swimming.

Cooperative Means–Individual Ends
Individuals cooperate and help each other achieve their own goals. For example, two athletes can watch one another and provide feedback and cues so that both of them can improve their skills.

Cooperative Means–Cooperative Ends
Players cooperate with each other from the outset to the end. Everybody works toward a common goal, sharing the means as well as the ends. Volleyball is a good example. The objective is to keep the ball from hitting the floor for as long as possible. Each team is allowed only three hits before hitting the ball over the net, but the goal is not to make your opponents miss; rather, it is to hit the ball over in such a way to ensure that they do not miss.

Philosophy of Cooperative Games

Although games that emphasize both cooperative means and cooperative ends are rare, some significant steps have been taken to develop alternatives to competitive games and sports (Orlick, 1978; Orlick, McNally, & O'Hara, 1978). Orlick argues that our competitive sports and games have become rigid, judgmental, highly organized, and excessively goal-

■ RESEARCH ■

Cooperative Games

In a study by Orlick, McNally, & O'Hara (1978) 4-year-olds were exposed to 14 weeks of cooperative games, playing 2 days a week and using 12 different types of games. The children were asked to play together toward a common end rather than to compete against other teams or individuals. The games were designed to tie all participants into continuous action. Researchers compared the responses of children playing these cooperative games with the responses of children participating in regular physical education classes. They found, for example, that children exposed to cooperative games engaged in three times as much cooperative behavior during "free play" in the gymnasium as did the control group of children who had not experienced cooperative games. Responses to the cooperative games were characterized as sharing, concern for others, helping, and cooperation. Control-group children tended to focus on their own desires, making sure that they got what they needed or wanted. Comments from their teachers highlighted these differences:

"Now my kids think of everyone as involved." (cooperation group)

"Mine don't do that at all." (control group)

"There's a definite difference in my classes. If there are not enough chairs, the children will share." (cooperation group)

"If there are not enough chairs, they'll fight." (control group)

"The most cooperation is visible at clean-up time. It constantly amazes me how the majority will team up and help each other. There is now no discrimination as to whether the mess is theirs or made by someone else." (cooperation group)

It is important to note that it was only during the final 6 weeks that these positive changes occurred; during the program's first 8 weeks there were no differences. This underscores how important it is that such programs be systematically carried out over time.

oriented. There is little relief from the pressure of evaluation and the psychological distress of disapproval. Many competitive sports for young athletes are designed by principles of elimination. In many sports there is only one winner and everyone else loses. This perceived failure is one reason for the large percentage of dropouts from competitive youth sports (see chapter 22). Even worse, many young athletes are taught to delight in others' failures that enhance their own chances of victory. Children become conditioned to the importance of winning, making it more difficult to play simply for the fun of it, which is why most kids play sports in the first place. They don't learn how to help one another, be sensitive to another's feelings, or compete in a friendly, fun-filled way.

The beauty of cooperative games lies in part in their versatility and adaptability. Most cooperative games require little or no equipment or money. Anyone can play, and the rules of the game can be altered to fit the specific constraints of the situation. Furthermore, through cooperation children learn to share, empathize, and work to get along better. The

players in the game must help one another by working together as a unit, leaving no one out of the action, waiting for a chance to play. They have freedom to learn from mistakes rather than trying to hide them (these attributes are similar to those of unorganized sport noted earlier in this chapter). This is not to say that cooperative games are inherently better than competitive ones, but that because some of the structure, goals, and outcomes differ in them, participants should have the opportunity to choose between cooperative and competitive games or play both types.

Blending Cooperation and Competition

Professionals in the physical education field play a crucial role in the development of the attitudes young athletes and sport participants acquire. Coaches, for example, can convey a win-at-all-costs attitude that promotes overaggressive behavior or they can emphasize and reward fair play and skill development. One junior high school basketball coach who

111

wanted to emphasize sportsmanship over winning gave rewards for sportsmanlike behaviors, including the biggest trophy at the end-of-year awards dinner for the player who displayed the best sportsmanship. The sportsmanship award became the most coveted prize, and players worked hard during the season to earn or win it.

Cooperation enhances enjoyment of the activity, communication, and sharing of information. Often it produces superior performance to what competition yields. Consequently, focusing on cooperation as well as encouraging healthy competition in sport and physical activity appears to have many possible positive outcomes.

However, cooperation need not replace competition. We are advocating a blend of competition and cooperation in our sport and physical activity. The focus on winning at all costs is an imbalance reflecting the values of one large segment of our society. Sport experiences should instead emphasize a blending of competition and cooperation. Along these lines, we provide some guidelines for teachers and coaches on the use of competition and cooperation in sport and games:

- Individualize instruction to meet each person's needs.
- Structure games for children to include both competitive and cooperative elements.
- When competition leads to fierce rivalry, use superordinate goals to get the groups together.
- Provide positive feedback and encouragement to students and athletes regardless of the competition's outcome.
- Stress cooperation to produce trust and open communication.
- Provide opportunities for both the learning of sport skills and the practice of these skills in competition.

The Special Olympics is a specific example of blending competition with cooperation to produce an optimal learning environment. Specifically, what exists in the Special Olympics is carefully controlled competition where, in addition to outcome, the focus is on fellowship and pride in one's own physical accomplishments. Participants receive unconditional support from spectators, coaches, and peers, as well as from fellow competitors. The competitive outcome is important to the athletes, but it takes a backseat to the sheer pleasure and camaraderie of personal involvement. The parents of the participants judge their children on the basis of effort and personal progress—not on the basis of wins and losses, medals, trophies, or championships. In essence, the overall social and psychological development of the athletes is paramount (Coakley, 1994).

Cooperative Games in the Gymnasium and on the Playing Field

Now that we have discussed the benefits of blending cooperation and competition for young participants, we can turn to the need to foster cooperative learning in their physical education classes and on sport teams. Therefore we suggest specific ways here to implement cooperative games and activities into your future programs. First, it is important for coaches and physical educators to determine what they want to accomplish in their classes or on the athletic field. If they consider having fun, learning skills, reducing stress, providing maximum participation, and enhancing social relationships to be important outcomes, then integrating some cooperative games into programs and curricula is appropriate. This is not to say that cooperative games should be the main or only type of games taught, but they should be included to complement other activities and competitive events. Often, cooperative games require only a modification of the rules in existing sports and games. To implement a cooperative approach to learning you can follow these general principles:

- Maximize participation.
- Maximize opportunities to learn sport and movement skills.
- Do not keep score of games.
- Maximize opportunities for success.
- Give positive feedback.
- Provide opportunities for youngsters to play different positions.

These are some more specific examples of rule modifications that encourage cooperation:

- Volleyball—the goal is to keep the ball from hitting the ground; each team still gets only three hits.
- Soccer—there should be at least five passes to different players before a shot on goal can be attempted.
- Baseball—no strikeouts or walks are allowed; every batter must hit the ball into fair territory to complete an at-bat.

SUMMARY

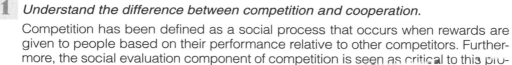

1 *Understand the difference between competition and cooperation.*

Competition has been defined as a social process that occurs when rewards are given to people based on their performance relative to other competitors. Furthermore, the social evaluation component of competition is seen as critical to this process because competition always involves a comparative judgment and performers are evaluated on how well they do. Cooperation is also seen as a social process through which performance is evaluated and rewarded in terms of the collective achievements of a group of people working together to reach a common goal.

2 *Describe the process of competition.*

Competition, in Martens's view, is a four-stage process. It involves an objective competitive stage, a subjective competitive stage, a response, and consequences. Understanding this framework helps you appreciate what determines and results from competitiveness and competitive behavior.

3 *Detail the psychological studies of competition and cooperation.*

Overwhelming evidence from psychological studies suggests that cooperative activities produce more open communication, sharing, trust, friendship, and even enhanced performance than competitive activities do. These differences were found in laboratory and field settings, as well as in a variety of experimental games. People will compete even when it is irrational to do so, and once competition breaks out, it's hard to stop it. How and why people choose to compete, athletes' evaluation of competition, the different potential responses to competition, and how competition affects athletes psychologically are just some of the questions still to be explored in research.

4 *Discuss the social factors influencing competition and cooperation.*

Our social environments in large part influence competitive and cooperative behaviors. For example, cross-cultural work has indicated that children's competitive and cooperative behaviors are shaped by the reinforcement patterns of adults as well as by the particular cultural and social expectations placed on them. In essence, coaches, teachers, and parents can influence the development of young participants by the degree to which they emphasize either the competitive or cooperative aspects of sport.

5 *Explain why competition can be both good and bad.*

Competition is not inherently good or bad. It can lead to positive outcomes (e.g., enhanced self-esteem, confidence, having fun) or to negative outcomes (e.g., cheating, preoccupation with winning, excessive aggression). Especially in youth sports, the quality of adult guidance is critical in determining whether competition positively or negatively affects the participants.

6 *Better understand how to balance competitive and cooperative efforts.*

Recent research has investigated the role of both competition and cooperation in sport and physical activity. Cooperative games are viable alternatives that can provide complements to more traditional competitive games that dominate our culture. In addition, unorganized sport participation provides youngsters with opportunities for personal growth, decision making, responsibility, and social interactions. We can all learn a great deal through participation in competitive sports. However, an overemphasis on competition can undermine some of the values of competitive sport. Simply put, physical educators, coaches, and parents must work together to provide athletes the most enjoyable, meaningful, and educational sport experience.

KEY TERMS

competition
cooperation
objective competitive situation
subjective competitive situation
Sport Orientation Questionnaire (SOQ)

competitiveness
win orientation
goal orientation
response
consequences

REVIEW QUESTIONS

1. Discuss some of the common themes emerging from the psychological studies on competition and cooperation and their implications for sport and physical education.

2. Describe the classic field experiments by Sherif and Sherif conducted at summer camps for boys. How were competition and hostility created and finally eliminated? What implications does this have for sport competition?

3. Describe how the prisoner's dilemma game helps us understand competition and cooperation.

4. Discuss some of the findings from the cross-cultural studies on competition and cooperation and their relevance to physical education teachers and coaches.

5. Discuss Martens's definition of the objective competitive situation. Do you agree or disagree with this definition? Why? Why did Martens define competition in this way?

6. Describe the four stages of Martens's model of competition, including examples of each stage.

7. Discuss the three different competitive orientations from the work of Gill and Deeter.

8. Compare and contrast the five different component structures of games.

9. Discuss Orlick's basic philosophy of cooperative games. Make up three games that have cooperative means and cooperative ends, and explain how they are cooperative.

10. Discuss the effects of competition on deviance, academic achievement, and social or occupational mobility.

CRITICAL THINKING QUESTIONS

1. Winning isn't everything—it's the only thing. Do you agree or disagree? Provide research and personal or anecdotal examples to support your point of view.

2. You are hired as the new physical education teacher for an elementary school. Based on your reading, you feel that at this age level, competition and cooperation should be blended to enhance personal growth and development. Discuss the specific games, activities, and sports you would devise to achieve this goal.

3. You are a parent and have a 7-year-old child. You want to get her involved in sports but are unsure whether she should play organized or unorganized sports. Discuss the pros and cons of organized versus unorganized sport competition. Which would you want your child to focus on and why?

© Human Kinetics

Feedback, Reinforcement, and Intrinsic Motivation

After reading this chapter you should be able to

1 explain how positive and negative feedback influence behavior,

2 understand how to implement behavior modification programs,

3 describe the relationship between intrinsic motivation and external rewards,

4 detail different ways to increase intrinsic motivation, and

5 describe the flow state and how to achieve it.

People thirst for feedback. An exerciser feels like a klutz and hopes for a pat on the back, some telling instruction, and a camera to capture the moment she finally gets the steps right. Similarly, a youngster trying to learn how to hit a baseball after a series of missed swings feels great when he finally connects with the next pitch. You are probably taking this course because you think you might want to help people like that exerciser or young athlete make sport and physical activity a lifetime habit. To create an environment that fosters pleasure in growth and mastery, professionals use motivational techniques based on the principles of reinforcement. **Reinforcement** is the use of rewards and punishments that increase or decrease the likelihood of a similar response occurring in the future. The principles of reinforcement are among the most widely researched and accepted in psychology. Their roots are firmly grounded in the theories of behavior modification and operant conditioning. The late B.F. Skinner, the most widely known and outspoken behavior theorist, argued that teaching rests entirely on the principles of reinforcement.

> *For example, Skinner would argue that teaching is the arrangement of reinforcers under which students learn. They learn without teaching in their natural environment, but teachers arrange special reinforcements which expedite learning, hastening the appearance of behavior which would otherwise be acquired slowly or making sure of the appearance of behavior which might otherwise never occur. (1968, pp. 64–65).*

And to provide students, athletes, and exercisers with constructive feedback requires first understanding the basic principles of reinforcement.

Principles of Reinforcement

Although there are many principles related to changing behavior, two basic premises underlie effective reinforcement: First, if doing something results in a good consequence (such as being rewarded), people will tend to try to repeat the behavior to receive additional positive consequences; second, if doing something results in an unpleasant consequence (such as being punished) people will tend to try not to repeat the behavior so they can avoid more negative consequences.

Imagine a physical education class on soccer skills where a player makes a pass to a teammate that leads to a goal. The teacher says, "Way to pass the ball to the open man—keep up the good work!" The player would probably try to repeat that type of pass in the future to receive more praise from the coach. Now imagine a volleyball player going for a risky jump serve and hitting the ball into the net. The coach yells, "Use your head—stop trying low-percentage serves!" Most likely, this player would not try this type of serve again, wanting to avoid the criticism from the coach.

Reinforcement principles are more complex than you might think, however, in the real world. Often the same reinforcer will affect two people differently. For example, reprimanding one participant in an exercise class might make her feel she is being punished, whereas it might provide attention and recognition for another person.

A second difficulty is people cannot always repeat the reinforced behavior. For instance, a point guard in basketball scores 30 points, although his normal scoring average is 10 points a game. He receives praise and recognition from the fans and media for his high scoring output and naturally wants to repeat this behavior. However, he is a much better passer than a shooter: When he tries hard to score more points, he actually hurts his team and lowers his shooting percentage because he attempts more low-percentage shots.

You must also consider all the reinforcements available to the individual, as well as how he or she values them. For example, someone in an exercise program receives great positive reinforcement from staying in shape and looking good. But because of his participation in the program he spends less time with his spouse and children, which is an aversive consequence that outweighs the positive reinforcer, so he drops out of the program. Unfortunately, coaches, teachers, and exercise leaders are often unaware of these competing motives and reinforcers.

> *The principles of reinforcement are complex because people react differently to the same reinforcement, that may not be able to repeat a desired behavior, and receive different reinforcers in different situations.*

Approaches to Influencing Behavior

There are positive and negative ways to teach and coach. The positive approach focuses on rewarding appropriate behavior (e.g., catching people doing something correctly), which increases the likelihood of desirable responses occurring in the future. Conversely, the negative approach focuses on punishing undesirable behaviors, which should lead to a future reduction of these inappropriate behaviors. The positive approach is designed to strengthen desired behaviors by motivating participants to perform them and by rewarding them when they occur. The negative approach, however, focuses on errors and thus attempts to eliminate unwanted behaviors through punishment and criticism. Thus, the primary motivation in this approach is fear.

Most coaches combine the positive and negative approaches in attempting to motivate and teach skills to their athletes (Smith, Zane, Smoll, & Coppel, 1983). However, sport psychologists agree that the predominant approach with sport and physical activity participants should be positive. As philosopher Henry David Thoreau remarked, "There are few exceptions where it is better to punish a sin than to reward a virtue." Still, it is easy to fall into the trap of constantly correcting and looking for what goes wrong—and inadvertently ignoring what goes right.

Positive Reinforcement

Sport psychologists highly recommend a positive approach to motivation to avoid the potential negative side-effects of using punishment as the primary approach. Research demonstrates that athletes who play for positive-oriented coaches like their teammates better, enjoy their athletic experience more, like their coaches more, and have greater team cohesion (Smith & Smoll, 1997). So let's examine some of the principles underlying the effective use of positive reinforcement.

Choose Effective Reinforcers

Rewards should meet the needs of those receiving them. It is best to know the likes and dislikes of the people you work with and choose reinforcers accordingly:

- Social reinforcers—praise, smile, pat on the back, publicity
- Material reinforcers—trophies, medals, ribbons, T-shirts
- Activity reinforcers—playing a game rather than drilling, playing a different position, taking a trip to play another team, getting a rest
- Special outings—going to a professional game, throwing a team party, hearing a presentation from a professional athlete

A physical education teacher might have students complete a questionnaire, like the one you see included on page 118, in order to determine what type of rewards they most desire. This information could help a teacher pinpoint the type of reinforcer to use for each student. Similarly, athletic trainers might develop a list of the type of reinforcements athletes react most favorably to when recovering from difficult injuries. Sometimes you might want to reward the entire team or class, rather than a particular individual, or to vary the types of rewards (it can become monotonous to receive the same reinforcement repeatedly).

These kinds of rewards you give are called *extrinsic* because they come from external sources (outside the individual), such as the coach or the teacher. Other rewards are called *intrinsic* because they reside within the participant. Intrinsic examples are taking pride in accomplishment and feeling competent. Although coaches, teachers, and exercise leaders cannot directly offer intrinsic rewards, they can structure the environment to promote intrinsic motivation. We will further discuss the relationship between extrinsic rewards and intrinsic motivation later in this chapter.

Schedule Reinforcements Effectively

Appropriate timing and frequency (that is, choosing the best time to reinforce desired behaviors and deciding how often to give rewards) can ensure that rewards are effective. During the initial stages of training or skill development, desirable responses should be reinforced often, perhaps on an almost

117

Reward Preferences Questionnaire

Please answer these questions and return the questionnaire to the coach.

Social rewards

Place a check beside the kinds of approval that you like others to show.

____ Facial signs (e.g., smiles, nods, winks)

____ Hand and body signs (e.g., clapping hands, holding thumbs up, clasping hands overhead)

____ Physical contact (e.g., a pat on the back, a handshake, a hug)

____ Praise about yourself (e.g., you're smart, very helpful, a nice person)

____ Praise about your athletic skills (e.g., you have a great throwing arm, backhand, jumpshot)

____ Other (be specific) _____

Activity rewards

What activities would you like to do more often during practice? Explain why you would like to do them.

1. _____

2. _____

3. _____

4. _____

(Examples: Have free-swim time; shoot baskets for fun; help the coach set up equipment; help the coach score time trials; lead the group; demonstrate skills; change playing positions for fun)

Outings as rewards

Place a check beside the things you would like to do with the whole team.

____ See a film about sports

____ Tour a sports museum

____ Have a local professional athlete visit with the team

____ Go to a competition or sports event of professionals or high-ranking amateurs

____ Visit a practice session for professional athletes

____ Have a team party or dance

____ Other events or activities (be specific) _____

_____

Material rewards

Place a check beside the things you would like to have or own.

____ Team sweater

____ Trophies

____ Team uniform

____ Personal chart that shows your progress from week to week

____ Team jacket

____ Other _____

Adapted from Martin and Lumsden (1987).

In the early stages of learning, continuous and immediate reinforcement are desirable; in the later stages of learning, however, intermittent, immediate reinforcement is more effective.

continuous schedule. A continuous schedule requires rewarding after every correct response, whereas on a partial schedule behavior is rewarded intermittently.

Research has indicated that continuous feedback not only acts as a motivator but also provides the learner with information about how she is doing. However, once a particular skill or behavior has been mastered or is occurring at the desired frequency, the schedule can be gradually reduced to be intermittent (Martin & Pear, 1992). Behavior reinforced intermittently rather than continuously will persist longer in the absence of further reinforcements; individuals get "used to" continuous reinforcement and eventually shut it from their minds.

Thus, although continuous reinforcement is desirable for early learning, an intermittent reinforcement schedule is better once the behavior has been mastered. Intermittent reinforcement is less time-consuming and increases the likelihood that the behavior will persist. In teaching complex skills, a teacher or coach might break the skill down into "subskills" and focus the reinforcement on each subskill until it's mastered.

All things being equal, the sooner after a response that a reinforcement is provided, the more powerful the effects on behavior. This is especially true when people are learning new skills, when it is easy to lose confidence if the skill isn't performed correctly. Once someone masters a skill, it is less critical to reinforce immediately, although it is still essential that the correct behaviors be reinforced at some point.

Reward Appropriate Behaviors

Choosing the proper behaviors to reward is also critical. Obviously you cannot reward someone every time he does something right. You have to decide on the most appropriate and important behaviors and concentrate on rewarding them. Many coaches and teachers tend to focus their rewards purely on the outcome of performance (e.g., winning), but there are other behaviors that could and should be reinforced, which we will now discuss.

Reward Successful Approximations
When individuals are acquiring a new skill, especially a complex one, they inevitably make mistakes. It may take days or weeks to master the skill, which

With difficult skills, shape the behavior of the learner by reinforcing close approximations of the desired behavior.

can be disappointing and frustrating for the learner. It is helpful, therefore, to reward small improvements as the skill is learned. This technique, called shaping, allows people to continue to improve as they get closer and closer to the desired response (Martin & Hyrcaiko, 1983). Specifically, individuals are rewarded for performances that approximate the desired performance. This spurs their motivation and provides direction for what they should do next. For example, if players are learning the overhand volleyball serve, you might first reward the proper toss, then the proper motion, then good contact, and finally the execution that puts all the parts together successfully. Similarly, an aerobics instructor might reward participants for learning part of a routine until they have mastered the entire program. Or a physical therapist might reward a client for improving the range of motion in her shoulder (after surgery) through adhering to her stretching program, even though she still has room for improvement.

Reward Performance, Not Only Outcome
Coaches who emphasize winning tend to reward players based on outcome. A baseball player hits a hard line drive down the third base line, but the third baseman makes a spectacular diving catch. In his next at-bat the same batter tries to check his swing and hits the ball off the end of the bat, just over the outstretched arm of the second baseman, for a base hit. Rewarding the base hit but not the out would be sending the wrong message to the player. If an individual performs the skill correctly, that's all he or she can do. The outcome is sometimes out of the player's control, so the coach should focus on the athlete's performance instead of the performance's outcome.

It is especially important to use an individual's own previous level of performance as the standard for success. For example, if a young gymnast's best score on her floor routines was 7.5 and she received a 7.8 for her most recent effort, then this mark should be used as the measure of success and she should be rewarded for her performance. This kind of reinforcement also encourages a task goal orientation (see Chapter 3), which creates more positive affect and thus leads to enhanced performance.

Reward Effort
It is imperative that coaches and teachers recognize effort as part of performance. Not everyone can be

© Human Kinetics

successful in sports. When sport and exercise participants (especially youngsters) know that they will be recognized for trying new and difficult skills—and not just criticized for performing incorrectly—they do not fear trying. All they can do is try as hard as possible, and if this is recognized, then they have nothing to fear. Former UCLA basketball coach John Wooden encapsulates this concept of focusing on effort instead of winning:

> *You cannot find a player who ever played for me at UCLA that can tell you he ever heard me mention winning a basketball game. He might say I inferred a little here and there, but I never mentioned winning. Yet the last thing that I told my players, just prior to tip-off, before we would go out on the floor was, when the game is over, I want your head up—and I know of only one way for your head to be up—and that's for you to know you did your best. . . . This means to do the best you can do. That's the best; no one can do more. . . . You made that effort.*

Reward Emotional and Social Skills

With the pressure to win, it is easy to forget the importance of fair play and being a good sport. Athletes who demonstrate good sportsmanship, responsibility, judgment, and other signs of self-control and cooperation should be recognized and reinforced. This becomes ever more important as our youngsters look up to sport heroes as role models and, unfortunately, are often disappointed. As leaders of sport and physical activity, we have a tremendous opportunity and responsibility to encourage positive emotional and social skills. We should not overlook the chance to reward such behaviors, especially in younger participants.

Provide Feedback

Help participants by giving them information and feedback about the accuracy and success of their movements. This type of feedback is typically provided after the completion of a response. For example, an athletic trainer working with an injured athlete on increasing her flexibility while

> *Knowledge of results helps people improve performance by providing specific feedback regarding the correctness (or incorrectness) of their response and by enhancing their motivation.*

rehabilitating from a knee injury asks the athlete to bend her knee as far as possible. The trainer then tells the athlete that she has improved her flexibility from 50 degrees to 55 degrees since the week before. Similarly, a fitness instructor might give participants specific feedback about proper positioning and technique when lifting weights.

When you give feedback to athletes, students, and exercisers, it is important that the feedback be sincere and contingent on some behavior. Whether it is praise or criticism, the feedback needs to be tied to ("contingent on") a specific behavior or set of behaviors. It would be inappropriate, for example, to tell a student in a physical education class who is having difficulty learning a new gymnastic skill, "Way to go, keep up the good work!" Rather, the feedback should be specific and tied to performance. Inform the athlete how to perform the skill correctly, such as saying, "Make sure you keep your chest tucked close to your body during the tumbling maneuver." Such feedback, when sincere, demonstrates that you care and are concerned with helping the learner.

Benefits of Feedback

Feedback about performance can benefit participants in several ways, and two of the main functions are to motivate and to instruct. Motivational feedback allows performers to learn specifically what they have been doing incorrectly and to have a benchmark for improving future performance. For example, a point guard in basketball who thinks she is a nifty playmaker might be motivated to improve her ball-handling skills when she finds out that she has twice as many turnovers as assists. A second way that feedback can be motivating is by serving as a valuable reinforcement to the performer, which would in turn stimulate positive or negative feelings. For example, individuals receiving specific feedback indicating poor performance might become dissatisfied with their current level of performance. This feedback can motivate them to improve, but they should also experience feelings of self-satisfaction that function as positive feedback when subsequent feedback indicates improvement. A third motivational function of feedback relates to establishing goal-setting programs. Clear, objective knowledge of results is critical to productive goal setting (see Chapter 15) because, in essence, effective goals are specific and measurable. Thus, individuals benefit from getting specific feedback to help them set their goals.

Instructional feedback provides information about (a) the specific behaviors that should be performed, (b) the levels of proficiency that should be achieved, and (c) the performer's current level of proficiency in the desired skills and activities. When skills are highly complex, the instructional component of knowledge of results can be particularly important. Breaking down complex skills into their component parts allows for a more effective learning environment and gives the learner specific information on how to perform each phase of the skill.

Types of Feedback

Verbal praise, facial expressions, and pats on the back are easy, effective ways to reinforce desirable behaviors. Statements such as "Well done!" "Way to go!" "Keep up the good work!" and "That's a lot better!" can be powerful reinforcers. However, this reward becomes more effective when you identify the specific behaviors you are pleased with. For instance, a track coach might say to a sprinter, "Way to get out of the blocks—you really pushed off strongly with your legs." Or an aerobics instructor might say to a participant who is working hard, "I like the way you're pumping your arms while stepping in place." This coach and instructor have identified exactly what the participants were doing well.

Punishment

Positive reinforcement should be the predominant way to change behavior; in fact, most researchers suggest that 80% to 90% of reinforcement should be positive. Despite this near consensus among sport psychologists about what fosters motivation in athletes, some coaches use a negative approach emphasizing punishment as the primary motivator (Rushall, 1983). In our society punishment is perhaps the most widespread means of controlling behavior. For example, the judicial system predominantly uses punishment when someone breaks the laws. Similarly, school achievement for athletes is often prompted by a fear of punishment, such as having one's eligibility taken away due to poor grades.

Punishment certainly can control and change negative behavior, and it has advocates among coaches and teachers who take a negative approach

© Terry Wild Studio

to learning and performance. Some coaches assume that by punishing athletes for making mistakes, they can eliminate these errors: They assume that if players fear making mistakes, they will try harder not to make them. Novice coaches tend to emulate their fear-oriented older counterparts (especially if the coach was perceived as successful). However, successful coaches who used a negative approach usually were also masters of strategy, teaching, or technical analysis. Often those were the attributes—not their negative approach—that made them successful. Although punishment has potential negative side effects, especially if it's used too often, there are occasions when punishment might be necessary to eliminate unwanted behaviors. Here are some guidelines for maximizing the effectiveness of punishment:

- Be consistent by giving everyone the same type of punishment for breaking similar rules.

- Punish the behavior, not the person. Convey to the individual that it's his or her behavior that needs to change.

- Allow athletes to have input in making up punishments for breaking rules.

- Do not use physical activity as a punishment.

- Make sure the punishment is not perceived as a reward or simply as attention.

- Impose punishment impersonally—do not berate the person or yell. Simply inform him of his punishment.

- Do not punish athletes for making errors while they are playing.

- Do not embarrass individuals in front of teammates or classmates.

- Use punishment sparingly, and enforce it when you use it.

■ MORE INFORMATION ■

Negative Approaches to Motivation: What Not to Do

Unfortunately, many coaches attempt to motivate their athletes predominantly through fear, threats, criticism, and intimidation. Although these methods often are effective in the short-term, they typically backfire in the long-term. These are some typical (*not* recommended) ways that coaches have tried taking a negative approach to motivation:

- Intimidation. An athlete is not playing well in practice so in front of the team the coach tells him, "If you don't start playing better immediately, you'll be sitting at the end of the bench and won't see any playing time at all."
- Criticism. An athlete makes an error during a game. "I can't believe how uncoordinated you are. Can't you do anything right?"
- Criticism with sarcasm. An athlete makes a mental mistake during a competition. "Aren't you thinking out there? My 8-year-old daughter is smarter than you."
- Physical abuse. A coach is unhappy with his team's focus and effort during practice. "I guess you guys will have to learn the hard way. You'll all be running sprints in the 90° weather until you drop."
- Guilt. A coach felt her team gave up when they fell behind early in the game. "You should feel ashamed. You let down not only yourselves, but the entire school and community."

Clear evidence suggests that punishment and criticism can help eliminate undesirable behaviors (Smith, 1993). The evidence is equally compelling, however, that these modes of teaching have serious drawbacks that can undermine the effectiveness of punishment in eliminating negative behaviors. Punishment usually works by arousing a fear of failure. An athlete who fears failure is not motivated by and does not enjoy the fruits of victory; rather he or she is only trying to avoid the agony of defeat.

The fear of failure usually causes a decrease in performance: An athlete becomes prone to choke under pressure. This occurs because the athlete focuses more on the consequences of losing and making mistakes than on what needs to be done to be successful. For example, a basketball player who worries that the coach will pull her from the game if she misses a shot or turns the ball over will likely become tentative and hesitant in her play. This is counterproductive: Basketball requires confidence, assertiveness, and some risk taking. Playing it safe (because you're afraid of making a mistake) ultimately leads to poor performance. In fact, research has indicated that athletes having a high fear of failure not only perform more poorly in competition but are also more likely to get injured, enjoy the sport experience less, and drop out (Smith & Smoll, 1990).

Second, using punishment can unwittingly reinforce the undesirable behavior by drawing attention to it. In some cases, criticism may be the only way a student gets attention from the teacher. Singling out a student who disrupts the class provides the student with the attention he craves. The punishment reinforces and strengthens the very behavior it was intended to eliminate.

A third problem with emphasizing punishment is that it can create an unpleasant, aversive learning environment. Punishment can produce hostility and resentment between the coach and the athletes. Over time, students and athletes may lose motivation as they become discouraged by frequent criticism. Furthermore, the undesirable behaviors may not even be eliminated; rather, they may be suppressed only while the threat of punishment is present. In many cases, individuals are not taught the correct alternative behaviors but only how to avoid punishment. For example, an exerciser may work hard in an aerobics class when the leader is watching her but slacken off when she is not being watched. People don't reach their potential in such situations because they haven't really developed the *internal motivation* to consistently work hard.

Potential drawbacks of punishment and criticism include arousing fear of failure, acting as reinforcers, and hindering the learning of skills.

Two Sides to Motivation

Indiana basketball coach Bobby Knight has a reputation for yelling, screaming, and using physical intimidation to get his players to perform up to their potential. Players have been known to quit the team and transfer schools because they can't tolerate Knight's constant criticism and verbal abuse. However, Knight is also known as a brilliant defensive coach and tactician. He uses his strong sense of discipline to teach fundamental basketball skills. Many of his former players have spoken out about the "other side" of Coach Knight, which includes caring for his players. In fact, Knight has an excellent record for players' graduating on time, and he is known to help them in their personal lives even after they graduate. It is probably not the fear and intimidation that makes Bobby Knight a successful coach—rather, it is his ability to combine this discipline with other aspects of coaching.

© Anthony Neste Photography

Modifying Behavior in Sport

The systematic application of the basic principles of positive and negative reinforcement to help produce desirable behaviors and eliminate undesirable behaviors has been given various names in the sport psychology literature: *contingency management* (Siedentop, 1980), behavioral coaching (Martin & Lumsden, 1987), and behavior modification (Donahue, Gillis, & King, 1980). These terms all refer to attempts to structure the environment through the systematic use of reinforcement, especially during practice. In general, behavioral techniques are used in sport and physical activity settings to help individuals stay task-oriented and motivated throughout a training period. In what follows we'll highlight a few studies that have used behavioral techniques in sport settings and then offer some guidelines for designing behavior programs.

Evaluating Behavioral Programs

The evidence to date suggests that systematic reinforcement techniques can effectively modify vari-

ous behaviors, including specific performance skills, coaching and teaching behaviors, and error reduction. Behavioral techniques have successfully changed attendance at practice; increased output by swimmers in practice (Koop & Martin, 1983); improved fitness activities (Leith & Taylor, 1992) and gymnastic performance (Wolko, Hrycaiko, & Martin, 1993); reduced errors in tennis, football, and gymnastics (Allison & Ayllon, 1980); and improved golf performance (Simek, O'Brien, & Figlerski, 1994). Other programs have effectively used behavioral techniques to decrease off-task behaviors by figure skaters (Hume, Martin, Gonzalez, Cracklen, & Genthon, 1985) and to change or develop healthier attitudes toward sportsmanship and team support. Let's look closely at a few examples of successful behavioral programs.

Feedback and Reinforcement in Football

In a classic study that provides a first good example, Komaki and Barnett used feedback and praise to improve specific football performance skills (1977). Barnett, who coached a Pop Warner football team, wanted to know if his players were improving in the

Using Feedback During Practice Sessions

Although many coaches provide extensive feedback to their athletes during their practices, unfortunately, the types of feedback they provide often do not maximize learning and time on task. Here are some suggestions for providing feedback during practices to maximize its effectiveness.

- Feedback should contain information relevant to performing the skill correctly.
- Feedback should be appropriate to the performance or behavior (e.g., excessive praise for success at an easy task or for mediocre performance is inappropriate).
- Feedback should be given as immediately as possible (however, during competition it is advised to wait a little before providing feedback; this allows the performer to clear his or her mind and be more receptive to the feedback.
- Feedback should promote the performer's taking personal responsibility for performance and behavior.
- Feedback should be short, clear, and geared to the performer's age level.

basic offensive plays. He and Komaki targeted three specific plays run from the wishbone offense (a formation that requires specific positioning of the running backs and quarterback) and the five players (center, quarterback, and running backs) responsible for their proper execution. For their study they broke each play into five stages. For instance, one play included a (a) quarterback-center exchange, (b) quarterback-right halfback fake, (c) fullback blocking end, (d) quarterback decision to pitch or keep, and (e) quarterback action.

After collecting data during an initial baseline period (10 practices or games), the coach systematically reinforced and provided feedback for Play A, Play B, and Play C. This feedback included

- demonstrating the correct behaviors at each stage,
- a checklist of parts that were successfully executed, and
- praise and recognition for performing each stage correctly.

To test the effectiveness of the behavioral program, the authors compared the percentage of stages performed correctly for each play during the baseline and reinforcement (about 2 weeks) periods. After 2 weeks correct performances increased on Play A from 62% at baseline to 82%, on Play B from 54% to 82%, and on Play C from 66% to 80%.

Behavioral Coaching in Golf

Another behavioral program targeted the performance of novice golfers (O'Brien & Simek, 1983). This study used a type of behavioral change program known as **backward chaining.** In this approach, the last step in a chain is first established (e.g., putting the ball into the hole), then paired with the next-to-last step (e.g., driving or chipping the ball onto the green), and so forth, finally progressing back to the beginning of the chain. In the case of golf, the last step in the chain would be putting on the green into the hole. Putting the ball in the hole in the smallest number of strokes is the goal in golf, and the successful putt should therefore be reinforced. As the next step, chipping onto the green is the focus, and putts are made as reinforcement. Then comes the fairway shot, followed by a successful chip and equally successful putt. The final step involves driving the ball off the tee box, followed in turn by successful completion of the previous three steps.

This behavioral approach using backward chaining was compared with traditional coaching methods used in training novice golfers. Results revealed that golfers receiving the backward chaining instruction scored some 17 strokes lower than golfers in the traditionally coached control group. In essence, the behavioral coaching group scored almost one stroke per hole (18 holes) better than the traditional coaching group, an amazing improvement.

Recording and Shaping in Basketball

Another behavioral program targeted both performance and nonperformance behaviors (Siedentop,

125

© Terry Wild Studio

1980). A junior high school basketball coach was distressed that his players criticized each other so often in practice while failing to concentrate on shooting skills. The coach decided to award points for daily practice in layups, jump shooting, free-throw drills, and for being a team player (which meant that you encouraged your teammates during play and practice). In this system, points were deducted if the coach saw an instance of a "bad attitude." An "Eagle effort board" was posted in a conspicuous place in the main hall leading to the gymnasium, and outstanding students received an "Eagle effort" award at the postseason banquet.

The program produced some dramatic changes: After just a few weeks, jump shooting improved from 37% to 51%, layups increased from 68% to 80%, and foul shooting improved from 59% to 67%. But the most dramatic improvement was in the team player category. Before implementing the behavioral program, the coach had detected 4 to 6 instances of criticism during each practice session, along with 10 to 12 instances of encouragement among teammates. After only a few sessions, over 80 encouraging statements were recorded during a practice session. (Recorders noted there were probably more statements of encouragement, but they couldn't record all of them quickly enough!) At the end of the season the coach commented, "We were more together than I ever could have imagined."

Characteristics of Effective Behavioral Programs

Although the previous examples demonstrated that behavioral change programs can alter behavior, actually changing behavior in sport and exercise settings can be a tricky proposition. Effective behavioral programs have certain major characteristics:

■ They emphasize specific, detailed, and frequent measurement of performance and behavior, and use these measures for evaluating the effectiveness of the program.

■ They recognize the distinction between developing new behavior and maintaining existing behavior at acceptable levels, and they offer positive procedures for accomplishing both.

■ They encourage participants to improve against their own previous level of performance. Thus, a

126

■ APPLICATION ■

Improving Attendance: A Behavioral Approach

A swimming team was showing poor attendance and punctuality at practices. To solve the problem, the swim coach made an attendance board with each swimmer's name. She placed the board prominently on a wall by the swimming pool where everyone could see it (see Figure 6.1). In the first phase of the program, swimmers who came to practice received a check on the board next to their names. In the second phase, swimmers had to show up on time to receive a check. In the final phase, swimmers had to show up on time and swim for the entire session to receive a check. Results indicated a dramatic increase in attendance at each phase of the study with increases of 45%, 63%, and 100% for the three phases, respectively (McKenzie & Rushall, 1974).

Then a public program board was developed on which swimmers could check off each lap of a programmed workout. The group increased its performance output by 27%, equivalent to an additional 619 yards for each swimmer during the practice session! The public nature of the attendance and program boards clearly served a motivational function: Every swimmer could see who was attending, who was late, who swam the entire period, and how many laps each swimmer completed. Coaches and swimmers commented that peer pressure and public recognition helped make the program successful, along with the attention, praise, and approval of coaches after swimmers' checks were posted on the board.

	Show up					Show up on time					Show up on time and swim entire practice			
Swimmer	M	T	W	T	F	M	T	W	T	F	M	T	W	T	F
Antonio															
Marcus															
Maria															
Ken															
Othello															
Karen															
Josh															
Kira															
Kathleen															
Bob															

Figure 6.1 *Swimming attendance board.*

recreational athlete recovering from injury does not try to compare her recovery rate against that of professional athletes, but rather against what the physical therapist feels is optimal for her particular circumstance.

■ They emphasize behavioral procedures that have been demonstrated by research to be effective (this is more a science than an art).

■ They emphasize that the coach, teacher, or leader should carefully monitor self-behavior in a systematic fashion (e.g., videotape, behavioral checklist) so that ineffective behaviors can be eliminated.

■ They encourage the leader to get feedback from participants regarding the effectiveness of the different aspects of the behavioral intervention.

Implementing Behavioral Programs

Clearly, behavioral techniques can produce positive changes in a variety of behaviors. As behavioral techniques are applied, the following guidelines can increase the effectiveness of your intervention programs.

Target the Behaviors

When you initiate a program, identify only a couple of behaviors to work with. If participants focus on changing just a couple of behaviors, they avoid being overwhelmed and confused by trying to do too much too fast. Furthermore, it is difficult to observe simultaneously what all the participants are doing, and by tracking only one or two behaviors you can more accurately record the targeted behaviors and reinforce them fairly. Social and emotional behaviors are appropriate targeted behaviors in addition to the typical performance improvement. Target the behaviors after you make a careful assessment of the particular needs of the individuals involved in the program.

Define Targeted Behaviors

Try to define behaviors in a way that makes them readily observable and easy to record. Attendance, foul shooting percentage, the number of laps done, and correct execution of a skill are relatively objective, concrete behaviors. But such behaviors as hustle and effort are more difficult to pinpoint, quantify, and measure. Individuals need to be told specifically what types of behaviors are expected of them so they can modify their behavior accordingly.

Record the Behaviors

Record observable behaviors on a checklist to give participants feedback. Checklists should be simple and straightforward to maximize efficiency and effectiveness. Head coaches, teachers, and exercise leaders are usually too busy to record the behaviors in question, but often assistant coaches, managers, trainers, or teacher aides can be enlisted to help. If so, you will need to teach them how to record the behaviors to ensure their reliability in the recording.

Provide Meaningful Feedback

Detailed feedback will enhance motivation. If someone can see a simple set of checkmarks on an easy-to-read graph that clearly displays her progress, it encourages self-praise, attention, a teacher's or coach's praise, and knowledge of improvement, which all help in motivation. Public display of this feedback can stimulate peer interaction that might also reinforce increased output. However, some people find this type of display embarrassing and aversive. The focus should always be on self-improvement; avoid creating unhealthy competition among teammates. A team meeting might be appropriate to help determine the exact location and nature of the public display.

State the Outcomes Clearly

Athletes and students want to be clear on what behaviors are required and what will be the result of their performing or not performing these behaviors. If being eligible to start in the next game is the reward for certain practice behaviors, the coach should clarify this outcome, along with which specific behaviors the athletes need to demonstrate.

Tailor the Reward System

Many athletes and students are already fairly well motivated, but they need a systematic program to direct their motivation. The less motivated that athletes and students are, the more they might initially need to rely on external rewards. But the strongest kind of motivation over the long haul is internal motivation, which should always be encouraged. The key point is to consider individual differences when you implement behavioral change programs.

Intrinsic Motivation and Extrinsic Rewards

The world of sport uses extrinsic rewards extensively. Most leagues have postseason banquets in which such awards as medals, trophies, ribbons, money, and jackets are given to participants. Elementary school teachers frequently give stickers and toys to reward good behavior in their students. Exercise participants, too, frequently get T-shirts and other rewards for regular attendance and participation in classes. Advocates of extrinsic rewards argue that rewards will increase motivation, enhance learning, and increase the desire to continue participation. As noted throughout this chapter, the systematic use of rewards can certainly produce some desired changes in behavior in sport, physical education, and exercise settings. However, if rewards are used incorrectly, some negative consequences also can result.

We know that motivation has two sources: extrinsic and intrinsic. With extrinsic rewards the motivation comes from other people through positive and negative reinforcements. But individuals also participate in sport and physical activity for intrinsic reasons. People who have intrinsic motivation strive inwardly to be competent and self-determining in their quest to master the task at hand. They enjoy competition, like the action and excitement, focus on having fun, and want to learn skills to the best of their ability. Individuals who participate for the love of sport and exercise would be considered intrinsically motivated, as would those who play for pride. For example, when Steve Ovett, British elite middle-distance runner, was asked why he ran competitively, he answered, "I just did it because I wanted to . . .

[get] the best out of myself for all the effort I'd put in." (Hemery, 1991, p.142). The practical question concerns what happens when we combine extrinsic rewards and intrinsic motivation.

Do Extrinsic Rewards Undermine Intrinsic Motivation?

Intuitively, it seems that combining extrinsic and intrinsic motivation would produce more motivation. For instance, adding extrinsic rewards such as trophies to an activity that is intrinsically motivating (e.g., intramural volleyball) should increase motivation accordingly. Certainly you would not foresee these extrinsic rewards as decreasing intrinsic motivation. But let's look further at the effect of extrinsic rewards on intrinsic motivation.

Most early researchers and practitioners saw intrinsic and extrinsic motivation as additive: the more, the better. Some people, however, noted that extrinsic rewards could have an undermining effect on intrinsic motivation. For example, Albert Einstein commented about exams, "This coercion had such a deterring effect that, after I passed the final examination, I found the consideration of any scientific problems distasteful to me for an entire year" (Bernstein, 1973, p. 88). When people see themselves as the cause of their behavior, they consider themselves intrinsically motivated. Conversely, when people perceive the cause of their behavior external to themselves (i.e., "I did it for the money"), they consider themselves extrinsically motivated. And, often, the more an individual is extrinsically motivated, the less he or she will be intrinsically motivated (deCharms, 1968).

What Research Says

In the late 1960s researchers as well as theorists began to systematically test the relationship between extrinsic rewards and intrinsic motivation. Edward Deci (1971, 1972) found that participants who were rewarded with money for participating in an interesting activity subsequently spent less time at it than did people who were not paid. In his quite original and now classic study, Deci paid participants to play a Parker Brothers mechanical puzzle game called SOMA, which is composed of many different shaped

> *Being paid for working on an intrinsically interesting activity can decrease a person's intrinsic motivation for the activity.*

blocks that can be arranged to form various patterns. In a later play period these participants spent significantly less time (106 seconds) with the SOMA puzzles than the time (206 seconds) spent by individuals who had not been rewarded for playing with the puzzles.

In another early study called "Turning Play Into Work," Lepper and Greene (1975) used nursery school children as subjects and selected an activity that was intrinsically motivating for these children—drawing with felt pens. Each child was asked to draw under one of three reward conditions. In the "expected reward" condition, the children agreed to draw a picture in order to receive a Good Player certificate. In the "unexpected reward" condition, the award was given to unsuspecting children after they completed the task. In the "no-reward" condition, the children neither anticipated nor received an award. One week later, the children were unobtrusively observed for their interest in the same activity in a free-choice situation. The children who drew with the felt pen for expected rewards showed a drop in intrinsic motivation, whereas the other two groups continued to use the felt pens just as much as they had before the experiment. When the expected reward was removed, the prime reason for the first group's using the felt pen was also removed, although they had initially been intrinsically motivated to use the felt pen (Lepper, Greene, & Nisbett, 1973). This study demonstrates potential long-term effects of extrinsic rewards and the importance of studying how the reward is administered.

Not all studies have found that extrinsic rewards produce a decrease in intrinsic motivation. To the contrary, recent *general* psychological studies of the relationship between extrinsic rewards and intrinsic motivation have concluded that external rewards undermine intrinsic motivation under certain select circumstances, such as recognizing someone merely for participating without tying it to the quality of performance (Cameron & Pierce, 1994; Eisenberger & Cameron, 1996). However, research conducted specifically *within the sport and exercise domains* reveals a number of instances where extrinsic rewards do indeed undermine and reduce intrinsic motivation (Vallerand, Deci, & Ryan, 1987). Thus, it is important to understand under what conditions extrinsic rewards can negatively affect intrinsic motivation.

Cognitive Evaluation Theory

To help explain the potential different effects of rewards on intrinsic motivation, Deci and his

Figure 6.2 *Cognitive evaluation theory.*

colleagues developed a conceptual approach called **cognitive evaluation theory** (Deci, 1975; Deci & Ryan, 1985). According to this useful theory, any events that affect individuals' perceptions of competence and feelings of self-determination ultimately will also affect their levels of intrinsic motivation. These events (e.g., distribution of rewards, the quantity and quality of feedback and reinforcement, and how situations are structured) have two functional components: a controlling aspect and an informational aspect. Both the informational and controlling aspects can produce increases or decreases in intrinsic motivation, depending on how they impact on one's competence and self-determination (see Figure 6.1).

Controlling Aspect of Rewards

The controlling aspect of rewards relates to an individual's perceived **locus of causality** (i.e., what is the cause of a person's behavior) in the situation. If a reward is seen as controlling one's behavior, then the person feels that the cause of their behavior (an

external locus of causality) resides outside his- or herself, and thus intrinsic motivation decreases.

People often feel a direct conflict between being controlled by someone's use of rewards and their needs for self-determination. That is, people who are intrinsically motivated feel they do things because they *want to*, rather than for external reward. When people feel

How the recipient perceives rewards is critical in determining whether they will increase or decrease intrinsic motivation.

- *Rewards that are perceived to control a person's behavior or suggest the individual is not competent decrease intrinsic motivation.*

- *Rewards that emphasize the informational aspect and provide positive feedback about competence increase intrinsic motivation.*

controlled by a reward (e.g., "I'm only playing for the money"), the reason for their behavior resides outside of themselves. For example, many college athletes feel controlled by the pressure to win, compete for scholarships, and conform to coaching demands and expectations. With the change to free agency in many professional sports, a number of athletes report feeling controlled by the large sums of money they earn—along with fan, media, and community pressure to perform up to the level of their multimillion dollar salaries. This in turn has led to their experiencing less enjoyment in the activity itself.

However, if a reward is seen as contributing to an internal locus of causality (i.e., the cause of one's behavior resides inside the person), intrinsic motivation will increase. In these situations individuals feel high levels of self-determination, perceiving their behavior as determined by their own internal motivation. For example, sport and exercise programs that provide individuals with opportunities for input about the choice of activities, personal performance goals, and team or class objectives and rules should result in higher intrinsic motivation since they increase personal perceptions of control (Vallerand et al., 1987).

Informational Aspect of Rewards

The informational aspect affects intrinsic motivation by altering how competent someone feels. When a person receives a reward for achievement, such as the Most Valuable Player award, this provides positive information of competence and should lead to increased intrinsic motivation. In essence, for rewards to enhance intrinsic motivation, they should be contingent on specific levels of performance or behavior.

Moreover, rewards or events that provide negative information about competence should result in lower levels of perceived competence and intrinsic motivation. For example, if a coach's style is predominantly critical, some participants may internalize it as negative information about their value and worth. This would lead to a decrease in their enjoyment and intrinsic motivation. Similarly, striving for an award and *not* receiving it would decrease feelings of competence and lower intrinsic motivation.

Functional Significance of the Event

In addition to the controlling and informational aspects of rewards, a third major element to cognitive evaluation theory is termed the functional significance of the event (Deci & Ryan, 1985). In essence,

every reward potentially has both controlling and informational aspects. How the reward will affect intrinsic motivation depends on whether the recipient perceives it to be more controlling or more informational. For example, on the surface it would seem positive to recognize individuals or teams with trophies. However, although the reward's message seems to be about the athletes' competence, the players may perceive that the coach is giving them these rewards to control their behavior (i.e., make sure they don't join another team next year). It is the message behind the reward that is crucial: It must be made clear to the participant that the reward provides positive information about her competence and is not meant to control her behavior. In general, perceived choice and positive feedback bring out the informational aspect, whereas rewards, time deadlines, and surveillance make the controlling aspect salient.

Consider the example provided by Weiss and Chaumeton (1992) of a high school wrestler. According to the coach, the wrestler had a great deal of talent and potential, had won most of his matches, and had received positive feedback from the coach, teammates, and community. In addition, as a team captain, he had participated in developing team rules and practice regimens. Despite the amount of positive information conveyed about his wrestling competence, which should have produced an internal locus of control, the coach was baffled by the wrestler's lack of positive affect, effort, persistence, and desire. It was only later that the coach found out that the boy's father had exerted considerable pressure on him to join the wrestling team and was now living vicariously through his son's success—while still criticizing him when he felt his son's performance wasn't up to par. Thus, the wrestler perceived the controlling aspect, emanating from his overbearing father, as more important than the positive feedback and rewards he was getting through his wrestling performance. The result was a perceived external locus of causality with a subsequent decrease in intrinsic motivation.

How Extrinsic Rewards Affect Intrinsic Motivation in Sport

Magic Johnson was once asked if he received any outrageous offers while being recruited by various college basketball teams. He responded, "I received my share of offers for cars and money. It immediately turned me off. It was like they were trying to buy me, and I don't like anyone trying to buy me." Notice that what Magic Johnson was really referring to was the controlling aspect of rewards. He did not like anyone trying to control him through bribes and other extrinsic incentives. With the outrageous multimillion dollar long-term contracts that are currently being offered many professional athletes, the natural question is whether athletes will lose their motivation and drive to perform at top level. Let's look at what some of the research has found.

Scholarships and Intrinsic Motivation

One of the first assessments of how extrinsic rewards affect intrinsic motivation in a sport setting was Dean Ryan's study of scholarship and nonscholarship collegiate football players (1977, 1980). Players on scholarship reported that they were enjoying football less than their nonscholarship counterparts. Moreover, scholarship football players exhibited less intrinsic motivation every year they held their scholarship, so their lowest level of enjoyment occurred during their senior year. Ryan later surveyed male and female athletes from different schools in a variety of sports (1980). Again, scholarship football players reported less intrinsic motivation than nonscholarship football players. However, male wrestlers and female athletes from six different sports who were on scholarship reported higher levels of intrinsic motivation than those who were not on scholarship.

These results can be explained by the distinction between the controlling and informational aspects in rewards. Scholarships can have an informational function—they tell athletes that they are good. This would be especially informative to wrestlers and women, who receive far fewer scholarships than other athletes. Remember that in 1980 few athletic scholarships were available to women and wrestlers. Compare this with some 80 scholarships awarded to Division I football teams, which would make the informational aspect of receiving a football scholarship less positive confirmation of outstanding competence.

Football is the prime revenue-producing sport for most universities. Consider how football scholarships

Athletic scholarships can either decrease or increase athletes' levels of intrinsic motivation, depending on which is more emphasized—the controlling or the informational aspect.

(as well as scholarships in other revenue-producing sports) can be used. Some coaches use scholarships as leverage to control the players' behavior. Players often feel they have to perform well or lose their scholarships. Sometimes players who are not performing up to the coaches' expectations are made to participate in distasteful drills, are threatened with being dropped from the team, or get no playing time. Bob Knight, head basketball coach at Indiana University, has had a reputation of using threats, intimidation, and verbal abuse to keep his athletes motivated and performing at high levels (although it should be noted that over the years coach Knight has done many positive things for his players, both on and off the basketball court). While this may have proved effective for coach Knight, this same approach has sometimes backfired; some athletes have reported losing motivation and transferring to other schools. By holding scholarships over their heads, coach Knight has sometimes turned what used to be play into work. Under these conditions, the scholarship's controlling aspect is more important than its informational aspect, which evidently decreases intrinsic motivation among these scholarship players.

Given the changing trends in both men's and women's collegiate sport during the 1980s and 1990s, a more recent study (Amorose, Horn, & Miller, 1994) investigated the role that scholarships have on intrinsic motivation. It found that among 440 male and female athletes in Division I, the players on scholarship had lower levels of intrinsic motivation, enjoyment, and perceived choice than their nonscholarship cohorts. This occurred with both the men and women, indicating that the growth of women's collegiate sports may have raised the pressure to win to the level experienced in men's collegiate athletics. Making more scholarships available to women athletes has reduced the informational aspect of these awards, and the concomitant pressure to win has enhanced the controlling aspect of scholarships, thus resulting in decreased intrinsic motivation.

Competition and Intrinsic Motivation

Competitive success and failure can also affect intrinsic motivation. Specifically, competitive events contain both controlling and informational events, and thus they can influence both a perceived locus of causality and perceived competence of the participants. By manipulating the success and failure subjects perceive on a motor task they perform, several researchers have revealed that people have higher

> *Competitive success tends to increase intrinsic motivation, whereas competitive failure tends to decrease intrinsic motivation.*

levels of intrinsic motivation after success than after failure (Vallerand, Gauvin, & Halliwell, 1986a; Weinberg & Jackson, 1979; Weinberg & Ragan, 1979). Success and failure have high informational value in competition, and males exhibited significantly higher levels of intrinsic motivation after success than after failure. In contrast, females did not vary much across success and failure conditions, which suggests that competitive success is more important for males than for females (Deaux, 1985). When males succeed, they tend to feel good and exhibit high intrinsic interest in the task, but when they lose, they also quickly lose interest and intrinsic motivation. Females appear less threatened by the information contained in competitive failure, likely because their egos are not typically as invested in display success as are their male counterparts. Recent changes in women's sports, however, suggest we should reexamine whether the participants still have these kinds of perceptions.

We tend to focus on who won or lost a competition, which represents the objective outcome. However, sometimes an athlete plays well but still loses to a superior opponent, whereas other times someone plays poorly but still wins over a weak opponent. These subjective outcomes also appear to determine an athlete's intrinsic motivation. People who perceive that they performed well show higher levels of intrinsic motivation than those with lower perceptions of success (McAuley and Tammen, 1989). Winning and losing are less important in determining intrinsic motivation than is how well people *perceive* (subjectively) they performed. The old adage, "It's not whether you win or lose, but how you play the game," applies in determining how a performance affects intrinsic motivation. In fact, coaches and parents can enhance the intrinsic motivation of young athletes by providing subjective feedback focusing on what they did well, despite an objective loss.

In essence, the focus of one's performance appears to be more important than the actual outcome. Vallerand, Gauvin, and Halliwell (1986b) investigated children, looking at the focus on comparative performance (e.g., winning and losing) and perceived performance. Those youngsters who were asked to

compete against another child (interpersonal competition) on a motor task exhibited less intrinsic motivation than those who were instructed to simply compete against themselves (mastery). The lesson for teachers and coaches is to have participants focus more on their own relative performance—which is more under their control—than on comparative performance against others.

Feedback and Intrinsic Motivation

Feedback and intrinsic motivation involves how positive and negative information from significant others affects your own perceived competence and subsequent intrinsic motivation. Vallerand (1983) first investigated varying the amounts of positive feedback to adolescent hockey players who were performing in simulated hockey situations. Players were given 0, 6, 12, 18, or 24 positive statements from coaches while performing various hockey skills. The groups who received feedback scored higher in perceived competence and intrinsic motivation than did the no-feedback group, although there were no differences among the various feedback groups. Therefore, the absolute quantity of positive feedback seems less important than receiving at least some type of positive feedback.

A second study using a balance task also found that positive feedback produced higher levels of intrinsic motivation than did getting negative feedback or receiving no feedback (Vallerand & Reid, 1984). Positive feedback in youth fitness testing (as compared to no feedback or negative feedback) also is found to increase perceived competence and intrinsic motivation (Whitehead & Corbin, 1991). These results underscore the importance of a positive approach to increase the competence and intrinsic motivation participants feel for the task.

Increasing Intrinsic Motivation

Inasmuch as rewards do not inherently undermine intrinsic motivation, coaches, physical educators, and exercise leaders do well to structure and use rewards and other strategies in ways that increase perceptions of success and competence and, by extension, the intrinsic motivation of the participants. Read these suggestions for increasing intrinsic motivation and analyze how the process in each leads from the use of rewards to a participant's getting information that will increase his intrinsic motivation and perception of competence.

Provide for Successful Experiences

Perceived success strengthens feelings of personal competence. For example, lowering the basket for young basketball players and structuring practice to provide successful experiences will enhance feelings of competence. Give positive feedback about what participants are doing right.

Give Rewards Contingent on Performance

Tie rewards to the performance of specific behaviors to increase their informational value. Reward based on proper execution of plays, good sportsmanship, helping other teammates, or mastering a new skill so as to provide information about the individual's competence. Make clear to the participants that the rewards are specifically for doing things well and that you are not trying to control them in any way. Emphasize the informational aspect of the rewards.

Use Verbal and Nonverbal Praise

Many people forget how powerful praise can be. Praise provides positive feedback and helps athletes continue to strive to improve. This is especially important for athletes who are second string and get little recognition and for students who are not particularly skilled in sport and physical activity. For example, overweight participants in an exercise class need plenty of positive feedback to stay motivated and feel good about themselves. A simple pat on the back or "good job" can acknowledge each athlete's contribution to the team or achievement of a personal goal.

Vary Content and Sequence of Practice Drills

Practices in sport and exercise can get tedious and boring. One way to break the monotony and maintain motivation levels is to vary the kinds of drills and how they are sequenced. Such variety can also give young athletes an opportunity to try new positions or assignments. They not only have more fun but gain an awareness and appreciation of the demands of different positions and of their abilities to handle them. Similarly, exercise leaders should strive to vary the content and format of their classes to keep motivation high (dropout rates in exercise programs all too frequently reach over 50%).

Involve Participants in Decision Making

Allow participants more responsibility for making decisions and rules. Doing so will increase their perception of control and lead to feelings of personal accomplishment. For example, they might suggest how to organize a practice session, make up team or class rules, establish a dress code, or, if they are ready, proceed with game strategy. They might plan a new or innovative drill for practice. People perceive they have greater competency when they are active in the learning process.

Set Realistic Performance Goals

Not all participants are highly skilled or apt to be winners in competition. However, people can learn to set realistic goals based on their individual abilities. These goals need not depend on objective performance outcomes; rather, they might include specified number of minutes played, keeping emotional control, or simply improving over a previous performance. Base performance goals on a personal level of performance (e.g., to improve your time in the mile run from 7:33 to 7:25), leaving participants in control of their performance (i.e., they don't depend on how well an opponent plays) and making success more likely. In turn, reaching performance goals is a sign of competence that affects motivation positively. A more detailed discussion of how to set goals is presented in chapter 15.

Flow—A Special Case of Intrinsic Motivation

Some of the most innovative studies of enhancing intrinsic motivation come from the work of Mihaly Csikszentmihalyi (1990). Whereas many researchers have tried to determine which factors undermine intrinsic motivation, Csikszentmihalyi investigated exactly what makes a task intrinsically motivating. He examined rock climbing, dancing, chess, music, and amateur athletics—all activities that people do with great intensity but usually for little or no external reward. He determined several common elements that make these activities intrinsically interesting. These essential elements of the flow state include the following:

■ Balance of skill and challenge. A key part of Csikszentmihalyi's definition of flow is the balance between one's perceived skill and challenge. An easy

win or lopsided loss will rarely get one into flow. As one hockey player noted, "When I have a competitor to push me to my limits and provide a real challenge is when I can get into the zone."

■ Complete absorption in the activity. The participant is so involved in the activity that nothing else seems to matter. A basketball player states, "The court—that's all that matters. . . . Sometimes I think of a problem, like fighting with my girlfriend, and I think that's nothing compared to the game. You can think about a problem all day but as soon as you get in the game, the hell with it. . . . When you're playing basketball, that's all that's on your mind."

■ Merging of action and awareness. You are aware of your actions but not of the awareness itself. This mental state is captured by a volleyball player who states, "The only thing that goes through my mind is performing well. I really don't have to think, though. When I'm playing [volleyball], it just comes to me. It's a good feeling. And when you're on a roll, you don't think about it at all. If you step back and think why you are so hot, all of a sudden you get creamed."

■ Total concentration. Performers report that they feel like a beam of concentrated energy. Crowd noises, opponent reactions and other distractions simply don't matter. The focus of attention is clearly on the task at hand. A tennis player demonstrates this total focus: "All that mattered was the tennis court and the ball. I was so into the zone and focused that the ball looked like a watermelon."

■ Loss of self-consciousness. Performers report that their ego is completely lost in the activity itself. A rock climber captures this feeling well: "In rock climbing one tends to get immersed in what is going on around him—in the rock, in the moves that are involved . . . search[ing] for handholds . . . proper position[ing] of the body—so involved he might lose the consciousness of his own identity and melt into the rock."

■ A sense of control. This element of flow refers to the fact that you are not actively aware of control; rather, you are simply not worried by the possibility of lack of control. A racquetball player demonstrates this sense of control: "At times when I have super concentration in a [racquetball] game, nothing else exists—nothing except the act of participating and swinging at the ball. The other player must be there to play the game, but I'm not concerned with him. I'm not competing with him at that point. I'm attempting to place the ball in the perfect spot, and it has no bearing on winning and losing."

◾ No goals or rewards external to the activity. You participate purely because of the activity itself, without seeking any other reward. A chess player makes this point by saying, "The most rewarding part of chess is the competition, the satisfaction of pitting your mental prowess against someone else. . . . I've won trophies and money, but considering expenses of entry fees, chess association, et cetera, I'm usually on the losing side financially."

◾ Effortless movement. This element refers to the fact that you're performing so well but yet you're not really thinking about it and don't appear to be trying too hard. A figure skater captures this element well: "It was just one of those programs that clicked. It's just such a rush, like you feel it could go on and on and on, like you don't want it to stop because it's going so well. It's almost as though you don't have to think, it's like everything goes automatically without thinking. It's like you're in automatic pilot, so you don't have any thoughts."

These elements represent the essential features of optimal performances, which athletes have described as "hot," "in a groove," "on a roll," or "in the zone," a special state where everything is going well and you're hitting on all cylinders. Csikszentmihalyi calls this holistic sensation flow, in which people feel they are totally involved or on automatic pilot. He argues that the flow experience occurs when your skills are

equal to your challenge. Intrinsic motivation is at its highest and maximum performance is achieved. However, if the task demands are greater than your capabilities, you become anxious and perform poorly. Conversely, if your skills are greater than the challenges of the task, you become bored and perform less well.

Figure 6.2 shows that flow is obtained when both capabilities (skills) and challenge are high. For example, if an athlete has a high skill level and the opponent is also highly skilled (e.g., high challenge), then the athlete may achieve *flow*. But if an athlete with less ability is matched against a strong opponent (high challenge), it will produce *anxiety*. Combining low skills and low challenge results in *apathy*, whereas high skills and low challenge results in *boredom*. By structuring exercise classes, physical education, and competitive sports to be challenging and creative, you foster better performance, richer experiences, and longer involvement in physical activity.

How People Achieve Flow

If they knew how, coaches and teachers would likely want to help students and athletes achieve this narrow framework of flow. So the logical question is how does one get into a flow state? Research studying athletes from different sports (Jackson, 1992; 1995) found that the following factors were most important for getting into flow:

◾ Motivation to perform. Being motivated to perform—and to perform well—is important to getting

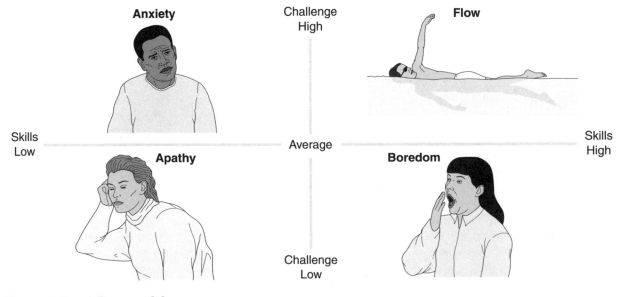

Figure 6.3 *A flow model.*
Adapted from Kimiecik and Stein, 1992.

into flow. When individuals lack such motivation, flow is much more difficult to achieve. The balance between challenge and skill may be the most relevant area to focus on to help ensure the individual is optimally motivated. Having goals and a challenging but realistic situation are essential to achieving optimal motivation.

■ Achieving optimal arousal level before performing. Being relaxed, controlling anxiety, and enjoying the activity contribute to flow. Some individuals clearly preferred to be more relaxed, whereas others wanted to be more energized. However, several athletes speak of finding a balance between calmness and arousal. As one skater said, "Relaxation and confidence—but you have to be on edge; you can't be too relaxed. You have to be concerned about something" (Jackson, 1992, p. 171).

■ Maintaining appropriate focus. Keeping a narrow focus, staying in the present, focusing before the performance, and focusing on key points in one's activity are critical to maintaining proper focus. Csikszentmihalyi (1990) refers to concentration on the task at hand as one of the most frequently mentioned dimensions of the flow experience. One skater asserts the positive result of focusing fully on the upcoming performance this way: "The fact that you're so focused, you're able to concentrate easily" (Jackson, 1992, p. 172).

■ Precompetitive and competitive plans and preparation. Along with confidence and positive attitude, athletes mentioned the planning theme most often in describing factors that influence their achieving flow states. Following precompetitive routines, feeling totally ready, having a competitive plan, and anticipating potential unusual events are clearly important components of preparation. For example, a javelin thrower stated, "The fact that I've done everything possible on my mental and physical side makes me feel confident. Every facet is covered. . . . That reassures my conscious mind that I've done everything—then I just have to let myself switch off and let it happen (Jackson, 1995, p. 144).

■ Optimal physical preparation and readiness. Having done the necessary training and preparation beforehand, working hard, and feeling that you are physically ready and able to have good practice sessions before competing are all critical to getting into and maintaining a flow state. Attention to rest, training, and nutrition also appears important for setting optimal conditions for the flow state to occur. In addition, athletes report that feeling they were physically prepared helped boost their confidence and

ability to stay in a flow state for a longer period of time.

■ Optimal environmental and situational conditions. Although people can *set the tone* for achieving a flow state by altering their own internal climate, athletes also cited influences of environmental and situational *conditions* that affected their ability to achieve a flow state. Such conditions as a good atmosphere, positive feedback from the coach, no outside pressures, and optimal playing conditions enhance the probability of flow occurring.

■ Confidence and mental attitude. Confidence is a major help to achieving a flow state; conversely, self-doubt and putting pressure on oneself are perceived as factors that can disrupt flow. Confidence seems to be a salient factor, regardless of the person's actual ability level. Believing you can win, positive thinking, blocking negatives, and enjoying what you're doing all help build confidence. But maybe most critical is the belief that you can meet the challenge you face. As one athlete stated, "I think probably the most important thing for me is the feeling that I've got the ability to be in that situation" (Jackson, 1995, p. 144).

■ Team play and interaction. In team sports, getting into flow sometimes depends (or at least is influenced by) on your teammates. Positive team interactions such as good passing, playing as a unit, and open communication are helpful in achieving flow. In addition, trusting your teammates and having a shared sense of purpose are also important for cohesive team interactions.

■ Feeling good about performance. The factor for getting into flow that athletes mentioned most often was feeling good about their performance and movements. In essence, receiving feedback from their movements and being in control of their bodies gives athletes a sense of ease in moving. Anyone who has participated in sport knows that sometimes things just feel right, smooth, effortless, and in sync. These feelings are usually related to getting into a flow state.

Controllability of Flow States

Can individuals control these thoughts and feelings connected with flow? The athletes interviewed by Jackson (1992; 1995) varied in their responses regarding the controllability of their flow states. Overall, 79% perceived flow to be controllable, whereas 21% felt it was out of their control. Athletes who felt that flow was controllable made comments like these: "Yeah, I think you can increase it. It's not a conscious effort. If you try to do it, it's not going to work.

I don't think it's something you can turn on and off like a light switch" (Jackson, 1992, p. 174). A triathlete noted, "I think I can set it up. You can set the scene for it, maybe with all that preparation. It should be something that you can ask of yourself and get into, I think, through your training and through your discipline" (Jackson, 1995, p. 158).

Some athletes, while considering flow to be controllable, placed qualifiers on whether it would actually occur. A javelin thrower captured this perception in his remark, "Yeah, it's controllable, but it's the battle between your conscious and subconscious, and you've got to tell your conscious to shut up and let the subconscious take over, which it will because it's really powerful" (Jackson, 1995, p. 158). A rugby player felt that flow was not controllable in team sports: "It all comes back to the team—everybody, all the guys knotted in together and it just rolls along for 5, 10 minutes, half an hour, going very well, but then someone might lose concentration or go off beat or something and then you'd be out of that situation you were just in, and you can't have any control over that" (Jackson, 1995, p. 159).

Jackson's studies suggest that although athletes cannot control flow, they still can increase the prob-ability of its occurring by following the guidelines stated here and focusing on things within their control, such as their mental preparation.

Factors That Prevent and Disrupt Flow

Although it's important to understand how to enhance the likelihood of flow's occurrence, it is equally important to understand what factors may prevent or disrupt it (Jackson, 1995). These factors are identified in Table 6.1. Despite some consistency in what prevents and what disrupts flow's occurrence, individuals do experience differences between these situations. The factors athletes cited most often as *preventing* flow were less than optimal physical preparation, readiness, and environmental or situational conditions; the reasons they gave most often as *disrupting* the flow state were environmental and situational influences.

Professionals can try to structure the environment and provide feedback to maximize the possibility of athletes reaching and maintaining a flow state. However, participants themselves must be aware of the factors that influence the occurrence of the flow state so that they can mentally and physically prepare for competition and physical activity accordingly. They should distinguish factors that are under their control and that they can change (e.g., physical or mental preparation, focus of attention, negative self-talk) from those they can't control (e.g., crowd responses, coach feedback, weather and field conditions, be-

havior of competitors). For example, an athlete can't control a hostile crowd, but she can control how she reacts both mentally and emotionally to the crowd. Similarly, a physical therapist can't control patients' attitudes or how crowded a clinic is, but he can strive to maintain a positive attitude in his interactions with clients.

Table 6.1 Factors That Disrupt and Prevent Flow

FACTORS THAT PREVENT FLOW FROM OCCURRING	FACTORS THAT DISRUPT FLOW

Non-optimal physical preparation and readiness
    Injury
    Fatigue
    Not feeling good physically
	Non-optimal environmental and situational influences
	    Stoppage in play
	    What opposition is doing
	    Negative refereeing decisions
	    Inappropriate, negative, or no feedback

Non-optimal environmental or situational conditions
    External stresses
    Unwanted crowd response
    Uncontrollable influences of the event
	Problems with physical readiness or physical state
	    Lack of physical preparation
	    Injury during the competition
	    Fatigue

Lacking confidence or a negative mental state
    Negative thinking
    Self-doubt
    No control of mental state
	Problems with team performance or interactions
	    Negative talk on the field
	    Team not playing well
	    Lack of team interactions

Inappropriate focus
    Thinking too much
    Worrying about what others are doing
    Frustration with teammates' effort
	Inappropriate focus
	    Worrying about competitor's ability
	    Daydreaming
	    Loss of concentration

Problem with precompetitive preparation
    Poor precompetitive preparation
    Distraction before competition
    Interruption to precompetitive preparation
	Doubting or putting pressure on self
	    Self-doubt
	    Putting pressure on self

Lacking motivation to perform
    No goals
    Lack of challenge
    Low arousal or motivation	

Non-optimal arousal level before competition
    Not being relaxed
    Feeling too relaxed	

Negative team play and interactions
    Team not performing well
    Not feeling part of the team
    Negative talk within the team	

Performance going poorly
    Unforced errors
    Poor technique
    Things not going as planned	

SUMMARY

1 *Explain how positive and negative feedback influence behavior.*

In discussing two basic approaches to reinforcement—positive and negative control—we recommended a positive approach, although punishment is sometimes necessary to change behavior. Several factors can make reinforcements more effective, including the choice of effective reinforcers, the schedule of reinforcements, and choice of appropriate behaviors—and performance such as social and emotional skills—to reinforce. Punishment has potential negative effects, such as creating a fear of failure or creating an aversive learning environment.

2 *Understand how to implement behavior modification programs.*

In systematically using the principles of reinforcement to structure sport and exercise environments the main goal is to help individuals stay task-oriented and motivated throughout a training period.

3 *Describe the relationship between intrinsic motivation and external rewards.*

Extrinsic rewards have the potential to undermine intrinsic motivation. Cognitive evaluation theory has demonstrated that extrinsic rewards can either increase or decrease intrinsic motivation, depending on whether the reward is more informational or controlling. Two examples of the effect of extrinsic incentives in sport are scholarships and winning and losing. If you want to enhance a participant's intrinsic motivation, the key is to make rewards more informational.

4 *Detail different ways to increase intrinsic motivation.*

Coaches, teachers, and exercise leaders can enhance intrinsic motivation through several methods, such as using verbal and nonverbal praise, involving participants in decision making, setting realistic goals, making rewards contingent on performance, and varying the content and sequence of practice drills.

5 *Describe the flow state and how to achieve it.*

A special state of flow epitomizes intrinsic motivation. This flow state contains many common elements, but a key aspect is that there is a balance between an individual's perceived abilities and the challenge of the task. Several factors, such as confidence, optimal arousal, focused attention, help us achieve a flow state; other factors, such as a self-critical attitude, distractions, and lack of preparation, can prevent or disrupt flow states.

KEY TERMS

reinforcement	behavior modification
intrinsic rewards	backward chaining
shaping	extrinsic rewards
feedback	intrinsic motivation
motivational feedback	cognitive evaluation theory
instructional feedback	locus of causality
behavioral coaching	flow

REVIEW QUESTIONS

1. Discuss the two principles of reinforcement and why they are more complex than they first appear.

2. Discuss the differences between the positive and negative approaches to teaching and coaching. Based on the research, which one is more beneficial and why?

3. Discuss three of the potential negative side effects of using punishment.

4. Discuss the different types of reinforcers and the effectiveness of continuous and intermittent reinforcement schedules.

5. Discuss three things other than success that a coach or physical educator might reinforce.

6. Discuss what you believe to be the three most important guidelines for implementing behavioral programs in sport and exercise settings.

7. For an individual who is intrinsically motivated, the introduction of extrinsic rewards will increase motivation. Discuss the accuracy of this statement and why you agree or disagree.

8. Discuss cognitive evaluation theory as a way to help explain the relation between extrinsic rewards and intrinsic motivation. Compare the informational with the controlling aspect of rewards.

9. Discuss the results of Ryan's studies on scholarships and intrinsic motivation. What are the implications of the findings?

10. Explain the effects of success and failure on intrinsic motivation, including findings from research studies. What implications do these findings have for the practitioner?

11. Discuss three ways to increase intrinsic motivation.

12. Discuss the concept of flow. What are its major characteristics? In what sort of activity is flow most likely to occur?

13. Discuss three factors that help people get into flow and three barriers that inhibit it.

CRITICAL THINKING QUESTIONS

1. You are taking over as a coach of a team that has a history of losing and that recently had a tyrannical coach. Intrinsic motivation is therefore low. What would you do to build intrinsic motivation with this team? What types of rewards would you use? Be sure to incorporate research findings and theory to support your methods.

2. You have been preparing for the Olympic games for the past four years. But you'll only have one chance to perform well in the Olympic trials if you want to make the team. Therefore, you feel you absolutely must be at your best if you want to make the team. Describe what you would do to help yourself get into a flow state so you can exhibit a peak performance at the Olympic trials.

Part IV

Understanding Group Processes

This part consists of four chapters, all focusing on group interaction. Group issues are especially important to professionals in our field because of the amount of time we spend working in or with groups. In chapter 7 you'll learn how groups are formed and how they function. In addition, you will learn why some people loaf in groups and how to reduce this social-loafing phenomenon in sport and exercise settings. Chapter 8 examines whether a tight-knit (cohesive) group is necessary for optimal performance and discusses ways to develop cohesion.

This part's final two chapters focus on leadership (chapter 9) and communication (chapter 10). Groups do not thrive unless someone exerts leadership, and effective leadership requires effective communication. You'll learn the essentials of good communication and leadership and ways to build these skills in others.

© Human Kinetics

Group and Team Dynamics

After reading this chapter you should be able to

1 discuss how a group becomes a team,

2 understand how groups are structured,

3 explain how to create an effective team climate,

4 describe how to maximize individual performance in team sports, and

5 better understand the concept of social loafing.

It isn't necessarily the talent on a team that makes it great, people have said, but how that talent is blended. Michael Jordan makes just this point in the following quote: "Talent wins games, but teamwork wins championships." We often see talented teams perform poorly, failing to use the resources of their individual members, whereas other teams with less talent and fewer resources succeed. Surely a team intends to take advantage of the various abilities, backgrounds, and interests of its members, but it takes considerable effort to build effective teamwork. Pat Riley, one of the most successful coaches in the National Basketball Association, highlights this idea:

Teamwork is the essence of life. If there's one thing on which I'm an authority, it's how to blend the talents and strengths of individuals into a force that becomes greater than the sum of its parts. My driving belief is this: great teamwork is the only way to reach our ultimate moments, to create the breakthroughs that define our careers, to fulfill our lives with a sense of lasting significance. . . . However, teamwork isn't simple. In fact, it can be a frustrating, elusive commodity. That's why there are so many bad teams out there, stuck in neutral or going downhill. Teamwork doesn't appear magically just because someone mouths the words. It doesn't thrive just because of the presence of talent or ambition. It doesn't flourish simply because a team has tasted success. (Riley, 1993, pp. 15–16)

Riley's comments make it obvious that teamwork, player-coach interactions, and group dynamics play an important role in the success of teams and groups. Team members must interact, work toward shared goals, adapt to environmental demands, and balance individual needs with those of team members (Hardy & Crace, 1997). In fact, most sport activities, even so-called individual sports, require groups or teams, and competition almost always involves more than one person. Group physical activities include multiperson forums such as exercise groups, fitness clubs, and physical education classes. In addition, sports medicine and athletic training teams work together in helping athletes prepare for competition and recover from injury. In short, almost any position in the sport and exercise field requires understanding the processes and dynamics of groups.

Why Study Groups?

In a classic text on group dynamics Cartwright and Zander wrote in *Group Dynamics: Research and Theory* (1968),

Whether one wishes to understand or improve human behavior, it is necessary to know a great deal about the nature of groups. Neither a coherent view of people nor an advanced social technology is possible without dependable answers to a host of questions concerning the operation of groups, how individuals relate to groups, and how groups relate to larger society.

As they asserted, to understand behavior in sport and physical activity, we must understand the nature of sport and exercise groups. We'll begin by defining what we mean by the terms *group* and *team*.

What Is the Difference Between a Group and a Team?

You may think it's easy to define what a group or team is, but it can be quite complex. For example, an instructor might call a badminton class, karate club, and exercise class "groups," whereas she might instead call groups of people who play soccer or volleyball "teams." To further complicate matters, several people might decide to meet at noon to play basketball or get together to go to the volleyball game on Thursday nights. In essence, a collection of individuals is not necessarily a group—and a group is not necessarily a team. So, how are groups and teams similar and what distinguishes a group from a team?

Members of a group or a team might both like and be attracted to other members of the group or team. They might actually share some common goals (e.g., all people in a fitness class might want to lose weight and tone muscle). There are some shared characteristics, then, among members of groups and teams. However, the key distinguishing characteristics between a group of individuals and a team is the interaction among its members, especially as it relates to shared, common goals. That is, team members have to depend on and support each other in the

The distinguishing characteristics of sport and exercise groups are a collective identity, a sense of shared purpose or objectives, structured modes of communication, personal or task interdependence (or both), and interpersonal attraction.

pursuit of common goals. Let's take a closer look at how a group becomes a team.

How a Group Becomes a Team

As we noted, a group of individuals does not necessarily form a team. Although all teams are groups, not all groups can be considered teams. In general, a team is any group of people who must interact with each other to accomplish shared objectives. In fact, most definitions of teams incorporate the fundamental elements of interdependency of team members and common goals (O'Brien, 1995). Becoming a team, however, is really an evolutionary process. Teams are constantly developing, changing in their attempts to respond to both internal and external factors.

In fact, groups go through a four-stage developmental sequence to move from a mere collection of individuals to a team (Tuckman, 1965). Although most groups go through all four stages, the duration of each stage and the sequence they follow might vary for different groups in the process of team development. For example, a coach's understanding of team formation in sport or a head athletic trainer's knowledge of her student trainers could lead to using different strategies that promote harmony among members of their respective teams. Furthermore, the knowledge of these stages will facilitate your ability to effectively function in groups despite the fact that groups may move through a stage quickly or even skip it. The four stages to the model are these: forming, storming, norming, and performing.

Forming

In this first stage of team development, forming, team members familiarize themselves with other team members. Members of a team engage in social comparisons, assessing one another's strengths and weaknesses. For example, athletes might compare the amount of playing time they receive to other athletes' playing time, whereas members of a fitness class might compare how much individual attention they receive from the fitness leader. Individuals also try to determine if they belong in the group and, if so, in what role. For instance, the first workouts in a new season tend to be unpolished as teammates become accustomed to one another, compete for positions, and learn how to communicate. After each athlete has found her place within the structure of the team, interpersonal relationships are formed and tested, including relationships between leaders (i.e., coaches) and team members. Athletes lacking a strong team identification will have difficulty forming positive relationships with other team members. Coaches should develop strategies to facilitate group member familiarity and to ease team interaction at the early stages of team formation, even prior to the first practice if possible.

Storming

The second stage of team formation, storming, is characterized by resistance to the leader, resistance to control by the group, and interpersonal conflict. Great emotional resistance emerges as each group member experiences conflict due to the demands placed on him or her. This stage is typically evident when routines are established with regard to practice just prior to the start of an athletic season, as team rules are developed and enforced, and during later periods when teams are losing. Infighting can occur as individuals and the leader establish their roles and status within the group. This conflict can extend to the physical; fights and other altercations may even break out as teammates vie for a spot on the team. Most of this infighting is social and interpersonal in nature. In this stage, coaches need to communicate with athletes objectively and openly. Their evaluations of each athlete's strengths and weaknesses, as well as his role on the team, will help relieve uncertainty, a chief source of stress for athletes. Relieving stress should reduce the hostilities. In addition, although some storming is probably inevitable, the coach should communicate her displeasure if it becomes excessive and undermines positive team interactions.

Norming

During norming, the third stage, hostility is replaced by solidarity and cooperation. Conflicts are resolved and a sense of unity forms. Instead of watching out for their individual well-being, the athletes work together to reach common goals. Group cohesion (see chapter 8) occurs during this stage, as members pull together and build team unity. This pulling together can be a catalyst for improved satisfaction among team members; it can also set the grounds for future success. Team roles stabilize, and a respect develops for each player's unique contribution to the team. Instead of competing for status or recognition, players strive for economy of effort and task effectiveness. For athletic teams, norming typically occurs as a season begins and a common opponent can be identified. Coaches can facilitate this process by praising team members for quality performance, effort, and improvement, while at the same time emphasizing each player's unique contribution to the team's success (Anshel, 1994).

© Human Kinetics

Performing

In this final stage, **performing,** team members band together to channel their energies for team success. The team focuses on problem solving, using group process and relationships to work on tasks and test new ideas. Structural issues are resolved, and interpersonal relationships have stabilized. Roles are well defined, and the players help one another to succeed; the primary goal is team success. Rather than feeling threatened by a teammate's success, team members respect and encourage the accomplishments of others. It is important that the coach avoid activities that promote intrateam competition and interpersonal aggression. Instead, feedback should be provided to players regarding their special contributions, and a cooperative climate should be encouraged.

Structure of a Group

Every group develops its own structure, which begins to emerge even at the group's first meeting. A group's

structure depends largely on the interactions of its members—how they perceive one another and what they expect of themselves and each other. For a group of individuals to become an effective team, certain structural characteristics must develop. Two of the most important are group roles and group norms.

Group Roles

A **role** consists of the set of behaviors required or expected of the person occupying a certain position in a group. Teachers, parents, athletic trainers, corporate executives, and health professionals, for example, all have specific roles within their professions and within society. Coaches, for example, are expected to perform such behaviors as teaching, organizing practices, interacting with other school officials, and being a good role model. Similarly, head athletic trainers are expected to perform such behaviors as assigning and evaluating student trainers as well as providing clinical evaluations for serious injuries.

148

Team Building on a College Swim Team

A college swim team coach noticed that his team was not meshing. New members didn't know their teammates and there was little camaraderie. To develop a team concept, the coach scheduled get-togethers, including picnics, soccer games, and other special events. He asked team members to interview each other and report to the rest of the team what they had learned. The idea was to develop team awareness, communication, and interdependence so that when a swimmer felt competitive stress, he could obtain some psychological security by knowing that team members would understand his responses to the situation.

© Terry Wild Studio

A team, like any other group, plays formal and informal roles. Formal roles are dictated by the nature and structure of the organization. Athletic director, coach, team captain, exercise leader, and the like are examples of specific formal roles within a sport or an exercise organization. Point guard in basketball, setter in volleyball, goalie in hockey, and other formal positions all have specific performance roles within a team. Each of these roles carries specific associated expectations. Usually, individuals are either trained or recruited to fill specific roles, such as when a football coach recruits a place kicker, or a high school baseball coach converts an outfielder to a catcher.

Informal roles evolve from interactions among group members. For example, the power and social structure of gangs evolve through informal means (see William Whyte's classic 1943 work on the social structure of street gangs). In contact and collision sports a common informal role is the *enforcer*—someone who assures that no teammate gets bullied, roughed up, or physically intimidated. Another informal team role is the *mediator*, a diplomatic player who mediates disputes among teammates or even between a coach and players. The idea of the existence of informal roles on a team was investigated by Rees and Segal (1984). They asked college football players to name the team members who (a) were the best players and (b) contributed to team harmony. Results revealed that these roles described two distinct groups of players. The best players, as you might expect, were starters. However, the players who contributed most to team harmony were seniors, and many of them were not starters. Thus, there seems to

Two different types of roles exist within any group or team: formal roles (e.g., coach or team captain) that are dictated by the structure of the organization; informal roles that evolve from the group's dynamics.

be an informal role for certain players (in this case seniors) to help keep the team together by maintaining positive social interactions among the players.

You can improve a team's effectiveness by making sure players understand ("role clarity") and accept their roles ("role acceptance"). Probably one of the reasons for the long-term outstanding success of the Chicago Bulls has been that players accepted their particular roles. Although Michael Jordan and Scottie Pippen were obviously the leaders and most talented players, they had significant ability (as had coach Phil Jackson) to get the other players to believe in and fulfill specific roles, such as rebounder (Dennis Rodman), defensive specialist (Ron Harper), and shooter (Steve Kerr).

People in a specific role usually have a different perspective of the role's requirements than do other members of the group. For example, if a soccer coach wants a player to concentrate on defense, passing, and positioning instead of scoring, then this needs to be clearly communicated to the player. Unclear roles hurt a team's performance. If two players on the same basketball team each think her role is to direct the team's offense, conflict will likely result over who

© Glenn James/NBA Photos

brings the ball up court. Similarly, an athletic trainer and team doctor must agree on their roles, so that athletes and coaches know whom to see for injury evaluation and whom to see for decisions on playing availability. Sometimes, individuals' performances can blur their roles on a team. A National Hockey League coach once observed that the worst thing that could happen to a team is to have its "enforcer" score a few goals in consecutive games. The enforcer would then begin to think of his role as a scorer, to the detriment of the team as a whole.

An effective goal-setting program (see chapter 15) can clarify roles. Helping players set goals in spe-

cific areas gives them direction and focus. If a football coach wanted a defensive lineman to focus on stopping the run instead of on sacking the quarterback, setting a specific goal would clarify the lineman's role. In fact, open communication can clarify everyone's role for everyone else. If a coach groups players and tells each one exactly what she expects of her individually and describes how her role fits in to the team concept, then everyone should know not only her own role but the roles of all her teammates.

Role acceptance is also important to enhance a group's structure. Players who don't start or get significant playing time can easily feel left out and confused about their contribution to the team. Coaches can help players accept their roles by minimizing the status differences among roles and emphasizing that the success of the team depends on each individual's contribution. When their responsibilities are perceived as important contributions to team success, players are more willing to accept and carry out their roles. For many years, Dean Smith, basketball coach at the University of North Carolina, has fostered the acceptance of the role of his reserves by playing them in actual games as a "second unit" for a short period of time. They all knew they were going to play in the game (even if for a short period), and they developed pride in trying to keep or extend a lead (or reduce a deficit) while giving the starters a rest.

Group Norms

A **norm** is a level of performance, pattern of behavior, or belief. Norms can be either formally established or informally developed by a group. Each norm carries specific expectations and behaviors that group members are expected to follow. Individuals usually receive pressure to adhere to their group's norms, whether the norm is seen as relevant or irrelevant. For example, rookies (especially with professional teams) are often expected to "carry the bags" for the veterans; although this may not appear functional, it is often the norm to indoctrinate new players onto the team.

On a sport team, the norm might involve practice behaviors, dress and hairstyle, the interactions between rookies and veterans, or who takes control in critical situations. Deviation from the expected behaviors might result in informal or formal sanctions. For example, Ken Griffey is obviously the leader of the Seattle Mariners and a player whom other players look up to, especially in big games. If a rookie decided to take charge and exert leadership in critical games, he would be violating the norm and would most assuredly receive some kind of censure. Similarly, in the movie, *Chariots of Fire*, the British sprinter Harold Abrahams was chided by his Cambridge colleagues for hiring a professional trainer since this meant he was too serious about his running and not really an amateur any longer.

In industrial settings, a group will establish a level or rate of performance called the norm for productivity. Anything falling below or above this level is not supported by the group. A norm for productivity can also apply to both fitness and sport settings. For example, in a corporate fitness program, members of a fitness club may all exercise at lunch for 30 minutes; this then becomes expected of new members. In a sport setting, the captain or top performer on a team is often a role model who sets the norm of productivity. For example, when Dan Gable, Olympic gold medalist, was wrestling at Iowa State, he put in unbelievable hours of practice time. And because Gable was considered the best wrestler in his weight classification in the country, his teammates adopted his standards.

Because norms can have powerful effects on behavior, it is imperative for a coach, teacher, or exercise leader to establish positive group norms or standards. This is especially critical since it has been demonstrated, for example, that an arbitrary norm can persist for even four or five generations after the original members have been removed from the group. One good method to create positive norms is to enlist the formal and informal leaders of a team to set positive examples. Dan Gable took the initiative and set the norm himself. But often the coach or teacher will need to encourage leaders to set high standards of achievement. Whenever possible, include all team members in decision making about norms adopted by the team. Some additional methods for sport leaders to establish and enforce group norms were developed by Zander (1982):

- Show individual team members how the group's standards (norms) can contribute to more effective team performance and team unity.
- Assess adherence to team standards, then reward those who adhere and sanction those who do not.
- Point out to each team member how his or her contribution toward developing and maintaining the standards contributes to the team's success.

Creating an Effective Team Climate

Team climate develops from how players perceive the interrelationships among the group members. Although the coach will certainly have his or her own perception of the team, it is the players' perceptions and evaluations that set the team's climate. Still, the coach has the strongest influence on establishing team climate. Some factors of team climate are more easily changed than others, but they all can affect the effective functioning of a group (Zander, 1982).

Social Support

Social support refers to "an exchange of resources between at least two individuals perceived by the

■ RESEARCH ■

The Pressure of Social Norms

Norms can have an enormous influence on individual members of a group, as demonstrated by the classic experiment conducted by Solomon Asch (1956). Seven students were asked to judge which of three lines was like the standard line (see Figure 7.1). The standard line was 5 inches in length, while the comparison lines were 5 inches, 4 inches, and 6-1/4 inches. All but one of the subjects (the "naive" subject) was told beforehand by the experimenter to give incorrect responses. Subjects answered aloud, one at a time, with the naive subject going next to last. Although it was clear that the comparison line was the correct answer, one-third of the naive subjects conformed to the group norm, even with as few as three other subjects. Thus, even when someone knows the correct response, she feels pressure to conform to the norms of the group by choosing a response she knows to be incorrect.

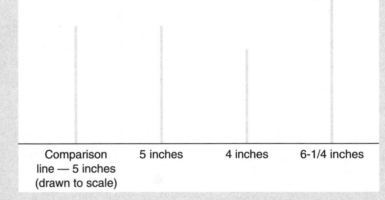

Comparison
line — 5 inches
(drawn to scale)   5 inches   4 inches   6-1/4 inches

Figure 7.1 *Typical comparison lines used in Asch's study of group effects on individual judgments.*

Social suport functions to:
- *provide appraisal, information, reassurance, and companionship;*
- *reduce uncertainty during times of stress;*
- *aid in mental and physical recovery; and*
- *improve communication skills.*

provider or the recipient to be intended to enhance the well-being of the recipient" (Shumaker & Brownell, 1984, p. 13). Research has indicated that social support of teammates, coaches, parents, and friends is positively related to athletes' performance and feelings of group cohesion (Westre & Weiss, 1991). For example, injured athletes often form groups to help support each other in the rehabilitation process. Positive support is also important when an athlete feels she is not performing well or realizing her potential. Conversely, negative responses from team members or coaches—such as harsh criticism, sarcasm, and lack of attention—can devastate some athletes. Mike Krzyzewski, men's basketball coach at Duke University, says the first thing he does at the beginning of the season is make sure all his players fit into the team concept and support each other. Creating an effective team climate that involves mutual support and respect is number one on his list in preparing his teams for the rigors of competition.

Proximity

People are more likely to bond when they are near each other. Although physical proximity alone will usually not develop a team concept, close contact with teammates promotes interaction, which in turn can hasten the group's development. Locker rooms, team training tables, and road trips ensure close proximity. Some college coaches promote team unity by having athletes live together in a residence hall. In youth sports, car or bus trips and fund-raisers, such as car washes, often help build a positive team climate as they provide opportunities for players to get to know one another better. These interactions, combined with a similarity of attitudes, can help establish team identity.

■ APPLICATION ■

Building an Effective Team Climate Through Social Support

Social support is a multidimensional concept and Rosenfeld and Richman (1997) have identified seven types of social support. Let's identify these social supports and offer suggestions for enhancing each aspect of social support to help in team building.

1. Listening Support

Listening support is the perception that someone else, an other, is listening without giving advice or being judgmental. These are some guidelines for enhancing listening support:

- Provide group social events for staff, athletes, and assistant coaches to allow them to step out of their typical roles.
- Emphasize the value of regular, informal contacts between athletes, coaches, trainers, and other support personnel.
- Provide communication training including skills for active listening.

2. Emotional Support

Emotional support is the perception that an other is providing comfort and caring and indicating that he or she is on the support recipient's side. These are guidelines for enhancing emotional support:

- Stress the importance of emotional support to the emergent and prescribed leaders.
- Encourage the team's giving emotional support to injured players by visiting them.
- Train student athletic trainers in the importance of emotional support and encourage them to provide this for one another.

3. Emotional-Challenge Support

Emotional-challenge support is the perception that an other is challenging the support recipient to evaluate his or her attitudes, values, and feelings. These are guidelines for enhancing emotional-challenge support:

- Encourage emotionally challenging verbal exchanges between players during practice and competitions (e.g., "You've been practicing that technique for the past several weeks; relax and let it happen.").
- Challenge team members to do their best through individual and team meetings focusing on achieving team and individual goals.

4. Reality-Confirmation Support

Reality-confirmation support is the perception that an other, who is similar to and sees things the same way as the support recipient does, is helping to confirm the support recipient's perspective. These are guidelines for enhancing reality-confirmation support:

- Arrange small group meetings where athletes discuss dealing with pressure, preparing for competition, adjusting to college life, and other such issues.
- Create shared opportunities between experienced and inexperienced athletic trainers, such as a buddy or mentor system pairing older and younger student trainers.
- Use value-clarification exercises to promote sharing.

continued

153

Building an Effective Team Climate Through Social Support
(continued)

5. Task-Appreciation Support

Task-appreciation support is the perception that an other is acknowledging the support recipient's efforts and expressing appreciation for the work he or she does. These are guidelines for enhancing task-appreciation support:

- Recognize preseason and daily goal attainment of specific skill improvements.
- Provide award ceremonies for both sport and academic performances.
- Provide specific feedback highlighting task achievements (e.g., "I thought you handled the injury situation in an intelligent and timely way.").

6. Task-Challenge Support

Task-challenge support is the perception that an other is challenging the support recipient's way of thinking about a task or an activity in order to stretch, motivate, and lead the support recipient to greater creativity, excitement, and involvement. These are guidelines for enhancing task-challenge support:

- Encourage team members to provide task-challenge support for one another as a team responsibility and norm.
- Videotape fitness participants to allow them to review their level of activity—and receive positive feedback from the fitness staff.

7. Personal-Assistance Support

Personal-assistance support is the perception that an other is providing services or help, such as running an errand or driving the support recipient somewhere. These are guidelines for lending personal-assistance support:

- Encourage teammates to help each other with non-sport related needs.
- Encourage each team member to get to know as many other team members on a personal level as possible and to demonstrate interest and caring about their teammates.

Distinctiveness

When a group feels distinct, its feelings of unity and oneness increase. Street gangs use distinctive dress and special initiation rites to set themselves apart from other gangs. In sport, distinctiveness is traditionally achieved through team uniforms and mottoes, special initiation rites, or special privileges. Athletes differ from other people in their intensive physical training programs, reduced time for social activities, and close relationships with team members. Some teams, such as the Boston Celtics and New York Yankees, Notre Dame's football team, UCLA's basketball team, and Iowa's wrestling team, overtly foster distinctiveness (e.g., the Celtics are known for their kelly green uniforms, which are distinct from all other teams'). By making team members feel unique and distinct from other teams, a coach helps develop and mold a team concept. In exercise classes, Carron and Spink (1993) increased group distinctiveness and built group cohesion in part by providing group T-shirts and special slogans for participants. Similarly, personal trainers might develop special logo shirts for people training at the same workout facility.

Fairness

An important component of team climate is trust, and at the core of trust is athletes' perceptions that they are being treated fairly. Athletes should feel that their play, effort, and contributions to the team's success are evaluated objectively and evenly. The fairness with which a coach treats athletes influences their level of commitment, motivation, and satisfaction. Athletes interpret fairness on three central issues (Anshel, 1994):

- The degree of compatibility between the coach's and the players' assessments of the players' skills and contributions to the team.
- How the coach communicates his or her views to the athletes.
- The athletes' perceptions that the coach is trying to help them improve and be happy.

Fairness, or lack of it, can bring a team close together or tear it apart. Coaches should deal with athletes honestly, openly, and fairly. Athletes need to feel they are treated fairly, even if they are not entirely happy with certain decisions. Some coaches do not pay much attention to their athletes' feelings of fairness. This is unfortunate, given the degree to which these feelings can transfer into negative actions, such as disruptive behavior or even quitting the team.

Similarity

Similarity among team members in commitments, attitudes, aspirations, and goals is important to developing a positive team climate. As Zander (1982) notes,

> *Birds of a feather flock together and create a more distinct entity when they do. People too form a better unit if they are alike, and an effective leader develops oneness within a set by encouraging likeness among members. To do this, they recruit persons who will interact well because of similar purpose, background, training, experience, or temperament. . . . Persons whose beliefs do not fit together will have a hard time forming a strong group. (p. 3)*

Team members usually differ in ethnicity, race, socioeconomic background, personality, and ability. But research has shown that factors such as socioeconomic background and playing experience are not necessarily important in building a team concept (Widmeyer & Williams, 1991). However, it is up to the coach to get a diverse bunch of athletes working together for common and shared purposes. Specifically, what the coach must do is to develop similarity in attitudes, such as shared group performance goals, expectations for individual behavior, codes of conduct for games and practices, and clarity about various team roles. The more this group of individuals feels the similarity among its members, the greater the probability of its developing a strong team concept. This concept of highlighting similarity holds true as well for an athletic director or a school principal trying to unify a diverse group of coaches or teachers who must work together.

Assessing Team Climate

Coaches find it useful to know how their athletes are feeling. The team climate questionnaire shows sample questions from a checklist to measure athletes' feelings about being on the team and their perceptions of the coach's behavior and attitudes.

Athletes' responses give the coach valuable information about the team's climate and possible ways to enhance its cohesion. Because it is valuable to look at changes occurring over the course of a season,

Team Climate Questionnaire

Read each statement and indicate how often it occurs, using the numbers on the following scale:

1 = Never occurs
2 = Sometimes occurs
3 = Usually occurs
4 = Always occurs

_____ 1. I can make many of the decisions that affect the way I play.

_____ 2. I can count on the coach to keep things I say confidential.

_____ 3. Members of the coaching staff pitch in to help each other out.

_____ 4. I have enough time to do the things the coach asks me to learn and perform.

_____ 5. I can count on my coach to help me when I need it.

athletes should respond to the checklist at preseason, and then coaches should periodically monitor changes throughout the season. Players should be told that this is not a test and that there are no right or wrong answers. Keep the responses anonymous so athletes are more likely to respond honestly.

Individual and Team Performance in Sport

Coaches are responsible for getting individual players to play together as a team, and they must understand how interactions among team members affect performance on the athletic field (or court). Most coaches and sport psychologists agree that a group of the best individuals usually does not make the best team. In essence, summing the abilities of individual team members does not accurately describe team performance. Take the 1997 NCAA men's basketball tournament. The two finalists, Kentucky and Utah, had lost their top players, all-Americans Keith Van Horn and Ron Mercer (who had been selected very high in the first round of the NBA draft). Yet, with less talent, they were able to reach the pinnacle of college basketball because of the teamwork and individual sacrifice of the returning players. Simply stated, a good team is more than the sum of its parts. How well a team works together is a key factor in the equation.

Steiner's Model

Ivan Steiner developed a model to show the relation between individual abilities or resources on a team and how team members interact (1972). Steiner's model is shown by this equation:

Actual productivity = potential productivity
– losses due to faulty group processes.

Potential productivity refers to a team's possible best performance, given each player's ability, knowledge, and skill (both mental and physical) as well as the demands of the task. Thus, a hockey team with six outstanding players who can shoot, play defense, pass, and skate would be considered to possess excellent group resources. According to Steiner's model, individual ability is probably the most im-

The abilities of individual team members are often not good predictors of how a team will perform.

portant resource for sport teams—thus, the team made up of the best individuals will usually achieve the most success.

However, Steiner's model implies that a team's actual productivity will not usually match its potential productivity. Only when a team effectively uses its available resources to match the demands of the task will its actual productivity or performance approach its potential performance. Specifically, a group's actual performance usually falls short of its potential productivity because of faulty group processes. In a team situation, group process refers to the complex interactions that help the team transform its individual resources into a collective performance. A volleyball team, for example, would have to have precise teamwork between setters, spikers, and blockers to achieve its potential.

There are two kinds of losses due to faulty group processes: motivation losses and coordination losses. Motivation losses occur when team members do not give 100% effort. Perhaps players feel that one or two stars can "carry the load"; thus, they slacken their efforts. Coordination losses occur when the timing between teammates is off or when ineffective strategies are used. For example, in a doubles match in tennis, if the ball is hit right down the middle of the court and neither player goes for it because each thinks the other will take it, that is a loss of coordination. Similarly, a soccer team that does not keep proper spacing and stay in position is not working well together.

Sports that require complex interaction or cooperation (e.g., basketball, soccer, football, or volleyball) are more susceptible to coordination losses than are sports requiring fewer interactions and less coordination (e.g., swimming or track and field). Basketball, soccer, and volleyball coaches typically spend much time and effort to fine-tune coordination, timing, and team movement patterns. Swimming coaches, on the contrary, spend most of their time developing individual swimming technique; they allot less time to integrative skills, such as the transitions between relay team members.

How Individual Skills Relate to Group Performance

Comrey and Deskin (1954) were two of the first researchers to investigate the relation between individual and group performance to see how faulty group processes reduce productivity. Using a pegboard assembly task and subjects performing alone and in groups, they found that no matter what level

156

© Human Kinetics

of motor skills individuals brought to the task, when two or more people tried to interact in precise ways, their ability to anticipate one another's movements and time their own actions accordingly was at least as important as their individual performance qualities. Other researchers have used laboratory tasks as well, finding that individual skills are only moderately good predictors of group performance.

Researchers in laboratories have studied the relationship between individual and group performance, but what about its application to real-world sports? Along these lines, Jones (1974) studied professional teams and players (tennis, basketball, football, and baseball), focusing on the statistics of individual players, such as their runs batted in and batting averages in baseball; points, assists, rebounds, and steals in basketball; singles rankings in tennis; and yards gained in football. He wanted to see how these statistics related to team success across a competitive

season, and he found a positive relationship between a team's effectiveness and individual performance success for all four sports. This relationship was strongest in baseball, which has the least number of interactions; it was weakest in basketball, which has the most complex interactions. Thus, it appears that where more cooperation and interaction are necessary, the importance of individual ability decreases and the importance of group process increases. In terms of Steiner's model, teams with fewer interactions (as in baseball) are less likely to suffer losses in productivity due to faulty group process, whereas highly interactive teams (as in basketball) must be more sensitive to decreases in performance due to faulty group interactions.

When teams of only two people play, they apparently work together best if they are close in ability. One investigation revealed that the best predictor of success was the averaged ability of the two players

157

(i.e., summing the abilities of the two-person team), but a large difference in ability between partners had a negative effect on performance (Gill, 1979). The closer teammates are in ability, the more likely they are to fully put to use their combined abilities. In tennis, when a superior player is paired with an inferior player, the better player will often try to do too much (i.e., play above her ability level) and wind up making mistakes. Similarly, experienced teams will quickly identify and target a weaker player and hit the majority of shots at that person. In short, teams are usually as good as their weakest player. In tennis, for example, the top singles players rarely win at doubles (Martina Hingis is an exception). Usually, the top doubles teams are made up of two very good players who complement each other (such as Mark Woodforde and Todd Woodbridge)—and not of one star and another adequate player who have trouble combining their skills.

The Ringlemann Effect

Clearly, individual abilities do not neatly sum up to group or team performance. This is consistent with Steiner's model, which noted that potential productivity could be reduced by faulty group processes. But what causes these losses, and how much potential productivity is lost? The answers to these questions began to emerge from an obscure, unpublished study on individual and group performance (the **Ringelmann effect**) on a rope-pulling task that Ringelmann conducted nearly 100 years ago (cited by Ingham, Levinger, Graves, & Peckhan, 1974). He observed individuals and groups of two, three, and eight people pulling on a rope. If there were no losses due to faulty group processes, then it could be assumed that each individual pulled 100 pounds. So groups of two, three, and eight would be able to pull 200, 300, and 800 pounds, respectively. However, the relative performance of each individual showed a progressive decline as the number of people in the group increased. That is, two-person groups pulled only 93% of their individual potential, three-person groups 85%, and eight-person groups only 49%.

Since some of the early methodology and descriptions had been incomplete in Ringelmann's study, Ingham et al. (1974) attempted to replicate Ringelmann's findings while extending the work.

> *The phenomenon by which individual performance decreases as the number of people in the group increases is known as the Ringlemann effect.*

They first had individuals and groups of two, three, four, five, and six persons perform the rope-pulling task. Results were similar to Ringelmann's study: Groups of two performed at 91% of their potential and groups of three, at 82% of their potential. However, contrary to what Ringelmann found, increases in group size did not lead to corresponding decreases in efficiency. Rather, there was a general leveling off, where groups of six pulled at an average of 78% of their potential (see a comparison of the Ringelmann and Ingham studies in Table 7.1).

In study 2, Ingham and his colleagues then wanted to determine whether the losses resulting from increased group size were due to poor coordination or reduced motivation. To separate these two, coordination was eliminated as a factor by testing only one subject at a time, blindfolding the subject, and having trained helpers pretend to pull on the rope (subjects thought the other members of the group were pulling on the rope, though they were not). Any decrease in performance was then attributed to a loss in motivation rather than a loss in coordination (because only the real subject was actually pulling the rope). The results were almost identical to their first study—average performance dropped to 85% in the three-person groups, with no further decrease in individual performance as group size increased (see Table 7.1). They concluded that the differences between actual and potential performance were not due to a decrease in coordination but to a decrease in motivation.

Two other experiments used shouting and clapping as group tasks and found that the average sound each person produced decreased from the solo performance to 71% in two-person groups, 51% in four-person groups, and 40% in six-person groups. When the scientists controlled for coordination, they found that two-person groups performed at 82% of their potential and six-person groups at 74% of their potential (Hardy & Latane, 1988; Latane, Williams, & Harkins, 1979).

Social Loafing

Psychologists call the phenomenon social loafing in which individuals within a group or team put forth less than 100% effort due to losses in motivation. Research has found social loafing effects in swimming, track, and cheerleading, as well as in a wide variety of laboratory motor tasks (see Hanrahan & Gallois, 1993, for a review). Numerous explanations have been proposed to account for the social loafing phenomenon, and the four that have received the most attention are highlighted in the box on p. 160. In testing these explanations research has shown that the

158

Table 7.1

Progressive Decline in Individual Rope-Pulling Performance Expressed as a Percentage of Individual Performance

Study	Group size							
	1	**2**	**3**	**4**	**5**	**6**	**7**	**8**
Ringlemann study	100	93	85					49
Ingham (study 1)	100	91	82	78	78	78		
Ingham (study 2)	100	90	85	86	84	85		

losses in individual productivity due to social loafing are greatest when the contributions of individual group members are not identified, are dispensable, or are disproportionate to the contributions of other group members. For example, offensive linemen in football might not block so hard if the running play is going in the opposite direction of where they are blocking. However, if they know that coaches will be reviewing the film of the game on Monday morning and their lack of effort could be identified, they may block harder on each play, regardless of the play's direction. Thus, if individual contributions to the group product are monitored directly, social loafing should be reduced. In addition, when individuals perceive that their contributions are essential to the group's productivity, social loafing should be reduced.

Let's look at some specific examples, along with supporting research, of what both athletes and coaches can do to reduce social loafing.

Emphasize the Importance of Individual Pride and Unique Contributions

When a coach stresses the team concept, some players might not recognize the importance of their own contributions to the team. All players should be challenged to examine their responsibility to the team and how they can improve for the team's benefit. In essence, each individual's unique contribution to the team's success should be communicated and highlighted whenever possible. In addition, each athlete should assume responsibility for his or her own efforts and not assume that a teammate will take care of things.

Increase the Identifiability of Individual Performances

The most consistent finding across research studies points to identifiability as the most acceptable explanation for the social loafing phenomenon. As a result, when team members believe that their individual performances are identifiable (i.e., known to others), social loafing may be eliminated because players no longer feel anonymous (Williams, Harkins, & Latane, 1981). Studies of swimmers found that they swam faster in relays than in individual events only when individual times in relays were announced (i.e., there was high identifiability). However, swimmers swam slower in relays than individual events when individual times were not announced in relays (i.e., there was low identifiability). Coaches, teachers, and exercise leaders should monitor individual efforts consistently and give feedback to participants who are learning new skills, as well as in practice and competition. By evaluating participants' efforts as individuals, coaches, teachers, and exercise leaders make the participants aware of their concern and assure them that they are not lost in the crowd. For example, a fitness leader might call out the names of individuals doing a specific exercise or movement particularly well.

Videotaping or using observational checklists at team-sport practices and games can also provide increased identifiability. For example, at Ohio State University, the late Woody Hayes increased the identifiability of football linemen by filming and specifically grading each player on each play, providing "lineman of the week" honors and awarding helmet decals to players who showed individual effort and performance. It's important to include practices as well as games in your evaluation because many players don't get a lot of actual game time.

Determine Specific Situations Where Loafing May Occur

Through videotaping or other observations, coaches can determine what situations seem to elicit loafing. However, social loafing is sometimes appropriate! For example, a basketball center gets a rebound and throws an outlet pass to the guard but does not follow the ball down the floor. She is taking a rest on the offensive end, in effect, to make sure she is ready on the defensive end, which may be appropriate if she is tired. In fact, Bill Russell, MVP center for the

■ MORE INFORMATION ■

What Causes Social Loafing?

- Sucker effect. Athletes might believe that teammates are less motivated than they are, and not wanting to play the role of a sucker, choose to put forth less effort.
- Minimizing strategy. Individuals may feel they are "lost in the crowd" and are not able to secure their fair share of the positive consequences of working hard.
- Allocation strategy. Athletes may feel that they don't really have to try hard because their teammates are there to take up the slack.
- Free rider. Athletes may feel that they can hide in the crowd and thereby avoid the negative consequences of not trying hard.

© Human Kinetics

champion Boston Celtics, popularized this exact strategy as he focused his efforts on the defensive end, letting his teammates run the fast break at the offensive end. This type of social loafing might be viewed as social engineering since it involves managing one's motivation and actions to match the task demands. In this case, resting actually helps the team achieve its goal of winning.

To better understand when social loafing might be appropriate, coaches should carefully analyze the dynamics and strategies involved in their sport. If changes need to be made, coaches should structure the practice sessions and competitions so that each player can economize efforts without interfering with team performance. For example, during a particularly tough part of the season, coaches might incorporate low-intensity practices into the schedule or complement high-intensity practices with fun activities. This will help keep players sharp and minimize their loafing.

Conduct Individual Meetings to Discuss Loafing

It is important to discuss loafing with each player individually. A player may have reasons for motivational loss that are more complex than feeling lost in the crowd or assuming someone else will get the job done. Good communication is

160

essential to learn why an athlete is not giving full effort. For example, athletes may have other commitments that place them under stress and require energy and time expenditure. Thus, the athlete may be economizing effort just to get through the day physically and mentally. But it's important to note that merely being warned about social loafing is not enough to prevent its occurring (Huddleston, Doody, & Ruder, 1985). Rather, coaches must devise specific strategies to reduce the probability of social loafing.

Walk a Mile in a Teammates' Shoes

It is important not only for athletes to know their own role on the team but also the roles their teammates play. One of the best ways for players to gain an appreciation of their teammates and how their performance affects others on the team is to learn about teammates' positions. Talking about the unique challenges of other positions will help each player better understand the impact they have on other positions when they loaf. Coaches can help here by requiring athletes to spend a small period of time rotating to other positions to better understand their teammates' contribution and to experience its potential effect on other positions.

Break Down the Team Into Smaller Units

Forming subgroups within a team allows for greater recognition of responsibility to others and helps develop a cohesive unit. Coaches should carefully monitor these subgroups and constantly reinforce the overall notion of team pride. Subgroup formation (e.g., in football, defensive backs, offensive linemen, receivers) can enhance feelings of group cohesion, which in turn leads to increased effort and commitment. Be careful, however, since placing too great an emphasis on subgroups at the expense of the larger group can result in the formation of destructive social cliques.

■ MORE INFORMATION ■

The Transition and Disengagement Process for Teams

Most of this chapter has been devoted to the formation of groups and teams. However, individuals often leave teams, and teams themselves often dissolve. Recent work by Danish, Owens, Green, & Brunelle (1997) has studied how disengagement and transition affect teams. Transition or disengagement can result through injury, retirement, graduation, being cut, transferring schools, being traded, or the team's even being disbanded. We should understand how individuals and their teams are affected by these transitions. The following four steps have been devoted to facilitate team transitions following the disengagement of an athlete. A trained sport psychologist can be specifically helpful in facilitating this process:

1. *Clarify role differentiation.* This step begins by having team members chart the role of each player, highlighting the position of the absent athlete. Then athletes are asked to clarify the role of each team member in relation to such areas as team unity, team spirit, cooperation, and resolving conflict.

2. *Increase individual awareness of disengagement.* The next step is to have athletes think about how disengagement affects them personally. It is especially important that athletes accept the responsibility of the possible shifting of their roles within the team.

3. *Facilitate group interaction.* The third step is to provide the team with opportunities to work together and talk about team interaction. This can help athletes deal with the absence of a teammate and with integrating a new teammate into the position formerly held by that absent athlete. For example, an activity could be devised where team members practice different positions (e.g., players who focus on offense might play defense positions and vice versa) so that they can break free of prior assumptions based on the role of the absent athlete and also work on integrating the new athlete.

4. *Negotiate closure and new group development.* The final step is to provide the team with an open format to recognize possible changes in group dynamics and reformulate team goals based on the current team members. In this way, the disengagement process can be seen as a challenge rather than a threat.

161

SUMMARY

1 *Discuss how a group becomes a team.*

There are four stages that groups go through to move from a mere collection of individuals to a team. These include forming, storming, norming, and performing. A leader's knowledge of these stages can help him or her structure the environment to support individuals in the group through each stage.

2 *Understand how groups are structured.*

A group's structure depends largely on the interactions of its members. Two of the most important structural characteristics of groups are group roles and group norms. Roles consist of the set of behaviors required or expected of the person occupying a certain position in a group. Norms are levels of performance, patterns of behaviors, or beliefs held by the group.

3 *Explain how to create an effective team climate.*

Team climate develops from how players perceive the interrelationships among the group members. Some of the critical factors affecting team climate are social support, proximity, distinctiveness, fairness, and similarity.

4 *Describe how to maximize individual performance in team sports.*

Individual skills are only moderately related to ultimate team success. Thus getting greater contributions from each player is critical for high-level team performance. Through the use of videotaping, helping players understand their roles, and increasing identifiability, you can maximize an individual's sense of contributing to the team effort.

5 *Better understand the concept of social loafing.*

Social loafing is the phenomenon whereby individuals within a group put forth less than 100% effort due to losses in motivation. In essence, there is a diffusion of responsibility, and individuals feel that others within the group will pick up the slack.

KEY TERMS

group	norm
team	social support
forming	potential productivity
storming	motivation losses
norming	coordination losses
performing	Ringlemann effect
role	social loafing

REVIEW QUESTIONS

1. Discuss why most definitions of a group agree that a collection of individuals is not necessarily a group.

2. Describe the four stages of team development and the key events that characterize each stage.

3. List some formal and informal roles in a sport you're familiar with. Who decides on these roles? What are the defining characteristics that identify each role?

4. What might happen to a team when the roles are clearly defined yet only partially accepted (i.e., only some of the players are willing to accept their roles)?

5. Provide examples of some norms you have experienced while participating in sport or exercise programs. Was there a norm for productivity? If so, how was this norm developed?

6. Explain at least three techniques you might use to improve a team's climate.

7. Discuss an experience you have had where Steiner's model of productivity was applicable and actual productivity was less than potential productivity. Was the loss due to a lack of coordination or motivation?

8. Describe the Ringelmann effect. What implications do his findings have for a coach, physical educator, or exercise leader?

9. Discuss three potential explanations for social loafing. How would you identify social loafing? How could your team captains help you alleviate or overcome social loafing?

CRITICAL THINKING QUESTIONS

1. You are an exercise leader and you want to build more unity within your class or group because you feel this will increase people's desire to come to class and participate. What kinds of things would you do (and why) to help build this sense of group or team unity.

2. You are a coach of a team sport and you see that not everyone is really hustling on every play. What would you say to your players to get them to realize they are loafing and that the team needs them to stop loafing? What kinds of things could you do to minimize or prevent this loafing from occurring?

Group Cohesion

After reading this chapter you should be able to

1 define task and social cohesion,
2 describe the conceptual model of cohesion,
3 discuss how cohesion is measured,
4 understand the cohesion-performance relationship,
5 better understand factors associated with cohesion, and
6 identify guidelines for building team cohesion.

Players and coaches often attribute a team's success or failure to how well the members work together as a cohesive unit. When a highly favored team is upset by a less talented team, its coach may say, "We just didn't play well as a team. Everyone seemed concerned about his own individual statistics instead of doing what was needed to win the game." On the other hand, when the Pittsburgh Pirates won the World Series in 1979, the team's motto was "We are family," suggesting that players owed the success to their ability to get along and work together toward a common goal. Superstar hockey players Wayne Gretzky and Mark Messier, to look at another example, focused on the team goal of winning for the New York Rangers in 1994 rather than simply on their personal statistics. Although other sport and exercise professionals, such as exercise or aerobics leaders, receive less attention in the media, they also try to build cohesion in their classes. Their purpose in fostering this spirit might be to enhance exercise adherence, inasmuch as adhering to an exercise program and promoting lifelong healthy lifestyles are the main goals of these exercise types of programs.

Yet we cannot always attribute success to team cohesion. Some teams win despite an apparent lack of cohesion. The Oakland Athletics in the early 1970s and the New York Yankees in the late 1970s won the World Series amidst a lack of harmony in their ball clubs, which had frequent battles among players and between players and coaches (Billy Martin and Reggie Jackson, for example). Similarly, Dennis Rodman of the Chicago Bulls has often been at odds with his teammates because of his unusual and provocative antics, but on the court all he wants to do is win, which has allowed him to play within the team concept. However, when Rodman has been disruptive on the court, coach Phil Jackson would bench him; he wasn't helping the team achieve its goal—winning an NBA championship. This quote by Michael Jordan captures the idea that a team can play well and be cohesive on-court, regardless of what occurs off-court:

Naturally there are going to be some ups and downs, particularly if you have individuals trying to achieve at a high level. But when we stepped in between the lines, we knew what we were capable of doing. When a pressure situation presented itself, we were plugged into one another as a cohesive unit. That's why we were able to come back so often and win so many close games. And that's why we were able to beat more talented teams.

Although Michael Jordan is widely considered the greatest basketball player ever to play at the professional level, he learned that individual brilliance and talent are not enough to win championships. A team needs all its players working together as a cohesive unit during competitions. Let's first examine the cohesion-performance relationship by defining cohesion and exploring its different aspects.

Defining Cohesion

In 1950, Festinger, Schacter, and Back defined cohesion as "the total field of forces which act on members to remain in the group" (p. 164). They felt that two distinct forces act on members to remain in a group. The first class of forces, attractiveness of the group, refers to the individual's desire for interpersonal interactions with other group members and a desire to be involved in the group's activities. Being with the group and interacting with others in it gives the members a sense of satisfaction. The second class of forces, means control, refers to the benefits that a member can derive by being associated with the group. For example, playing for a highly ranked college football team might increase an athlete's recognition and value in the draft.

Between 1950 and 1970, several other definitions of group cohesion were proposed, their common thread being that cohesion comprises basic *task* and *social* dimensions. Task cohesion reflects the degree to which members of a group work together to achieve common goals. In sport, a common goal would be winning a championship, which in part depends on the team's coordinated effort or teamwork. Social cohesion, on the other hand, reflects the degree to which members of a team like each other and enjoy each other's company. Social cohesion is often equated with interpersonal attraction. In an exercise class, for example, a common goal would be enhanced fitness, and it has been shown that adherence to the exercise program increases as the social cohesion of the group increases (Spink & Carron, 1992).

Task cohesion refers to the degree that group members work together to achieve common goals and objectives, whereas social cohesion reflects the interpersonal attraction among group members.

Task or Social Cohesion

The New York Yankees in the late 1970s were a classic case of a team that apparently did not get along well together (low social cohesion) yet was able to win pennants and several World Series (high task cohesion). The major personality conflicts in the "Bronx Zoo" (as some people called it) were George Steinbrenner, manager Billy Martin, and star outfielder Reggie Jackson. Steinbrenner and Martin had strong personalities that often clashed (in fact Steinbrenner fired Martin three times). Steinbrenner wanted to make managerial decisions instead of focusing on front office decisions. But Martin wanted complete control over what happened on the field and felt that Steinbrenner was usurping his authority. To add to the stew, Reggie Jackson was outspoken and strong-willed, frequently and openly disagreeing with both Martin's and Steinbrenner's decisions. As this circus unfolded throughout the season, other players were inevitably drawn into the melee.

It seemed unlikely that such a team could hang together for even a single season, yet for several years the Yankees were probably the most successful team in professional baseball. The key to understanding the team's success is to understand the difference between social and task cohesion. That is, despite the team's infighting and bickering (i.e., low social cohesion), it had a strong desire to win and be the best (i.e., high task cohesion). When Reggie Jackson came to bat, he would try his hardest, both for Reggie Jackson and for the success of the team. Similarly, in making managerial decisions, winning was always foremost in Billy Martin's mind, regardless of what he thought about Reggie Jackson or George Steinbrenner. Thus, the shared common goal of winning the World Series overcame the lack of interpersonal attraction among players and management.

The distinction between task and social cohesion is important conceptually and helps explain how teams can overcome conflict to succeed. Take the examples of the New York Yankees and Oakland Athletics, teams that certainly appeared to be low in social cohesion (team members fought, formed cliques, and exchanged angry words). However, these teams obviously had a high degree of task cohesion—they wanted to win the World Series. It didn't matter if Reggie Jackson didn't get along with manager Billy Martin because they shared the goal of winning. In terms of working together effectively, the teams had excellent field work and could turn double plays, hit cut-off men, and advance runners as good as or better than any other teams.

To reflect these task and social components of cohesion, Carron refined the definition of cohesion in 1982, proposing "a dynamic process which is reflected in the tendency for a group to stick together and remain united in the pursuit of its goals and objectives" (p. 124).

A Conceptual Model of Cohesion

Carron's definition is more useful for sport and exercise settings than the earlier one of Festinger et al. He later developed a conceptual system as a framework for systematically studying cohesion in sport and exercise (see Figure 8.1).

Carron's model outlines four major antecedents or factors affecting the development of cohesion in sport and exercise settings: environmental, personal, team, and leadership factors.

Environmental Factors

Environmental factors, which are the most general and remote, refer to the normative forces holding a group together. Some examples are players being under contract to the management, athletes holding scholarships, family expectations of athletes, regulations specifying the minimum playing time in a youth sport program, and exercisers paying an extra fee for their class. These influences can hold a group together, although other factors such as age, proximity, or eligibility requirements can also play an important role. For example, having individuals in close proximity to each other with opportunities for interaction and communication foster group development. In addition, the size of a group also affects cohesion, with smaller groups being more cohesive than larger groups (Carron & Spink, 1995). Groups that are more distinctive and separate from others (accomplished by such things as their having

167

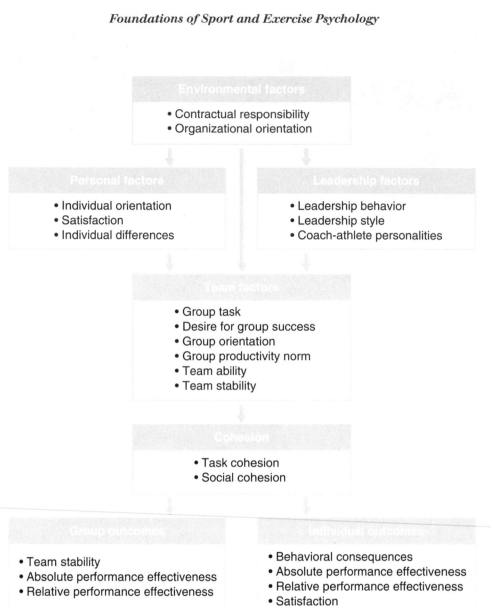

Figure 8.1 *Carron's conceptual model for cohesion in sport teams.*
Adapted from Carron, 1982.

Personal Factors

Personal factors refer to the individual characteristics of group members, such as participation motives. While environmental factors are fairly constant and usually apply to all teams within a given league, a great deal of variation occurs in personal factors. Bass, for example, identified three primary motives: task motivation, affiliation motivation, and self-motivation (1962). Task motivation and affiliation motivation are closely associated with task and social cohesion, respectively. If you have high task motivation, you would contribute to a group's task cohesion. Similarly, ath-

special team uniforms, initiation rites, and unique group names) also enjoy higher levels of cohesion.

letes high in affiliation motivation would contribute to social cohesion. Self-motivation refers to the attempt to obtain personal satisfaction by performing up to one's level of ability, and it seems to contribute to both social and task cohesion. In addition, such factors as social background, satisfaction, gender, attitudes, commitment, and personality have differential influences on cohesion. For example, Widmeyer and Williams (1991) found that member satisfaction was the best predictor of both social and task cohesion in the sport of golf.

Leadership Factors

Leadership factors include the leadership style and behaviors that professionals exhibit and the relation-

168

© Human Kinetics

ships they establish with their groups (these factors will be discussed more thoroughly in chapter 9). Research has indicated that the role of leaders is vital to team cohesion. Specifically, clear, consistent, unambiguous communication from coaches and captains regarding team goals, team tasks, and team members' roles significantly influences cohesion (Carron, 1993; Westre & Weiss, 1991). In addition, the compatibility between the leader and group members is also important to enhance feelings of cohesion.

Team Factors

Team factors refer to group task characteristics (individual versus team sports), group productivity norms, desire for group success, and team stability. For example, Carron (1982) argues that teams that stay together a long time and have a strong desire for group success also exhibit high levels of group cohesion. In addition, shared common experiences, such as a series of successes or failures, are important in developing and maintaining cohesion because they act to unify a team to counter the threat of opposing teams (Brawley, 1990).

Measuring Cohesion

To determine the relationship between cohesion and performance we must be able to measure cohesion. Two types of measures have been developed: questionnaires and sociograms.

Questionnaires

Most early research on cohesion utilized the Sport Cohesiveness Questionnaire developed by Martens, Landers, and Loy (1972). This questionnaire has 7 items that measure either interpersonal attraction or direct ratings of closeness or attraction to the group. Unfortunately, no reliability or validity measures were established on the Sport Cohesiveness Questionnaire, and most items address only social cohesion. To account for the multidimensional nature of cohesion, Yukelson, Weinberg, and Jackson developed a 22-item tool called the Multidimensional Sport Cohesion Instrument (1984). It includes four broad dimensions of team cohesion: (a) attraction to the group, (b) unity of purpose, (c) quality of teamwork, and (d) valued roles.

169

■ CLOSE-UP ■

The Disease of Me

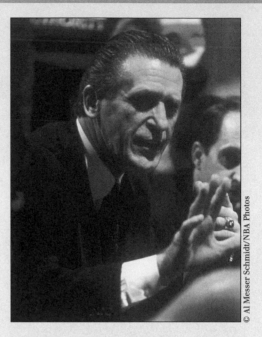

When highly successful basketball coach Pat Riley was hired by the New York Knicks, he felt the team suffered from something he called "the disease of me." The team was plagued with too many self-centered individuals looking out only for themselves, players not liking one another, and players not respecting one another. Based on his mission statement "Success Through Unselfishment," Riley and the organization sought to reinstill a sense of team cohesion so that individuals were willing to sacrifice self-interests for the betterment of the team. Riley attempted to accomplish this goal through positive peer pressure, reinforcing appropriate team-oriented behaviors, team goal setting, and open discussions focusing on mutual respect, trust, and responsibility. The productivity of the team was the focus, and each player was asked to put his unique talents toward the good of the team. As a result, the team pulled together to play well throughout the season and was particularly impressive during the playoffs (Riley, 1993).

© Al Messer Schmidt/NBA Photos

The first factor, attraction to the group, reflects social cohesion. The final three factors can be collectively considered as relating to task cohesion since they all have to do with working together as a team in pursuit of common goals. While the Multidimensional Sport Cohesion Instrument was designed for basketball teams, its versatility allows it to be used with other team sports.

More recently, the Group Environment Questionnaire (GEQ) was developed, distinguishing between the individual and the group and between task and social concerns (Widmeyer, Brawley, & Carron, 1985). It is conceptually based and systematically developed in terms of establishing reliability and validity (Brawley, Carron, & Widmeyer, 1987; Carron, Widmeyer, & Brawley, 1985).

The GEQ has been successfully utilized in numerous studies investigating group cohesion in sport as well as fitness settings (e.g., Widmeyer & Williams, 1991; Prapavessis, Carron, & Spink, 1997; Spink & Carron, 1993). For example, using the GEQ, level of cohesion has been shown to be related to team performance, increased adherence, group size, attributions for responsibil-

The Group Environment Questionnaire focuses on how attractive the group is to individual members and on how the members perceive the group. The GEQ is accepted for assessing team cohesion.

ity for performance outcomes, reduced absenteeism, member satisfaction, and intrateam communication.

The model on which the development of the GEQ was based has two major categories: a member's perception of the group as a totality (group integration) and a member's personal attraction to the group (individual attraction to the group). The members' perceptions of the group as a unit and their perceptions of the group's attraction for them can be focused on task or social aspects. Thus, there are four constructs in the model:

■ Group integration—task

■ Group integration—social

170

Group Environment Questionnaire (GEQ): Sample Items

	Strongly disagree								Strongly agree
Attraction to group—task subscale									
I like this team's style of play.	1	2	3	4	5	6	7	8	9
Attraction to group—social subscale									
Some of my best friends are on this team.	1	2	3	4	5	6	7	8	9
Group integration—task subscale									
We all take responsibility for any loss or poor performance by our team.	1	2	3	4	5	6	7	8	9
Group integration—social subscale									
Our team would like to spend time together in the off-season.	1	2	3	4	5	6	7	8	9

Note. The GEQ is scored by adding up all questions for each subscale. The higher the score, the higher the individual feels about that particular aspect of group cohesion (scoring reverses for negatively worded items). For example, an attraction to the group-task scores can range from 4 to 36. Comparisons can be made among individuals or among groups.

Adapted from Carron, Brawley, and Widmeyer, 1985.

- Individual attractions to group—task
- Individual attractions to group—social

These beliefs and perceptions are thought to act together in creating a group's and an individual group member's sense of cohesion. In essence, there are both social and task aspects about the group as a whole and the individuals within the group. The relationship of these four constructs is presented in Figure 8.2.

Sociograms

Questionnaires have been the most popular way to measure group cohesion, but they do not show how particular individuals relate to each other, whether cliques are developing, and if some group members are socially isolated. A sociogram is a tool to measure social cohesion. It discloses affiliation and attraction among group members, including

- the presence or absence of cliques,
- members' perceptions of group closeness,
- friendship choices within the group,

- the degree to which athletes perceive interpersonal feelings similarly,
- social isolation of individual group members, and
- extent of group attraction.

To generate information for the sociogram you ask individual group members specific questions, such as, "Name the three people in the group you would most like to invite to a party and the three people you would least like to invite," "Name the three people you would most like to room with on road trips and the three you would least like to room with," and "Name three people you would most like to practice with during the off-season and three whom you would least like to practice with." Confidentiality must be assured, and you should encourage honesty in responses.

Based on the responses to the questions, a sociogram is created (see an example in Figure 8.3), which should reveal the pattern of interpersonal relationships in a group. In creating a sociogram, the most frequently chosen individuals are placed toward the center of the sociogram and less frequently chosen individuals are placed outside. Notice that the arrows in Figure 8.3 indicate the direction of choice. Reciprocal choice is represented by arrows going in

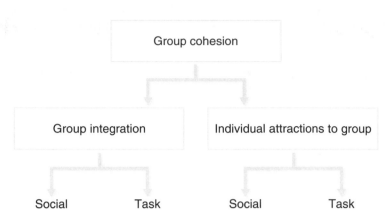

Figure 8.2 *Conceptual model of group cohesion for the GEQ.*
Adapted from Carron, Widmeyer, and Brawley, 1985.

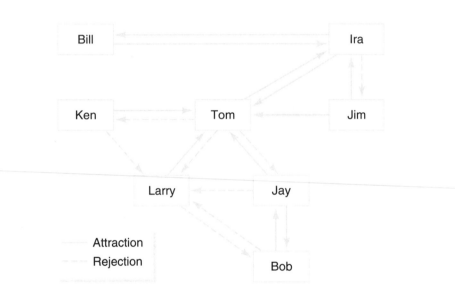

Figure 8.3 *Sociogram for measuring cohesion on a baseball team.*

both directions between two individuals. In the baseball team represented in the figure, you can see that Tom is the person everyone seems to like. Larry is isolated from the team and is disliked by several members, so there is a problem that the coach should address. Jay and Bob form a closed unit and are not really involved with the rest of the team. Knowing about these relationships might help the coach deal with interpersonal problems before they become disruptive.

The Relationship Between Cohesion and Performance

Fans, coaches, and sport psychologists seem to have an enduring fascination with how team cohesion re-

lates to performance success. On an intuitive level, you might assume that the higher the level of a team's cohesion, the greater its success. Why else spend so much time trying to develop team cohesion? In fact, in a review of 30 studies Widmeyer, Carron, and Brawley (1993) found that 83% reported a positive relationship between cohesion and performance, with higher team cohesion associated with greater team success. In addition, another review using 66 empirical studies assessing the cohesion-performance relationship in a variety of settings, found positive relations in 92% of the studies, with the strongest relations found in sport teams (Mullen & Cooper, 1994). There are, however, several studies which found a negative cohesion-performance relationship. In fact, several reviews of the research literature have noted the somewhat contradictory nature of the results regarding cohesion and performance success (e.g., Carron, Spink, & Prapavessis, 1997). The inconsistencies that have been found can best be understood by considering the measurement of cohesion, characteristics of the task, and direction of causality.

Type of Measurement

Think back to the breakdown of task and social cohesion. Almost all the studies reporting a negative relation between cohesion and performance used only an interpersonal attraction measure, such as a sociogram or the interpersonal attraction items from the Sport Cohesion Questionnaire (e.g., Landers & Lueschen, 1974; Lenk, 1969). In essence, teams high in interpersonal attraction were more likely to be unsuccessful.

When both task cohesion and social cohesion were assessed, however, mixed results were found. That is, positive relationships between cohesion and performance were found for task measures of cohesion but not for social measures, such as friendship and interpersonal attraction (e.g., Widmeyer & Martens, 1978). Much of the research before 1985 used some measure of social cohesion but often had no measure of task cohesion, which probably accounts for the inconsistent findings.

Task Demands

A second explanation for the confusing cohesion-performance results involves the diversity of task demands that sport teams face. The explanation can

be attributed to the original work of Landers and Laschen (1974), who noted that task structure and demands need to be considered when assessing the cohesion performance relationship. Specifically, they characterize the nature of interactions among team members along a continuum, from being interactive to coactive (see Figure 8.4). **Interactive sports** require team members to work together and coordinate their actions. Players on a soccer team, for example, have to constantly pass the ball to each other, maintain certain positions, coordinate offensive attacks, and devise defensive strategies to stop opponents from scoring. **Coactive sports** require little, if any, team interaction and coordination to achieve their goals. For instance, members of a golf or bowling team have little to do with each other in terms of coordinated activity. Baseball is a good example of a sport that is both interactive and coactive: Batting or catching a fly ball is coactive, whereas making a double play or hitting the cut-off man is interactive.

The distinction between interactive and coactive tasks further helps us understand the varied cohesion-performance results. Positive cohesion-performance relations are reported most often for team sports that require extensive interaction, coordina-

> *Cohesion increases performance for interacting sports (e.g., basketball) but decreases or shows no effect on performance for coacting.*

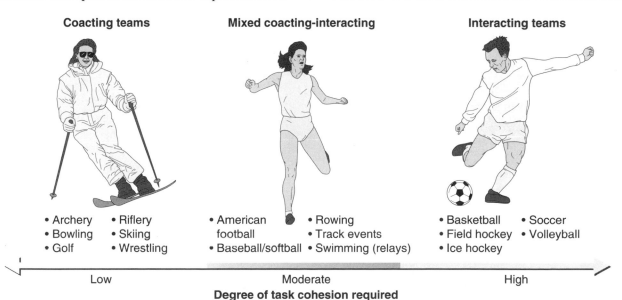

Coacting teams   **Mixed coacting-interacting**   **Interacting teams**

- Archery   • Riflery
- Bowling   • Skiing
- Golf   • Wrestling

- American football   • Rowing
- Baseball/softball   • Track events
                       • Swimming (relays)

- Basketball   • Soccer
- Field hockey • Volleyball
- Ice hockey

Low   Moderate   High
Degree of task cohesion required

Figure 8.4 *Examples of task cohesion required in different sports.*
Adapted from Cratty, 1983.

© Human Kinetics

tion, and cooperation among team members, such as basketball (Widmeyer, Brawley, & Carron, 1990), hockey (Dawe & Carron, 1990), and volleyball (Ruder & Gill, 1982). On the other hand, sports such as bowling (Landers & Lueschen, 1974), riflery (McGrath, 1962), and rowing (Lenk, 1969) are predominantly coactive, requiring independent performance with little interaction and integration. Typically they show no relation between cohesion and performance or even a negative relation.

From an intuitive perspective these findings make sense, especially when we consider task cohesion. For instance, in basketball, a team's success depends on all its members working closely together. Good team defense requires switching assignments, calling out screens, and blocking out for rebounding. A smooth offense requires distribution of passes, movement without the ball, screens away from the ball, and proper spacing among teammates. These maneuvers require close teamwork, with members understanding their roles and having common goals.

Now think of a track-and-field team. Although each athlete's score on a particular event will be part of the team score, the athletes do not really have to work with each other to achieve their goals (except for runners in a relay team). Pole vaulters, long jumpers, hurdlers, sprinters, and middle-distance runners each compete at their own specialty. As long as the athletes on the track-and-field team do their best, how well they get along matters little to the team's performance.

Direction of Causality

The **direction of causality** refers to whether cohesion leads to performance success or performance success leads to cohesion. In other words, will a team that works together on and off the field be successful, or do players like each other more and work together well because they are successful? Researchers have investigated these questions from two perspectives:

■ Cohesion leads to performance; that is, cohesion measures precede performance.

■ Performance leads to cohesion; that is, performance measures precede cohesion.

At first the researchers relied heavily on correlational data in trying to predict performance from

174

cohesion. They assessed early-season cohesion and tried to determine if it would predict later-season success (Widmeyer & Martens, 1978). Or, attempting to study the causal effects of performance on cohesion, they measured performance early in the season and tried determining if this would predict cohesion later in the season (Ruder & Gill, 1982).

Direction of causality or cause-effect relationships have proven difficult to establish due to many uncontrolled factors, such as previous team success, coaching, or talent. To assess the performance and cohesion relation more directly, a couple of researchers employed a cross-lagged panel design, which incorporates time factors into the measurement. Using this design, Carron and Ball tested cohesion in 12 intercollegiate hockey teams at early season, midseason, and end of season (1977). They also assessed team performance in terms of win-loss percentage at midseason and at the end of the season (see Figure 8.5). None of the correlations were significant as far as cohesion predicting later performance. However, significant correlations were found between early performance and later cohesion. That is, the relation between early-season performance and later-season co-

hesion is stronger than the relationship between early-season cohesion and later-season performance. The same stronger effects of performance on cohesion were found in a study of intercollegiate female field hockey players (Williams & Hacker, 1982). However, additional research suggests that the relation between cohesion and performance is circular. Performance seems to affect later cohesion, and these changes in cohesion then affect subsequent performance (Landers, Wilkinson, Hatfield, & Barber, 1982; Nixon, 1977).

In summary, then, the cohesion-performance relationship is complex. We currently think that increased cohesion leads to greater performance and that better performances bring teams together and lead to increased cohesion. Hence, the relationship is circular. Still, the performance-cohesion relationship appears stronger than the cohesion-performance relationship.

Other Factors Associated With Cohesion

Although researchers have focused predominantly on the relation between cohesion and performance,

■ MORE INFORMATION ■

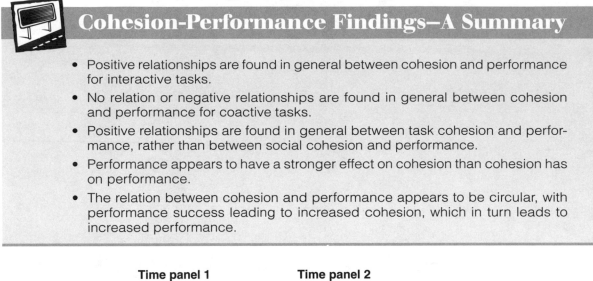

Cohesion-Performance Findings—A Summary

- Positive relationships are found in general between cohesion and performance for interactive tasks.
- No relation or negative relationships are found in general between cohesion and performance for coactive tasks.
- Positive relationships are found in general between task cohesion and performance, rather than between social cohesion and performance.
- Performance appears to have a stronger effect on cohesion than cohesion has on performance.
- The relation between cohesion and performance appears to be circular, with performance success leading to increased cohesion, which in turn leads to increased performance.

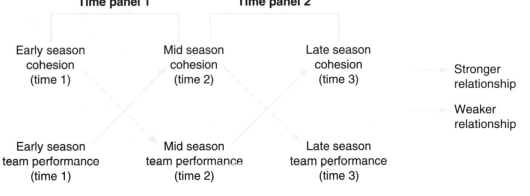

Figure 8.5 *Cross-lagged correlations for cohesion and performance in Carron and Ball's study of hockey players.*
Adapted from Carron and Ball, 1977.

The relation between cohesion and performance appears to be circular, with performance success leading to increased cohesion, which in turn leads to increased performance.

other potentially important factors are also associated with cohesion. We will review these factors here.

Team Satisfaction

Satisfaction and cohesion are highly similar except that cohesion is about groups, whereas satisfaction is an individual construct. Although consistently strong relations have been found between cohesion and satisfaction (e.g., Widmeyer & Williams, 1991), two different models are used to explain the relation among cohesion, satisfaction, and performance.

One model (A) hypothesizes a circular relation, with team cohesion leading to success, which leads to feelings of satisfaction, which tend to strengthen and reinforce team cohesion. The other model (B) hypothesizes that performance success leads to higher cohesion, which in turn leads to greater satisfaction. Thus, both the models suggest that there is indeed a relation among satisfaction, cohesion, and performance. However, model A suggests that cohesion directly enhances performance whereas model B argues that performance success leads to cohesion. But in either case, leaders do well in building group cohesion because being in a cohesive group is satisfying and also indirectly and directly enhances performance.

Conformity

Psychological research has found that the more cohesive the group, the more influence the group has on its individual members. This means there will be greater pressure on individual members to conform to the attitudes and behavior of the group. Group members might feel pressured about clothing style, hairstyle, practice habits, or game behavior. For example, when the Detroit Pistons won consecutive NBA titles in 1989 and 1990, they were known as the "bad boys," and the norm was to play rough, tough, aggressive, intimidating basketball. Rookies and new players had to adapt to this norm and style of basketball to fit in with the team. Similarly, those joining health clubs might feel pressured to purchase designer exercise clothing so they don't look out of place.

Highly cohesive groups demonstrate a greater conformity to the group's norm for productivity. A norm for productivity can be either high or low, and thus conformity to this norm may result in a member having higher or lower productivity. For example, the best performance occurs when the group norm for productivity is high and group cohesion is high, whereas the poorest performance occurs when the group norm is low and group cohesion is high. In either case, conformity and compliance of individual members is enhanced by the group's cohesion. One of the reasons the Chicago Bulls have been so successful in the 1990s is that Michael Jordan and Scottie Pippen set such a high group norm for productivity, which helped raise the level of their teammates' contributions to the team success.

Social Support

Research on social support suggests there is a positive relationship between the social support an individual receives and her or his evaluations of group cohesion. For example, social support provided by coaches has been positively related to athletes' perceptions of task cohesion within high school football teams (Westre & Weiss, 1991), cohesion and satisfaction within college basketball teams (Weiss & Friedrichs, 1986), and higher performance within

The more cohesive a group is, the greater an influence it will have on individual members to conform to the group's norms.

- *Teams higher in cohesion can better resist disruption than teams lower in cohesion.*
- *Teams that stay together longer tend to be more cohesive, which leads to improvements in performance.*

collegiate football teams (Garland & Barry, 1990).

Although many people view social support as simply providing some sort of emotional support for others, seven distinguishable forms of social support have been identified (Rosenfeld & Richman, 1997), which were presented in detail in chapter 7 of this text. Rosenfeld and Richman provide numerous suggestions concerning enhancing these areas of social support. However, the key point is that coaches and leaders should understand the importance of social support and how and when to employ the different types of social support to enhance group cohesion.

Stability

Stability refers both to the turnover rate for group membership and to how long group members have been together. It seems logical that teams which remain relatively constant across a certain period of time would be more stable, cohesive, and ultimately successful. In fact, Carron (1993) suggests that team cohesion and stability are related in a circular fashion. That is, the longer the team has been together, the more likely it is that cohesion will develop, and the more cohesive the team becomes, the less likely it is that members will choose to leave. Let's look at some research that has investigated this issue.

A study of 18 German Federation Soccer teams across a single season showed that teams with few lineup changes were more successful than those that changed constantly (Essing, 1970). A study of major league baseball teams supported this finding (Loy, 1970). A third study tried to determine if there is an optimal time to keep a group of players together to maximize cohesion and subsequent success. It found that in major league baseball, teams with a half-life of 5 years were the most successful (a team's half-life was defined as the time it took for the starting roster to reduce to half its original size; Donnelly, Carron, & Chelladurai, 1978).

More recent studies examined the relation between cohesion and a sport group's resistance to disruption (e.g., personnel changes or internal conflict) among elite sport athletes, recreational sport athletes, and fitness classes. Brawley, Carron, and Widmeyer (1988) compared the groups that exhibited either high or low cohesion on their perceived resistance to disruption. There was a reliable positive relationship between group cohesion and group resistance to disruption: The groups that were higher in cohesion exhibited a higher resistance to disruption than teams lower in cohesion. Establishing positive group norms for productivity is one way to keep individuals working together as a unit over time.

Group Goals

Most people think individuals set their own goals. But in group situations, such as occur with sport teams or exercise groups, goals are often set for the group as a whole. A group's goals are not merely the sum of the personal goals of group members; they are shared perceptions that refer to a desirable state for the group as a unit. The question is, What relation is there among group goals, cohesion, and performance? One study of volleyball, hockey, basketball, and swimming teams revealed the following:

- Members who perceived that their team engaged in group goal setting for competition had higher levels of cohesion.

- The higher the level of satisfaction with team goals, the higher the level of team cohesion.

- Although individual group members' perceptions of cohesion changed across a season, cohesion was still related to team satisfaction and group goals throughout the season (Brawley, Carron, & Widmeyer, 1993).

Other studies (Widmeyer, Silva, & Hardy, 1992; Widmeyer & Williams, 1991) have found that a stated team goal—and its acceptance—was the most important contributor to task cohesion and the second most important for social cohesion. In addition, as commitment to, clarity of, and importance of the goal increased for players, group cohesion also increased. And having individuals participate in developing team or group goals also increases group cohesion.

On a practical note, athletes who perceive that a team goal encourages them to increase effort and practice drills designed to achieve that goal (e.g., in volleyball moving quickly from defensive to offensive sets) will likely feel satisfied with their team's practice goals. You might expect this to happen as team members received feedback that the drills were correctly completed (i.e., the goal was reached) and perceived that the team's effort was high and its attention was focused. In this way the group's goals can enhance its feelings of unity and cohesion.

In setting up a team goal-setting program, Widmeyer and Ducharme (1997) suggest the following guidelines:

- Establish long-term goals first that are specific and challenging.

- Establish clear paths to the long-term goals through the use of short-term goals.

© Human Kinetics

- Involve all team members in establishing goals.
- Carefully monitor progress toward team goals.
- Reward team progress toward team goals.
- Foster collective efficacy concerning team goal attainment.

Enhancing Cohesion

Now that sport psychologists better understand the nature of group cohesion and what factors help enhance cohesion and subsequent performance, some researchers have begun to focus on specific interventions for enhancing cohesion in sport and exercise groups.

Exercise Settings

With dropout rates from formal exercise programs at about 50%, researchers have been investigating ways to reduce this discouraging statistic. One innovative approach has focused on team building and how group cohesion might enhance adherence to exercise programs. It has been found that dropouts from exercise programs have less regard for their exercise class's

Exercise classes with high feelings of group cohesion have fewer dropouts and late arrivals than do classes low in cohesiveness. Exercise leaders can help increase a class's cohesiveness.

task and social cohesion than have participants who stay with the program (Carron & Spink, 1993; Spink & Carron, 1992, 1993). Exercisers with higher feelings of cohesion attend class more regularly and are more punctual than exercisers with lower cohesion.

In another innovative study, sport psychologists attempted to build cohesion in exercise classes through a team approach (Spink & Carron, 1993). Instructors were trained in team-building strategies to enhance adherence by improving group cohesion. They learned that distinctiveness contributes to a sense of group identity, unity, and cohesion. Some emphasized distinctiveness by having a group name, making up a group T-shirt, or handing out neon headbands (see Table 8.1 for strategies to enhance

Table 8.1

Specific Strategies Suggested by Fitness Class Instructors to Enhance Group Cohesiveness

Factor	Example of intervention strategies used
Distinctiveness	Have a group name. Make up a group T-shirt. Hand out neon headbands or shoelaces. Make up posters and slogans for the class.
Individual positions	Divide pool into areas by fitness level. Have signs to label parts of the group. Use specific positions for low-, medium-, and high-impact exercisers. Let participants pick their own spot and encourage them to keep it throughout the year.
Group norms	Have members introduce each other. Encourage members to become fitness friends. Establish a goal to lose weight together. Promote a smart work ethic as a group characteristic.
Individual sacrifices	Ask two or three people for a goal for the day. Ask regulars to help new people. Ask people who aren't concerned with weight loss to make a sacrifice for the group on some days (more aerobics) and people who are concerned to also make a sacrifice on other days (more mat work).
Interaction and communication	Use partner work and have them introduce themselves. Introduce the person on the right and left. Work in groups of five and take turns showing a move.

Adapted from Carron and Spink, 1993.

cohesion). Their classes showed higher levels of cohesion and significantly fewer dropouts and late arrivals than the classes not exposed to team building. This suggests that cohesion is an important ingredient in exercise settings as well as in traditional sport settings.

To further test the effects of team building on cohesion, Carron and Spink (1995) devised an intervention for small and large exercise classes. The team-building program actually offset the negative impact that increased size can have on perceptions of cohesion. Specifically, there were no differences in perceptions of cohesion for participants from small (fewer than 20 participants) and large (more than 40) exercise groups that had been exposed to a team-building intervention. In essence, a sense of cohesion can still be maintained even in relatively large groups if an appropriate team-building program is implemented.

Sport Settings

Other research recently has focused on team building in sport settings (Prapavessis, Carron, & Spink, 1997). In this case, the intervention began with elite male soccer coaches attending a workshop during the off-season, in which were established specific strategies for implementing a team-building program. The coaches then became active agents in the development of practical strategies to be used in the team-building program. Specifically, based on the specific principles outlined in Table 8.2, the coaches were asked to develop applied techniques and procedures that could be used for team building with their teams during the 6 weeks prior to the season. Although results did not find significant improvement differences in cohesion between the team building and control

---

Table 8.2

Principles Underlying the Team-Building Program in a Sport Setting

Categories	Principle
TEAM STRUCTURE	
Role clarity and acceptance	When group members clearly understand their roles in the group, cohesion is enhanced. When group members are satisfied and accept their roles in the group, cohesion is enhanced.
Leadership	Task and social cohesion in the group are influenced by the behavior of the team leaders. A participatory style of coaching leadership contributes to enhanced cohesion.
Conformity to standards	Conformity to group social and task norms contributes to enhanced cohesion. Group norms are highly resistant to change.
TEAM ENVIRONMENT	
Togetherness	When group members are repetitively put in close physical proximity, feelings of cohesion increase.
Distinctiveness	The presence of group distinctiveness contributes to group cohesion.
TEAM PROCESSES	
Sacrifices	When high status members make sacrifices for the group, cohesion is enhanced.
Goals and objectives	Group goals are more strongly associated with team success than individual goals. Member participation in goal setting contributes to enhanced cohesion.
Cooperation	Cooperative behavior is superior to individualistic behavior for individual and group performance. Cooperative behavior is superior to competitive behavior for individuals and group performance. Cooperative behavior contributes to enhanced cohesion.

Adapted from Prapavessis, Carron, and Spink, 1997.

■ MORE INFORMATION ■

A Team-Building Model

In an attempt to guide coaches, teachers, and instructors, Carron and colleagues (Carron & Spink, 1993; Prapavessis et al., 1997; Spink & Carron, 1993) have developed a team-building model that has been successfully implemented in sport and exercise settings. This four-stage process model employs a sport psychologist in the first three stages in a workshop format; then coaches or leaders apply the workshop strategies to their group members in stage four.

- Introductory stage. A brief overview of the benefits of group cohesion is conveyed, emphasizing the relationship between cohesion and exercise adherence (exercise group) and perceptions of cohesion and enhanced team dynamics (sport teams).

- Conceptual stage. A conceptual model is presented, with group cohesion as an output or product of conditions in three categories: the group's environment, the group's structure, and the group's processes. It is important to understand that the specific factors within each category may differ across situations because the importance of fundamental group processes are different across groups. For example, role acceptance and role clarity are important factors in team sports, whereas they are not an important consideration in exercise groups. Some of the key aspects in team building during the conceptual stage are highlighted in Tables 8.1 and 8.2. Finally, coaches or leaders are presented with research-based generalizations that undergird the team-building intervention.

- Practical stage. In this stage, coaches or leaders attempt to generate as many specfic strategies as possible in an interactive brainstorming session to use for team building in their groups. Examples of some of the strategies generated by fitness instructors are presented in Table 8.1. Having coaches or leaders generate specific intervention strategies is desirable because these people differ in personality and preferences—and the nature of groups differs. An intervention strategy that might be effective for one group might be ineffective for another.

- Intervention stage. The specific team-building strategies are introduced by the coaches to their respective teams or exercise groups. It is good to have trained assistants monitor the team-building sessions on a weekly basis to ensure that these strategies are being implemented.

conditions, the authors felt that the coaches in the control conditions were using many of the strategies from the cohesion intervention to enhance their own team's cohesion. Therefore, future research should continue to investigate how team-building interventions can supplement and complement what coaches already do to enhance cohesion.

Guidelines for Building Team Cohesion

Cohesion doesn't always enhance group performance, but it can certainly create a positive environment that elicits positive interactions among group members. Sport psychologists (e.g., Anshel, 1990; Carron et al., 1997; Yukelson, 1997) have pinpointed guidelines for developing group cohesion. Their ideas

are appropriate to competitive sport, teaching, and exercise settings.

What Coaches or Leaders Can Do

As long as communication is effective and open, coaches and leaders can foster group cohesion in several ways. We'll discuss here what these leaders can do to help build cohesion and then turn to what participants themselves can do.

Communicate Effectively

An effective group or team leader needs to create an environment where everyone is comfortable expressing thoughts and feelings (see chapter 10 for more discussion of communication). Open lines of communication can alleviate many potential problems. Here Terry Orlick describes communication's critical role in group cohesion:

Harmony grows when you really listen to others and they listen to you, when you are considerate of their feelings and they are considerate of yours, when you accept their differences and they accept yours, and when you help them and they help you. (1990, p. 143)

Team building requires a climate of openness, where airing problems and matters of concern is not just considered appropriate but is also encouraged. One technique Yukelson (1997) gives to help individuals communicate and express their feelings positively and assertively is known as the DESC Formula. This technique consists of *describing* (the situation), *expressing* (feelings), *specifying* (changes you want to take place), and noting the *consequences* (what to expect if agreement is not reached).

Leaders should ensure that everyone pulls together and is committed to the group's goals, which include improved interpersonal relations. This improvement is important because increased communication has a circular relation with increased group cohesiveness (Carron, 1993). As communication about task and social issues increases, cohesiveness develops. As a result, group members are more open with each other, volunteer more, talk more, and listen better. The group leader plays a major role in integrating the group into a unit that communicates openly and performs with a sense of pride, excellence, and collective identity (Yukelson, 1993; 1997).

Explain Individual Roles in Team Success

Coaches should clearly outline individual roles to team members, stressing the importance of each player's role to the team's success. The more team members there are who perceive their roles as unimportant, the more apathetic the team will become. It's not easy to keep everyone on a football team happy and involved when some players never get to play in real games. Coaches need to carefully explain to these athletes what their roles are on the team and give them opportunities to contribute.

When players understand what is required of their teammates, they can begin to develop support and empathy. The coach can help this process by having players observe and record the efforts of their teammates in different positions. Also, during practice, the coach might assign a player to a position other than her usual one. For example, a spiker in volleyball who is upset at the setter's poor passes could be asked to set during practice. This way she can see how hard it is to set the ball in just the right spot for the spiker.

Develop Pride Within Subunits

In sports where subunits naturally exist, such as football, hockey, and track-and-field sports, coaches should foster pride within these groups. Players need the support of their teammates, especially those playing the same position. The offensive linemen for the Washington Redskins in the 1980s called themselves "the hogs" because they did all the dirty work. The linemen took pride in this name and in what they contributed to the team's overall success. And the running backs and quarterback really appreciated the linemen's contributions—after all, their success depended on how well those hogs blocked.

Set Challenging Group Goals

Setting specific, challenging goals has a positive impact on individual and group performance (see chapter 15). Goals set a high norm for productivity and keep the team focused on what it needs to accomplish. As players reach goals, they should collectively feel encouraged to take pride in their accomplishments and strive toward new goals. These goals need to be clearly defined for them to foster group cohesion in their pursuits. The goals should

---

■ MORE INFORMATION ■

Barriers to Group Cohesion

- A clash of personalities in the group
- A conflict of task or social roles among group members
- A breakdown in communication among group members or between the group leader and members
- One or more members struggling for power
- Frequent turnover of group members
- Disagreement on group goals and objectives

Figure 8.6 *T-shirts can help build unity in a group and make members feel special.*

be performance-based (relating to players' abilities), rather than outcome-based (winning).

Encourage Group Identity

A coach or leader can encourage team identity (by ordering team jackets and scheduling social functions, for example), but these should not interfere with the development of subunit identity. The two should work hand in hand. Groups should be made to feel special and in some sense different from other groups.

Avoid Formation of Social Cliques

As compared to subunits, which are groups of athletes working at a similar position or task, social cliques usually benefit only a few athletes—at the expense of alienating most team members. Players often form cliques when the team is losing, their needs are not being met, or when coaches treat athletes differently, setting them apart from each other (e.g., starters vs. substitutes). Cliques tend to be disruptive to a team, and coaches should quickly determine why they are forming and take the steps to break them up. Changing roommate assignments on trips

and encouraging team functions are ways to battle the development of cliques.

Avoid Excessive Turnover

Excessive turnover decreases cohesion and makes it difficult for members to establish close rapport. They feel unfamiliar with each other and uncertain about the group's longevity. Of course, high school and college teams will lose players to graduation each year. In this case, the veteran players should be asked to help integrate the new players into the team. Team expectations can be shared in a warm, sincere, open manner, making the new players feel at ease with their new team and teammates. Similarly, exercise groups often have turnover as people drop out, and it's important to make newcomers feel welcome and part of these groups as well.

Conduct Periodic Team Meetings

Throughout the season coaches should conduct team meetings to allow positive and negative feelings to be honestly, openly, and constructively expressed. A team can resolve its internal conflicts, mobilize its resources, and take intelligent action only if it has a means for consensually validating its own experience. Teams can talk about learning from mistakes, redefining goals, and maintaining good sportsmanship. Or they can simply express positive or negative feelings. The group leader or coach should steer the group to deal constructively with problems.

If there are no particular problems or issues but the goal is simply to enhance feelings of cohesion, then a technique known as *group disclosures* might be appropriate (Yukelson, 1997). Participants discuss individuals and teams they admire the most along with the attributes and characteristics that contribute to the success of these individuals and groups. Then individuals are asked to share things they admire about each other and what they have learned from each other.

Know the Team Climate

Inside any formal organization lies an informal, interpersonal network that can greatly affect the organization's functioning. A coach or leader should identify the group members who have high interpersonal prestige and status in the group. They can be the links for communication, for example, between the coaching staff and players, helping coaches to stay in touch with the team's attitudes and feelings. These liaisons or links give coaches and athletes vehicles for expressing ideas, opinions, and feelings regarding what's happening on the team. For example, a Player Counsel has been implemented at Penn State University (Yukelson, 1997) that holds regularly scheduled breakfast or lunch meetings with team leaders and representatives from each class (e.g., freshman, junior) or subgroup (e.g., offense, defense, specialty teams). These meetings help keep coaches informed of prevailing attitudes, wants, and feelings that exist in the group.

Know Something Personal About Each Group Member

Participants appreciate it when the coach or leader makes a special effort to know about their lives outside the context of the team. Even simple things, such as knowing and remembering a birthday or an exceptional grade in class, shows an athlete that you care. Being aware of potentially negative personal events, such as a divorce in the family or breakup with a boyfriend or girlfriend, and making yourself available to listen also demonstrate that you care.

One way to get to know more about participants is by surveying their individual values (e.g., achieve-

ment, health and activity, creativity, family, concern for others, independence); values are central determinants of behavior. Crace and Hardy (1997) present a model to help leaders survey and understand individual values within their groups. This assessment, using the Life Values Inventory (Crace & Brown, 1996), allows coaches and leaders to (a) increase their awareness of individual characteristics from a values perspective, (b) understand the predominant values of the group, (c) identify the factors that promote and interfere with group cohesion from a values perspective, and (d) develop interventions and strategies to improve mutual respect and subsequent cohesion.

What Group Members Can Do

So far our guidelines have been targeted at coaches and leaders. But team unity is not only the coach's responsibility—group members can also promote team cohesion. Here are some ways group members can improve communication and build a strong, cohesive unit.

Get to Know Members of the Group

The better team members know each other, the easier it is to accept individual differences. Individuals should take time to get to know their teammates, especially the new members in the group.

Help Group Members Whenever Possible

Being a team means that individuals are mutually interdependent. Helping each other out creates team spirit and brings teammates closer together. For example, if a teammate is having trouble with free-throw shooting in basketball, you might offer to help him, especially if you are proficient in this aspect of the game.

Give Group Members Positive Reinforcement

Supporting teammates, instead of being negative and critical, goes a long way toward building trust and support. Team members should be especially sensitive, positive, and constructive when a teammate is going through adversity. The help and support given to this player also helps the team.

Be Responsible

Group members should not habitually blame others for poor performances. Blaming serves no useful purpose. When things are not going well, players should try to make positive, constructive changes and get themselves back on track.

Communicate Honestly and Openly With the Coach or Leader

Team members should communicate with the coach openly and honestly. The better everyone understands each other, the better the chances for team success and harmony.

Resolve Conflicts Immediately

If a team member has a complaint or a conflict with the coach or a teammate, she should take the initiative to resolve the situation and clear the air. Players should not just gripe, complain, and vent their feelings. It is important to respond to the problem quickly so that negative feelings don't build up, only to later explode.

Give 100% Effort at All Times

Working hard, especially in practice, helps bring the team together. Dedication and commitment are contagious. Setting a good example usually has a positive impact on a team's unity.

SUMMARY

1 *Define task and social cohesion.*

Team cohesion is a dynamic process reflected in the group's tendency to stick together while pursuing its goals and objectives. By measuring cohesion, researchers have found that it is multidimensional and comprises both task and social cohesion. Task cohesion refers to working together as a team to achieve goals, whereas social cohesion refers to the interpersonal attraction among team members.

2 *Describe the conceptual model of cohesion.*

Carron's model of cohesion indicates that four areas affect the development of cohesion: environmental (team size, scholarships), personal (motivation, social background), team (team norms, team stability), and leadership factors (leadership style, leader's goals). It is important to note that these factors interact, not existing in isolation, to impact on both task and social cohesion.

3 *Discuss how cohesion is measured.*

Cohesion has been traditionally measured through simple questionnaires. However, newer instruments such as the Group Environment Questionnaire take into account the multidimensional nature of cohesion. In addition to questionnaires, sociograms can be used to specifically focus on the social aspects of cohesion within a team or group.

4 *Understand the cohesion-performance relationship.*

Researchers have been examining the relationship between cohesion and performance in sport for more than 30 years. However, this relationship is complex, and studying it must involve three important factors: (a) measurement of cohesion, (b) type of task, and (c) direction of causality. Generally speaking, task cohesion is more closely related to performance than is social cohesion, and cohesion is more important for interactive sports than for coactive sports. In addition, the cohesion-performance relation appears to be circular, with team success enhancing cohesion, which leads in turn to success.

5 *Better understand factors associated with cohesion.*

Cohesion is positively related to other important constructs, such as satisfaction, conformity, social support, group goals, and stability. This knowledge is important to consider when coaches, teachers, and exercise leaders want to enhance cohesion in their teams or groups.

6 *Identify guidelines for building team cohesion.*

Researchers have recently developed and outlined interventions for both sport and exercise settings to enhance task and social cohesion. However, it is important that both coaches or leaders and group members assume responsibility for developing group cohesion.

KEY TERMS

cohesion

attractiveness of the group

means control

task cohesion

social cohesion

environmental factors

personal factors

leadership factors

team factors

interactive sports

coactive sports

direction of causality

stability

REVIEW QUESTIONS

1. Discuss the definitions of cohesion, including the difference between task and social cohesion.

2. Discuss how measuring cohesion has developed via questionnaires.

3. The cohesion-performance relation has produced inconsistent findings in the research literature. Explain how the types of instruments used to measure these two factors and the demands of the task have affected this relation.

4. Does cohesion lead to winning or does winning lead to cohesion? In light of the research literature, discuss this question and its implications for coaches.

5. Although researchers have focused on the cohesion-performance relationship, cohesion appears to be related to several other potentially important variables. Discuss the relation of cohesion and conformity and of cohesion and satisfaction.

6. Discuss how cohesion is related to social support. Discuss three different types of social support and how you would develop these to enhance group cohesion.

7. Although it is often considered the job of a coach to build team cohesion, athletes can also help in the process. If you were an athlete on a team lacking in cohesion, what might you do to build your team's unity?

8. Describe the conceptual model used for setting up team-building interventions in sport and exercise settings providing specific examples for each of the four stages.

9. How could you enhance group cohesion among participants in exercise classes?

CRITICAL THINKING QUESTIONS

1. You are a new coach who has inherited a high school team that had a great deal of dissension and in-fighting last season. Using the guidelines provided, discuss (supported by research where appropriate) what you would do before and during the season to build both task and social cohesion in your team.

2. You are a new physical education teacher, and you want to better understand the personal relationships among your students so you can maximize your teaching strategies. You feel that a sociogram might be a good way to achieve this goal. Explain how a sociogram can help you understand the interpersonal attraction and cohesion of your class. Draw a hypothetical sociogram of your class (limit it to 15 people) and explain what information this gives you regarding the development of cohesion.

3. You are asked to devise a program for a local YMCA to help its coaches develop greater cohesion among their players, which has been a problem in the past. Using Carron's conceptual model of cohesion, which focuses on four major antecedents of cohesion, what kind of program would you develop and what information would you impart to these coaches?

© Nathaniel S. Butler/NBA Photos

Leadership

After reading this chapter you should be able to

1 describe the differences between leaders and managers;

2 understand the trait, behavioral, and interactional approaches to studying leadership;

3 explain the Multidimensional Model of Sport Leadership;

4 discuss research investigating leadership in sport settings; and

5 discuss the four components of effective leadership.

Who can forget the numerous fourth-quarter comebacks of the Chicago Bulls led by Michael Jordan resulting in six NBA championships? Or the final series of hockey's Stanley Cup in 1994 when the Rangers were led by their captain, Mark Messier, to their first title in 54 years?

In the world of sports, coaches such as John Wooden, Tara VanDerveer, Pat Head Summitt, Bill Parcells, and Tommy Lasorda, and players including Rebecca Lobo, John Elway, Ken Griffey, Jr., and Wayne Gretzky have shown great leadership capacity. Although not so visible to the public, great leaders emerge as well in settings of physical education, fitness, and athletic training, often meeting professional practice objectives and increasing the efficiency of all who are involved. It is easy to think of people who are great leaders, but it is much more difficult to determine what makes them leaders. For decades psychologists have studied leadership. In fact, more than 3,500 studies on leadership have been published, and researchers are still investigating the factors associated with effective leadership. Let us begin by discussing what leadership is and what leaders actually do.

What Is Leadership?

Leadership might broadly be considered "the behavioral process of influencing individuals and groups toward set goals" (Barrow, 1977, p. 232). This definition is useful because it encompasses many dimensions of leadership. In sport and exercise these dimensions include decision-making processes, motivational techniques, giving feedback, establishing interpersonal relationships, and directing the group or team confidently.

A leader knows where the group or team is going (i.e., its goals and objectives) and provides the direction and resources to help it get there. Coaches who are good leaders provide not only a vision of what to strive for but also the day-to-day structure, motivation, and support to translate vision into reality. Coaches, teachers, and exercise specialists are leaders who seek to assure each participant maximum opportunities to achieve success. And successful leaders also try to ensure that individual success helps achieve team success.

Distinguishing a Leader From a Manager

A manager is generally concerned with planning, organizing, scheduling, budgeting, staffing, and re-

> *A manager takes care of such things as scheduling, budgeting, and organizing, whereas a leader is concerned more with the direction of an organization, including its goals and objectives.*

cruiting. Although leaders often perform these same functions (or delegate them to others), they act in some other critical ways. For example, leaders help determine the direction that the organization or team pursues, including its goals and objectives. They try to provide the resources and support to get the job done. Many coaches become excellent managers as they tackle operations that keep things running smoothly. But this is different from providing the leadership needed for players and teams to grow and mature. "Too many teams are overmanaged and underled" (Martens, 1987, p. 33).

How Leaders Are Chosen

Usually leaders and coaches are appointed by someone in authority. For example, in health clubs owners choose the managers, and in schools the principal chooses the teachers. Similarly, in college sports, the athletic director (with some feedback from a search committee) commonly selects coaches.

Sometimes, however, leaders simply emerge from the group and take charge, such as with captains and coaches of intramural or club teams. Many leaders who emerge are more effective than appointed leaders because they have the respect and support of team or group members. They probably have special leadership skills or high ability in the particular sport or exercise.

Researchers have tried to identify these special leadership skills, hoping to be able to predict and select those people likely to become leaders. They have also researched if certain factors in a situation produce effective leadership and if an environment might be structured to better develop leadership abilities. We will review early research into industrial and organizational leadership and the studies it stimulated in sport settings. Then we will discuss how sport psychologists have studied leadership effectiveness.

Trait Approach

In the 1920s researchers tried to determine what characteristics or personality traits were common to great leaders in business and industry. They considered

Team Leadership

It's the fifth game of the 1997 NBA final between the Chicago Bulls and Utah Jazz, and the series is even at 2–2. Utah has won the last two home games and is playing at home again where they are undefeated in the play-offs. Michael Jordan, who many consider the greatest player to ever play the game, is sick with an intestinal virus and has stayed in bed all day since he is so weak. He looks sick out on the court, his every movement appearing strained. But somehow he manages to conserve his energy and focus on what he has to do to win. Miraculously, he not only scores 38 points but also hits the key 3-point shot to win the game, and Chicago goes on to win the championship in 6 games on its home floor (Michael Jordan being voted MVP of the playoffs). Teammate Scottie Pippen comments on Jordan's performance: "What you saw out here tonite was an unbelievable display of courage and leadership. Michael is the leader of the team and he brought everyone along with him. He led by example, and his desire to win and be the best rubbed off on all of us."

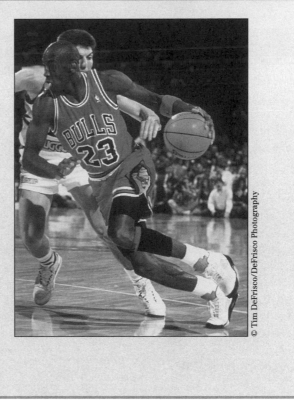

© Tim DeFrisco/DeFrisco Photography

leadership traits to be relatively stable personality dispositions, such as intelligence, assertiveness, independence, and self-confidence. These researchers were proponents of the trait theory and argued that successful leaders have certain personality characteristics that make it likely for them to be leaders, no matter what situation they are in. This would mean, for example, that Michael Jordan would be a great leader not only on the basketball court but also in other sports and aspects of life such as business and community affairs.

The trait approach lost favor after World War II, when Stogdill (1948) reviewed more than a hundred trait-theory studies of leadership and found only a couple of consistent personality traits. Although certain traits might be helpful for a leader to have, they are certainly not essential. Nor do they guarantee successful leadership.

Researchers also attempted to identify successful coaches according to the trait view. For example, one profile of typical coaches was tough-minded, authoritarian, willing to bear the pressure of fans and the media, emotionally mature, independent in their thinking, and realistic in their perspective (Ogilvie & Tutko, 1966; 1970). The study, however, did not provide documented evidence to support this coaching profile.

In fact, no particular set of traits seems to characterize effective sport leadership. For example, Charles Barkley is a leader on the basketball floor, although he would not fit any typical psychological profile of effective leadership. Because an ideal leadership style among coaches and athletes has not been found, little sport research today uses the trait approach to leadership theory.

Behavioral Approach

Researchers next focused on discovering universal behaviors of effective leaders. These *behaviorists* argued that anyone could be taught to become a leader by simply learning the behaviors of other effective leaders. Thus, unlike trait theory, the behavioral approach argues that leaders are made, not born.

Leaders have a variety of personality traits. There are no specific traits that make a leader successful.

Leaders in Non-Sport Settings

To describe how leaders in non-sport (business, military, educational, and government) organizations behave or go about doing their jobs, researchers at the Ohio State University developed the Leader Behavior Description Questionnaire (LBDQ). Using it, they found that most of what leaders do falls into two categories: being considerate (consideration) and initiating structure. Consideration refers to friendship, mutual trust, respect, and warmth between the leader and subordinates. Leaders who scored high on consideration had good rapport and communication with others. Initiating structure refers to such behaviors as setting up rules and regulations, channels of communications, procedural methods, and well-defined patterns of organization to achieve goals and objectives. Leaders who scored high on initiating structure were active in directing group activities, communicating, scheduling, and experimenting with new ideas. These two categories are distinct but also compatible. For instance, successful leaders tend to score high on both consideration and initiating structure.

Leaders in Sport

Leaders in sport and exercise settings work both through interpersonal relationships and by providing direction, goals, and structure to their teams or classes. For example, when a coach takes over a new team, she must establish open lines of communication, good interpersonal relations, and clear goals and objectives. To study leadership behaviors in sport, psychologists devised several sport-specific questionnaires. We will describe two useful methodologies and some of their findings.

Instruction and Demonstration

Former UCLA basketball coach John Wooden is a coaching legend in basketball, winning an unprecedented 10 of 12 NCAA basketball championships. He has coached, among other greats, Kareem Abdul-Jabbar and Bill Walton. What has been John Wooden's secret?

Tharp and Gallimore (1976) sought to answer this question by using the event recording technique. In event recording an investigator lists several typical coaching behaviors and then records when and how often these behaviors occur. Usually more than one rater records the behaviors. Having two or more raters verifies that people can consistently observe the same behavior, improving the study's reliability. For example, if three raters watch a coach during a game and agree that she used punishment five times, the conclusion would be considered more reliable than if only one rater observed the coach's behavior.

Using the event recording technique for 30 hours of observation, Tharp and Gallimore identified 10 categories of behavior that Wooden exhibited. Most of his behaviors involved giving instructions (what to do and how to do it); he also often encouraged intensity and effort. In communicating, for example, he spent about 50% of his time in verbal instruction, 12.7% in hustling players to intensify instruction, 8% in scolding and reinstructing with a combination statement, 6.9% in praising and encouraging, and 6.6% in simple statements of displeasure (i.e., scolding).

Studying Wooden, the researchers noted that his demonstrations rarely lasted longer than 5 seconds, but they were so clear that they left an image in memory, much like a textbook sketch. Wooden models with his body most often during patterned offensive drills, half-court scrimmages when he will whistle down play. He promptly demonstrates the correct way (modeling positive) to perform the activity and then imitates the incorrect way (modeling negative) the player has just performed (Tharp & Gallimore, 1976, p. 77).

More recently, Cote, Salmela, and Russell (1995) investigated coaching behaviors using a qualitative interview approach. They interviewed 17 elite gymnastic coaches to find out how they used their expert knowledge during training. These are the behaviors the elite coaches most often exhibited: (a) providing a supportive environment through positive feedback; (b) giving technical instruction regarding gymnasts' progressions; (c) teaching mental skills such as dealing with stress, developing proper motivation, and becoming self-sufficient; (d) providing opportunities that simulated the mental and technical demands of competition; (e) providing manual training to ensure

Successful leaders tend to score high on both initiating structure and consideration.

Coach Wooden focused his coaching on telling players what to do and how to do it. He accomplished this through short demonstrations modeling the correct behavior.

© Terry Wild Studio

safety; and (f) stressing conditioning to ensure the physical readiness of the gymnast.

Both the observational study of John Wooden and the interviews of elite gymnastic coaches consistently showed a reliance on positive, supportive feedback and on technical, corrective feedback in helping athletes improve. The key to providing effective sport leadership, therefore, is to focus on the positive while providing clear feedback and technical instruction.

Reactive and Spontaneous Behaviors

Researchers have wanted to investigate coaching behaviors in general to develop guidelines for training coaches (Smith, Smoll, & Hunt, 1977; Smoll, Smith, Curtis, & Hunt, 1978). They have used a mediational model in which players' attitudes toward their coaches and sport experience are affected by their perception and recall of the coaches' behaviors. To objectively assess the actual behavior of coaches in natural field settings, the Coaching Behavior Assessment System (CBAS) was developed. For this system several carefully trained observers record the behaviors of the coaches, noting on portable tape recorders the situations in which the behaviors oc-

curred. These behaviors turn out to be either reactive or spontaneous (see Table 9.1). **Reactive behaviors** are responses to a specific player behavior, as when a coach instructs after an error. **Spontaneous behaviors,** on the other hand, are initiated by the coach. For example, a coach might yell encouragement to his players as they go onto the field.

Other studies have used the CBAS to assess specific coaching behaviors and how they affect young athletes. These behaviors relate in general to a leadership style that emphasizes a positive approach to coaching. In fact, about two-thirds of all observed coaching behaviors were found to be positive, falling into the categories of

- positive reinforcement ("You really got down on that ground ball. Keep up the good work."),
- general technical instruction ("Keep your head down when you complete your golf swing."), and
- general encouragement ("Keep up the good work!").

Players demonstrate greater self-esteem at the end of a season when they have played for coaches who

Table 9.1

Categories of Coaching Behavior From the Coaching Behavior Assessment System

Class I. Reactive behaviors

RESPONSES TO DESIRABLE PERFORMANCE

Reinforcement	A positive, rewarding reaction (verbal or nonverbal) to a good play or good effort
Nonreinforcement	Failure to respond to a good performance

RESPONSES TO MISTAKES

Mistake-contingent encouragement	Encouragement given to a player following a mistake
Mistake-contingent technical instruction	Instruction or demonstration to a player on how to correct a mistake he or she has made
Punishment	A negative reaction, verbal or nonverbal, following a mistake
Punitive technical instruction	Technical instruction following a mistake given in a punitive or hostile manner
Ignoring mistakes	Failure to respond to a player mistake

RESPONSES TO MISBEHAVIOR

Keeping control	Reactions intended to restore or maintain order among team members

Class II. Spontaneous behaviors

GAME-RELATED

General technical instruction	Spontaneous instruction in the techniques and strategies of the sport (not following a mistake)
General encouragement	Spontaneous encouragement that does not follow a mistake
Organization	Administrative behavior that sets the stage for play by assigning duties or responsibilities

GAME-IRRELEVANT

General communication	Interactions with players unrelated to the game

Adapted from Smoll and Smith, 1980.

frequently use mistake-contingent encouragement and reinforcement. They rate their teammates and their sport more positively when they have played for coaches who use high amounts of general technical instruction. In one study, low self-esteem players who had supportive and instructive coaches expressed the highest level of attraction toward the coaches, while the low self-esteem players who had less supportive and instructive coaches expressed the least amount of attraction to the coaches. Conversely, high self-esteem players were not affected to the same extent by variations in the level of their coaches' support and instruction. In essence, it's particularly important for coaches to be supportive of low self-esteem youngsters to maximize the potential positive

experiences of competitive sport (Barnett, Smoll, & Smith, 1992).

Many coaches learn this positive approach to coaching young athletes by attending a workshop focusing on how to communicate positively with young athletes. The youngsters who work with these coaches report that they like their teammates more, feel their coaches are knowledgeable, rate their coaches better as teachers, have a greater desire to play again the next year, and have higher levels of enjoyment than other young players whose coaches did not attend the workshop.

In another study (Barnett, Smoll, & Smith, 1992) found that Little League players whose coaches attended a workshop designed to facilitate positive coach-athlete interaction had a dropout rate of 5% during the next season, whereas a control group of players had a 29% dropout rate. Not surprisingly, therefore, not only does facilitating positive interactions between coaches and young athletes assure that the athletes enjoy the experience more, it also keeps them involved and participating in the sport. Based on their extensive research program, Smith and Smoll (1996; 1997) have developed leadership guidelines for coaching youth sport athletes.

Interactional Approach

Trait and behavioral approaches emphasize personal factors at the expense of considering the interaction between people and their situational constraints (see chapter 2). Many researchers in industry and general psychology have proposed interactional models of leadership (see Horn, 1993, for a review of the literature). These interactional theories have important implications for effective leadership in sport and exercise settings.

1. As we have seen, no one set of characteristics ensures successful leadership. Investigators believe that great leaders have had in common personality traits appropriate to leadership roles and distinct from nonleadership roles. However, leaders have not been predicted solely by their personality traits.

2. Effective leadership fits the specific situation. Some leaders function better in certain situations than in others. Coaches have been fired from team positions, for example, when administrators thought they weren't providing effective leadership, only to be hired by another team where they were immediately successful. These coaches probably did not suddenly change their leadership styles or the way they coached—rather, their leadership styles and behavior fit better in their new settings.

3. Leadership styles can be changed. If you hear someone say, "Some people just have what it takes," don't believe him. In fact, coaches and other leaders can alter their styles and behaviors to match a situation's demands. Here are two examples of leadership styles and how they might change to fit a situation. **Relationship-oriented leaders** develop interpersonal relationships, keep open lines of communication, maintain positive social interactions, and assure that everyone is involved and feeling good (like the consideration function described earlier; Fiedler, 1967). On the other hand, **task-oriented leaders** primarily work to get the task done and meet their objectives (like the initiating structure function described earlier). Their focus is performance and productivity, rather than on creating good interpersonal relations.

People can change from a relationship-oriented style to a task-oriented style and vice versa, depending on the situation. Fiedler's research demonstrates that a task-oriented leader is more effective in either very favorable or unfavorable situations. However, a relationship-oriented leader is more effective in moderately favorable situations. A physical education teacher in an inner-city school that lacks facilities, leadership, and community support might have to be very task-oriented. Getting things done and setting goals would override developing positive interpersonal relations. Conversely, a physical education teacher in a lower-middle-class school where the facilities are poor but the community support is good (moderately favorable situation) might be more effective if she is a relationship-oriented leader. Thus, sport and exercise professionals need to be flexible in leadership styles, tailoring them to meet the demands of the situation. If a coach feels more comfortable with one type of leadership style than another, he should seek out situations where this style would be more effective.

Highly skilled players are typically already task-oriented, and coaches who have a more relationship-oriented style appear to be more effective with these players. Conversely, less skilled players need more continuous instruction and feedback, and a task-oriented coach would be more appropriate for them. This does not mean that less skilled individuals do not need or want a caring, empathic coach or that more highly skilled participants do not need specific feedback and instruction. It is a matter of what should be emphasized. Getting the task done and providing a supportive environment are both necessary for effective leadership.

A relationship-oriented leader focuses on developing and maintaining good interpersonal relationships; a task-oriented leader focuses on setting goals and getting the job done.

The effectiveness of an individual's leadership style stems from matching the situation.

■ CLOSE-UP ■

Coaching Leadership

Doug Collins had an up-and-down career as an NBA coach after a wonderful career as a player. Collins was then hired as the coach of the Chicago Bulls. A fiery, emotional leader, he also tends to be autocratic, taking just the right approach for the relatively young team. His volatile personality in fact helped motivate the somewhat immature and unpredictable team. However, these same personality characteristics and his autocratic approach became a liability as the Bulls matured as a team; they began to tune him out (McCallum, 1991). Several years later, Collins emerged as the coach of the Detroit Pistons, another young team in need of direction and a strong hand. Collins provided this sense of direction and purpose, bringing with him an emotional volatility. Once again, this was the right approach, and it helped the Pistons turn around, after several seasons of losing records, and start to contend for the division title. However, after a couple of successful seasons Collins's fiery style was at odds with a maturing team, and he was fired.

Jerry Faust was one of the most successful high school football coaches in the country when he became head coach at the University of Notre Dame. Faust could not maintain Notre Dame's standard of winning and was fired after several seasons. After coaching high school players, he may not have altered his coaching behavior to fit the maturity level of college athletes. The maturity level of participants needs to be considered to determine the most effective leadership style, and this, too, is a matter of an interactional approach to leadership. For example, younger athletes especially need relationship-oriented leadership for their best performance, personal growth, and development. Unfortunately, traditional sport practices, which emphasize autocratic behaviors, may actually hinder the development of athletic maturity:

> *People on the high school level talk about sport programs and how they develop a kid's self-discipline and responsibility. I think the giveaway that most of this stuff preached on the lower level is a lie is that when you go to college and professional levels, the coaches still treat you as an adolescent. They know damn well that you were never given a chance to become responsible or self-disciplined. Even in the pros you are told when to go to bed, when to turn your lights off, when to wake up, when to eat, and what to eat.*

All-pro football player George Sauer (as cited in Sage, 1978, p. 225)

Multidimensional Model of Sport Leadership

The leadership models we have discussed so far were derived outside of sport settings, such as in industry and the military, and have provided excellent frameworks for understanding leadership. Yet, they are not specific to sport or physical activity. Chelladurai (1978, 1990) developed the Multidimensional Model of Sport Leadership specifically for athletic situations. His leadership model conceptualizes leadership as an interactional process. That is, he argues that leader effectiveness in sport is contingent on situational characteristics of both the leader and the group members. Thus, effective leadership can and will vary depending on the characteristics of the athletes and constraints of the situation (see Figure 9.1).

According to Chelladurai, an athlete's satisfaction and performance (box 7 in the figure) depend on three types of leader behavior: required (box 4), preferred (box 6), and actual behaviors (box 5). The situation (box 1), leader (box 2), and members (box 3) lead to these three kinds of behavior, so they are called antecedents.

If we put this model in interactional terms, leader characteristics are the personal factor, whereas situ-

> *Optimal performance and satisfaction are achieved when a leader's required, preferred, and actual behaviors are consistent.*

194

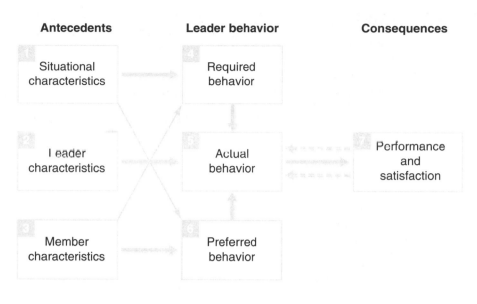

Figure 9.1 *The multidimensional model of leadership for sports.*
Adapted from Chelladurai, 1980.

ational characteristics and member characteristics are the situational factors. Chelladurai hypothesizes that a positive outcome—that is, optimal performance and group satisfaction—occurs if the three aspects of leader behavior agree. If the leader behaves appropriately for the particular situation and these behaviors match the preferences of the group members, they will achieve their best performance and feel satisfied. For example, a supervisor tells an exercise leader to concentrate on good communication and relations with the participants in her class (i.e., to be relationship-oriented), and the participants want this kind of behavior in a leader: They perform optimally and find satisfaction. We'll now take a closer look at the three types of leader behavior and how the antecedent conditions affect them.

Required Leader Behavior

The situation demands that a leader behave in certain ways. In other words, the organizational system itself dictates behaviors, and people are expected to conform to the established norms. For example, physical education teachers are expected to behave in certain ways in front of their students, fellow teachers, and parents (e.g., high school physical education teachers shouldn't attend the same parties as their students). Similarly, coaches are expected to behave in specific ways with reporters, other coaches, and spectators. Some of the situational characteristics that affect leader behavior include the goals and formal organizational structure of the team and larger sys-

tem (e.g., those of professional teams or of high school teams), the group task (e.g., individual or team sports), social norms, and cultural values.

Preferred Leader Behavior

Group members also have preferences for specific leader behaviors. Personality variables (such as the need for achievement, for affiliation, and for competence in the task) as well as age, gender, and experience influence a member's preference for coaching and guidance, social support, and feedback. An adult in rehabilitation after surgery for the anterior cruciate ligament (knee reconstruction), for example, probably expects to have more input into program planning than a young athlete does. In addition, situational characteristics can also affect a member's preferences. If an organization or school has an expectation that a coach conduct himself in a certain manner, then this expectation is typically shared by both the coach and players.

Sometimes group members become used to certain behaviors and grow to prefer them. For instance, the owner of the Los Angeles Raiders football team, Al Davis, has traditionally advocated a loose leadership style, allowing players individualism off the field as long as they perform well on the field. Players on his team have grown to prefer this style of leadership. Conversely, Pat Riley, the highly successful professional basketball coach, is demanding and intense, but players tend to adopt his style because he has shown it to be successful.

195

Actual Leader Behavior

Actual leader behaviors are simply the behaviors the leader exhibits, such as initiating structure or being considerate. According to Chelladurai, the leader's characteristics, such as personality, ability, and experience (box 2 in Figure 9.1) affect these behaviors directly. Actual behavior is believed to be indirectly affected by group preferences and what the situation dictates. A professional sports team, for example, usually has winning as a goal, and its coach would likely adopt task-oriented behaviors. Although winning is among a high school team's goals, the experience itself is also valued, and a coach would likely adopt consideration-oriented behaviors. Characteristics of both the situation and group members would influence the coaches.

Research on the Multidimensional Model of Sport Leadership

Researchers have tested both the accuracy and the usefulness of Chelladurai's multidimensional model,

applying the model in interesting ways. We'll briefly discuss a couple of these applications. (For a more detailed analysis of the Multidimensional Model of Sport Leadership, see Chelladurai, 1993, and Horn, 1993).

Leadership Scale for Sports

The Leadership Scale for Sports (LSS) was developed to measure leadership behaviors, including the athletes' preferences for specific behaviors, athletes' perceptions of their coaches' behaviors, and coaches' perceptions of their own behavior (e.g., Chelladurai & Saleh, 1978; Chelladurai, Malloy, Imamura, & Yamaguchi, 1987; Chelladurai, Imamura, Yamaguchi, Oinuma, & Miyauchi, 1988). The scale has been translated into several languages and has received extensive testing in recent years. The LSS has five dimensions:

■ Training (instructional behaviors)—A coach who is oriented toward training and instruction scores high in trying to improve the athletes' performances by giving technical instruction on skills, techniques, and strategies; by emphasizing and facilitating rigorous training; and by coordinating the activities of team members.

© Human Kinetics

■ Democratic behavior (decision-making style)—A coach with a democratic style allows athletes to participate in decisions about the group's goals, practice methods, and game tactics and strategies.

■ Autocratic behavior (decision-making style)—An autocratic coach uses independent decision making and stresses personal authority in working with the decisions. Input from athletes is generally not invited.

■ Social support (motivational tendencies)—A coach who scores high in social support shows concern for the welfare of individual athletes and attempts to establish warm relationships with them. Unlike a coach who stresses positive feedback during performance, social support–oriented coaching behaviors are independent of (not contingent on) the athlete's performance, and they typically extend beyond the athletic arena.

■ Positive feedback (motivational tendencies)—A coach who scores high in positive feedback consistently praises or rewards athletes for good performance. Positive feedback is contingent on the performance and limited to the athletic context.

Antecedents of Leadership

Some studies have concentrated on the conditions, or antecedents, that affect leader behavior, whereas others have focused on the consequences of leader behavior—that is, how it affects member performance and satisfaction (see Chelladurai, 1993 for a detailed discussion). Personal and situational factors that affect leader behavior have produced many insights, including the following:

Age and Maturity

As people get older and mature athletically, they increasingly prefer coaches who are more autocratic and socially supportive. More mature athletes are typically more serious about their sport, and they want

■ MORE INFORMATION ■

Decision Styles in Coaching

Coaching effectiveness largely depends on making good decisions and the degree to which those decisions are accepted by athletes. Chelladurai and others (Chelladurai & Arnott, 1985; Chelladurai & Haggerty, 1978; Chelladurai, Haggerty, & Baxter, 1989) have developed a model of decision making that applies in sport settings and have conducted research investigating the use and effectiveness of different decision styles. Five primary styles of decision making are used in sport:

- Autocratic style. The coach solves the problem her- or himself using the information available at the time.
- Autocratic/consultive style. The coach obtains the necessary information from relevant players and then comes to a decision.
- Consultive/individual style. The coach consults the players individually and then makes a decision. The decision may or may not reflect the players' input.
- Consultive/group style. The coach consults the players as a group and then makes a decision. The decision may or may not reflect the players' input.
- Group style. The coach shares the problem with his players; then the players jointly make the decision without any influence from the coach.

Although the autocratic and consultative-group decision styles are the ones that most coaches prefer, the choice of the most effective decision style for a particular situation depends on the following factors:

- Coach's information. How much information does the coach have (relative to the players) to make a good decision?
- Problem complexity. How complex is the problem?
- Coach's power. How much influence does the coach have over his or her players?
- Acceptance requirement. How important is it that the athletes accept the coach's decision?
- Team integration. How cohesive are team members?
- Quality requirement. How important is it for a coach to make an optimal decision (e.g., naming a starting point guard or a team mamager)?

a coach who gets things done and is highly organized but who also is supportive of the players.

Gender

Males prefer training and instructive behaviors and an autocratic coaching style more than females do. Hence, coaches should be more directive with males and provide plenty of instructional feedback. Females prefer democratic and participatory coaching that allows them to help make the decisions. Coaches and other group leaders should allow females opportunities for input.

Nationality

Athletes from the United States, Great Britain, and Canada do not differ notably in the coaching styles they prefer. Japanese university athletes prefer more social support and autocratic behaviors than do Canadian athletes, and they perceive their coaches to be more autocratic. Thus, cultural background may influence leadership preferences.

Type of Sport

Athletes who play highly interactive team sports, such as basketball, volleyball, and soccer, prefer an autocratic coaching style more than do athletes in coacting sports, such as bowling. Thus, the volleyball team would typically prefer an autocratic coach more than would a track team.

Determining what makes effective sport leadership is clearly not a simple process. Not only is effective leadership style influenced by a variety of personal and situational factors, but it can also have varied consequences for the leader and group members.

Consequences of Leadership

According to Chelladurai (1990; 1993), when a coach leads in a style that matches the group members' preferences, optimal performance and satisfaction result. Using Chelladurai's model to investigate the consequences of how a sport leader behaves, researchers have proposed several guidelines, which we now present.

Satisfaction

When a coach reports developing the same decision style that his or her athletes prefer and perceive, coaching effectiveness will be rated highly. Similarly, athletes' not getting the coaching style they prefer clearly will affect their satisfaction. Especially with behavior related to training and instruction, as well as positive behaviors, the greater the discrepancy, the less the satisfaction. Generous social support, rewarding of behavior, and democratic decision making are generally associated with high satisfaction among athletes.

Cohesion

Coaches perceived as high in training and instruction, democratic behavior, social support, and posi-

tive feedback, along with being low in autocratic behavior, had teams that were more cohesive (Gardner, Shields, Bredemeier, & Bostrom, 1996; Pease & Kozub, 1994; Westre & Weiss, 1991).

Performance

Frequent social support is related to poorer team performance (i.e., win-loss record). The increased social support did not cause the team to lose more, however; more likely, losing teams need more social support from leaders to sustain motivation.

Four Components of Effective Leadership

We have emphasized that personal traits alone do not account for leadership. Yet research has identified some common and consistent components of effective leaders, including qualities of great leaders and leadership styles. Research has also identified general strategies to produce more effective leadership in physical education, sport, and exercise settings, including manipulating situational factors and promoting certain group member characteristics. Four general components that we will discuss in this section are a leader's qualities, leadership style, situational factors, and the followers' qualities.

The four components of effective leadership (see Figure 9.2) are really a composite of many different approaches to the study of leadership. No one approach is best—they all make some contribution to understanding what makes effective leadership. Consistent with the interactional model, the four components together show that behavior is best understood as an interaction between personal and situational factors.

Leader's Qualities

Although there isn't one distinct set of essential core personality traits that assure a person will become a leader, successful leaders appear to have many qualities in common. In his recent book *Finding a Way to Win* (1995) Bill Parcells, successful football coach and winner of two Super Bowls, discusses what he believes to be the keys to successful leadership:

■ Integrity. A leader's philosophy must have a sound structure, be rooted in his basic values, be communicated and accepted throughout the organization, be resistant to outside pressure, and it must remain in place long enough to allow for success.

■ Flexibility. Traditions are made to be broken. If you're doing something just because it's always been done that way, then you may be missing an opportunity to do better.

■ Loyalty. The first task of leadership is to promote and enforce collective loyalty, also known as teamwork.

■ Confidence. If you want to build confidence in your players and coaching staff, give them responsibility and decision-making capabilities and support them in their attempts.

■ Accountability. Accountability starts at the top. You can't build an accountable organization without leaders who take full responsibility.

■ Candor. When sending a message, it's not enough to be honest and accurate. The impact of the message will hinge on who's receiving it—and what they are willing to take in at that time.

■ Preparedness. Well-prepared leaders plan ahead for all contingencies, including the ones they consider unlikely or distasteful.

■ Resourcefulness. At its most basic level, resourcefulness is simply resilience, a refusal to quit or give in even when all seems bleak.

■ Self-discipline. There is always a way to compete, even against superior forces, but it requires strict adherence to a calculated plan.

■ Patience. Patience is rarest—and most valuable—when an organization is performing poorly. It's not enough to know what changes must be made; it's equally important to decide when to make them.

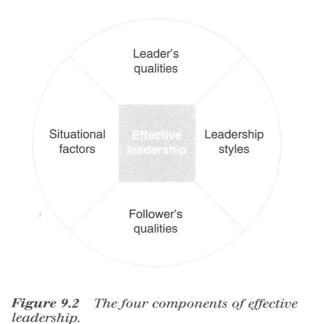

Figure 9.2 *The four components of effective leadership.*
Reprinted from Martens, 1987.

In addition to the points that Bill Parcells makes, researchers have identified several additional characteristics of successful leaders, including intelligence, optimism, intrinsic motivation, and empathy. It should be noted that these are requisite or necessary qualities to become a leader but still they are not sufficient—that is, the presence of all these qualities doesn't guarantee a leader. And these qualities will be needed in greater or lesser amounts depending on the preferences of group members and the specific situation.

Leadership Styles

We have talked about democratic or autocratic coaching styles. As you might expect, the democratic style coach is typically athlete-centered, cooperative, and relationship-oriented. Conversely, the autocratic style coach is usually win-oriented, tightly structured, and task-oriented. A coach need not act entirely one way or the other. She or he can effectively integrate and blend both democratic and autocratic leadership styles. In essence coaching does not have to be solely democratic or autocratic in style; rather, a coach can have positive interactions with athletes while remaining focused on achieving excellence (Blake & Moulton, 1969). Different leadership behaviors are more optimal in various situations, as you have seen through the Multidimensional Model of Sport Leadership and Leadership Scale for Sports. The challenge is determining what style best suits the circumstances and whether an individual is flexible enough to adapt his or her dominant style to a particular leadership situation. The appropriate coaching style depends most on situation factors and member characteristics.

Situational Factors

A leader should be sensitive to the specific situation and environment. Several situational factors are relevant to planning for effective leadership in sport (Martens, 1987), including considering these:

■ Is it a team or individual sport? Team sport athletes typically prefer more autocratic leaders than do individual sport athletes.

■ Is it an interactive (e.g., basketball) or coactive (bowling) sport? Interactive team athletes prefer more task-oriented leaders than do coactive team athletes.

■ What is the size of the team? As the group size increases, it becomes more difficult to effectively use a democratic leadership style.

■ How much time is available? When little time is available, a task-oriented leader is more desirable.

■ Does the group have a particular leadership tradition? A group that has a tradition with one style of leadership will typically have difficulty in changing to another style of leadership.

Follower's Qualities

The characteristics of the followers (athletes in sport settings) are also important in determining the effectiveness of a leader. The need for a mesh between the characteristics and style of leaders and participants shows how important the interactional process is to effective leadership. For example, older and more experienced athletes usually prefer an autocratic coaching style, and female athletes prefer a democratic coach. Specific characteristics (such as gender, experience or maturity, nationality, ability level, and personality) of the participants that interact with leadership to determine its effectiveness in sport and exercise were discussed earlier in assessing the Multidimensional Model of Sport Leadership.

SUMMARY

1 *Describe the differences between leaders and managers.*

Leaders influence individuals and groups toward set goals. They affect participants by establishing interpersonal relationships, providing feedback, influencing the decision-making process, and providing motivation. A leader knows where the group needs to go and provides the direction and resources to help it get there. Managers are more concerned with planning, organizing, scheduling, budgeting, staffing, and recruiting activities.

2 *Understand the trait, behavioral, and interactional approaches to studying leadership.*

The trait approach assumes that great leaders possess a set of universal personality traits which are essential for effective leadership. The behavioral approach assumes that a relatively universal set of behaviors characterizes successful leaders. The interactional approach posits the interaction of the situation and a leader's behaviors as what determines effective leadership. This approach assumes there is not one best type of leader but rather that leadership style and effectiveness depend on fitting the situation and qualities of the group's members.

3 *Explain the Multidimensional Model of Sport Leadership.*

The Multidimensional Model of Sport Leadership considers group performance and member satisfaction to depend on how well three types of leader behavior—required, preferred, and actual—mesh with the antecedent characteristics of the situation, the leader, and the members. Positive outcomes, performance, and group satisfaction typically occur if the three types of leader behavior are congruent. That is, if a coach or other leader uses behaviors prescribed for the particular situation that are consistent with the preferences of the members, optimal performance and member satisfaction will result.

4 *Discuss research investigating leadership in sport settings.*

Research has found that several personal and situational factors affect leader behavior in sport and exercise. These antecedents include such specifics as age and maturity, gender, nationality, and type of sport. The consequences of the leader's behavior can be seen in terms of the satisfaction, performance, and cohesion of the group. For example, satisfaction of athletes is high when there is a good match between their preferred coaching style and the coach's actual coaching style.

5 *Discuss the four components of effective leadership.*

Effective leadership in sport depends on the qualities of the leader, leadership style, situational factors, and characteristics of the followers. But it is how these four interact that really determines what makes a leader more effective.

KEY TERMS

leadership
manager
leadership traits
reactive behaviors
spontaneous behaviors

relationship-oriented leaders
task-oriented leaders
Multidimensional Model of Sport Leadership
Leadership Scale for Sports

REVIEW QUESTIONS

1. Compare and contrast the trait, behavioral, and interactional approaches to leadership.
2. Discuss three practical implications and principles that can be drawn from the psychological literature on leadership.
3. Describe three major results of the Coaching Behavior Assessment System and how it applies to coaching and teaching.
4. Discuss event recording as a technique for studying leadership behaviors in sport along with the findings regarding Coach John Wooden.
5. Describe the major tenets of Chelladurai's Multidimensional Model of Sport Leadership, including the three antecedents and three types of leader behaviors.
6. List three findings each from studies about the antecedent conditions and the consequences of leadership behaviors in sport.
7. Discuss the four components of effective leadership. What implications do these have for leaders in coaching, teaching, or exercise settings?
8. Describe five decision styles used by coaches and three factors that affect their effectiveness.
9. According to successful football coach Bill Parcells, what are five characteristics of effective leaders?

CRITICAL THINKING QUESTIONS

1. You have taken your first coaching and teaching position with a local high school. Describe how you might apply some of the principles and findings derived from Chelladurai's model to your coaching and teaching. Be specific about how you might alter your approach to your athletes and students in the class, in practice, and in competitions.
2. You are hired as the director of a Little League program in your city. You want to make sure that your volunteer coaches are effective leaders for the young athletes. You decide to hold a coaching clinic that all the volunteer coaches must attend. Describe what principles and information you would include in your clinic to help ensure that these novice coaches would be effective leaders.

201

Communication

After reading this chapter you should be able to

1 describe the communication process,

2 describe how to send messages more effectively,

3 describe how to receive messages more effectively,

4 identify what causes breakdowns in communication,

5 explain in detail the process of using confrontation, and

6 discuss how to offer constructive criticism.

Communication, integral to our daily lives, certainly is a critical element in the sport environment. Do you remember Jason, the Little League baseball player from chapter 4 who came to bat in the last inning with two teammates on and two outs? Now it's the championship game, Jason's team is losing 3–2, and once again there's a lot of pressure. The count goes to 2 and 2, and then Jason is fooled, swings at a bad pitch, and misses. The head coach says:

Jason, I can't believe you actually swung at that pitch. How many times have I told you to lay off bad pitches? That was just stupid. You let us all down and we may never get another chance to win the championship.

Right after that, the assistant coach comes up to Jason and says:

Don't worry about it, Jason. It's just a game. The pitcher made a really good pitch, and you had to protect the plate with two strikes on you. Maybe next time you could choke up on the bat a little more and shorten your swing. But I know you tried your best out there.

Jason received very different messages from his coaches about his performance, and of course the two messages had far different effects. Thanks to the assistant coach, Jason will not hang his head because he knows he has done his best. Next time he'll choke up on the bat a bit more and come through. If Jason had received only the head coach's message, who knows if there would even be a next time?

This scene underscores how important communication is in sport and exercise settings. No matter how brilliant a coach is in planning strategy and knowing the technical aspects of the game, success still depends on being able to communicate effectively not only with athletes, but also with parents, officials, assistant coaches, the media, and other coaches. Having to communicate in varied arenas holds true also for physical education teachers and exercise leaders. In essence, it's not what you know, but how well you can communicate information to others.

Good communication skills are among the most important ingredients contributing to performance enhancement and the personal growth of sport and exercise participants. One of the biggest problems in communication is that we often expect others to be mind readers. We expect them to understand our feelings without our ever expressing them. This expectation of mind reading and extraordinary short-

hand interpretation also is common when coaches, athletes, teachers, and parents expect that a simple gesture or unspoken thought will be enough for others to understand their feelings and unique perspective.

So it should not be surprising that breakdowns in communication often are at the root of problems as coaches talk to athletes or teachers to students. These remarks probably sound familiar: "I just can't talk to him." "If I've told her once, I've told her a thousand times." "When I talk to her, it goes in one ear and out the other." On the other side, athletes and students often have these kinds of things to say about coaches and teachers: "He never explains why he does things." "She's so hard to approach." "He's always shouting and yelling." Clearly, there are problems on both sides of communication. Repairing these communication gaps is essential in the learning and coaching environment.

The Communication Process

All one-way communication follows the same basic process. As the first step, one person decides to send a message to another. Then the sender translates (**encodes**) thoughts into a message. As the third step, the message is channeled (usually through spoken words but sometimes through nonverbal means, such as sign language) to the receiver. Next, the receiver interprets (**decodes**) the message. Finally, the receiver thinks about the message and responds internally, such as becoming interested, getting mad, feeling relieved, and so on. This process is outlined in Figure 10.1.

Purposes of Communication

Although the same process occurs in all communications, the purposes of the communication can vary. You might communicate to persuade a person in an aerobics class that she can lose weight by exercising regularly, evaluate how well a gymnast performs her routine on the balance beam, inform students of how to perform a new volleyball skill, psych up your team for a tough opponent, or deal with a conflict between two of the players on your team.

Communication may incorporate several purposes at once. For example, let's say an aerobic dance instructor wants to include harder and more vigorous movements in the class's exercise regimen. She would try motivating and persuading (to convince) the class of the benefits of this added exercise and then inform them how to perform the new skill.

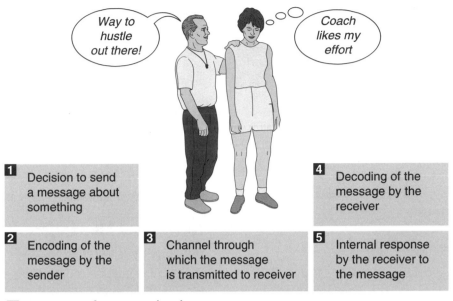

Figure 10.1 *The process of communication.*
Reprinted from Martens, 1987.

Types of Communication

Communication occurs in two basic ways: interpersonally and intrapersonally. Usually when we talk about communicating, we mean interpersonal communication, which involves at least two people and a meaningful exchange. The sender intends to affect the response of a particular person or persons. The message or content may be received by the person for whom it was intended, by persons for whom it was not intended, or both. Sometimes that message gets distorted so that the sender's intended response does not get transmitted.

An important part of interpersonal communication involves nonverbal communication, or nonverbal cues. Research has indicated that this type of communication is also critical to imparting and receiving information. In one study, subjects watching a tennis match were shown only the players between points—they never saw a player actually hit a ball or play a point. Still, about 75% of the time they could pick out who was winning the match. The nonverbal cues that players exhibited between points were strong enough to communicate who was ahead or behind.

Intrapersonal communication ("self-talk") is the communication we have with ourselves. We talk a lot to ourselves, and this inner dialogue is important. What we say to ourselves usually helps shape and predict how we act and perform. For instance, perhaps a youngster

in a physical education class is afraid of performing a new skill, the tennis serve, and tells himself that he can't do it and will look foolish if he tries. This intrapersonal communication increases the chances that he will not execute the skill properly. Self-talk can also affect motivation. If someone is trying to lose weight and tells herself that she's looking slimmer and feeling good, she is improving her motivation with her self-talk. (See chapter 16 for more on self-talk.)

Sending Messages Effectively

Effective communication is often the difference between success and failure for teachers, coaches, and exercise leaders. Thus, it is important to understand how to send effective messages, both verbally and nonverbally. Fortunately, research has indicated that we can teach effective communication skills to sport and exercise participants.

John Madden, long-time successful coach of the Los Angeles Raiders (and more recently a football commentator), succinctly summarizes the nature of successful communication in sport context:

Communication between a coach and his players was being able to say good things, bad things,

> *As much as 50% to 70% of human communication is nonverbal.*

> *Inner dialogue, or intrapersonal communication, affects motivation and behavior.*

and average things. Conversely, it's being able to listen to good, bad, and average things. . . . I tried to talk to each player. Sometimes it was merely a quick "How ya' doin'?" Sometimes it was a conversation. But by [my] talking to them every day, they didn't feel something was up when I would stop to talk to them. (Syer, 1986, pp. 99–110).

In the following discussion we will briefly discuss interpersonal and intrapersonal communication, but our focus will be on nonverbal communication, which is subtle but critical to the imparting and receiving of information.

Verbal Messages

Verbal messages should be sent clearly and received and interpreted correctly. Bill Parcells, successful football coach of the New York Giants, New England Patriots, and New York Jets understands the importance of both the effective sending and receiving of a message: "When sending a message, it's not enough to be honest and accurate. The impact of the message will hinge on who's receiving it and what they're willing to take in at that time" (Parcells & Coplon, 1995, p.117). In essence, we have to pick the right time and place to deliver our communication. Unfortunately, coaches and parents often pick the most inappropriate time to deliver their communication (e.g., right after a game or in front of the team).

Breakdowns occur because messages are sent ineffectively, not received, or are misinterpreted. Sometimes the problem is simply the lack of trust between coach and athlete or teacher and student (Burke, 1997). More often, the problem is with the transmission of the message. Some people talk too much, rambling on about things that bore or distract others, whereas others talk too little, not communicating enough information.

Nonverbal Messages

People are often unaware of the many nonverbal cues they use in communicating. They also often ignore the nonverbal cues coming their way, which are a

> *Nonverbal messages are harder to hide and consciously control than verbal messages are, so they are often more accurate indicators of how a person feels.*

© Human Kinetics

rich source of information. Understanding various kinds of nonverbal communication improves both sending and receiving messages (see Yukelson, 1998, for an in-depth discussion of nonverbal communication).

Nonverbal messages are less likely to be under conscious control, and therefore they are harder to hide. They can give away our unconscious feelings and attitudes. People tend to believe nonverbal messages. For example, just before starting an aerobics class an exercise leader asks a young woman how she is feeling. The young woman shrugs, looks down, frowns, and mutters, "Oh, fine." Although her words say everything is okay, the leader knows otherwise from the nonverbal messages being conveyed.

Although nonverbal messages can be powerful, they are often difficult to interpret accurately. Thus, we have to be cautious in giving them meaning and we have to try to correctly judge the context.

Physical Appearance

Often our first impression of a person comes from physical appearance. We might think of someone as fat, skinny, handsome, sloppy, attractive, or homely. A detail can pack a large message. For example, 20 years ago a male athlete who walked into a coach's office wearing an earring would likely have been quickly escorted out. Now it is more accepted for males to wear earrings, and a different message is conveyed. Dress and hairstyles convey powerful information. However, sometimes what we wish to convey is misinterpreted by others.

Posture

How we carry ourselves also sends a message. Slumped posture conveys low self-image or depression, whereas erect posture conveys control and energy. Our gait and the way we walk carry messages. Someone who shuffles along with his head down and his hands in his pockets conveys sadness, whereas a bouncy step suggests a sense of control and confidence.

Athletes often recognize frustrated or discouraged opponents by how they move. When they see an opposing player hanging his head, they know it's time to "go in for the kill." Tennis greats Pete Sampras and Steffi Graf knew the importance of posture and never let on to their opponents how they were feeling: Whether they made a great shot or blew an easy one, they looked and acted the same. This made Graf and Sampras tougher to beat because opponents could not tell when they were down.

Gestures

People's gestures often convey messages, whether or not they want them to. For instance, folding your arms across your chest usually expresses that you're not open to others, whereas locking your hands behind your head connotes superiority. Coaches often express themselves through gestures—sometimes if they verbalize their thoughts to officials they risk getting thrown out of the game!

Body Position

This refers to the personal space between you and others and to the position of your body with respect to others. Body position is really an aspect of **proxemics,** which is the study of how people communicate by the way they use space.

An example of body position language is the coach's surrounding him- or herself with starting players, rather than with reserves. Many coaches stand next to starting players, connoting favoritism. John Thompson, basketball coach for Georgetown University, makes it a habit to sit instead among the reserves to make them feel like valued members of the team.

Touching

Touching is another powerful form of nonverbal communication that can be used to calm or to express affection or other feelings, depending on the situation. We have become freer in recent years with the use of touching in sport, including more embracing between males than was socially acceptable years ago. A gentle pat on the back or an arm around the shoulder can often effectively communicate caring and empathy. However, with the increased sensitivity regarding the issue of sexual harassment, coaches and teachers have to be especially careful in their use of touching. You must make sure that the touching is appropriate and welcomed by the athlete or student. Touching should be restricted to public places to minimize any misinterpretation of the meaning of your touching.

Facial Expression

Your face is the most expressive part of your body. When listening to others, people often study facial expressions and eye movements to try to find deeper meaning in their messages. Eye contact is particularly important in communicating feelings. Getting eye contact usually means your listener is interested in your message. When people feel uncomfortable or embarrassed, they tend to avoid direct eye contact and look away. The smile is the universal bridge across language barriers and one of the most efficient ways of communicating. Smiles and other facial expressions can both invite verbal communication and give feedback about how effective your communication has been.

Voice Characteristics

The sound of a voice can powerfully reinforce or undercut verbal communication. As the adage goes, "It's not what you say but how you say it." The voice's quality often betrays true feelings, moods, and attitudes, revealing what we might never state verbally. Voice characteristics include pitch (high or low), tempo (speed), volume (loud or soft), rhythm (cadence), and articulation (enunciation).

These are guidelines for sending effective verbal and nonverbal messages (Martens, 1987):

1. Be direct. People who avoid straightforward communicating assume others know what they want or feel. Rather than expressing their message directly, they hint at what they have in mind—or they tell someone else, hoping the message will get to the person indirectly.

2. Own your message. Use "I" and "my," not "we" or "the team," when referencing your messages. You disown your messages when you say, "The team feels . . ." or "Most people think you are. . . ." What you're saying is what *you* believe, and using others to bolster what you have to say implies cowardice in expressing your own messages.

3. Be complete and specific. Provide the person to whom you are speaking with all the information he or she needs to fully understand your message. Watch for leaps in logic, unknown assumptions, and unstated intentions.

4. Be clear and consistent. Avoid double messages. "I really want to play you, Mary, but I don't think this is a good game for you. I think you're a fine athlete, but you'll just have to be patient." This is an example of a double message—acceptance and rejection—and it probably leaves Mary confused and hurt. Double messages send contradictory meanings, and usually the person sending them is afraid to be direct.

5. State your needs and feelings clearly. Because our society frowns on those who wear their emotions on their sleeves, we tend not to reveal our feelings and needs to others. Yet to develop close relationships, you must share your feelings.

6. Separate fact from opinion. State what you see, hear, and know, and then clearly identify any opinions or conclusions you have about these facts. You say to your son when he returns home late one night, "I see you've been out with the Williamson kid again." In the context in which you say it, your son will receive the message but not be certain of what

exactly your concern is about the Williamson boy. A better way to send this message would be to say, "That was the Williamson kid, wasn't it?" (verifying a fact), and then, "I'm concerned that you spend time with him. I'm afraid he'll get you into trouble" (stating your opinion). Although your son may not be pleased with your opinion, at least he'll understand it.

7. Focus on one thing at a time. Have you ever begun discussing how to execute a particular skill and abruptly switched to complaining about how the team hasn't been practicing well? Organize your thoughts before speaking. Disjointed messages do not transmit well.

8. Deliver messages immediately. When you observe something that upsets you or that needs to be changed, don't delay sending a message. Sometimes holding back can result in your exploding later about a little thing. Responding immediately also makes for more effective feedback than a delayed response.

9. Make sure your message does not contain hidden agendas, which means that the stated purpose of the message is not the same as the real purpose. Hidden agendas and disguised intentions destroy relationships. To determine if your message contains hidden agendas, ask yourself these two questions: Why am I saying this to this person? Do I want him or her to hear this, or is something else involved?

10. Be supportive. If you want another person to listen to your messages, don't deliver them with threats, sarcasm, negative comparisons, or judgments. Eventually the person will avoid communicating with you or simply tune you out whenever you speak. Your cumulative messages need to demonstrate support.

11. Be consistent with your nonverbal messages. Perhaps you tell your player it is okay to make an error, but your body gestures and facial expressions contradict your words. Conflicting messages confuse your athletes and hinder future communication.

12. Reinforce with repetition. That is, you should repeat your message. "Am I understanding you that . . . ?" "That's correct." Repeat key points to reinforce what you are saying. However, don't overrepeat, as this results in the other person not listening. You can also reinforce messages by using additional channels of communication—show a picture or video along with explaining the skill, for example.

13. Make your message appropriate to the receiver's frame of reference. Messages can be much better understood if you tailor them to the experiences of the person with whom you are communicating. It is inappropriate, for example, to use complex language when speaking to young athletes. They do not have the vocabulary to understand what you're saying.

14. Look for feedback that your message was accurately interpreted. Watch for verbal and nonverbal signals that the person to whom you are speaking is receiving the message you intended. If no signal is given, ask questions to solicit the feedback: "Do you understand what I am telling you, Susan?" or "Are you clear about what you should do?"

Receiving Messages Effectively

So far we've focused on the sender side of communication. However, people spend 40% of their communication time listening (Sathre, Olson, & Whitney, 1973). Yet although students learn writing and speaking skills, they seldom receive any formal training in listening. Before you read about how to improve listening skills, complete the short listening skills test on p. 211 to learn what specific skills you need to improve.

Active Listening

The best way to listen better is to listen actively. Active listening involves attending to main and supporting ideas, acknowledging and responding, giving appropriate feedback, and paying attention to the speaker's total communication. Active listening also involves nonverbal communication, such as direct eye contact and nodding to confirm that you understand the speaker. In essence, the listener shows concern for the content and the intent of the message and for the feelings of the messenger or sender.

If you really want people to confide in you, you should make a concerted effort to listen to them. Some people think they are showing that they are available to others when they really are not. A coach may say of his policy, "Sure, my athletes can come to see me anytime they want. I have an open-door policy," but his athletes may feel, "Aw, the coach doesn't really listen to us. All he's interested in is telling us what to do." Good listening shows sensi-

tivity and encourages an open exchange of ideas and feelings.

An active listener often paraphrases what the speaker has said. These are some typical lead-ins for a paraphrase:

- What I hear you saying is. . .
- Let me see if I've got this right. You said. . .
- What you're telling me is. . .

Asking specific questions to allow the person to express his or her feelings is also part of active listening, as is paraphrasing. Here are some examples:

> Statement. *"I am thinking about increasing my exercise times from 3 days a week to 5 days a week, but I'm not sure this is the best thing to do right now."*

> Question. *"What do you gain or lose by increasing your exercise times?"*

> Paraphrase. *"It sounds as though you're struggling with trying to balance getting fit with other demands in your life."*

By paraphrasing a person's thoughts and feelings, you let her know that you're listening and you care. Often this leads to more open communication and exchange, as the speaker senses that you're interested. When you ask questions, avoid using the interrogative *why?* which can seem judgmental. Rosenfeld and Wilder (1990) offer some additional suggestions for improving active listening skills:

- Don't mistake hearing for listening. Hearing and listening are distinct activities. Hearing is simply receiving sounds, whereas listening is an active process. Hearing someone does not mean you're listening to the meaning of their message. It is frustrating to the speaker when a receiver hears but doesn't listen. If you find yourself not listening, practice focusing your concentration on the speaker.

Active listening enhances communication because the speaker feels that he or she is being heard, acknowledged, and provided with appropriate feedback.

■ APPLICATION ■

Improving Communication

Here are some ways to improve coach-athlete and teacher-student communications:

- Convey rationales as to why you expect (or why you don't expect) certain behaviors from your participants.

- Use a communication style that is comfortable for you. Don't try to copy the communication style of another coach or teacher just because that individual's style happens to be successful for him or her. Rather communicate consistently with your own personality and teaching style.

- Learn how to become more empathic by placing yourself in the shoes of your athletes. Show genuine concern for them as people and work with them to find appropriate solutions jointly.

- Use the positive approach when communicating, which includes the liberal use of praise, encouragement, support, and positive reinforcement.

- Always acknowledge the greetings of others—a hello and a smile are easy ways to communicate positive feelings.

- If you have an open-door policy for your students and athletes, show that you are sincere about it.

- Be consistent in administering discipline.

Note. Adapted from Yukelson, 1997, 1998.

■ Mentally prepare to listen. Listening sometimes requires mental preparation. For example, before having an important discussion with your coach, develop a mental game plan for the exchange. That is, rehearse in your mind attending very carefully to the meaning of the speaker's message. You should try to save difficult discussions for when your energy level is high so you can sustain intensity and listen actively.

Supportive Listening

Being a supportive listener communicates that you are "with" the speaker and value his message. Here are some tips for **supportive listening:**

1. Use supportive behaviors as you listen. These communicate the message that the other person is acknowledged, understood, and accepted. Supportive listening behaviors

- describe the other's behavior, instead of trying to evaluate or attack it;

- focus on immediate thoughts and feelings;

- are not calculated or manipulative;

- are empathic, not indifferent; and

- remain open to new ideas, perspectives, and the possibility of change.

Along with these behaviors use active attending behaviors, such as nodding your head and making clear, direct eye contact.

2. Use confirming behaviors as you listen. Part of effective communication is letting people know you are with them in the conversation and understand their message, even if you do not agree with it. Interrupting or failing to either verbally or nonverbally acknowledge what someone is saying is disconcerting to the speaker. Use confirming behaviors along with supportive behaviors to show you are paying attention, accept-

210

Listening Skills Test

Rating scale	Never	Seldom	Sometimes	Often
1. You find listening to others uninteresting.	1	2	3	4
2. You tend to focus attention on the speaker's delivery or appearance instead of the message.	1	2	3	4
3. You listen more for facts and details, often missing the main points that give the facts meaning.	1	2	3	4
4. You are easily distracted by other people talking, chewing gum, rattling paper, and so on.	1	2	3	4
5. You fake attention, looking at the speaker but thinking of other things.	1	2	3	4
6. You listen only to what is easy to understand.	1	2	3	4
7. Certain emotion-laden words interfere with your listening.	1	2	3	4
8. You hear a few sentences of another person's problems and immediately start thinking about all the advice you can give.	1	2	3	4
9. Your attention span is very short, so it is hard for you to listen for more than a few minutes.	1	2	3	4
10. You are quick to find things to disagree with, so you stop listening as you prepare your argument.	1	2	3	4
11. You try to placate the speaker by being supportive through head-nodding and uttering agreement, but you're really not involved.	1	2	3	4
12. You change the subject when you get bored or uncomfortable with it.	1	2	3	4
13. As soon as someone says anything that you think reflects negatively on you, you defend yourself.	1	2	3	4
14. You second-guess the speaker, trying to figure out what he or she *really* means.	1	2	3	4

Now add up your score. The following subjective scale will give you some help in determining how well you listen.

14–24	Excellent
25–34	Good
35–44	Fair
45–56	Weak

Reprinted from Martens, 1987.

ing, and understanding. This is especially important for coaches and teachers and other sport and exercise leaders. Participants usually look up to the leader, and a lack of attention on the leader's part can therefore be particularly disappointing to the participant.

3. Use both verbal and nonverbal listening behaviors. Nonverbal behaviors that communicate interest and attention include

- standing no more than a few feet from the person,
- maintaining eye contact,
- making appropriate facial gestures,
- facing the speaker, and
- maintaining an open posture.

Verbal behaviors should communicate an understanding and acknowledgment of what the speaker is saying and feeling.

Aware Listening

Be aware that people react differently to the way you communicate. Here are tips for aware listening:

1. Be flexible. There is no one best listening strategy. Different situations require different strategies (think of the interactional model). People prefer or feel more comfortable with one style of listening than another. Some people simply like to talk, and they may appear unconcerned about your understanding. Others will give you time to think about what they've said and provide opportunities for feedback.

2. Be alert for barriers and breakdowns in communication. *Barriers* involve "noise," such as other people talking while you are trying to listen to a specific person. For example, coaches and athletes often have to listen above the roar of a crowd. It is useful to develop strategies to deal with noise, such as using nonverbal signals. Breakdowns occur when messages are misinterpreted or misdirected. Often, we do not know a breakdown has occurred until something bad happens that can be traced back to the breakdown. We'll discuss breakdowns at greater length in what follows.

Breakdowns in Communication

Communicating effectively requires skill and effort from both parties. The process can be complicated and often breaks down. Breakdowns can result from either sender or receiver failures.

Sender Failures

Senders may transmit a message poorly. Ambiguous messages, for example, are ineffective communications. Say a coach tells an athlete that if she continues to do well in practice, she will be in the starting lineup when the season opens. Over the next few weeks, the coach compliments the athlete regularly but says nothing about her not starting. So two days before the start of the season the athlete is taken aback when she is listed as a reserve. In this case, the coach should have been more specific about the criteria for starting and should have given the athlete ongoing feedback.

Inconsistent messages also cause communication breakdowns. Nothing is more frustrating than hearing one thing today and the opposite tomorrow. Consistency is critical to building trust and rapport. For example, if a coach is always supportive during practice but is harsh and critical during games, athletes get confused and may even fall apart during competitions.

Often inconsistency results when verbal and nonverbal channels conflict. A physical education teacher might offer encouraging words to a student attempting a new skill, while her body language and facial expression convey disappointment and impatience. Inconsistent communication produces insecurity and anxiety in those receiving it. Physical educators want to establish credibility in their communications, and consistency is a good route toward this goal. And it's necessary to be consistent not only with each participant but also among participants. For example, say a coach tells her team that anyone late to practice will not play in the next game. If the coach then enforces this policy when a couple of reserves are late for practice, she must also enforce it if the star player is late.

Receiver Failures

Ineffective communication is a double-edged sword. Receivers as well as senders can contribute to miscommunication. As an illustration, let's look at Mary, an exercise leader. She is talking to Cindy, a member of her aerobics class who has missed several classes. "Cindy, I've missed you the past several weeks," says Mary. "If you don't keep up your regular exercise, you'll get fat again. In fact, I already see those love handles." Mary's intent was to motivate Cindy to stop missing exercise classes, but Cindy heard only the "getting

■ MORE INFORMATION ■

Barriers to Effective Communication

- Receiver not paying attention to the sender
- Lack of trust between the individuals attempting to communicate
- Socialization and hereditary differences, causing misinterpretations between the sender and receiver
- Differences in the mental set or perception between people
- Embarrassment interferes
- Tendency to tell people what they want to hear
- Difficulties in expression or reluctance to communicate

Note. From Dawson, 1985.

fat" and "love handles" part. Overweight for many years, she is sensitive to comments about her weight. What she heard Mary saying was that she was getting fat, and she started feeling depressed because she had worked so hard to lose the weight. Had Mary been more aware of Cindy's tendency toward sensitivity, however, she could have simply told Cindy that she missed her in class and was glad to see her back and exercising. Thus, in this case there was a problem in both the sending and the receiving.

Along with misinterpreting the message, failing to listen is another way receivers can cause problems. For example, a teacher might convey information very well, but if her students are looking out the window or thinking about an upcoming party, communication will break down. The receiver shares responsibility with the sender and should make every effort to listen to the message being sent.

Confrontation

Many times, the nature of the communication is inherently difficult. For example, when coaches have to inform players that they are being cut from the team, removed from the starting lineup, punished for a rule violation, or talked to for having made a critical performance error, athletes can often get angry, upset, and defensive. If these types of communications are not handled carefully, then communication breakdowns can occur, often leading to confrontations.

A confrontation is usually a face-to-face discussion among people in conflict. Despite its negative connotations, confrontation when properly used can

Use active and supportive listening techniques to avoid breakdowns that prevent effective communication.

help both parties understand the issues more clearly without feeling undue stress, guilt, or inadequacy. Confrontations are useful not only for major conflicts but also for minor conflicts to help "clear the air."

When to Avoid or to Use Confrontation

Avoid confrontations when you are angry. It has been said that someone who speaks when he is angry will make the best speech he will forever regret. Many people feel uncomfortable with confrontations because they anticipate a negative, stressful encounter. When athletes and coaches or students and teachers have a confrontation, there is, in addition, a difference in power and that also can be problematic. Thus, oftentimes participants avoid the meeting and let things fester. Other people jump to arguments and escalate feelings of hostility. Neither approach produces a productive resolution of the problem.

In what situations should you use confrontation? Decide by considering the purposes a confrontation might serve. It should not be to put other people "in their place" but should lead to carefully examining the behavior and its consequences. For example, if a fitness instructor feels that her supervisor was wrong in reprimanding her in front of a client "just because" she used a different lifting technique than usual, then the instructor should

Assertiveness Training

Athletes, exercisers, and students often would benefit from being more assertive in their communications with their coaches, teachers, and fitness instructors. But this is not always easy for people, who may have difficulty being assertive for a variety of reasons including a fear of losing social approval, lack of awareness, lack of confidence to speak up, and fear of the risk in making oneself known. For example, some freshmen might fear that if they speak up in team meetings, they will look bad in the eyes of the upperclassmen or be perceived as disruptive.

Connelly and Rotella (1991) describe a role-playing technique that has effectively helped individuals learn to communicate and express themselves more assertively. The technique is known as the DESC Formula (Describe, Express, Specify, Consequences). First, athletes are asked to describe a situation or another person's behavior to which they are reacting (e.g., "When you criticize my performance in front of other teammates . . ."). Then they express their feelings regarding the other person's behavior that was just described ("I get angry and frustrated when you talk and criticize behind my back"). Next they specify what changes they want to take place ("I would appreciate it if you did not talk behind my back"). Finally they identify consequences to expect if the response is not met (e.g., "If you don't get off my case, I will ask coach to meet with us to straighten this out").

---

meet with the supervisor to resolve their differences, rather than letting them fester and turn into a full-blown incident.

How to Use Confrontation

Once you decide that confrontation can be useful and appropriate, you need to know how to confront. There are some general guidelines to make confrontations more productive and less stressful (Anshel, 1993; Martens, 1987), which we will now discuss.

Express Feelings Constructively

People often use anger to release strong emotional feelings and tension—and this venting of feelings might make them feel better for the moment. But usually the subsequent response to anger is guilt, an upset stomach, or a headache. Also, when people are angry, they tend to make irrational and cruel statements without thinking about the consequences of what they are saying.

We cannot eliminate anger from our emotional makeup, but we can learn how to deal with it. A first step is realizing that getting angry isn't necessarily bad. It's what someone does with this anger that makes it constructive or destructive:

■ Do not attack a person's character or personality in anger. Communication should aim to improve future situations. Providing specific information and instruction—instead of attacking char-

acter—can produce more desirable behavior change and still maintain a positive working relationship.

■ When you feel angry or upset, try to identify the exact feelings by name. For example, "I am annoyed with you," or "Your behavior disappoints me." Sometimes just recognizing feelings can ease them before you fly off the handle.

■ Take time to gather yourself. If you let your anger speak, your message will probably not be constructive to anyone. Try turning away or taking a very brief walk. Sometimes getting away from the situation for a moment gives you time to cool down and evaluate.

Think

Before you start screaming commands or blurting out insults, think of the consequences. Will what you are about to say produce a successful confrontation? That is, will it get across your message without embarrassing and shaming the other person? Take a deep breath and back off for even a few seconds. This can make the difference between a positive interchange and a disaster.

Understand

Ask yourself if you are accurately understanding the person and situation. To help, ask directed questions to get information, establish facts, and clarify perceptions—not to instill guilt or cause embarrassment. Let the person know that you are

trying to understand his or her position. Understanding is not always easy in the midst of a confrontation, but allowing the person to express feelings without your being judgmental will often lead to a resolution.

Be Empathetic

Being aloof, antagonistic, or sarcastic does not convey that you care—it only produces distrust and resentment. Your goal in a confrontation should be to resolve the problem mutually without dominating or intimidating someone. Putting yourself in the other person's shoes is the essence of empathy. It is asking yourself how you would feel under similar circumstances. If you were receiving a message, how would you feel if you were criticized and yelled at? Unfortunately, many adults in leadership positions don't know how it feels to be on the receiving end of destructive comments. Professionals must think about how their comments and critiques will feel to re-

cipients. This doesn't mean to never criticize, but instead to be sincere and sensitive to how others are feeling.

Be Tentative

In most sport situations, tentativeness can lead to indecision and harm performance, but this is not the case in confronting a person. Being a little tentative helps the person to consider what you are saying. If you come on too strong, the person might feel under attack. Tentative does not mean being "wishy-washy." It simply means that you are inviting the person to examine the problem as you see it.

Proceed Gradually

Beginning the confrontation with accusations and critical remarks gets things off to a poor start. Instead, give the other person time to absorb what you say and understand the nature of the problem. Throwing too much information at someone too rapidly causes overload and confusion.

■ APPLICATION ■

Dos and Don'ts When Initiating Confrontation (Martens, 1987)

Dos

- Do convey that you value your relationship with the person.
- Do go slowly and think about what you want to communicate.
- Do try to understand the other person's position.
- Do listen carefully to what the other person is trying to communicate.

Don'ts

- Don't communicate the solution. Rather, focus on the problem. We are often overly anxious to tell others what they must do, instead of letting them figure it out.
- Don't stop communicating. Even if the confrontation isn't going as you planned, keep communicating about the problem in a constructive manner.
- Don't use "put-downs." Sarcasm and attacks usually alienate people. A confrontation is not a competition, and the idea is not to win it. The idea is to solve a problem together.
- Don't rely on nonverbal hints to communicate your thoughts. You need to be direct and forthright in communicating. Now is not the time for subtle nonverbal cues.

Constructive Criticism

Although we generally want to be positive, there are times when criticism is necessary. Unfortunately, many people take criticism as a threat to self-esteem. When they feel threatened, their immediate response is to become defensive. They concentrate on defending themselves, instead of on listening to the message. Some exemplary research and application of the research indicates that the "sandwich approach" is the most effective way to give criticism (Smith & Smoll, 1996; Smoll & Smith, 1996). The sandwich approach is a technique to offer constructive feedback in a sensitive yet effective manner. It consists of three sequential elements:

1. A positive statement
2. Future-oriented instructions
3. A compliment

Let's take a closer look. After a participant makes a mistake, he or she typically anticipates a negative remark from the coach or teacher. Often the person will tune out the anticipated unpleasant message and never hear it. To assure the individual attends to the first comment, it should be positive. Appropriate positive statements might be "Nice try, Janet," "Good effort, Marty," or "What a tough pitch to hit!" Once the person is receptive to the opening (positive) statement, he or she will also pay attention to the second part, the instructional feedback.

The key aspect of the sandwich approach is the future-oriented instruction. After gaining the person's attention, provide the critical instructional feedback—behaviors or strategies to use the next time the person performs the skill. The reason for keeping the instruction future-oriented is to keep the person from thinking about the error immediately (thinking about an error will often result in repeating it). The feedback should be positive to keep the individual focused on it. The message should be what to do next time—not a comment that ridicules, embarrasses, or criticizes. For instance,

- after a ground ball goes through a player's legs, say, "Next time you get a hard grounder, just get down on one knee and block the ball with your body," or
- after a student trying a new skill on the balance beam falls off, say, "You really need to concentrate on keeping your eyes

■ APPLICATION ■

The Athlete-Coach Meeting

Athletes may want to meet with their coach to discuss some of their feelings (whether positive or negative), and this should be done in a thoughtful manner. Here are some guidelines to help prepare for such a meeting (Anshel, 1993):

- Plan the content of the meeting, deciding on one or two specific issues.
- Make sure you are on time for the meeting.
- Make your opening statement positive to avoid putting the coach immediately on the defensive; this positive statement can help create some good feelings.
- Keep your conference confidential unless the coach agrees to make it public. In most cases, the details of the meeting should be left in the coach's office.

looking forward to help maintain your balance."

The final part of the sandwich is a compliment. After the instructional feedback, make sure the individual still feels good about the performance. Ending the interaction on a positive note makes it more likely that the instruction will be remembered. It also helps build trust and rapport; the individual realizes that making a mistake isn't the end of the world and that people can learn from their errors.

Let's look at two examples of the complete sandwich. (a) Max drops a pass from the quarterback that would have been a sure touchdown. "All right, Max. That was a good pass pattern. Next time make sure you watch the ball into your hands. Hang in there, way to go, you're on the right track." (b) Sally keeps getting out of step during her aerobics dance class. "Sally, you're really working hard out there. Next time try to slow down and not get ahead of the music. You're looking good. Keep up the good work."

SUMMARY

1 *Describe the communication process.*

Effective communication takes work and effort. Basically we communicate in two ways: interpersonally and intrapersonally. However, it is important to understand that communication is a process. Interpersonal communication involves both verbal and nonverbal communication, whereas intrapersonal communication is really communicating with ourselves via self-talk.

2 *Describe how to send messages more effectively.*

It is important to understand how to send effective messages, both verbally and nonverbally, because effective communication is essential for positive interactions. In nonverbal communication, such factors as physical appearance, posture, gestures, body positioning, and touching are critical. Effective verbal communication includes such characteristics as being clear and consistent, being direct, delivering messages immediately, and being consistent.

3 *Describe how to receive messages more effectively.*

Active listening is the most useful way to receive messages more effectively. It involves attending to main and supporting ideas, acknowledging and responding, and giving appropriate feedback, as well as using nonverbal cues, such as eye contact and nodding one's head to show understanding.

4 *Identify what causes breakdowns in communication.*

Effective communication is complex, and breakdowns often occur either in sending or receiving a message. Senders who convey messages that are ambiguous or inconsistent can cause communication breakdowns. Similarly, receivers who do not pay close attention to the messages can also cause ineffective communication.

5 *Explain the process of using confrontation.*

Confrontation is a way of communicating, and although most people view confrontation as negative, it can lead to a mutual solution. Part of successfully resolving a problem is recognizing when and why a confrontation may be appropriate. The critical component is to express your feelings in a constructive manner.

6 *Discuss how to offer constructive criticism.*

Constructive criticism can be provided through what is known as the "sandwich approach." This involves a positive statement, future-oriented instructions, and a compliment. This type of criticism avoids the negativism usually accompanying most critical remarks; it allows the person to focus on the positive aspects of their behavior.

KEY TERMS

encodes	active listening
decodes	supportive listening
interpersonal communication	aware listening
nonverbal communication	confrontation
intrapersonal communication	sandwich approach
proxemics	

REVIEW QUESTIONS

1. Discuss the five steps comprising the communication process.
2. Compare and contrast interpersonal and intrapersonal communication, providing specific examples of each type.
3. Describe three types of nonverbal communication, giving examples from applied settings.
4. Define active listening. How can practitioners enhance their listening skills?
5. Discuss three breakdowns in communication, including examples of each type.
6. Describe the five-step process you would use when confronting someone.
7. Discuss the sandwich approach to constructive critiques after a mistake.
8. How would you help athletes become more assertive in their communication?

CRITICAL THINKING QUESTIONS

1. As a paid consultant you are asked to devise a guide for teachers and coaches at a local high school to help them communicate more effectively with their students and athletes. Based on what you know about effective communication, what are the most important guidelines you would include in your guide? In addition, what barriers are most likely to undermine effective communication?

2. As a coach, you have just had a brief confrontation with an athlete about breaking some team rules. He has stormed out of practice mad and upset. Soon you are to meet with the athlete and likely will have to confront him about his behavior—and possibly punish him for his actions. How would you prepare for this meeting and what principles would you employ to have this confrontation be a positive meeting? How might the athlete best prepare for this encounter?

Part V

Enhancing Performance

One of the main questions asked by sport and exercise psychologists is, How can we use psychological techniques to help people perform more effectively? In fact, this question has been a major focus of sport psychology since the field's early days. In this part we'll try to convey what progress has been made toward answering this question.

Chapter 11 introduces you to psychological skills training. Here you'll discover that psychological skills are like physical skills and can be taught, learned, and practiced. You'll learn how to enhance performance in your students, athletes, and exercisers by teaching mental skills.

Chapters 12 through 16 then focus on specific topics to develop psychological skills training for performance enhancement. In chapter 12 we'll examine arousal regulation and reduction, which will equip you to help athletes psych up rather than psych out. You'll become familiar with a variety of health-related stress-management techniques as well. Chapter 13 discusses the topic of imagery (or visualization). You will learn how to augment physical practice with mental practice techniques and strategies. Self-confidence is the focus of chapter 14. Here the relationship between confidence and performance is emphasized, as well as confidence-building methods you can use. One of the best ways to build confidence is by effectively setting goals. Thus, in chapter 15 you'll learn about effective goals and goal-setting skills for enhancing confidence, other psychological skills, and performance. Finally, the section ends with chapter 16 and a discussion of the all-important topics of attention and concentration. Here we'll focus on how you can improve performance through enhanced concentration and attentional skills.

© Human Kinetics

Introduction to Psychological Skills Training

After reading this chapter you should be able to

1 define psychological skills training,
2 describe the myths surrounding psychological skills training,
3 identify the knowledge base for psychological skills training,
4 discuss three phases of psychological skills training programs,
5 develop a psychological skills training program, and
6 understand the problems of implementing a psychological skills training program.

How many times have you seen athletes attribute their poor performances to such reasons as losing concentration or tightening up under pressure, the mental side of their game? Yet, a mistake coaches and athletes alike commonly make is to attempt to correct a poor performance simply through more practice time. Often, however, a lack of physical skills is not the real problem—rather, a lack of mental skills is the cause. Let's take a look at a scenario that makes this point.

Jim's high school basketball team is behind 67–66 with 1 second left on the clock when Jim is fouled in the act of shooting and awarded two shots. The opposing coach calls a time-out to try to ice Jim and let the pressure build. Jim's coach tells him to just relax and shoot the foul shots as he does in practice. But Jim knows how important the game is to his teammates, his coach, the school, his friends, and his family in the audience. He starts to think about how awful he would feel if he let everybody down, and this worrying starts to affect him physically. As he approaches the free-throw line, the muscles in his shoulders and arms tighten up. As a result, he rushes his shots, lacks rhythm in his release, misses both free throws, and his team loses the game.

The next day in practice, Jim's coach tells him to work more on his free-throw shooting, recommending that he stay after every practice to shoot 100 free throws. The coach feels that the extra practice will help Jim perfect his free-throw technique so that he won't choke at the next big game.

However, Jim's problem did not have to do with the mechanics of shooting a free throw. The real problem was that he got too tense and couldn't stay relaxed to shoot his free throws smoothly and rhythmically, just like in practice. Having Jim rehearse free throws will not help him overcome the pressures of shooting when the game is on the line. Jim needs to develop skills to relax physically and mentally under great pressure. These skills (as well as others) can be developed through psychological skills training (PST). So let's start by taking a closer look at what PST is really all about.

What Is PST?

Psychological skills training (PST) refers to systematic and consistent practice of mental or psychological skills. Coaches and athletes all know that physical skills need to be regularly practiced and refined through literally thousands and thousands of repetitions. Similar to physical skills, psychological skills such as maintaining and focusing concentration, regulating arousal levels, enhancing confidence, and maintaining motivation also need to be systematically practiced. In the example, Jim needed to practice the psychological skill of relaxation so he could deal with the pressure of shooting free throws under intense game pressure. Just telling an athlete to relax won't produce the desired response unless the player already knows how to relax through prior practice and training.

Why PST Is Important

All sport and exercise participants fall victim to mental letdowns and mistakes. Which of the following sport and exercise experiences have you had, or have you known others to have?

- You walked off a playing field in disgust after losing a game you felt you should have won.
- You choked at a critical point in a competition.
- You felt depressed because you weren't recovering quickly enough from an injury.
- You lacked the desire or motivation to exercise.
- Your mind wandered during a competition.
- You became angry and frustrated with your performance and put yourself down.

Chances are you have had at least one of the experiences on this list. Conversely, most sport performers also know what it feels like to be "in the zone," where everything seems to come together effortlessly and performance is exceptional. Mental and emotional components often overshadow and transcend the purely physical and technical aspects of performance. In any sport a player's success (or failure) results from a combination of physical (e.g., strength, speed, balance, coordination) and mental (e.g., concentration, confidence, anxiety management) abilities. Most coaches consider that sport is at least 50% mental (see Figure 11.1), and certain sports, such as golf, tennis, and figure skating, are consistently viewed as being 80% to 90% mental. Jimmy Connors, known for his mental tenacity and toughness, has often stated that professional tennis is 95% mental. Tiger Woods started his amazing run at winning the Master's by 18 strokes with a subpar first nine holes. He said that after the disastrous first nine holes he knew he just needed to remain focused and get his "mental game" back together because it would be the key to his success. Still, many serious athletes typically allot 10 to 20 hours weekly to physical practice and little, if any, time to mental practice. This proportion doesn't make sense.

Figure 11.1 *Mental and physical skills figure importantly in performance success.*

Psychological factors account primarily for day-to-day performance fluctuations.

A "B" tennis player usually plays against other "B" players, similar in ability. Likewise, a nationally ranked swimmer will probably compete against other high-caliber swimmers. Of course athletes sometimes are clearly overmatched in physical skills or, conversely, are clearly superior to their opponents. In these cases, the outcome probably results from differences in physical skills and abilities. In most competitions, however, players win or lose depending on how they (and their opponents) perform that particular day. Physical ability being fairly equal, the winner is usually the athlete who has better mental skills. Consider fluctuations in your own day-to-day performance. How is it that on some days you can't do anything wrong, whereas on other days you can't do anything right? You know you haven't lost your physical skills—it's your mental skills that fluctuate.

Why Sport and Exercise Participants Neglect PST

If psychological skills are so important for success, the logical question is, Why do people spend so little time working on developing psychological skills to enhance performance? There are three basic reasons why PST is neglected by many coaches and participants.

Lack of Knowledge

Many people don't really understand how to teach or practice PST skills. For example, some coaches teach concentration by shouting, "Concentrate out there!" or "Will you get your mind on what you're supposed to be doing?" The implicit assumption is that the player knows how to concentrate but is just not doing it. Another common practice (remember Jim's errant free throws?) is telling a player to "just relax" as he goes into an important performance. But this is not easily done without having had training in relaxation skills. A track-and-field coach would not expect a 100-meter runner to perform well in the 440

225

if she hadn't been running that distance in practice. Similarly, relaxation and concentration must be practiced to become effective tools to use in competition. We do not mean to criticize coaches and athletes. Unfortunately, many of them have not had access to techniques for teaching and learning psychological skills.

A recent survey of junior tennis coaches found that they felt they were fairly knowledgeable in sport psychology, although their knowledge of mental skills training did not come from books or formal courses. Rather, they were influenced by actual experience in working with players or by attending clinics (Gould, Medbery, Damarjian, & Lauer, 1999a). The importance of actual experience as a primary teaching mechanism for coaches was also apparent in earlier research on elite athletes (Gould, Giannini, Krane, & Hodge, 1990). Since researchers have not always conveyed their knowledge to practitioners, however, coaches have suggested that mental training information could be made more user friendly by (a) focusing on the development of "hands-on" concrete examples and exercises, (b) developing more mental skills training resources, particularly in audio and video formats, and (c) by engaging and actively involving coaches in actual mental skills coach education (Gould, Medbery, Damarjian, & Lauer, 1999b).

PST programs establish a scientific basis for the effective development of psychological skills. Applied sport psychology has been evolving rapidly since the 1980s. The days of simply telling players, "Don't choke," "Get psyched up," "Be confident," "Stay loose," "Be mentally tough," or "Concentrate" are on their way out. We are learning that such advice needs action-oriented approaches and plans for improving mental skills in order to enhance performance.

Misunderstandings About Psychological Skills

People don't enter the world equipped with mental skills—it is a misconception that champions are born rather than made. Despite common assumptions that Steffi Graf, Tiger Woods, Ken Griffey, Jr., Wayne Gretzky, and other such athletes were blessed with a congenital mental toughness and competitive drive as part of their personality, it doesn't quite work that way. Yes, we are all born with certain physical and psychological predispositions, but skills can be learned and developed, depending on the experiences we encounter in our lives. No great athlete ever

Psychological skills training is often neglected due to a lack of knowledge, perceived lack of time, or a belief that psychological skills are innate and can't be taught.

achieved stardom without endless hours of practice, honing and refining physical skills and techniques. Although some athletes do possess exceptional physical skills, they had to work hard to develop their talents to become champions. For example, as physically talented and gifted as Michael Jordan is, his competitors say his most impressive trait is his competitiveness. Staying calm under pressure, maintaining concentration despite distractions, and keeping confident in the face of failure are simply not innate. Rather, they are skills that need systematic practice and integration with physical skills.

Lack of Time

A third reason coaches and athletes cite for not practicing psychological skills is too little time. In fact, the study of junior tennis coaches (noted earlier) found that lack of time was given as the most important roadblock to teaching mental skills to their players (Gould et al., 1999a). These coaches say their players barely have adequate time to practice physical skills, much less mental ones. Yet people reason that they lost a particular game or competition because "I wasn't up for the game today," "I just couldn't seem to concentrate," "I got too tight and choked," or "I lost confidence in my game." You would think that if coaches thought their teams lost because of poor concentration, they would make time to practice concentration skills. Instead they typically add time to physical practice. The issue is one of priorities. If you believe that mental skills are important and you know how to practice them, you will find time for them.

Myths About PST

Several myths circulate about the use of psychological techniques in optimizing performance (Gould & Eklund, 1991). These myths (i.e., not grounded in fact or empirical data), only confuse what sport psychology consultants can—and cannot—do to help athletes maximize their performance.

Myth 1: PST Is for "Problem" Athletes Only

Many people wrongly think that all sport psychologists work with athletes who have psychological problems. This is not the case (see chapter 1). Clinical sport psychologists are typically licensed to practice clinical psychology in a particular state and trained to treat various mental disorders, including some sport-related problems such as substance abuse, eating disorders, and severe depression. However, only about 10% of athletes exhibit behaviors and mental disorders that require the expertise of a clinical sport psychologist. Rather, most athletes' psychological needs can be addressed by educational sport psychologists who focus on helping develop mental skills in athletes who have a normal range of functioning. (It's important to note that neither type of sport psychologist is better or more essential than the other. Both clinical and educational sport psychologists have unique roles to help people improve performance and psychological well-being.) Table 11.1 gives examples of the different PST needs addressed by educational and clinical sport psychologists.

Myth 2: PST Is for Elite Training Only

PST is not only for the elite. It is appropriate for all athletes, including young, developing athletes (Hellstedt, 1987; Orlick & McCaffrey, 1991; Weiss, 1991) and special populations such as people who are mentally retarded (Travis & Sachs, 1991), physically challenged (Asken, 1991), or hearing-impaired (Clark & Sachs, 1991). Dedicated professionals work to help improve performance and personal growth. Popular magazines and news media tend to focus on Olympic and professional athletes who work with sport psychology consultants, but many other groups receive sport psychology consultation as well.

Myth 3: PST Provides "Quick Fix" Solutions

Many people mistakenly think that sport psychology offers a quick fix to psychological problems. Sometimes athletes and coaches expect learning how to concentrate or to stay calm under pressure to be accomplished in one or two lessons. Actually, psychological skills take time and practice to develop. And PST is not magical—it won't turn an average player into a superstar. However, it will help athletes reach their potential and maximize their abilities.

Myth 4: PST Is Not Useful

Some people still think that sport psychology is hocus-pocus, having nothing positive to offer. However, substantial scholarly research—and anecdotal reports from athletes and coaches—indicates that psychological skills do in fact enhance performance (e.g., Greenspan & Feltz, 1989; Weinberg & Comar, 1994). Advances and new methods are sometimes scary, and people may have extreme reactions to or expectations of them. Sport psychology is neither a magic elixir nor useless bunk. People in the physical activity professions should have realistic expectations of what psychological skills training can and cannot do to enhance performance and well-being.

> *Psychological skills can be learned, but they must be practiced over time and integrated into a person's daily training regimen.*

Table 11.1

Topics Addressed by Sport Psychologists

Educational sport psychologists	Clinical sport psychologists
Goal setting	Eating disorders
Imagery	Substance abuse
Arousal regulation	Personality disorders
Concentration	Severe depression/anxiety
Mental preparation	Psychopathology

The PST Knowledge Base

PST has developed a knowledge base primarily from two sources. One source is original research studies conducted with elite athletes, and the other is the experience of coaches and athletes. Let's take a look at each of these sources.

Research on Elite Athletes

Several studies that have compared successful and less successful athletes in terms of psychological skills consistently showed that more successful athletes had better concentration, higher levels of self-confidence, more task-oriented thoughts (rather than outcome-oriented; see chapter 3), and lower levels of anxiety (Gould, Eklund, & Jackson, 1992a; 1992b). Successful athletes also had more positive thoughts and used

More successful players differ from less successful ones in how developed their psychological skills are.

more positive imagery to visualize success. They tended to be more determined and show more commitment than their less successful counterparts.

Experiences of Athletes and Coaches

Increasingly, researchers are asking coaches and athletes about the content and core sport psychology topics to be included in PST programs. For example, Gould, Tammen, Murphy, and May (1991) surveyed elite coaches and athletes from the U.S. Olympic Committee's National Governing Body sport programs. The coaches and athletes rated relaxation training, concentration, imagery, team cohesion, concentration and attention training, and self-talk strategies as very important topics.

In another study Canadian Olympic athletes who performed up to their potential had developed plans for competition, performance evaluation, and dealing with disruptions. They could overcome adversity and performance blocks by sticking to their plans and could channel performance anxiety and arousal positively. In addition, they set daily goals, were high

© Tim DeFrisco/DeFrisco Photography

in confidence, and practiced positive imagery. These Canadian Olympians who achieved peak performance demonstrated a total commitment to pursuing excellence, one not evidenced by their less successful counterparts. They set daily training goals, used simulations in practice to replicate competitive environments, and used imagery to help focus attention and visualize successful outcomes (Orlick & Partington, 1988).

Both Olympic and professional athletes consistently deal with anxiety, coping with training stress and fatigue, developing mental plans, maintaining motivation, staying focused, and enhancing confidence. Other issues they report include interactions with friends and family, communication problems with coaches and fellow athletes, dealing with the media, and dealing with injuries.

In summary, coaches and athletes would find these topics useful in PST programs:

- Arousal regulation
- Imagery (mental preparation)
- Confidence building
- Increasing motivation and commitment (goal setting)
- Attention or concentration skills (self-talk, mental plans)

The specific topics that you might choose for your PST program will depend on the particular athletes, their orientations and experience, and other personal factors that they bring to the competitive situation.

PST Effectiveness

To learn how effective PST programs can be in improving sport performance requires the accumulation of well-controlled, outcome-based intervention studies conducted in competitive environments. These kinds of studies are costly and time-consuming, and they depend on the willingness of coaches and athletes to participate and the researcher's ability to adequately control the environment.

Greenspan and Feltz (1989) reviewed 23 published studies of the effectiveness of various psychological interventions (e.g., stress inoculation, imagery, relaxation, reinforcement, systematic desensitization) in competitive settings including skiing, boxing, golf, karate, tennis, figure skating, volleyball, gymnastics, and basketball. They concluded that, in general, educationally based psychological interventions effectively improve competitive per-

Psychological skills training that is educationally based enhances sport performance.

formance in collegiate and adult athletes. As a follow-up to Greenspan and Feltz, Weinberg and Comar (1994) examined 45 studies employing psychological interventions in competitive sport settings. Positive performance effects were apparent in 38 (85%) of the studies, although causality could only be inferred in 20 of them. It's interesting that a greater percentage of the more recent studies found positive effects of psychological interventions; this is likely due to the more in-depth, multimodal approach taken in recent years, which combines different types of psychological skills (e.g., imagery, relaxation, self-talk, goal setting) into a packaged approach. Applied sport psychologists have begun to understand that to be effective a psychological intervention must be carried out in an individualized, systematic manner over time, often using a variety of psychological techniques to form an integrated program. Despite these initial, encouraging reports, we still need additional controlled studies on elite athletes, young sport participants, and recreational athletes to draw more definitive conclusions.

Three Phases of PST Programs

Although PST programs take many forms to match participants' individual needs, they generally follow a set structure with three distinct phases: education, acquisition, and practice. We'll now discuss what each of these phases involves.

Education Phase

Because many sport participants are unfamiliar with how mental skills can enhance performance, the first phase of any PST program is educational. In the education phase participants quickly recognize how important it is to acquire PST and how the skills affect performance. This is usually easy to accomplish: Simply ask participants how important they think the mental side of sport performance is. Most will say that it is very important. Then ask, "How often do you practice developing mental skills compared with practicing physical skills?" Usually the answer is "Hardly ever." Next explain how psychological skills can be learned, just like physical skills.

■ MORE INFORMATION ■

Mental Skills Training: From Sport to Business and Life

Many corporations have started to bring in successful coaches and athletes to talk to their employees about becoming more mentally tough and staying motivated. For example, coaches and athletes such as Rick Pitino, Lou Holtz, Pat Riley, Pat Head-Summit, Dan Jansen, and Ken Griffey, Jr. have been hired as motivational speakers in the corporate sector. Most speakers bring in their own particular philosophy, which usually has a catchy acronym. For example, Pat Riley uses the acronym TEAM (*to*getherness, *e*steem, *a*ttitude, and *m*ental toughness). The implicit assumption is that these qualities would be appropriately transferable from the athletic field to the corporate boardroom.

On a more empirical level, some sport psychologists have argued that the mental skills learned on the athletic field are really life skills, which transferred usually to enhance one's everyday life. For example, Danish, Nelson, and Owens (1996) have developed a program they call Sports United to Promote Education and Recreation (SUPER). This is a sports-based

life-skills intervention designed to teach sport and life skills to adolescents. Participants are taught a variety of skills to improve their athletic performance, some physical and some mental. They are then asked to recognize situations both in and out of sports requiring these skills and to apply them in sport and nonsport settings. Examples of skills learned in sport that could transfer to other aspects of life include goal setting, communicating, handling both success and failure, performing under pressure, working with a team, reacting to feedback, and meeting deadlines and challenges. You'll find more detail about the development of life skills in chapter 22.

The education phase may last as little as an hour or as long as several hours over the course of a few days. The gist of what you should explain is the importance of developing psychological skills. For example, in teaching the skill of regulating arousal states, you would explain the causes of anxiety and the relation of arousal and performance. You would tell athletes to learn to find their own optimal level of arousal. Some arousal is desirable, but skilled athletes have learned how to turn this tension or anxiety into positive energy, rather than debilitating tension that can deter performance. Learning to control arousal states is critical: Give players you work with examples of well-known athletes in the particular sport to reinforce the importance of developing mental skills.

Acquisition Phase

The acquisition phase focuses on strategies and techniques for learning the different psychological skills. Both formal and informal meetings are devoted to the learning of these skills. For example, when developing arousal-regulation skills, formal meetings might focus on positive coping statements to replace negative self-statements that surface under stressful competitive conditions. You would follow these formal sessions with individual sessions to teach athletes how to use positive coping in actual competitive settings. Here you would tailor specific strategies to an athlete's unique needs and abilities (Seabourne, Weinberg, Jackson, & Suinn, 1985). For example, anxiety reduction strategies should be

> *Psychological skills should be learned–and practiced. Expect improvement as you develop these skills and refine them over time.*

matched to the specific problem the individual is experiencing. One athlete might worry too much about failure (cognitive anxiety): For her, a cognitively based strategy to change thought patterns might be most appropriate (Meichenbaum, 1977). Another athlete might suffer from increased muscle tension (somatic anxiety): For him, a physically based relaxation technique, such as progressive relaxation (Jacobson, 1938), could be the best choice.

Practice Phase

The practice phase has three primary objectives: (a) to automate skills through overlearning; (b) to teach people to systematically integrate psychological skills into their performance situations; and (c) to simulate skills you will want to apply in actual competition.

To develop skills in arousal regulation, for example, an athlete would begin the practice phase after becoming proficient in relaxation and cognitive coping skills. You could guide the athlete through an imagined competitive situation requiring relaxation and coping skills. During the practice phase, a performer might progress from guided imagery practice to self-directed imagery to using imagery in a practice session, as if it were a real competition. Finally, the athlete would incorporate arousal-control strategies into preparing for and participating in actual competitions.

During the practice phase it is helpful to keep a logbook in which the athlete records the frequency and perceived effectiveness of the arousal-control strategies used in practice and competition. A log helps to systematically chart progress and provide feedback for areas of improvement. For example, after every practice athletes record how tense they felt, the relaxation procedure used, and if their relaxation techniques helped.

Who Should Conduct PST Programs?

Ideally, a PST program should be planned, implemented, and supervised by a qualified sport psychology consultant. However, unless you are at the high-

> *Tailor training programs to meet individual needs. You can provide general information to the group or team, but be specific when developing an individual's PST program.*

est level of competition, it is often not feasible to have a consultant administer the program. Usually a sport psychology consultant sets up the program and then either monitors it periodically or trains the coaching staff to implement it.

The selection of a qualified sport psychology consultant is critical. In 1991 the Association for the Advancement of Applied Sport Psychology (AAASP) adopted certification criteria for people in applied sport psychology. Basically, certification requires a person to have extensive backgrounds in both the sport and psychological sciences and some practical, supervised experience in implementing PST with athletes and teams. AAASP certification ensures a certain experience, background, and competence in applied sport psychology. In fact, the U.S. Olympic Committee now requires sport psychologists to have AAASP certification to practice applied sport psychology with their Olympic athletes. However, it is important to also consider the specific fit between the skills, abilities, and orientations of the sport psychology consultant *and* the needs and goals of the sport coaches and athletes.

Coaches, of course, see athletes on a daily basis, whereas a sport psychologist does not. Thus coaches are in a position to administer psychological interventions over the course of a season. In working with the minor league player development program for the Houston Astros, Smith (a sport psychologist) worked with Johnson (a coach) in developing an innovative consultation model that we present in the box on p. 232 (Smith & Johnson, 1990). However, the dual role of a coach–sport psychologist can present an ethical dilemma. Specifically, an athlete might have difficulty revealing very personal information that the sport psychologist–coach might perceive negatively (i.e., the coach is in a position to determine the playing time of the athlete). Therefore, it is recommended that the coaching and sport psychologist roles be separated whenever possible. On the other hand, all coaches, teachers, and exercise leaders should be using psychological skills and strategies on a regular basis even though they should not act in the role of a sport psychologist.

When to Implement a PST Program

It is best to initiate a PST program during the off-season or preseason when there is more time to learn new skills and athletes are not so pressured with winning. Some athletes report that it can take several months to a year to fully understand new psychological skills and integrate them into actual competitions. Mental training is an ongoing process that needs to be integrated with physical practice over time.

Many coaches and athletes want to start a PST program in the middle of the season, usually because of some precipitating situation, such as a batter in a hitting slump. They become desperate to find a solution, but mental training in such a situation is rarely effective. A high jumper wouldn't change jumping technique right before a big meet; she would want extensive practice over several weeks or months. Similarly, athletes cannot expect to learn new psychological skills overnight.

The time needed for practicing mental skills will vary according to what is being practiced and how well it is to be learned. If a new psychological skill is being learned, special 10- to 15-minute training sessions 3 to 5 days a week may be necessary. The first or last 10 to 15 minutes of practice is often a good time for training. (Session content will determine whether it is better held at the beginning or end of practice.) As athletes become more proficient, they may be able to integrate the mental training more with physical training and may need fewer special

training sessions. Once a skill has been effectively integrated into physical practice, it should be tried during simulated competition before being used during actual competition. Homework assignments can also be given, but unless the athletes are self-directed, it is better to supervise most mental training practice.

If a sport psychology consultant (who is not typically present on a daily basis) implements the training, some scheduling adjustments may be necessary. Under such circumstances, fewer and longer mental training sessions are usually held. Sport psychology consultants typically start with some group sessions to explain general principles and their philosophy. They then follow up by meeting athletes individually (Botterill, 1990; Halliwell, 1990). It is critical that athletes be assigned training exercises to practice between meetings with the sport psychology consultant. And the coach can help assure compliance and feedback by conducting the training exercises—or at least providing time for athletes to practice.

Ideally, PST continues as long as athletes participate in their sport. Tiger Woods, Jackie Joyner-Kersee, Wayne Gretzky, Martina Hingis, Greg Louganis, Tara Lipinski—all highly skilled and physically talented athletes—have all been known for continually integrating the mental aspects of their sports into physical practice.

CLOSE-UP

Smith and Johnson: An Example of Service Delivery

A sport psychology consultant can train one or more qualified individuals within a sport organization to provide psychological services to athletes or coaches. The consultant then oversees the program, providing ongoing supervision of the actual trainers.

Smith (a sport psychology consultant) trained Johnson (a coach with a master's degree in psychology who works in the minor league organization of the Houston Astros). In an intensive 6-week training program before spring training, Johnson received extensive reading materials on sport psychology and met with Smith for several days about using psychological interventions in sport. Smith also accompanied Johnson to spring training for 10 days of hands-on training plus a series of orientation workshops for staff and players. Weekly and sometimes daily telephone supervision continued throughout the remainder of spring training and the regular season, along with two additional 4-day blocks of personal contact. Smith helped oversee the program, but Johnson implemented the day-to-day development of psychological skills.

> *The learning of psychological skills should progress from practices and simulations to actual competitions.*
>
> ---
>
> *Mental training should continue throughout an athlete's sport participation.*

Although PST is an ongoing process, an athlete's first exposure to it in a formal program should last 3 to 6 months. Learning, practicing, and integrating new mental skills requires this much time. The specific sport, time available, existing mental skills, and commitment of the participants also are factors in determining how much time to allot to the formal program.

Designing and Implementing a PST Program

You have learned why PST is important, who should conduct the program, when to implement it during the season, and how much time to spend on it. We'll now outline some key aspects of developing and implementing PST programs.

Discussing Your Approach

It is important to spell out to participants exactly what kind of PST services can be provided. You should explain the distinction between educational and clinical sport psychology consultants. Psychological skills training is an educational approach to mental training. If more serious mental problems are encountered (e.g., substance abuse, eating disorders), explain that the sport psychology consultant will make a referral to a qualified therapist or counseling center.

Emphasizing the educational approach also helps dispel the idea that seeing a sport psychology consultant means something must be "wrong" with a person. Younger athletes especially can be sensitive to the idea that they "have to see a psychologist." You can explain that most people applaud the extra effort of an athlete who stays after practice to work with the coach on a particular move or to improve technique. Similarly, an athlete recognizing the need to work on concentration skills should also be applauded.

■ MORE INFORMATION ■

Characteristics of Effective and Ineffective Sport Psychology Consultants

By interviewing athletes, researchers (Gould, Murphy, Tammen, 1991; Orlick & Partington, 1987) have found consistent characteristics of effective and ineffective sport psychology consultants.

Effective Consultants

- were accessible and could establish rapport with athletes,
- were flexible and knowledgeable enough to meet the needs of individual athletes,
- were likable and had something very concrete or practical to offer,
- conducted several follow-up sessions with athletes throughout the season, and
- were trustworthy and fit in with the team.

Ineffective Consultants

- had poor interpersonal skills,
- lacked sensitivity to the needs of individual athletes,
- lacked specific psychology knowledge to apply to the sport setting,
- demonstrated inappropriate application of consulting skills at competitions, and
- relied on a "canned" approach when implementing psychological skills.

■ APPLICATION ■

Performance Profiling: Individualizing Psychological Interventions

The technique of performance profiling has been recently developed to both identify important PST objectives and help maximize the motivation of athletes to implement and adhere to a psychological skills training program (Butler & Hardy, 1992; Jones, 1993). Areas of change (e.g., improving concentration and coping with pressure) are identified by the athlete, so this approach provides a degree of self-determination not always evident in some other approaches to psychological skills training. For example, a female volleyball player might be asked to identify the characteristics or qualities of elite female volleyball players. The volleyball player would list all the qualities on a piece of paper (this could also be done with teams asking athletes to generate qualities of elite athletes through brainstorming in small groups). When the volleyball player stopped writing, a coach or sport psychologist might then assist the player in identifying other characteristics by mentioning qualities noted by other elite performers who had employed this technique in the past. The player would then rate herself on all the qualities she identified, and her responses would be translated into a "Performance Profile" (see Figure 11.2), providing a visual representation of the player's strengths and potential areas of improvement.

Figure 11.2 *A performance profile. Darkened sections indicate the degree to which an athlete feels he or she has the mental skills of top performers in the sport.*
Adapted from Butler and Hardy, 1992.

If you asked participants to name the mental skills they would like to develop, they might list such diverse topics as positive mental attitude, mental toughness, aggressiveness, self-motivation, character, leadership, self-confidence, anxiety management, concentration, competitiveness, and communication skills. It isn't possible to develop all these skills, nor does each athlete need to. What is important is to assess each person's specific strengths and weaknesses in psychological skills so that programs can be individualized.

Assessing Athletes' Mental Skills

In first evaluating athletes' psychological strengths and weaknesses, bear in mind that not only psychological factors influence performance. A baseball player, for example, may attribute his slump to being overly anxious when in reality his problem is biomechanical, concerning a "hitch in his swing." Thus, input from coaches, biomechanists, physiologists, and teachers is often useful. Two clues that athletes might benefit from mental training are that they perform better in practice than in competition or perform more poorly in important competitions than in unimportant ones.

An oral interview and written psychological inventories can provide useful subjective and objective information. Taylor (1995) summarizes the strengths and limitations of both subjective and objective assessments in evaluating athletes mental skills (see Table 11.2). The exact format and integration of both objective and subjective assessments depend on the expertise of the sport psychologist as well as on the rapport and trust between athlete and the sport psychologist. However, in general, we recommend the semistructured interview, which includes general questions with opportunities to use the athlete's responses to form follow-up questions (Orlick, 1990). The interview is a good time to determine the areas in which the athlete needs help and to start building the trust critical to any therapeutic relationship (see the Sample Interview Items).

You should also try some psychological inventories to assess various skills. These are some of the ones most popular with sport psychology consultants:

- Test of Attentional and Interpersonal Style (Nideffer, 1976)
- Sport Anxiety Scale (Smith, Smoll, & Schutz, 1990)
- Psychological Skills Inventory for Sport (Mahoney, Gabriel, & Perkins, 1987)

- Trait-State Confidence Inventory (Vealey, 1986)

Some sport and situation-specific inventories have also been developed, such as the Baseball Test of Attentional and Interpersonal Style (Albrecht & Feltz, 1987), the Officials Stress Test (Goldsmith & Williams, 1992), and the Gymnastics Efficacy Measure (McAuley, 1985). In addition to evaluating the athlete's mental skills, you should consider the unique physical, technical, and logistical demands of the sport itself in order to maximize the effectiveness of the psychological intervention (Taylor, 1995). For example, sports (e.g., the 100-meter dash) that involve explosiveness and anaerobic output will differ greatly from those (e.g., marathon running) that require endurance and aerobic output. Furthermore, sports (e.g., archery) that rely on fine motor skills would differ from ones (e.g., power lifting) involving gross motor skills. Sports also differ in the amount of continuous play; for example, golf has many long breaks between shots whereas soccer is continuous in action except at half-time.

Once the interview and psychological inventories have been completed, the evaluator should give written feedback to each athlete to highlight his or her specific psychological strengths and weaknesses in sport performance. This assessment should conclude with a section identifying the type of psychological skills appropriate for each athlete. It is important to provide people with the opportunity to react to the consultants' evaluations and to agree on how to proceed. If a sport psychology consultant works with an entire team, it is essential that the coach, who is more likely to know the team's mental strengths and weaknesses, is also involved in the assessment.

Beware of anyone who presents a "canned" mental training program that does not provide individual assessment and ignores the specific needs of athletes.

Sample Interview Items

Tell me about your involvement in your sport, summarizing what you consider important events, both positive and negative. (This is a good starting point because it lets athletes talk about themselves and become comfortable.)

Describe in detail the thoughts and feelings surrounding your best and worst performances. What do you believe is your greatest psychological strength? Your biggest weakness?

Try to describe any psychological problems you are having now. What is your relationship with your coach? Do you feel comfortable talking to your coach?

Table 11.2
Assessing Athletes' Needs

Types	Strengths	Limitations
Subjective assessment Interviewing (client)	Trust and rapport Self-perceptions, beliefs, and attitudes In-depth knowledge about sport participation & life issues	Self-presentational bias Lack of self-awareness Poor insight
Interviewing (others)	New perspective of athlete Consensus	Subjectivity bias Alternative agenda
Observation	Unambiguous behavioral data Comparison of behavioral with expressed perceptions Patterns of behavior Relationship between practice and competitive performance Cross-situational consistency	Observer bias Representativeness of observed behaviors Observational time limitations
Objective assessment Sport-specific General Trait vs. state	Impartial evaluation Confirmation of subjective assessment Sport-specificity Uncover new issues Time-efficient Ease of administration	Resistance by athlete Self-presentational bias Non–sport-specific inventories Nondiagnostic inventories Lack of relationship with performance Traits only measured Restricted test usage

Adapted from Taylor, 1995.

It takes more time and effort to individualize the programs, but the more attention paid to individual needs, the more likely the program will succeed. A sample needs assessment is provided in the case study on p. 237.

Determining Which Psychological Skills to Include

After the assessment comes the decision about which psychological skills to emphasize during the program. This decision should be based on the coaches' and athletes' answers to these questions:

- How many weeks of practice or preseason are available?
- How much practice time will be devoted weekly to PST?
- How interested are the athletes in receiving PST?
- Will there still be time to practice mental skills after the competitive season begins?

When there isn't sufficient time and commitment for a comprehensive training program, rather than superficially working on all the needed skills, it is better to prioritize objectives and emphasize a few skills initially.

The first thing to do is differentiate between psychological skills and psychological methods (Vealey, 1988). Skills are qualities to be obtained; methods are procedures or techniques employed to develop these skills. The basic PST methods include four traditional techniques for developing skills, including arousal regulation (see chapter 12), imagery (see chapter 13), goal setting (see chapter 15), and attention or concentration (see chapter 16).

Vealey emphasizes that productive physical practice and understanding the physical and mental processes influencing performance will foster psychological skills. Using these methods, she proposes several skills that a well-rounded PST program can develop (see Table 11.3). These skills reflect areas of personal growth and performance enhancement. Foundation skills are the most basic personal skills, such as self-esteem; they lay the foundation for skills that are related to performance (such as regulating arousal and

■ CASE STUDY ■

Needs Assessment for a Soccer Player

The following is an actual case study conducted by one of the authors and represents an actual needs assessment. The assessment includes both an in-depth interview and psychological sport-specific questionnaire. This assessment would be shared with the athlete prior to the start of the actual psychological skills training program.

Motivation

Your motivation and drive to do well are extremely high. You are a self-starter and are motivated to improve yourself. You hang in there even when the going gets tough, and you can be counted on to give 100% effort. This area is definitely one of your key strengths.

- You are concerned with developing and maintaining self-discipline.
- You stick to tasks (even difficult ones) until they're completed.
- Whenever you reach a goal, you set a higher one.
- You persist even in the face of failure.
- You have a strong desire to achieve.
- You exhibit commitment to the tasks you undertake. The only potential problem I see is that your motivation and drive for success might make you push yourself harder than you should. This could result in increased anxiety and might actually undermine your performance.

Anxiety

You show some strengths and some potential areas for improvement in this area. Unlike many athletes, you seem more relaxed during games than during practice. It is possible that you feel you must play well in practice to increase the possibility of playing time during the game. Perhaps you get so involved in the game that you don't have time to think and, therefore, you just react. Given your present position as a midfielder, which emphasizes speed and quickness, you can probably function well on instinct since ball handling is at a minimum. Here are specific situations that cause you some anxiety:

- You worry about performing up to your level of ability.
- You worry about making mistakes.
- You worry about not performing well.

These worries may be tied to the pressure you put on yourself because you tend to be a perfectionist. Being a perfectionist is a double-edged sword—it can push you toward higher achievement but at the same time cause stress—because it is impossible to be perfect. Over time, this could take the fun out of the game for you.

Concentration

You appear able to focus well while you're playing and to block out distractions, such as crowd noises. Your concentration sometimes is compromised from distractions that you create. That is, the inability to forget mistakes and other negative thoughts interferes with your concentration. This, in turn, takes away from the fluid, automatic, and relaxed fashion in which you would like to be performing. Sometimes, too much thinking can be counterproductive in a fast-moving sport such as soccer (especially indoor soccer).

continued

Needs Assessment for a Soccer Player
(continued)

Confidence

This is probably the area that you will want to work on the most. Although anxiety, concentration, and confidence are all interrelated, I believe that in your case, confidence controls the other two. One overriding concern is the adjustment from outdoor to indoor soccer. It's likely that you now have to think about some of the things you previously did by instinct, and this can decrease confidence. Second, with minimum playing time, it's hard to develop your confidence and get into the flow of the game. These probably converge in causing you not to be confident on the ball, which used to be one of your strengths. Your confidence should improve as you feel more secure and familiar with the indoor game, but there are ways to speed up the process. Some specific areas where your confidence is lacking include the following:

- Your ability to make critical decisions during competition
- Your ability to perform under pressure
- Your ability to execute the skills necessary to be successful

And here are some of the areas in which your confidence is high:

- Your ability to relate successfully to teammates and coaches
- Your physical conditioning
- Your ability to improve your skills
- Your ability to control your emotions
- Your ability to put forth the effort to succeed

Summary

Strengths

- Strong desire to succeed
- Confidence in your ability to succeed
- Ability to relax during competitions
- Confidence in your ability to relate well to teammates and coaches
- Your physical conditioning

Areas for improvement

- Forgetting about mistakes
- Maintaining confidence despite early errors
- Remaining relaxed during practice
- Worrying about performing up to your ability
- Perfectionistic attitude

Recommendations

- Learn thought stopping
- Change negative to positive self-talk
- Focus on having fun while competing hard
- Develop cue words to help concentration
- Learn relaxation techniques
- Think confidently

Table 11.3

Psychological Skills Developed in PST Programs

Foundation skills	Performance skills	Facilitative skills
Volition	Optimal physical arousal	Interpersonal skills
Self-awareness	Optimal mental arousal	Lifestyle management
Self-esteem	Optimal attention	
Self-confidence		

Adapted from Vealey, 1988.

focusing attention). Finally, facilitative skills focus on growth and change to help people gain control of their lives, both inside and outside sport (Vealey, 1988).

Whatever methods and skills are included in the PST program, they will be more effective if psychological objectives that are appropriate to the individual accompany them (Butler & Hardy, 1992; Seabourne et al., 1985). The objectives should be easily understood and defined in measurable terms (see Table 11.4 for an example). Such definitions clarify the objective and expected outcomes. They give a clear foundation for planning how to accomplish the objectives and assessing how effective the strategies were in achieving objectives.

Designing a Schedule

Needs have been assessed, psychological-skill objectives identified, and specific strategies delineated to achieve the objectives. Now comes the training schedule. Maybe 1 or 2 days a week before or after practice could serve as a formal meeting time for educating participants on imagery, anxiety management, attentional control, goal setting, and other psychological skills. In general, it is better to hold frequent, short meetings rather than less frequent, long meetings.

Informal meetings allow the sport psychology consultant to impart information and build rapport. Many athletes who hesitate to sign up for a formal meeting are willing instead to talk informally. Informal meetings can occur during social events, on bus or plane rides to competitions, at the hotel, at meals, or any other time and place. These informal meetings complement the structured meetings and individualize content to each athlete.

Formal and informal meetings with coaches and athletes are opportunities for the PST consultant to enhance communication and build rapport.

A critical point in setting up a training schedule is determining when to start and how long the training should last. As we noted earlier, it is best to develop psychological skills just before the season begins or during the off-season when coaches and athletes can focus on developing skills, instead of on practice, games, travel, and winning. But the key is to systematically schedule PST into the daily practice regimen.

Evaluating the Program

Evaluating psychological skills development and change is an important but often overlooked element of PST programs. There are ethical obligations to evaluate the effectiveness of the program (Smith, 1989), but practical considerations as well:

■ An evaluation provides feedback for gauging the program's effectiveness and for then modifying the program as necessary.

■ An evaluation allows participants to suggest changes in how the program is conducted.

■ An evaluation is the only way to objectively judge if the program has achieved its goals.

Ideally, the evaluation should include interviews and written rating scales to supply both qualitative and quantitative feedback. Also useful to coaches and athletes is objective performance data. For example, if one of the program goals was to help a basketball player relax while shooting free throws under pressure, then free-throw percentage in critical situations (e.g., last 5 minutes of a game when there is less than a 5-point difference in the score) would be a good statistic for evaluation. The following questions are useful for evaluating the effectiveness of a PST program:

■ What techniques appeared to work best?

■ Was enough time allotted to practice the psychological skills?

Table 11.4

A Sample of Psychological Skills, Objectives, and Outcomes

Objective 1: Positive mental attitude	Objective 2: Coping with mistakes and failures	Objective 3: Handling the high-stress situation
Don't make negative statements at games or practices.	Accept that mistakes and failures are necessary to the learning process.	Learn to interpret the situation as a challenge, not a threat.
Change "I can't" statements to "I can" statements.	Don't make excuses. Accept responsibility in order to help turn failures into successes.	Recognize too much tension. Achieve appropriate differential relaxation.
Always give 100%.	Stay positive even after a mistake.	Keep thoughts positive and focused on the task.
Don't talk while coaches talk.	Support teammates—even when they are making mistakes.	Imagine goal of performing well under high-stress situations.
Hustle during all plays and drills.	Keep focused on the task rather than dwelling on mistakes.	Focus on appropriate cues.

Adapted from Gould, 1983.

- How useful were the team sessions?
- How useful were the individual sessions?
- Was the consultant available?
- Was the consultant knowledgeable, informative, and easy to talk with?
- Should anything be added to or deleted from the program?
- What were the major strengths and weaknesses of the program?

Partington and Orlick (1987a; 1987b) developed a sample sport psychology evaluation form and data on what makes a consultant effective from both the coaches' and athletes' points of view. Sport psychologists are continually learning, and their programs will continue to change and evolve in the future.

Common Problems in Implementing PST Programs

By attending to some common problems athletes, coaches, and consultants have encountered in implementing PST programs, you can avoid hampering your program's effectiveness. We've already touched on some of these problems in various contexts. We'll now provide some specific examples.

Lack of Conviction

Many people resist change, no matter what the change happens to be. Thus, consultants often have to convince coaches and athletes that developing psychological skills will facilitate individual and team success. One good "selling point" is the example of highly visible athletes known for their psychological skills. Diver Greg Louganis, for instance, exemplified exceptional psychological skills at the 1988 Olympics after he had hit his head on the board during a dive. He sustained an injury that required sutures, yet Louganis was able to regain his composure, successfully execute his next dive, and win a gold medal. He had clearly acquired psychological skills of concentration and anxiety management.

Lack of Time

Coaches frequently claim there isn't enough time in their situation to practice mental skills. However, time can usually be found if mental skills training is made a priority. This is another reason to first convince coaches and athletes of the benefits of PST. It is important to get a commitment to set specific times during or after practice to devote to PST. If you value acquiring mental skills, it makes sense to set time aside to practice them.

The Sport Psychology Consultant Evaluation Form

Name _____ Consultant's name _____

Please rate your sport psychology consultant on each of the following characteristics by using a number from 0 to 10 as shown on the scale below.

Not at all										Yes, definitely
0	1	2	3	4	5	6	7	8	9	10

Ratings

1. *Consultant characteristics:*

    Had useful knowledge about mental training that seemed to apply directly to my sport. _____

    Seemed willing to provide an individual mental-training program based on my input and needs. _____

    Seemed open, flexible, and ready to cooperate with me. _____

    Had a positive, constructive attitude. _____

    Proved to be trustworthy. _____

    Was easy for me to relate to (i.e., I felt comfortable and that he or she understood me). _____

    Provided clear, practical, concrete strategies. _____

2. How effective was this consultant? _____

	Hindered										Helped
Effect on you:	−5	−4	−3	−2	−1	0	+1	+2	+3	+4	+5
Effect on the team:	−5	−4	−3	−2	−1	0	+1	+2	+3	+4	+5

3. Do you have any recommendations to improve the sport psychology consultation service? Please write suggestions on the back of this sheet.

Adapted from Partington and Orlick, 1987.

Lack of Sport Knowledge

Coaches sometimes point out that a consultant lacks sport-specific knowledge. Having some playing or coaching experience indeed helps the consultant understand the specific problems athletes experience and talk about them in the sport's jargon. This helps build the trust and rapport essential for an effective consultant-athlete relationship. However, although it is good to have sport-specific experience, it is not absolutely essential as long as consultants acquaint themselves with the nature of the sport and its competitive environment. They can view videotapes, watch practices, and attend competitions to learn about the sport.

Lack of Follow-Up

Some coaches and consultants implement a PST program enthusiastically but provide little follow-up once the program is under way. Psychological skills, like any skills, must be practiced to be learned well enough to use under pressure. Following up throughout the season—by making time for PST and meeting with athletes to discuss their progress—is important.

A sport psychology consultant should be aware of these potential problems and be ready to deal with them if necessary. Many consultants make mistakes in their first years of consulting because they aren't aware of the nuances of setting up and implementing PST programs. Homework and planning should be prerequisites for any sport psychology consultant to work with athletes and teams. However, good preparation, careful thought, and a sense of commitment can lead to a rewarding experience. After all, helping individuals reach their potential both inside and outside the world of sport is what it's all about.

■ MORE INFORMATION ■

PST Is Not Just for Enhancing the Performance of Athletes

In this chapter, primary attention has been focused on PST for athletes and performance enhancement. Although this emphasis reflects the general body of sport psychological PST knowledge, physical educators, athletic trainers, and fitness instructors should also use a PST approach with their students or clients. Some examples of their using PST techniques and principles include the following:

- A physical educator might use relaxation training to teach a hyperactive child to learn to calm down.
- A trainer might use mental imagery to help rebuild confidence in an athlete rehabilitating from a knee injury.
- A therapist might use self-monitoring and thought stopping to help a person quit smoking.
- A physical therapist might use goal setting to help maintain motivation for an individual out with a prolonged, serious injury.
- A fitness instructor might use positive self-statements to enhance self-esteem in an overweight client.

In any of these settings, PST would be appropriate. The important thing is that these are merely psychological skills that can be learned, practiced, and applied in a wide variety of settings.

SUMMARY

1 *Define psychological skills training.*

Psychological skills training refers to learning to systematically and consistently practice mental or psychological skills. Coaches and athletes all know that physical skills need to be regularly practiced and refined through literally thousands and thousands of repetitions. Similar to physical skills, psychological skills, such as maintaining and focusing concentration, regulating arousal levels, enhancing confidence, and maintaining motivation, also need systematic practice.

2 *Describe the myths surrounding psychological skills training.*

A number of myths (not grounded in fact or empirical data) have developed regarding the use of psychological skills training. Some of these myths are that (a) PST is only for "problem" athletes, (b) PST is only for elite athletes, (c) PST provides "quick fix" solutions to complex problems, and (d) PST is only hocus-pocus and does not really work.

3 *Identify the knowledge base for psychological skills training.*

The knowledge base for PST has basically developed from two sources: research studies and practical experience. Original research studies have been conducted with athletes demonstrating superior psychological skills (as compared with less successfully performing athletes). The second source relates to coaches and athletes whose sport experience has convinced them of the importance of psychological skills in maximizing performance and that they should be integrated in athletes' daily training regimens.

4 *Discuss three phases of psychological skills training programs.*

Although PST programs take many forms to fit participant needs, they generally follow a set structure with three distinct phases. These phases are education (learning the importance of PST), acquisition (learning the mental skills), and practice (using the mental skills during training—before using them in competition).

5 *Develop a psychological skills training program.*

A first step is psychological needs assessment to determine the specific components of a PST program. The program should be tailored to an individual's specific personality, situation, and needs. The initial PST program should probably last 3 to 6 months and start during the preseason or off-season. There are advantages to having a sport psychology consultant implement a PST program, but it's also possible for a coach or for other trained personnel to conduct it.

6 *Understand the problems of implementing a psychological skills training program.*

There are a number of potential problems to be aware of when implementing PST programs. These include an athlete's lack of conviction, perceived lack of time to fit it in the training program, lack of sport-specific knowledge (when program is administered by a sport psychology consultant), and lack of follow-up and evaluation.

KEY TERMS

psychological skills training (PST)
education phase
acquisition phase

practice phase
skills
methods

REVIEW QUESTIONS

1. Discuss three reasons why PST training is important.
2. Discuss three reasons why coaches and athletes often neglect PST and why the myths concerning PST training are false.
3. Provide specific examples of how PST derives its knowledge base from research with elite athletes and athlete-coach experiences.
4. Describe the three phases of PST training: education, acquisition, and practice.
5. What empirical evidence is there that PST enhances sport performance?
6. Who should conduct PST programs? Include AAASP criteria for certification as part of your answer.
7. When is the best time to implement PST programs and why?
8. How much time should individuals spend practicing PST and why?
9. How would you assess an individual's psychological strengths and weaknesses in an interview and through written psychological inventories?
10. Describe how Vealey breaks down PST programs into psychological methods and psychological skills. Give examples of each.
11. Why is it important to evaluate PST effectiveness? What specific questions would you use to evaluate effectiveness?

CRITICAL THINKING QUESTIONS

1. You are a coach and you decide that you want to implement a PST program starting in the off-season. How will you do it? What are some of the potential pitfalls you should be aware of and what would you do to overcome them?

2. You want to start a PST program with your team and you decide to hire a sport psychologist to help administer the program. Discuss how you, the coach, would interact with the sport psychologist. What would be your role in the PST program? Discuss the limitations and advantages of this approach.

© Human Kinetics

Arousal Regulation

After reading this chapter you should be able to

1 understand how to increase self-awareness of arousal states;

2 use somatic, cognitive, and multimodal anxiety-reduction techniques;

3 identify coping strategies to deal with competitive stress;

4 describe on-site relaxation tips to reduce anxiety;

5 understand the matching hypothesis; and

6 identify techniques to raise arousal for competition.

We live in a world where stress has become almost part of our daily lives. Certainly the pressure to perform at high levels in competitive sport has increased in recent years with all the media attention and money available through sports. In essence, our society values winning and success, and coaches and athletes feel pressure to be successful. People who don't cope effectively with the pressure of competitive sport, however, may experience not only decreases in performance but also mental distress and even physical illness. Continued pressure sometimes causes burnout in sport and exercise (see chapter 21), and it can lead to ulcers, migraine headaches, and hypertension.

Depending on the person and the situation, however, there are various ways of coping with the pressure of competitive sports. The following quotes show how a few athletes have approached the pressure of competition.

> *The thing that always worked best for me whenever I felt I was getting too tense to play good tennis was to simply remind myself that the worst thing—the very worst thing that could happen to me—was that I'd lose a bloody tennis match. That's all!*
>
> **Rod Laver, former top professional tennis player**

> *I love the pressure. I just look forward to it.*
>
> **Daly Thompson, Olympic decathlon gold medalist**

> *The relaxation technique that I have adopted over the past year is a type of mantra. I count down from three to zero, and when I get to zero I can produce a calmer approach. I use this if I have to stand there and wait around for the judges and I feel a rush of nervousness that's too much.*
>
> **James May, Commonwealth Games gymnastics gold medalist**

Not only do athletes respond differently to pressure, the type of sport or task they perform also becomes a critical factor in how they react. For example, a golfer preparing to knock in a 20-foot putt would control arousal differently than would a wrestler taking the mat. Similarly, one specific relaxation procedure might work better for controlling cognitive anxiety, whereas another might be more effective for coping with somatic anxiety. The relation between arousal and performance can be complicated (see chapter 4), and athletes in competitive sport need to learn to control their arousal. They should be able to increase it—to psych up—when they're feeling lethargic and decrease it when the pressure to win

causes them anxiety and nervousness. The key is for individuals to find their optimal levels of arousal—to psych up without psyching out and to relax without losing intensity and focus.

In this chapter we will discuss in detail a variety of arousal-regulation techniques that should help individuals in sport and exercise settings reach their optimal levels of arousal. The first step in this process is to learn how to recognize or become aware of anxiety and arousal states.

Self-Awareness of Arousal

The first step toward controlling arousal levels is to be more aware of them during practices and competitions. This typically involves self-monitoring and recognizing how emotional states affect performance. As an athlete you can probably identify certain feelings associated with top performances and other feelings associated with poor performances. To increase awareness of your arousal states, we recommend the following process.

First, think back to your best performance—some athletes refer to this special state as "playing in the zone." Try to visualize the actual competition as clearly as possible, focusing on what you felt and thought at that time. Don't rush: Take at least 5 minutes to relive the experience. Now complete the items on p. 247. Because you are reconstructing your best performance, for "played extremely well," you would circle the number 1. For the second item, if you felt moderately anxious, you might circle number 4. There are no right or wrong answers; the goal is to simply become more aware of the relation between your psychological states and performances. After completing the checklist for your best performance, repeat the process for your worst performance.

Now compare how you responded in this exercise to the two performances you brought to mind. Most people find that their thoughts and feelings are distinctly different when comparing playing well and playing poorly. This is the beginning of awareness training. If you want to better understand the rela-

> *You must increase your awareness of your psychological states before you can control your thoughts and feelings. How individuals cope with anxiety is more important than how much anxiety they experience.*

© Mary Langenfeld/Langenfeld Photos

Checklist of Performance States

Played extremely well	1	2	3	4	5	6	Played extremely poorly
Felt extremely relaxed	1	2	3	4	5	6	Felt extremely anxious
Felt extremely confident	1	2	3	4	5	6	Felt extremely unconfident
Felt in complete control	1	2	3	4	5	6	Had no control at all
Muscles were relaxed	1	2	3	4	5	6	Muscles were tense
Felt extremely energetic	1	2	3	4	5	6	Felt extremely fatigued
Self-talk was positive	1	2	3	4	5	6	Self-talk was negative
Felt extremely focused	1	2	3	4	5	6	Felt extremely unfocused
Felt effortless	1	2	3	4	5	6	Felt great effort
Had high energy	1	2	3	4	5	6	Had low energy

tion between your thoughts, feelings, and performance, monitor yourself by completing the checklist immediately after each practice or competitive session over the next few weeks. Of course, your psychological state will vary during a given session. If you feel one way during the first half of a basketball game, for example, and another way during the second half, simply complete two checklists. You are only estimating your feeling states—absolute precision is virtually impossible. If you are diligent with this procedure, however, you will quickly enhance your awareness, which is a giant step toward reaching your optimal level of arousal consistently. Remember that the most important thing is to

Anxiety-Reduction Techniques

Excess anxiety can produce inappropriate muscle tension, which in turn can diminish performance. When the muscles become too tense, your movements appear awkward, jerky, rigid, and uncoordinated. And it is all too easy to develop excess muscle tension. The common thinking is "The harder you try, the better you will perform." This reasoning is incorrect.

As a quick, practical exercise, rest your dominant forearm and hand palm down on a desktop or table. Tense all the muscles in your hand and wrist and then try to tap your index and middle fingers quickly back and forth. Do this for about 30 seconds. Now try to relax the muscles in your hands and fingers and repeat the exercise. You will probably discover that muscular tension slows your movements and makes them less coordinated, as compared with muscles that are relaxed.

Besides sometimes producing inappropriate muscle tension, excess anxiety can also produce inappropriate thoughts and cognitions. Have you ever felt really anxious before or during an important sport performance, becoming distracted and thinking negative thoughts, such as "I hope I don't blow this shot" or "I hope I don't fail in front of all these people"?

As noted in chapter 4, anxiety can affect us both physically (somatic anxiety) and mentally (cognitive anxiety).

We'll now present some relaxation procedures commonly used in sport and physical activity settings. Some of these techniques focus on reducing cognitive anxiety, some on somatic anxiety. Still others are multimodal in nature, using a variety of techniques to cope with both somatic and cognitive anxiety. It is interesting to note that virtually all these techniques were designed to help people cope with stressful events they encounter in everyday life—only recently have they been applied to sport and exercise situations.

Somatic Anxiety-Reduction Techniques

The first group of techniques work primarily to reduce physiological arousal associated with increased somatic anxiety.

Progressive Relaxation

Edmund Jacobson's progressive relaxation technique (1938) forms the cornerstone for many modern relaxation procedures. This technique involves tensing and relaxing specific muscles. Jacobson named the technique *progressive relaxation* because the tensing and relaxing progresses from one major muscle group to the next, until all muscle groups are completely relaxed. Progressive relaxation rests on a few assumptions: (a) It is possible to learn the difference between tension and relaxation; (b) tension

RESEARCH

Trying Harder Isn't Always Better

A college track coach would ask his runners to run 400 meters all out (i.e., give 110%). A few days later, the same runners were asked to run at 95% of their capacity. Interestingly enough, the runners ran faster at 95% than at 110%. Why this happened involves the effect that muscle tension can have on skilled performance. Specifically, when running at 110% runners were using all their energies and muscular capacities. However, running—like most other sport activities—is performed most effectively when some muscles are contracting while others are relaxing. Thus, by using all of their muscles, agonists and antagonists, the runners were using muscles that prevented them from running as fast as they could. Running at 95%, they expended a great deal of muscular effort but relaxed the antagonist muscles that hinder maximum performance.

Consider a baseball pitcher who is overthrowing his fast ball, that is, trying too hard to throw the ball fast. Not only does the pitch not go as fast, it is also less accurate. Trying to throw the ball as fast as he can, the pitcher uses all the muscles in his arm. However, for accuracy, as well as speed, some of the muscles in the arm (particularly the flexor muscles like the biceps) need to relax as the extensor muscles (such as the triceps) do most of the work.

and relaxation are mutually exclusive—it is not possible to be relaxed and tense at the same time; and (c) relaxation of the body through decreased muscle tension will, in turn, decrease mental tension. Jacobson's technique has been modified considerably over the years, but its purpose remains to help people learn to feel tension in their muscles and then be able to let go of this tension.

The tension-relaxation cycles develop an athlete's awareness of the difference between tension and lack of tension. Each cycle involves maximally contracting one specific muscle group and then attempting to fully relax that same muscle group, all the while focusing on the different sensations of tension and relaxation. With skill, an athlete can detect tension in a specific muscle or area of the body, like the neck, and then relax that muscle. Some people even learn to use the technique during breaks in an activity, such as a time-out. The first few sessions of progressive relaxation take an athlete up to 30 minutes. With practice, less time is necessary, the goal being the ability to relax on-site during competition.

Ost (1988) developed an applied variant of relaxation technique that he based on progressive relaxation to teach an individual to relax even within 20 to 30 seconds. The first phase of training involves a 15-minute progressive relaxation session practiced twice a day, in which muscle groups are tensed and relaxed. The individual then moves on to a release-only phase that takes 5 to 7 minutes to complete. The time is next reduced to a 2-to-3 minute version with the use of a self-instructional cue, "relax." This time is further reduced until only a few seconds are required, and then the technique is practiced in specific situations (noted as "application training" in Figure 12.1). For example, a golfer who becomes tight and anxious when faced with important putts could use this technique in between shots to prepare for these difficult putts.

Breath Control

Proper breathing is often considered key to achieving relaxation, and breath control is another physically oriented relaxation technique. Breath control, in fact, is one of the easiest, most effective ways to control anxiety and muscle tension. When you are calm, confident, and in control, your breathing is likely to be smooth, deep, and rhythmical. When you're under pressure and tense, your breathing is more likely to be short, shallow, and irregular.

Unfortunately, many athletes have not learned proper breathing. Performing under pressure they often fail to coordinate their breathing with the performance of the skill. Similarly, in athletic rehabilitation settings, rhythmic breathing is important to maximize the effectiveness of stretching and lifting movements. Research has demonstrated that breathing in and holding your breath increases muscle tension, whereas breathing out decreases muscle tension. For example, most discus throwers, shot-putters, and baseball pitchers learn to breathe out during release. Some athletes are even known as "grunters" because they exhale audibly each time they perform. As pressure builds in a competition, the natural

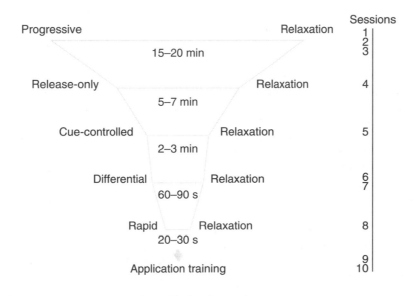

Figure 12.1 *Different components of applied relaxation.*
Reprinted from Hardy, Jones, and Gould, 1996.

249

■ APPLICATION ■

Instructions for Progressive Relaxation

In each step you'll first tense a muscle group and then relax it. Pay close attention to how it feels to be relaxed as opposed to tense. Each phase should take about 5 to 7 seconds. For each muscle group, perform each exercise twice before progressing to the next group. As you gain skill, you can omit the tension phase and focus just on relaxation. It is usually a good idea to record the following instructions on tape; you might even invest a few dollars in buying a progressive relaxation recording.

1. Find a quiet place, dim the lights, and lie down in a comfortable position with your legs uncrossed. Loosen tight clothing. Take a deep breath, let it out slowly, and relax.

2. Raise your arms, extend them in front of you, and make a tight fist with each hand. Notice the uncomfortable tension in your hands and fingers. Hold that tension for 5 seconds, then let go halfway and hold for an additional 5 seconds. Let your hands relax completely. Notice how the tension and discomfort drain from your hands, replaced by comfort and relaxation. Focus on the contrast between the tension you felt and the relaxation you now feel. Concentrate on relaxing your hands completely for 10 to 15 seconds.

3. Tense your upper arms tightly for 5 seconds and focus on the tension. Let the tension out halfway and hold for an additional 5 seconds, again focusing on the tension. Now relax your upper arms completely for 10 to 15 seconds and focus on the developing relaxation. Let your arms rest limply at your sides.

4. Curl your toes as tight as you can. After 5 seconds relax the toes halfway and hold for an additional 5 seconds. Now relax your toes completely and focus on the spreading relaxation. Continue relaxing your toes for 10 to 15 seconds.

5. Point your toes away from you and tense your feet and calves. Hold the tension hard for 5 seconds, then let it out halfway for another 5 seconds. Relax your feet and calves completely for 10 to 15 seconds.

6. Extend your legs, raising them about 6 inches off the floor, and tense your thigh muscles. Hold the tension for 5 seconds, let it out halfway and hold for another 5 seconds before relaxing your thighs completely. Concentrate on your feet, calves, and thighs for 30 seconds.

7. Tense your stomach muscles as tight as you can for 5 seconds, concentrating on the tension. Let the tension out halfway and hold for an additional 5 seconds before relaxing your stomach muscles completely. Focus on the spreading relaxation until your stomach muscles are completely relaxed.

8. To tighten your chest and shoulder muscles, press the palms of your hands together and push. Hold for 5 seconds, then let go halfway and hold for another 5 seconds. Now relax the muscles and concentrate on the relaxation until your muscles are completely loose and relaxed. Concentrate also on the muscle groups that have been previously relaxed.

9. Push your back to the floor as hard as you can and tense your back muscles. Let the tension out halfway after 5 seconds, hold the reduced tension and focus on it for another 5 seconds. Relax your back and shoulder muscles completely, focusing on the relaxation spreading over the area.

10. Keeping your torso, arms, and legs relaxed, tense your neck muscles by bringing your head forward until your chin digs into your chest. Hold for 5 seconds, release the tension halfway and hold for another 5 seconds, and then relax your neck completely. Allow your head to hang comfortably while you focus on the relaxation developing in your neck muscles.

continued

Instructions for Progressive Relaxation
(continued)

11. Clench your teeth and feel the tension in the muscles of your jaw. After 5 seconds, let the tension out halfway and hold for 5 seconds before relaxing. Let your mouth and facial muscles relax completely, with your lips slightly parted. Concentrate on totally relaxing these muscles for 10 to 15 seconds.

12. Wrinkle your forehead and scalp as tight as you can, hold for 5 seconds, and then release halfway and hold for another 5 seconds. Relax your scalp and forehead completely, focusing on the feeling of relaxation and contrasting it with the earlier tension. Concentrate for about a minute on relaxing all of the muscles of your body.

13. Cue-controlled relaxation is the final goal of progressive relaxation. Breathing can serve as the impetus and cue for effective relaxation. Take a series of short inhalations, about one per second, until your chest is filled. Hold for 5 seconds, then exhale slowly for 10 seconds while thinking to yourself the word relax or calm. Repeat the process at least five times, each time striving to deepen the state of relaxation that you're experiencing.

© Kristin Olenick/MK Productions

tendency is to hold one's breath, which increases muscle tension and interferes with the coordinated movement necessary for maximum performance. With practice, however, breathing is one physiological system that is simple to control. Learning to take a deep, slow, complete breath will usually trigger a relaxation response.

As with any skill, breath control takes practice to develop. It involves breathing from the diaphragm instead of the chest. To practice a deep, complete breath, imagine that the lungs are divided into three levels. Focus on filling the lower level of the lungs with air, first by pushing the diaphragm down and forcing the abdomen out. Then fill the middle portion of the lungs by expanding the chest cavity and raising the rib cage. Finally, fill the upper level of the lungs by raising the chest and shoulders slightly. This breath should be held for several seconds and then exhaled slowly by pulling the abdomen in and lowering the shoulders and chest. By focusing on the lowering (inhalation) and raising (exhalation) of the diaphragm, you'll experience a greater sense of stability, centeredness, and relaxation. To help enhance the importance and awareness of the exhalation phase, individuals can learn to inhale to a count of four and exhale to a count of eight. This 1:2 ratio of inhalation to exhalation helps slow breathing and deepens the relaxation by focusing on the exhalation phase (Williams & Harris, 1998).

The best time to use breath control during competition is when there is a time out or break in the action (e.g., before serving in tennis, just prior to putting a golf ball, preparing for a free throw in basketball). The slow and deliberate inhalation-exhalation sequence will help you maintain composure and control over your anxiety during particularly stressful times. By focusing on your breathing, you are less likely to be bothered by irrelevant cues or distractions, such as spectator or opponent antics. Deep breathing also helps relax shoulder and neck muscles; it allows you to feel strong, centered, and ready for action. Finally, deep breathing provides a short mental break from the pressure of competition and can renew your energy.

Biofeedback

In most relaxation procedures one of the goals is to become aware of muscular tension and reactions in other autonomic nervous systems, such as the heart or respiration rate. Biofeedback is a physically oriented technique specifically designed to teach people to control physiological or autonomic responses. It ordinarily involves an electronic monitoring device that can detect and amplify internal responses not ordinarily known to us. These electronic instruments provide visual or auditory feedback of physiological responses such as muscle activity, skin temperature, or heart rate, although most studies have used muscle activity as measured by electromyography (Zaichkowsky & Takenaka, 1993).

For example, a tennis player might feel muscle tension in her neck and shoulders before serving on important points in a match. Electrodes could be at-

© Human Kinetics

Biofeedback training can help people become more aware of their autonomic nervous system and subsequently to control their reactions.

tached to specific muscles in her neck and shoulder region, and she would be asked to relax these specific muscles. Excess tension in the muscles would then cause the biofeedback instrument to make a loud and constant clicking noise. The tennis player's goal would be to quiet the machine by attempting to relax her shoulder and neck muscles. Relaxation could be accomplished through any relaxation technique, such as visualizing a positive scene or using positive self-talk. The key point is that the lower the noise level, the more relaxed the muscles are. Such feedback attunes the player to her tension levels and whether they are decreasing or increasing.

Once the tennis player learns to recognize and reduce muscle tension in her shoulders and neck, she then needs to be able to transfer this knowledge to the tennis court. This can be done by interspersing sessions of nonfeedback (time away from the biofeedback device) within the training regimen. Gradually, the duration of these nonfeedback sessions is increased, and the tennis player depends less on the biofeedback signal while maintaining an awareness of physiological changes. With sufficient practice and experience, the tennis player can learn to identify the onset of muscle tension and control it so that her serve remains effective in clutch situations.

Research has indicated that rifle shooters can improve their performance by training themselves, using biofeedback, to fire between heartbeats (Daniels & Landers, 1981; Wilkinson, Landers, & Daniels, 1981). In addition, biofeedback has been effective for improving performance among recreation, collegiate, and professional athletes in a variety of sports (Crews, 1993; Zaichkowsky & Fuchs, 1988; 1989). Although it should be noted that not all studies of biofeedback have demonstrated enhanced performance, the technique has been shown to consistently reduce anxiety and muscle tension. Biofeedback appears to be effective in increasing awareness of tension levels, and it provides a useful mechanism for coping with precompetitive anxiety.

Cognitive Anxiety-Reduction Techniques

Some relaxation procedures focus more directly on relaxing the mind than progressive relaxation and deep breathing do. It is argued that relaxing the mind will in turn relax the body. Both physical and mental techniques can produce a relaxed state although they work through different paths. We'll now discuss some of the techniques for relaxing the mind.

Relaxation Response

Herbert Benson, a physician at the Harvard Medical School, popularized a scientifically sound way of relaxing that he called the relaxation response (Benson & Proctor, 1984). Benson's method applies the basic elements of meditation but eliminates any spiritual or religious significance. Many athletes have used meditation to mentally prepare for competition, asserting that it improves their ability to relax, concentrate, and become energized. However, to date few controlled studies have investigated the effectiveness of the relaxation response in enhancing performance. The state of mind produced by meditation is characterized by keen awareness, effortlessness, relaxation, spontaneity, and focused attention—many of the same elements that describe peak performance.

The relaxation response requires four elements:

1. A quiet place, which assures that distractions and external stimulation are minimized.

2. A comfortable position that can be maintained for a while. Sit in a comfortable chair, for example, but do not lie down in bed—you do not want to fall asleep.

3. A mental device, which is the critical element in the relaxation response. It involves focusing your attention on a single thought or word and repeating it over and over. Select a word, such as relax, calm, or easy, that does not stimulate your thoughts and repeat the word while breathing out. Every time you exhale, repeat your word.

4. A passive attitude, which is important but can be difficult to achieve. You have to learn to let it happen, allowing the thoughts and images that enter your mind to move through as they will, making no attempt to attend to them. If something comes to mind, let it go and refocus on your word. Don't worry about how many times your mind wanders; continue to refocus your attention on your word.

The relaxation response teaches you to quiet the mind, concentrate, and reduce muscle tension.

© Human Kinetics

Learning the relaxation response takes time. You should practice it about 20 minutes a day. You will discover how difficult it is to control your mind and focus on one thought or object. But staying focused on the task at hand is important to many sports. The relaxation response teaches you to quiet the mind, which will help you to concentrate and reduce muscle tension. However, it is not an appropriate technique to use right before an event or competition.

Autogenic Training

Autogenic training consists of a series of exercises designed to produce sensations, specifically of warmth and heaviness. Used extensively in Europe but less in North America, the training was developed in Germany in the early 1930s by Johannes Schultz and later refined by Schultz and Luthe (1969). Basically, it is a technique of self-hypnosis, thus a mental technique. Attention is focused on the sensations you are trying to produce. As in the relaxation response, it is important to let the feeling happen without interference. The autogenic training program is based on six hierarchical stages, which should be learned in order:

1. Heaviness in the extremities
2. Warmth in the extremities
3. Regulation of cardiac activity
4. Regulation of breathing
5. Abdominal warmth
6. Cooling of the forehead

Phrases such as "My right arm is heavy," "My right arm is warm and relaxed," "My heartbeat is regular and calm," "My breathing rate is slow, calm, and relaxed," and "My forehead is cool" are all examples of commonly used verbal stimuli in autogenic training. One reason that autogenic technique has not caught on in North America is that it takes a long time. It usually takes several months of regular practice, 10 to 40 minutes a day, to become proficient, to experience heaviness and warmth in the limbs, and to produce the sensation of a relaxed, calm heartbeat and respiratory rate accompanied by warmth in the abdomen and coolness in the forehead.

■ CASE STUDY ■

Relaxation Training

An elite racquet sport player (who had won numerous international championships) sought out a sport psychologist to help her cope with her propensity to "panic under pressure"—that is, when the score is close at the end of a match. The following is an overview of the relaxation training that sport psychologist (Jones, 1993) provided her. Note that this relax-

© Anthony Neste Photography

ation training method is similar to one that Ost (1988) presented, except that the relaxation response, rather than progressive relaxation, serves as the starting point.

• **Phase 1.** This initial phase involves about 20 minutes of taped instructions in which the athlete generally learns the relaxation response. This includes (a) concentrating on breathing, (b) introduction of a mental device (repeating the word "one" or some other single-syllable word such as "ease") on each exhalation, (c) relaxing music, (d) counting down from 10 to 1 on each exhalation, (e) counting up from 1 to 7 on each inhalation. After two sessions of this form of relaxation in the presence of the sport psychologist, the athlete practices using the tape at least once daily for the next two weeks finally being able to achieve a deep state of relaxation.

• **Phase 2.** In this phase the period of relaxation was reduced to approximately 5 minutes. In this version, the athlete continued to listen to the taped instructions but the music was excluded and the mental device of "one" was changed to "relax." In addition, the counting procedure was changed to counting down from 5 to 1 and then up from 1 to 3. This was practiced every day for two weeks with the 20 minute tape used twice a week. During the second week, the athlete also practiced the 5-minute relaxation without the aid of the tape. By the end of the tape the athlete was proficient at reaching the desired level of relaxation without the tape.

• **Phase 3.** This phase involved having the athlete concentrate on each inhalation and silently saying to herself "relax" on each exhalation. The sport psychologist put the athlete in different physically taxing, uncomfortable situations (e.g., shuttle runs to exhaustion) in which she was asked to "relax" as best as possible. While doing this, the relaxation technique was reduced to approximately 5–20 seconds, requiring four or five breaths. The athlete was now practicing three versions of the original relaxation technique: (a) the 20-minute version used for deep relaxation, but not to be used on match days, (b) the 5-minute version which was used for gaining composure and could be used on competition days, and (c) the "quick" version which required only a few seconds and could be used on court to maintain composure.

• **Phase 4.** The athlete practiced the quick relaxation technique as much as possible during practice situations and practice matches. The athlete used a cue to trigger her quick relaxation which was simply to focus on the trademark on her racquet and to relax as she walked across court to either serve or receive serve. She then used this technique in competitive matches when she played a poor shot, or just before she played a critical point.

Multimodal Anxiety-Reduction Packages

The anxiety-reduction techniques just presented focus on either the cognitive or the somatic aspects of anxiety. Multimodal stress-management packages, however, can alleviate both cognitive and somatic anxiety while providing systematic strategies for the rehearsal of coping procedures under simulated stressful conditions. The two most popular ones are cognitive-affective stress-management training (SMT), developed by Ronald Smith (1980), and stress-inoculation training (SIT), developed by Donald Meichenbaum (1985).

Cognitive-Affective Stress-Management Training

Cognitive-affective stress-management training (SMT) is one of the most comprehensive stress-management approaches. SMT is a skills program designed to teach a person a specific integrated coping response using relaxation and cognitive components to control emotional arousal. Bankers, business executives, social workers, and college administrators have all applied SMT, and athletes have also found this technique to be effective (Crocker, Alderman, Murray, & Smith, 1988). Athletes have proved to be an ideal target population: They acquire the coping skills (e.g., muscular relaxation) somewhat more quickly than other groups, face stressful athletic situations frequently enough to permit careful monitoring of their progress, and perform in ways that can be readily assessed.

The theoretical model of stress underlying SMT (see Figure 12.3) includes both cognitively based and physiologically based intervention strategies (derived from the work of Ellis, 1962; Lazarus, 1966; and Schachter, 1966). This model accounts for the situation, the person's mental appraisal of the situation, the physiological response, and the actual behavior. The program offers specific intervention strategies, such as relaxation skills, cognitive restructuring, and self-instructional training, to help deal with the physical and mental reactions to stress. Combining mental and physical coping strategies eventually leads to an integrated coping response.

Smith's cognitive-affective SMT program has four separate phases:

1. Pretreatment assessment. During this phase the consultant conducts personal interviews to assess what kinds of circumstances produce stress, the player's responses to stress, and how stress affects performance and other behaviors. The consultant also assesses the player's cognitive and behavioral skills and deficits and administers written questionnaires to supplement the interview. This information is used to tailor a program to the player.

2. Treatment rationale. During the treatment rationale, or educational phase, the focus is on helping the player understand his or her stress response by analyzing personal stress reactions and experiences. It is important to emphasize that the program is educational, not psychotherapeutic, in design. Participants should understand that the program is designed to increase their self-control and that the level of coping ability they achieve depends on their efforts.

3. Skill acquisition. The major objective of the SMT program is to develop an integrated coping response (see Figure 12.2) by acquiring both relaxation and cognitive intervention skills. In the skill acquisition phase participants receive training in muscular relaxation, cognitive restructuring, and self-instruction. The muscular relaxation comes from progressive relaxation. Cognitive restructuring is the attempt to identify irrational or stress-inducing self-statements, which are typically related to the fear of failure and disapproval (e.g., "I know I'll mess up," "I couldn't stand to let my teammates and coaches down," or "If I'm not successful, I won't be worth anything"). These statements are then restructured into more positive thoughts (e.g., "I'll still be a good person whether I win or lose," "Don't worry about losing—just play one point at a time"). (Changing negative self-statements into positive self-statements is discussed in more detail in chapter 16.) Self-instructional training teaches people to provide themselves with specific instructions to improve concentration and problem solving. This training teaches specific, useful self-commands, especially helpful for stressful situations. Examples of such commands might be "Don't think about fear, just think about what you have to do," "Take a deep breath and relax," and "Take things one step at a time, just like in practice."

4. Skill rehearsal. To facilitate the rehearsal process, the consultant intentionally induces different levels of stress (typically by using films, imaginary rehearsals of stressful events, and other physical and psychological stressors), even high levels of emotional arousal that exceed actual competitions (Smith, 1980). These arousal responses are then reduced through the use of coping skills the participant has acquired. The procedure of induced affect can produce high levels of arousal, so only trained clinicians should employ this component of the technique.

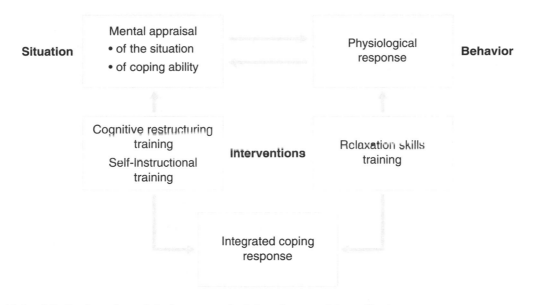

Figure 12.2 *Mediational model of stress underlying the cognitive-affective stress-management program, together with the major intervention strategies used in developing the integrated coping response.* Adapted from Smith, 1980.

Stress-Inoculation Training

One of the most popular multifaceted stress management techniques used both inside and outside the sport environment is stress-inoculation training (Meichenbaum, 1985). The approach for SIT has a number of similarities to SMT, so only a brief outline of SIT will be provided. However, it should be noted that recent research has found SIT to be effective in reducing anxiety and enhancing performance in sport settings (Kerr & Leith, 1993), as well as in helping athletes cope with the stress of injury (Kerr & Goss, 1996).

Stress-inoculation training gets its name because the individual is exposed to and learns to cope with stress in increasing amounts, thereby enhancing his or her immunity to stress. SIT teaches skills for coping with psychological stressors and for enhancing performance by developing productive thoughts, mental images, and self-statements. Individuals using SIT are taken through the following three stages: (a) the *conceptualization stage*, in which awareness of the effects of positive and negative thoughts, self-talk, and imagery is developed (e.g., individuals are taught how negative self-statements such as "You stink tonight" can undermine self-confidence); (b) the *rehearsal stage*, in which participants learn the use of such coping skills as imagery and positive self-statements (e.g., individuals learn to image positive outcomes to stressful events); and (c) the *application stage*, in which people practice their coping skills in low-stress situations, gradually progressing to moderate- and high-stress situations. The use of a stage approach and the strategies of self-talk, cognitive restructuring, and relaxation make both SIT and SMT effective multimodal approaches for anxiety reduction.

Matching Hypothesis

You now have learned about a variety of relaxation techniques, and it is logical to ask when these techniques should be used to achieve maximum effectiveness. In attempting to answer this question researchers have explored what is known as the matching hypothesis. This hypothesis states that an anxiety-management technique should be matched to a particular anxiety problem. That is, cognitive anxiety should be treated with mental relaxation, and somatic anxiety should be treated with physical relaxation. This individualized approach is similar to the stress model developed by McGrath (see chapter 4). A series of recent studies (Maynard & Cotton, 1993; Maynard, Hemmings, & Warwick-Evans, 1995; Maynard, Smith, & Warwick-Evans, 1995) have provided support for the matching hypothesis.

These studies by Maynard and his colleagues have shown a somatic relaxation technique (progressive relaxation) to be more effective than a cognitive one (positive thought control) in reducing somatic anxiety. Conversely, the cognitive relaxation technique was more effective than the somatic one in reducing cognitive anxiety. The reductions in somatic and cognitive anxiety were associated with some subsequent (not quite consistent) increases in performance.

However, "crossover" effects (where somatic anxiety relaxation techniques produce decreases in cognitive anxiety and where cognitive anxiety relaxation techniques produce decreases in somatic anxiety) also occurred in these studies. In one study using a cognitive relaxation technique, the intensity of cognitive anxiety decreased by 30%, whereas the intensity of somatic anxiety also decreased, though by 15%. Similarly, when a somatic relaxation procedure was used, the intensity of somatic anxiety decreased by 31%, and the intensity of cognitive anxiety decreased as well, though by 16%. In other words, somatic relaxation techniques had some positive benefits for reducing cognitive anxiety and cognitive relaxation techniques had some positive benefits for reducing somatic anxiety. These "crossover" effects have led some researchers to argue that SMT and SIT are the more appropriate programs to employ, inasmuch as these multimodal anxiety-reduction techniques can work on both cognitive and somatic anxiety.

Based on the current state of knowledge, we recommend that if an individual suffers primarily from cognitive anxiety, a cognitive relaxation technique should be used. If somatic anxiety is the primary concern, focus on somatic relaxation techniques. Finally, if you are not sure what type of anxiety is most problematic, then use a multimodal technique.

Coping With Adversity

Athletes should learn a broad spectrum of coping strategies to use in different situations, and for different sources of stress (Hardy, Jones, & Gould, 1996). Successful athletes vary in their coping strategies, but all have skills that work when they need them most. Consider the strategies of two athletes:

> [My strategy is] having tunnel vision. . . . I eliminate anything that's going to interfere with me. I don't have any side doors, I guess, for anyone to come into. I make sure that nothing interferes with me.
>
> **Olympic wrestler (cited in Gould, Eklund, & Jackson, 1993, p. 88)**

> I did a lot of visualization. A lot of that. . . . It's a coping strategy. It felt like you did more runthroughs. You went through the program perfectly [many] times. So, it gave you a sense of security and understanding about what was to take place and how it was supposed to go. It just gives you a calmer, more serene way.
>
> **U.S. national champion figure skater (cited in Gould, Finch, & Jackson, 1993, p. 458)**

Although the relaxation techniques we have discussed have helped individuals reduce anxiety in sport and exercise settings, this wrestler and figure skater demonstrate how athletes also use more specific coping strategies to help deal with potential adversity and stress in competitions. The stressors particular to competitions include the fear of injury, performance slumps, the expectations of others, crowd noises, external distractions, and critical points within the competition. Let's first take a look at how coping is defined before discussing specific coping strategies employed in sport.

Definition of Coping

Although many definitions of coping have been put forth in the psychological literature, the most popular definition views coping "as a process of constantly changing cognitive and behavioral efforts to manage specific external and/or internal demands or conflicts appraised as taxing or exceeding one's resources" (Lazarus & Folkman, 1984, p. 141). This view has the advantage of considering coping as a dynamic process involving both cognitive and behavioral efforts to manage stress, a definition that is consistent with McGrath's (1970) model of stress (presented in chapter 4). In addition, it emphasizes an interactional perspective, with both personal and situational factors combining to influence the coping responses. In fact, although individuals appear to exhibit similar coping styles across situations, the particular coping strategies they use depend on both personal and situational factors (Bouffard & Crocker, 1992).

Categories of Coping

The two most widely accepted coping categories are **problem-focused coping** and **emotion-focused coping.** Problem-focused coping involves efforts to alter or manage the problem that is causing the stress for the individual involved. It includes such specific behaviors as information gathering, goal setting, employing time-management skills, problem solving, and adhering to an injury-rehabilitation program. Emotion-focused coping involves regulating the emotional responses to the problem that causes stress for the individual. It includes such specific behaviors as meditation, relaxation, and cognitive efforts to change the meaning (but not the actual problem or environment) of the situation. Lazarus and Folkman (1984) suggest that problem-focused coping is employed more often when situations are amenable to change, and emotion-focused coping is utilized more often when situations are not amenable to change.

Coping in Sport

Compared with the general psychology literature, there is a paucity of research in sport psychology on coping, although such studies have been on the increase in the 1990s (e.g., Anshel, Brown, & Brown, 1993, Anshel & Weinberg, 1995a; Crocker, 1992; Madden, 1995). In a series of in-depth qualitative interviews, Gould, Eklund, & Jackson (1992a; 1992b) assessed the coping strategies that elite athletes use. Despite a wide variety, at least 40% of the athletes reported using the following strategies:

- Thought control (blocking distractions, using coping thoughts such as "I can do it")

- Task focus (narrow focus, concentrating on goals)

- Rational thinking and self-talk (taking a rational approach to oneself and the situation)

- Positive focus and orientation (belief in one's ability, changing negative assessments of the situation to positive ones)

- Social support (encouragement from coach, family, and friends)

- Precompetitive mental preparation and anxiety management (mental practice, precompetition routines, narrow focus, relaxation strategies)

- Time management (making time for personal growth and daily goals)

- Training hard and smart (work ethic, taking responsibility for one's training)

Hardy, Jones, and Gould (1996) have listed the following findings as a summary of the research on coping in sport:

- Athletes use a wide variety of coping strategies, often in combination.

- Athletes use both emotion- and problem-solving strategies for coping, as well as adaptive and nonadaptive ones. Although many athletes cope successfully with the pressure of competition, others (even elite athletes) have difficulty with stress and use inappropriate or maladaptive coping techniques.

On-Site Relaxation Tips

In addition to the well-developed and carefully structured techniques we've discussed so far, other on-site procedures can also help you cope with competitive stress. These techniques are not backed with scientific, empirical research but come from applied experience with athletes (Kirschenbaum, 1998; Weinberg, 1988). You should choose the strategies that best work for your situation.

Smile When You Feel Tension Coming On

A simple and effective cue is to smile in the face of tension. It is difficult if not impossible to be mad or upset when you are smiling. By smiling you take the edge off an anxiety-producing situation. It keeps things in perspective so you can forget about the pressure and enjoy the competition.

Have Fun—Enjoy the Situation

Athletes highly skilled in their sport convey a sense of enjoyment and fun. Most of them look forward to and even relish pressure situations. For example, Al Oerter, four-time Olympic gold medalist in the decathlon, says, "I love competing in the Olympics. That's what training is all about." Similarly, former tennis great Billie Jean King says, "I like the pressure, the challenge—it's exciting; I choose to be here!" Enjoying the game also helps keep young players from burning out. Try to keep winning and losing in perspective and focus on enjoying the experience without undue concern for the outcome.

Set Up Stressful Situations in Practice

Practicing under simulated pressure can be good preparation for actual pressure situations. As you become more accustomed to playing under pressure, you will not be as negatively affected by it. You can create pressure in many ways during practice. Some college basketball coaches invite other students to practices, asking them to scream and boo so that the players feel how it is to play on an opponent's home floor with the crowd against them. Football coaches will set the stage for a 2-minute drill by telling the team there are 2 minutes left in the game, they are down by 2 points on their own 20-yard line, and there are 2 time-outs left: The offense must then move the ball into field goal range.

© Terry Wild Studio

Slow Down, Take Your Time

Many athletes report that when they are feeling frustrated and mad, they start to perform too quickly. It is as if the easiest way to cope with all the anger and pressure is to hurry up and finish. For example, tennis players and golfers tend to rush their shots when they get anxious. Conversely, some athletes take too much time between shots, and their thinking disrupts performance. You can find the middle ground if you develop highly consistent preshot routines and perform them regularly before each golf shot or tennis serve, regardless of the situation and pressure (see chapter 16).

Stay Focused on the Present

Thinking about what just happened or what might happen usually only increases anxiety. You can be sure that worrying about a fly ball you just dropped will not help you catch the next one that comes your way. In fact, worry makes you more anxious and increases your chances of missing. Similarly, thinking about what might happen on the next point or shot only increases pressure and anxiety (see chapter 16 for methods of focusing on the present).

Come Prepared With a Good Game Plan

Indecisiveness produces anxiety. Making decisions can be stressful, and in competition athletes and coaches have to make literally hundreds of decisions during the course of a game or match. Think of the decisions that point guards in basketball, football quarterbacks, golfers, baseball pitchers, tennis players, or soccer players have to make. But if they come prepared with a specific game plan or strategy, decision making is easier. For example, deciding what pitch to throw from behind in the count often causes baseball pitchers stress. Some pregame scouting, however, can give pitchers a good idea of the best pitches to use if they fall behind to certain batters.

Arousal-Inducing Techniques

So far we have focused on anxiety-management techniques to reduce excess levels of anxiety. There are times, however, when you need to pump yourself up

260

because you are feeling lethargic and underenergized. Perhaps you have taken an opponent too lightly and she has surprised you. Or you're feeling tired in the fourth quarter. Or you're lethargic about your rehabilitation exercises. Be aware that certain behaviors, feelings, and attitudes signal that you are underactivated:

- Moving slowly; not getting set
- Mind wandering; becoming easily distracted
- Lack of concern about how well you perform
- Lack of anticipation or enthusiasm
- Heavy feeling in the legs; no bounce

You don't have to experience all these signs to be underactivated. The more you notice, however, the more likely you need to increase arousal. Although these feelings can appear at any time, they usually indicate you are not physically or mentally ready to play. Maybe you didn't get enough rest, played too much (i.e., overtrained), or are playing against a significantly weaker opponent. The more quickly you can detect these feelings, the quicker you can start to get yourself back on track. Here are suggestions for generating more energy and activating your system.

Increase Breathing Rate

Breath control and focus can produce energy and reduce tension. Short, deep breaths tend to activate and speed up the nervous system. Along with the accelerated breathing rate, you may want to say "energy in" with each inhalation and "fatigue out" with each exhalation.

Act Energized

At times when you feel lethargic and slow, acting energetically can help recapture your energy level.

To take the steps to increase or decrease your arousal level, first become aware of how activated or aroused you feel.

For example, football players often bang against each other's shoulder pads in the locker room before games to get themselves pumped up. Many athletes like to jump rope or take a little jog just before starting a competition to "get the butterflies out."

Use Mood Words and Positive Statements

The mind can certainly affect the body. For example, saying or thinking mood words (e.g., strong, forward, tough, aggressive, move, quick, fast, hard) can be energizing and activating. Positive self-statements can also energize you. Some examples include "Hang in there," "I can do it," "Get going," and "Get tough."

Listen to Music

Energetic music can be a source of energy just before a competition, and many athletes use cassettes with headphones before a game. And listening to upbeat music while exercising can generate enthusiasm and emotion.

Use Energizing Imagery

Imagery is another way to generate positive feelings and energy (see chapter 13). Imagery invoves visualizing something that is energizing to you. A sprinter, for example, might imagine a cheetah running swiftly over the plains. A swimmer might imagine moving through the water like a shark.

Complete a Precompetitive Workout

A precompetitive workout typically occurs 4 to 10 hours before the athletic performance. When feeling a little lethargic, it's not uncommon for athletes to come out to practice and stretch several hours earlier to help activate them for a performance later in the day.

SUMMARY

1 *Understand how to increase self-awareness of arousal states.*

The first step toward controlling arousal levels is to become aware of the situations in competitive sport that cause you anxiety and how you respond to these events. To do this athletes can be asked to think back to their best and worst performances and then recall their feelings at these times. In addition, it is also helpful to use a checklist to monitor your feelings during practices and competitions.

2 *Use somatic, cognitive, and multimodal anxiety-reduction techniques.*

A number of techniques have been developed to reduce anxiety in sport and exercise settings. The ones used most often to cope with somatic anxiety are progressive relaxation, breath control, and biofeedback. The most prevalent cognitive anxiety-reduction techniques include the relaxation response and autogenic training. Two multimodal anxiety management packages that use a variety of techniques are (a) cognitive-affective stress management and (b) stress-inoculation training.

3 *Identify coping strategies to deal with competitive stress.*

The two major categories of coping are known as problem-focused coping and emotion-focused coping. Problem-focused coping involves efforts to alter or manage the problem that is causing stress, such as goal setting or time management. Emotion-focused coping involves regulating the emotional responses to the problem causing the stress. Having an array of coping strategies allows athletes to effectively cope with unforeseen events in a competition.

4 *Describe on-site relaxation tips to reduce anxiety.*

In addition to several well-developed and carefully structured techniques, on-site techniques have been identified to help sport and exercise participants cope with feelings of anxiety. These on-site tips usually involve having participants remember that they are out there to have fun and enjoy the experience.

5 *Understand the matching hypothesis.*

The matching hypothesis states that anxiety-management techniques should be matched to the particular anxiety problem. That is, cognitive anxiety should be treated with mental relaxation, and somatic anxiety should be treated with physical relaxation.

6 *Identify techniques to raise arousal for competition.*

Sometimes energy levels need to be raised. Increased breathing, imagery, music, positive self-statements, and simply acting energized can all help increase arousal. The ability to regulate your arousal level is indeed a skill. To perfect that skill you need to systematically practice arousal-regulation techniques, integrating them into your regular physical practice sessions whenever possible.

KEY TERMS

progressive relaxation
breath control
biofeedback
relaxation response
autogenic training
cognitive-affective stress-management training (SMT)

stress-inoculation training (SIT)
matching hypothesis
coping
problem-focused coping
emotion-focused coping

REVIEW QUESTIONS

1. Discuss two ways to help athletes increase awareness of their psychological states.
2. Discuss the four basic tenets of progressive relaxation and give some general instructions for using this technique.
3. Describe the four elements of the relaxation response and how to use it.
4. Describe the approach taken, skills included, and phases of Meichenbaum's stress-inoculation training.
5. How does biofeedback work? Provide an example of its use in working with athletes.
6. Describe the theoretical model of stress underlying the development of the cognitive-affective stress-management technique.
7. Discuss the four phases of cognitive-affective stress-management, comparing and contrasting cognitive structuring and self-instructional training.
8. Define coping as suggested by Lazarus and Folkman. What are the advantages of defining coping in this way?
9. Describe and give contrasting examples of emotion-focused and of problem-focused coping. Under what circumstances is each type of coping used in general?
10. Describe five different coping strategies that elite athletes used in Gould et al.'s studies.
11. Discuss three strategies for on-site reductions in anxiety and tension.
12. An athlete is having trouble getting psyched up for competition. How would you help her get energized?

CRITICAL THINKING QUESTIONS

1. You are getting ready to play the championship game to end your volleyball season in two weeks. You know that some of your players will be tense and anxious, especially as it's the first time your team has reached the final game. But you have a few players who are always slow starters and seem lethargic at the start of competitions. What kinds of techniques and strategies would you employ to get your players ready for this championship game?
2. Think back to a time that you were really anxious before a competition and when your anxiety had a negative effect on your performance. Now you know all about relaxation and stress-management techniques as well as several specific coping strategies. If you had this same situation again, what would you do (and why) to prepare yourself to cope more effectively with your excess anxiety?

© Mary Langenfeld/Langenfeld Photos

Imagery

After reading this chapter you should be able to

1   define imagery and identify its uses,
2   discuss factors influencing the effectiveness of imagery,
3   describe how imagery works,
4   identify the different types of imagery,
5   explain how to develop a program of imagery training, and
6   explain when to use imagery.

Only in the last two decades have researchers been systematically studying the potential uses and effectiveness of imagery in sport and exercise settings. But athletes have been using imagery to help their performance for a long time. This quote by all-time golf great Jack Nicklaus demonstrates his use of imagery:

> *Before every shot I go to the movies inside my head. Here is what I see. First, I see the ball where I want it to finish, nice and white and sitting up high on the bright green grass. Then, I see the ball going there; its path and trajectory and even its behavior on landing. The next scene shows me making the kind of swing that will turn the previous image into reality. These home movies are a key to my concentration and to my positive approach to every shot.*

—*Jack Nicklaus (1976)*

Nicklaus obviously believes that rehearsing shots in his mind before actually swinging is critical to his success. In fact, he has said that hitting a good golf shot is 10% swing, 40% stance and setup, and 50% the mental picture of how the swing should occur. In the 1960s former Olympic athlete Dwight Stones used to visualize his high jumps before performing them. Sometimes in his mind's eye or imagination he missed the jump—so he kept practicing in his head until he cleared the bar. Then, and only then, did he attempt the jump. Gold medalist Jean Claude Killy mentally rehearsed his slalom races before actually skiing down the mountain. He would run through the course in his head, seeing each turn, feeling his body respond to each mogul and shift in direction. Nicklaus, Stones, and Killy are three of the many athletes who, for quite some time, have used imagery to enhance performance.

As scientific evidence accumulates supporting the effectiveness of imagery in sport and exercise settings, many more athletes and exercisers have begun using imagery to not only help their performances but also make their experiences in sport and exercise settings more enjoyable. We will discuss the many uses of imagery in sport and exercise settings as well as what factors make it more effective. Many people misunderstand the term, so let's start by defining what exactly we mean by imagery.

What Is Imagery?

You probably have heard several different terms that describe an athlete's mental preparation for compe-

Through imagery you can recreate previous positive experiences or picture new events to prepare yourself mentally for performance.

tition, including visualization, mental rehearsal, imagery, and mental practice. These terms all refer to creating or recreating an experience in the mind. The process involves recalling from memory pieces of information stored from experience and shaping these pieces into meaningful images. These experiences are essentially a product of your memory, experienced internally by recalling and reconstructing previous events. Imagery is actually a form of simulation. It is similar to a real sensory experience (e.g., seeing, feeling, or hearing), but the entire experience occurs in the mind.

All of us use imagery to recreate experiences. Have you ever watched the batting technique of a great baseball player and tried to copy the swing? Have you ever mentally reviewed the steps and music of an aerobic dance workout before going to the class? We are able to accomplish these things because our minds can remember events and recreate pictures and feelings of them.

Our minds can also imagine (or "image") and picture events that have not yet occurred. Although imagery relies heavily on memory, we can build an image from several parts of memory. For example, an athlete rehabilitating from a shoulder separation could see herself lifting her arm over her head, even though she has not yet been able to do this. Many football quarterbacks view films of the defense they will be facing and then, through imagery, see themselves using certain offensive sets and strategies to offset the specific defensive alignments. Tennis great Chris Evert would carefully rehearse every detail of a match, including her opponent's style, strategy, and shot selection. Here is how she described using imagery to prepare for a tennis match:

> *Before I play a match, I try to carefully rehearse what is likely to happen and how I will react in certain situations. I visualize myself playing typical points based on my opponent's style of play. I see myself hitting crisp, deep shots from the baseline and coming to the net if I get a weak return. This helps me mentally prepare for a match, and I feel like I've already played the match before I even walk on the court.*

© Terry Wild Studio

Imagery can, and should, involve as many senses as possible. Even when imagery is referred to as "visualization," the kinesthetic, auditory, tactile, and olfactory senses are all potentially important. The **kinesthetic sense** is particularly important to athletes because it involves the sensation of bodily position or movement that arises from the stimulation of sensory nerve endings in muscles, joints, and tendons. In essence, the kinesthetic sense is the feeling of our body as it moves in different positions. Using more than one sense helps to create more vivid images, thus making the experience more real.

Let's look at how you might use a variety of senses as a baseball batter. First, you obviously use **visual sense** to watch the ball as the pitcher releases it and it comes toward the plate. You employ kinesthetic sense to know where your bat is and to transfer your weight at the proper time to maximize power. You use **auditory sense** to hear the sound of the bat hit the ball. You can also use your **tactile sense** to note how the bat feels in your hands. Finally, you might use your **olfactory sense** to smell the freshly mowed grass.

Besides using your senses, learning to attach various emotional states or moods to your imagined expe-

riences is also important. Recreating emotions (e.g., anxiety, anger, joy, or pain) through imagery can help control these states. For instance, an aerobic dance instructor might get angry after making a mistake during her routine. Later, using imagery, she might imagine getting angry but then controlling that anger by redirecting her thoughts back to her routine. In one case study, a hockey player had difficulty dealing with officiating calls that went against him. He would get angry, lose his cool, and then not concentrate on his assignment. The player was instructed to visualize himself getting what he perceived to be a bad call, and then to use the cue words "stick to ice" to remain focused on the puck. A soccer player who tore an Achilles tendon, in another case, felt angry when he thought he wasn't recovering quickly enough and would get down and not work hard at his exercises. But through imagery he turned his anger into a positive emotion that stimulated him to work even harder toward rehabilitation.

Does Imagery Work?

To determine if imagery indeed does enhance performance, sport psychologists have looked at three different kinds of evidence: anecdotal reports, case studies, and scientific experiments.

Anecdotal reports, people's reports of isolated occurrences, are numerous (Jack Nicklaus's and Chris Evert's remarks are examples). Many of our best athletes and national coaches include imagery in their daily training regimen, and ever more athletes report using imagery to help recover from injury. A study conducted at the United States Olympic Training Center (Murphy, Jowdy, & Durtschi, 1990) found that 100% of sport psychology consultants and 90% of Olympic athletes used some form of imagery, with 97% of these athletes feeling it helped their performance. In addition, 94% of the coaches of Olympic athletes used imagery during their training sessions, with 20% using it at every practice session. Orlick and Partington (1988) reported that 99% of Canadian Olympians also used imagery. A highly successful swimmer reports on his use of imagery:

> *My visualization has been refined more and more as the years go on. That is really what got me the world record and Olympic medals. I see myself swimming the race before the race really happens, and I try to be on the splits. I concentrate on attaining the splits I have set out to do. About 15 minutes before the race I always visualize the race in my mind and see how it will go. . . . In my mind I go up and down the pool, rehearsing all parts of the race, visualizing how I actually feel in the water (Orlick & Partington, 1988, pp. 118–119).*

Although anecdotal reports might be the most interesting pieces of evidence supporting imagery effectiveness, they are also the least scientific. A more scientific approach is the use of case studies, which closely observe, monitor, and record an individual's behavior over a period of time. Case studies have been used to closely monitor how imagery over time might help improve performance. The first such case study concerned a field-goal kicker from Colorado State University, Clark Kemble (Titley, 1976). During the 1973 season, Kemble missed a few relatively easy field goals at crucial times in the game, sometimes causing his team to lose in the final seconds. Afterward, during the off-season, Kemble diligently used imagery to visualize himself making field goals in important games under all types of game conditions and to see himself bounce back from a missed field-goal attempt. During the next two seasons he went on to kick many field goals near the ends of games to help Colorado State win, and he was also

perfect on extra points. To top that off, he kicked a 63-yard field goal to break the NCAA record!

Some multiple-baseline case studies (i.e., an approach studying just a few people over a long period of time, with multiple assessments documenting changes in behavior and performance) have investigated the effects of imagery on performance. Many other studies have focused on psychological intervention packages, approaches that utilize a variety of psychological interventions (e.g., self-talk, relaxation, concentration training) along with imagery. For example, Suinn (1993) has utilized a technique known as visuo-motor behavior rehearsal (VMBR) which combines relaxation with imagery. Research has demonstrated increases in the neuromuscular activity of skiers in the muscles used for skiing when they used VMBR, and similar performance increases for karate performers who used VMBR (Seabourne, Weinberg, Jackson, & Suinn, 1985). Other studies using imagery as part of a psychological intervention package have shown positive performance results with golfers, basketball players, figure skaters, and tennis players, although the improvements could not be attributed to imagery alone (see Perry & Morris, 1995 for a review).

Evidence from scientific experiments in support of imagery also is impressive and clearly demonstrates the value of imagery in learning and performing motor skills (Feltz & Landers, 1983; Murphy, 1994; Richardson, 1967a; 1967b; Weinberg, 1981). Among experimental evidence, several studies have demonstrated the effectiveness of imagery in basketball, football, swimming, karate, skiing, volleyball, tennis, and golf.

Factors Affecting the Effectiveness of Imagery

Several factors seem to determine to what extent imagery can improve performance. It is important to keep these in mind if you want to maximize imagery effectiveness.

Nature of the Task

Symbolic learning theory (discussed in detail later in this chapter) has shown that tasks involving mostly cognitive components, such as decision making and perception, show the greatest positive benefits from imagery rehearsal (Feltz & Landers, 1983). The performer practicing mentally "can think about what kinds of things might be tried, the consequences of each action can be predicted to some extent based

> *The nature of the task and the skill level of the performer affect how imagery will enhance performance. Novice and highly skilled performers who use imagery on cognitive tasks show the most positive effects.*

on previous experiences with similar skills, and the performer can perhaps rule out inappropriate courses of action" (Schmidt, 1982, p. 520). In addition, the performer can rehearse the temporal and spatial regularities of a skill. For instance, to make the right decision to finish off a fast break, a basketball point guard might visualize running a break and note the changing positions of the offensive and defensive players.

Skill Level of the Performer

Another important potential factor to consider in the effectiveness of imagery is the performer's skill level. Experimental evidence shows that imagery significantly helps performance for both novice and experienced performers, although there are somewhat stronger effects for experienced players (Feltz & Landers, 1983). Imagery may help novice performers learn cognitive elements relevant to successful performance of the skill. After a physical education teacher demonstrates serving a volleyball, for example, she might have the students picture themselves performing the serve. For experienced performers imagery appears to help refine skills and prepare for making decisions and perceptual adjustments rapidly. For example, Olympic gold medalist Greg Louganis used imagery to help himself prepare to make minute changes in his dive based on his body positioning during different phases. He pictured himself making a perfect dive and feeling different points of the dive.

Imaging Ability

Research has indicated that imagery is more effective when individuals are higher in their ability to imagine or image (to develop the imagery). In addition, imaging ability has been shown to be an important factor in distinguishing between elite and non-elite, or successful and less successful performers (Murphy, 1994). Good imaging ability has been defined mostly in terms of the vividness and controllability of images (see more discussion later in this chapter on developing imagery vividness and

controllability). It is important to let individuals know that imagery is a skill and, therefore, the vividness and controllability of one's imagery can be improved with practice (Rodgers, Hall, & Buckholtz, 1991). Sport psychologists working with Olympic athletes have found that although some athletes had difficulty getting controllable and vivid images, through systematic practice they were able to significantly improve the quality of their imagery.

Using Imagery Along With Physical Practice

It is important to remember that imagery does not take the place of physical practice. In fact, a combination of physical and mental practice is not better than physical practice alone within the same time frame if the mental component takes time away from physical practice (Hird, Landers, Thomas, & Horan, 1991). In essence, imagery needs to be added to your normal physical practice, but it shouldn't replace it. However, mental practice does improve performance more than no practice at all. Therefore, imagery should be viewed as a way to train the mind in conjunction with physically training the body, not as a replacement for physical practice. In essence, imagery might be thought of as a vitamin supplement to physical practice, one that could give individuals an edge in improving performance (Vealey & Walter, 1993). However, when an individual is injured, fatigued, or overtrained, then imagery might be employed as a substitute for physical practice.

How Imagery Works

How can just thinking about jumping over the high bar, hitting a perfect tennis serve, healing an injured arm, or sinking a golf putt actually help athletes accomplish these things? We can generate information from memory that is essentially the same as an actual experience; consequently, imagining events can have a similar effect on our nervous system to what the real, or actual, experience would. "Imagined stimuli and perceptual or 'real' stimuli have a qualitatively similar status in our conscious mental life" (Marks, 1977, p. 285). Think for a moment about dreaming. Perhaps someone dreams a big slobbering dog is chasing him; he awakes in a cold sweat to find that the dog was only in his imagination. Sport psychologists have proposed three theoretical explanations of this phenomenon.

Psychoneuromuscular Theory

The **psychoneuromuscular theory** originated with Carpenter (1894), who proposed the **ideomotor principle** of imagery. According to his principle, imagery facilitates the learning of motor skills because of the nature of the neuromuscular activity patterns activated during the imaginal process. That is, vividly imagined events innervate the muscles somewhat as does physically practicing the movement. These slight neuromuscular impulses are identical to those produced during actual performance, but reduced in magnitude (indeed, these impulses may be so minor that they do not actually produce movement). Thus, although the magnitude of the muscle activity is reduced during imagery, the activity is a mirror image of the actual performance pattern.

The first scientific support of this phenomenon came from the work of Edmund Jacobson (1931), who reported that the imagined movement of bending the arm created small muscular contractions in the flexor muscles of the arm. In research with downhill skiers, Suinn (1972; 1976) monitored the electrical activity in the skiers' leg muscles as they imag-

ined skiing the course and found that the muscular activity changed during their imaginings. Muscle activity was highest when the skiers were imagining themselves skiing rough sections in the course, which would actually require greater muscle activity (also see studies by Hale, 1982, and Harris & Robinson, 1986).

When you vividly imagine performing a movement, you use similar neural pathways to those you use in actual performance of the movement. Let's take the example of trying to perfect your golf swing. The goal is to make your swing as fluid and natural as possible to achieve a consistent and accurate drive off the tee. To accomplish this, you take a bucket of balls to the driving range and practice your swing, trying to automate it (i.e., groove your swing). In effect, you are strengthening the neural pathways that control the muscles related to your golf swing. You can also strengthen these neural pathways by imagining that you are executing a perfect swing. Through the imagery, your body believes that you are actually practicing the swing, so in effect you are programming your muscles and preparing your body to perform. Although there is some research to support

270

this explanation of how imagery works, more definitive research is necessary to empirically substantiate that imagery actually works as predicted by the psychoneuromuscular theory.

Symbolic Learning Theory

Sackett (1934) argued that imagery can help individuals understand their movements. His symbolic learning theory suggests that imagery may function as a coding system to help people understand and acquire movement patterns. That is, one way individuals learn skills is by becoming familiar with what needs to be done to successfully perform them. By creating a motor program in the central nervous system, a mental blueprint is formed for successfully completing the movement. For example, in a doubles match in tennis if a player knows how her partner will move on a certain shot, she will be able to better plan her own course. Similarly, a volleyball player should be familiar with the defensive team's position to decide where best to place his shots.

In a thorough review of more than 60 studies in the literature, Feltz and Landers (1983) found that subjects using imagery or some other form of mental practice consistently performed better on tasks that were primarily cognitive (mental) in nature than on those that were more purely motoric. For example, lifting weights or kicking a soccer ball are predominantly motoric, whereas playing chess or a quarterback's deciding which receiver to throw the ball to are mostly cognitive. The research that was reviewed thus supports the symbolic learning theory. Of course, most sport skills have both motor and cognitive components; imagery can be effective to an extent, therefore, in helping players with a variety of skills.

Psychological Skills Hypothesis

Sport psychologists have more recently argued that imagery also works through its developing and refining psychological skills, and the psychological

Three theories are that imagery works by producing muscle activity, providing a mental blueprint, or improving other psychological skills. All three theories have received some support in the literature–therefore, imagery works in a variety of ways.

skills hypothesis would predict that imagery can improve concentration, reduce anxiety, and enhance confidence—all important psychological skills for maximizing performance. And imagery is a convenient, effective tool to practice and learn a variety of psychological skills. For instance, several intervention techniques (such as stress-inoculation training and stress-management training), which focus primarily on reducing or coping with anxiety, employ imagery as a key component in the process. People visualize themselves successfully coping with stress in tough situations. A golfer, for example, might visualize herself standing over a 10-foot putt that would win a tournament. In the past, she has tightened up and missed. Now, in her mind, she sees herself taking a deep breath and relaxing her muscles as she goes through her preshot routine. With a relaxed body and mind, she visualizes sinking the putt and winning the tournament.

Bioinformational Theory

Probably the best-developed theoretical explanation for the effects of imagery is Lang's bioinformational theory (1977; 1979). Based on the assumption that an image is a functionally organized set of propositions stored by the brain, the model states that a description of an image contains two main types of statements: response propositions and stimulus propositions. *Stimulus propositions* are statements that describe specific stimulus features of the scenario to be imagined. For example, a weightlifter at a major competition might imagine the crowd, the bar he is going to lift, locker-room conditions, and the people sitting or standing on the sidelines. *Response propositions,* on the other hand, are statements that describe the imager's response to the particular scenario, and they are designed to produce physiological activity. For example, having a weightlifter *feel* the weight in his hands as he gets ready for his lift, along with feeling a pounding heart and a little tension in their muscles, would be response propositions.

The crucial point to emphasize here is that response propositions are a fundamental part of the image structure in Lang's theory. In essence, the image is not only a stimulus in the person's head to which he or she responds. In fact, imagery instructions that contain response propositions elicit far greater physiological responses than do imagery instructions that contain only stimulus propositions (Hale, 1982). From a practical point of view, imagery scripts should contain both stimulus and response

■ MORE INFORMATION ■

Response vs. Stimulus Propositions: Lang's Bioinformational Theory

To be most effective, imagery scripts should contain both stimulus and response propositions. Here are examples of each:

Script Weighted With Stimulus Propositions

It is a beautiful autumn day and you are engaged in a training program, running down a street close to your home. You are wearing a bright red tracksuit and as you run, you watch the wind blow the leaves from the street onto a neighbor's lawn. A girl on a bicycle passes you, and you see she is delivering newspapers. You swerve to avoid a pothole in the road and you smile at another runner passing you in the opposite direction.

Script Weighted With Response Propositions

It is a crisp autumn day and you are engaged in a training run, going down a street close to your home. You feel the cold bite of air in your nose and throat as you breathe in large gulps of air. You are running easily and smoothly, but you feel pleasantly tired, and can feel your heart pounding in your chest. Your leg muscles are tired, especially the calf and thigh ones, and you can feel your feet slapping against the pavement. As you run you can feel a warm sweat on your body.

© Caroline Woodham

---

propositions, which are more likely to create a vivid image than stimulus propositions alone.

Triple Code Model

Another fairly recent model, which also recognizes the primary importance of psychophysiology in the imagery process, goes a step further in stating that the meaning the image has to the individual must also be incorporated into imagery models. Specifically, Ahsen's (1984) triple code model (ISM) of imagery highlights understanding three effects that are essential aspects or parts of imagery. The first part is the image (I) itself. "The image is a sensation but it is internal at the same time. It represents the outside world and its objects with a degree of sensory realism which enables us to interact with the image as if we were interacting with the real world"(Ahsen, 1984, p. 34). The second part is the somatic response (S): The act of imagination results

in psychophysiological changes in the body (this part is similar to Lang's bioinformational theory). The third aspect of imagery (mostly ignored by other models) is the meaning (M) of the image. According to Ahsen, every image imparts a definite significance, or meaning, to the individual imager, and that the same set of imagery instructions will never produce the same imagery experience for any two people.

Individual differences can be seen in Murphy's (1990) description of how figure skaters differed in their imagery when they were asked to relax and concentrate on "seeing a bright ball of energy, glowing golden, floating in front of me, which I inhale and take down to the center of my body." One skater imagined a glowing energy ball "exploding in my stomach [and] leaving a gaping hole in my body." Another skater said that the image of the ball of energy "blinded me so that when I began skating I could not see where I was going and crashed into the wall of the rink." In essence, Ahsen's triple code model recognizes the powerful reality of images for the individual and also encourages us, as we help people with imaging, to seek the *meanings* of the images to them.

In summary, the five explanations—psychoneuromuscular, symbolic learning, psychological skills, bioinformational, and triple code—all assert that imagery can help program an athlete both physically and mentally, and they all have found support from research (although the validity of the psychoneuromuscular theory has been questioned recently). You might regard imagery as a strong mental blueprint of how to perform a skill, which should result in quick and accurate decision making, increased confidence, and improved concentration. In addition, the increased neuromuscular activity in the muscles helps players make movements more fluid, smooth, and automatic.

Uses of Imagery

Athletes can employ imagery in many ways to improve both physical and psychological skills, including concentration, confidence, control over emotional responses, acquiring and practicing sport skills and strategies, and coping with pain or injury.

Improve Concentration

By visualizing what you want to do and how you want to react in certain situations, you can prevent your mind from wandering. You can imagine yourself in situations where you often lose your concentration (e.g., after missing an easy shot in basketball, forgetting a step in an aerobic dance class, or dropping a pass in football) and then imagine yourself remaining composed and focused on the next play or step.

Build Confidence

If you have had trouble with serving in recent matches, for example, you might imagine hitting hard, accurate volleyball serves to build up your self-confidence. An official who has her confidence shaken when the crowd starts booing her calls against the home team could visualize herself taking control and maintaining confidence and impartiality on subsequent calls. Seeing yourself perform well in your

Imagery can enhance a variety of skills to improve performance and can facilitate the learning of new techniques and strategies.

mind makes you feel you can perform under adverse circumstances. A recent study (Moritz, Hall, Martin, & Vadocz, 1996) found that athletes high in confidence have different image content than athletes low in confidence. Specifically, compared with athletes low in confidence, highly confident athletes used more mastery imagery (e.g., I imagine myself to be focused during a challenging situation) and arousal imagery (e.g., I imagine the excitement associated with competing) and had better ability with kinesthetic and visual imagery.

Control Emotional Responses

You can visualize situations that have caused problems in the past, such as choking under pressure or getting angry because of your own errors or officials' calls. You can then picture yourself dealing with these events in a positive way, such as taking a deep breath and focusing on your breathing as you concentrate on the task at hand. Along these lines, Pat Head Summitt, the highly successful women's basketball coach at the University of Tennessee, uses imagery for relaxation before important games when players tend to get too "pumped" and play out of control. Recent research has also revealed that arousal imagery produces higher levels of cognitive anxiety (Vadocz, Hall, & Moritz, 1997). Competitive state anxiety can be both facilitative and debilitative, so an athlete who is having trouble getting up for a competition might want to use arousal imagery, whereas an athlete who finds anxiety a problem will probably only make things worse by engaging in arousal imagery.

Acquire and Practice Sport Skills

Probably the best-known use of imagery is for practicing a particular sport skill. Athletes practice putting a golf ball, executing a takedown in wrestling, throwing the javelin, doing a routine on the balance beam, or swimming the backstroke—all in their minds. You can practice skills to fine-tune them or you can pinpoint weaknesses and visualize correcting them. A physical education teacher might have his students imagine the proper execution of a backward roll as they wait in line for their turn (imagery can be particularly useful during waiting periods). An aerobics instructor might have her students imagine a sequence of movements as they listen to the music before physically attempting the steps (see Figure 13.1). This practice can take the form of a preview or a review. A participant can look forward to and visualize what to do in an upcoming competition or event; a player can review a past performance,

Figure 13.1 *Imaging is a way to practice movement skills.*

focusing on specific aspects of the movement that were done particularly well.

Acquire and Practice Strategy

Imagery can be used to practice and learn new strategies or review alternative strategies for either team or individual sports. A quarterback, for example, might visualize different defenses and what plays he would call to counteract them. A hockey goalie might imagine what he would do on a breakaway as three players converge on the goal. A softball pitcher might visualize how to pitch to different batters on the opposing team, based on their strengths and weaknesses. To prepare himself mentally to bat, Hank Aaron, the all-time leading home run hitter, used to visualize the different types of pitches a particular pitcher might throw him.

Cope With Pain and Injury

Imagery is also useful for coping with pain and injury. It can help speed up recovery of the injured area and keep skills from deteriorating all the while (Ievleva & Orlick, 1991). It is hard for athletes to go through an extended layoff. But instead of feeling sorry for themselves, they can imagine doing practice drills and thereby facilitate recovery. (We'll further discuss using imagery during injury rehabilitation later in this chapter.)

Solve Problems

Imagery can also be utilized to discover or solve problems in performance. If an individual is not performing up to past or expected levels, the player can use imagery to critically examine all aspects of the performance to find the potentially confounding factor.

If a gymnast is experiencing trouble on a particular aspect of her floor routine, for example, she can visualize what she is doing now and possibly compare it to what she has done in the past when she was performing the moves successfully.

Functions of Imagery

Imagery has a myriad of specific uses. In addition, Pavio (1985) has distinguished between two of its functions: the motivational and cognitive functions. He suggests that imagery plays both cognitive and motivational roles in mediating behavior, each capable of being oriented toward either general or specific behavioral goals (see figure 13.2). On the motivational side, imagery can represent emotion-arousing situations as well as specific goals and goal-oriented behaviors. On the cognitive side, imagery can be focused on the strategies used in the performance situation or on the motor skills necessary for success.

Types of Imagery

Athletes usually take either an internal or external perspective for viewing their imagery (Mahoney & Avener, 1977). Which perspective is used depends on the athlete and the situation. Gymnasts who qualified for the 1976 U.S. Olympic team, for example, reported using internal imagery more frequently than external imagery. We'll look briefly at each perspective.

Internal Imagery

Internal imagery refers to imagining the execution of a skill from your own vantage point. As if you had a camera on your head, you see only what you would see if you actually executed the particular skill.

	Motivational	**Cognitive**
Specific	**Goal-oriented responses** (e.g. , imaging oneself winning an event and receiving a medal)	**Skills** (e.g., imaging performing on the balance beam successfully)
General	**Arousal** (e.g., including relaxation by imaging a quiet place)	**Strategy** (e.g., imaging carrying out a strategy to win a competition)

Figure 13.2 *Cognitive and motivational functions of imagery.* Adapted from Pavio, 1985.

As a softball pitcher, for instance, you would see the batter at the plate, the umpire, the ball in your glove, and the catcher's target, but not the shortstop, second baseman, or anything else out of your normal range of vision. Because internal imagery is done from a first-person perspective, the images would emphasize the feel of the movement. As a softball pitcher, you would feel your fingers gripping the ball, the stretch of your arm during the backswing, the shift of weight, and finally the extension of your arm upon release.

External Imagery

In external imagery you view yourself from the perspective of an external observer. It is as if you are watching yourself in the movies or on videotape. For example, if a baseball pitcher imagined pitching from an external perspective, he would see not only the batter, catcher, and umpire, but also all the other fielders. However, there would be little emphasis on the kinesthetic feel of the movement because the pitcher is simply watching himself perform it.

Regarding performance results, few differences have been established between external and internal imagery. Studies show no differences in performance generally between individuals given internal imagery instructions compared with those told to use external imagery. It was virtually impossible to characterize participants as strictly internal or external imagers because people's images varied considerably, both within and between images (Epstein, 1980; Mumford & Hall, 1985). In fact, most Olympic athletes surveyed by Murphy, Fleck, Dudley, & Callister (1990) indicated that they use both internal and external imagery.

However, although the research is inconclusive, some evidence suggests that internal imagery might indeed yield better results than external imagery. One study found that internal imagery produced more electrical activity in the biceps muscle than external imagery did when subjects imagined flexing their arm (Hale, 1982). Internal imagery makes it easier to bring in the kinesthetic sense, feel the movement, and approximate actual performance skills. For example, using an internal perspective, a golfer might become more aware of how her body feels and looks during her swing.

In summary, many people switch back and forth between internal and external imagery. As one Olympic rhythmic gymnast reported, "Sometimes you look at it from a camera view, but most of the time I look at it as what I see from within, because that's the way it's going to be in competition" (Orlick & Partington, 1988, p. 114). The important thing appears to be getting a good, clear, controllable image, regardless of whether it is from an internal or external perspective. It may be better sometimes to use external imagery (e.g., to correct a play that went wrong in football after watching game films), although at other times internal imagery might be better (e.g., practicing the golf swing just before hitting a drive).

Keys to Effective Imagery

Like all psychological techniques, imagery skill is acquired through practice. Some participants are

Whether a person uses an internal or external image appears to be less important than choosing a comfortable style that produces clear, controllable images.

When using imagery, involve as many senses as possible and recreate or create the emotional feelings associated with the task or skill you're trying to execute.

pretty good at it, whereas others may not even be able to get an image in their minds. There are two keys to good images—vividness and controllability. We'll consider each of these in turn.

Vividness

Good imagers use all of their senses to make their images as vivid and detailed as possible. It is important to recreate or create as closely as possible the actual experience in your mind. The closer images are to the real thing, the better they transfer to actual performance. Pay particular attention to environmental detail, such as the layout of the facilities, type of surface, and closeness of spectators. Experience the emotions and thoughts of the actual competition. Try to feel the anxiety, concentration, frustration, exhilaration, or anger associated with your performance. All of this detail will make the imagined performance more real.

If you have trouble getting clear, vivid images, first try to imagine things that are familiar to you, such as the furniture in your room. Then use the arena or playing field where you normally play and practice. Here you will be familiar with the playing surface, grandstands, background, colors, and other environmental details. You can practice getting vivid images with the three vividness exercises that follow. (We also recommend trying the exercises in *Put Your Mother on the Ceiling* by Richard DeMille, 1973.)

Vividness Exercises

1. *Imagining home.* Imagine that you are home in your living room. Look around and take in all the details. What do you see? Notice the shape and texture of the furniture. What sounds do you hear? What is the temperature like? Is there any movement in the air? What do you smell? Use all your senses and take it all in.

2. *Imagining a positive performance of a skill.* Select a particular skill in your sport and visualize yourself performing it perfectly. Perform the skill over and over in your mind, and imagine every feeling and movement in your muscles. For example, in serving a tennis ball, start by seeing yourself in the

ready position, looking at your opponent and the service court. Then pick the spot where you want the serve to go. See and feel how you start the service motion and release the ball at the perfect height, the toss going just where you want. Feel your back arch and your shoulder stretch as you take the racquet back behind your head. Feel your weight start to transfer forward and your arm and racquet reach high to contact the ball at just the right height and angle. Feel your wrist snap as you explode into the ball. Now see and feel the follow-through with your weight coming completely forward. The ball goes exactly where you want it to, forcing a high floating return from your opponent. You close in on the net and put the ball away with a firm crosscourt volley.

3. *Imagining a positive performance.* Recall as vividly as possible a time when you performed very well. If you can recall a finest hour in recent memory, use that. Your visualization will cover three specific areas of recall: visual, auditory, and kinesthetic.

First, visually recall a picture of how you looked when you were performing well. Notice that you look different when you're playing well compared with when you're playing poorly. You walk differently; you carry your head and shoulders differently. When an athlete is confident on the inside, it shows on the outside. Try to get as clear a picture as possible of what you look like when you are playing well. Review films of successful performances to help crystallize the image.

Now reproduce in your mind the sounds you hear when you are playing well, particularly the internal dialogue you have with yourself. There is often an internal silence that accompanies your best performances. Listen to it. What is your internal dialogue like? What are you saying to yourself, and how are you saying it? What is your internal response when you face adversity during play? Recreate all the sounds as vividly as you can.

Finally, recreate in your mind all the kinesthetic sensations you have when playing well. How do your feet and hands feel? Do you have a feeling of quickness, speed, or intensity? Do your muscles feel tight or relaxed? Stay focused on the sensations associated with playing well.

Controllability

Another key to successful imagery is learning to manipulate your images so they do what you want them to. Many athletes have difficulty controlling their images and often repeat their mistakes. A base-

> *Tailor imagery programs to the exerciser's or athlete's individual needs, abilities, and interests.*

ball batter might visualize his strikeouts; a tennis player, her double faults; a hockey goalie, a puck going past him for a goal; or a gymnast, falling off the uneven parallel bars. Controlling your image helps you to picture what you want to accomplish instead of seeing yourself make errors. The key to control is practice. The following quote by an Olympic springboard diver shows how practice can help overcome an inability to control one's images:

> *It took me a long time to control my images and perfect my imagery, maybe a year, doing it every day. At first I couldn't see myself; I always saw everyone else, or I would see my dives wrong all the time. I would get an image of hurting myself, or tripping on the board, or I would see something done really bad. As I continued to work on it, I got to the point where I could see myself doing a perfect dive and the crowd at the Olympics. But it took me a long time. (Orlick & Partington, 1988, p. 114)*

You can practice by doing the following controllability exercises.

Controllability Exercises

1. *Controlling performance.* Imagine working on a specific skill that has given you trouble in the past. Take careful notice of what you were doing wrong. Now imagine yourself performing that skill perfectly while seeing and feeling your movements. For example, a basketball player might see and feel herself shooting a free throw perfectly, getting nothing but net.

Now, think about a competitive situation in which you have had trouble in the past. Taking the basketball example, you might see yourself shooting two free throws at the end of a game with your team down by one point. See yourself remaining calm as you sink both shots.

2. *Controlling performance against a tough opponent.* Picture yourself playing a tough opponent who has given you trouble in the past. Try to execute a planned strategy against this person just as you would for a competition. Imagine situations in which you are getting the best of your opponent. For example, a quarterback might imagine different de-

fenses and see himself calling the correct audible at the line of scrimmage to beat each defense. Then, he would actually see himself carrying out the successful play. Whatever your sport, make sure you control all aspects of your movements as well as the decisions you make.

3. *Controlling emotions.* Picture yourself in a situation where you tense up, become angry, lose concentration, or lose confidence (e.g., missing a field goal, blowing a breakaway layup, missing an empty net in soccer, or missing a jump and falling on the ice). Recreate the situation, especially the feelings that accompany it. Feel the anxiety, for example, of playing in a championship game. Then use anxiety-management strategies (see chapter 12) to feel the tension drain from your body and to instead focus on what you need to do to execute your skills. Try to control what you see, hear, and feel in your imagery.

Developing an Imagery Training Program

Now that you know the fundamentals and principles underlying the effectiveness of imagery and how to improve vividness and controllability, you have the basics you need to set up an imagery training program. To be effective, imagery should become part of the daily routine. It is important to tailor imagery programs to the needs, abilities, and interests of each athlete or exerciser.

Imagery Evaluation

The first step in setting up imagery training is to evaluate the athlete's or student's current level of imagery skill. Because imagery is a skill, individuals differ in how well they can do it. Measuring someone's ability in imaging is not easy, however, because imagery is a mental process—and therefore not directly observable. Although psychologists have tried different techniques, basically they use questionnaires to try to discern the different aspects of imagery content. Tests of imagery date back to 1909 when the Betts Questionnaire on Mental Imagery was first devised. Later the Vividness of Movement Imagery Questionnaire (Isaac, Marks, & Russell, 1986 was developed to measure visual imagery as well as the kinesthetic sensations accompanying the imagery. In addition, Hall, Mack, Pavio, and Hausenblas (1997) developed the Sport Imagery Questionnaire that asks individuals how often they use various types of imagery (e.g., imaging sport skills, strategies of

Sport Imagery Questionnaire

Read the following descriptions of four general sport situations. For each one, imagine the situation and provide as much detail from your imagination as possible (using all the senses—seeing, hearing, feeling, tasting, and smelling) to make the image as real as you can. Think of a specific example of the situation (e.g., the skill, the people involved, the place, the time). Now close your eyes and take a few deep breaths to become as relaxed as you can. Put aside all thoughts. Keep your eyes closed for about 1 minute as you try to imagine the situation as vividly as you can. Your accurate appraisal of your images will help you determine which exercises you will want to emphasize in the basic training exercises.

After you have completed imagining the situation, rate the four dimensions of imagery by circling the number that best describes the image you had.

1 = No image present
2 = Not clear or vivid, but a recognizable image
3 = Moderately clear and vivid image
4 = Clear and vivid image
5 = Extremely clear and vivid image

For each situation, pick the number that answers each of these four questions:

a. How vividly did you see yourself doing this activity?	1	2	3	4	5
b. How clearly did you hear the sounds of doing the activity?	1	2	3	4	5
c. How well did you feel yourself making the movements?	1	2	3	4	5
d. How clearly were you aware of your mood?	1	2	3	4	5

PRACTICING ALONE

Select a specific skill in your sport such as hitting a backhand, vaulting over the bar, swimming the breaststroke, or kicking a goal. Now imagine yourself performing this skill at the place where you normally practice (e.g., gymnasium, pool, field, rink, court) without anyone else present. Close your eyes for about 1 minute and try to see yourself at this place, hear the sounds, feel your body perform the movement, and be aware of your state of mind or mood.

a. _____   c. _____

b. _____   d. _____

PRACTICING WITH OTHERS

You are doing the same activity but now you are practicing the skill with your coach and your teammates present. This time, however, you make a mistake that everyone notices.

a. _____   c. _____

b. _____   d. _____

WATCHING A TEAMMATE

Think of a teammate's or an acquaintance's performing a specific skill unsuccessfully in competition, such as dropping a pass, falling off the balance beam, or missing an empty net.

a. _____   c. _____

b. _____   d. _____

(continued)

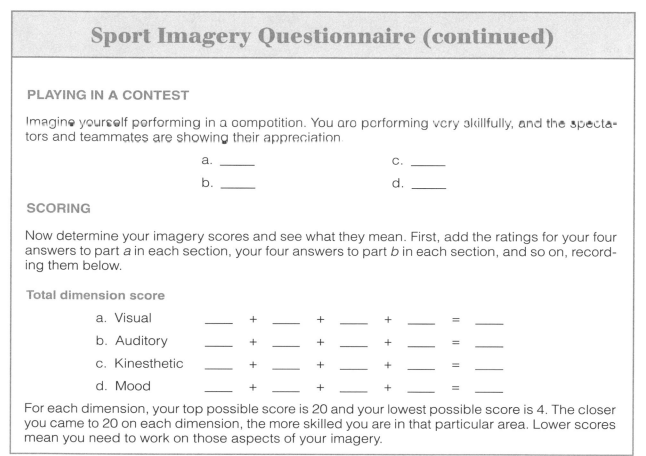

---

play, staying focused, or the arousal that may accompany performance).

These imagery questionnaires can be used to evaluate different aspects of imagery ability and use; the practitioner chooses the most appropriate instrument for a specific situation. As an example and to see how good your own imagery skills are, complete the Sport Imagery Questionnaire (Martens, 1982b) given on p. 278, which measures how well athletes can use all their senses while imaging. There are no right or wrong answers to the questionnaire; the evaluation should take you 10 to 15 minutes.

After compiling feedback from the questionnaire, players and coaches can determine which areas to incorporate into the athlete's daily training regimen. The imagery program need not be complex or cumbersome, and it should fit well into the individual's daily training regimen. What follows are tips and guidelines for implementing a successful program in imagery training.

Proper Setting

People who are highly skilled in the use of imagery can perform the technique almost anywhere. But these people are rare. For the beginner it's best to practice in a setting with no distractions. Some people like to practice imagery in their rooms before going to sleep, others in the locker room before competition, and others during a break at school or work. As skills develop, people learn to use imagery amid distractions and even in actual competition.

Relaxed Concentration

Imagery preceded by relaxation is more effective than using imagery alone (Weinberg, Seabourne, & Jackson, 1981). So before each imagery session, relax by using deep breathing, progressive relaxation, or some other relaxation procedure that works for you. Relaxation is important for two reasons: (a) It lets you forget everyday worries and concerns and concentrate on the task at hand, and (b) it results in more powerful imagery because it won't have to compete with other events.

Realistic Expectations and Sufficient Motivation

Some athletes are quick to reject such nontraditional training as imagery, believing that the only way to improve is through hard physical practice, drills, and blood and sweat. They are skeptical that thinking about and visualizing a skill can help improve its performance. Such negative thinking and doubt undermine the effectiveness of imagery. Other athletes believe that imagery can help them become the next Tiger Woods or Martina Hingis, as if imagery is the magic that can transform them into the players of their dreams. The truth is simply that imagery can improve athletic skills if you work at it systematically. Excellent athletes are usually intrinsically motivated to practice their skills for months and even years. A similar dedication and motivation is needed to develop psychological skills. Yet many athletes do not commit to practice imagery systematically. Remember that efforts in a systematic imagery program are rewarded in the near future.

Vivid and Controllable Images

Try to use all your senses and to feel the movements as if they were actually occurring. Many Olympic teams visit the actual competition sites months in advance so they can visualize themselves performing in that exact setting, with its color, layout, construction, and grandstands. Moving and positioning your body as if you were actually performing the skill can make the imagery and feeling of movement more vivid. For example, instead of lying down in bed to image kicking a soccer goal, stand up and kick your leg as if you were actually performing the skill. Imagery can be used during quick breaks in the action, so it is important to learn to image with your eyes open as well as closed. Work on controlling images to follow your instructions and produce the desired outcome.

Positive Focus

Focus in general on positive outcomes, such as kicking a field goal, getting a base hit, completing a successful physical therapy session, scoring a goal, or doing a perfect routine. Sometimes using imagery to recognize and analyze errors is beneficial (Mahoney & Avener, 1977) because nobody is perfect and we all make mistakes every time we play. It is also important, however, to be able to leave the mistake behind and focus on the present. Try using imagery to prepare for the eventuality of making a mistake and effectively coping with the error.

For trouble with a particular mistake or error, we suggest the following: First try to imagine the mistake and determine the correct response. Then immediately imagine performing the skill correctly. The image of the correct response (along with the feeling of that response) should then be repeated several times, and this should be followed immediately with actual physical practice. This will help you absorb what it looks like and how it feels to perform the skill well.

Imagining successful outcomes helps program the body to execute skills. The better that athletes can visualize successful performances, the stronger their motor programs will become. But errors and mistakes are part of competition, so they should be prepared to deal with them effectively. This is highlighted in the following quote by a three-time Olympian:

> *It's as if I carry around a set of tapes in my mind. I play them occasionally, rehearsing direct race strategies. Usually I imagine the race going the way I want—I set my pace and stick to it. But I have other tapes as well—situations where someone goes out real fast and I have to catch him, or imaging how I will cope if the weather gets really hot. I even have a "disaster" tape where everything goes wrong and I'm hurting badly, and I imagine myself gutting it out. (Murphy & Jowdy, 1992, p. 242)*

Videotapes

Many athletes can get good, clear images of their teammates or frequent opponents but have trouble imaging themselves. This is because it is difficult to visualize something you have never seen. The challenge is to capture that perfect shot, pass, jump, kick, or routine and lock it in for use with mental practice. A videotape can provide just this feedback—a picture of how you look performing at your best. Seeing yourself on videotape for the first time is quite eye-opening, and people typically ask, "Is that me?"

A good procedure is to film athletes practicing, carefully edit the tape (usually in consultation with the coach or athlete) to identify the perfect or near-perfect skills, and then duplicate the sequence repeatedly on the tape. The athlete observes her skills in the same relaxed state prescribed for imagery training. After watching the film for several minutes, she closes her eyes and images the skill.

A program called Sybervision (DeVore & DeVore, 1981) shows professional athletes in different sports hitting the basic shots perfectly. Along with repeated footage of these perfect movements, the tape also brings in auditory cues, such as the thwack of the bat as Rod Carew hits the ball. This approach still awaits detailed scientific scrutiny, but it appears to offer promise.

Using Imagery to Cope With Adversity

Al Oerter holds the distinctions of winning four gold medals in the discus in four different Olympics (Carl Lewis is the only other Olympian to achieve this remarkable feat). In two of his gold medal performances Oerter won the gold on his last throw, and in the others he had to overcome injuries and poor weather conditions to win. In speaking about how he prepared for the Olympics and overcoming potential obstacles, this is what Oerter said:

"I used to imagine that it was the day of the Olympic trials, the day that I had spent the last four years preparing for, and that it was raining. Pouring rain. The throwing area was slippery, conditions were atrocious, and I had to go out and throw anyway. And I imagined myself throwing well. I visualized myself throwing strongly, with good technique despite the rain. Or sometimes I would imagine that I was down to my last throw in the Olympic finals. The Russian was competing right ahead of me, and with his last throw he set a world record. So to win the gold medal, I now had to set a new world record! On my last throw of the Games, I would imagine that I did just that; I would see myself setting a new world record. Those were the things I visualized. I thought about what might go wrong, and I imagined responding to the challenge." (Murphy, 1996, p. 67).

Image Execution and Outcome

Imagery should include both the execution and end result of the skills. Many athletes image the execution of the skill and not the outcome, or vice versa. Athletes need to be able to feel the movement and control the image so they see the desired outcome. For instance, divers must first be able to feel their body in different positions throughout the dive. Then they should see themselves making a perfectly straight entry into the water.

Image in Real Time

A final principle is to image in real time (Nideffer, 1985). In other words, the time spent imaging a particular skill should be equal to the time the skill actually takes to occur. If a golfer normally takes 20 seconds as part of a preshot routine before putting, then his image of this routine should also take 20 seconds. Because athletes tend to image faster than the actual time it takes to perform the skill, it is a good idea to time the skill. Imaging in real time makes the transfer from imagery to real life easier.

When to Use Imagery

Although imagery can be used virtually any time, it appears to be most useful before and after practice, before and after competition, during breaks in the action in both practice and competition, during personal time, and when recovering from injury. In the

following sections, we'll describe how imagery can be used during each of these times.

Before and After Practice

One way to schedule imagery systematically is to include it before and after each practice session. Limit these sessions to about 10 minutes; most athletes have trouble concentrating any longer than this on imagery (Murphy et al., 1990). To focus concentration and get ready before practice, athletes should visualize the skills, routines, and plays they expect to perform. After each practice individuals should then review the skills and strategies they worked on. Because they have just finished working out, the feel of the movement should be fresh in their minds, which will help create clearer, more detailed imagery than usual.

Before and After Competition

Imagery can focus athletes on the upcoming competition if they review in their minds exactly what they want to do, including different strategies for different situations. Imagery before a contest helps finctune actions and reactions. Optimally timing this precompetition imagery is individual: Some athletes like to visualize right before the start of a competition, whereas others like to image an hour or two beforehand. Some athletes image at two or three different times before the competition. What's important is that the imaging fit comfortably into the pre-event routine. It should not be forced or rushed.

After competition athletes can replay the things they did successfully and get a vivid, controllable image. Similarly, students in physical education classes can imagine themselves correcting an error in the execution of a skill they just learned and practiced. They can also replay unsuccessful events, imagining performing successfully or choosing a different strategy.

Imagery can also be used to strengthen the blueprint and muscle memory of those skills already performed well. Larry Bird was a great shooter, but he still practiced his shooting every day. Good performance of a particular skill does not mean that imaging will not maintain or improve it further; its usefulness continues as long as one is performing his or her skill.

During Breaks in the Action

Most sporting events have some extended breaks in the action during which an athlete can use imagery to prepare for what's ahead. Many sports have a certain amount of "dead time" after each shot, and this is an ideal opportunity to use imagery.

During Personal Time

Athletes can use imagery at home (or in any other appropriate quiet place). It may be difficult to find a quiet spot before practicing, and there may be days when the athlete does not practice at all. In such cases

athletes should try to set aside 10 minutes at home so that they do not break their imagery routine. Some people like to image before they go to sleep; others prefer doing it when they wake up in the morning.

When Recovering From Injury

Athletes have been trained to use imagery with relaxation exercises to reduce anxiety about an injury. They have used imagery to rehearse emotions they anticipate experiencing upon return to competition. Through imagery, athletes can mentally rehearse physical and performance skills, thereby staying sharp and ready for return.

Positive images of healing or full recovery have been shown to enhance recovery. Ieleva and Orlick (1991) found that positive healing and performance imagery were related to faster recovery times. (Similarly, terminally ill cancer patients have used imagery to see themselves destroying and obliterating the cancerous cells. In a number of cases, the cancer has reportedly gone into remission; see Simonton, Matthews-Simonton, & Creighton, 1978). Imagery can also help athletes, such as long-distance runners, fight through a pain threshold and focus on the race and technique instead of on their pain.

> *For imagery to be effective, it should be built into the daily routine.*

MORE INFORMATION

How Different Professionals Use Imagery

As we have seen, imagery can be used in all sports and activities. Remember that imagery has many uses, not only to enhance performance. The following are examples of how coaches and sport professionals in several activities can use imagery to enhance performance:

- *Physical education.* After finishing a period of vigorous physical activity, ask students to stretch, sit down, and imagine themselves feeling relaxed and calm. Have them practice while they wait in line to participate in an activity.
- *Volleyball.* Before matches, reserve a quiet, dark room for players to visualize themselves performing against a specific opponent.
- *Exercise class.* During a cool-down period, ask participants to visualize how they want their bodies to look and feel.
- *Basketball.* Before practice have players imagine their specific assignments for different defenses and offensive sets.
- *Tennis.* During changeovers instruct players to visualize what type of strategy and shots they want to use in the upcoming game.
- *Swimming.* After every practice give swimmers 5 minutes to pick a certain stroke and imagine doing it perfectly or visualize it during rest periods between intervals.

SUMMARY

1 *Define imagery and identify its uses.*

Imagery refers to creating or recreating an experience in the mind. It is a form of simulation that involves recalling from memory pieces of information stored there from all types of experiences and shaping them into meaningful images. Imagery has many uses including reducing anxiety, building confidence, enhancing concentration, recovering from injury, and practicing specific skills and strategies.

2 *Discuss factors influencing the effectiveness of imagery.*

Consistent with the interactional theme seen throughout the text, imagery effectiveness is affected by both situational and personal factors. These include the nature of the task, the skill level of the performer, and the imaging ability of the person.

3 *Describe how imagery works.*

A number of theories or explanations attempt to explain how imagery works. These include the psychoneuromuscular theory, symbolic learning theory, psychological skills hypothesis, bioinformational theory, and triple code theory. All five explanations have some support from research findings, and they basically propose that physiological and psychological reasons account for imagery effectiveness.

4 *Identify the different types of imagery.*

There are basically two types of imagery: internal and external. People need not use one or the other exclusively. Whatever kind of imagery is comfortable to the individual should be practiced systematically, just like physical skills. Both types of imagery involve not only the visual sense but also kinesthetic, auditory, tactile, and olfactory senses.

5 *Explain how to develop a program of imagery training.*

Motivation and realistic expectations are critical first steps in setting up a program of imagery training. In addition, evaluation, using such an instrument as the Sport Imagery Questionnaire, should occur before the training program begins. Basic training in imagery includes exercises in vividness and controllability. Athletes should initially practice imagery in a quiet setting and in a relaxed, attentive state. They should focus on developing positive images, although it is also useful to occasionally visualize failures to develop coping skills. Both the execution and outcome of the skill should be imaged, and imaging should occur in real time.

6 *Explain when to use imagery.*

Imagery can be used before and after practice and competition, during breaks in the action, and during personal time. Imagery can also benefit the injury rehabilitation process.

KEY TERMS

imagery
kinesthetic sense
visual sense
auditory sense
tactile sense
olfactory sense
anecdotal reports
case studies
multiple-baseline case studies
psychological intervention packages
scientific experiments

psychoneuromuscular theory
ideomotor principle
symbolic learning theory
psychological skills hypothesis
bioinformational theory
triple code model
internal imagery
external imagery
vividness
controllability

REVIEW QUESTIONS

1. What is imagery? Discuss recreating experiences that involve all the senses.
2. What are three uses of imagery? Provide practical examples for each.
3. Compare and contrast the psychoneuromuscular and symbolic learning theories as they pertain to imagery.
4. Describe some anecdotal and some experimental evidence supporting the effectiveness of imagery in improving performance, including the nature of the task and ability level.
5. Compare and contrast internal and external imagery and their comparative effectiveness.
6. Describe two exercises each to improve vividness and controllability of imagery.
7. What is the importance of vividness and controllability in enhancing the quality of imagery?
8. Discuss three of the basic elements of a successful imagery program, including why they are important.

CRITICAL THINKING QUESTIONS

1. Think of a sport or physical activity you enjoy (or used to enjoy). If you were to use imagery to help improve your performance as well as enhance the experience of your participation, describe how you would put together a training program for yourself. What would be the major goals of this program? What factors would you have to consider to enhance the effectiveness of your imagery?
2. As an exercise leader you want to use imagery with a class, but the students are a little skeptical of its effectiveness. Using anecdotal, case study, and experimental evidence, convince them that imagery would be a great addition to making the class experience more positive.

© Photo: Action Images

Self-Confidence

After reading this chapter you should be able to

1 define and understand the benefits of self-confidence,

2 understand how expectations affect performance and behavior,

3 explain the theory of self-efficacy,

4 explain how you would assess self-confidence, and

5 describe strategies for building self-confidence.

If you listen to interviews with athletes and coaches after competitions, you will inevitably hear them discussing the critical role that self-confidence (or a lack of self-confidence) played in their mental success (or failure). Research, too, indicates that the most consistent factor distinguishing highly successful from less successful athletes is confidence (Jones & Hardy, 1990). In interviews with 63 of the highest achievers from a wide variety of sports, nearly 90% stated that they had a very high level of self-confidence. What this means is that top athletes, regardless of the sport, consistently display a strong belief in themselves and their abilities. Let's look at how Olympic decathlon gold medalist Daly Thompson and all-time tennis great Jimmy Connors view confidence.

> *I've always been confident of doing well. I know whether or not I'm going to win. I have doubts, but come a week or ten days before the event, they're all gone. I've never gone into competition with any doubts. I've always had confidence of putting 100% in and at the end of the day, I think regardless of where you come, you can't do any more than try your best.*
>
> **— Daly Thompson (cited in Hemery, 1986, p. 156)**

> *The whole thing is never to get negative about yourself. Sure, it's possible that the other guy you're playing is tough and that he may have beaten you the last time you played, and okay, maybe you haven't been playing all that well yourself. But the minute you start thinking about these things you're dead. I go out to every match convinced that I'm going to win. That's all there is to it.*
>
> **—Jimmy Connors (cited in Weinberg, 1988, p. 127)**

Even elite athletes sometimes have self-doubts, however, although they still seem to hold the belief they can perform at high levels. Former world-class middle-distance runner Herb Elliot stated, "I think one of my big strengths has been my doubts of myself; if you're very aware of the weaknesses and are full of your own self-doubts, in a sense, that's quite a motivation" (Hemery, 1986, p. 155). So sometimes there is a struggle between feeling self-confident and recognizing your weaknesses. Let's begin by defining what we mean by self-confidence.

Defining Self-Confidence

Although we hear athletes and exercisers talk about confidence all the time, it is not an easy term to define precisely. Sport psychologists define self-confidence as the belief that you can successfully perform a desired behavior. The desired behavior might be kicking a soccer goal, staying on an exercise regimen, recovering from a knee injury, serving an ace, or hitting a home run. But the common factor is that you believe you will get the job done.

Vealey (1986) views self-confidence as both a trait and a state. Trait self-confidence is defined as the belief or degree of certainty individuals usually possess about their ability to be successful in sport. State self-confidence is the belief of certainty individuals possess at a particular moment about their ability to be successful in sport. Although someone might have a general or overall level of self-confidence, this can change from situation to situation or even within a competition. Here is how a college basketball player described self-confidence and its sometimes transient nature:

> *The whole thing is to have a positive mental approach. As a shooter, you know that you will probably miss at least 50% of your shots. So you can't get down on yourself just because you miss a few in a row. Still, I know it's easy for me to lose my confidence fast. Therefore, when I do miss several shots in a row I try to think that I am more likely to make the next one since I'm a 50% shooter. If I feel confident in myself and my abilities, then everything else seems to fall into place.*

Confident athletes believe in themselves. Most importantly, they believe in their ability to acquire the necessary skills and competencies, both physical and mental, to reach their potential. Less confident players doubt whether they are good enough or have what it takes to be successful.

When you doubt your ability to succeed or expect something to go wrong, you are creating what is called a self-fulfilling prophecy—which means that expecting something to happen actually helps cause it to happen. Unfortunately, this phenomenon is common in both competitive sport and exercise programs. Negative self-fulfilling prophecies are psychological barriers that lead to a vicious cycle: The expectation of failure leads to actual failure, which lowers self-image and increases expectations of future failure. For example, a baseball batter in a slump begins to expect to strike out, which leads to increased anxiety and decreased concentration, which in turn usually result in lowered expectancies and poorer performance.

A great example of someone overcoming a negative self-fulfilling prophecy is the story of how Roger

© Human Kinetics

Bannister broke the 4-minute mile. Before 1954 most people claimed there was no way to run a mile in less than 4 minutes. Many runners were timed at 4:03, 4:02, and 4:01, but most runners agreed that to get below 4 minutes was physiologically impossible. Roger Bannister, however, did not. Bannister felt certain that he could break the 4-minute barrier under the right conditions—and he did. Bannister's feat was impressive, but what's really interesting is that in the next year more than a dozen runners broke the 4-minute mile. Why? Did everyone suddenly get faster or start training harder? Of course not. What happened was that runners finally believed it could be done. Until Roger Bannister broke the barrier, runners had been placing psychological limits on themselves because they felt it just wasn't possible to break the 4-minute mile.

Benefits of Self-Confidence

Self-confidence is characterized by a high expectancy of success. It can help individuals to arouse positive emotions, facilitate concentration, set goals, increase effort, focus their game strategies, and maintain momentum. We'll discuss each of these briefly.

Confidence Arouses Positive Emotions

When you feel confident, you are more likely to remain calm and relaxed under pressure. This state of mind and body allows you to be aggressive and assertive when the outcome of the competition lays in the balance.

Confidence Facilitates Concentration

When you feel confident, your mind is free to focus on the task at hand. When you lack confidence, you tend to worry about how well you are doing or how well others think you are doing. A preoccupation with avoiding failure will impair concentration by making you more easily distracted.

Confidence Affects Goals

Confident people tend to set challenging goals and pursue them actively. Confidence allows you to reach for the stars and realize your potential. People who are not confident tend to set easy goals and never push themselves to the limits (see goal setting in chapter 15).

Confidence Increases Effort

How much effort someone expends and how long she will persist in pursuit of that goal depend largely

© Photo: Action Images

on confidence (Weinberg, Yukelson, & Jackson, 1980). When ability is equal, the winners of competitions are usually the athletes who believe in themselves and their abilities. This is especially true where persistence is essential, such as running a marathon, playing a 3-hour tennis match, or enduring painful rehabilitation sessions.

Confidence Affects Game Strategies

People in sport commonly refer to "playing to win" or, conversely, "playing not to lose." These phrases sound similar but they produce very different styles of play. Confident athletes tend to play to win: They are usually not afraid to take chances and so they take control of the competition to their advantage. When athletes are not confident, they play not to lose: They are tentative and try to avoid making mistakes. For example, a confident basketball player who comes off the bench will try to make things happen by scoring, stealing a pass, or getting an important rebound to ignite the team. A less confident player will try to avoid making a mistake, like turning over the ball or failing to take an open shot. They are content not to mess up and less concerned with making something positive happen.

Confidence Affects Psychological Momentum

Athletes and coaches refer to momentum shifts as critical determinants of winning and losing (Miller & Weinberg, 1991). Being able to produce positive momentum or reverse negative momentum is an important asset. Highly skilled athletes are better able to rebound from adversity (i.e., being behind) than are their less elite counterparts (Ransom & Weinberg, 1985). And confidence appears to be a critical ingre-

Psychological Momentum: Illusion or Reality?

Most coaches and athletes speak about the concept of psychological momentum and how it is often elusive; you have it one minute and the next minute you don't. Competitions often seem to sway back and forth: One team or player is "on a roll" and then, just as quickly, the other team or player gets rolling. Researchers have found that this feeling of momentum might be more an illusion than a reality. For example, a study investigated the "hot hand" phenomenon in basketball, which traditionally has meant that when a player has hit a few shots in a row, he or she is likely to continue making baskets. But using records from professional basketball teams, researchers mathematically analyzed the probability of making a shot after having made several shots in a row. They discovered that a player was just as likely to miss the next basket as to make the next basket after having several successful shots in a row (Gillovich, Vallone, & Tversky, 1985). Other psychologists learned that after scoring three consecutive points and having momentum, volleyball teams were just as likely to win as to lose the next point (Miller & Weinberg, 1991). Researchers continue to investigate this elusive concept of psychological momentum.

dient in this process. People who are confident in themselves and their abilities have a never-give-up attitude. They view situations in which things are going against them as challenges and react with increased determination. For example, Wayne Gretzky, Michael Jordan, Steffi Graf, and Tiger Woods exude the confidence to reverse momentum when the outlook looks bleak.

Optimal Self-Confidence

Although confidence is a critical determinant of performance, it will not overcome incompetence. Confidence can take an athlete only so far. The relation between confidence and performance can be represented by the form of an inverted-U with the highest point skewed to the right (see Figure 14.1). Performance improves as the level of confidence increases—up to an optimal point, whereupon further increases in confidence produce corresponding decrements in performance.

Optimal self-confidence means being so convinced that you can achieve your goals that you will strive hard to do so. It does not necessarily mean you will always perform well, but it is essential to reaching your potential. You can expect to make some errors and bad decisions, and you might lose concentration occasionally.

People strive for an individual, optimal confidence level but sometimes become either overconfident or underconfident.

But a strong belief in yourself will help you deal with errors and mistakes effectively and keep you striving toward success. Each person has an optimal level of self-confidence, and performance problems can arise with either too little or too much confidence.

Lack of Confidence

Many people have the physical skills to be successful but lack confidence in their ability to perform these skills under pressure—when the game or match is on the line. For example, a volleyball player consistently hits strong and accurate spikes during practice. In the match, however, her first spike is blocked back in her face. She starts to doubt herself and becomes tentative and conservative in subsequent spikes, thus losing her effectiveness.

Self-doubts undermine performance: They create anxiety, break concentration, and cause indecisiveness. Individuals lacking confidence focus on their shortcomings rather than on their strengths, distracting themselves from concentrating on the task at hand. Sometimes athletes in the training room doubt their ability to fully recover from injury. Exercisers often have self-doubts about the way they look or their ability to stay with a regular exercise program. But, as noted earlier, for some individuals a little self-doubt keeps them motivated and prevents complacency or overconfidence.

Overconfidence

Overconfident people are actually falsely confident. That is, their confidence is greater than their

289

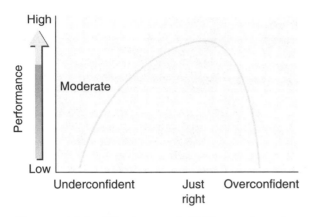

Figure 14.1 *The inverted-U illustrating the confidence-performance relationship.*

abilities warrant. Their performance declines because they believe that they don't have to prepare themselves or exert the effort to get the job done. This occurs when a top-rated team takes another team for granted, its members thinking that all they have to do is show up to win. You cannot be overconfident, however, if your confidence is based on actual skill and ability (and, in other words, as long as you give proper credit to your competitor). As a general rule, overconfidence is much less a problem than underconfidence. When it does occur, however, the results can be just as disastrous.

In the mid-1970s Bobby Riggs lost a famous "battle of the sexes" tennis match against Billie Jean King. Riggs explained the loss this way:

> *It was mainly a case of overconfidence on my part. I overestimated myself. I underestimated Billie Jean's ability to meet the pressure. I let her pick the surface and the ball because I figured it wouldn't make a difference, that she would beat herself. Even when she won the first set, I wasn't worried. In fact, I tried to bet more money on myself. I miscalculated. I ran out of gas. She started playing better and better. I started playing worse. I tried to slow up the game to keep her back but she kept the pressure on. (Tarshis, 1977, p. 48)*

A more common situation is when two players or teams of different abilities play each other. The better player or team often approaches the competition overconfidently. They slight preparation and play haphazardly, which may well cause them to fall behind early in the competition. The opponent, meanwhile, starts to gain confidence, making it even harder for the overconfident players to come back and win the competition. This scenario happens even to the

best athletes, but they will usually not let it happen often.

False overconfidence is seen sometimes when athletes attempt to cover self-doubts. Most coaches encourage athletes to be confident, so players usually aren't comfortable showing self-doubt. Thus, they fake overconfidence to hide actual feelings of self-doubt. It would be more constructive to express these feelings to the coach and have the coach devise a program to help athletes remove their doubts and gain back their self-confidence. Of course, this means that the coach or teacher must create an atmosphere that encourages open communication from their students or athletes.

How Expectations Influence Performance

Since self-confidence is the belief that you can successfully perform a desired behavior, it becomes clear that one's expectations play a critical role in the behavior-change process. Research has shown that giving people a sugar pill for extreme pain (telling them that it's morphine) can produce as much relief as a painkiller. In essence, the powerful effect of expectations on performance is evident in many aspects of daily life, including sport and exercise. Keeping expectations high and maintaining confidence under adversity are important not only for athletes and exercisers but also for officials. Here is what a professional tennis umpire has said on the subject:

> *The chair umpire in tennis is a job that requires individuals who have confidence in themselves and are not easily shaken. The players hit the ball so hard and fast and close to the lines that it is virtually impossible to be absolutely certain of all the calls. But . . . you can't start to doubt yourself, because once you do, you start to lose control of the match. In the end the players will respect you and your calls more if you show them that you are confident in your judgment and your abilities.*

Self-Expectations and Performance

There have been some interesting studies to demonstrate the relation of expectations and performance.

Positive expectations for success have been shown to produce positive effects in many fields of life, including sport.

290

> *Expecting to beat a tough opponent or successfully perform a difficult skill can produce exceptional performance as psychological barriers are overcome.*

> *Your expectations of others affect not only your own behavior but the feelings and behavior of others.*

In one study, subjects were each paired with someone they thought clearly stronger in arm strength and then instructed to arm wrestle (Nelson & Furst, 1972). Remarkably, in 10 of the 12 contests, the objectively weaker subject (whom both subjects believed was stronger) won the competition. Clearly, the most important factor was not actual physical strength but who the competitors expected to win.

In another study two groups of subjects were told that they were lifting either more weight or less weight than they really were (Ness & Patton, 1979). For example, someone who had already lifted 130 pounds was told he was given 130 pounds again, when in fact he was given 150 pounds, or vice versa. A third group of subjects was told nothing about how much weight they were lifting. Subsequently, subjects lifted the most weight when they thought they were lifting less—that is, when they believed and expected they could lift the weight.

In a study conducted on the 1976 U.S. men's Olympic gymnastics team (Mahoney & Avener, 1977), researchers interviewed gymnasts to assess their level of confidence. The gymnasts with self-doubts tended to perform worse during the qualifying meet than those who expressed no self-doubts. Among the 12 finalists, the gymnasts who exhibited the strongest expectations of success in the meet tended to perform the best. More recent studies have also found that self-confidence was a critical factor in discriminating between successful and less successful performers (Jones, Hanton, & Swain, 1994; Mahoney, Gabriel, & Perkins, 1987). In summary, these studies demonstrate the critical role that self-expectations play on an athlete's performance.

Coaching Expectations and Athletes' Performance

The idea that a coach's expectations could affect athletes' performances evolved from a classic study: Rosenthal and Jacobson (1968) informed teachers that a standardized test of academic ability had identified certain children in each of their classes as "late bloomers" who could be expected to show big gains in academic achievement and IQ over the course of the school year. In fact, these children had been selected at random, so there was no reason to expect they would show greater academic progress than their classmates. But at the end of the school year, these so-called late bloomers did in fact achieve greater gains in IQ scores than the other children did. Rosenthal and Jacobson suggested that the false test information made the teachers expect higher performance from the targeted students, which led them to give these students more attention, reinforcement, and instruction. The students' performance and behavior thus conformed to the teachers' expectations that they were gifted students.

Studies in physical education classrooms (Martinek & Johnson, 1979) and competitive sport environments (Chase, Lirgg, & Feltz, 1997; Solomon, Striegel, Eliot, Heon, & Maas, 1996) also indicate that teachers' and coaches' expectations can alter their students' and athletes' performances. These studies found that head coaches provided more of all types of feedback to athletes of whom they had high expectations and that these athletes viewed their coaches more positively. In addition, the coaches' expectations were a significant predictor of their athletes' performances. This process is a form of the self-fulfilling prophecy, but it does not occur in all situations: Some teachers and coaches let their expectations affect their interaction with students and athletes, but others do not.

A sequence of events that occurs in athletic settings seems to explain the expectation-performance relationship (Horn, 1986).

Step 1. Coaches Form Expectations

Coaches usually form expectations of their athletes and teams. Sometimes these expectations come from an individual's race, physical size, gender, or socioeconomic status. These expectations are called person cues. The exclusive use of person cues to form judgments about an athlete's competence could certainly lead to inaccurate expectations. Coaches also use performance information, such as past accomplishments, skill tests, practice behaviors, and other coaches' evaluations. When these sources of information lead to an accurate assessment of the athlete's ability and potential, there's no problem. However, inaccurate expectations (either too high or too low), especially when they are inflexible, will typically lead to inappropriate behaviors on the part of the coach.

291

This brings us to the second step in the sequence of events—the self-fulfilling prophecy.

Step 2. Coaches' Expectations Influence Their Behaviors

Among teachers and coaches who behave differently if they have high or low expectancies of a given student or athlete, behaviors usually fit into one of the following categories:

Frequency and Quality of Coach-Athlete Interaction

- Coach spends more time with high-expectancy athletes he or she expects more of.
- Coach shows more warmth and positive affect toward these high-expectancy athletes.

Quantity and Quality of Instruction

- Coach lowers his or her expectations of what skills some athletes will learn, thus establishing a lower standard of performance.
- Coach allows the athletes he or she expects less of correspondingly less time in practice drills.
- Coach is less persistent in teaching difficult skills to these "low-expectation" athletes.

Type and Frequency of Feedback

- Coach provides more reinforcement and praise for "high-expectation" athletes after a successful performance.
- Coach provides less beneficial feedback to "low-expectation" athletes, such as praise after a mediocre performance.
- Coach gives "high-expectation" athletes more instructional and informational feedback.

Here is an example of how a coach's expectations might affect his or her behavior.

During the course of a volleyball game, Kira (whose coach has high expectations of her) attempts to spike the ball despite the fact that the setup was poor, pulling her away from the net. The spike goes into the net, but the coach says, "Good try, Kira, just try to get more elevation on your jump so you can contact the ball above the level of the net." When Janet (whom the coach expects less of) does the same thing, the coach says, "Don't try to spike the ball when you're not in position, Janet. You'll never make a point like that."

Step 3. Coaches' Behaviors Affect Athletes' Performances

In this step the coaches' expectation-biased treatment of athletes affects performance both physically and psychologically. It is easy to understand that athletes who consistently receive more positive and instructional feedback from coaches will show more improvement in their performance and enjoy the competitive experience more. Look at these ways athletes are affected by the negatively biased expectations of their coaches:

- Low-expectation athletes exhibit poorer performances due to less effective reinforcement and playing time.
- Low-expectation athletes exhibit lower levels of self-confidence and perceived competence over the course of a season.
- Low-expectation athletes attribute their failures to lack of ability, thus substantiating the notion that they aren't any good and have little chance of future success.

Step 4. Athletes' Performances Confirm the Coaches' Expectations

Step 4 of course communicates to coaches that they were correct in their initial assessment of the athletes' ability and potential. Few coaches observe that their own behaviors and attitudes help produce this result. And not all athletes will allow a coach's behavior or expectations to affect their performance or psychological reactions. Some athletes look to other sources, such as parents, peers, or other adults, to form perceptions of their competency and abilities. The support and information from these other people can often help athletes resist the biases communicated by a coach.

Clearly, sport and exercise professionals, including trainers and rehabilitation specialists, need to be aware of how they form expectations and how their behavior is affected. Early on, both teachers and coaches should determine how they form expectations and whether their sources of information are reliable indicators of an individual's ability. Initial assessments can be mistaken. Coaches and teachers should also monitor the quantity and quality of reinforcement and instructional feedback they give so that they make sure all participants get their fair share. Such actions help ensure that each participant has a fair chance to reach his or her potential and enjoy the athletic experience.

Self-Efficacy Theory

Self-efficacy, the perception of one's ability to perform a task successfully, is really a situation-specific

© Eric Berndt/Unicorn Stock Photos

Self-efficacy theory provides a model to study the effects of self-confidence on sport performance, persistence, and behavior.

form of self-confidence. For our purposes, we'll use the terms interchangeably. Psychologist Albert Bandura (1977a; 1986) brought together the concepts of confidence and expectations to formulate a clear and useful conceptual model of self-efficacy. Bandura's theory of self-efficacy has been adapted to explain behavior within several disciplines of psychology, and it has formed the theoretical basis adopted for most performance-oriented research in self confidence and sport. The theory was originally developed within the framework of a social-cognitive approach to behavior change that placed self-efficacy as a common cognitive mechanism for mediating motivation and behavior. Consistent with the orientation of this textbook, self-efficacy theory takes an interactional approach, viewing one's self-efficacy

as interacting with environmental determinants to produce behavior change.

Bandura's self-efficacy theory has several underlying premises, including the following:

- If someone has the requisite skills and sufficient motivation, then the major determinant of his or her performance is self-efficacy. Self-efficacy alone is not enough to be successful—an athlete must also want to succeed and have the ability to succeed.

- Self-efficacy affects an athlete's choice of activities, level of effort, and persistence. Athletes who believe in themselves will tend to persevere, especially under adverse conditions.

- Although self-efficacy is task-specific, it can generalize or transfer to other similar skills and situations.

- Self-efficacy is related to goal setting, with those exhibiting high self-efficacy being more likely to set challenging goals.

According to Bandura's theory, one's feelings of self-efficacy are derived from six principal sources of information: performance accomplishments, vicarious experiences, verbal persuasion, imaginal experiences, physiological states, and emotional states. The fact that these six sources of efficacy are readily applicable in sport and exercise contexts is largely responsible for the theory's popularity among sport and exercise psychologists. These six categories or sources are not mutually exclusive in terms of the information they provide, although some are more influential than others. The relation between the major sources of efficacy information, efficacy expectations, and performance is diagrammed in Figure 14.2. We'll discuss each source in the sections that follow.

Performance Accomplishments

Performance accomplishments (particularly clear success or failure) provide the most dependable basis for self-efficacy judgments because they are based on one's mastery experiences. If experiences are generally successful, they will raise the level of self-efficacy. However, repeated failures will result in expectations of lower efficacy. For example, if a field-

goal kicker has kicked the winning field goal in several games as time was running out, he will have a high degree of self-efficacy that he can do it again. Similarly, an athlete rehabilitating from a wrist injury will persist in exercise after seeing steady improvement in her range of motion and wrist strength. Research into diving and gymnastics shows that performance accomplishments increase self-efficacy, which in turn increases subsequent performance (McAuley, 1985) as well as exercise adherence (McAuley, 1992; 1993a). Coaches and teachers can help participants experience the feeling of successful performance by using such tactics as guiding a gymnast through a complicated move, letting young baseball players play on a smaller field, or lowering the basket for young basketball players.

Vicarious Experiences

Physical educators, exercise leaders, athletic trainers, and coaches all often use vicarious experiences, also known as demonstration or modeling, to help students learn new skills. This can be a particularly important source of efficacy information for

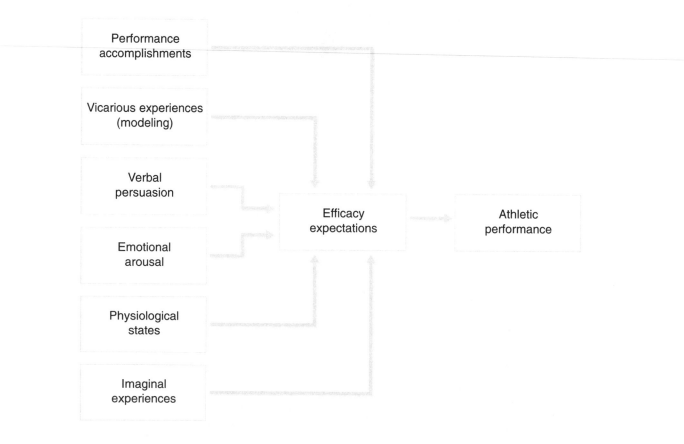

Figure 14.2 *Relations among sources of efficacy information, efficacy expectations, and athletic performance.*
Adapted from Feltz, 1984.

Sources of Sport Self-Confidence

Recently researchers have identified nine sources of self-confidence specific to sport. Many of these are similar to the six sources Bandura earlier identified in his self-efficacy theory. The nine sources fall into the three general categories of achievement, self-regulation, and climate:

- Mastery—developing and improving skills
- Demonstration of ability—showing ability by winning and outperforming opponents
- Physical and mental preparation—staying focused on goals and prepared to give maximum effort
- Physical self-presentation—feeling good about my body and weight
- Social support—getting encouragement from teammates, coaches, and family
- Coaches' leadership—trusting the coaches' decisions and believing in their abilities
- Vicarious experience—seeing other athletes perform successfully
- Environmental comfort—feeling comfortable in the environment where I will perform
- Situational favorableness—seeing breaks going my way and feeling everything is going right

---

performers lacking experience with the task at hand, relying on others to judge their own capabilities. For example, seeing a team member complete a difficult move on the uneven parallel bars can reduce anxiety and help convince other gymnasts that they, too, can accomplish this move. Although vicarious experiences are usually not as potent as actual performance accomplishments in building self-efficacy, they have been effective in improving performance. For example, people watching skilled models who were similar to the observers themselves enhanced their self-efficacy and performance (Gould & Weiss, 1981; Lirgg & Feltz, 1991). Coaches view their own modeling of self-confidence as an important, additional source of confidence for their athletes (Gould, Hodge, Peterson, & Giannini, 1989; Weinberg, Grove, & Jackson, 1992). In essence, coaches perceive that if they act confidently, then their athletes will feel more confident.

According to Bandura (1965; 1974; also see McCullagh, Weiss, & Ross, 1989), modeling can be best understood through a four-stage process: attention, retention, motor reproduction, and motivation. In order to learn through watching, careful attention must first be given to the model. Our ability to attend to depends on respect for the person observed, interest in the activity, and how well we can see and hear. The best teachers and coaches do not overload you with information, expect you to focus your attention on all the specific elements of the skill, or show the skill only one quick time. Rather, they focus on a few key points, demonstrate several times, and let you know exactly what to look for.

For effective modeling to occur, the observed act must be committed to memory. This retention can be accomplished through mental practice techniques, analogies (e.g., tell the athlete to liken the tennis serve motion to throwing a racquet), or by having individuals verbally repeat the key points aloud (Remember the hokey-pokey dance in elementary physical education? "Put your right foot in, take your right foot out."). The key is to help the observer remember the modeled act.

Even if people attend to the demonstrated physical skills and remember how to do them, they still may not be able to perform if they have not learned motor reproduction, that is, how to coordinate their muscle actions with their thoughts. For example, you could know exactly what a good approach and

■ APPLICATION ■

Tips for Giving
Effective Demonstrations

Effective modeling is one of the primary sources of self-efficacy. Try to determine whether each tip fits the category of attention, retention, motor reproduction, or motivation.

- Inform learners of the importance of the skill to the game or activity.
- Point out a high-status model (e.g., professional athlete) who effectively uses the skill to be modeled.
- Make sure participants do not face any distractions and that they can all see and hear.
- Make eye contact with the learner as you convey instructions about the modeled act.
- Demonstrate complex skills from several angles (e.g., tennis serve for both left- and right-handed individuals).
- Focus learner attention on only three or four key points of the skill.
- Repeat demonstrations of complex skills.
- Make sure instructions always slightly precede the skill or segment of the skill being demonstrated.
- Have the learners mentally rehearse what was shown immediately after observing the demonstration.
- Practice the skill immediately after it has been demonstrated and mentally rehearsed.
- Have observers name the subunits or parts of the skill.
- Always follow slow-motion demonstrations by giving at least one demonstration performed at full speed.
- Reinforce correct performance of the modeled act.

With children, focus on fewer key points and emphasize mental practice.

---

delivery in bowling looks like and even be able to mimic the optimal physical action, but without physical practice to learn the timing, you will not roll strikes. When modeling sport and exercise skills, you must make sure you have taught lead-up skills, provided optimal practice time, and considered the progression of how to best order related skills.

The final stage in the modeling process is motivation, and it affects all the other stages. Without being motivated, an observer will not attend to the model, try to remember what was seen, and practice the skill. The key, then, is to motivate the observer through praise, through the promise of earning rewards, by imparting the importance of learning the modeled activity, or by utilizing models who will motivate them.

Verbal Persuasion

Coaches, teachers, and peers often use persuasive techniques to influence behavior. An example would be a baseball coach telling a player, "I know you're a good hitter, so just hang in there and take your swings. The base hits will eventually come." Similarly, an exercise leader might tell an exercise participant to "hang in there and don't get discouraged, even if you have to miss a couple of days." This type of encouragement is important to participants and can be helpful in improving self-efficacy. When a psychological barrier is present, coaches and instructors sometimes even resort to deception to persuade performers that they can perform certain skills. For example, if a high jumper has a mental block about high-jumping six feet, in practice the coach might

Collective Efficacy:
A Special Case of Self-Efficacy

A recent focus of research has been on the concept of collective, or team, efficacy. Collective efficacy refers to a belief or perception shared by members of the team regarding their aggregate capabilities. In short, it's each individual's perception of the efficacy of the team as a whole. Research (Lirgg & Feltz, 1994) has demonstrated that athletes' belief in the team's total (collective) efficacy was positively related to performance; adding up each individual's personal self-efficacy, however, was *not* related to team performance. In essence, coaches should be more concerned with building the efficacy of the team as a whole rather than with each individual player's self-efficacy. Creating a belief in the team and its ability to be successful as a group appears to be critical to success. Many of the great teams (Chicago Bulls, New York Yankees, Montreal Canadians, San Francisco 49ers) have had this sense of team efficacy during their winning years. Therefore, in order to enhance performance and productivity—whether you are a coach, teacher, exercise leader, or head athletic trainer—it seems crucial that you get your team, group, or class to believe in themselves as a unit (as opposed to simply believing in themselves individually).

© Anthony Neste Photography

raise the bar to six feet but tell the athlete it's really 5 feet 10 inches. Using deception is tricky, however, and can undermine credibility and trust.

Verbal persuasion to enhance confidence can also take the form of self-persuasion. Janel Jorgensen, silver medalist in the 100-meter butterfly in the 1988 Olympic Games, explains:

> *You have to believe it's going to happen. You can't doubt your abilities by saying, Oh I'm going to wake up tomorrow and I'm going to feel totally bad since I felt bad today and yesterday. You can't go about it like that. You have to say O.K., tomorrow I'm going to feel good. I didn't feel good today. That's that. We will see what happens tomorrow. (Ripol, 1993, p. 36)*

Imaginal Experiences

Individuals can generate beliefs about personal efficacy or inefficacy by imagining themselves or others behaving effectively or ineffectively in future situations. The key to using imagery as a source of

confidence is to see oneself demonstrating mastery (Moritz et al., 1996). A detailed discussion of the use of imagery in sport and exercise settings is provided in chapter 13.

Physiological States

Physiological states influence self-efficacy when individuals associate aversive physiological arousal with poor performance, perceived incompetence, and perceived failure. Thus, when people become aware of unpleasant physiological arousal (e.g., racing heartbeat), they are more likely to doubt their competence than if they were experiencing pleasant physiological arousal (smooth, rhythmical breathing). For instance, some athletes may interpret increases in their physiological arousal or anxiety (such as the heart's beating fast or their breathing being shallow) as a fear that they cannot perform the skill successfully (lowered self-efficacy), whereas others might perceive them as a sign that they are ready for the upcoming competition (enhanced self-efficacy).

Emotional States

Although physiological cues are important components of emotions, emotional experiences are not simply the product of physiological arousal. Thus, emotions or moods can be an additional source of information about self-efficacy. For example, an injured athlete who is feeling depressed and anxious about her rehabilitation would probably have lowered feelings of self-efficacy. Conversely, an athlete who feels energized and positive would probably have enhanced feelings of self-efficacy.

Assessing Self-Confidence

Now that you understand the relation of confidence and performance and that effectiveness can be hampered by overconfidence or underconfidence, the next step is to identify confidence levels in a variety of situations. Athletes might do this by answering the following questions:

- When am I overconfident?
- How do I recover from mistakes?
- When do I have self-doubts?

Sport Confidence Inventory

Read each question carefully and think about your confidence with regard to each item as you competed during the last year or season. For each item indicate by what percentage of time you feel you have had too little, too much, or just the right degree of confidence. Below is an example to give you some confidence in filling out the inventory correctly.

	Underconfident (%)	Confident (%)	Overconfident (%)
You are a pole vaulter:			
How confident are you each time you attempt to clear 17 feet?	20	70	10

The three answers should always add up to 100%. You may distribute this 100% in any way you think is appropriate. You may assign all 100% to one category, split it between two categories, or, as in the example, divide it among all three categories.

How confident are you with respect to . . .	Underconfident (%)	Confident (%)	Overconfident (%)
1. your ability to execute the skills of your sport or exercise?	_____	_____	_____
2. your ability to make critical decisions during the contest?	_____	_____	_____
3. your ability to concentrate?	_____	_____	_____
4. your ability to perform under pressure?	_____	_____	_____
5. your ability to execute successful strategy?	_____	_____	_____
6. your ability to put forth the effort needed to succeed?	_____	_____	_____
7. your ability to control your emotions during competition?	_____	_____	_____
8. your physical conditioning or training?	_____	_____	_____
9. your ability to relate successfully to your coach(es)?	_____	_____	_____
10. your ability to come back when behind?	_____	_____	_____

Adapted from ACEP, 1989.

- Is my confidence consistent throughout the event?
- Am I tentative and indecisive in certain situations?
- Do I look forward to and enjoy tough, highly competitive games?
- How do I react to adversity?

The Sport Confidence Inventory presents a more formal and detailed self-confidence inventory to assess confidence levels.

To score your overall confidence, add up the percentages in each of the three columns and then divide by 10. The higher your score in the "Confident" column, the more likely you are to be at your optimal level of confidence during competition. High scores in the "Underconfident" or "Overconfident" columns present some potential problem areas. To determine specific strengths and weaknesses, look at each item. The scale assesses confidence both in physical and mental terms. You can use this questionnaire to inform yourself or others of areas you need to work on.

Building Self-Confidence

Many people believe that you either have confidence or you don't. Confidence can be built, however, through work, practice, and planning. Jimmy Connors is a good example. Throughout his junior playing days, his mother taught him to always hit out and go for winners. Because of this playing style he lost some matches he should have won. Yet Connors said he never could have made it without his mother and grandmother. "They were so sensational in their support, they never allowed me to lose confidence. They just kept telling me to play the same way, and they kept assuring me that it would eventually come together. And I believed them" (Tarshis, 1977, p. 102).

Confidence can be improved through performance accomplishments, acting confidently, thinking confidently, imagery, physical conditioning, and preparation. We will consider each of these in turn.

Performance Accomplishments

We have already discussed the influence of performance accomplishments on self-efficacy, but we'll elaborate on some of those points here. The concept is simple: Successful behavior increases confidence and leads to further successful behavior. The suc-

cessful accomplishment might be beating a particular opponent, coming from behind to win, fully extending your knee during rehabilitation, or exercising continuously for 30 minutes.

Of course, when a team loses 8 games in a row, it will be hard-pressed to feel confident about winning the next game, especially against a good team. Confidence is crucial to success, but how can you be confident without previous success? It appears to be a "Catch-22" dilemma: "We're losing now because we're not feeling confident, but I think the reason the players don't feel confident is that they have been losing."

You are certainly more likely to feel confident about performing a certain skill if you can consistently execute it during practice. That's why good practices and preparing physically, technically, and tactically to play your best enhance confidence. For the most part, performance accomplishments build confidence, and confidence then improves subsequent performance. Nothing elicits confidence like experiencing in practice what you want to accomplish in the competition.

Similarly, an athlete rehabilitating a shoulder separation needs to experience some success in improving range of motion to keep up her confidence that she will eventually regain full range of motion. Short-term goals can help her feel she has made progress and can enhance her confidence (also see chapter 15).

A coach should structure practices to simulate actual performance conditions. For example, if foul shooting under pressure has been a problem in the past, each player could shoot an extra 100 free throws during practice. However, that would not simulate actual game action. It would be better for each player to sprint up and down the floor several times before shooting any free throw (since this is what happens during a game). Furthermore, to create pressure a coach might require each player to make five free throws in a row or to continue this drill until they do so. This can create a little pressure and fatigue (just like in the game). As the players start to consistently make their free throws under these conditions, it will build confidence that they can do the same thing in a game.

Performance accomplishments represent the most powerful way to build confidence. Manipulate or create situations that allow participants to experience success and a sense of accomplishment.

■ APPLICATION ■

Dos and Don'ts for Building Self-Confidence

Dos

- Do maintain a high positive precompetitive environment.
- Do have high expectations of all your participants.
- Do set realistic but challenging short- and long-term goals.
- Do provide lots of contingent, positive feedback and praise.
- Do structure the environment to provide for early success.
- Do try to find individuals doing something right (as opposed to just looking for their mistakes).

Don'ts

- Don't use sarcasm and put-downs to motivate people.
- Don't allow teammates or group members to belittle other team or group members.
- Don't criticize individuals for inconsequential mistakes or errors.
- Don't embarrass and criticize individuals at the first sign of a mistake.
- Don't criticize the person, criticize the behavior.

Acting Confidently

Thoughts, feelings, and behaviors are interrelated: The more an athlete acts confidently, the more likely she is to feel confident. This is especially important when you begin to lose confidence and your opponent, sensing this, begins to gain confidence. Acting confidently is also important for other sport and exercise professionals. An aerobics instructor should project confidence when leading her class if she wants to have a high-spirited workout. An athletic trainer should act confidently when treating athletes so they feel trust and confidence during the rehabilitation process.

Athletes should try to display a confident image during competition. They can demonstrate their confidence by keeping their head up high—even after a critical error. Many people give themselves away through body language and movements that indicate they are lacking confidence.

Acting confidently can also lift spirits during difficult times. If someone walks around with slumped shoulders, head down, and a pained facial expression, he communicates to all observers that he is down, which works to pull him even further down. It is best to keep your head up, shoulders back, and facial muscles loose to indicate that you are confident and will persevere. This will keep opponents guessing.

Thinking Confidently

Confidence consists of thinking you can and will achieve your goals. As a collegiate golfer noted, "If I think I can win, I'm awfully tough to beat." A positive attitude is essential to reaching potential. Athletic performers need to discard negative thoughts ("I'm so stupid," "I can't believe I'm playing so bad," "I just can't beat this person," or "I'll never make it") and replace them with positive thoughts ("I'll keep getting better if I just work at it," "Just keep calm and focused," "I can beat this guy," or "Hang in there and things will get better"). Thoughts and self-talk should be instructional and motivational rather than judgmental. Correcting one's technique, encouragement, and cues to perform the skill more successfully should be the focus of self-talk (see chapter 16). In fact, positive self-talk not only can provide specific performance cues but also keep motivation and energy high. Although sometimes difficult to do, positive self-talk results in a more enjoyable and successful athletic experience, making it well worth using.

Imagery

As you can recall from chapter 13, one use of imagery is to help build confidence. You can see yourself

300

■ CLOSE-UP ■

Fast Is What You Think It Is

Kenyon College's Gregg Parini won the 1980 NCAA Division III 50-yard freestyle in 21.49 seconds but worried the next winter about successfully defending his title. Gregg's coach thought a major barrier preventing Gregg from going faster was his conception of what is fast. So he told Gregg that a major difference between swimmers going 20-plus seconds and those going 19-plus was their positive thinking. After all, what's the difference between a 20-plus and 19-plus? One second in a race that covers half the distance of a football field—that's almost nothing.

The coach suggested to Gregg that he was limiting himself by what he thought was fast for a Division III swimmer. Twenty-one plus was fast enough to win Division III, so that's what Gregg swam. Then, the coach asked him what he'd be shooting for if he were swimming in Division I. "Twenty-plus" was Gregg's reply. Gregg won the 1981 Division III Nationals in 20.83 (Bell, 1982, pp. 44–45). Gregg since has been named Division III coach of the year at Denison University.

© CLEO Photography

doing things that you either have never been able to do or have had difficulty doing. For example, a golfer who consistently has been slicing the ball off the tee can imagine himself hitting the ball straight down the fairway. A long-distance runner can see herself beating an arch rival after losing to her in the last five races. A football quarterback can visualize different defensive alignments and then try to counteract these with specific plays and formations. Simi-

larly, trainers can help injured athletes build confidence by having them imagine getting back on the playing field and performing well.

Physical Conditioning

Being in your best possible physical shape is another key to feeling confident. Athletes in most sports now train year-round to improve strength, endurance, and flexibility. Training and following good nutritional habits help you know that you can stay out there as long as necessary to get the job done.

Preparation

Jack Nicklaus has said in interviews, "As long as I'm prepared, I always expect to win." The flip side of this is that you can't expect to win if you're unprepared. Being prepared gives you confidence that you have done everything possible to ensure success. A plan gives you confidence because you know what you're going to try to do. Many athletes enter a competition without a strategy. But there should always be a plan of attack, which requires that you have at least a general idea of what you want to accomplish and how you will do it.

Most successful Olympic athletes have detailed plans and strategies of what they want to do. They also have alternative strategies (Gould, Eklund, & Jackson, 1992c; Orlick, 1986). For example, a miler should go into every race with both a plan on how to run the race and an adjustment strategy if the pace of the race dictates such a move. A good plan considers not only your own abilities but also your opponent's.

Good preparation also includes a set precompetition routine. Knowing exactly what will happen and when it will happen gives you confidence and puts your mind at ease. Being sure when you will eat, practice, stretch out, and arrive at the competition helps build confidence that extends to the competition itself. (See chapter 16 for more on precompetition routines.)

SUMMARY

1 *Define and understand the benefits of self-confidence.*

Self-confidence has been defined as the belief that you can successfully perform a desired behavior. High levels of self-confidence can enhance positive emotions, concentration, setting more challenging goals, increasing effort, and developing effective competitive strategies.

2 *Understand how expectations affect performance and behavior.*

Expectations can have a critical affect on performance. Expecting to win or expecting to lose can greatly impact one's performance in a competition. Coaches' or teachers' expectations can also have a tremendous influence on the performance and behavior of students and athletes. Coaches and teachers have been shown to act differently depending on whether they have high or low expectations of a player or student.

3 *Explain the theory of self-efficacy.*

Self-efficacy theory takes an interactional approach to the study of self-confidence, viewing one's self-efficacy as interacting with an environmental determinant to produce behavioral change. The theory views self-efficacy as the major determinant of performance as long as one has the requisite skills and is motivated to perform. The sources of self-efficacy include performance accomplishments, vicarious experiences, verbal persuasion, imaginal experiences, physiological states, and emotional states.

4 *Explain how you would assess self-confidence.*

You can assess self-confidence by asking some key questions such as How do you deal with adversity? How do you recover from a mistake? How easily do you lose your confidence? Do you get tentative in pressure situations? You can also measure self-confidence more formally through psychological confidence inventories. One such inventory asks you to rate yourself as being underconfident, overconfident, or confident about different aspects of your performance.

5 *Describe strategies for building self-confidence.*

Strategies for enhancing one's self-confidence include acting confidently, thinking confidently, using imagery, being in good physical condition, and preparing mentally and physically for upcoming performances.

KEY TERMS

self-confidence
trait self-confidence
state self-confidence
self-fulfilling prophecy
person cues
performance information

self-efficacy
vicarious experiences (modeling)
attention
retention
motor reproduction
motivation

REVIEW QUESTIONS

1. What is self-confidence? How is it related to expectations?

2. Describe two studies that demonstrate the important role that expectations can have on performance.

3. Discuss the implications that Rosenthal's and Jacobson's study on expectation effects has for coaches and physical education teachers.

4. What is self-efficacy? How does it affect behavior?

5. Discuss the six sources of self-efficacy. What evidence supports that these various sources influence efficacy?

6. Discuss Bandura's four-stage modeling process.

7. Discuss three characteristics of confidence and how these are related to athletic performance.

8. Describe the relationship between self-confidence and athletic performance, including the ideas of overconfidence and underconfidence.

9. Discuss three strategies for building self-efficacy, and describe how they affect sport performance.

10. Name three dos and don'ts for coaching when attempting to build self-confidence in athletes.

11. Is psychological momentum an illusion? Discuss this statement, citing relevant research to support your answer.

CRITICAL THINKING QUESTIONS

1. You are a new coach for a high school basketball team. You have just selected your team after rigorous tryouts. You feel that you have a wide range of talent and ability on the team, and you want to be able to develop the younger talent. But you also know how easy it is to fall into the trap of creating differential expectations of the various athletes. Using the four-step process for how coaches' expectations might influence their own behavior and that of their athletes, what specific types of feedback or instruction would you use to keep the expectations of all your athletes high? How would you also structure practices to help keep athlete expectations high?

2. Sometimes we create psychological barriers for ourselves by not believing that we can accomplish something. Discuss three situations in your life (or a close friend's or family member's) when a psychological barrier was created. How could you handle things differently to create a more positive expectation?

© Human Kinetics

Goal Setting

After reading this chapter you should be able to

1 define what goals are and identify major types of goals,

2 describe the latest research and theory of goal setting,

3 describe basic goal-setting principles,

4 explain group goals and how to use them,

5 explain how to design a goal-setting system, and

6 identify common problems in goal setting and how to overcome them.

I want to lose 10 pounds.

I want to fully recover from my injury by August 15.

My goal is to make the starting lineup.

I want to be able to bench-press my own weight.

I intend to improve my golf game and win the club tournament.

My objective is to become a high school varsity basketball coach.

People often set goals like these in sport and exercise activities. You may be wondering, then, Why devote an entire chapter to goal setting if people already set goals on their own?

The problem is not getting people to identify goals. It is getting them to set the right kind of goals—ones that provide direction and enhance motivation—and helping them learn how to stick to and achieve their goals. As most of us have learned from the New Year's resolutions we've made, it is much easier to set a goal than to follow through on it.

Seldom are goals to lose weight or to exercise set realistically in terms of commitment, difficulty, evaluating progress, and specific strategies to achieve them. Most people do not need to be convinced that goals are important; they need instruction on setting effective goals and designing a program to achieve them.

Defining Goals

Many people define a goal as an objective, a standard, an aim of some action, or a level of performance or proficiency. Some people talk about very subjective aims or objectives such as having fun, doing the best they can, or enjoying themselves. Others focus on more objective aims, such as lifting certain amounts of weight, running so many laps, or scoring a set number of points during a basketball game—that is, reaching a particular standard in an event or on a task. (McClements, 1982).

Types of Goals

Sport and exercise psychologists usually distinguish between subjective goals and objective goals, spend-

An objective goal is the desire to attain a specific standard of proficiency on a task, usually within a specified time.

ing most of their time helping their clients or students set and achieve objective goals. Subjective goals are general statements of intent (e.g., "I want to do well," "I want to have fun"), but are not stated in measurable, objective terms. In contrast, objective goals focus on "attaining a specific standard of proficiency on a task, usually within a specified time" (Locke, Shaw, Saari, & Latham, 1981, p. 145). Attempting to attain a specified level of weight loss within 3 months, a certain team win-loss record by the end of the season, and a lower performance time by the next competition are all examples of objective goals. Our definition of objective goals includes outcome, performance, and process goals (Burton, 1984; Hardy, Jones, & Gould, 1996; Martens, 1990).

Outcome Goals

Outcome goals typically focus on a competitive result of an event, such as winning a race, earning a medal, or scoring more points than an opponent. Thus, achieving these goals depends not only on your own efforts but also on the ability and play of your opponent. You could play the best tennis match of your life and still lose—and thus fail to achieve your outcome goal of winning the match.

Performance Goals

Performance goals focus on achieving standards or performance objectives independently of other competitors, usually making comparisons with one's own previous performances. For this reason performance goals tend to be more flexible and within your control. Running a mile in 6 minutes and 21 seconds or improving the percentage of successful slice first serves from 70% to 80% would be examples of performance goals.

Process Goals

Process goals focus on the actions an individual must engage in during performance to execute or perform well. For example, a swimmer may set a goal of maintaining a long, stretched-out arm pull in her freestyle stroke, or a basketball player may set a goal of squaring up to the basket and releasing the ball at the peak of his jump. Interestingly, recent research

Outcome goals in sport focus on achieving a victory in a competitive contest, whereas performance goals focus on achieving standards based on one's own previous performances, not the performances of others.

© Anthony Neste Photography

by Kingston and Hardy (1997) has shown that process goals are particularly effective in positively influencing golfer's self-efficacy, cognitive anxiety, and confidence.

Outcome, Performance, and Process Goals in Behavior Change

It is important that athletes and exercisers set outcome, performance, and process goals: All three play important roles in directing behavioral change. Outcome goals can facilitate short-term motivation away from the competition (thinking about how it felt to lose to an arch rival may motivate one to train in the off-season). Focusing on outcome goals just before or during competition, however, often leads to increased anxiety and irrelevant, distracting thoughts (e.g., an athlete worries too much about the score of the game and doesn't focus enough on the task at hand).

Performance and process goals are important because you usually can make much more precise adjustments to these goals (e.g., increase the goal from

80% to 82%) than you can to outcome goals, which often have fewer levels (i.e., you win or lose a game). Achieving a performance or process goal also depends much less on your opponent's behavior. For these reasons, performance and process goals are particularly useful for athletes at the time of competition, although they should be used in practice as well.

Under special circumstances too much focus on a specific performance goal (e.g., running a personal-best five-minute mile) can create anxiety, although this is less likely to occur than with an outcome goal. It is often difficult, in addition, to prioritize specific performance and process goals unless one also considers long-term outcome goals. For cxample, you would design quite a different fitness program if someone's outcome goal is to bulk up and gain 20 pounds than you would if an individual wanted to lose 20 pounds. All three types of goals, then, have purpose. The key is knowing when to focus on each type of goal and not falling into the trap of focusing all one's attention on outcome goals.

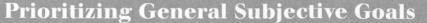

■ CASE STUDY ■

Prioritizing General Subjective Goals

Whereas most sport psychology research has focused on studying objective goals, the importance of subjective goals must not be overlooked. In the popular or commercial literature about personal productivity and business management, for example, considerable attention has been paid to identifying and clarifying one's personal values and priorities and then using these general, subjective goals to formulate more specific goals that guide day-to-day behavior (Smith, 1994). The following case makes this point.

Kim is an undergraduate student with a major in Exercise and Sport Science. Her goals are to graduate with excellent grades, get into graduate school, and become a physical therapist. Already a good student, she runs on the cross-country team, works in the training room, holds a part-time job, participates in several campus social groups, and tries to get home whenever she can. Kim has struggled lately because she has not achieved her goals. After talking to the athletic deparment sport psychologist, Kim realizes that the problem is not with the specific goals she sets (e.g., get an A in biomechanics, run a specified time on her home cross-country course) but with her global priorities or subjective goals. She is trying to do too much and needs to prioritize her activities. After considerable reflecting, Kim develops the following list of governing values and then prioritizes each subjective goal, using an A (most important), B (somewhat important), and C (less important) rating. She subsequently uses this list of general priorities each week to formulate more specific weekly goals, making sure she first devotes most of her attention to achieving goals in the high-priority areas. This ensures that Kim spends most of her time accomplishing her highest priority goals—not the ones that *seem* critical on a particular day but aren't in actuality of highest priority.

Goal	Priority
Do well in school	A
Run cross-country	B
Volunteer in the training room	B
Participate in campus social activities	C
Visit home	C
Work a part-time job	C

Is Goal Setting Effective?

Psychologists (especially business psychologists) have studied goal setting as a motivational technique, focusing on whether setting specific, difficult goals improves performance more than setting no goals or setting the more general goal of simply doing your best. These reviewers have concluded that goal setting works and works well (Locke et al., 1981; Locke & Latham, 1990; Mento, Steel, & Karren, 1987). In fact more than 90% of the studies show that goal setting has a consistent and powerful effect on behavior, whether it's used with elementary school children or professional scientists, whether with brainstorming or with loading logs onto trucks. Goal setting is a behavioral technique that works!

Not only has the general psychological research shown goal setting to work, but moreover a meta-analysis (a statistical review of the literature, which combines the results of independent studies and indicates whether results were significant across all the studies) of 36 studies in sport and exercise psychology has reached a similar conclusion (Kyllo & Landers, 1995). Goal setting is a successful technique specifically for improving sport and exercise performance.

Goal-setting researchers (including those summarized by Kyllo & Landers) have found the following factors most consistently enhance the effectiveness of goal setting in sport and exercise settings: having moderately difficult goals, both short- and long-term goals, specific goals, publicly acknowledged goals, commitment to goal attainment, participant's input in the goal-setting process, and focusing on performance goals.

Goal-Setting Research

Researchers have examined the relation between various types of goals (e.g., specific or general, long-term or short-term) and physical fitness tasks (e.g., the number of sit-ups performed within 3 minutes, performance times in a swimming event, free-throw shooting in basketball; see Weinberg, 1992, for a detailed review). In one study, college students in an 8-week basketball course set either specific or general goals for fundamental basketball skill tasks (e.g., defensive footwork, free-throw shooting, dribbling). Setting specific rather than general goals enhanced performance, though not on all tasks. Specifically, goal setting appeared to enhance performance on low-complexity tasks better than on high-complexity tasks (Burton, 1989a).

Although the empirical goal-setting research in sport and exercise settings over the past 15 years has helped provide us with a better understanding of what makes goals more effective, we really have not found out much about the *process* of goal-setting, including how people set goals, what goals are most important to them, what barriers impede goal attainment, and how different types of individuals differ

Goal setting is an extremely powerful technique for enhancing performance, but it must be implemented correctly.

in their goal setting. However, research using questionnaires and interviews with collegiate and youth athletes (Weinberg, Burton, Yukelson, & Weigand, 1993; Weinberg, Burke & Jackson, 1997) has more recently revealed much about athletes' preferences and goal-setting strategies, including the following:

- Almost all athletes used some type of goal setting to enhance performance, finding their goals to be moderately to highly effective.
- Improving performance, winning, and enjoyment (having fun), in this order, were the three most important goals for athletes.
- Athletes commented that they preferred goals that were difficult, very difficult, and moderately difficult—these were, in order, the top three preferences for goal difficulty.
- Major barriers to achieving goals include a lack of time, stress, fatigue, academic pressures, and social relationships.
- Females set goals more often and found them to be more effective than males did (except for outcome goals).
- Athletes did not systematically write down their goals, although they thought about them a great deal.
- The more experience that athletes had with setting goals, the better they became in developing effective goal-setting strategies.
- The number-one reason athletes gave for setting goals was to provide them direction and keep them focused on the task at hand.

Although researchers in both general psychology and sport psychology have produced considerable evidence that goal setting is a powerful technique for enhancing performance, it is not a foolproof method. It must be implemented with thought, understanding of the process, and planning. Systematic programs are necessary, as well as monitoring the process, to determine when and where goal setting is most effective in a program.

Why Goal Setting Works

Researchers have two ways to explain how goals influence behavior: (a) the direct mechanistic view and (b) the indirect thought-process view. The **direct mechanistic view** specifies that goals influence performance in one of four direct ways (Locke & Latham, 1985):

309

1. Goals direct attention to important elements of the skill being performed.
2. Goals mobilize performer efforts.
3. Goals prolong performer persistence.
4. Goals foster the development of new learning strategies.

First, goals direct performers' attention to important elements of the skill, which may not normally be attended to. For example, when soccer players set specific goals to improve their games, they focus on the particular skills that need improving such as corner kicks, movement off the ball, and winning 50/50 balls.

Goals also mobilize effort and persistence by providing incentives. For instance, a swimmer may not want to practice on a given day, finding it difficult to muster her efforts to do so. However, by dividing the distance she needs to swim into 10 equal parts, or goals, she has incentives that seem reasonable. Similarly, safely losing 50 pounds may seem like an insurmountable goal requiring considerable persistence. However, by setting a subgoal of losing 1 to 2 pounds weekly and charting subgoal accomplishment, you are much more likely to stay motivated and persist with the weight-loss program.

Goal setting has a hidden advantage, too, in its encouragement of new learning strategies. A goalie in ice hockey, for instance, may learn new strategies for clearing the puck after a save when he sets his goal of stopping more shots on goal. Similarly, a basketball player with a goal of improving her free-throw percentage from 70% to 80% might refine her preshot routine, change the biomechanics of her shot, or practice more shots even when she feels tired.

The indirect thought-process view proposes that goals influence performance indirectly by affecting a performer's psychological state, including such factors as confidence level, anxiety, and satisfaction (Burton, 1984; Garland, 1985). Burton (1989b) contends that athletes who set outcome goals experience more anxiety and lower self-confidence in competition because their goals are not within their complete control. In contrast, athletes who set performance goals experience less anxiety and enhanced self-confidence because their goals do not depend on their opponents' behavior, only on their own.

In Burton's (1989b) study, intercollegiate swimmers participated in a 5-month goal-setting program emphasizing performance (as contrasted with outcome) goals. All the swimmers learned to set performance goals. More importantly, swimmers who were high (as compared to low) in goal-setting ability demonstrated less anxiety, higher confidence, and improved performance. In other words, goals apparently influence performance indirectly through effects on psychological state. Thus, the effects of goal setting on psychological states should be monitored.

Principles of Goal Setting

A number of basic goal-setting principles can be identified from research and practice (Gould, 1998; Murphy, 1996). The correct application of these principles provides a strong foundation for designing a goal-setting program.

Principles of Goal Setting

1. Set specific goals.
2. Set moderately difficult but realistic goals.
3. Set long- and short-term goals.
4. Set performance and process, as well as outcome, goals.
5. Set practice and competition goals.
6. Record goals.
7. Develop goal-achievement strategies.
8. Consider the participant's personality and motivation.
9. Foster an individual's goal commitment.
10. Provide goal support.
11. Provide evaluation of and feedback about goals.

In the following sections, we'll discuss each of these principles.

Set Specific Goals

Specific goals affect behavioral change more effectively than general "do your best" goals or having no goals at all. However, many teachers, coaches, and exercise leaders still simply tell their students or clients to do their best. Goals should be stated in very specific, measurable, and behavioral terms. For example, a goal to improve your golf game is too vague. A better goal would be to lower your golf handicap from 14 over par to 11 by improving the accuracy of your short-iron approach shots to the

Specific goals, as compared to general "do-your-best" goals, are most effective for producing behavioral change.

© Photo: Action Images

green. Similarly, a goal to lower your cholesterol level is broad and imprecise compared with lowering your cholesterol level from 290 to 200 by eliminating an evening snack of high-fat potato chips and beginning an exercise program of walking 4 days a week. To be effective, goals must be stated in specific terms.

Set Moderately Difficult but Realistic Goals

Effective goals are difficult enough to challenge a participant, yet realistic enough to achieve. In fact, in their meta-analysis Kyllo and Landers (1995) found that "moderately difficult" goals lead to best performance. Goals are of little value if no effort is needed to achieve them, and participants soon lose their interest in the goal-setting program. But goals that are too difficult to achieve lead to frustration, reduced confidence, and poor performance. The secret is to strike a balance between goal challenge and achieveability, which is no easy task. Professionals must know the capabilities and commitment of the individuals they are working with. As professional experience is gained, it's easier to judge capabilities and how long improvement will take to occur.

If someone does not have extensive experience with the activity or the individuals involved in her program, it is better to err on the side of setting goals that can be more easily achieved. That way, participants will not become frustrated. As soon as it becomes clear that the goals are being easily mastered, however, more challenging moderately difficult goals should be set.

Set Long- and Short-Term Goals

Major behavioral change does not occur overnight. Thus, both long- and short-term goals should be set. Focusing only on long-term goals does not improve performance (Kyllo & Landers, 1995). Think of a staircase with a long-term goal or dream at the top, the present level of ability at the lowest step, and a sequence of progressively linked, short-term goals connecting the top and bottom of the stairs. Figure 15.1a depicts a goal-setting staircase used with a group of 8- to 11-year-old figure skaters. The skaters had a long-term goal of achieving the next test level (performing a prescribed set of skills) but were not ready to test at the time. Thus, the coach charted a progression of skills, or short-term goals, that would prepare the young skaters to achieve the next test level. The goal-setting staircase was posted, and each time a skater mastered a particular skill, a gold skate sticker was placed on the graph—until all the subgoals were accomplished and the long-term test goal was achieved.

This short- and long-term goal-setting staircase has been successfully adapted and used with elite athletes as well, including several World and Olympic champions. It also can be easily adapted for exercise programs. For example, Figure 15.1b depicts a goal-setting staircase (depicted in the form of climbing the mountain of behavioral change) for an individual beginning an exercise program designed to improve overall health and fitness. As was the case in the figure-skating example, the key is to develop a progression of short-term goals that lead to a long-term objective.

Short- and long-term goals should be linked. Terry Orlick (1986) developed the form on p. 314 that links an athlete's long-term goals with a series of more immediate, short-term physical and psychological goals. The form also creates a progression of goals, starting with some that can be achieved immediately and leading to more difficult and distant objectives. Orlick's approach is useful in a variety of sport and exercise settings.

Set Performance and Process Goals, as Well as Outcome, Goals

It is difficult not to think about winning or how your performance compares with others. After all, winning and losing receive much more attention from others than do an individual's personal goal achievements. Not surprisingly, then, athletes often cite as their goals such outcomes as winning games, winning championships, or beating particular opponents.

Ironically, the best way to win a championship or beat a particular opponent is to focus on performance or process goals. Placing too much emphasis on outcome goals creates anxiety during competition, and the athlete spends undue time worrying instead of focusing on the task at hand.

The key, then, is to continually emphasize performance and process goals. For every outcome goal an athlete sets, there should be several performance and process goals that would lead to that outcome. For example, if you are working with the members of a junior high school softball team who want to win the city championship, you should emphasize the relevant performance goals of improving field-

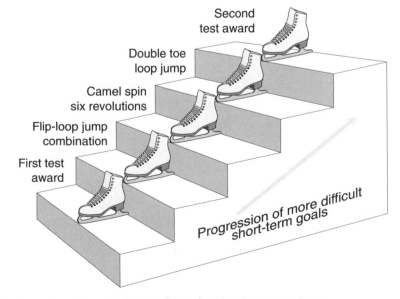

Figure 15.1a   *(a) A goal-setting staircase for a beginning exerciser;*

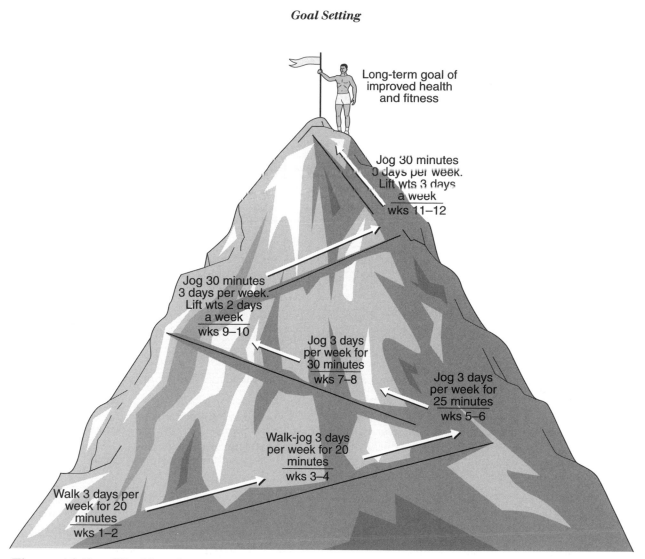

Figure 15.1b *Climbing the mountain of change in lifestyle—a progression of short-term goals leading to improved health and fitness.*

ing percentage, the team's batting average, and stolen bases. In addition, you should emphasize process goals, such as the players' improving their sliding technique and pitchers improving their pickoffs, both in practice and then in games. Encourage efforts to achieve these goals and chart progress toward them throughout the season.

Set Practice and Competition Goals

It is important that goals be set for both practices and competitions. Too often, however, athletes and coaches focus only on competition goals. Setting prac-

For every outcome goal an athlete sets, he should set several performance and process goals that will lead to that outcome.

tice goals is important because of the large amount of time athletes spend practicing (especially compared to competing) and the potential the long hours of practice have of becoming boring to some individuals. Setting practice goals, then, is a good way to get a competitive edge by focusing on making improvements that one may not normally work on and by maintaining motivation. Interestingly, in studying how successful Olympic athletes compared with less successful ones, Orlick and Partington (1988) found that the setting of practice goals for quality practice was one factor that differentiated the two groups. As examples of a practice goal, a downhill skier may aim to ski three flat sections of the course on a given day or a tennis player to come more often to the net.

Record Goals

The old adage "Out of sight, out of mind" has its use for goal-setting procedures. Several sport psychologists

Short- and Long-Term Goals

1. Dream goal (long-term)—What is your long-term dream goal? What is possible in the long term if you stretch all your limits?

2. Dream goal (this year)—What is your dream goal for this year? What is possible if all your limits are stretched this year?

3. Realistic performance goal (this year)—What do you feel is a realistic performance goal that you can achieve this year (based on your present skill level, your potential for improvement, and your current motivation)?

4a. Goal of self-acceptance—Can you make a commitment to accept yourself and to learn from the experience, regardless of whether you achieve your ultimate performance goal this year?

4b. If you do not meet your desired performance goal, to what extent will you still be able to accept yourself as a worthy human?

   Complete   0   1   2   3   4   5   6   7   8   9   10   Complete and full
   self-rejection   self-acceptance

5. Can you set an on-site goal of best *effort* (giving everything you have that day) and be satisfied with achieving that single goal?

6. Focused psychological goal (this year)—What do you feel is an important goal for you to focus on this year in terms of your psychological preparation or mental control? Some examples are a *specific* goal related to psychological readiness for the event, focus control within the event, distraction control, confidence, coping with hassles or setbacks, and improving interpersonal harmony or relationships.

7. Daily goal—(a) Set a personal goal for *tomorrow's* training session. Write down one thing you would like to do, accomplish, or approach with a special focus or intensity. (b) Can you set a personal goal before going to *each* training session this year?

8. What do you think you or others could do to increase the harmony among team members this year?

Reprinted from Orlick, 1986.

(Botterill, 1983; Harris & Harris, 1984; McClements, 1982) have recommended that once goals are set, they should be recorded and placed where they can be easily seen. Unfortunately, many athletes do not write goals down in any systematic fashion (Weinberg et al., 1993).

There is a gamut of ways to record goals. Athletes or exercisers can simply write down their goals on 3-by-5 cards—or they can formulate complex behavioral contracts. No one strategy is optimal. However, the more efficient the method of recording, the more useful it is. For example, writing down goals on a card and posting the card in a locker or on the bedroom mirror at home is more effective and time efficient than an in-depth, behavioral contract that is signed and placed in a drawer never to be looked at again. Athletes who use training logs often find it useful to include sections where they record goals and their progress toward them.

Develop Goal-Achievement Strategies

Setting goals without developing corresponding goal-achievement strategies is like driving a car to a strange city without consulting a map. You must have strategies to accompany the goals you set. Chipping a bucket of golf balls onto a practice green 3 days a week is a strategy to achieve the goal of lowering your handicap by three shots. Participating in a walking program that burns 2,500 calories a week is a strategy to achieve a weight-loss goal of 20 pounds in 5 months. Strategies should be specific and indicate how much and how often they are to be performed.

Athletes and exercisers should build flexibility into their goal-achievement strategies. Instead of saying they will lift weights on Monday, Wednesday, and Friday, it is better to say they will lift 3 days a week. That way, if an individual cannot lift on one of the designated days, he can lift on another day and still achieve his goal.

© Jay Foreman/Unicorn Stock Photos

Consider Participants' Personalities and Motivations

When you help athletes and exercise participants set and achieve goals, it is important to consider their personalities. An individual's motivation and goal orientations influence the goals she adopts and how well the goal-setting process functions. High achievers (see chapter 3 on achievement motivation), whose personalities are characterized by high levels of the motive to achieve success and low levels of the motive to avoid failure, will readily seek out and adopt challenging but realistic goals. In contrast, low achievers with high levels of the motive to avoid failure and low levels of the motive to achieve success will avoid challenging goals and seek to adopt cither very easy or very difficult goals.

Similarly, children in the social-comparison stage of achievement tend to focus on competitive and outcome goals. Competitive people also focus on outcome goals, whereas task-oriented athletes and exercisers will be much more open to performance and process goals.

Understanding and recognizing these personality differences will help you know what to expect from the people you help set goals for. High achievers and task-oriented athletes and exercisers should respond well to your goal-setting efforts. For low achievers and outcome-oriented participants, you will need to repeatedly emphasize the importance of setting realistic performance and process goals. You will also need to monitor them to ensure they do not gravitate back to more familiar outcome goals.

Extra efforts to focus on performance and process goals will also be necessary with young children. Goal setting should be easier once youngsters reach the integrated stage and feel comfortable focusing on personal improvement.

Foster an Individual's Goal Commitment

A person will not achieve a goal without commitment to achieving it. Instructors should promote **goal commitment** by encouraging progress and providing consistent feedback. Teachers or coaches should not set their students' or athletes' goals for them, either directly or indirectly. Instead, make your participants part of the goal-setting process by

315

soliciting their input and letting them set their own goals.

Provide Goal Support

Other people also can support athletes, students, and exercisers in their goal setting. Too often this **goal support** does not occur. For example, a high school lacrosse coach whose team is competing for the district championship may have her athletes set a series of performance goals. Meanwhile, the athletes' parents, teachers, and friends frequently ask the players about winning the championship. Educating these significant others about the importance of performance and process (rather than outcome) goals can be accomplished through letters to parents, staff meeting announcements, and stories in the school newspaper.

Spousal support is a critical factor affecting exercise adherence (Dishman, 1988). Thus, many corporate fitness specialists have found it useful to involve spouses in weight-loss and conditioning programs and invite them to support the achievement of the participant's goals. Finally, fitness professionals need to show a genuine inter-

est in the people with whom they work. They should review their participants' goals, ask about their progress, empathize with their struggles, and foster a caring, upbeat, and encouraging atmosphere.

Provide Evaluation of and Feedback About Goals

Feedback about performance progress is absolutely essential if goals are going to effectively change performance and behavior. Yet all too often coaches and exercise leaders fail to provide evaluation and feedback about a participant's goals.

Goal evaluation strategies should be initiated at the start of the goal-setting program and continually implemented as the program progresses. Evaluation can take many forms (see Table 15.1 for some examples). The key is to be consistent. Too often, people spend considerable time defining and setting goals only to have their work wasted because they don't follow through with essential evaluation and feedback.

> *Enlist support from significant others to make goal setting effective.*

> *Goal evaluation and feedback are essential parts of facilitating behavior change.*

Table 15.1
Forms of Goal Evaluation

Goal	Goal evaluation strategy
Lose 20 pounds in 6 months	Client informs fitness instructor of his or her weight weekly.
Increase free-throw shooting percentage from 65% to 72% by the end of the season	Team manager charts free-throw percentage statistics after each game and calculates year-to-date free-throw average.
Attend injury rehabilitation clinic 3 days a week until recovery	Attendance is posted weekly at rehabilitation center and coach is notified of attendance.
Improve concentration levels during practice	Coach gives player weekly report card, rating practice concentration on a 0 (low)-to-10 (high) scale.
Improve class cooperation in elementary school physical education class	Teacher tallies cooperative acts on behavioral checklist during week and charts the improvement of various classes on gym bulletin board.

Group Goals

To date, sport and exercise psychologists have focused mostly on the individual goals of exercisers and athletes and how these goals influence behavioral change. Group and team goal setting has received far less attention until quite recently (Widmeyer & Ducharme, 1997). To understand the effects of goals on groups, you must know more than the individual goals of the group members.

A group's or team's goal is "the future state of affairs desired by enough members of a group to work towards its achievement" (Johnson and Johnson, 1987, p. 132). **Group goals** are defined as attaining specific standards of group (not individual) proficiency, usually within a specified time. Hence, common group goals might include winning the state high school basketball league championship, having the lowest dropout rate of any cardiac rehabilitation program in the state, or improving school physical fitness scores on a standardized physical fitness test.

Having a team or group meeting to develop a list of shared group goals is not enough to bring about behavioral change, however. Setting group goals is only the first step in the process (Widmeyer & Ducharme, 1997). In addition to identifying group goals themselves, it is critical to identify the task that the group must perform in order to accomplish its goals, as well as the process of how the group will interact to achieve the goals. Not surprisingly, then, group or team goals are linked to change in behavior via increases in motivation and cohesion.

Widmeyer and Ducharme (1997) have outlined six principles of effective team goal setting. Following these principles will allow you to effectively set and achieve goals with the groups you help:

1. Establish long-term goals first.
2. Establish clear paths of short-term goals en route to long-term goals.
3. Involve all members of the team in establishing team goals.

© Terry Wild Studio

317

4. Monitor progress toward team goals.

5. Reward progress made toward team goals.

6. Foster collective team confidence or efficacy concerning team goals.

Designing a Goal-Setting System

Just as a basketball coach develops a game plan from individual plays, the fitness professional should develop a goal-setting system or plan from the 11 basic goal-setting principles we discussed earlier. Although there are many different goal-setting systems, most of them include three basic stages: (a) preparation and planning, (b) education and acquisition, and (c) implementation and follow-up. We'll discuss each of these stages separately.

Preparation and Planning

An effective instructor, trainer, or coach does not want to enter a physical activity setting unprepared. Thought and preparation must precede effective goal setting. The time spent on preparing the goal-setting process saves hours of work once the program is implemented.

Assess Abilities and Needs

The first step is to assess the participant's abilities and needs. Based on his knowledge of the athlete, the fitness professional should identify the areas he thinks most need improvement. When little is known about the athlete's background, it can also be useful to develop a list of all the skills needed in her activity. Then the athlete is asked to rate her ability relative to each of the skills identified.

Set Goals in Diverse Areas

Too often people consider only performance-related goals. Goals can and should be set in a variety of areas including individual skills, team skills, fitness levels, playing time, enjoyment, and psychological skills. It is important to set goals in a variety of areas because students, athletes, and exercisers participate in physical activity for diverse reasons (e.g., skill improvement, fun, achievement). Moreover, many factors influence individual and team performance in physical activity settings, so goals should not only be set for skill improvement and performance, but in other areas as well. Table 15.2 lists sample goals for a number of diverse areas in physical activity.

Identify Influences on Goal-Setting Systems

Goals can't be set in a vacuum. The athlete's potential, commitment, and opportunities for practice must be assessed before goals can be set. For instance, it does little good to establish after-hours practice goals for an athlete who is not committed or disciplined enough to do them on his own. It would be more

Table 15.2
Areas in Which Goals Can Be Set

Goal area	Goal
Individual skills	I will decrease my time by .4 seconds in the 400-meter dash by increasing my speed in the initial 100 meters through a more explosive start.
Team skills	Our high school wrestling team will increase the percentage of successful takedowns achieved from 54% to 62% by midseason.
Fitness	A homemaker will lower his or her resting heart rate from 71 beats per minute to 61 beats per minute by participating in a 50-minute aerobic dance class at least 3 days per week for the next 5 months.
Playing time	A junior in high school will earn a varsity football letter by participating in at least 16 different game quarters during the season.
Enjoyment	A veteran professional tennis player will get more pleasure from touring by identifying and visiting one new restaurant and historic site in each tour city.
Psychological skills	A diver will attempt to regain her confidence on an inward 2-1/2 dive by visualizing a successful dive before each practice attempt and repeating at least one positive self-statement.

> *Goals will not be effective unless they are tied to specific and realistic strategies for achieving them.*

effective for this person to have goals that he can achieve during regular practice times—or, better yet, to set a goal of becoming more independent and disciplined enough to practice on his own.

Plan Goal-Achievement Strategies

Strategies must be planned that participants can use to achieve their goals. Goals are not effective unless they are tied to specific and realistic strategies.

Education and Acquisition

Once the preparation and planning stage has been completed, the coach, teacher, or exercise leader can begin educating the athlete directly on the most effective ways to set goals. This involves imparting basic goal-setting information and principles.

Schedule Meetings

A formal meeting or a series of brief, less formal meetings should be scheduled before practices or classes. In these meetings the coach and athlete can identify examples of effective and ineffective goals. Participants should not be expected to be able to list goals right on the spot. Instead, they can be introduced to goal setting and given time to think about their goals and the process. The coach or instructor can schedule a follow-up meeting or subsequent practice to discuss specific goals.

Focus on One Goal at a Time

Unless an athlete has had considerable experience in setting goals, it is better to set only one goal at a time. The coach can help each individual select one goal from his or her list. The athlete will then focus on correctly defining that particular goal and outlining realistic strategies to achieve it. After participants have learned to set and achieve a single goal, they might be ready to try multiple goals.

Implementation and Follow-Up

Once participants have learned to set goals, the next step is to list the goals that have been identified as appropriate. The coach or instructor will need to assist in the goal evaluation and follow-up process.

Identify Appropriate Goal-Evaluation Procedures

You want to avoid designing a goal-setting system that is impossible for you as a coach, teacher, or fit-

ness instructor to keep up with. For example, anticipate the busiest time of your year and estimate how much time you will have available for goal evaluation and follow-up.

Moreover, be sure to identify the most effective system for managing goal evaluation and follow-up. Many coaches streamline the evaluation process by having managers keep and post practice and game statistics related to player goals. Similarly, some physical educators schedule periodic skills tests during class when students receive feedback about their performance progress toward their goals. In these cases, the feedback process costs the instructor or coach little time.

Provide Support and Encouragement

Throughout the season the coach or exercise leader should ask participants about their goals and publicly encourage their goal progress. Showing enthusiasm about the goal-setting process supports the athletes and exercise participants, helping to keep them motivated to fulfill their goals.

Plan for Goal Reevaluation

Goal setting is not a perfect science, and sometimes the goals that have been set don't work out. For example, a tennis player sets a goal to hit 40% of her first serves in, but she discovers that with practice she has little trouble hitting 50% of her first serves in. In such a case, her goal must be modified to challenge her. Other athletes will set initial goals that are too difficult, which should be made easier. Injuries and illness might also require an athlete to modify his goals. It is necessary to reevaluate goals intermittently. Modifying and reestablishing goals is a normal part of the process.

Common Problems in Goal Setting

Goal setting is not a difficult psychological technique to understand, but this doesn't mean that problems will not arise in implementing a goal-setting program (Gould, 1998; Murphy, 1996). Some common problems include convincing students, athletes, and exercisers to set goals; failing to set specific goals; setting too many goals too soon; failing to adjust goals when they are not being achieved; failing to

> *Goal setting is not a perfect science. Plan for specific reevaluation of goals.*

set performance and process goals; and not initiating goal-setting evaluation and follow-up procedures. By understanding and anticipating these problems you can reduce their effects and even circumvent some problems altogether. Anticipating problems and understanding how to avoid them are major components of effective goal setting.

Convincing Students, Athletes, and Exercisers to Set Goals

Based on years of experience as a sport psychologist working at the U.S. Olympic Training Center, Shane Murphy identified several common obstacles to individuals' formal goal setting (Murphy, 1996). These include the notion that goal setting takes too much time, their previous negative (failure) experiences setting goals; the perception that they will become a public failure if they do not reach certain goals; and the feeling that goal setting is too structured and will not work with "spontaneous" people. Murphy points out that goal setting actually saves time because one becomes much better organized. He argues that goal failure typically results from an overemphasis on setting goals outside of one's control (i.e., they choose outcome goals rather than performance goals, though focusing on process and performance goals causes one less worry about failure), and he reassures athletes that writing out and working toward specific goals does not mean losing spontaneity or becoming rigid. Anticipating these reactions and being able to effectively disarm them will help you, too, convince those whom you work with to engage in goal setting.

Failing to Set Specific Goals

The most frequent problem people in sport and exercise settings have is failing to set specific goals. Even when activity participants are told how important it is to state goals in specific, behavioral terms, they often identify goals in a general, vague way. For example, "improving my tennis serve" might be the stated goal, instead of "improving the accuracy of good serves from 60% to 70% by developing a more consistent ball toss."

It is important for the physical fitness professional to monitor initial goals and give feedback about their specificity. Additionally, we need to teach people to form a numerical goal that includes an improved percentage or number for assessing the behavior. Finally, when establishing sport skill goals, people should be asked to include specific characteristics of improved technique in their goal statements (e.g.,

Initially set only one or two goals. Participants can set more goals once they have gained experience in the process.

"improve downhill running by shortening stride length," or "improve the percentage of strikes thrown by bending my back more").

Setting Too Many Goals Too Soon

Novices at setting goals tend to take on too many goals at once. Their desire to improve leads them to become overzealous and unrealistic. On the practical side, monitoring, tracking, and providing individualized feedback across time becomes virtually impossible for the fitness leader when participants have too many goals. Plus, when too many goals are set at once, they are all almost invariably abandoned.

Inexperienced goal setters should set only one or two goals at a time. Making the goals short term (e.g., achieved within 2 weeks rather than 5 months) keeps them in the foreground and maximizes the performer's enthusiasm. Tracking the goals and providing feedback are also easier over a shorter time period. Once the individual has gained experience, however, he or she can set multiple or simultaneous goals.

Failing to Adjust Goals

Adjusting goals, especially lowering them, once they have been set can be difficult. For example, swimmers who had no difficulty adjusting goals upward, found after an injury or illness that adjusting goals downward was extremely difficult from a psychological perspective (Burton, 1989b).

Two things can alleviate this problem. First, right from the start of the goal-setting program discuss the need to adjust goals upward and downward. That way, participants can view adjustments as a normal part of the process, rather than as indicating a problem on their part. Second, if goals must be lowered due to illness or injury, make the adjustment part of a new staircase of goals (see Figure 15.2) that ultimately surpasses the original goal. In that way, the person can view the lowered goal as a temporary setback to be ultimately overcome.

■ APPLICATION ■

SMART Goals

A good tip for helping athletes or exercisers remember characteristics of effective goals is to think of the word SMART and remember the following principles (Smith, 1994):

- Specific—goals should indicate precisely what is to be done
- Measurable—make sure you can quantify your goal.
- Action-oriented—goals should indicate something that needs to be done.
- Realistic—make sure the goal can be achieved given various constraints.
- Timely—make sure the goal can be achieved in a reasonable time.

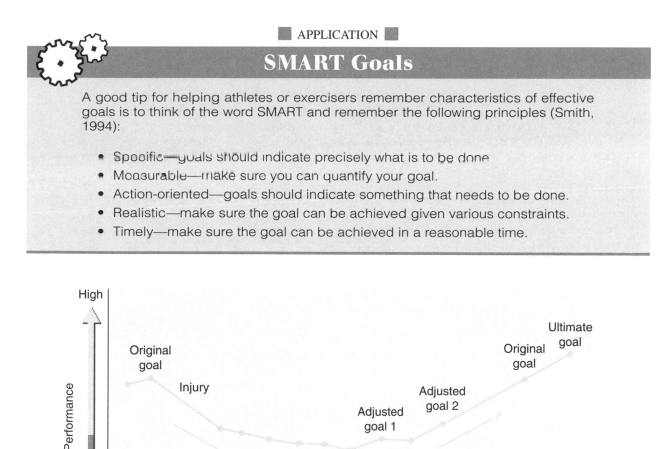

Figure 15.2 *Adjusting goals downward–maintaining a positive perspective through a stepwise approach.*

Failing to Set Performance and Process Goals

Many athletes in competitive sports fail to set performance and process (rather than outcome) goals. It is important to emphasize performance and process goals throughout the athletic season, and both coaches and exercise leaders should remain alert that they do not unconsciously stress outcome goals. Instead, they should evaluate the players' performance goals as thoroughly after a win as after a loss.

Not Providing Follow-Up and Evaluation

A problem teachers, coaches, and exercise leaders have all too frequently is setting goals at the start of a season and then not effectively using them throughout the season or year. A lack of follow-up and evaluation is one of the major factors in the failure of goal-setting programs. It is imperative to develop a follow-up and evaluation plan for goals and to examine it critically for ease and efficiency. It must be simple to implement. Goal setting without follow-up and evaluation is simply a waste of time and effort!

SUMMARY

1 *Define what goals are and identify major types of goals.*

Goals are objectives or aims of actions. They may be subjective or objective and directed toward performance (self-comparisons for improvement), process (actions that lead to improved performance), or outcome (beating or surpassing others). All these types of goals can be useful. The key is knowing when to focus on each goal type and not focusing all one's attention on outcome goals.

2 *Describe the latest research and theory of goal setting.*

The research on goal setting demonstrates that goals are a powerful means for effecting behavior changes, either directly or indirectly. Goals influence behavior directly by bringing a performer's attention to important elements of the skill or task. They also can increase motivation and persistence, and can facilitate the development of new learning strategies. Furthermore, goals influence behavior indirectly by causing changes in important psychological factors, such as self-confidence, anxiety, and satisfaction.

3 *Describe basic goal-setting principles.*

Basic goal-setting principles include developing helpful kinds of goals: specific, moderately difficult but realistic, both short- and long-term, both practice and competition, and both performance and process goals. Some other basic principles of effective goal setting are recording the goals, developing concomitant goal-achievement strategies, considering a participant's personality and motivation, fostering commitment to the goals, providing support to the goal setter, and providing evaluation and feedback of performance toward goals.

4 *Explain group goals and how to use them.*

Group goals focus on attaining specific standards of group proficiency, usually within a specified time. Setting group goals is important because having goals has been linked to increases in a group's motivation and cohesion. When establishing group goals you should (a) establish long-term goals first; (b) establish clear, short-term goals as paths to long-term goals; (c) involve all members of the group in establishing its goals as a team; (d) monitor progress toward team goals; (e) reward progress toward team goals; and (e) foster collective team confidence or efficacy concerning its team goals.

5 *Explain how to design a goal-setting system.*

A significant number of goal-setting principles form the foundation of a three-stage system (preparation and planning, education and acquisition, and follow-up). The preparation and planning stage focuses on assessing individual abilities and needs, setting goals in diverse areas, identifying influences on goal-setting systems, and planning goal-achievement strategies. The education and acquisition stage involves scheduling meetings and limiting the number of goals one initially focuses on. Finally, the implementation and follow-up stage involves the use of appropriate goal-evaluation procedures, goal support and encouragement, and goal reevaluation.

6 *Identify common problems in goal setting and how to overcome them.*

Failing to convince students, athletes, and exercisers to set goals; failing to set specific goals; setting too many goals too soon; failing to adjust goals flexibly as the situation requires; failing to set performance and process goals, and not initiating goal-setting follow-up and evaluation are common goal-setting problems that a good program must address.

KEY TERMS

goals
subjective goals
objective goals
outcome goals
performance goals
process goals
direct mechanistic view

indirect thought-process view
practice goals
goal-achievement strategies
goal commitment
goal support
group goals

REVIEW QUESTIONS

1. What is the difference between a subjective and an objective goal? Between a performance, a process, and an outcome goal?

2. Compare and contrast the "direct mechanistic" and "indirect thought-process" explanations of goal setting.

3. Identify a basic goal-setting principle or guideline that relates to each of the following areas: goal specificity, goal difficulty, short- and long-term goals, performance and process compared with outcome goals, writing down goals, strategies for achieving goals, participant personality, individual commitment, goal support, and goal evaluation.

4. What are the different advantages of outcome, performance, and process goals?

5. What is a goal-setting staircase and why is it important?

6. What are the three basic stages to consider in designing a goal-setting system? What should happen during each stage?

7. Identify six common problems with goal setting.

8. Why is it important to adjust goals periodically?

CRITICAL THINKING QUESTIONS

1. Using what you have learned in this chapter, design a goal-setting program for a fellow student who wants to begin an exercise program to lose 25 pounds.

2. In the box on p. 308 the importance of prioritizing general subjective goals is discussed. Identify your most important subjective goals, listing and prioritizing them. How can you use these goals to guide your day-to-day actions?

© Mary Langenfeld/Langenfeld Photos

Concentration

After reading this chapter you should be able to

1 define concentration and explain how it is related to performance,

2 identify different types of attentional focus,

3 describe some attentional problems,

4 explain how self-talk works,

5 explain how to assess attentional ability, and

6 discuss how to improve attentional focus.

We hear the word *focus* more and more when athletes and coaches discuss getting ready to play and when they evaluate actual performance. Staying focused for an entire game or competition is often the key to victory (or, if you lose that focus, the ticket to failure). Even in competitions lasting hours or days (such as golf), a brief loss of concentration can mar total performance and affect outcome. It is critical to concentrate during a competition, even through adverse crowd noise, weather conditions, and irrelevant thoughts.

This intense focus throughout an event is evident in the recollections of Olympic swimming gold medalist Michelle Smith: "I was never more focused in a race. No looking about, tunnel vision all the way . . . my concentration was so intense that I almost forgot to look up to see my time after touching the finishing pads" (cited in Roche, 1995, p. 1). On the other hand, the temporary loss of focus can spell defeat, as George Foreman commented after defeating Michael Moorer in the World Boxing Association championship: "They urged me to pile up some points, but I knew I could only win the fight by a knock-out. I waited and waited, until Moorer briefly lost his concentration and gave me an opening" (cited in K. Jones, 1994, p. 1).

Many athletes mistakenly believe that concentrating is important only during actual competition. All-time tennis great Rod Laver in effect says that the old adage "Practice makes perfect" is apt when it comes to developing concentration skills:

> "If your mind is going to wander during practice, it's going to do the same thing in a match. When we were all growing up in Australia, we had to work as hard mentally as we did physically in practice. If you weren't alert, you could get a ball hit off the side of your head. What I used to do was force myself to concentrate more as soon as I'd find myself getting tired, because that's usually when your concentration starts to fail you. If I'd find myself getting tired in practice, I'd force myself to work much harder for an extra ten or fifteen minutes, and I always felt as though I got more out of those extra minutes than I did out of the entire practice." (Tarshis, 1977, p. 31)

Although many things can affect your concentration, one of the most common and problematic occurrences is high anxiety. Getting upset and anxious when things aren't going your way is a sure way to lose concentration, and Shaquille O'Neal pinpoints this common problem, which he experienced after missing three dunks and going 0 for 5 from the foul line: "I wasn't even concentrating, I was so upset. I simply lost my cool."

In this chapter we will explain how to effectively cope with the pressures of competition and to maintain concentration despite momentary setbacks, errors, and mistakes. We start by describing what concentration is and how it is related to performance. We should note that the terms *concentration* and *attention* will be used interchangeably throughout the chapter, inasmuch as researchers tend to use the term *attention* and practitioners seem to prefer *concentration*.

What Is Concentration?

Attention and its role in human performance have been subjects of debate and examination for more than a century, beginning with the following classic description that William James wrote:

> *Everyone knows what attention is. It is taking possession by the mind, in clear and vivid form, of one out of what seems several simultaneously possible objects or trains of thought. Focalization, concentration of consciousness are the essence. It implies withdrawal from some things in order to deal effectively with others. (1890, pp. 403–404)*

James's definition focuses on one particular aspect of concentration (selective attention), although a more contemporary definition views attention more broadly as the concentration of mental effort on sensory or mental events (Solso, 1995). Thus, a useful definition of concentration in sport and exercise settings would typically contain three parts: (a) focusing on the relevant cues in the environment (selective attention), (b) maintaining that attentional focus over time, and (c) having awareness of the situation.

Focusing on Relevant Environmental Cues

Part of concentration refers to focusing on the relevant environmental cues, or selective attention. Irrelevant cues are either eliminated or disregarded.

> *Concentration is the ability to maintain focus on relevant environmental cues. When the environment changes rapidly, attentional focus must also change rapidly. Thinking of the past or the future raises irrelevant cues that often lead to performance errors.*

This is referred to as selective attention because you are selecting what cues to attend to and what cues to disregard. Let's return to the example we have used before of a basketball player shooting two free throws at the end of a game, with only 2 seconds of play left and her team down by a point. What cues in our basketball player's environment are relevant or irrelevant? A relevant cue might be making sure she goes through her own normal preshot routine: bouncing the ball three times, taking a deep breath, looking up at the basket, and focusing on the front of the rim. Irrelevant cues might include the players lined up for the rebound and the hometown fans behind the backboard waving their hands and making a lot of noise. The ability to focus on the preshot routine and rim, while eliminating all extraneous noise and movements, is critical to the successful execution of the foul shot.

Maintaining Attentional Focus

Maintaining attentional focus for the duration of the competition is also part of concentration. Many athletes have instants of greatness, yet few can sustain a high level of play for an entire competition. Chris Evert was never the most physically talented player on the women's tour, but nobody could match her ability to stay focused throughout a match. She was virtually unaffected by irrelevant cues (such as bad line calls), missing easy shots, crowd noise, and her opponent's antics. Concentration helped make her a champion.

Maintaining focus over long time periods is no easy task. Tournament golf, for example, is usually played over 72 holes. Say that after playing great for 70 holes, you have 2 holes left in the tournament and lead by a stroke. On the 17th hole, just as you prepare to hit your drive off the tee, an image of the championship trophy flashes in your mind. This momentary distraction causes you to lose your focus on the ball and hook your drive badly into the trees. It takes you three more strokes to get on the green, and you wind up with a double bogey. You lose your lead and wind up in second place. Thus, one lapse in concentration over the course of 72 holes cost you the championship.

Now consider a runner competing in a marathon. You might think that in a race of 2 or 3 hours a few attentional lapses wouldn't matter much. Nothing could be farther from the truth. Studies of the cognitive strategies of elite marathon runners found that the most successful marathoners used a combination of an associative attentional strategy (monitoring bodily functions and feelings, such as heart rate, muscle tension, and breathing rate) and a dissociative attentional strategy (distraction and tuning out) during the race (Silva & Applebaum, 1989). Further study revealed that although both strategies were being utilized, increased running pace was accompanied by a predominantly associative cognitive strategy (Schomer, 1986). In essence, attentional flexibility seems to be critical, and athletes shift their attention between an external and internal focus,

■ CLOSE-UP ■

Attentional Focus

A quarterback in football has to distinguish between what is relevant and irrelevant. When he stands behind the center and looks over the defense, he first must recognize the specific defensive formation to determine if the play that was called will work. If he believes the linebackers are all going to blitz, he might decide to change the long pass he originally called to a quick pass over the middle. Of course, the linebackers are probably trying to fool the quarterback into thinking they are going to blitz when they really aren't—a cat-and-mouse game occupying the quarterback's attentional focus.

Now the quarterback has the ball and has dropped back to throw a pass. Seeing one of his men open, he is about ready to release the ball when, out of the corner of his eye, he notices a 250-pound lineman getting ready to slam into him. Is this lineman a relevant or irrelevant cue for the quarterback? If he can release the ball before being tackled by the lineman, then the lineman is an irrelevant cue, even though the quarterback knows he will be hit hard right after he releases the ball. However, if the quarterback determines that the defensive lineman will tackle him before he can release the ball, then the lineman becomes a relevant cue that should signal the quarterback to "scramble out of the pocket" and gain more time to find an open receiver.

depending on the stage of the race and how they feel at a particular moment. Less successful marathoners used a dissociative strategy almost exclusively throughout the race. Dissociative attentional strategies "tune out" physiological feedback from the body to help deal with the boredom and fatigue of the marathon. However, this lack of attentional focus to what's happening in the body (i.e., relevant cues) can often result in being unprepared for important changes, such as muscle cramps or "hitting the wall," when you suddenly feel you can go no farther.

Situation Awareness

One of the least understood but most interesting and important aspects of attentional focus in sport is an athlete's ability to understand what is going on around him or her. Known as situation awareness, in essence this ability allows players to size up game situations, opponents, and competitions to make appropriate decisions based on the situation, often under acute pressure and time demands. For example, Boston Celtic announcer Johnny Most gave one of the most famous commentary lines in basketball, when in the seventh game of the 1976 NBA playoffs between the Boston Celtics and Philadelphia 76ers and with five seconds left, he screamed repeatedly, "and Havlicek stole the ball!" John Havlicek later described how his situation awareness helped him make this critical play. The 76ers were down by a point and were taking the ball in from an out-of-bounds. He was guarding his man, with his back to the passer, when the referee handed the ball to the player inbounding the ball. A team has five seconds to put the ball into play when throwing it in from out of bounds, and Havlicek started counting to himself 1001, 1002, 1003. When nothing had happened, he knew that the passer was in trouble. He turned halfway to see the passer out of the corner of his eye, still focusing on his own man. A second later he saw a poor pass being made and reacted quickly enough to deflect the ball to one of his own players who ran out the clock. The Celtics won the game—and went on to win the NBA championship. Had Havlicek not counted, he would not have had a clear sense of the most important focus at that instant (Hemery, 1986).

Along these lines we all know of athletes who seem to be able to do just the right thing at the right time. Some that come to mind are Larry Bird, Martina Hingis, Karch Kiraly, and Teresa Edwards. Their awareness of the court and competitive situation always makes it seem as if they are a step ahead of everyone else. In fact, research has indicated that experts (high-ability athletes) are able to analyze situ-ations more quickly and use more anticipatory cues than their nonexpert counterparts (Abernathy, 1993). Being able to size up a situation to know what to do—and possibly what your opponent is about to do—is a key attentional skill.

Concentration and Optimal Performance

As noted at the outset of the chapter, athletes and coaches certainly recognize the importance of proper attentional focus in achieving high levels of performance. And research from several sources substantiates their experience. For example, Garfield and Bennett (1984) investigated the components of exceptional performance and found eight physical and mental capacities that elite athletes associate with peak performance. Three of these eight are associated with high levels of concentration. Specifically, athletes describe themselves as (a) being absorbed in the present and having no thoughts about the past or future, (b) being mentally relaxed and having a high degree of concentration and control, and (c) being in a state of extraordinary awareness of both their own bodies and the external environment.

Researchers comparing successful and less successful athletes have consistently found that attentional control is an important discriminating factor. In general, their studies reveal that successful athletes are less likely to become distracted by irrelevant stimuli; they maintain a more task-oriented attentional focus, as opposed to worrying or focusing on the outcome. Some researchers have argued that peak performers have developed exceptional concentration abilities appropriate to their sport. These observations led Gould, Eklund, and Jackson (1992c) to conclude that optimal performance states have a characteristic that is variously referred to as concentration, the ability to focus, a special state of involvement, or awareness of and absorption in the task at hand.

Another line of research demonstrating the key role of proper attentional focus relates to differences between expert and novice athletes. Neither physical characteristics nor perceptual-motor factors fully account for the differences between expert and nov-

It is important to focus on only the relevant cues in the athletic environment and eliminate distractions.

ice performers. Rather, a growing body of evidence suggests that "knowledge-based" factors, such as where an athlete directs his attention, can account for performance differences between expert and novice athletes in a variety of sports (Moran, 1996). For example, these studies consistently show that expert badminton and squash players are able to use earlier cues than novices can to predict the flight of the ball and shuttle. In particular, experts are attuned to movements of the player's arm and racquet, whereas novices typically rely on racquet cues alone. The use of earlier cues led to faster decision times and superior accuracy among the experts. This capacity to use "advance cues" to make predictions about the likely flight of the ball or movement of players appears to be a distinctive characteristic of expert athletes.

Eye movement patterns also confirm that expert players have a different focus of attention than have novice performers. Researchers have found this phenomenon in a variety of individual and team sports such as basketball, volleyball, tennis, soccer, baseball, and karate (for a review see Moran, 1996). Think about the no-look passes that

Magic Johnson was famous for making. Most good point guards in basketball, such as Dawn Staley, John Stockton, and Mark Jackson, now throw these kind of passes. In reality, these point guards "see the floor" and anticipate where players will go (this skill gets better the more you play with teammates and become familiar with their movement patterns). Thus, the no-look pass is accomplished by using advance cues to predict the future movement of one's teammates.

Types of Attentional Focus

Most people think concentration is an all-or-none phenomenon—you either concentrate or you don't. However, researchers have discovered that various types of attentional focus are appropriate for specific sports and activities. To date, the most useful research on the role of attentional style in sport has developed from the theoretical framework of Nideffer (1976; 1981), who views attentional focus along two dimensions: width (broad or narrow) and direction (internal or external).

© Terry Wild Studio

■ MORE INFORMATION ■

To Watch or Not Watch the Ball: That Is the Question

Anyone who has played a sport involving a ball has probably often heard the admonishment, Keep your eye on the ball. Tennis players learn "Watch the ball right onto the racquet," and baseball players "Never take your eyes off the ball if you want to catch it." However, researchers indicate that these long-held beliefs are not necessarily correct. For example, they have found that the eyes can be removed from the flight of the ball at some stage without incurring a performance decrement (Savelsbergh, Whiting, & Pijpers, 1992). In addition, contrary to popular belief, top professional tennis players do not watch the ball approaching them as they prepare to return serve because it is virtually impossible for someone to track a ball traveling at speeds of 120 to 130 miles per hour (Abernathy, 1991). The same is true for baseball hitters trying to hit 90-mile-per-hour fastballs. Instead, these expert players use advance cues—such as the server's racquet and toss or the pitcher's motion—to make informed judgments on where the ball will be going and what type of serve or pitch is coming toward them. This is not to say that watching the ball is unimportant. Rather, optimal performance is inevitably enhanced by an athlete's ability to predict the flight of a ball from cues.

■ A broad attentional focus allows a person to perceive several occurrences simultaneously. This is particularly important in sports where athletes have to be aware of and sensitive to a rapidly changing environment (i.e., they must respond to multiple cues). Two examples are a basketball point guard leading a fast break and a soccer player dribbling the ball up field.

■ A narrow attentional focus occurs when you respond to only one or two cues, such as when a baseball batter prepares to swing at a pitch or a golfer lines up a putt.

■ An external attentional focus directs attention outward to an object, such as a ball in baseball or a puck in hockey, or to an opponent's movements, such as in a doubles match in tennis.

■ An internal attentional focus is directed inward to thoughts and feelings, such as when a coach analyzes plays without having to perform, a high jumper prepares to start his run-up, or a bowler readies her approach.

By combining width and direction of attentional focus, four different categories emerge, appropriate to various situations and sports (see Figure 16.1).

Shifting Attentional Focus

Often it is necessary to shift attentional focus during an event. Let's take a golf example. As a golfer prepares to step up to the ball before teeing off, she needs to assess the external environment: the direction of the wind, the length of the fairway, the positioning of water hazards, trees, and sand traps. This requires a broad-external focus. After appraising this information, she might recall previous experience with similar shots, note current playing conditions, and analyze the information she's gathered to select a particular club and determine how to hit the ball. These considerations require a broad-internal focus.

Once she has formulated a plan, she might monitor her tension, image a perfect shot, or take a deep, relaxing breath as part of a preshot routine. She has moved into a narrow-internal focus. Finally, shifting to a narrow-external focus, she addresses the ball. At this time, her focus is directly on the ball. This is not the time for other internal cues and thoughts, which would probably interfere with the execution of the shot. Golfers have ample time to shift attentional focus because they themselves set the pace.

Shifting attention is also necessary, and often more difficult, when time pressures during a competition are intense. Hemery (1986) describes how this might occur during the running of a 400-meter hurdles race. The hurdler's primary attention is narrow and external because of the need to focus and concentrate on the upcoming hurdle. However, the focus can change rapidly. For example, he uses a broad-internal focus to constantly review the stride lengths required to reach the next hurdle in the proper position for a rapid balanced clearance. He assesses the effects of the

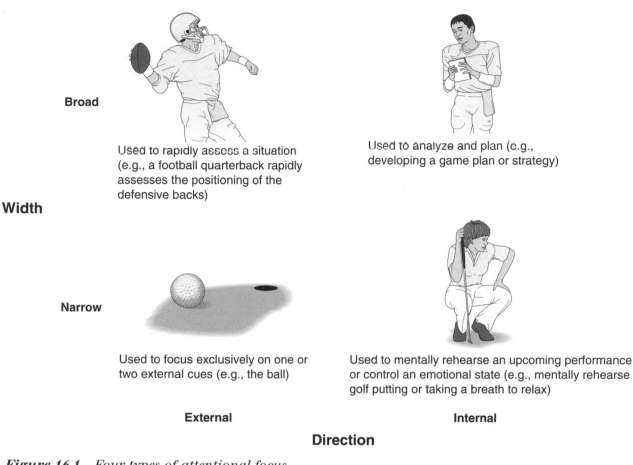

Width

Broad

Used to rapidly assess a situation (e.g., a football quarterback rapidly assesses the positioning of the defensive backs)

Used to analyze and plan (e.g., developing a game plan or strategy)

Narrow

Used to focus exclusively on one or two external cues (e.g., the ball)

Used to mentally rehearse an upcoming performance or control an emotional state (e.g., mentally rehearse golf putting or taking a breath to relax)

External　　　　　　　　　　　　　　**Internal**

Direction

Figure 16.1　Four types of attentional focus.

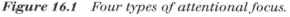

wind, track conditions, and pace on the stride pattern for clearing the next hurdle. He uses a broad-external focus to assess where he is in relation to all the other competitors in the race, and a narrow-internal focus for personal race judgment and effort distribution. At any one instant, any one of these factors could be critical.

Attentional Problems

Many athletes recognize that they have problems concentrating for the duration of a competition. Usually, their concentration problems are caused by inappropriate attentional focus. They are not focusing on the proper cues; rather, they become distracted by thoughts, other events, and emotions. We'll now discuss some of the typical problems athletes have in controlling and maintaining attentional focus, dividing them into distractions that are internal and those that are external.

Internal Distracters

Some distractions come from within ourselves—our thoughts, worries, and concerns. Jackson (1995) has

shown through interviews with elite athletes that worries and irrelevant thoughts can cause performers to lose concentration and develop an inappropriate focus of attention. Let us look at some of these internal distracters that present attentional problems.

Attending to Past Events

Some people cannot forget about what has just happened—especially a bad mistake. Focusing on past events has been the downfall of many talented athletes, as looking backward prevents them from focusing on the present. For example, archers who are preoccupied with past mistakes tend to produce poorer performances than those whose minds are focused on the present (Landers, Boutcher, & Wang, 1986).

Attending to Future Events

Concentration problems can also involve attending to future events. Younger athletes especially tend toward future-oriented thinking, usually focusing on the consequences of certain actions. Such thinking often takes the form of "what if" statements:

■ MORE INFORMATION ■

Can You Identify the Proper Attentional Focus?

See if you can identify the proper attentional focus of a football quarterback under time duress. Fill in the name of the proper focus in the blank spaces here (the answers, which correspond to the numbers in the blanks, are given afterward).

As the quarterback calls the play, he needs a _____ focus to analyze the game situation, including the score, what yard line the ball is on, the down, and time left in the game. He also considers the scouting reports and game plan that the coach wants him to execute in calling the play. As the quarterback comes up to the line of scrimmage his focus of attention should be _____ while he looks over the entire defense and tries to determine if the originally called play will be effective. If he feels that another play might work better, he may change the play by calling an "audible" at the line of scrimmage. Next the quarterback's attention shifts to a _____ focus to receive the ball from the center. Mistakes sometimes occur in the center-quarterback exchange because the quarterback is still thinking about the defense or what he has to do next (instead of making sure he receives the snap without fumbling).

If a pass play was called, the quarterback drops back into "the pocket" to look downfield for his receivers. This requires a _____ perspective so the quarterback can evaluate the defense and find the open receiver while still avoiding onrushing linemen. Finally, after spotting a specific receiver, his focus becomes _____ as he concentrates on throwing a good pass.

Within a few seconds, the quarterback shifts attentional focus several times to effectively understand the defense and pick out the correct receiver. Examples of different types of attentional focus are shown in Figure 16.1.

Answers

1. broad-internal
2. broad-external
3. narrow-external
4. broad-external
5. narrow-external

■ What if we lose the game?

■ What if I strike out again?

■ What if I make another error?

■ What if I get injured?

■ What if I let my teammates down?

■ What if I can't adhere to my new exercise program?

This kind of future-oriented thinking and worry negatively affects concentration, mistakes and poor performance becoming more likely. For example, Pete Sampras was leading 7–6, 6–4, and serving at 5–2 in the 1994 Australian Open finals. He double-faulted and lost two more games before holding out by 6–4 in the third set. Interviewed afterward, Sampras explained that his lapse in concentration was caused by speculating about the future. "I was thinking about winning the Australian Open and what a great achievement [it

would be], looking ahead and just kind of taking it for granted, instead of taking it point by point."

Sometimes future-oriented thinking has nothing at all to do with the situation. Your mind wanders without much excuse. For example, athletes report thinking during the heat of competition about such things as what they need to do at school the next day, what they have planned for that evening, their girlfriend or boyfriend, and what they are going to wear on an upcoming date. These irrelevant thoughts are often involuntary—suddenly the players just find themselves thinking about things that have nothing to do with the present exercise or competition. Such concentration lapses are very frustrating and certainly affect performance.

Choking Under Pressure

Emotional factors such as the pressure of competition often play a critical role in creating internal sources of distraction, and we often hear the word **choking** to describe an athlete's poor performance under pressure. Tennis great John McEnroe underscores the point that choking is part of competition:

When it comes to choking, the bottom line is that everyone does it. The question isn't whether you choke or not, but how—when you choke you are going to handle it. Choking is a big part of every sport, and a part of being a champion is being able to cope with it better than everyone else.

—John McEnroe (in Goffi, 1984, pp. 61–62)

Although most players and coaches have their own ideas about what choking is, providing an objective definition of choking is not easy. For example, read the three scenarios that follow and determine whether the athlete choked.

A basketball game is tightly fought, the lead shifting after each basket. Finally with 2 seconds left and her team down by 2 points, steady guard Julie Lancaster gets fouled in the act of shooting and is awarded two foul shots. Julie is a 90% free-throw shooter. She steps up to the line, makes her first shot but misses her second, and her team loses. Did Julie choke?

Jane is involved in a close tennis match. After splitting the first two sets with her opponent, she is now serving for the match at 5–4, the score 30–30. On the next 2 points, Jane double-faults to lose the game and even the set at 5–5. However, Jane then comes back to break serve and hold her own serve to close out the set and match. Did Jane choke?

Bill Moore is a baseball player with a batting average of .355. His team is playing a one-game playoff to decide who will win the league championship and advance to the district finals. Bill goes 0 for 4 in the game, striking out twice with runners in scoring position. In addition, in the bottom of the ninth he comes up with the bases loaded and one out and all he needs to do is hit the ball out of the infield to tie the game. Instead he grounds into a game-ending—and game-losing—double play. Did Bill choke?

When people think of choking, they tend to focus on the bad performance at a critical time of the game or competition, such as a missed shot, dropped pass, poor kick, or bad throw. However, choking is much more than the actual behavior—it is a process that leads to impaired performance. The fact that you missed a free throw to lose a game does not necessarily mean you choked. The more important questions to answer are why and how you missed the free throw.

Let's take a closer look at the process characteristic of what we have come to call choking. Behaviorally, we infer that athletes are choking when their performance progressively deteriorates and they cannot regain control over performance without outside assistance. In other words, we infer choking from a pattern of behavior. An example is the gymnast who allows an early mistake of falling off the balance beam to upset her and cause additional errors once she's back on the beam. Similarly, we can infer that a baseball player is choking when he drops an easy fly ball and then makes matters worse by overthrowing the cutoff man. Choking usually occurs in a situation of emotional importance to the athlete. For example Jana Novotna was serving at 4–1 in the third set of the 1993 Wimbledon finals against Steffi Graf and was one point away from a seemingly insurmountable 5–1 lead. But she proceeded to miss an easy volley, later served three consecutive double faults, and hit some wild shots, allowing Graf to come back to win 6–4. Wimbledon is considered by many the most prestigious tournament to win, and thus the pressure for Novotna was extremely high.

The choking process is shown in figure 16.2. Sensing pressure causes your muscles to tighten. Your heart rate and breathing increase; your mouth gets dry and your palms get damp. But the key breakdown occurs at the attentional level: Instead of focusing externally on the relevant cues in your environment (e.g., the ball, the opponent's movements), your attention becomes narrow and internal as you focus on your own worries and fears of losing and failing. At the same time, the increased pressure reduces your flexibility to shift your attentional focus—you have problems changing your focus as the situation dictates. Impaired timing and coordination, fatigue, muscle tension, and poor judgment and decision making soon follow. The box on p. 334 provides a practical example of the choking process.

Overanalyzing Body Mechanics

Another type of inappropriate attention is focusing too much on body mechanics and movements. Of course an internal-narrow focus is always bad. When you're learning a new skill, you should focus internally to get the kinesthetic feel of the movement. If you're learning to ski downhill, for instance, you might focus on the transfer of weight, the positioning of your skis and poles, and simply on avoiding a fall or running into other people. As

you attempt to integrate this new movement pattern, your performance is likely to be uneven. This is what practice is all about—focusing on improving your technique by getting a better feel of the movement.

The problem arises when internal-narrow thinking continues after you have learned the skill. At this

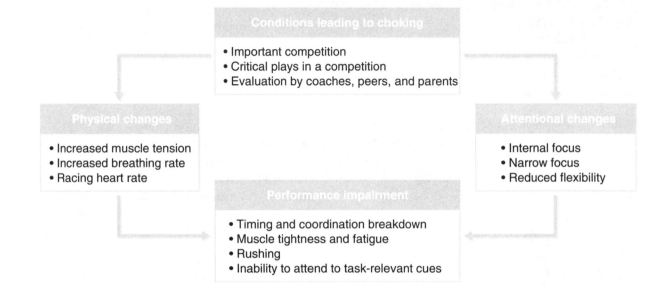

Conditions leading to choking
• Important competition
• Critical plays in a competition
• Evaluation by coaches, peers, and parents

Physical changes
• Increased muscle tension
• Increased breathing rate
• Racing heart rate

Attentional changes
• Internal focus
• Narrow focus
• Reduced flexibility

Performance impairment
• Timing and coordination breakdown
• Muscle tightness and fatigue
• Rushing
• Inability to attend to task-relevant cues

Figure 16.2 *The choking process.*
Adapted from Nideffer, 1993.

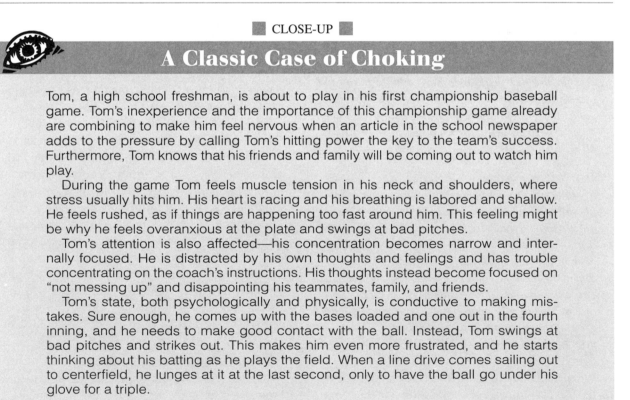

■ CLOSE-UP ■

A Classic Case of Choking

Tom, a high school freshman, is about to play in his first championship baseball game. Tom's inexperience and the importance of this championship game already are combining to make him feel nervous when an article in the school newspaper adds to the pressure by calling Tom's hitting power the key to the team's success. Furthermore, Tom knows that his friends and family will be coming out to watch him play.

During the game Tom feels muscle tension in his neck and shoulders, where stress usually hits him. His heart is racing and his breathing is labored and shallow. He feels rushed, as if things are happening too fast around him. This feeling might be why he feels overanxious at the plate and swings at bad pitches.

Tom's attention is also affected—his concentration becomes narrow and internally focused. He is distracted by his own thoughts and feelings and has trouble concentrating on the coach's instructions. His thoughts instead become focused on "not messing up" and disappointing his teammates, family, and friends.

Tom's state, both psychologically and physically, is conductive to making mistakes. Sure enough, he comes up with the bases loaded and one out in the fourth inning, and he needs to make good contact with the ball. Instead, Tom swings at bad pitches and strikes out. This makes him even more frustrated, and he starts thinking about his batting as he plays the field. When a line drive comes sailing out to centerfield, he lunges at it at the last second, only to have the ball go under his glove for a triple.

> *Once a skill is learned well, an overemphasis on body mechanics is detrimental to performance.*

point the skill should be virtually automatic, and your attention should be primarily on what you're doing and one or two key cue words to keep you focused. If you are skiing in a competition for the fastest time, you should not be focusing on body mechanics. Rather, you should be externally focused on where you're going, skiing basically on automatic pilot.

This doesn't mean that no thinking occurs once a skill is well learned. But an emphasis on technique and body mechanics during competition is usually detrimental to performance because the mind gets in the way of the body. The more you analyze, the more likely you are to break the natural, smooth movements characteristic of high levels of performance, especially when rapid decisions and reactions are imperative.

Fatigue

Remembering our definition of attention, which involves mental effort, it is not surprising that concentration can be lost simply through fatigue. A high school football coach makes this point by saying, "When you get tired, your concentration goes. This results in impaired decision making, lack of focus and intensity, and other mental breakdowns. This is why conditioning and fitness are so important." In essence, fatigue reduces the amount of processing resources available to the athlete to meet the demands of the situation.

External Distracters

External distracters may be defined as stimuli from the environment that divert people's attention away from the relevant cues relating to their performance. Unfortunately for performers, a variety of potential distractions exist.

Visual Distracters

One of the difficult aspects of remaining focused throughout an exercise bout or competition is that there are so many visual distracters in the environment competing for your attention. One successful diver described it this way:

> *I started to shift away from the scoreboard a year and a half before the Olympics because I knew that every time that I looked at the scoreboard my heart went crazy. . . . At the Olympics, I really focused on my dives rather than on other divers. . . . Before that I used to just watch the event and watch the Chinese and think "Oh, how can she do that? She's a great diver." I thought "I'm as good as anyone else, let's stop thinking about them and focus on your own dives." That was an important step in my career.*

> —*Sylvie Bernier, 1984 Canadian Olympic diving champion (Orlick, 1990, p. 91)*

People who have a broad-external focus seem to notice everything happening in their vicinity, even things that have nothing to do with the activity. Spectators, for example, can distract them. Perhaps they start thinking about the audience and want to impress friends and family. But in trying to impress others, they might attempt things beyond their capabilities. A basketball player might try long-range shots outside her normal shooting range, or a baseball player might try for a home run instead of just making good contact with the ball.

Spectators affect some people's concentration and subsequent performance by making them try too hard. We all want to look good when playing in front of people we know and care for, so we often start to press, tighten up, and try too hard. This usually results in poorer play instead of better, which makes us feel embarrassed and causes us to tighten up even more. Of course, some people actually play better in front of audiences they know. For many others, knowing people in the audience is a powerful distraction. Other visual distracters reported by athletes include the leader board in professional golf tournaments, the scoreboard which has scores of other games, and the television camera crews at courtside.

Auditory Distracters

Most sport competitions take place in environments where various types of noise may act as a distracter to one's focus. Common auditory distracters include crowd noise, airplanes flying overhead, announcements on the public address system, mobile telephones, beepers or other electronic paging devices, and loud conversations among spectators. Accordingly, athletic success may hinge on an athlete's ability to ignore such distracters while focusing on the most relevant cues to complete the task at hand. It is interesting that noise and sounds are part of most team sports (e.g., basketball, soccer, hockey, baseball), though very quiet environments are expected for most individual sports (e.g., golf, tennis). Thus, a loud sound from the crowd is typically more disturbing to a golfer who expects near silence than to a hockey player who probably expects the sound.

Gamesmanship

In many sport situations competitors use strategic ploys in an effort to disrupt the concentration of their opponents; this is typically referred to as gamesmanship. The great boxer Mohammed Ali was a genius when it came to gamesmanship, and his barbs and constant talking inevitably distracted his opponents. When he was fighting Ernie Terrell, for example, he called out "What's my name" every time he landed a punch on him. A more subtle type of gamesmanship occurs when one athlete gives a "compliment" to her opponent. But this so-called compliment is really meant to have the opponent engage in a form of self-analysis, which will ultimately undermine her performance. A basketball player might say to an opponent who has just hit several shots in a row, "You're really following-through nicely on your jump shot." What this will typically do is have the player start to think about her jump shot and mechanics, thereby disrupting the rhythm of a previously effortless and smooth release. Other types of gamesmanship include physical and verbal intimidation, stalling (wasting time), and using insults. Finally, while gamesmanship can certainly be an external distracter, exhibiting such behavior is a question of ethics, which will be discussed in chapter 24.

Self-Talk

The previous section focused on a variety of internal and external distractions typically present in the competitive environment. Self-talk is another potential internal distracter (though it can also be a way to deal with distractions). Anytime you think about something, you are in a sense talking to yourself. This self-talk can take many forms, but for convenience we will categorize it into two types: positive and negative. Positive self-talk is an asset that enhances self-esteem, motivation, attentional focus, and performance. By using a specific set of verbal cues, performers can keep their minds appropriately focused on task-relevant cues. Self-talk that helps you focus on the present and keeps your mind from wandering is considered positive. It usually has either a motivational component (e.g., "I can do it" or "Just

hang in there a little longer") or an instructional component (e.g., "Keep your eyes on the ball" or "Bend your knees"). Legendary golfer Sam Snead has used the word *oily* to remind himself to concentrate on his fluid swing, and gold medalist swimmer Nelson Diebel has used the word *now* to motivate him to kick extra hard at certain points in a race.

Negative self-talk is critical and self-demeaning and gets in the way of a person's reaching goals; it is counterproductive and anxiety producing. Saying things like, "That was a stupid shot," "You stink," or "How can you play so bad?" does not enhance performance or create positive emotions. Rather, it creates anxiety and fosters self-doubt.

How Self-Talk Works

Thoughts play a critical role in shaping emotional responses to events. Most people assume that events themselves determine their emotional and physical responses, but this is not the case. Events in and of themselves do not cause depression, anger, anxiety, hopelessness, or frustration—it is how the event is interpreted that determines the response. This is what the famous philosopher Epictetus meant in saying, "We are not disturbed by things, but rather the view we take of them." Table 16.1 displays the relationship among an event, self-talk, and response. As the relationship shows, self-talk plays a key role in reactions to situations, and these reactions affect future actions and feelings.

Uses of Self-Talk

Although positive self-talk is crucial for concentration, the uses of self-talk extend into several other areas as well. We will now discuss some ways that athletes use cue words as self-talk to help their performances.

Skill Acquisition

When learning skills, people use self-talk as cue words to focus participants' attention. For example, an aerobics instructor might use simple cue words, such as *turn, stretch, pull,* or *reach* to focus attention on the next movement for learning a new routine.

Breaking Bad Habits

When breaking a bad habit, you need to decide on the best self-instructional cue (or cues) to make the new response automatic. The greater the change, the more self-instruction is necessary. A golfer who doesn't keep her head down throughout the execution of her shot might use a cue word such as *stay* or *ball* to remind herself to keep her head down.

Table 16.1
Process of Self-Talk

Event (environmental stimulation)	Self-talk (perception, evaluation)	Response (emotional, physiological, behavioral)
Missing an important shot in a tennis match	"What an idiot I am—I'll never win now."	Anger, hopelessness, increased muscle tension
Missing an important shot in a tennis match	"Keep your eye on the ball—this match isn't over."	Better concentration, optimism, calmness
A setback in rehabilitating a knee injury	"I'll never get back in the starting lineup."	Hopelessness, anger, frustration
A setback in rehabilitating a knee injury	"This type of injury just takes time to heal, so I need to continue to work hard."	Optimism, motivation, increased effort

---

Initiating Action

Self-talk can be motivating. Runners can increase their speed by using such cue words as *quick* or *fast*. A tennis serve might be cued by *smooth, reach,* or *forward,* whereas a swimmer getting out of the blocks might use such words as *explode, stretch,* or *push.*

Sustaining Effort

Although getting started is sometimes difficult, staying motivated and continuing to work hard can be just as tough. Positive, motivational self-talk (e.g., "Keep it up," "Stay with it," and "Hang in there") can help sustain effort when the body is fatigued.

Self-Talk and Performance Enhancement

Although both practitioners and researchers have argued the potentially important benefits of positive self-talk in enhancing task performance, it has only been relatively recently that empirical research has corroborated this assumption. Van Raalte, Brewer, Rivera, and Petitpas (1994) conducted an interesting descriptive analysis of audible "self-talk" and observable gestures that junior tennis players exhibited during competition. Several important findings emerged from their study, including the following: (a) More negative (i.e., self-critical) than positive (i.e., encouraging) self-talk was apparent among the players, and these negative self-statements were mainly displayed after mistakes; (b) negative self-talk was associated with poor performance on the court; (c) the players exhibited little instructional self-talk (e.g., "Move your feet"); and (d) there was no significant association between audible, positive self-talk and performance. Thus, this sample of youth tennis players seemed to focus on the negative, and

the self-talk they uttered proved to undermine their performance.

A variety of other athletic samples, however, have found that different types of positive self-talk (i.e., instructional, motivational, mood, self-affirmations) can be effective in enhancing performance. These studies have been conducted, for example, with cross-country skiers (Rushall, Hall, & Rushall (1988), beginning tennis players (Ziegler, 1987), sprinters (Mallett & Hanrahan, 1997), and figure skaters (Ming & Martin, 1996). The study with figure skaters is particularly impressive because self-report follow-ups a year after the intervention found that the participants continued to utilize the self-talk during practices and believed it enhanced their competitive performance.

Techniques for Improving Self-Talk

Several techniques or strategies can improve self-talk. Two of the most successful involve thought stopping and changing negative self-talk to positive self-talk.

Thought Stopping

One way to cope with negative thoughts is to stop them before they harm performance. **Thought stopping** involves concentrating on the undesired thought briefly and then using a cue or trigger to stop the thought and clear your mind. The trigger can be a simple word like *stop* or a trigger like snapping your fingers or hitting your hand against your thigh. What makes the most effective cue depends on the person.

Initially, it's best to restrict thought stopping to practice situations. Whenever you start thinking a negative thought, just say "stop" (or whatever cue you choose) aloud and then focus on a task-related cue. Once you have mastered this, try saying "stop" quietly to yourself. If there is a particular situation that produces negative self-talk (like falling during a figure-skating jump), you might want to focus on that one performance aspect to stay more focused and aware of the particular problem. Old habits die hard, so you should practice thought stopping on a continuing basis.

Changing Negative Self-Talk to Positive Self-Talk

It would be nice to eliminate all negative self-talk, but in fact almost everyone has negative thoughts from time to time. When they come, one way to cope with them is to change the negative thoughts into positive self-talk, which redirects attentional focus to provide encouragement and motivation.

First, list all the types of self-talk that hurt your performance or produce other undesirable behaviors. The goal here is to recognize what situations produce negative thoughts and why. Then try to substitute a positive statement for the negative one. When this is accomplished, create a chart with negative self-talk in one column and your corresponding positive self-talk in another (see Table 16.2).

Use the same guidelines to practice changing self-talk from negative to positive as you used for thought stopping. That is, use it in practice before trying it in competition. Because most negative thoughts occur under stress, you should first try to halt the negative thought and then take a deep breath. As you exhale, relax and repeat the positive statement.

Let's now look at some other skills connected with attention or concentration—specifically, how to assess attentional strengths and weaknesses.

Assessing Attentional Skills

Before trying to improve concentration, you should be able to pinpoint problem areas, such as undeveloped attentional skills. Nideffer's distinctions of attentional focus as internal or external and broad or narrow is useful in this regard. Nideffer argues that people have different attentional styles that contribute to differences in the quality of performance.

Test of Attentional and Interpersonal Style

Nideffer (1976) devised the Test of Attentional and Interpersonal Style (TAIS) to measure a person's attentional style, or disposition. The TAIS has 17 subscales, six of them measuring attentional style (the others measure interpersonal style and cognitive control). Notice in Table 16.3 that three of the scales indicate aspects of effective focusing (broad-external, broad-internal, and a narrow focus) and three assess aspects of ineffective focusing (external overload, internal overload, and a reduced focus).

Table 16.2

Negative and Positive Self-Talk

Negative self-talk	*change to*	Positive self-talk
"You idiot—how could you miss such an easy shot?"		"Everyone makes mistakes—just concentrate on the next point."
"I'll never recover from this injury."		"Healing takes time. Just continue to exercise every day."
"He robbed me on the line call—that ball was definitely in."		"There's nothing I can do about it. If I play well, I'll win anyway."
"I'll take it easy today and work out hard tomorrow."		"If I work hard today, then the next workout will be easier."
"That was a terrible serve."		"Just slow down and keep your rhythm and timing."
"I'll never stay with this exercise program."		"Just take one day at a time and make exercise fun."
"I never play well in the wind."		"It's windy on both sides of the court. This just requires extra concentration."

Table 16.3
Attentional Scales of the TAIS

Scale	Description
Broad-external	High scores indicate an ability to integrate many external stimuli simultaneously.
External overload	High scores indicate a tendency to become confused and overloaded with external stimuli.
Broad-internal	High scores indicate an ability to integrate several ideas at one time.
Narrow focus	High scores indicate an ability to narrow attention when appropriate.
Reduced focus	High scores indicate chronically narrowed attention.
Internal overload	High scores indicate a tendency to become overloaded with internal stimuli.

Effective and Ineffective Attentional Styles

People who concentrate well (**effective attenders**) deal well with simultaneous stimuli from external and internal sources (see Figure 16.3). They have high scores on broad-external and broad-internal focusing and can effectively switch their attention from a broad to a narrow focus as is necessary. Effective attenders are also low on the three measures of ineffective attention we just mentioned, which means they can attend to many stimuli (both internal and external) without becoming overloaded with information. They also can narrow their attentional focus when necessary without omitting or missing any important information.

In contrast, people who don't concentrate well (**ineffective attenders**) tend to become confused and overloaded by multiple stimuli, both internal and external. When they assume either a broad-internal or broad-external focus, they have trouble narrowing their attentional width. For example, they may have trouble blocking out crowd noises or movement in the stands. Furthermore, the high score on the reduced-focus scale indicates that when they assume a narrow focus, it is so narrow that important information is left out. A soccer player, for example, might narrow his attentional focus to the ball and fail to see an opposing player alongside him who steals the ball! For ineffective attenders to perform better in sport competition, they must learn to switch their direction of attention at will and to narrow or broaden attention as the situation demands.

TAIS as a Trait Measure

Nideffer's Test of Attentional and Interpersonal Style is a trait measure of a person's generalized way of attending to the environment. It does not consider situational factors. Recall the interactional paradigm from chapter 3, a model that more completely describes human behavior than the more traditional trait approach does. If a soccer coach used the TAIS to measure the attentional style of players without taking into consideration that different positions require different types of attentional focus, he would gain little pertinent information for enhancing performance.

If the TAIS had sport-specific measures of attentional styles, it would be more useful because questions assessing attentional abilities would be directed at the specific skills employed in a particular sport. Sport-specific attentional style measures have been developed for tennis (Van Schoyck & Grasha, 1981) and pistol shooting (Etzel, 1979). Using sport-specific measures of attentional focus can help identify specific attentional weaknesses for athletes and coaches to work on. Despite the usefulness of the TAIS for practitioners in assessing attentional style, the test has been criticized by researchers in terms of its validity and some of its underlying assumptions. Researchers argue that other measures should be utilized for assessing attentional capacities, and we will next discuss a couple of these alternatives.

> *Effective attenders can attend to several stimuli without getting overloaded and can narrow attentional focus without leaving out important information. Ineffective attenders are easily confused by multiple stimuli.*

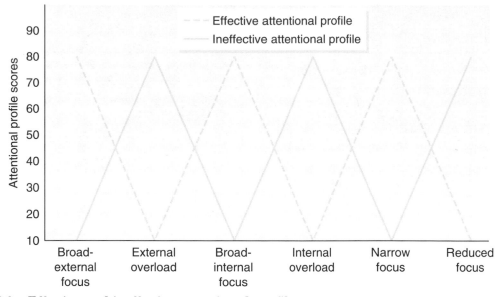

Figure 16.3 *Effective and ineffective attentional profiles.*

Psychophysiological Measures

Although practitioners have relied mostly on questionnaire measures of attentional style, such as the TAIS, researchers have also used psychophysiological assessments to help measure attentional processes. The psychophysiological indicators of attention they have used most often in sport and exercise environments are brain waves, as measured by an electroencephalogram (EEG), and heart rate measures. In general, physiological measures of attention have been administered most frequently to performers of "closed" skills (i.e., those that are self-paced, repetitive, and performed in a relatively unchanging environment, such as golf, bowling, pistol shooting, and archery).

Electroencephalogram Measures

In the studies using EEG, brain-activity patterns of pistol and rifle shooters and archers have typically been assessed "preshot." One consistent finding is that the accuracy of shooting performance tends to be associated with alpha frequencies (usually associated with relaxed wakefulness) in the left cerebral hemisphere. In particular, there is an increase in alpha activity in the left hemisphere in the few seconds prior to releasing the arrow or pulling the pistol's trigger. This increase in alpha activity suggests that elite shooters have gained such control over their attentional processes that they can voluntarily reduce cognitive activity in their left hemisphere. This, in turn, can lead to a lowering of task-irrelevant cognitive distractions that might otherwise disrupt shooting performance (Summers & Ford, 1995).

Heart Rate Measures

The notion that heart rate is related to attentional processes stems from work in the 1960s, when Lacey (1967) explained that the deceleration in heart rate during the preparatory period in shooting was caused by the shooters directing their attention outward at that time—focusing not only on the visual target but also on the best way to stabilize and align the gun. These observations have been supported by more recent research (e.g., Landers, Han, Salazar, Petruzello, Kubitz, & Gannon, 1994), which indicates that cardiac deceleration just prior to performance can be explained by the shooters' focusing their attention on external cues that prime them to respond. In addition, the extent of this cardiac deceleration is related to the proficiency of the athlete: Expert athletes display greater deceleration than do their lower-ability counterparts. This suggests that expert athletes know how to regulate their physiological processes in order to prepare optimally for skilled performance.

Understanding a person's attentional style and skills is a first step toward improving concentration skills. In the next section we suggest specific methods for improving attentional focus and shifting between types of attention.

Tips for Improving Concentration On-Site

Being able to maintain a focus on relevant environmental cues is critical for effective performance. In describing ways to improve concentration, we'll focus first on things that can be done on the field of play. Then we'll suggest exercises that can be practiced at other times and in other places.

Use Simulations in Practice

Anyone who has played competitive sport understands that the competitive environment includes numerous factors that are not present to the same degree (if at all) in the training environment. Such environmental factors as a noisy and antagonistic crowd, the presence of officials, and the behavior of the opposition undoubtedly make the competitive environment much different from practice. In addition, psychological factors, such as competitive anxiety, motivation, and confidence, are all likely to vary between practice and competition. All these factors represent potential distractions to the athletes and may impair performance.

You can prepare yourself to cope with distractions by systematically practicing with typical distractions present. Some basketball coaches, for instance, have loud crowd noises piped in, wanting the players to get used to playing and shooting in that environment.

Similarly, some tennis coaches have people stand around and talk or walk by the court from time to time to simulate the environment at match play. Football coaches continually practice variations of the two-minute drill so players will be physically and psychologically prepared for this pressure situation in the game. This type of practice is known as **simulation training** because the coaches are trying to simulate an actual competitive environment.

In working with Canadian Olympic athletes, Orlick and Partington (1988) found that these successful athletes emphasized the importance of simulation training as part of their preparation. "The best athletes made extensive use of simulation training. They approached training runs, routines, plays, scrimmages in practice as if they were at the competition, often wearing what they would wear and preparing like they would prepare" (p. 114). Besides the physical preparation, elite athletes also reported using simulations to prepare mentally. For example, British Olympic javelin thrower Steve Backley stated that he sometimes structured his training in such a way as to put himself under the same sort of pressure that he expected to encounter on the qualifying

day of a major competition. "I'd have three throws to get over 75 to 76 meters, and I'd mark out the distance and actually go through the process of trying to simulate the pressure" (Jones & Hardy, 1990, p. 270).

Fans in individual sports such as tennis and golf tend to follow proper etiquette, keeping quiet and still during play and remaining passive. Conversely, team-sport spectators often cheer loudly for the home team and even boo the visiting team. Thus, team-sport athletes are exposed more to distractions and learn to play in spite of them. Individual-sport athletes rarely face distractions in competition or practice, and are thus less prepared to deal with them.

Although practicing with distractions can help develop focus, many athletes avoid situations they find aversive. For example, if a baseball player does not like to bat when it's cold because it stings his hands, he will usually avoid practicing under such conditions. But what happens when he must bat in cold weather during an actual game? The more you practice under adverse conditions, the better prepared you will be to cope with these conditions during competition. Here's an example of how Jimmy Connors blocked out heat and humidity during a match to maintain his focus:

> *It was hot out there—really hot—but I knew that if I started thinking too much about the sun, I wouldn't do my best. I didn't worry about it while I was on the court, but when I was sitting down, with the sun bearing down, it started to get to me a little. So I just blocked it out and pretended it wasn't there. That's what you have to do in tennis—not let yourself think about anything that can have a negative effect on your game. (Tarshis, 1977, p. 45)*

Use Cue Words

Put simply, cue words are used to trigger a particular response. They can be instructional (e.g., *follow-through, shoulders back, watch the ball, stretch*) or motivational or emotional (e.g., *strong, move, relax, hang in there, get tough*). The key is to keep the cue word simple and let it automatically trigger the desired response. For example, a gymnast performing a floor routine might use the cue word *forward* to

Cue words should be either instructional or motivational to help focus on the task at hand.

make sure that she pushes ahead at a certain point during her performance. Similarly, a sprinter might say *explode* to make sure that he gets off the starting blocks well. Or, a figure skater might say *glide* to make sure she keeps her balance between jumps. It is important that these cue words be used in practice so that they become familiar and well learned before being used in competition.

Cue words are particularly useful when you are trying to vary or change a movement pattern—whether it be changing your golf swing, batting stance, aerobic dance routine, or service motion. In the training room, athletes could use cue words like *relax* or *easy* when stretching injured muscles and joints.

Attentional cues are also helpful for trying to break a bad habit. For instance, if a miler tends to tighten up in the last lap of a race and her stride becomes shorter, thus spoiling her rhythm, a cue such as *smooth, stretch*, or *relax* might help her keep focused on relaxing and lengthening her stride. Similarly, a hockey player might use the cue *stick to ice* to remind himself to keep his stick on the ice until he has control of the puck.

Employ Nonjudgmental Thinking

One of the biggest obstacles athletes face in maintaining concentration is the tendency to evaluate performance and classify it as good or bad. That is, they assign a positive or negative value to what they do. Such judgments tend to elicit personal, ego-involved reactions.

The process of evaluating and judging what you do on the athletic field or in exercise class usually results in performance declines. After you become judgmental about a portion of your performance or behavior, it is common to start generalizing. For example, a soccer player who misses a couple of opportunities to score a goal might think, "I always miss the easy ones," "I'm just a choke artist," or "I just can't kick one when I need to." Such thoughts and judgments make you lose your fluidity, timing, and rhythm. Your brain starts to override your body, causing excess muscle tension, excess effort, concentration lapses, and impaired decision making. Suppose someone in an exercise class misses a few workouts and thinks, "I just don't have what it takes to stay with the program." Such thinking undermines her motivation to adhere to an exercise program (more about this in chapter 18).

Instead of judging the worth of a performance and categorizing it as either good or bad, you should learn to look at your actions nonjudgmentally. This doesn't mean you should ignore errors and mistakes but that you should see your performance as it is, without adding judgments. For instance, a baseball pitcher realizes he doesn't have good control today—he has walked four batters in the first 3 innings and thrown more balls than strikes. He knows that the manager is getting edgy and that if he continues this pattern, he'll soon be taken out of the game. This observation could lead him to generalize that he's a bad pitcher and doesn't have control over his pitches. This thinking could lead to anger, frustration, and discouragement.

Instead, this pitcher might evaluate how he is pitching and simply notice that most of his pitches out of the strike zone have been high, rather than low. This would tell him, for example, that he is not following through properly and so the ball is getting away from him on delivery. In response, he could focus on getting a good wrist snap and following through to keep the ball from rising on him. In this way he has used his performance evaluation constructively, which translates into better performance and a more enjoyable experience.

Establish Routines

Routines can focus concentration and be extremely helpful to mental preparation for an upcoming performance. Researchers have argued that preperformance routines work by helping athletes to divert their attention from task-irrelevant thoughts to task-relevant thoughts. In essence, routines increase the likelihood that individuals will not be distracted internally or externally prior to and during performance. The effectiveness of routines has substantial support (see Cohn, Rotella, & Lloyd on golf, 1990; Feltz & Landers on mental rehearsal, 1983; Gould, Eklund, & Jackson on wrestling, 1992b; Kirschenbaum, Ordman, Tomarken, & Holtzbauer on bowling, 1982; Moore & Stevenson on tennis, 1994; Orlick on skiing, 1986; and Wrisberg & Pein on basketball, 1992).

The mind often starts to wander during breaks in the action. Such times are ideal for routines. For example, a tennis player during changeovers might sit

Routines can be used before or during an event to focus attention, reduce anxiety, eliminate distractions, and enhance confidence.

in a chair, take a deep breath, and image what she wants to do in the next game. Then she might repeat two or three cue words to help her focus attention before taking the court. Routines can help structure the time before performance and between performances so that an athlete can be mentally focused when it's time to perform.

Athletes have routines varying from short and simple to complex and lengthy. Some border on superstition, such as wearing a lucky pair of socks, tying their shoelaces a certain way, or walking to the pitcher's mound without stepping on the foul lines. The routine needs to be comfortable to the individual and help sharpen focus as the time of performance nears. Preperformance routines structure the athlete's thought processes and emotional states, keeping the focus of attention in the present and on task-related cues. (See Table 16.4 for examples of preperformance routines for tennis and golf.)

Develop Competition Plans

In-depth interviews with elite athletes in a variety of sports clearly indicate the importance to them of establishing precompetition and competition plans to help maintain their attentional focus (Gould et al., 1992a; Orlick & Partington, 1988). These plans help athletes not only prepare for their events but also to prepare for what they would do in different circumstances, both before and during their competition. In most cases athletes design these detailed plans of action to facilitate attentional focus on the *process* of performance (as opposed to factors over which they have no direct control, such as other competitors and final outcome). These remarks by an Olympic kayaker highlight this focus on a detailed plan:

My focus was very concentrated throughout the race. We have a start plan, and in it I concentrate only on the first few strokes. . . . Then I concentrate on the next little bit of the race. . . . Then it's getting to the end, [and] we have to really push. Almost every 3 seconds or so toward the end I'd have to say, "Relax" and let my shoulders and my head relax, and I'd think about putting on the power and then I'd feel the tension creeping up again so I'd think about relaxing again, then power, then relax.

—*Orlick and Partington, 1988, p. 116*

Inherent in competition plans is a focus on process goals. In other words, the plans focus on what is under the control of the athlete rather than on the

Table 16.4

Sport-Specific Examples of Preperformance Routines

GOLF SHOT

1. Take a deep breath.

2. Look at the fairway's lie and assess weather conditions and possible hazards.

3. Look at the target and decide on the shot required.

4. Picture your target and the shot you want to hit. Imagine not only your swing but also the trajectory of the ball and its final resting place.

5. Address the ball, adjusting and readjusting your position until you feel comfortable.

6. Feel the shot with your whole body.

7. Again picture the desired shot and, while feeling the shot, think *target*.

8. Think *target* and swing.

TENNIS SERVE

1. Determine positioning and foot placement.

2. Decide on service type and placement.

3. Adjust racquet grip and ball.

4. Take a deep breath.

5. Bounce the ball for rhythm.

6. See and feel the perfect serve.

7. Focus on ball toss and serve to programmed spot.

■ CLOSE-UP ■

The Lucky Chair

Tennis players Tom Okker and Ray Moore were preparing to face each other in the semifinals of the Paris Indoor Championships. As they emerged from the locker room they began briskly walking side by side. By the time they were halfway to the umpire's chair, their brisk pace seemed like a race. "You bet it was a race," said Moore later. "It was a race to see who could reach the lucky chair first. Of course, neither of us wanted to admit it. I had played well in the tournament, beating Vilas and Tanner, and on both occasions I had sat to the left of the umpire. Okker had been using that side during matches as well. Neither of us wanted to risk breaking the routine, so here we were engaged in this farce of trying to reach a certain spot on the court before the other guy, when we were supposed to be walking side by side. At the last moment, that bloody Okker broke all the rules and sprinted the last couple of yards, so of course I had no chance. I mean the man's quick as a hare. I was livid." (Weinberg, 1988, p. 167).

© Human Kinetics

outcome of the competition. For example, the kayaker's process goals related to maintaining relaxed muscles in his shoulders and neck and to focusing on his stroke. A soccer player may focus instead on her positioning and footwork, and a volleyball player on the position of her arms when striking the ball. In any case, detailed, specific plans can help an athlete focus and maintain attention throughout the competition.

Practice Eye Control

Eye control is still another method to focus concentration. The eyes tend to wander (just as minds do). Rather than fixing only on the task at hand (task-relevant cues), they see such distractions (task-irrelevant cues) as motions in the crowd, antics by opponents, signals that officials are giving, outbursts from coaches, and behavior in teammates. Many a race has been lost near the end by looking at the opposition instead of focusing on the finish line. A player watching the runners take off on a hit-and-run in baseball instead of staying focused on the pitch is an attentional error. Similarly, a gymnast looking around at other competitors while preparing to start her own floor exercise is an inappropriate attentional focus.

The key to eye control is to make sure your eyes do not wander to irrelevant cues. Some things that athletes have used to enhance eye control is focusing on the floor, the equipment, or a spot on the wall. How many times have you heard athletes in tennis, golf, baseball, soccer, or volleyball say "Watch the ball." You hear it a lot because, as you know from experience, keeping your eyes on the ball is easier said than done.

For example, a basketball player on the free-throw line shooting in front of a hostile crowd may want to keep his head down and eyes on the floor until he is ready to look up at the basket and focus on the rim. A tennis player may want to focus between points on the strings of her racquet to keep from looking at the opponent or the crowd. Preparing to dive, a diver might focus on a spot on the wall. The key is to pick something that can maintain your focus of attention and prevent your eyes from wandering.

Stay Focused in the Present

The importance of keeping focused in the present cannot be overemphasized. Because the mind is so open to incoming messages, it is hard to keep a present focus. The mind wants to replay that missed

shot and review that error in judgment or blown assignment. It also wants to look ahead to what might happen in the future. But past- and future-oriented thinking usually creates attentional problems.

Staying in the present requires a focused concentration throughout the event. It's okay to take a brief mental break occasionally during stops in the action. But it is important then to have a cue word, like *focus,* to help bring you back into the present when it's time to start competing again.

Overlearn Skills

To perform at high levels, athletes report that overlearning of the skills involved in their sport helps concentration in the competitive situation. In interviews, athletes consistently stated that the skill they were required to perform in competition had to be overlearned to the extent that they could stay focused despite any distractions that might be present (Hardy, Jones, & Gould, 1996). Overlearning helps make the performance of a skill automatic. This, in turn, frees up one's attention to concentrate on other aspects of the performance environment.

Research, too, has found that overlearning facilitates the concurrent performance of more than one task by enabling athletes to establish automatic attentional processes. For example, a basketball point guard doesn't have to focus much attention on dribbling the ball once it is automatic; the focus then turns to the movement and positioning of the other players on the court, allowing her to throw the most effective pass. In the same way that physical skills must be overlearned in order to be performed automatically, there is also evidence that elite performers have made their psychological skills automatic (Gould, Eklund & Jackson, 1993).

Exercises for Improving Concentration

Besides the eight areas we have given to improve concentration on the field, other techniques can increase concentration skills. These exercises can be adapted to any sport.

Exercise 1: Learning to Shift Attention

This exercise can be practiced in its entirety or broken down into separate exercises (Gauron, 1984). Before starting the exercise, sit or lie down in a comfortable position and take a few deep breaths from the diaphragm. Begin the technique once you feel comfortable and relaxed.

1. Pay attention to what you hear. Take each separate sound and label it, such as voices, footsteps, or the radio. Next, listen to all the sounds around you without attempting to label or classify them. Simply dismiss your thoughts and listen to the blend of sounds as if you were listening to music.

2. Now become aware of body sensations, such as the feeling of the chair, floor, or bed supporting you. Mentally label each sensation as you notice it. Before moving on to another sensation, let each sensation linger for a moment while you examine it closely, considering its quality and source. Finally, try to experience all of these sensations at once without labeling any of them. This will require a broad-internal focus.

3. Turn your attention to your thoughts and emotions. Let each emotion or thought simply arise; do not try to specifically think about anything. Remain relaxed and at ease, no matter what you are thinking or feeling. Now try to experience each of your feelings and thoughts one at a time. Finally, see if you can just let go of all these thoughts and emotions and relax.

4. Open your eyes and pick an object across the room and directly in front of you. While looking straight ahead, see as much of the room and as many objects there as your peripheral vision allows. Now try to narrow your focus of attention to just the object centered in front of you. Continue to narrow your focus until that is the only object in view. Now expand your focus little by little, widening your perspective until you can again see everything in the room. Think of your external focus as a zoom lens; practice zooming in and out, narrowing or broadening your attentional focus according to your preference.

By shifting your focus across internal-external and broad-narrow dimensions, this exercise helps you experience different attentional styles. The exercise also demonstrates why different perspectives are needed to perform the various skills required in different sports.

Exercise 2: "Parking" Thoughts

This exercise is concerned with effectively eliminating negative, intruding thoughts by "parking" them in a safe and nondistracting place until after the performance. Parking is typically accomplished by some form of self-talk instruction or visualization. This technique can be especially effective for athletes who bring outside issues into the competition. After identifying these unwanted thoughts in their minds, athletes are instructed to write them down on paper and then place this paper in some other place (this is the parking component). Upon completion of the performance, the athlete can go back and deal with the issue by "unparking" it. The benefit is that the athlete has been able to compete without the distracting thought continually intruding; after the performance it can be dealt with in an appropriate manner.

Exercise 3: Learning to Maintain Focus

Find a quiet place with no distractions. Choose an object to focus on (you might choose something related to the sport that you play, such as a hockey puck, soccer ball, baseball, or volleyball). Hold the object in your hands. Get a good sense of how it feels, its texture, color, and any other distinguishing characteristics. Now put the object down and focus your attention on it, examining it in great detail. If your thoughts wander, bring your attention back to the object.

Record how long you can maintain your focus on the object. It isn't easy to stay focused on one object. Once you are able to maintain focus for at least 5 minutes, start practicing with distractions present. Chart how long you can maintain your attention under these conditions. You will enhance your performance capabilities if you can become proficient at maintaining your concentration despite distractions and disruptions.

Exercise 4: Searching for Relevant Cues

The grid exercise has been used extensively in Eastern Europe as a precompetition screening device. It can give you a sense of what it means to be totally focused. The exercise requires a block grid containing two-digit numbers ranging from 00 to 99 (see Figure 16.4). The object is to scan the grid and within a set period of time (usually 1 or 2 minutes) mark a slash through as many sequential numbers as possible (00, 01, 02, 03, etc.). The same grid can be used several times by just starting with a higher number (e.g., 33, 41, 51, etc.) than in your previous attempt. You can make new grids using any combination of numbers. People who intensely concentrate, scan, and store relevant cues reportedly score in the upper 20s and into the 30s in terms of how many numbers they find in sequence within 1 minute.

This exercise will help you learn to focus your attention and scan the environment for relevant cues (which is especially important in fast-moving sports such as basketball, hockey, and soccer), and you can modify it for different situations. For instance, you can scan the grid amidst different types of distractions, such as people talking or loud music. As your concentration improves, you will be better able to block out such distractions and focus exclusively on the task. And isn't this what most athletes want to accomplish in terms of concentration: complete absorption and the elimination of all distractions?

Exercise 5: Rehearsing Game Concentration

Using imagery or mental rehearsal is another good practice for concentration. For example, a football

32	42	39	34	99	19	84	44	03	77
37	97	92	18	90	53	04	72	51	65
95	40	33	86	45	81	67	13	59	58
69	78	57	68	87	05	79	15	28	36
09	26	62	89	91	47	52	61	64	29
00	60	75	02	22	08	74	17	16	12
76	25	48	71	70	83	06	49	41	07
10	31	98	96	11	63	56	66	50	24
20	01	54	46	82	14	38	23	73	94
43	88	85	30	21	27	80	93	35	55

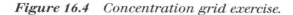

Figure 16.4 *Concentration grid exercise.*

referee might picture making calls on different pass plays, in which both offensive and defensive players make contact just as the ball is arriving. Sprinters might see themselves get a great start off the blocks, hit their strides, and then stay loose and relaxed in the last 20 yards of the race (where sprinters often tighten up).

SUMMARY

1 *Define concentration and explain how it is related to performance.*

Concentration in sport and exercise settings usually involves focusing on the relevant cues in the environment, maintaining that focus over time, and being aware of the changing situation. Athletes who describe their best performances inevitably mention that they are completely absorbed in the present, focused on the task at hand, and are acutely aware of their own bodies and the external environment. Research, too, has shown that a key component of optimal performance is the performer's ability to focus attention and become fully absorbed in the game. Expert performers use various attentional cues, picking these cues up more quickly than do novices, to help themselves perform their skills more quickly and more effectively.

2 *Identify different types of attentional focus.*

Nideffer identified four different types of attentional focus: broad-external, narrow-external, broad-internal, and narrow-internal. Different sports or tasks within sports require these different types of attention for effective performance.

3 *Describe some attentional problems.*

Attentional problems can be categorized as coming from internal or external distracters. Internal distracters include attending to past events, attending to future events, fatigue, and overanalyzing body mechanics. External distracters include visual factors, such as the audience, and auditory ones, such as the crowd noise, as well as the opponent's gamesmanship itself.

4 *Explain how self-talk works.*

Self-talk takes many forms, but it can be simply categorized as positive and negative. Positive self-talk is an asset that can enhance self-esteem, motivation, and attentional focus. Negative self-talk is critical and self-demeaning, and it tends to produce anxiety, which undermines concentration.

5 *Explain how to assess attentional ability.*

Attentional style can be measured by the Test of Attentional and Interpersonal Style (TAIS), and strengths and weaknesses can then be assessed for developing programs to improve an individual's focus. Attentional processes can also be measured by brain wave activity and heart rate.

6 *Discuss how to improve attentional focus.*

Practicing simple techniques and exercises both on and off the court will help improve concentration skills. These include such activities as using simulations, employing cue words, using nonjudgmental thinking, developing competitive plans, and establishing routines.

KEY TERMS

attention
concentration
selective attention

attentional focus
associative attentional strategy
dissociative attentional strategy

situation awareness
broad attentional focus
narrow attentional focus
external attentional focus
internal attentional focus
internal distracters
choking
external distracters
visual distracters

auditory distracters
gamesmanship
self-talk
thought stopping
effective attenders
ineffective attenders
simulation training
cue words
eye control

REVIEW QUESTIONS

1. How did William James originally define concentration more than 100 years ago? How has its definition evolved since then? Why is the ability to focus on relevant cues in the environment and maintain that focus essential to the definition of a proper attentional focus?

2. Explain the old saying, "Fatigue makes cowards of us all." Include a description in your explanation of an athletic situation in which fatigue is common and concentration requirements are high.

3. Why is concentration not an "all-or-none" phenomenon? Use sports examples to explain the different types (according to Nideffer) of concentration and the situations for which they are appropriate.

4. Providing an example from a sport, discuss the kinds of shifts in attentional focus that Nideffer describes.

5. What are some attentional problems that affect focus and impair performance? Be sure to distinguish between internal and external distracters.

6. When is it appropriate to have an internal-narrow focus on body mechanics and movements? When is this type of focus inappropriate? What impact do physical and psychological skill development have on an appropriate attentional focus during competition?

7. Nideffer's Test of Attentional and Interpersonal Style (TAIS) is a trait measure of a person's generalized way of attending to the environment. What are the limitations inherent in a trait measure of an athlete's perceptions? What could be done to make the TAIS a better assessment tool?

8. What have we learned about attentional processes from psychophysiological assessments of brain waves and heart rate?

9. What steps would you take in setting up an athletic practice using concentration-enhancing techniques? Explain why each technique is likely to get participants to focus on the relevant stimuli.

10. Discuss why routines work as preparation for performance and when is the best time to perform a routine.

11. Describe the different types and uses of self-talk. Give a practical example of thought stopping to enhance performance.

CRITICAL THINKING QUESTIONS

1. You are asked to write an article about choking for an applied journal in your sport. They want you to define what it is (and isn't), when it occurs, why it occurs, and how you could help athletes avoid it. Write the article.

2. You are coaching a high school team (pick your sport), and the team has a habit of losing concentration at critical times during the competition. You want to work with your athletes to enhance their concentration skills and keep their attention focused throughout the competition. Describe the drills, exercises, and strategies you would use with the team to help its members build concentration skills.

Part VI

Enhancing Health and Well-Being

In the past 20 years we have witnessed an increased interest in health, exercise, and wellness, including exercise and health psychology. With greater attention has come better understanding of the roles that psychological factors play in health and exercise.

This sixth part begins with two chapters that specifically address exercise. In chapter 17 we examine the psychological benefits of exercise, such as reduced depression and anxiety, and tell you how to maximize these benefits. Chapter 18 discusses exercise motivation and ways to keep people exercising regularly. New models and approaches to improving exercise adherence are presented, along with practical tips to improve health and well-being through consistent exercise.

The next three chapters deal with more general health-related concerns. Chapter 19 focuses on the psychological antecedents and consequences of athletic- and exercise-induced injuries and the role of psychological factors in injury rehabilitation. In chapter 20, we'll examine three of today's most critical concerns—substance abuse, eating disorders, and gambling. We'll prepare you to recognize the signs of such problems and help those who are afflicted receive the specialized assistance they require. Finally, chapter 21 examines the potential negative effects of athletic and exercise participation, including close looks at burnout and overtraining. The prevalence, causes, and treatment of burnout and overtraining will be discussed.

© Photophile

Exercise and Psychological Well-Being

After reading this chapter you should be able to

1 explain the effects of exercise on anxiety and depression;
2 describe the relationship between exercise and mood states;
3 discuss the effects of exercise on psychological well-being;
4 describe the relation among exercise, personality changes, and cognitive functioning;
5 discuss the "runner's high"; and
6 explain positive and negative addiction to exercise.

Much of technology was meant to make our lives easier. In fact, the advent of car phones, fax machines, computers, the internet, and other communication devices has made our world increasingly complex and pressured. Ever more demands seem to be built into our daily existence, and noise, smog, inflation, unemployment, racism, sexism, drug abuse, gambling, and random violence add still more stress to our lives. These demands have affected the mental health and psychological well-being of our society.

About 16 million Americans suffer from depression and between 12 and 14 million suffer from anxiety or stress reactions. Although people typically deal with these mood disturbances through psychological counseling, drug therapy, or both, more and more individuals are looking to exercise to promote their psychological well-being. In fact, many researchers, clinicians, and lay people have observed that physical activity enhances feelings of well-being, in particular by reducing anxiety and tension and increasing vigor (Landers, 1994).

Epidemiological data add credibility to these obvservations of the beneficial influences of exercise. This epidemiological data refers to statistics and information about the distribution and determinants of health problems or health-related events in populations as they apply to the control of health problems. For example, Stephens (1988) analyzed data from 56,000 subjects and concluded that "the level of physical activity is positively associated with good mental health in the household population of the United States and Canada, when mental health is defined as positive mood, general well-being, and relatively infrequent symptoms of anxiety and depression" (p. 41). The positive effects of exercise on physical well-being are well documented, and these effects include changing the course of such illnesses as osteoporosis, hypertension, coronary heart disease, and cancer (Blair, 1995).

In this chapter we look at the psychological benefits of exercise in four broad areas: the reduction of stress and depression, enhancing of mood, improvement in the self-concept, and higher quality of life. Let's begin with how exercise helps reduce anxiety and depression.

Exercise in the Reduction of Anxiety and Depression

Mental health problems account for some 30% of the total days of hospitalization in the United States and about 10% of total medical costs, with the So-cial Security Administration ranking them third as a cause of disability. The mental health problems that have received the most attention are anxiety and depression. Although millions of Americans suffer from anxiety disorders and depression, not all of them have psychopathological states; many simply have subjective distress, a broader description of unpleasant emotions. For these people, regular exercise appears to have some therapeutic value in reducing feelings of anxiety and depression. And participating in regular exercise for psychological well-being is more than an American phenomenon. For example, in a survey conducted in England, Londoners also found exercise to be one of the most effective things to do when feeling depressed.

So far, most studies of the relation of exercise and reductions in anxiety and depression have been correlational, so we cannot conclusively state that it was exercise that caused or produced the change in mood state. Rather, exercise appears to be *associated with* positive changes in mood states and reductions in anxiety and depression.

The effects of exercise on anxiety and depression can be classified as acute or chronic. Acute effects refer to immediate and possibly, but not necessarily, temporary effects arising from a single bout of exercise. They are usually measured to assess psychological states directly after exercise. Sport psychologists have also studied the long-term, or chronic effects of exercise, investigating the validity of the old motto, "A sound mind in a sound body." Research on the chronic effects of exercise has focused on changes over time in both anxiety and depression.

The vast majority of research investigating the relation between exercise and psychological well-being has used aerobic exercise. Although it was once believed that exercise needed to be of a certain or sufficient duration and intensity to produce positive psychological effects, more recent research has indicated that high-intensity aerobic activity is not absolutely necessary to produce these positive benefits (e.g., Hobson & Rejeski, 1993). In fact, activities such as weight or strength training, yoga, and other nonaerobic exercises have produced positive effects on psychological well-being. However, aerobic exercise seems to maximize these positive effects on

Although a cause-effect relation has not been established, regular exercise is associated with reductions in anxiety and depression.

354

mood and psychological state, and thus has been the focus of most research in this area.

Reduction of Anxiety

Studies of how exercise influences the reduction of anxiety can be categorized into investigations of either the (a) acute (short-term) or (b) chronic (long-term) effects.

Acute Effects

Most research into the acute effects of exercise has focused on its reducing state anxiety. It should be noted that when researchers refer to the tranquilizing effect of exercise on anxiety, they usually mean somatic anxiety, not cognitive anxiety. One of the earlier studies (Bahrke & Morgan, 1978) compared the effects of walking on a treadmill for 20 minutes at 70% of maximal heart rate with meditating or with resting quietly; it found these three treatments all lowered state anxiety scores. The researchers concluded that exercise, like rest or meditation, acts as a time-out or diversion from the usual routine and that the physical aspect of exercise is not the main factor in lowering state anxiety. (We will return later in the chapter to this idea that exercise acts simply as a time-out.)

Exercise intensity, however, appears to be important in determining how well exercise reduces state anxiety. In a series of seven experiments summarized by Morgan (1987), reductions in state anxiety were found only when exercise was performed at 70% of maximal heart rate. Exercise bouts of low or moderate intensity were not effective in reducing state anxiety.

How long does the tranquilizing effect of exercise last? Raglin and Morgan (1987) found that state anxiety was reduced for 2 hours after the exercise bout—whereas subjects in a control rest condition returned to baseline levels within 30 minutes. Another study evaluated men and women before and after 45 minutes of aerobic exercise. Both sexes experienced significant decreases in state anxiety levels immediately after the exercise, but levels returned to the preexercise range within 4 to 6 hours (Seeman, 1978). After 24 hours the mean state anxiety levels were identical to the values before the exercise session. These findings suggest that regular exercise on a daily basis might reduce anxiety and prevent the onset of chronic anxiety.

Chronic Effects

Although researchers have focused on the acute effects of exercise in reducing anxiety, there have been some additional studies investigating the possible association of long-term exercise and reduced anxiety. Investigations into these chronic effects of exercise have involved programs that typically last about 2 to 4 months, with two to four exercise sessions per week. Two studies (Long, 1984; Long & Haney, 1988) compared different anxiety-reduction techniques, such as stress inoculation and progressive relaxation, with jogging as stress-management interventions. In both studies the jogging groups and stress-management groups exhibited significant

---

■ MORE INFORMATION ■

Aerobic and Anaerobic Exercise

Aerobic exercise is physical activity that increases the activity of pulmonary and cardiovascular systems. During aerobic exercise the body uses and transports oxygen to the working muscles to maintain the activity. Aerobic exercise includes such activities as brisk walking, running, swimming, step aerobics, cycling, aerobic dance, cross-country skiing, and rowing. The American College of Sports Medicine has suggested that for most healthy adults to receive cardiovascular benefits from exercise, the exercise must be performed at least 20 to 30 minutes (duration) 3 to 5 times a week (frequency) at 60% to 90% of maximal heart rate (intensity). However, it should be noted that some individuals could improve their aerobic capabilities with intensities substantially below 50% of maximal heart rate. Furthermore, each individuals' threshold for frequency, duration, and intensity must be exceeded to achieve gains in aerobic capacity, and this threshold is likely to increase as aerobic capacity improves. Anaerobic exercise, in contrast, is either of short duration or of insufficient intensity to require much transporting of oxygen to the working muscles. Anaerobic activities include weightlifting, golf, bowling, and baseball.

decreases in state anxiety over the course of the intervention period as compared with waiting-list controls. But, more important, these reductions in state anxiety were maintained in follow-ups of up to 15 weeks (see Figure 17.1).

In one interesting study participants were randomly assigned to either a regimen of high-intensity aerobic training or moderate-intensity training, with a strengthening-and-stretching regimen serving as a placebo condition (Moses, Steptoe, Mathews, & Edwards, 1989). All three regimens were equated for frequency (four sessions per week) and duration (10 weeks) of sessions. The moderate-intensity aerobic exercise group exhibited a decrease in anxiety, whereas the other two groups showed no changes in anxiety. The high-intensity aerobics group showed the greatest gains in fitness. These results suggest that greater physiological gain does not necessarily lead to greater psychological gain.

More recently, some literature reviews using the statistical technique called meta-analysis (e.g., Long & Stavel, 1995; McDonald & Hodgdon, 1991; Petruzzello, Landers, Hatfield, Kibitz, & Salazar, 1991), as well as narrative reviews (Martinsen & Stephens, 1994; Mutrie & Biddle, 1995), were conducted to determine the relationship between exercise and anxiety reduction. These reviews show general consensus about the positive effects of exercise in reducing anxiety, including the following:

- Although consistent reductions in state anxiety occur with both aerobic and anaerobic exercise, most research has focused on aerobic exercise to reduce anxiety.

- Exercise is associated with moderate reductions in both state and trait anxiety.

- Longer training programs (sessions conducted over weeks, rather than hours or days) are more effective than shorter ones in producing positive changes in well-being.

- Reductions in state anxiety after exercise may be due less to the physical activity than to the "time-out" from daily stresses and hassles.

- Reductions in anxiety after exercise occur independently of age and health status.

- Exercise training is particularly effective for individuals who have elevated levels of stress.

- All durations of exercise significantly reduced anxiety, although larger effects were found for periods up to 30 minutes.

- State anxiety returns to preexercise anxiety levels within 24 hours.

- Exercise is associated with reductions in muscle tension.

Exercise in the Reduction of Depression

Depression is a well-documented source of human suffering, and about one in four Americans suffers from clinical depression at any given time. Although depression is treated through prescription drugs or

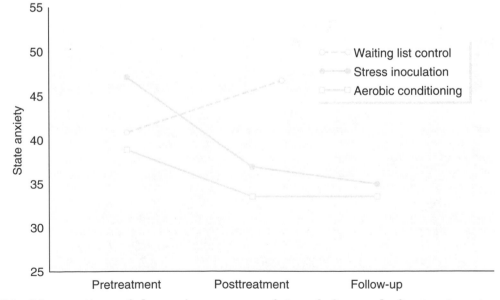

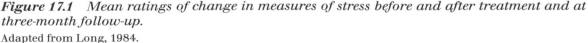

Figure 17.1 *Mean ratings of change in measures of stress before and after treatment and at three-month follow-up.*
Adapted from Long, 1984.

therapy most of the time, a recent Gallup poll identified exercise as a close second behind religion as an effective alternate means of relieving depression. In addition, physical inactivity has been shown to be related to higher levels of depression. Many people have an intuitive appreciation of the beneficial relationship of exercise on depression, but researchers have expended a great deal of effort also to investigate this important relationship.

One early attempt to evaluate the influence of exercise on depression (Morgan, Roberts, Brand, & Feinerman, 1970) looked at groups of middle-aged men who participated in various 6-week training programs (e.g., jogging, swimming, circuit training, and cycling), comparing them to controls who remained sedentary for the 6 weeks. The exercise groups became more physically fit, whereas the control group did not. Participants (from both exercise and control groups) without a history of clinical depression did not exhibit changes in depression levels. However, all 11 of the participants who manifested depression at the outset of the study did experience a decrease in depression after physical training. These results are consistent with several other research studies that

have found that exercise appears most helpful in relieving depression for subjects who are clinically depressed.

In another interesting early study, depressed subjects (as diagnosed by the National Institute of Mental Health) were randomly divided into (a) running, (b) time-limited psychotherapy, or (c) time unlimited psychotherapy groups. The runners met individually with a running therapist three times a week for 45 minutes. The psychotherapy subjects also met individually with a therapist, in 10-minute sessions for the time-limited therapy, and without a time limit for the time-unlimited therapy. After 10 weeks, the runners showed a significant decrease in depression scores, comparable to the best outcomes obtained by either psychotherapy group (Griest, Klein, Eischens, & Faris, 1978).

Consistent agreement also appears among other studies about the relationship between exercise and depression; these include several narrative (e.g., Martinsen & Stephens, 1994; Morgan, 1994; Mutrie & Biddle, 1995) and statistical reviews (McDonald & Hodgdon, 1991; North, McCullagh, & Tran, 1990), and also population surveys. People

© Photophile

requiring medical or psychological care show the greatest effect from exercise, but all participants, men and women, show positive effects across all age groups and across various ranges of health status. All modes of exercise are effective, but the greater the duration of the exercise program, the greater the antidepressant effect. However, exercise *intensity* is not related to changes in depression. Exercise is as effective as psychotherapy, although exercise plus psychotherapy form a better antidepressant than exercise on its own. It is important to note that these relationships between exercise and depression are correlational: exercise, in essence, is associated with, but does not cause, changes in depression.

In summary, here are some factors that seem to maximize the effectiveness of exercise on depression:

■ A pleasing and enjoyable activity

■ Aerobic or rhythmical breathing

■ An absence of interpersonal competition

■ A closed, predictable, and spatially certain environment (e.g., running)

■ Moderate intensity

■ Duration of at least 20 to 30 minutes

■ Regular inclusion in the weekly schedule

—Adapted from Berger (1996)

Exercise and Mood Changes

Mood can be defined as a state of emotional or affective arousal of varying, and not permanent, duration. Feelings of elation or happiness lasting a few hours or even a few days are examples of moods. Confidence or self-esteem, on the other hand, represent more a personality trait. Mood changes have been studied in a variety of settings, and considerable experiential and anecdotal evidence supports the existence of changes in mood states related to exercise. For example, psychologists and psychiatrists rate exercise as the most effective technique for changing a bad mood; they are more likely to use exercise than other techniques to energize themselves

> *Mood is generally defined as a state of emotional or affective arousal of varying, impermanent duration.*

(Thayer, Newman & McClain, 1994). Beyond anxiety and depression, other findings have emerged from research about the relation between various forms of exercise and changes in mood states, such as decreases in fatigue and anger, as well as increases in vigor, clear thinking, energy, alertness, and an increased sense of well-being.

Researchers (Thayer et al., 1994) have also identified various techniques to alter mood, categorizing and evaluating the effectiveness of these methods used by men and women (ranging in age from 16 to 89 years). Mood regulating, they say, has three interrelated components: changing a bad mood, raising one's energy level, and reducing tension. The researchers concluded, "Of all the separate behavioral categories described to self-regulate mood, a case can be made that exercise is the most effective. This behavior was self-rated as the most successful in changing a bad mood, fourth most successful in raising energy, and third most successful at tension reduction" (p. 921). Although we know that exercise is related to positive changes in mood states, there still is little evidence to suggest that exercise itself causes the benefits. Perhaps, for example, those experiencing more desirable ("better") moods simply exercise more often.

How Exercise Enhances Psychological Well-Being

The evidence we've reviewed so far suggests a positive relation between exercise and psychological well-being (Table 17.1 summarizes the psychological benefits of exercise). Several hypotheses, both psychological and physiological, have been proposed to explain how exercise works to enhance well-being. However, no one theory or hypothesis has support as the sole or primary mechanism producing these positive changes. In fact, it is likely that the positive changes in psychological well-being are due to an interaction of both physiological and psychological mechanisms. Therefore we will simply list the potential psychological and physiological mechanisms that researchers propose may account for exercise's having a positive affect on psychological well-being.

Physiological Explanations

■ Increases in cerebral blood flow

■ Changes in brain neurotransmitters (e.g., norepinephrine, endorphins, serotonin)

■ Increases in maximal oxygen consumption and delivery of oxygen to cerebral tissues

■ RESEARCH ■

Chronic Exercise and Mental Health

The National Institute of Mental Health convened a panel to discuss the possibilities and limitations of physical activity for coping with stress and depression (Morgan & Goldston, 1987). In terms of chronic exercise and mental health, the panel concluded the following:

- Physical fitness is positively associated with mental health and well-being.
- Exercise is associated with the reduction of stress emotions such as state anxiety.
- Anxiety and depression are common symptoms of failure to cope with mental stress, and exercise has been associated with a decreased level of mild to moderate depression and anxiety.
- Long-term exercise is usually associated with reductions in traits such as neuroticism and anxiety.
- Severe depression usually requires professional treatment, which may include medication, electroconvulsive therapy, psychotherapy, or a combination of these, with exercise as an adjunct.
- Appropriate exercise results in reductions in various stress indicators, such as neuromuscular tension, resting heart rate, and some stress hormones.
- Current clinical opinion holds that exercise has beneficial emotional effects across ages and genders.
- Physically healthy people who require psychotropic (mood altering) medication may safely exercise under close medical supervision.

Table 17.1

Psychological Benefits of Exercise in Clinical and Nonclinical Populations

Increases	Decreases
Academic performance	Absenteeism at work
Assertiveness	Alcohol abuse
Confidence	Anger
Emotional stability	Anxiety
Intellectual functioning	Confusion
Internal locus of control	Depression
Memory	Headaches
Perception	Hostility
Positive body image	Phobias
Self-control	Psychotic behavior
Sexual satisfaction	Tension
Well-being	Type A behavior
Work efficiency	Work errors

Adapted from Taylor, Sallis, and Needle, 1985.

- Reductions in muscle tension
- Structural changes in the brain

Psychological Explanations

- "Time-out" or distraction from daily hassles
- Enhanced feeling of control
- Feeling of competency and self-efficacy
- Positive social interactions
- Improved self-concept and self-esteem

Exercise and Changes in Personality and Cognitive Functioning

In addition to examining the relationship among exercise and anxiety, depression, and mood, people have also asked whether exercise can change personality and mental (cognitive) functioning. We'll briefly review the research in these areas and offer some suggestions to practitioners.

Personality

A classic study to determine the effects of a fitness program on middle-aged men led to some information on how exercise might change personality (Ismail & Young, 1973). Over the course of the program, the men improved their fitness levels and reported feeling dramatic psychological effects. They reported higher levels of self-confidence, greater feelings of control, improved imagination, and a greater sense of self-sufficiency. Other studies have since been conducted investigating the relationship of exercise to various personality factors. In a review of these studies, McDonald and Hodgdon (1991) found that aerobic fitness training increased scores on self-sufficiency and intelligence and decreased scores on insecurity. In addition, studies using clinical populations found positive changes in various aspects of personality adjustment.

Exercise and Development of the Self

Exercise and physical activity can be related to a participant's self-concept, self-esteem, and self-efficacy (Fox, 1997). These concepts of the self are interrelated but yet distinct, although they all refer to how we feel about ourselves and our capabilities. Self-concept incorporates all aspects of what we think we are: it is central to our conscious lives. As such, many people consider self-concept the most important measure of psychological well-being.

Regular exercise has been shown to be related to increased self-esteem.

It is commonly believed that changes in the body as a result of physical fitness training can alter one's body image and thus enhance self-concept and self-esteem. In reviewing the research literature Sonstroem & Morgan (1989) found that exercise programs are associated with significant increases in self-esteem, and that increases are especially pronounced among individuals who were initially lower in self-esteem. Based on more recent research, Sonstroem (1997a, 1997b) qualified his earlier observations, saying that the increases in self-esteem found after exercise may result from perceptions of improvement or other program factors (either biological or psychological) rather than from fitness improvement itself. In addition, positive changes in self-esteem have been found more recently in "normal" populations as well as in individuals who initially had low self-esteem—although individuals lower in fitness or ability also demonstrated significant positive changes in self-esteem. According to the latest studies, changes in self-esteem have been maintained over a period of time (at least one year).

In a review of children's programs, Gruber (1986) discovered that positive changes in self-concept and self-esteem were associated with participation in directed play and physical education programs. Physical fitness activities were also found to be superior to other components of elementary school physical education programs in developing self-concept. Furthermore, diverse populations (adult females, college students, obese teenage males, seventh-grade males, elementary school children, and adult male rehabilitation clients) have shown improvement in self-esteem after fitness programs.

Despite these positive findings, other research studies have *not* found positive relationships between exercise and self-concept. Perhaps this relationship varies according to exercise mode or a host of environmental conditions. In essence, self-concept is multidimensional, and certain aspects of self-concept (e.g., physical) might be more affected by exercise than others (e.g., social) (Fox, 1997; Marsh, 1997). Certainly a strong self-concept is critical to the healthy psychological development and adjustment of children, and exercise can be an important ingredient in helping children and adults feel good about themselves. Berger (1996) has proposed that exercise programs designed to enhance self-esteem and self-concept should emphasize experiences of success, feelings of increased physical competence, and attainment of goals.

Exercise and Hardiness

Hardiness is a personality style that enables a person to withstand or cope with stressful situations. Stress produces minimal debilitating effects in a hardy personality. You are hardy if you have these three traits:

- A sense of personal control over external events,
- A sense of involvement, commitment, and purpose in daily life, and
- The flexibility to adapt to unexpected changes by perceiving them as challenges or opportunities for further growth (Gentry & Kosaba, 1979).

Exercise can help protect against stress-related illness, especially for hardy people.

Some research has focused on how exercise combined with hardiness can reduce some of the negative effects of stress. One study found that business executives who scored high in both hardiness and exercise remained healthier than those who scored high in only one or the other component. Another study learned that exercise combined with social support resulted in the least amount of illness in individuals with hardy personalities (Kosaba, Maddi, Puccetti, & Zola, 1985). In essence, a hardy personality and exercise in combination are more effective in preserving health than either one alone.

Cognitive Functioning

For a long time we have assumed that motor development is important to the development of intelligence in children (Piaget, 1936) and that learning potential will vary with a person's physical fitness level. Since the 1970s researchers have looked for evidence that would validate these two assumptions. Although the findings are still somewhat inconsistent, there is some research support for the relationship between exercise and cognitive functioning.

© Jay Foreman/Unicorn Stock Photos

Narrative reviews, for example, have not clearly or conclusively proved the beneficial effect of exercise on cognitive functioning (Chodzko-Zajko & Moore, 1994; Tomporowski & Ellis, 1986). Statistical reviews of more than 100 studies (Etnier, Salazar, Landers, Petruzzello, Han, & Nowell, 1997; Thomas, Landers, Salazar, & Etnier, 1994) found that exercise had a modest positive relationship with improved cognitive functioning. Chronic exercise, in comparison with acute exercise, showed greater effects on cognitive performance: That is, exercise programs conducted over longer periods of time are associated with gains in cognitive functioning (this does not demonstrate a cause-effect relationship necessarily).

Exercise and Quality of Life

Researchers have also been investigating the more global and encompassing question of how regular exercise affects our quality of life (Berger, 1996;

Sheppard, 1996). The nebulous phrase quality of life is defined as a person's evaluative reactions to his or her life, either in terms of satisfaction or negative effect. Quality of life tends to be affected by psychosocial events and health behaviors, so that as we age, physical activity becomes increasingly important due to its positive relationship with both physical and mental health.

This is what research can already tell us about the relationship between exercise and quality of life:

- Physically active individuals tend to be in better health, report more stamina, have more positive attitudes toward work, and report a greater ability to cope with stress and tension.

- College students participating in an endurance-conditioning program report significantly higher quality of life than do nonexercisers.

- Older adults who are physically active report greater life satisfaction—due to less dependence on others—and better overall physical health.

RESEARCH

Does Exercise Enhance Sleep?

Insomnia, which afflicts about a third of the adult population, is associated with increased mortality, psychiatric disturbances, and decreased productivity and performance. Sleeping pills are the most common treatment for insomnia, but they typically have numerous potential negative side effects and are therefore seldom recommended for long-term use. Exercise is an alternative treatment that has received recent attention. Because it elicits physical fatigue and has well-established physiological and psychological calming effects, the notion that exercise promotes sleep may seem like common sense. However, research has indicated that the effects of exercise on sleep are not as compelling or large as has commonly been believed. For example, reviews of the exercise-and-sleep literature suggest these conclusions regarding a single bout of exercise (O'Connor & Youngstedt, 1995; Youngstedt, O'Connor, & Dishman, 1997):

- It has no effect on the time it takes an individual to fall asleep.
- It produces small (although statistically significant) increases in total sleep time (10 minutes on average) and in the amount of slow-wave sleep (4 minutes).
- It produces small (although statistically significant) decreases in rapid-eye-movement (REM) sleep (7 minutes on average).

It is important to note that these studies focused exclusively on good sleepers. Thus, although the effects of acute exercise are small, they still are noteworthy: Even sleeping pills have little influence on good sleepers. Interestingly, a few recent studies using insomniacs (see Youngstedt, 1997, for a review of them) have been promising, indicating that exercise can promote sleep in an individual with insomnia. More research is necessary to provide definitive answers about the exercise-sleep relationship, and it is a promising area of inquiry.

Special Cases of Exercise and Psychological Well-Being

There are several "special cases" in the exercise psychology literature that describe unique relationships between physical activity and psychological functioning. Two of these are the "runner's high" and exercise addiction (positive or negative).

Runner's High

Many regular exercisers report feeling better psychologically, emotionally, and spiritually after exercising. This phenomenon is so pervasive among runners that the feeling has been dubbed the runner's high, and it includes a sense of mental alertness and awareness; a feeling of liberation; a lift in the legs; suppressed pain or discomfort; and the sense of ease, perfect rhythm, and exhilaration.

Defining the Runner's High

Sachs found 27 different adjectives or phrases used in the literature to describe the runner's high (1984), including euphoria, spirituality, power, gracefulness, effortless movement, a glimpse of perfection, and

> *The runner's high is a euphoric sensation, usually unexpected, of heightened well-being, an enhanced appreciation of nature, and the transcendence of time and space.*

 ■ CLOSE-UP ■

Personal Examples of the Runner's High

The first half hour is pure agony—exaggerated body pain and philosophical crisis. Thirty minutes out and something lifts. Legs and arms become light and rhythmic. The fatigue goes away and feelings of power begin. "I think I'll run 25 miles today. I'll double the size of the research grant request. I'll have that talk with the dean and tolerate no equivocating. . . ." Then, another switch, from fourth gear into overdrive. . . . Sometime into the second hour comes the spooky time. Colors are bright and beautiful, water sparkles, clouds breathe, and my body, swimming, detaches from the earth. A loving contentment invades the basement of my mind, and thoughts bubble up without trails. I find the place I need to live if I'm going to live. (Black, 1979, p. 79)

[With] my first step I felt lighter and looser than ever before. My shirt clung to me, and I felt like a skeleton flying down a wind tunnel. My times at the mile were so fast that I almost felt like I was cheating. It was like getting a new body that no one else had heard about. My mind was so crystal clear that I could have held a conversation. The only sensation was the rhythm and the beat, all perfectly natural, all and everything part of everything else. . . . Distance, time, motion were all one. There were myself, the cement, a vague feeling of legs, and the coming dusk. I tore on. I could have run and run. Perhaps I had experienced a physiological change, but whatever, it was magic. I came to the side of the road and cried tears of joy and sorrow. Joy for being alive; sorrow for a vague feeling of temporalness, and a knowledge of the impossibility of giving this experience to anyone. (Mike Spino, 1971, p. 222)

spinning out. He consolidated these to define the runner's high as a euphoric sensation experienced during running, usually unexpected, in which the runner feels a heightened sense of well-being, enhanced appreciation of nature, and a transcendence of time and space. This definition resembles aspects of peak performance and especially of flow (Csikszentmihalyi, 1975; see chapter 6) in that the runner's high requires rhythmic, long-lasting, and uninterrupted activity.

Characteristics of the Runner's High

In a qualitative study, Sachs (1980) interviewed 60 runners to discover what conditions (internal to the runner and external in the environment) facilitate the runner's high. They told him that the runner's high cannot be reliably predicted but is facilitated by few distractions and cool, calm weather with low humidity. It requires long distances (6 or more miles) and at least 30 minutes of running at a comfortable pace—although there must be no concern with pace or time. The runners described the mood as a very positive psychological state with feelings of well-being, euphoria, relaxation, and effortlessness.

Individual Differences in the Runner's High

Not every runner who puts on running shoes experiences a runner's high. But Lilliefors (1978) surveyed runners and found that 78% of them reported a sense of euphoria during their runs. Forty-nine percent said the euphoria was occasionally spiritual in nature. Along these lines, Sachs (1980) found that 77% of the 60 runners he interviewed reported they had experienced the runner's high at least a few times. Several runners said they experienced the high in nearly 30% of their regular runs. On the other hand, only 10% of another group of runners whom Sachs had surveyed earlier (1978) had experienced the runner's high.

Addiction to Exercise

Some people develop exceptionally strong feelings about their running, as you can sense in the following quote by Cierpinski, the two-time gold medalist from East Germany: "I have run since infancy. . . . It's the passion of my life. Running as long as pos-

sible—I've made that into a sport. I have no other secrets. Without running I wouldn't be able to live." (Cierpinski, *Track and Field News,* 1980, p. 27)

The intense involvement with exercise, particularly running, has been described in such terms as compulsion (Abell, 1975), dependence (Sachs & Pargman, 1984), obsession (Waters, 1981), exercise fix (Benyo, 1990), and addiction (Glasser, 1976). In the exercise psychology literature, most writers use the term addiction to refer to an intense involvement in exercise.

What Is Exercise Addiction?

Exercise addiction is a psychological or physiological (or both) dependence on a regular regimen of exercise that is characterized by withdrawal symptoms after 24 to 36 hours pass without exercise (Sachs, 1981). Note in addition that exercise addiction incorporates both psychological and physiological factors. Some withdrawal symptoms commonly associated with the cessation of exercising include anxiety, irritability, guilt, muscle twitching, a bloated feeling, and nervousness. But these occur only if an individual is prevented from exercising for some reason (e.g., injury, work, or family commitments), as opposed to purposefully taking a day or two off.

Positive Addiction to Exercise

The concept of beneficial addiction to exercise, running in particular, was popularized by William Glasser in his book *Positive Addiction.* Glasser argues that positive addictions such as running and meditation promote psychological strength and increase life satisfaction (1976). This is in sharp contrast to negative addictions, such as heroin or cocaine, that inevitably undermine psychological and physiological functioning. Furthermore, Glasser notes, people can use a positive addiction to help themselves become stronger. He sees exercise as an addiction that increases an individual's psychological and physical strength, thereby enhancing his or her state of well-being and functioning. Rather than standard quantitative assessments and analyses, Glasser's work includes qualitative data from clinical and psychiatric assessments. For example, reports of the runner's high and the general "feel-good

Runners differ in how often they experience the runner's high, and each may require a slightly different set of conditions.

Positive addiction to exercise implies that a variety of physiological and psychological benefits occur with regular physical activity.

phenomenon" after exercise support Glasser's concept of positive addiction.

Exercise as a positive addiction means that a variety of psychological and physiological benefits discussed earlier will typically occur as a person continues to participate in regular physical activity. A positive addiction to exercise means that exercisers view their involvement in regular physical activity as important to their lives, and they can successfully integrate it with other aspects of their lives, including work, family, and friends. Exercise becomes a habit of daily activity, in essence, for most regular exercisers, and this level of involvement represents a "healthy habit."

Negative Addiction to Exercise

Although many exercisers develop a positive addiction to their exercise, for a small percentage of people exercise can control their lives (Benyo, 1990; Morgan, 1979a). Exercise then becomes a negative addiction that eliminates other choices in life. Lives become structured around exercise to such an extent that home and work responsibilities suffer and relationships take a backseat. This condition apparently reflects personal or social maladjustment and parallels other addictive processes characterized by increasing dose dependence and withdrawal symptoms under deprivation. Chan (1986) describes how people typically become addicted to exercise:

> *The typical addict is . . . female or male, and began exercising in adulthood as a way to lose weight and become more physically fit. As these individuals improve their heart rate, lose weight, and feel better physically, they also begin to feel better about themselves. They develop a sense of control over their bodies—something they had been unable to do through dieting—and this feeling of control generalizes to a sense of control over their lives. In other words, they feel more powerful and more self-confident. (p. 430)*

Negative addiction to exercise is characterized by a dependence on exercise. The addiction can result in problems at home, work, and in relationships. Not being able to exercise can cause severe depression.

For an activity to be classified as addictive it should meet these criteria:

1. The activity is noncompetitive and of one's own choice. About an hour each day is devoted to the activity.
2. The activity requires little skill or mental effort.
3. The activity is not dependent on others and is usually done alone.
4. The activity can be done without self-criticism.
5. The exerciser believes the activity is valuable.
6. The exerciser believes that persistence in the activity will lead to improvement.

Symptoms of Negative Addiction to Exercise

Several case studies of addicted runners reveal they are totally consumed by the need to run, this being the driving force in their lives. Exercise addicts who are forced to stop running for a while often become depressed, anxious, and extremely irritable. Interpersonal relations in the home, work, and social settings decay, accompanied by restlessness, insomnia, and general fatigue. Tics, muscle tension and soreness, decreased appetite, and constipation or irregularity often develop. The true exercise addict continues even when the exercise is medically, vocationally, and socially contraindicated (Benyo, 1990). These are the primary symptoms for exercise dependency:

1. Stereotyped pattern of exercise with a regular schedule of once or more daily
2. Giving increasing priority, over other activities, to maintaining the pattern of exercise
3. Increased tolerance to the amount of exercise performed
4. Withdrawal symptoms related to mood disorder following cessation of the exercise
5. Relief of withdrawal symptoms by further exercise
6. Subjective awareness of a compulsion to exercise
7. Rapid reinstatement of the previous pattern of exercise and withdrawal symptoms after a period of abstinence

Many addicted exercisers recognize their own symptoms of negative addiction. The toll of strenuous training often shows itself in a decreased ability to concentrate, listlessness, fatigue, lapses in judgment, and impaired social activity and work productivity. Because exercise addicts tend to be well-educated, many negatively addicted people can acknowledge these symptoms and recognize the effects that exercise is having on their lives (Sachs & Pargman, 1984). Still, accepting help is another matter. Exercise addicts often feel that though exercise may control their lives, it enhances their existence. Runner and physician George Sheehan demonstrated this perspective when he wrote:

> *The world will wait. Job, family, friends will wait; in fact, they must wait on the outcome. . . . Can anything have a higher priority than running? It defines me, adds to me, makes me whole. I have a job and family and friends that can attest to that. (1979, p. 49)*

When an Addicted Exerciser Can't Exercise

What happens when an addicted exerciser is injured and cannot exercise? The exerciser will probably suffer withdrawal symptoms including tension, restlessness, irritability, depression, interpersonal problems, and feelings of guilt. In one study (Chan & Grossman, 1988), injured runners who were prevented from running suffered greater overall tension, anxiety, depression, confusion, anger, and hostility—along with lower self-esteem and vigor—than their still-running counterparts. The authors concluded that these withdrawal symptoms were similar to those commonly noted in withdrawal from other addictions. One way to cope with an injury is to try other activities. A runner who injures her lower leg might still swim and possibly ride a bicycle. However, the substitution will likely not satisfy the true addict. As one woman said when she pulled an Achilles tendon and had to substitute bicycling for running, "It was like methadone maintenance for a heroin addict." In such cases, other types of psychological therapy might be appropriate.

There are a number of things an exerciser can do to help guard against falling into the trap of negative addiction, including the following:

■ Schedule rest days or take them when necessary.

■ Work out regularly with a slower partner.

■ Use year-long schedules with built-in down times.

■ If you're injured, stop exercising until you are rehabilitated and healed.

■ Train hard-easy: Mix in low intensity and less distance with days of harder training.

■ If you're interested in health benefits, exercise 3 or 4 times a week for 30 minutes.

■ Set realistic short- and long-term goals.

Exercise as an Adjunct to Therapy

Literally millions of Americans still suffer from some sort of depression or anxiety disorder every year, even though research has demonstrated that exercise can help reduce such negative psychological states and that aerobic exercise is related to enhanced self-esteem, improved mood, and higher levels of work productivity. Not surprisingly, the use of physical interventions, including some form of exercise, has received increased attention since the late 1970s (Folkins & Sime, 1981; Griest et al., 1978), and many physicians and mental health professionals now routinely recommend exercise for their patients (Rooney, 1993).

Exercise therapy has long been shown to produce physiological benefits in a broad variety of rehabilitation settings, but its benefits on mental health and psychological well-being are only more recently being discovered. For example, since depression has been shown to be a predictor of future heart attacks in cardiac patients, exercise that reduces depression would be extremely beneficial in this population. Researchers (Tennant et al., 1994) have shown that exercise in cardiac rehabilitation in fact decreased anger and hostility, depression, anxiety, or emotional disturbances. Large-scale epidemiological studies have also found that regular exercise programs are related to positive mental health, especially for more at-risk populations (e.g., Weyerer, 1992), and experimental studies using exercise with institutionalized patients have shown improvements in mood and affect and decreases in depression (Martinsen, 1993). Therefore, there appears to be ample evidence supporting the use of exercise to improve psychological well-being in clinical and other special populations.

> *Running can be an inexpensive, time-efficient adjunct to traditional psychotherapies, and offers added health benefits such as increased cardiovascular efficiency and weight control.*

Guidelines for Using Exercise as Therapy

Here are a few important points for using exercise as part of therapy:

- Explore the client's exercise history (good and bad experiences).
- Provide a precise diagnosis of the psychological problem.
- Use an individualized exercise prescription for duration, intensity, and frequency of exercise.
- Evaluate the infuence of family and friends (to facilitate support).
- Develop a plan for any lack of adherence and irregular patterns of exercise.
- Make exercise practical and functional (e.g., bicycling to work, doing hard physical work).
- Encourage exercise as an *adjunct* to other forms of therapy. A multimodal therapeutic approach is more effective than the use of a single intervention.
- Include a variety of activities, which enhances adherence to the exercise regimen.
- Exercise therapy should be done only by qualified professionals. Although no exact criteria have been established, Buffone (1984) suggests that formal training and practical experience in both the psychological and sport sciences are necessary because exercise therapy takes a multidisciplinary approach to treatment.

Exercise for Enhancing Well-Being in HIV-Positive Populations

Since the first reported cases of HIV-1 infection in 1981, the number of individuals contracting the disease has grown exponentially, as has the number of deaths. Recently, the use of multiple drug therapies has shown promise toward controlling the disease. In addition, exercise has been targeted as a means of enhancing subjective well-being in HIV-1 individuals. Enhancing perceptions of well-being is particularly relevant for individuals with HIV-1 and AIDS: Perceived control over physical health is a primary concern of these people (and indeed most patients). If individuals with HIV-1 and AIDS feel some sense of control over their psychological health and well-being, this may profoundly affect how they deal and cope with the disease.

In a recent study (Lox, McAuley, & Tucker, 1995) HIV-1 individuals were randomly assigned to an aerobic training group, a resistance weight-training group and a stretching-flexibility control group. After 12 weeks of these interventions, results indicated that both the aerobic and weight-training exercise interventions had enhanced physical self-efficacy, improved moods, and higher satisfaction in life. Conversely, control participants experienced declines in each of these areas. The authors suggest that exercise may be one therapeutic modality capable of enhancing components of subjective well-being; it should therefore be considered a complementary therapy for treating the psychological and emotional manifestations associated with a positive HIV-1 diagnosis.

Of all the aerobic activities shown to enhance psychological well-being, running has received the most attention in both the professional and popular literature. Running provides a natural, practical, inexpensive, and time-efficient adjunct to traditional psychotherapies. For example, one classic study found that running was four times more cost-effective than more traditional verbal-oriented psychotherapies for treating depression (Griest et al., 1978). Running as an adjunct to therapy takes on added importance because of the high cost of health care and the trend toward cost-effective counseling. Running therapies add health benefits such as increased respiratory efficiency and cardiovascular endurance, and they improve muscle tone, weight control, and blood volume. Running as part of therapy can encourage a positive approach to health promotion as clients learn a healthier style of living through exercise.

Despite the psychological benefits of exercise, it should not be used in all cases of depression, stress, or other emotional disorders. For example, Buffone (1984) argues that aerobic exercise therapy should not be prescribed for obese people (40% or more over ideal body weight), those with severe heart disease, or those with high blood pressure that cannot be controlled by medication. Exercise may also be contraindicated for the severely depressed and those having a tenuous contact with reality or suicidal tendencies. Another caution is that for exercise to be effective the program must be adhered to, and dropout rates from regular exercise programs are approximately 50% (see chapter 18). Therefore, special care must be taken to support individuals who incorporate exercise as part of therapy.

SUMMARY

1 *Explain the effects of exercise on anxiety and depression.*

Many people suffer from problems due to depression and anxiety, and exercise has been shown to be related to reductions in these negative emotional states. Both the acute and chronic effects of exercise have been studied, and reductions in anxiety and depression are maximized with regular exercise of moderate intensity that is 20 to 30 minutes in duration, aerobic in nature, and enjoyable. However, it is important to note that the relationship between exercise and psychological well-being is correlational rather than causal in nature.

2 *Describe the relationship between exercise and mood states.*

Regular exercise has been shown to be related to changes in mood states, such as decreases in fatigue and anger and increases in vigor, alertness, and energy. These positive changes are maximized with low-intensity exercise, which can be either aerobic or anaerobic in nature.

3 *Discuss the effects of exercise on psychological well-being.*

Research has revealed a positive relationship between exercise and psychological well-being. These positive effects have been explained by both psychological (e.g., feelings of competency and a sense of control) and physiological (e.g., reductions in muscle tension, increases in cerebral blood flow) mechanisms.

4 *Describe the relation among exercise, personality changes, and cognitive functioning.*

Physical activity has also been shown to be positively related to changes in personality and cognitive functioning. Changes in personality (e.g., increased self-confidence) and intelligence, as well as changes in cognitive functioning (e.g., attentional control) have been linked to increases in exercise.

5 *Discuss the "runner's high."*

Many exercisers report feeling psychologically, emotionally, and spiritually better after exercise. This phenomenon is particularly pervasive among runners; thus it has been termed the runner's high. The feelings associated with the runner's high include a sense of mental alertness, liberation, a lift in the legs, suppressed pain or discomfort, ease, and exhilaration, and they are felt only after running a considerable distance (usually at least 5 miles) at a comfortable pace.

6 *Explain positive and negative addiction to exercise.*

The term "positive addiction" to exercise was popularized because running and other forms of exercise have been shown to be associated with positive psychological outcomes and increases in life satisfaction. However, for a small percentage of people this "healthy" habit of exercise can turn into a negative addiction in which the exercise starts to control their lives. This is typically associated with negative outcomes at home and at work.

KEY TERMS

acute effects
chronic effects
depression
mood
hardiness

quality of life
runner's high
exercise addiction
positive addiction
negative addiction

REVIEW QUESTIONS

1. What is the difference between anaerobic and aerobic exercise? Which is more critical for improving psychological well-being?

2. Discuss the research findings on the acute and chronic effects of exercise on anxiety and depression.

3. Discuss the research findings regarding the relationship between exercise and changes in mood, personality, and cognitive functioning.

4. Describe characteristics of the "runner's high."

5. List three plausible physiological and three plausible psychological explanations for how exercise enhances psychological well-being.

6. Compare and contrast the characteristics of positive and negative addictions. What are some steps for avoiding a negative addiction to exercise?

7. What are the guidelines you should remember in using exercise as an adjunct to other types of therapy?

8. Discuss how exercise might be related to the treatment of HIV-1.

9. Describe the research relating to how exercise can help enhance the quality of life.

10. What does research say about the relationship between exercise and sleep?

CRITICAL THINKING QUESTIONS

1. You have been asked to contribute to the Surgeon General's report on the relationship between exercise and psychological well-being. What key points would you include based on the empirical research in this area? What guidelines would you suggest for maximizing the effectiveness of exercise in enhancing positive psychological well-being?

2. The National Institute of Mental Health panel has arrived at several conclusions about exercise and mental health. You are an administrator in a YMCA program or fitness club and have learned that many participants are dropping out of your exercise programs. Although there are many reasons for this, you feel that one way to get them to return is through emphasizing the positive feelings that are often associated with exercise. What would you advise your exercise leaders to do to adjust the structure of their programs so they might maximize exercise's aspects of psychological well-being?

© Anthony Neste Photography

Exercise Behavior and Adherence

After reading this chapter you should be able to

1 discuss why people do or do not exercise,
2 explain the different models of exercise behavior,
3 describe the determinants of exercise adherence,
4 identify strategies for increasing exercise adherence, and
5 give guidelines for improving exercise adherence.

Judging from the looks of store windows, we're in the midst of a fitness craze. Athletic footwear appears in every color and for every sport. Sportswear is in vogue not only for sport and physical activity but also for leisure and even office work. Fitness clubs look crowded with firm, lean bodies and rippling muscle mass. It seems that almost everyone wants to get fit. But the fact is that most Americans do not regularly participate in physical activity (U.S. Department of Health and Human Services, 1996).

Let's look at some statistics to get a better idea of the level of exercise participation in the United States. The U.S. Department of Health and Human Services (1991) set national goals for participation in regular and vigorous physical activity at 90% for youth and 60% for adults by the year 2000. However, we are still far short of these goals. Here's where we stood as of 1996:

- Among adults 60% are sedentary (not engaging in leisure-time physical activity or engaging in it only irregularly).

- Among youths from 12 to 21 years of age 50% do not participate regularly in physical activity.

- Among children and adults 25% report no vigorous physical activity.

- Among adults only 15% participate in vigorous exercise regularly (three times a week for at least 20 minutes).

- Of sedentary adults only 10% are likely to begin a program of regular exercise within a year.

- Among both boys and girls physical activity declines steadily through adolescence.

- Among women physical inactivity is more prevalent than among men, as it is among blacks and Hispanics compared with whites, older adults compared with younger ones, and the less affluent compared with the more affluent.

- Daily attendance in physical education classes dropped from 42% to 25% from 1990 to 1995.

- Of people who start an exercise program 50% will drop out within 6 months.

Despite the physiological and psychological benefits of exercise, including reduced tension and depression, increased self-esteem, lowered risk of cardiovascular disease, better weight control, and en-

hanced functioning of the metabolic, endocrine, and immune systems (see chapter 17), only half the adults who begin exercise programs continue their participation. So let's start by looking at why people exercise—as well as the reasons they give for not exercising.

Reasons to Exercise

With half of the adult population sedentary, the first problem that exercise leaders and other health and fitness professionals face is how to get these people to start exercising. People are motivated for different reasons (see chapter 3), but a good starting place to get people to initiate an exercise program is to emphasize the diverse benefits of exercise (President's Council on Physical Fitness and Sport, 1996).

Weight Control

Our society values fitness, good looks, and thinness, so staying in shape and keeping trim concerns many people. However, an estimated 60 to 70 million American adults and 10 to 15 million American teenagers are overweight. For most people, the first thing they think to do when they face that they are overweight is diet. Although dieting certainly helps someone to lose weight, exercise plays an important and often underrated role. People worry that exercise increases appetite, but this isn't true of workouts of moderate and short duration. Some people assume that exercise does not burn enough calories to make a significant difference in weight loss, but this, too, is contrary to fact. For example, running 3 miles five times a week can produce a weight loss of 20 to 25 pounds in a year if caloric intake remains the same.

Weight loss can have important health consequences beyond looking and feeling good. Obesity and physical inactivity are primary risk factors for coronary heart disease. Thus, regular exercise will not only help in weight control and appearance but will also eliminate physical inactivity as a risk factor.

Exercise combined with proper eating habits can help you lose weight. But weight loss should be slow and steady, occurring as you change your exercise and eating patterns.

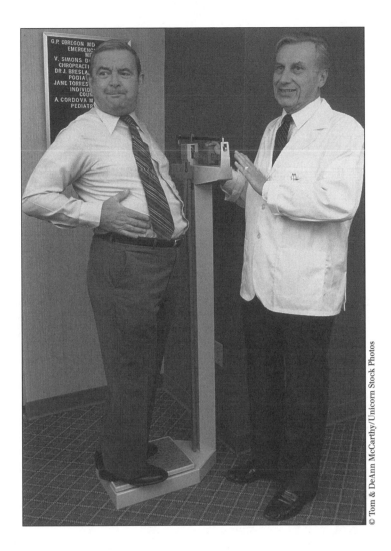

© Tom & DeAnn McCarthy/Unicorn Stock Photos

Reduced Risk of Cardiovascular Disease

Research has produced evidence that regular physical activity or cardiorespiratory fitness decreases the risk of mortality from cardiovascular disease in general and from coronary heart disease in particular. In fact, the decreased risk for coronary heart disease that is attributable to regular physical activity is similar in level to that of other lifestyle factors, such as restraining from cigarette smoking. In addition, regular exercise has been shown to prevent or delay the development of high blood pressure, and exercise reduces blood pressure in people with hypertension. Like obesity, hypertension is a prime risk factor in coronary heart disease. Statistics indicate that a blood pressure level of 110 mmHg systolic and 70 mmHg diastolic constitute optimal conditions for longevity. A rise in the systolic blood pressure to 150 mmHg increases the risk of heart disease more than twofold. Yet research has indicated that blood pressure can be reduced through regular exercise.

Reduction in Stress and Depression

As discussed in chapter 17, regular exercise is associated with an improved sense of well-being. Our society has recently seen a tremendous increase in the number of people suffering from anxiety disorders and depression. Exercise is one way to cope more effectively with the society we live in and our everyday lives.

Enjoyment

Although many people start exercise programs to improve their health and lose weight, it is rare for people to continue these programs unless they find the experience enjoyable. In general, people continue an exercise program because of the fun, happiness, and satisfaction it brings. The major reason for participation in organized youth sports is to have fun. Yet as people mature, the fun aspect of sport and physical activity seems to be overshadowed in favor of being productive, hard working, and successful.

Both the physiological and psychological benefits of exercising can be cited to help persuade sedentary people to initiate an exercise program.

People often cite time constraints for not exercising, but such constraints are more perceived than real and often reveal a person's priorities.

Building Self-Esteem

Exercise is associated with greater feelings of self-esteem and self-confidence. Many people get a sense of satisfaction from accomplishing something they couldn't do before. Something as simple as walking around the block or jogging a mile makes them feel good to be moving toward their goals. In addition, people who exercise regularly feel more confident about the way they look. They may get more recognition from a variety of sources.

Socializing

Often people start an exercise program for the chance to socialize and be with others. They can meet people, fight loneliness, and shed social isolation. Group experiences often lead to camaraderie and friendship. Aerobics class members, for example, who usually meet regularly to exercise have some fun while doing it. Many people who lead busy lives find the only time they have to spend with friends is when exercising together. Regular exercisers often find sharing the experience makes exercise more enjoyable. Almost 90% of exercise program participants prefer to exercise with a partner or group rather than alone. Exercising together gives people a sense of personal commitment to continue the opportunity and to derive social support from each other (Willis & Campbell, 1992).

Reasons for Not Exercising

Despite the social, health, and personal benefits of exercising, many people still choose not to exercise, usually citing lack of time, lack of energy, and lack of motivation as their primary reasons for inactivity (Canadian Fitness and Lifestyle Research Institute, 1996). It is interesting to note that these are all factors that individuals have within their control, as opposed to environmental factors, which are often out of their control. (Table 18.1 shows that virtually all the major and minor barriers to exercise are within the control of the individual.) This is consistent with research (McAuley, Poag, & Gleason, 1990) that found the

major reasons for attrition in an exercise program were internal and personally controllable causes (e.g., lack of motivation, time management), which are amenable to change. It is clear that understanding why people don't exercise can help fitness professionals develop better strategies to counteract these barriers.

Lack of Time

The most frequent reason given for inactivity is a lack of time. In fact, 69% of truant exercisers cited lack of time as a major barrier to physical activity (Canadian Fitness and Lifestyle Research Institute, 1996). However, a closer look at schedules usually reveals that this so-called lack of time is more a perception than a reality. The problem lies in priorities—after all, people seem to find time to watch TV, hang out, or read the newspaper. When fitness professionals make programs enjoyable, satisfying, meaningful, and convenient, exercising can compete well against other leisure activities. But professionals should also clarify the benefits of exercise to help motivate a sedentary person to start an exercise program.

Lack of Energy

Many people keep such busy schedules that fatigue becomes an excuse for not exercising. In fact, 59% of nonexercisers said that lack of energy was a major barrier to physical activity. Fatigue is typically more mental than physical and often stress-related. Fitness professionals should emphasize that a brisk walk, bicycle ride, or tennis game can relieve tension and stress and be energizing as well. If these activities are structured to be fun, the harried worker will look forward to them after a day filled with hassles.

Lack of Motivation

Related to a lack of energy is not having sufficient motivation to sustain physical activity over a long period. It takes commitment and dedication to maintain regular physical activity when someone's life is busy with work, family, and friends. It is easy to let other aspects of life take up all your time and energy and then feel little motivation for exercising.

Table 18.1
Barriers to Physical Activity

Barrier	Individuals who cite this as a barrier to participation (%)	Type of barrier
MAJOR BARRIERS		
Lack of time	69	Individual
Lack of energy	59	Individual
Lack of motivation	52	Individual
MODERATE BARRIERS		
Excessive cost	37	Individual
Illness/injury	36	Individual
Lack of facilities nearby	30	Environmental
Feeling uncomfortable	29	Individual
Lack of skill	29	Individual
Fear of injury	26	Individual
MINOR BARRIERS		
Lack of safe places	24	Environmental
Lack of child care	23	Environmental
Lack of a partner	21	Environmental
Insufficient programs	19	Environmental
Lack of support	18	Environmental
Lack of transportation	17	Environmental

Adapted from Canadian Fitness and Lifestyle Research Institute, 1992.

So keeping in mind the positive benefits of physical activity becomes even more important to maintaining your motivation.

Problem of Exercise Adherence

Once sedentary people have overcome inertia and started exercising, the next barrier they face is to continue their exercising program. Evidently many people find it easier to start an exercise program than to stick with it: about 50% of participants drop out of exercise programs within the first 6 months. Figure 18.1 illustrates this steep drop-off in exercise participation during the first 6 months of an exercise program, which then essentially levels off until 18 months. Exercisers often have lapses in trying to adhere to exercise programs, many of them discontinuing exercise for at least three months. For example, Sallis and colleagues (1990) found that in a

Exercise professionals should consistently provide sound, scientific information about exercise and physical activity to increase the likelihood of clients' adhering to a fitness program.

sample of more than 500 exercisers, 40% had experienced an exercise relapse, and 20% had experienced three or more relapses. The most frequent reason for relapse was injury, other reasons that followed being work demands, lack of interest, lack of time, family demands, end of sport season, bad weather, and stress.

In that exercise programs have a high relapse rate, they are like dieting, smoking cessation, or cutting down on drinking alcohol. People intend to change a habit that negatively affects their health and well-being. In fact, fitness clubs traditionally have their

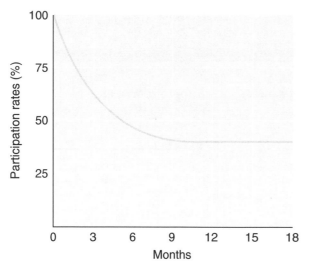

Figure 18.1 *Change in rate of exercise program participation over time.*

highest new enrollments in January and February, when sedentary individuals feel charged by New Year's resolutions to turn over a new leaf and get in shape. The marketing of exercise has accelerated in North America in a campaign of mass persuasion, with heavy advertising promoted by sportswear companies. So, how is it that when people start an exercise program, they fail to stick with it?

Models of Exercise Behavior

One start to answering this question is through the development of theoretical models that help us understand the process of exercise adoption and adherence. Some of these models and theories are discussed in this section.

Health Belief Model

The Health Belief Model stipulates that the likelihood of an individual's engaging in preventive health behaviors (such as exercise) depends on the person's perception of the severity of the potential illness as well as his or her appraisal of the costs and benefits of taking action (Becker & Maiman, 1975). An individual who feels that the potential illness is serious, that he or she is at risk, and that the pros of taking action outweigh the cons is likely to adopt the target health behavior.

Theory of Planned Behavior

The theory of planned behavior (Ajzen & Madden, 1986) is an extension of the theory of reasoned action (Ajzen & Fishbein, 1980). First, the theory of reasoned action states that intentions are the best predictors of actual behavior. Specifically, intentions are the product of an individual's attitude toward a particular behavior and what is normative regarding the behavior (subjective norm). This subjective norm is the product of beliefs about others' opinions and the individual's motivation to comply with others' opinions. For example, if you are a nonexerciser and believe that other significant people in your life (e.g., your spouse, children, friends) think you should exercise, then you may wish to do what these others want you to do. This results in a positive subjective norm for exercising, an intention to exercise, and then the actual exercise behavior.

As we just noted, the theory of reasoned action also posits that intentions are the best predictor of actual behavior. Planned behavior theory extends the theory of reasoned action by arguing that intentions cannot be the sole predictors of behavior, especially in situations in which people might lack some control over the behavior. So in addition to the notions of subjective norms and attitudes, planned behavior theory states that perceived behavioral control, that is, people's perceptions of their *ability* to perform the behavior, will also affect behavioral outcomes. For example, even if a person has a positive attitude and subjective norm regarding exercise, if the person believes that she does not have the ability or sufficient opportunities to exercise, then her intention to exercise will likely be weak.

Social Cognitive Theory

Social cognitive theory (Bandura, 1986) proposes that personal, behavioral, and environmental factors operate as reciprocally interacting determinants of each other. This model, therefore, is known as reciprocal determinism. Not only does the environment affect behaviors, but behaviors also affect the environment. In addition, such personal factors as cognitions or thoughts, emotions, and physiology are also important. Despite this interaction among different factors, probably the most critical piece to this approach is an individual's belief that he can successfully perform a behavior (self-efficacy). As shown in chapter 14, people's perceptions that they can successfully perform a behavior increase the likelihood that they will engage in the behavior. Self-efficacy has been shown to be a good predictor of behavior in a variety of health situations, such as smoking cessation, weight management, and recovery from heart attacks.

Transtheoretical Model

Although the previous models are useful in trying to grasp why people do or do not exercise, these constructs tend to focus on a given moment in time. However, the Transtheoretical Model (Prochaska, DiClemente, & Norcross, 1992) argues that individuals progress through stages of change, and movement across the stages is cyclic (see Figure 18.2), rather than linear, because many people do not succeed in their efforts at establishing and maintaining lifestyle changes.

These are the five stages in the Transtheoretical Model:

1. *Precontemplation stage.* In this stage individuals do not intend to start exercising in the next 6 months. They are "couch potatoes." People in this first stage may be demoralized about their ability to change, they may be defensive due to social pressures, or they may be uninformed about the long-term consequences of their behavior.

2. *Contemplation stage.* In this stage people seriously intend to exercise within the next 6 months. Despite their intentions, individuals usually remain in this second stage, according to research, for about 2 years. So the couch potato has a fleeting thought about starting to exercise but is unlikely to act on that thought.

3. *Preparation stage.* People in this stage are exercising some, perhaps less than three times a week, but not regularly. Hence, though our couch potato now exercises a bit, it is not regularly enough to gain major benefits. In the preparation stage individuals typically have a plan of action and have indeed taken action (in the past year or so) to make behavioral changes, such as exercising a little.

4. *Action stage.* Individuals in this stage exercise regularly (three or more times a week for 20 minutes or longer) but have been doing so for fewer than 6 months. This is the least stable stage; it tends to correspond with the highest risk for relapse. It is also the busiest stage, in which the most processes for change are being used. So our couch potato is now an active potato who could easily fall back into his or her old "couchly" ways.

5. *Maintenance stage.* Individuals in this stage have been exercising regularly for more than 6 months. Once they stay in this stage for 5 years, they are likely to maintain regular exercise throughout the life span except for time-outs because of injury or other health-related problems. At this stage, one is truly an active potato—and for a lifetime.

In a large work site promotion project (Marcus et al., 1992) participants were classified into the following categories: (a) 24% in precontemplation, (b) 33% in contemplation, (c) 10% in preparation, (d) 11% in action, and (e) 22% in maintenance. This approximate distribution pattern of the stages of change is found for other behaviors as well, such as smoking cessation and weight control. Researchers have found that when there is a mismatch between the stage of change and intervention strat-

Figure 18.2   Cyclic pattern of stages of changes.

egy, however, attrition is high. If an individual is in the contemplation stage, for example, and the intervention focuses on maintenance strategies instead of motivational strategies, dropouts will increase. Therefore, matching treatment strategies to an individual's stage of change is important to improve adherence and reduce attrition (see the box on p. 379).

The stages of change describe when people change, but the processes of change describe *how* people change. People use a range of strategies and techniques to change behaviors, and these strategies are their processes of change. We can divide processes into two categories: cognitive and behavioral. These processes are listed in Table 18.2. The cognitive processes tend to be used most during the preparation stage, whereas the behavioral processes tend to peak in the action stage.

In making decisions about exercise, people go through a kind of cost-benefit analysis called *decisional balance*. Specifically, when people are considering a change in lifestyle, they weigh the pros and cons of a given behavior (e.g., Should I begin exercising?). In one study, researchers found that in the precontemplation and contemplation stages the cons are usually greater than the pros. However, a crossover of the balance then occurs in the prepara-

tion stage, and the pros outweigh the cons in the action and maintenance stages (Prochaska et al., 1994). Therefore, it's important for exercise specialists to help individuals who are contemplating exercise realize all of the benefits of exercise to help them move from contemplation to preparation.

Determinants of Exercise Adherence

Theories help us understand the process of adopting—later maintaining—exercise habits and give us a way to study this process. Another way researchers have attempted to study adherence to exercise programs is through investigating the specific determinants of exercise behavior. In a broad sense, the determinants fall into the following two categories: personal factors and environmental factors.

We'll examine each category, highlighting the most consistent specific factors related to adherence and dropout rates. Table 18.3 summarizes the positive and negative influences on adherence, along with the variables that have no influence on exercise adherence (Dishman & Buckworth, 1997; Dishman & Sallis, 1994).

Table 18.2
Processes of Change for Exercise

Processes	Examples
COGNITIVE PROCESSES	
Consciousness-raising	I recall information people have personally given me on the benefits of exercise.
Dramatic relief	Warnings about health hazards of inactivity move me emotionally.
Environmental reevaluation	I feel I would be a better role model for others if I exercised regularly.
Self-reevaluation	I am considering the idea that regular exercise would make me a healthier, happier person to be around.
Social liberation	I find society changing in ways that make it easier for the exerciser.
BEHAVIORAL PROCESSES	
Counterconditioning	Instead of remaining inactive, I engage in some physical activity.
Helping relationships	I have someone on whom I can depend when I am having problems with exercising.
Reinforcement management	I reward myself when I exercise.
Self-liberation	I tell myself I am able to keep exercising if I want to.
Stimulus control	I put things around my home to remind me of exercising.

Adapted from Marcus et al., 1992.

378

■ RESEARCH ■

Matching the Exercise Intervention to the Individual

© Chevron Cooperation

Matching treatments to the specific characteristics and needs of individuals has become popular in the realms of smoking cessation and obesity treatment. When one looks at the large percentage of sedentary people in the population and the high dropout rates from programmed exercise programs, it appears the time is right to consider individualized treatment for the promotion of physical activity. In fact, this is the underlying theme of the transtheoretical model. That is, people are at different levels of readiness to change their behavior, and interventions using different techniques are needed to bring about the desired change.

To test this matching notion, Marcus and colleagues (1992) implemented an Imagine Action campaign, which was a community-wide program designed to increase physical activity. The participants, 610 adults, underwent a 6-week intervention consisting of stage-matched, self-help materials, resource materials, "fun walks," and "activity nights." The content of the stage-matched manuals was based on the exercise-adherence literature and informed by the Transtheoretical Model. The manuals for participants at different stages were as follows:

- "What's in It for You?"—contemplation stage, focused on the benefits and barriers to physical activity, along with specific suggestions for leading an increasingly active lifestyle (e.g., taking the stairs instead of the elevator).

- "Ready for Action"—preparation stage, focused on getting participants into action for 30 minutes, three to five times a week, and helping them overcome barriers to experience the benefits of physical activity (using such strategies as using short-term goals, applying time-management skills, and rewarding oneself for activity).

- "Keeping It Going"—action stage, focused on keeping up a regular regimen of physical activity among the individuals who, having exercised for only a short period, were at great risk of sliding back to the preparation stage, in which they would only exercise occasionally. Therefore, the manual attempted to troubleshoot situations that might lead to a relapse (e.g., illness, injury, boredom) and to help with goal setting, cross-training to prevent boredom, and gaining social support.

Following this intervention, 30% of those in contemplation at the baseline and 61% of those in preparation at the baseline progressed to action; an additional 31% in contemplation progressed to preparation. Only 4% of those in preparation and 9% of those in action regressed. These findings demonstrate that a low-cost, relatively low-intensity intervention can produce significant improvement in stage-of-exercise adoption. Furthermore, matching the intervention to the stage an individual is currently in appears to be effective in producing higher levels of regular exercise.

Table 18.3

Factors Associated With Participation in Supervised Exercise Programs

Determinant	Positive	Negative	Neutral
PERSONAL FACTORS			
Demographics			
Age		✔	
Blue-collar occupation		✔	
Education	✔		
Gender (male)	✔		
High risk for heart disease		✔	
Income/socioeconomic status	✔		
Overweight/obesity			✔
Cognitive/personality variables			
Attitudes			✔
Barriers to exercise		✔	
Enjoyment of exercise	✔		
Expect health and other benefits	✔		
Intention to exercise	✔		
Knowledge of health and exercise			✔
Lack of time		✔	
Mood disturbance		✔	
Perceived health or fitness	✔		
Self-efficacy for exercise	✔		
Self-motivation	✔		
Behaviors			
Diet			✔
Past unstructured physical activity during childhood			✔
Past unstructured physical activity during adulthood	✔		
Past program participation	✔		
School sports			✔
Smoking		✔	
Type A behavior pattern		✔	
ENVIRONMENTAL FACTORS			
Social environment			
Class size			✔
Group cohesion	✔		
Physician influence			✔
Past family influences	✔		
Social support friends/peers	✔		
Social support spouse/family	✔		
Social support staff/instructor	✔		
Physical environment			
Climate/season		✔	
Cost			✔
Disruptions in routine		✔	
Access to facilities: actual	✔		
Access to facilities: perceived	✔		
Home equipment			✔
Physical activity characteristics			
Intensity		✔	
Perceived effort		✔	
Group program	✔		
Leader qualities	✔		

Personal Factors

We can distinguish three types of personal characteristics that may influence exercise adherence: demographic variables, cognitive variables, and behaviors. We'll discuss these in order.

Demographic Variables

Demographic variables traditionally have had a strong association with physical activity. For example, education, income, male gender, and income or socioeconomic status all have been consistently and *positively* related to physical activity. Specifically, people with higher incomes, more education, and higher occupational status are more likely to be physically active. For example, of individuals earning less than $15,000 annually, 65% are inactive as compared with 48% of those earning more than $50,000. In addition, of those with less than a high school education, 72% are sedentary as compared with 50% of college-educated individuals (U.S. Centers for Disease Control and Prevention, 1993). Age and risk for heart disease, conversely, have been found to be *negatively* related to physical activity.

Cognitive and Personality Variables

Many cognitive variables have been tested over the years to determine if they help predict and are related to patterns of physical activity. Of all the variables tested, self-efficacy and self-motivation have been found to be the most consistent predictors of physical activity. Self-efficacy is simply the belief than an individual can successfully perform a desired behavior. Getting started in an exercise program, for example, is likely affected by the confidence one has in being able to perform the desired behavior (e.g., walking, running, aerobic dance, etc.) and keep the behavior up. Many people who haven't been exercising regularly feel awkward about physical activity and are very self-conscious about their bodies. Therefore, it is important to help people feel confident about their bodies through social support, encouragement, and tailoring activities to meet their needs and abilities. It is also important to provide beginning exercisers with a sense of success and competence in their exercise programs. This sense of success could lead to more confidence, and more confidence could in turn lead to a greater desire to continue participation. In essence, the relationship between confidence and exercise adherence appears to be circular in nature.

Self-motivation has also been consistently related to exercise adherence and has distinguished adherents from dropouts across many settings, including athletic conditioning and adult fitness centers, preventive medicine clinics, cardiac rehabilitation units, commercial spas, and corporate fitness gyms (Dishman & Sallis, 1994). Evidence suggests that self-motivation may reflect self-regulatory skills, such as effective goal setting, self-monitoring of progress, and self-reinforcement, which are believed to be important in maintaining physical activity. Combined with other measures, self-motivation can predict adherence even more accurately. For example, when self-motivation scores were combined with percent body fat, about 80% of subjects were correctly predicted to be either adherents or dropouts (Dishman, 1981).

In addition to self-efficacy and self-motivation, the cumulative body of evidence also supports the conclusion that beliefs and expectations of benefits from exercise are associated with increased physical-activity levels and adherence to structured physical-activity programs among adults (e.g., Marcus, Pinto, Simkin, Audrain, & Taylor, 1994). In fact, population-based educational campaigns can modify knowledge, attitudes, values, and beliefs regarding physical activity; these changes then can influence individuals' intentions to be active and finally their actual level of activity. Therefore it is important to inform people of the benefits of regular physical activity, along with giving them ways to overcome perceived barriers. An example of how to provide this type of information (see Marcus, Rossi, Selby, Niaura, & Abrams, 1992) is distributing exercise-specific manuals to participants, based on their current stage of physical activity (see box on p. 379).

Behaviors

Of the many behaviors studied as possible predictors of physical activity patterns in adulthood, some

Blue collar workers typically have lower exercise adherence rates than white collar workers. However, increased choices can increase their adherence rates.

Early involvement in sport and physical activity should be encouraged, because there is a positive relation between childhood exercise and adult physical activity patterns.

of the most interesting findings have involved a person's previous physical activity and sport participation. In supervised programs where activity can be directly observed, past participation in an exercise program is the *most reliable predictor* of current participation (Dishman & Sallis, 1994). That is, someone who has remained active in an organized program for 6 months is likely to remain active a year or two later. This prediction holds for adult men and women in supervised fitness programs, and it is consistent with observations in treatment programs for patients with coronary heart disease and obesity.

There is little evidence that mere participation in school sports in and of itself will predict adult physical activity. Similarly, there is little support for the notion that activity patterns in childhood or early adulthood are predictive of later physical activity. However, active children who receive parental encouragement for physical activity will be more active as adults than will children who are sedentary and do not receive parental support. Along these lines, an extensive survey of some 40,000 schoolchildren in 10 European countries revealed that children whose parents, best friends, and siblings take part in sport and physical activity are much more likely themselves to take part and continue to exercise into adulthood (Wold & Anderssen, 1992). These results underscore the importance of encouraging youngsters and getting them involved in regular physical activity and sport participation early in life as well as serving as positive role models.

Environmental Factors

Environmental factors can help or hinder regular participation in physical activity. These factors include the social environment (e.g., family and peers), the physical environment (e.g., weather, time pressures, and distance from facilities), and characteristics of the physical activity (e.g., intensity and duration of the exercise bout). Environments that promote increased activity—offering easily accessible facilities and removing real and perceived barriers to an exercise routine—are probably necessary for the successful maintenance of changes in exercise behavior. For example, adherence to physical activity is higher when individuals live or work closer to a fitness club, receive support from their spouse for the activity, and can manage their time effectively.

Social Environment

Social support is a key aspect of one's social environment, and such support from family and friends

> *Spousal support is critical to enhance adherence rates for people in exercise programs. Spouses should be involved in orientation sessions or in parallel exercise programs.*

has consistently been linked to physical activity and adherence to structured exercise programs among adults (U.S. Department of Health and Human Services, 1996). A spouse has great influence on exercise adherence, for example, and a spouse's attitude can exert even more influence than one's own attitude (Dishman, 1994). In the Ontario Exercise-Heart Collaborative Study (Oldridge et al., 1983) the dropout rate among patients whose spouses were indifferent or negative toward the program was three times greater than among patients whose spouses were supportive and more enthusiastic. Spousal support is generally defined as the demonstration of a positive attitude toward an exercise program and the encouragement of involvement in it. Expressing interest in program activities, enthusiasm for the spouse's progress, and a willingness to juggle schedules to facilitate the spouse's exercise program are examples of this support.

Exercise professionals can utilize a participant's family or spousal support. They might arrange an orientation session for family members, offer a parallel exercise program for them, or educate spouses on all aspects of the exercise program to foster their understanding of the goals. In Erling's and Oldridge's cardiac rehabilitation study, the dropout rate, which had been 56% before initiation of the spouse program, reduced to only 10% for patients with a spouse in the support program (1985). Encouragement for a friend, family member, or peer who is trying to get back or stay in an exercise program can be as simple as saying, "Way to go" or "I'm proud of you." Such personalized social reinforcement can exert a positive influence on exercise adherence.

Physical Environment

A convenient location is important for regular participation in community-based exercise programs. Both the perceived convenience and actual proximity to home or work site are consistent factors in whether someone chooses to exercise and adheres to a supervised exercise program (King, Blair, & Bild, 1992). The closer to a person's home or work the exercise setting is, the greater the likelihood of his or her beginning and staying with a program. In recent years

© Photophile

various community sites have been explored as potential locales for exercise programs, in addition to the more traditional home and work site settings. These have included such places as primary and secondary schools, senior centers, places of worship, and recreation centers. These different locations offer potentially effective venues for community-based physical-activity programs, especially when they are convenient to the participants (Smith & Biddle, 1995).

Still, the most prevalent and principal reason people give for dropping out of supervised clinical and community exercise programs is a perceived lack of time (Dishman & Buckworth, 1997). When time seems short, people typically drop exercise. How many times have you heard someone say, "I'd like to exercise but I just don't have the time." For many people, however, this perceived lack of time reflects a more basic lack of interest or commitment. Regular exercisers are at least as likely as the sedentary to view time as a barrier to exercise. For example, working women are more likely than nonworking women to exercise regularly, and single parents are more physically active than families with two parents. So it is not clear that time constraints truly predict or determine exercise participation. Rather, physical inactivity may have to do more with poor time-man-

agement skills than with too little time. And very busy people who lack an appreciation of the benefits of exercise allot it low priority in their hectic days.

Many sedentary people who lack motivation rationalize that they lack time—it becomes an easy excuse for not exercising. Still, exercise leaders should try to schedule programs at optimal times for busy people. Before and after the workday seem to be more popular than during lunch. Studies have shown that trying to squeeze an exercise class in during the lunch hour causes people to drop out. Therefore, helping new exercisers deal more effectively with time management might be especially beneficial.

Physical Activity Characteristics

The success or failure of exercise programs can depend on several structural factors. Some of the more important factors are the intensity of the exercise, whether the exercise is done in a group or alone, and qualities of the exercise leader.

Exercise Intensity and Duration

Discomfort while exercising certainly affects adherence to a program. High-intensity exercise is more stressful on the system than low-intensity exercise, especially for people who have been sedentary. People in walking programs, for example, continue

> *Exercise intensities should be kept at moderate levels to enhance the probability of long-term adherence to exercise programs.*

> *Although group exercising generally produces higher levels of adherence than exercising alone, tailoring programs to fit individuals and the constraints they feel can help them adhere to the program.*

their regimens longer than do people in running programs. One study showed that dropout rates (25% to 35%) with a moderate-level activity are only about half what is seen (50%) for vigorous exercise (Sallis et al., 1986). Furthermore, more recent research found that adherence rates in exercise programs were best when individuals were exercising at 50% or less of their aerobic capacity (U.S. Department of Health and Human Services, 1996). By lowering the intensity level and extending the workout's duration, in other words, a person can achieve nearly the same benefits as from a high-intensity workout. The best results seem to come from an exercise program with sessions between 20 and 30 minutes in duration. However, for people who are unable to set aside this time to exercise, accumulating shorter bouts of various exercise (e.g., taking the stairs) throughout the day is recommended.

More vigorous physical activity carries a greater risk for injury. In starting an exercise program many people try to do too much the first couple of times out and wind up with sore muscles, injuries to soft tissues, or orthopedic problems. Of course, they find such injury just the excuse they need to quit exercising. The message to give them is that you are much better off doing some moderate exercise, like walking or light aerobics, than trying to shape up in a few weeks by doing too much, too soon.

Comparing Group With Individual Programs

Group exercising leads to better adherence than exercising alone does (Dishman & Buckworth, 1996). Group programs offer enjoyment, social support, an increased sense of personal commitment to continue, and an opportunity to compare progress and fitness levels with others. One reason people exercise is for affiliation. Being part of a group fulfills this need and also provides other psychological and physiological benefits. There tends to be a greater commitment to exercise when others are counting on you. For example, if you and a friend agree to meet at 7 A.M. four times a week to run for 30 minutes, you are likely to keep each appointment so that you don't disappoint your friend. Although group programs are more effective in general than individual programs, cer-

tain people prefer to exercise alone for convenience. In fact, about 25% of regular exercisers almost always exercise alone. Therefore, it is important for exercise leaders to understand the desires of participants to exercise in a group or alone.

Leader Qualities

Although little empirical research has been conducted in this area, anecdotal reports and other related research suggest that program leadership is an important factor in determining the success of an exercise program. Not surprisingly, likable and knowledgeable leaders tend to foster high adherence rates. A good leader can compensate to some extent for other program deficiencies, such as a lack of space or equipment. By the same token, weak leadership can result in a breakdown in the program, regardless of how elaborate the facility.

This underscores the importance of evaluating not only a program's activities and facilities but also the expertise and personality of the program leader(s). Most people starting a program need extra motivation, and the leader's encouragement, enthusiasm, and knowledge are critical in this area. Good leaders also show concern for safety and psychological comfort, develop expertise in answering questions about exercise, and have personal qualities that participants can identify with.

An exercise leader may not be equally effective in all situations. Take the examples of Jane Fonda, Richard Simmons, and Arnold Schwarzenegger, all of whom have had a large impact on fitness programs. Although they are all successful leaders, they appeal to different types of people. Thus, someone trying to start an exercise program should find a good match in style with a leader who is appealing and motivating.

Strategies for Enhancing Adherence to Exercise

Presumably, you now know numerous factors that influence people to stay in or drop out of exercise programs. And you know that these reasons and factors are correlational, telling us little about the cause-

Exercise leaders influence the success of an exercise program so they should be knowledgeable, give lots of feedback and praise, help participants set flexible goals, and show concern for safety and psychological comfort.

effect relation between specific strategies and actual behavior. Therefore, sport psychologists have used information about the determinants of physical activity, along with the theories of behavior change discussed earlier, to develop and test the effectiveness of different strategies that may enhance exercise adherence. Recall that the Transtheoretical Model argues that the most effective interventions appear to match the stage of change the person is in to the particular intervention and therefore its proponents recommend that programs be individualized as much as possible. In making these individualized changes to enhance adherence to exercise, exercise leaders can use five different categories of strategies: (a) environmental approaches, (b) reinforcement approaches, (c) goal-setting and cognitive approaches, (d) decision-making approaches, and (e) social-support approaches. We'll discuss each of these approaches in some detail.

Environmental Approaches

Usually something in the physical environment acts as a cue for habits of behavior. The sight and smell of food is a cue to eat; the sight of a television after work is a cue to sit down and relax. If you want to promote exercise, one technique is to provide cues that will eventually become associated with exercise. There are some interventions that attempt to do just that.

Prompts

A prompt is a cue that initiates a behavior. Prompts can be verbal, physical, or symbolic. The goal is to increase cues for the desired behavior and decrease cues for competing behaviors. Examples of cues to increase exercise behavior include posters, slogans, Post-it notes, placement of exercise equipment in visible places, recruitment of social support, and performance of exercise at the same time and place every day. In one study, cartoon posters (symbolic prompts) were placed near elevators in a public building to encourage stair climbing (Brownell, Stunkard, & Albaum, 1980). In this study, the percentage of

people using the stairs rather than the escalators increased from 6% to 14% within one month after posters were put in place. The posters were removed, and after 3 more months stair use returned to 6% (see Figure 18.3). Removing a prompt can have an adverse effect on adherence behavior; signs, posters, and other materials should be kept in clear view of exercisers to encourage program adherence. Eventually, prompts can be gradually eliminated through a process called fading. Using a prompt less and less over time allows an individual to gain increasing independence without the sudden withdrawal of support, which occurred in the stair-climbing study.

Contracting

Another way to change exercise behavior is to have participants enter into a contract with the exercise practitioner. This contract typically specifies expectations, responsibilities, and contingencies for behavioral change. Contracts should include realistic goals, dates by which goals should be reached, and consequences for not meeting goals (Willis & Campbell, 1992). A different type of contract, in which participants sign a statement of intent to comply with the exercise regimen, has also been used effectively (Oldridge & Jones, 1983). Research has found that people who sign such a statement have significantly better attendance than those who refuse to sign. Thus, people's choosing not to sign a statement of intent to comply can be a signal that they need special measures to enhance their motivation.

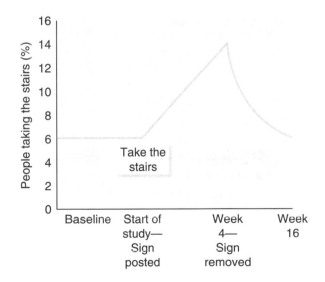

Figure 18.3 Effect of a motivational prop (a sign reading "take the stairs) on the percent of people taking the stairs in a public building.

Perceived Choice

Having a choice of activities to choose from appears to promote subsequent adherence. Thompson and Wankel (1980) found that people given a choice of activities had higher levels of adherence than those given no choice. This held true even when people only perceived that they had a choice (when in reality the experimenter was manipulating their choices of activities).

Reinforcement Approaches

Reinforcement, either positive or negative, is a powerful determinant of future action. To increase exercise adherence, incentives or rewards (e.g., T-shirts) can be given for staying with the program. We'll discuss a few reinforcement interventions in detail.

Rewards for Attendance and Participation

One example of positive reinforcement is rewarding attendance. In one particular study two rewards were given for attendance during a 5-week jogging program: a $1 weekly deposit-return, contingent on participation, and an attendance lottery coupon to win a prize, which was awarded for each class attended. The two interventions resulted in 64% attendance, whereas subjects in a control group attended only 40% of the classes (Epstein, Wing, Thompson, & Griffiths, 1980).

An approach that has proved effective in corporate programs is for the company to pay most (but not all) of the exercise program's cost. Researchers compared four methods of payment and found that program attendance was better when participants were either reimbursed based on attendance or split the fee with their employer. Interestingly, the lowest attendance was found when the company paid the entire fee (Pollock, Foster, Salisbury, & Smith, 1982).

> *Manipulating the environment by providing cues to exercise and perceived choices of activities can greatly enhance adherence to exercise programs.*
>
> ———————————■———————————
>
> *Rewards for attendance and participation can help improve adherence rates. However, rewards must be provided throughout the length of a program to promote adherence in the long term.*

Following this research the Campbell Soup Company required employees to pay $50 for the first year of participation. If they exercised three times a week or more during the second year, they paid only $25. If employees continued to exercise at this rate, they paid nothing the third year (Legwold, 1987). In general, the results have been encouraging for initial attendance or adherence but less so for long-term improvement. Additional incentives or reinforcement must be provided throughout the program to encourage adherence over longer time periods.

Feedback

Providing feedback to participants on their progress can have motivational benefits. For example, Scherf and Franklin (1987) developed a data documentation system for use in a cardiac rehabilitation setting in which the participants' body weight, resting heart rate, exercise heart rate, laps walked, laps run, and total laps after each session were recorded on individual forms. Staff members reviewed these records monthly with the participants and then returned record cards to the participants with appropriate comments. Individuals who met certain performance goals were then recognized in a monthly awards ceremony. This program resulted in better exercise participation and adherence as well as in higher levels of motivation and enthusiasm.

Giving feedback to individuals during a program session is apparently more effective than praising the whole group at the end. Specifically, a study that provided for giving feedback to runners individually produced higher levels of program attendance during the program than did group feedback, and, as you can see in Figure 18.4, adherence levels continued to be higher 3 months after the program's termination (Martin et al., 1984).

Self-Monitoring

Self-monitoring of physical activity has been a frequently employed behavioral management or reinforcement technique. Typically, it has involved individuals keeping written records of their physical activity (i.e., number of episodes each week, time spent per episode, and feelings during exercise). In one study, self-monitoring was combined with different schedules of calling participants to prompt them to walk. Frequent calls (placed once a week)

> *The more that feedback is individualized to meet specific needs, the more likely it is to succeed.*

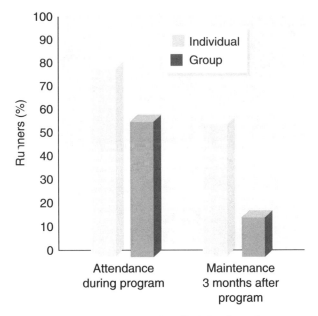

Figure 18.4 *Effect of individual and group feedback on exercise adherence.*

resulted in three times the number of reported episodes of physical activity as resulted from calling only every third week (Lombard, Lombard, & Winett, 1995). Combining self-monitoring with additional external prompts appears to work best in maximizing adherence to exercise programs.

Goal-Setting and Cognitive Approaches

Goal setting can be a useful motivational technique and strategy to improve exercise behavior and adherence. One study found that 99% of participants enrolled in an intermediate fitness class set multiple, personally motivating goals for their exercise participation (Poag-DuCharme & Brawley, 1994). Martin and his colleagues (1984) found that flexible goals which participants set themselves resulted in better attendance and maintenance behavior of the exercise (for a 3-month span) than did fixed, instructor-set goals. Specifically, attendance rates were 83% when subjects set their own goals, compared with 67% when instructors set the goals. Furthermore, 47% of those who set their own goals were still exercising 3 months after the program ended (compared with 28% of the people for whom the instructor set goals).

Time-based goals resulted in better attendance (69%) than did distance-based goals (47%). Moreover, longer term, or distal (6-week), goal setting produced better attendance (83% vs. 71%) and better 3-month exercise maintenance (67% vs. 33%) than did proximal (weekly) goal setting (Martin et al., 1984).

> *Exercise-related goals should be self-set rather than instructor-set, flexible rather than fixed, and time-based rather than distance-based.*
>
> ■
>
> *Dissociative strategies emphasizing external distraction produce significantly higher levels of exercise adherence than associative strategies focusing on internal body feedback.*

You can find more specific guidelines for using goal setting in chapter 15.

Thoughts or cognitions—what people focus their attention on—while exercising are also important to adherence to the exercise program. When the focus is on internal body feedback (e.g., how the muscles feel or the breathing), it is called association; when the focus is on the external environment (e.g., how pretty the scenery is), it is called dissociation (a distraction). Researchers found that people who dissociate have significantly better attendance (77%) than those whose thinking is associative (58%). In a study of a 12-week exercise program the dissociative subjects were also superior in long-term maintenance of exercise after 3 months (87% vs. 37%) and 6 months (67% vs. 43%) than associative subjects were (see Figure 18.5; Martin et al., 1984). Focusing on the environment instead of on how the individual feels may improve exercise adherence rates because thinking about other things reduces a person's boredom and fatigue.

Decision-Making Approaches

Whether to start an exercise program can often be a difficult decision. To help people in this decision-making process, psychologists developed a technique known as a decision balance sheet (Hoyt & Janis, 1975; Wankel, 1984; see Figure 18.6), which can make them more aware of potential benefits and costs of an exercise program. In devising a decision balance sheet, individuals write down the anticipated consequences of exercise participation in terms of gains to self, losses to self, gains to important others, losses to important others, approval of others, disapproval of others, self-approval, and self-disapproval.

In one study participants who completed a decision balance sheet attended 84% of the classes during a 7-week period, whereas controls attended only 40%

© Mary Langenfeld/ Langenfeld Photos

of the classes (Hoyt & Janis, 1975). In a variant of this study, Wankel and Thompson (Wankel, 1984) compared using a full balance sheet (identical to the one in the Hoyt and Janis study) to using a positive-only balance sheet, which deleted reference to any anticipated negative outcomes. Both types of balance sheets produced higher attendance rates than a control condition. Collectively, the evidence available demonstrates the effectiveness of involving participants in decisions before initiating an exercise program.

Social-Support Approaches

In our context, social support refers to an individual's favorable attitude toward another individual's involvement in an exercise program. Social and family interactions may influence physical activity in many ways. Spouses, family members, and friends can cue exercise through verbal reminders. Significant others who exercise may model and cue physi-

cal activity by their behavior and reinforce it by their companionship during exercise. Sometimes a family can adjust its routine to allow exercise time. Often people give practical assistance, providing transportation, measuring exercise routes, or lending exercise clothing or equipment. In any case, social support from family and friends has been consistently and positively related to adult physical activity and adherence to structured exercise programs (U.S. Department of Health and Human Services, 1996). We next provide several examples of specific social support programs.

Wankel (1984) developed a program to enhance social support that included the leader, the class, a buddy (partner), and family members. The leader regularly encouraged the participants to establish and maintain their home and buddy support systems, attempted to develop a positive class atmosphere, and ensured that class attendance and social support charts

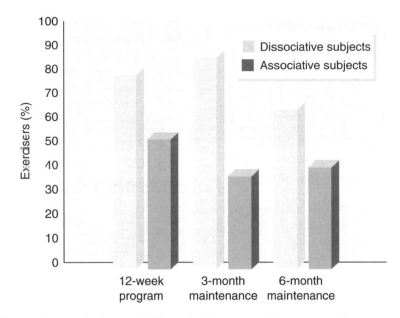

Figure 18.5 *Effects of associative and dissociative strategies on exercise program involvement.*

Gains to self

- Better physical condition
- More energy
- Weight loss

Losses to self

- Less time with hobbies

Gains to important others

- Healthier so I can play baseball with my kids
- Become more attractive to my spouse

Losses to important others

- Less time with my family
- Less time to devote to work

Approval of others

- My children would like to see me be more active
- My spouse would like me to lead a healthier lifestyle

Disapproval of others

- My boss thinks it takes time away from work

Self-approval

- Feel more confident
- Improved self-concept

Self-disapproval

- I look foolish exercising because I'm out of shape

Figure 18.6 *A decision balance sheet.*

Using small groups, personalized feedback, and a buddy system to enhance social support has been shown to increase exercise adherence.

were systematically marked. Results showed that participants receiving social support had better attendance than did the members of a control group.

King and Frederiksen (1984) set up three- or four-member groups and instructed people in them to jog with at least one group member throughout the study. In addition, the groups took part in team-building exercises to promote group cohesiveness. These small social-support groups increased attendance and improved exercise behavior. The fact that exercise adherence improves when a leader gives personalized, immediate feedback and praises attendance and maintenance of exercise (Martin et al., 1984) also shows the importance of social support.

Settings for Exercise Interventions

We have spent most of the chapter discussing theories for changing exercise behavior, determinants of physical activity, and strategies to enhance exercise adherence. But these interventions all must be implemented in a specific setting, and that particular setting can also be an important determinant of how effective the intervention is (King, 1994). The main settings for exercise interventions are (a) schools, (b) work sites, (c) home, (d) community, and (e) health-care facilities. Although successful interventions can be found in all sites, research reveals that community-based exercise interventions produce the most positive effects (U.S. Department of Health and Human Services, 1996).

Community-based approaches appear to offer the best ways of reaching large numbers of people through exercise programs. An example of such a successful, community-based program is the Community Health Assessment and Promotion Project (CHAPP), sponsored by the Centers for Disease Control. Designed to modify dietary and exercise behaviors in some 400 obese women from a predominantly black Atlanta community, the program features a working coalition of various community organizations (e.g., churches, YMCAs). CHAPP has seen participation rates of 60% to 70%, significantly higher than was typical in this community (Lasco et al., 1989).

Guidelines for Improving Exercise Adherence

Several elements have emerged as being keys to enhancing adherence to exercise. We'll consolidate these elements now into guidelines for the aspiring fitness professional.

- Match the intervention to the stage of change of the participant.
- Provide cues for exercises (signs, posters, cartoons).
- Make the exercises enjoyable.
- Tailor the intensity, duration, and frequency of the exercises.
- Promote exercising with a group or friend.
- Have participants sign a contract or statement of intent to comply with the exercise program.
- Offer a choice of activities to choose from.
- Provide rewards for attendance and participation.
- Give individualized feedback.
- Find a convenient place for exercising.
- Have participants reward themselves for achieving certain goals.
- Encourage goals to be self-set, flexible, and time-based, (rather than distance-based).
- Remind participants to focus on environmental cues (not bodily cues) when exercising.
- Use small group discussions.
- Have participants complete a decision balance sheet before starting the exercise program.
- Obtain social support from the participant's spouse, family members, and peers.
- Suggest keeping daily exercise logs.

■ APPLICATION ■

Promoting Physical Activity in School and Community Programs

Schools and communities have the potential to improve the health of young people by providing instruction, programs, and services that promote enjoyable, lifelong physical activity. To realize this potential, the following recommendations have been made (U.S. Department of Health and Human Services, 1997).

- Policy—establish policies that promote enjoyable, lifelong physical activity among young people (e.g., require comprehensive, daily physical education for students in kindergarten through grade 12).

- Environment—provide physical and social environments that encourage and enable safe and enjoyable physical activity (e.g., provide time within the school day for unstructured physical activity).

- Physical education—implement physical education curriculums and instruction that emphasize enjoyable participation in physical activity and that help students develop the knowledge, attitudes, motor skills, behavioral skills, and confidence needed to adopt and maintain physically active lifestyles.

- Health education—implement health education curriculums and instruction that help students develop the knowledge, attitudes, behavioral skills, and confidence needed to adopt and maintain physically active lifestyles.

- Extracurricular activities—provide extracurricular activities that meet the needs of all students (e.g., provide a diversity of developmentally appropriate competitive and noncompetitive physical activity programs for all students).

- Parental involvement—include parents and guardians in physical activity instruction and in extracurricular and community physical-activity programs; encourage them to support their children's participation in enjoyable physical activities.

- Personnel training—provide training for education, coaching, recreation, health-care, and other school and community personnel that impart the knowledge and skills needed to effectively promote enjoyable, lifelong physical activity among young people.

- Health services—assess physical activity patterns among young people, counsel them about physical activity, refer them to appropriate programs, and advocate for physical activity instruction and programs for young people.

- Community programs—provide a range of developmentally appropriate community sports and recreation programs that are attractive to all people.

- Evaluation—regularly evaluate school and community physical-activity instruction, programs, and facilities.

■ CASE STUDY ■

Increasing Exercise Adherence

Jennifer was just hired at a local fitness facility. The club owners told her that her major job would be to increase member participation in and adherence to exercise—that is, to get and keep people exercising. Jennifer reviewed her college books and notes, looking for programs and techniques to enhance exercise adherence. She then devised a plan she could implement after the first of the year, when attendance was typically highest.

First Jennifer called a meeting of all the fitness instructors at the club. She wanted both to get input from the instructors about keeping people exercising and to present her philosophy on exercise adherence so that her staff would know where she was coming from. She detailed the problems in keeping members coming back, made several suggestions for what could and would be done to change things, and emphasized that the instructors would all need to work together and support each other to put the new programs into action. Perhaps most importantly, she explained to her staff that people are in different stages when it comes to exercising (see transtheoretical model) and that it's important to individualize the exercise intervention as much as possible to correspond to the particular stage a person might be in at that time.

The first step was for the instructors to set aside time to meet with each member one-on-one for 30 minutes. Jennifer felt individualized meetings were critical for the instructors to find out more about all the members and determine what stage they were in. In these meetings members were asked to complete a decision balance sheet, noting the potential benefits and costs of partcipation in the exercise program. They were also asked what barriers might potentially block their way from staying with the program and what the club could do to help them in their quest to stay in shape. Finally, members were asked to set some flexible short- and long-term goals for themselves, which were written down for both the member and exercise leader.

This information helped Jennifer fine-tune the program and open up communication lines between the members and exercise leaders. Several themes emerged from these individual meetings, and Jennifer tried to tailor the club's program to meet the needs of the majority of the members. She then summarized and shared this information with her staff.

Jennifer soon scheduled exercise programs and classes at the times members said were convenient (because time and inconvenience were major factors in whether they exercised or not). The scheduling was flexible, and classes were held even if only a few members could attend at a given time. Classes included exercises that met the minimum guidelines developed by the American College of Sports Medicine for intensity and duration to receive health benefits. A variety of exercise classes and activities were planned so that each member could find something she or he enjoyed doing. The variety would also help keep them from getting bored (or injured).

Jennifer implemented a buddy system—each member was paired off with another member identified as having similar interests and a similar time schedule. This system was designed to acquaint members and allow them to set up exercise dates outside of class if they couldn't make a class meeting.

As an extension of the buddy system, Jennifer learned the names of members' spouses or significant others. When possible, these people were telephoned and told how important their support was for keeping the member motivated. Spouses were encouraged to start exercising themselves, with the assistance of the trained exercise leaders at the club.

continued

Increasing Exercise Adherence
(continued)

Finally, Jennifer planned contests in different categories, including best attendance record for the month, most consecutive days of attendance, and most enthusiasm (as chosen by the exercise leaders). Prizes included T-shirts, free dinners, free massages, and an extra month's membership free.

After 6 months, Jennifer evaluated the program and found that the attendance rate for formal exercise classes was up about 25%, and general club attendance had increased by about 20%. In addition, new memberships had increased by 30% over the previous year. Jennifer and the club owners were pleased with this progress. By using the input of the club members and her staff and the latest concepts from the research on exercise adherence, Jennifer made the program a success.

SUMMARY

1 *Discuss why people do or do not exercise.*

Although the notion of a fitness boom has been sold to the public, most adults still do not exercise regularly, and only a small percentage of those who do exercise actually work out enough to receive health benefits. Thus, the first problem is getting people started in an exercise program. People usually follow a program to derive the many benefits of exercise, including weight control, reduced risk of cardiovascular disease, reduction of stress and depression, enhanced self-esteem, and increased enjoyment. The major reasons why people drop out include a perceived lack of time, lack of energy, and lack of motivation.

2 *Explain the different models of exercise behavior.*

Theoretical models provide an introduction to understanding the process of exercise adoption and adherence to an exercise regimen, and the major models that have been developed in this area include the Health Belief Model, the theory of planned behavior, social cognitive theory, and the Transtheoretical Model. The Transtheoretical Model offers the advantage of accounting for the process by which individuals move through different stages of exercise adoption, exercise behavior, and exercise maintenance.

3 *Describe the determinants of exercise adherence.*

In a broad sense, the determinants of exercise behavior fall into two categories: personal factors and environmental factors. Personal factors include demographic variables (e.g., gender, socioeconomic status), cognitive and personality variables (e.g., self-efficacy, knowledge of health and exercise), and behaviors (e.g., smoking, diet). Environmental factors include the social environment (e.g., social support, past family influences), the physical environment (e.g., access to facilities, weather), and the characteristics of the physical activity itself (e.g., intensity, group or individual program).

4 *Identify strategies for increasing exercise adherence.*

Five types of approaches are useful to increase exercise adherence. These approaches are (a) environmental (e.g., prompts, contracting), (b) through reinforcement (e.g., rewards for attendance, feedback), (c) using goal setting and cognition (e.g., association or dissociation), (d) using decision making (e.g., decision balance sheet), and (e) through social support (e.g., classmates, family).

5 *Give guidelines for improving exercise adherence.*

To implement exercise programs that maximize participant adherence, a group leader should make the exercise enjoyable and convenient, provide social support, encourage exercising with a friend, provide rewards for attendance and participation, and offer participants a range of activities from which to choose.

KEY TERMS

Health Belief Model
theory of planned behavior
subjective norm
social cognitive theory
Transtheoretical Model
prompt

fading
self-monitoring
association
dissociation
decision balance sheet

REVIEW QUESTIONS

1. Why is it important to understand the reasons people start and adhere to exercise programs? Use data from the Department of Health and Human Services to discuss your answer.

2. Your friend is sedentary and should start a regular exercise program but doesn't consider it important. What are three reasons you would cite to convince your friend?

3. Why is exercise adherence a problem?

4. Discuss the major points regarding the Health Belief Model, theory of planned behavior, and social cognitive theory as they relate to exercise behavior.

5. Discuss the Transtheoretical Model of behavioral change for an exerciser, including the different stages of change.

6. How does the Transtheoretical Model support the notion of treatment-client matching?

7. Give three examples of the cognitive and behavioral processes of changing exercise behavior.

8. Discuss three personal factors and how they affect and predict adherence rates.

9. What are the relations among body fat, risk of cardiovascular disease, and adherence? What implications do these have for the practitioner?

10. Discuss three environmental (physical and social) factors as they relate to exercise adherence and the structuring of exercise programs.

11. Compare and contrast the environmental and reinforcement approaches to exercise adherence. Include different methods for each, and describe studies that have found these approaches effective.

12. Based on research about the effects of goal setting on adherence, how would you use goals in setting up an exercise program?

13. How is a decision balance sheet used to help people stick with an exercise program? What research studies demonstrate its effectiveness?

14. Discuss two studies of using social support for enhancing adherence.

CRITICAL THINKING QUESTIONS

1. You are hired as the new director of fitness by your local health and fitness club. The dropout rate has been large in the past. You know adherence to exercise is difficult, but your boss wants you to increase participation and adherence rates. How would you go about designing a program that would maximize adherence rates? Be specific about the principles you would use and programs you would implement.

2. A big company is getting ready to build a new physical fitness facility. They hire you as a consultant to discuss what to include in the building, where to build it, what equipment to purchase, and other factors to maximize participation by the public. Given what you know from research on the determinants of exercise adherence, what specific recommendation would you provide the company?

© Photo: Action Images

Athletic Injuries and Psychology

After reading this chapter you should be able to

1 discuss the role of psychological factors in athletic and exercise injuries,

2 identify psychological antecedents that may predispose people to athletic injuries,

3 compare and contrast explanations for the stress-injury relationship,

4 describe typical psychological reactions to injuries,

5 identify signs of poor adjustment to injury, and

6 explain how to implement psychological skills and strategies that can speed the rehabilitation process.

It was the start of the football season, and Minnesota Vikings' defensive tackle Keith Millard was one of the premier players in the NFL. Then, while rushing the Tampa Bay Buccaneers, quarterback Millard went down with a serious knee injury. Sportswriter Jill Lieber (1991) captured his reaction in an interview:

"My knee's shot. My knee's shot. There goes my whole career. It's over. I'm through." Agonizing over his misfortune, Millard buried his head in his hands and cried so hard that his 6 foot 5 inch, 265-pound body shook.... He was impossible to be around, lashing out at nurses, refusing to eat, slamming his crutches to the floor instead of learning how to use them. ... Embarrassed by how vulnerable he looked in bed, Millard was so uncomfortable when Viking coaches and players came to visit that he finally phoned Dan Endy of the team's public relations department and dictated a terse letter specifying no more visitors. ... When Millard began rehabilitating his knee at the Vikings' practice facility in mid-October, he acted tough and invincible and didn't let on to his teammates that the pain was excruciating. (pp. 37–38)

Millard did recover to play again. But his reactions after the injury clearly showed that he had been hurt psychologically as well as physically. Because of cases like Millard's, the psychology of athletic injuries has become an area of great concern and interest to a much broader population than elite athletes. It concerns anyone—whether an athlete, exercise enthusiast, or dancer—who has sustained a physical activity–related injury.

Psychological Factors in Athletic Injuries

It is conservatively estimated that 3 to 5 million adults and children are injured each year in the United States in sport, exercise, and recreational settings (Kraus & Conroy, 1984). Whether your goal is becoming a physical educator, high school coach, personal trainer, strength-and-conditioning specialist, athletic director, physical therapist, or athletic trainer, you can expect to encounter and work with your share of injured participants.

> *An estimated 3 to 5 million adults and children are injured each year in sport, exercise,1 and recreational outings. People with high levels of life stress have more sport- and exercise-related injuries.*

Physical factors are the primary causes of athletic injuries, but psychological factors can also contribute to them. Thus, fitness professionals should understand both the psychological reactions to injuries and how mental strategies can facilitate recovery.

Sport psychologists Jean Williams and Mark Andersen (1988; 1998) have helped clarify the role psychological factors play in athletic injuries. Figure 19.1 shows a simplified version of their model. You can see that the relation between athletic injuries and psychological factors is viewed as primarily stress-related. In particular, a potentially stressful athletic situation (e.g., competition, important practice, poor performance) can contribute to injury, depending on the athlete and how threatening he or she perceives the situation to be (see chapter 4). A situation perceived as threatening increases state anxiety, which causes a variety of changes in focus or attention and muscle tension (e.g., distraction and tightening up). This in turn leads to an increased chance of being injured.

Stress isn't the only psychological factor to influence athletic injuries, however. As you also see in Figure 19.1, personality factors, a history of stressors, and coping resources all influence the stress process and, in turn, the probability of injury. Furthermore, after someone sustains an injury these same factors influence how much stress the injury causes and the individual's subsequent rehabilitation and recovery. Moreover, you can see from Figure 19.1 that people who develop psychological skills (e.g., goal setting, imagery, and relaxation) may deal better with stress, reducing both their chances of being injured and the stress of injury, should it occur.

With this overview of the roles that psychological factors can play in athletic- and exercise-related injuries, we can now examine in more depth the pieces of the model.

How Injuries Happen

Physical factors, such as muscle imbalances, high-speed collisions, overtraining, and physical fatigue, are the primary causes of exercise and sport injuries. However, psychological factors may also play a role. Personality factors, stress levels, and certain predisposing attitudes have all been identified (Rotella & Heyman, 1986; Wiese & Weiss, 1987) as psychological antecedents to athletic injuries.

Personality Factors

Personality traits were among the first psychological factors associated with athletic injuries. Investi-

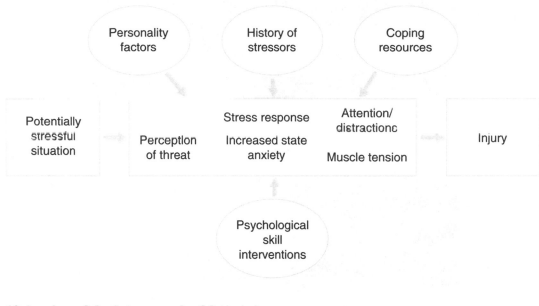

Figure 19.1 *A model of stress and athletic injury.*
Adapted from Anderson and Williams, 1988.

gators wanted to understand whether such traits as self-concept, introversion-extroversion, and tough-mindedness were related to injury. For example, would athletes with low self-concepts have higher injury rates than their high self-concept counterparts? Unfortunately, most of the research on personality and injury has suffered from inconsistency and the problems that have plagued sport personality research in general (Feltz, 1984b; also see chapter 2). Of course, this does not mean that personality is not related to injury rates; it means that to date we have not successfully identified and measured the particular personality characteristics associated with athletic injuries.

Stress Levels

Stress levels, on the other hand, have been identified as important antecedents of athletic injuries. Research has examined the relation between life stress and injury rates (Andersen & Williams, 1988; Williams & Andersen, 1998). Measures of these stresses focus on major life changes, such as losing a loved one, moving to a different town, getting married, or experiencing a change in economic status. Such minor stressors and daily hassles as driving in traffic have also been studied. Overall, the evidence suggests that athletes with higher levels of life stress experience more injuries. Thus, fitness and sport professionals should ask about major

changes and stressors in athletes' lives and, when such changes occur, carefully monitor and adjust training regimens and provide psychological support.

Stress and injuries are related in complex ways. A study of 452 male and female high school athletes (in basketball, wrestling, and gymnastics) examined the relation between stressful life events; social and emotional support from family, friends, and coaches; coping skills; and the number of days athletes could not participate in their sport due to injury (Smith, Smoll, & Ptacek, 1990). No relation was found among these factors across a school season. However, life stress was associated with athletic injuries in the specific subgroup of athletes who had both low levels of social support and low coping skills. These results suggest that when an athlete possessing few coping skills and little social support experiences major life changes, he or she is at a greater risk of athletic injury. Athletic trainers and coaches should be on the lookout for these at-risk individuals. This finding supports the Andersen and Williams model, emphasizing the importance of looking at the multiple psychological factors in the stress-injury relationship.

Recent research has also identified the specific stress sources athletes undergo when injured and when rehabilitating from injury (Gould, Udry, Bridges, & Beck, 1997b). Interestingly, the greatest sources of stress were not the result of the physical

© Terry Wild Studio

aspects of the injuries themselves. Rather, psychological reactions (e.g., fear of reinjury, feeling that hopes and dreams were shattered, watching others get to perform) and social concerns (e.g., lack of attention, isolation, negative relationships) were mentioned more often as stressors. For example, one elite skier commented:

I felt shut up, cut off from the ski team. That was one of the problems I had. I didn't feel like I was being cared for, basically. Once I got home, it was like they (the ski team) dropped me off at home, threw all my luggage in the house, and were [saying] like "See you when you get done." I had a real hard time with that.

Another injured skier said:

"It was hard, really hard . . . because it was an Olympic year and people took a lot of time that summer to get better. And then you come back in the fall and see everybody is skiing so good because they're all excited about the Olympic year and you just got back on snow."

Other stress concerns (stresses) these athletes experienced involved physical problems (e.g., pain, physical inactivity), medical treatment (e.g., medical uncertainty, seriousness of diagnosis), rehabilitation difficulties (e.g., dealing with slow progress, rehabbing on their own),

© Mary Langenfeld/ Langenfeld Photos

financial difficulties, career worries, and their sense of missed opportunities. Being familiar with what these stress sources are is important for the people working with injured athletes.

Teaching stress-management techniques (see chapter 12) may not only help athletes and exercisers perform more effectively but also reduce their risk of injury. In a recent experiment with elite gymnasts, for instance, Kerr and Goss (1996) found that participating in a stress-management training program reduced the amount of stress gymnasts experienced across the season. In addition, the data disclosed that the group of gymnasts who had the stress-management training had fewer injuries than their counterparts who did not have the training.

Explaining the Stress-Injury Relationship

Understanding why athletes who experience high stress in life are more prone to injury can significantly help you in designing effective sports-medicine programs to deal with stress reactions and in-

jury prevention. To date, two major theories have been advanced to explain the stress-injury relationship.

Attentional Disruption

One promising view is that stress disrupts an athlete's attention by reducing peripheral attention (Williams, Tonyman, & Andersen, 1991). Thus, a football quarterback under great stress might be prone to injury because he does not see a charging defender rushing in from his off side. When his stress levels are lower, the quarterback would have a wider field of peripheral vision and be able to see the defender in time to avoid a sack and subsequent injury.

It has also been suggested that increased state anxiety causes distraction and irrelevant thoughts. For instance, an executive who jogs at lunch after an argument with a colleague might be inattentive to the running path and step into a hole, twisting her ankle.

Increased Muscle Tension

High stress can be accompanied by considerable muscle tension that interferes with normal oordination and increases the chance of injury (Nideffer, 1983). For example, a highly stressed gymnast might experience more muscle tension than is desirable and fall from the balance beam, injuring herself.

Teachers and coaches who work with an athlete experiencing major life changes (e.g., a high school student whose parents are in the midst of a divorce) should watch the athlete's behavior closely. If he shows signs of increased muscle tension or abnormal attentional difficulties when performing, it would be wise to ease training and initiate stress-management strategies.

Other Psychologically Based Explanations for Injury

In addition to stress, sport psychologists working with injured athletes have identified certain attitudes that predispose players to injury. Rotella and Heyman (1986) observed that attitudes held by some coaches—such as "Act tough and always give 110%" or "If you're injured, you're worthless"—can increase the probability of athlete injury.

Act Tough and Give 110%

Slogans such as "Go hard or go home," "No pain, no gain," and "Go for the burn" typify the 110%-effort orientation many coaches promote. By rewarding such effort without also emphasizing the need to recognize and accept injuries, coaches encourage their athletes to play hurt or take undue risks (Rotella & Heyman, 1986). A college football player, for instance, may be repeatedly Rewarded for sacrificing his body on special teams. He becomes ever more daring, running down to cover kickoffs, until one day he throws his

> *Teach athletes and exercisers to distinguish the normal discomfort accompanying overload and increased training volumes from the pain accompanying the onset of injuries.*

body into another player and sustains a serious injury.

This is not to say that athletes should not play assertively and hit hard in football, wrestling, and rugby. But giving 110% should not be emphasized so much that athletes take undue risks—such as spearing or tackling with the head down in football—and increase their chances of severe injuries.

The act-tough orientation is not limited to contact sports. Many athletes and exercisers are socialized into believing that they must train through pain and that "more is always better." They consequently overstrain and are stricken with tennis elbow, shin splints, swimmer's shoulder, or other injuries. Hard physical training does involve discomfort, but athletes and exercisers must be taught to distinguish between the normal discomfort that accompanies overloading and increased training volumes and the pain that accompanies the onset of injuries.

If You're Injured, You're Worthless

Some people learn to feel worthless if they are hurt, an attitude that develops in several ways. Coaches may convey, consciously or otherwise, that winning is more important than the athletes' well-being. When a player is hurt, that player no longer contributes toward winning. Thus, the coach has no use for the player—and the player quickly picks up on this. Athletes want to feel worthy (like winners) so they play while hurt and sustain even worse injuries. A less direct way of conveying this attitude of injury meaning worthlessness is to say the "correct" thing (e.g., "Tell me when you're hurting! Your health is more important than winning.") but then act very differently when a player is hurt. The player is ignored, which tells him that to be hurt is to be less worthy. Athletes quickly adopt the attitude to play even when they are hurt. The case study on p. 404 shows how athletes should be encouraged to train hard without risking injury.

> *Most people experience a typical reaction to injury, but the speed and ease with which they progress through the stages can vary widely.*

Psychological Reactions to Exercise and Athletic Injuries

Despite their taking physical and psychological precautions, many people engaged in vigorous physical activity will sustain injuries. Even in the best-staffed, -equipped, and -supervised programs injury is inherently a risk. So it is important to understand psychological reactions to activity injuries.

Sport psychology specialists and athletic trainers have identified varied psychological reactions to injuries. Some people view an injury as a disaster, as did football player Keith Millard. Others may view their injury as a relief—a way to get a break from tedious practices, save face if they are not playing well, or even to have an acceptable excuse for quitting. While many different reactions can occur, some are more common than others. Sport and fitness professionals must observe these responses.

Emotional Responses

At first sport psychologists speculated that people react to exercise and athletic injury with a response similar to what those facing imminent death experience. That is, exercisers and athletes who have become injured often follow a five-stage grief response process (Hardy & Crace, 1990). These stages are

1. denial,
2. anger,
3. bargaining,
4. depression, and
5. acceptance and reorganization.

Although this grief reaction has been widely cited in articles about the psychology of injury, recent evidence shows that although injured individuals may exhibit many of these emotions in response to being injured, they do not follow a set, stereotypical pattern

■ CASE STUDY ■

Injury Pain and Training Discomfort

Sharon Taylor coaches a swimming team that has been plagued over the years by overuse injuries. Yet her team is proud of its hard work ethic. Incorporating swimming psychologist Keith Bell's guidelines (1980), Sharon has taught the team to view the normal discomfort of training (pain) as a sign of growth and progress, as opposed to something awful or intolerable. For her team, normal training discomfort is not a signal to stop but a challenge to do more.

Because Sharon's swimmers have taken their training philosophy too far and misinterpreted Bell's point, Sharon set a goal of having her swimmers distinguish between the discomfort of training and the pain of injury. At the start of the season she discussed her concerns and asked swimmers who had received overuse injuries the season before to talk about the differences between pushing through workouts (overcoming discomfort) and ignoring injury (e.g., not stopping or telling the coach when a shoulder ached). She changed the team slogan from "No pain, no gain" to "Train hard and smart." She also revamped the training cycling scheme to include more days off and initiated a team rule that no one could swim or lift weights on the days off. Sharon periodically discussed injury in contrast to discomfort with her swimmers during the season, and she reinforced correct behavior with praise and occasional rewards. And Sharon turned to parents of her swimmers, informing them of the need to monitor their children's chronic pains.

As the season progressed, the swimmers began to understand the difference between injury pain and the normal discomfort of hard training. At the end of the season most of her swimmers remained healthy and excited about the state meet.

---

or necessarily experience each emotion of these five stages (Brewer, 1994; Evans & Hardy, 1995; Udry, Gould, Bridges, & Beck, 1997). Sport psychologists now recommend that typical responses to injury should be viewed in a more flexible and general way—people do not move nicely through set stages in a predetermined order. Rather, many of them feel such emotions and thoughts simultaneously or revert back to categories once they have gone through them. While emotional responses to being injured have not proved to be as fixed or orderly as sport psychologists once thought, you can expect injured individuals to exhibit three general categories of responses (Udry, Gould, Bridges, & Beck, 1997):

1. *Injury-relevant information processing.* The injured athlete focuses on such information as the pain of the injury, awareness of the extent of injury, questions about how the injury happened, and the individual recognizes the negative consequences or inconvenience.

2. *Emotional upheaval and reactive behavior.* Once the athlete realizes that he or she is injured, the individual may become emotionally agitated, experience vacillating emotions, feel emotionally depleted, experience isolation and disconnection, and feel shock, disbelief, denial, or self-pity.

3. *Positive outlook and coping.* The athlete accepts the injury and deals with it, initiates positive coping efforts, exhibits a good attitude and is optimistic, and is relieved to sense progress.

In reaction to injury most athletes move through these general patterns, but the speed and ease with which they progress varies widely. One person may move through the process in a day or two; others may take weeks or even months.

Other Reactions

Athletes experience additional psychological reactions to injury (Petitpas & Danish, 1995). These are some of their other reactions:

1. *Identity loss.* Some athletes who can no longer participate because of an injury experience a loss of personal identity. That is, an important part of themselves is lost, seriously affecting self-concept.

2. *Fear and anxiety.* When injured, many athletes experience high levels of fear and anxiety. They worry whether they will recover, if reinjury will occur, and whether someone will replace them permanently in the lineup. Because the athlete

cannot practice and compete there's plenty of time for worry.

3. *Lack of confidence.* Given the inability to practice and compete and their deteriorated physical status, athletes may lose confidence after an injury. Lowered confidence can result in decreased motivation, inferior performance, or even additional injury if the athlete overcompensates.

4. *Performance decrements.* Because of lowered confidence and missed practice time, athletes may suffer postinjury performance declines. Many athletes have difficulty lowering their expectations after an injury, and may expect to return to a preinjury level of performance.

The loss of personal identity is especially significant to athletes who define themselves solely through sport. Individuals who suffer a career or activity-ending injury may require special, often long-term, psychological care.

Signs of Poor Adjustment to Injury

Most people work through their responses to injury, showing some negative emotions but not great difficulty in coping. A recent national survey of athletic trainers revealed that they refer 8% of their clients to psychological counseling (Larson, Starkey, & Zaichkowsky, 1996). How can you tell whether an athlete or exerciser exhibits a "normal" injury response or is having serious difficulties that require special attention?

The following list of symptoms are warning signs of poor adjustment to athletic injuries (Petitpas & Danish, 1995):

- Feelings of anger and confusion
- Obsession with the question of when one can return to play
- Denial (e.g., "The injury is no big deal.")
- Repeatedly coming back too soon and experiencing reinjury
- Exaggerated braggings about accomplishments
- Dwelling on minor physical complaints
- Guilt about letting the team down
- Withdrawal from significant others
- Rapid mood swings
- Statements indicating that no matter what is done, recovery will not occur

If a fitness instructor or coach observes someone with these symptoms, he or she should discuss the situation with a sports medicine specialist and suggest the specialized help of a sport psychologist or counselor.

Role of Sport Psychology in Injury Rehabilitation

Tremendous gains have been made in recent years in the rehabilitation of athletic and exercise-related injuries. An active recovery, less invasive surgical techniques, and weight training are among these advances in the methods for rehabilitation. New psychological techniques also facilitate the injury-recovery process, and professionals increasingly use a holistic approach to healing both the mind and body. Understanding the psychology of injury recovery is important for everyone involved in sport and exercise.

Psychology of Recovery

In a study of how psychological strategies help injury rehabilitation, Ievleva and Orlick (1991) tried to determine if athletes with fast-healing (fewer than 5 weeks) knee and ankle injuries demonstrated greater use of psychological strategies and skills than those with slow-healing (more than 16 weeks) injuries. The researchers conducted interviews, assessing attitude and outlook, stress and stress control, social support, positive self-talk, healing imagery, goal setting, and beliefs. They found that fast-healing athletes used more goal setting, positive self-talk strategies, and, to a lesser degree, healing imagery than did slow-healing athletes. This suggests that psychological factors play an important role in injury recovery. In essence, injury treatment should include psychological techniques to enhance the healing and recovery process.

Surveys of athletic trainers support this conclusion (Gordon, Milios, & Grove, 1991; Larson, Starkey, & Zaichkowsky, 1996; Wiese, Weiss, & Yukelson, 1991). Larson and his colleagues, for example, asked 482 athletic trainers to identify the primary characteristics of athletes who most or least successfully coped with their injuries. The trainers observed that athletes who more successfully coped with their injuries differed from their less successful counterparts in the following ways: They complied better with their rehabilitation and treatment programs; demonstrated a more positive attitude about their injury status and life in general; were more motivated, dedicated, and determined; and

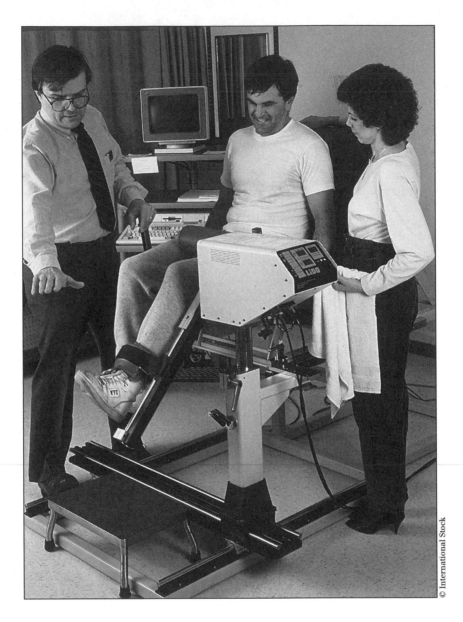

asked more questions and became more knowledgeable about their injuries. Some 90% of these trainers also reported that it was important or very important to treat the psychological aspects of injuries.

Implications for Injury Treatment and Recovery

Descriptive studies clearly show that a holistic approach is to be recommended, one that supplements physical therapy with psychological strategies to facilitate recovery from injuries. The psychological aspects of injury rehabilitation are derived from understanding responses to injury. However, understanding the process of injury response is not enough. Several psychological procedures and techniques facilitate the rehabilitation process, including building rapport with the injured athlete, educating her or him about the injury and recovery process, teaching specific psychological coping skills, preparing her or him to cope with setbacks, fostering social support, and learning from other injured athletes.

We'll discuss these in more detail in the following section. It is the sport psychologist's or trainer's responsibility to learn and administer these procedures as appropriate.

Build Rapport With the Injured Person

When athletes and exercisers become injured, they often experience disbelief, frustration, anger, confusion, and vulnerability. These emotions can make it difficult for helpers to establish rapport with the injured person. Showing empathy is helpful—that is, trying to understand how the injured person feels.

Showing emotional support and striving to be there for the injured party also help. Visit, phone, and show your concern for the person. This is especially important after the novelty of the injury has worn off and the exerciser or athlete feels forgotten. In building rapport, be careful not to be overly optimistic about a quick recovery. Instead, be positive and stress a team approach to recovery. ("This is a tough break, Mary, and you'll have to work hard to get through this injury. But I'm in this with you, and together we'll get you back.")

Educate the Injured Person About the Injury and Recovery Process

Especially when someone is working through a first injury, it is important to tell him what to expect during the recovery process. Help him understand the injury in practical terms. For example, if a high school wrestler suffers a clavicular fracture (broken collar bone), you might bring in a green stick and show him what his partial "green stick" break looks like. Explain that he will be out of competition for about 3 months. Equally important, you should tell him that in 1 month his shoulder will feel much better. Tell him he will likely be tempted to try to resume some normal activities too soon, which might cause a setback.

Outlining the specific recovery process is important. For instance, the athletic trainer may indicate that a wrestler can ride an exercise cycle in 2 to 3 weeks, begin range-of-movement exercises in 2 months, and follow this with a weight program until his preinjury strength levels in the affected area have been regained. Then and only then may he return to wrestling, first in drill situations and slowly progressing back to full contact. (For a comprehensive discussion of the progressive rehabilitation process, see Tippett and Voight's *Functional Progressions for Sport Rehabilitation*, 1994.)

Teach Specific Psychological Coping Skills

The most important psychological skills to learn for rehabilitation are goal setting, positive self-talk, imagery visualization, and relaxation training (Hardy

For complete recovery, both physical and psychological aspects of injury rehabilitation must be considered.

& Crace, 1990; Petitpas & Danish, 1995; Wiese & Weiss, 1987).

Goal setting can be especially useful for athletes rehabilitating from injury. For example, Theodorakis, Malliou, Papaioannou, Beneca, and Filactakidou (1996) found that setting personal performance goals with knee-injured participants facilitated performance, just as it did with uninjured individuals. They concluded that, combined with strategies designed to enhance self-efficacy, setting personal performance goals can be especially helpful in decreasing athlete's recovery time.

Some goal-setting strategies to use with injured athletes and exercisers are setting a date to return to competition; the number of times per week to come to the training room for therapy; and the number of range-of-motion, strength, and endurance exercises to do during recovery sessions. Highly motivated athletes tend to do more than is required during therapy, and they might reinjure themselves by overdoing it. Thus, it is important to emphasize the need to stick to goal plans and not do more when they feel better on a given day.

Self-talk strategies are important for counteracting the lowered confidence that can follow injury. Athletes should learn to stop their negative thoughts ("I am never going to get better") and replace them with realistic, positive ones ("I'm feeling down today, but I'm still on target with my rehabilitation plan—I just need to be patient and I'll make it back").

Visualization is useful in several ways during rehabilitation. An injured player can visualize herself in game conditions to maintain her playing skills and facilitate her return to competition. Or someone might use imagery to quicken recovery, visualizing the removal of injured tissue and the growth of new healthy tissue and muscle. This may sound far-fetched, but healing imagery often characterizes fast-healing patients (see study on the healing from knee injury, Ievleva

Build rapport with the injured party by:
- *taking her perspective (thinking how she must feel)*
- *providing emotional support, and*
- *being realistic but positive and optimistic.*

> *Highly motivated people tend to overdo. A recovering athlete should not exceed the program because she feels better on a given day.*

> *Prepare the injured person for coping with setbacks during the recovery process.*

& Orlick, 1991). The box below also describes how one sport psychologist used her knowledge of imagery and other sport psychological skills to battle cancer and extend her life (healing imagery originated from advances in nontraditional cancer treatments).

Relaxation training can be useful to relieve pain and stress, which usually accompany severe injury and the injury-recovery process. Athletes can also employ relaxation techniques to facilitate sleep and reduce general levels of tension.

Teach How to Cope With Setbacks

Injury rehabilitation is not a precise science. People recover at different rates, and setbacks are not uncommon. Thus, it is extremely important to prepare an injured person to cope with setbacks. Inform him or her during the rapport stage that setbacks will likely occur. At the same time, encourage the athlete to keep a positive attitude toward recovery. Setbacks are normal and not a cause for panic, so there's no reason to be discouraged.

Similarly, rehabilitation goals will need evaluation and periodic redefining. To help teach people coping skills, encourage them to inform significant others when they experience setbacks. By discussing their feelings, they can receive the necessary social support.

Foster Social Support

Social support of injured athletes can take many forms, including emotional support from friends and loved ones; informational support from a coach, such as "You're on the right track"; and even tangible support, such as money from parents (Hardy & Crace, 1991). Injured athletes need social support. They need to know that their coaches and teammates care, that people will listen to their concerns without judging them, and how others have recovered from similar injuries.

It is a mistake to assume that adequate social support occurs automatically. As previously noted, social support tends to be more available immediately after an injury and become less frequent during the later stages of recovery. Remember that injured

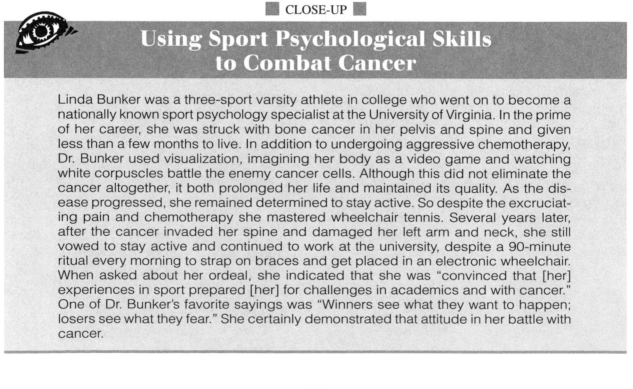

■ CLOSE-UP ■

Using Sport Psychological Skills to Combat Cancer

Linda Bunker was a three-sport varsity athlete in college who went on to become a nationally known sport psychology specialist at the University of Virginia. In the prime of her career, she was struck with bone cancer in her pelvis and spine and given less than a few months to live. In addition to undergoing aggressive chemotherapy, Dr. Bunker used visualization, imagining her body as a video game and watching white corpuscles battle the enemy cancer cells. Although this did not eliminate the cancer altogether, it both prolonged her life and maintained its quality. As the disease progressed, she remained determined to stay active. So despite the excruciating pain and chemotherapy she mastered wheelchair tennis. Several years later, after the cancer invaded her spine and damaged her left arm and neck, she still vowed to stay active and continued to work at the university, despite a 90-minute ritual every morning to strap on braces and get placed in an electronic wheelchair. When asked about her ordeal, she indicated that she was "convinced that [her] experiences in sport prepared [her] for challenges in academics and with cancer." One of Dr. Bunker's favorite sayings was "Winners see what they want to happen; losers see what they fear." She certainly demonstrated that attitude in her battle with cancer.

people benefit from receiving adequate social support throughout the recovery process.

Learn From Injured Athletes

Another good way to help injured athletes and exercisers cope with injury is to heed the recommendations they themselves make. Members of a U.S. ski team who sustained season-ending injuries made several suggestions for injured athletes, the coaches working with them, and sports medicine providers (Gould, Udry, Bridges, & Beck, 1996, 1997a). These are summarized in Table 19.1, and they should be considered both by injured athletes and those assisting them.

Table 19.1

Elite Skiers Recommendations for Coping With Season-Ending Injuries and Facilitating Rehabilitation

RECOMMENDATIONS FOR		
Other injured athletes	Coaches	Sports medicine personnel
Read body and pace self accordingly.	Foster coach-athlete contact and involvement.	Educate and inform athlete of injury and rehabilitation.
Accept and positively deal with situation.	Demonstrate positive empathy and support.	Use appropriate motivation and optimally push.
Focus on quality training.	Understand individual variations in injuries and injury emotions.	Demonstrate empathy and support.
Find and use medical resources.	Motivate by optimally pushing.	Have supportive personality (be warm, open, and not overly confident).
Use social resources wisely.	Engineer training environment for high quality, individualized training.	Foster positive interaction and customize training.
Set goals.	Have patience and realistic expectations.	Demonstrate competence and confidence.
Feel confident with medical staff coaches.	Don't repeatedly mention injury in training.	Encourage athlete's confidence.
Work on mental-skills training.		
Use imagery/visualization.		
Initiate/maintain competitive atmosphere and involvement.		

SUMMARY

1 *Discuss the role of psychological factors in athletic and exercise injuries.*

Psychological factors influence the incidence of injury, responses to injury, and injury recovery. Professionals in our field must be prepared to initiate teaching and coaching practices that help prevent the onset of injuries, assist in the injury-coping process when injuries are sustained, and provide supportive psychological environments to facilitate injury recovery.

2 *Identify psychological antecedents that may predispose people to athletic injuries.*

Psychological factors, including stress and certain attitudes, can predispose athletes and exercisers to injuries. Professional sport and exercise science personnel must recognize antecedent conditions, especially major life stressors, in individuals who have poor coping skills and little social support.

3 *Compare and contrast explanations for the stress-injury relationship.*

When high levels of stress are identified, stress-management procedures should be implemented and training regimens adjusted. Athletes must learn to distinguish between the normal discomfort of training and the pain of injury. They should understand that a "no pain, no gain" attitude can predispose them to injury.

4 *Describe typical psychological reactions to injuries.*

Injured athletes and exercisers exhibit various psychological reactions, typically falling into three categories: injury-relevant information processing, emotional upheaval and reactive behavior, and positive outlook and coping. Increased fear and anxiety, lowered confidence, and performance decrements also commonly occur in injured athletes.

5 *Identify signs of poor adjustment to injury.*

If you work with an injured athlete or exerciser, be vigilant in monitoring warning signs of poor adjustment to an injury. These include feelings of anger and confusion, obsession with the question of when one can return to play, denial (e.g., "The injury is no big deal"), repeatedly coming back too soon and experiencing reinjury, exaggerated braggings about accomplishments, dwelling on minor physical complaints, guilt about letting the team down, withdrawal from significant others, rapid mood swings, and statements indicating that no matter what is done, recovery will not occur.

6 *Exlain how to implement psychological skills and strategies that can speed the rehabilitation process.*

Psychological foundations of injury rehabilitation include building rapport with the injured individual; educating him or her about the nature of the injury and the injury-recovery process; teaching specific psychological coping skills, such as goal setting, relaxation techniques, and imagery; preparing him or her to cope with setbacks in rehabilitation; and fostering social support. Athletes themselves have also made specific injury-coping recommendations that are useful for other injured athletes, coaches, and sports medicine providers.

KEY TERMS

grief response   social support

REVIEW QUESTIONS

1. What is the Andersen and Williams (1988) stress-injury relationship model? Why is it important?

2. What three categories of psychological factors are related to the occurrence of athletic and exercise injuries?

3. Identify two explanations for the stress-injury relationship.

4. Describe three general categories of emotional reactions to athletic injuries.

5. What are common symptoms of poor adjustment to athletic and exercise injuries?

6. What strategies did Ievleva and Orlick (1991) find associated with enhanced healing in knee-injured athletes? Why are these findings important?

7. Give five implications for working with exercisers and athletes during injury treatment and recovery, briefly identifying and describing each.

CRITICAL THINKING QUESTIONS

1. A close friend suffers a major knee injury and needs surgery. What have you learned that can help you prepare your friend for surgery and recovery?

2. Design a persuasive speech to convince a sports medicine center to hire a sport psychology specialist. How would you convince the center's directors that patients or clients would benefit?

© Terry Wild Studio

Addictive and Unhealthy Behaviors

After reading this chapter you should be able to

1 define and discuss the prevalence of eating disorders in sport,
2 identify predisposing factors for developing eating disorders,
3 describe how to recognize disordered eating,
4 define and discuss the prevalence of substance abuse in sport,
5 explain why some athletes and exercisers take drugs,
6 discuss how to detect and prevent substance abuse, and
7 discuss the problem of compulsive sports gambling.

In 1988 Canadian sprinter Ben Johnson set a world and Olympic record in the 100-meter dash but was later disqualified when he tested positive for steroid use. Johnson left the Olympic games in shame. Former NFL great Lyle Alzado was never caught taking steroids, but after retirement he admitted using massive amounts of steroids throughout his career and attributed the cancer that ended his life prematurely to substance abuse. University of Maryland basketball star Len Bias did not use steroids. He tried cocaine only once—and died of cocaine-induced heart failure just before he was to have embarked on his NBA career. He died not because he was a drug addict but because he decided to celebrate with a recreational drug. Although tennis star Zina Garrison never abused drugs, she had another problem: food. In response to stress and other psychological problems she suffered from bulimia, an eating disorder that involves food binges and self-induced vomiting.

Elite gymnast Christy Henrich not only suffered from anorexia but she also died from it. Art Schlichter, former professional football quarterback who was touted while an All-American at Ohio State, progressed from being an occasional visitor at race tracks to betting with a bookie on pro sports and later on to being a full-fledged gambler. His addiction to gambling and the actions he took to secure the money to pay his losses landed him in prison.

Addictive and unhealthy behaviors certainly are not limited to elite athletes. Even high school and youth sport participants abuse drugs, steroids, alcohol, and smokeless tobacco; people also are known to start gambling at a young age. Like it or not, physical education, sport, and exercise professionals must be prepared to deal with these issues.

Substance abuse, eating disorders, and compulsive gambling are clinical problems requiring treatment by specialists. Still, nonspecialists must learn to detect signs of these conditions and refer afflicted exercisers, students, and athletes to specialists for the treatment they need. Let us begin with a discussion of eating disorders.

Anorexia nervosa is a psychobiological disease characterized by an intense fear of becoming obese, a disturbed body image, a significant weight loss, the refusal to maintain normal body weight, and amenorrhea.

Eating Disorders

Anorexia nervosa and bulimia are the two most common eating disorders. Before we discuss the prevalence and potential treatment of these conditions, here are some relevant definitions. According to the *Diagnostic and Statistical Manual of Mental Disorders* (American Psychiatric Association, 1994) anorexia nervosa includes the following characteristics:

- Weight loss leading to body weight maintained at least 15% below expected norms
- Intense fear of gaining weight or becoming fat, despite being underweight
- Disturbance in how one's body weight, size, or shape is experienced (e.g., feeling fat even when obviously underweight)
- In females, the absence of at least three consecutive menstrual cycles otherwise expected to occur

Anorexia is potentially fatal; it can lead to starvation and other medical complications, such as heart disease. In addition, it is a severe condition made worse because the affected individual often doesn't see himself or herself as abnormal.

The diagnostic criteria for bulimia include the following (American Psychiatric Association, 1994):

- Recurrent episodes of binge eating (rapid consumption of large quantities of food)
- A sense of lacking control over eating behavior during the binges
- Engaging in regular self-induced vomiting, use of laxatives or diuretics, strict dieting or fasting, or vigorous exercise in order to prevent weight gain
- An average minimum of two binge-eating episodes a week for at least three months
- Persistent overconcern with body shape and weight

Bulimia is an episodic eating pattern of uncontrollable food bingeing followed by purging; it is characterized by an awareness that the pattern is abnormal, fear of being unable to stop eating voluntarily, depressed mood, and self-deprecation.

■ CASE STUDY ■

Maggie's Weight-Loss Tragedy

Maggie is 26 years old and weighs 73 pounds. She was once a sleek, powerful all-conference athlete in soccer and an academic All-American. Before that she was a high school homecoming queen, voted most likely to succeed. Now Maggie is in intensive care at Tacoma University Hospital. Her doctors give her only a few weeks to live because heart complications resulting from her 15-year battle with anorexia and bulimia have gone well beyond the treatment phase. Ironically, even now Maggie sees herself not as emaciated and malnourished but as bloated and obese.

Maggie comes from an upper middle-class home and has two loving parents and a wonderful older sister. Yet ever since her early teenage years she has felt pressured to live up to her parents' high expectations—socially, academically, and athletically. Moreover, following in the footsteps of a highly successful sister has been no easy task.

No one ever chastised Maggie for failing or even voiced specific expectations. However, her parents and friends always seemed so pleased when she did well in school or on the athletic field, and constantly talked about the contributions she would make to her community. And Maggie always remembered how much her mom and dad bragged to the relatives about her achievements.

Inside, however, Maggie was not doing well. She was not confident, despite her many accomplishments and immense talent. In fact, she began to dread succeeding, because with each new accomplishment came higher expectations from her parents, coaches, teachers, and even peers. By the time Maggie entered college, she felt she had to be perfect.

Maggie also wanted to look like the swimsuit models who saturated popular magazines; she was very conscious of her weight. However, she was a short, mesomorphic woman who added muscle mass to her frame easily, especially when she lifted weights. She can still remember how hurt she was when she overheard one of her teammates refer to her as "thunderthighs." She dreaded every Monday when she had to be weighed in front of her soccer teammates. Finally, Coach Peterson challenged the team to develop speed by everyone's shedding a few pounds.

The more Maggie's coaches talked about weight, the more self-conscious she became about her appearance and eating. She tried the water diet, the grapefruit diet, and the protein diet, but she felt so hungry after practice and with the academic, social, and athletic stresses that she ate more. Although she was never overweight, her weight bounced around like a yo-yo.

Then one day Maggie found her solution: She would eat whatever she pleased whenever she wanted and then later, in private, either make herself throw up or take an abundance of laxatives. This made her feel she had some control over her weight, although her energy level was down and she often felt guilty about her uncontrolled eating. She also started exercising more, getting up and running 4 miles in the morning, going to practice in the afternoon, and then running again and working on the StairMaster in the evening.

Maggie hid her eating habits throughout her college days, but after college she slipped slowly into a pattern of eating less and less. Her weight dropped and she began to exercise more, despite developing a stress fracture from running. At first she felt good about her weight loss and her friends' comments about it. Later, when her weight dropped well below her optimal level, she did not believe her friends' and parents' concerns about her "low" body weight. If they asked about her eating habits and low weight she would change the subject and deny the problem. In fact, convinced she was still overweight, she wore baggy clothes to cover up the layers of fat she perceived. She dreaded looking in the mirror because she hated the obese person she saw.

One day Maggie fainted while visiting her parents, and when her dad picked her up to put her on the couch, he realized she was just skin and bones under all of those sweatshirts. Her parents insisted that she see the family doctor, who immediately recommended an institution, where Maggie was force-fed. Behavior therapy helped some, but suffering from her severe eating disorder for more than a decade caused permanent damage to Maggie's internal organs, and the prognosis remains bleak.

A bulimic person often becomes depressed because of low self-esteem, eats excessively in an effort to feel better (bingeing), then feels guilty about eating, and induces vomiting or takes laxatives to purge the food. Although a severe problem, bulimia is usually less severe than anorexia. The person with bulimia is aware he or she has a problem, whereas the anorexic is not. Bulimia can lead to anorexia, and some individuals are characterized as bulimarexic. Within each disorder are progressive stages of involvement. Let's now look at the prevalence of eating disorders in sport.

Prevalence of Eating Disorders in Sport

An accurate assessment of the prevalence of bulimia and anorexia in any population is difficult to achieve due to the secretive nature of these disorders. In the competitive sport environment an athlete also risks being dropped from a program or team if his or her eating problem is discovered. The accuracy of studies assessing eating disorders in sport is also questionable, the validity of many of the questionnaires utilized to measure eating problems being doubtful. Finally, many investigations have not specifically determined the prevalence of clinical eating disorders, but instead have focused on describing the frequency of eating-disordered behaviors. Although discovering the prevalence of various eating problems, such as quick weight loss to make the necessary weight in wrestling, is important (highlighted by the recent deaths of collegiate wrestlers), it should not be construed as an estimate of eating disorders. Because of these assessment problems, you should view even the data we present here with caution.

Various researchers (e.g., Brewer & Petrie, 1996; Brownell & Rodin, 1992; Swoap & Murphy, 1995) have tried to summarize the prevalence of eating disorders in sport. These are some of their general conclusions:

- Athletes appear to have a greater occurrence of eating-related problems than does the general population.

- A significant percentage of athletes engage in pathogenic eating or weight-loss behaviors (e.g., binge eating, rigorous dieting, fasting,

© Steve Lange

vomiting, use of diuretics), and these are important to examine even though they are subclinical in intensity.

■ Eating disorders among athletes and their use of pathogenic weight-loss techniques tend to have a sport-specific prevalence (e.g., they occur more among gymnasts and wrestlers than in archers or basketball players).

Although anorexia and bulimia are of special concern in sports emphasizing form (e.g., gymnastics, diving, and figure skating) or weight (e.g., wrestling), athletes with eating disorders have been found in a wide array of sports.

Predisposing Factors

It is important for coaches, physical education teachers, exercise leaders, athletic trainers and parents to understand the factors that might predispose an athlete to develop an eating disorder. Although some of these factors include genetics, personality, and family background, which are largely stable and unchangeable, other factors relating to the athletic and sociocultural environment are more unstable and amenable to change. Knowing these factors might help you prevent or reduce the probability of an eating disorder occurring in someone—or yourself. Swoap and Murphy (1995) outline the factors we now describe.

Weight Restrictions and Standards

Sports such as weightlifting, wrestling, and boxing commonly use weight classifications (based on body weight) to subdivide competitors. Oftentimes athletes try to "make weight" so they can compete at a lower weight classification, which presumably would give them an advantage against a lighter opponent. This can result in their trying to drop up to 10 or even 15 pounds immediately before weigh-ins, usually resulting primarily in rapid dehydration. Fasting, fluid restriction, and the use of diuretics, laxatives, and purging are all techniques to achieve this rapid weight loss. These techniques, especially if done repeatedly, and the resulting rapid dehydration can have both short- and long-term negative health consequences. Coaches and trainers should discourage these weight-loss methods, even those that are embedded in the sport culture.

Coach and Peer Pressure

Coaches and peers can play an important role in shaping the attitude and behaviors of athletes. Unfortunately coaches sometimes knowingly or unknowingly exert pressure on athletes to lose weight,

even when they know safe and effective weight-management procedures. Therefore, practice good preventive medicine by being careful about *how you comment* to the students, athletes, and clients with whom you work about weight gain or weight loss. You never know when an off-hand comment, even one meant in jest, could be taken the wrong way and contribute to an eating disorder. The following account from the *Austin American Statesman* newspaper describes a coach who promoted unhealthy attitudes toward weight and weight reduction:

> *The coach emphasized weight in training and competition and insisted that his swimmers remain under maximum weight limits. Those who failed to do so were required to participate in special workouts. According to current and former swimmers, the pressure to meet those guidelines were so intense that many routinely fasted, induced vomiting, used laxatives and diuretics, or exercised in addition to workouts. They did not want to be relegated to the group they called "The Fat Club." Primarily, the pressure came from the coach, until you started to internalize it. Then it became self-inflicted torture, almost to where some people would weigh themselves three or four times a day. (Halliburton & Sanford, 1989, pp. D1, D7)*

Many coaches also demonstrate relatively negative attitudes toward and limited knowledge about obesity (Griffin & Harris, 1996). Some of them tend to decide about the need for weight control based on appearance rather than objective indicators (e.g., body fat assessments). Besides coaches, peers can also pressure one another in weight-reducing behaviors. Athletes spend a lot of time with their teammates, both on and off the court or field, and often they influence the onset of unhealthy eating behaviors. In fact, it has been reported that athletes learn these behaviors from observing teammates.

Performance Demands

Over the last 20 years, there has been an increased focus on the relationship between body weight or body fat and performance. In fact, research has indicated that there is a correlation between a low-percent body fat and high levels of performance in a number of sports (Wilmore, 1992). This has led many coaches and athletes to focus on weight control in an attempt to reach their optimal weight. However, at times this type of information has been inappropriately applied, often pushing athletes well below their optimal body weight. Lower body fat does not always mean better performance. Individual

417

differences are critical here and strict weight standards are therefore inappropriate. As Wilmore (1992) suggests, there is typically a range of values for body fat related to optimal performance, and ideal levels vary between males and females as well.

Judging Criteria

In sports where physical attractiveness, especially for females, is considered important for success (gymnastics, figure skating, diving), coaches and athletes may perceive that judges tend to be biased toward certain body types. Very slender body builds are often seen as desirable, and this is typically communicated to the athletes in informal ways. Specifically, anecdotal reports reveal that comments about losing a few pounds to look better are unfortunately communicated from judges to athletes. These, of course, have sometimes led athletes to disordered eating to achieve the desired look and body type. The following quote by a national champion figure skater describes how appearances are perceived to be tied to judging criteria:

Skating is such an appearance sport. You have to go up there with barely anything on. . . . I'm definitely aware of [my weight]. I mean I have

Fitness professionals must be able to recognize the physical and psychological signs of eating disorders.

dreams about it sometimes. So it's hard having people look at my thigh and saying "Oops, she's an eighth of an inch bigger" or something. It's hard. . . . Weight is continually on my mind. I am never, never allowed to be on vacation. (Gould, Jackson, & Finch, 1993, p. 364)

Recognition and Referral of an Eating Problem

Physical educators, exercise leaders, athletic trainers, and coaches are in an excellent position to spot individuals with eating disorders. Thus, they must be able to recognize the physical and psychological signs and symptoms of these conditions (see Table 20.1). Often, unusual eating patterns are among the best indicators of problems. Anorexics often pick at their food, push it around their plates, eat predominantly low-calorie foods, and then lie about their

Table 20.1

Physical and Psychological-Behavioral Signs of Eating Disorders

Physical signs	Psychological-behavioral signs
Weight too low	Excessive dieting
Considerable weight loss	Excessive eating without weight gain
Extreme weight fluctuations	Excessive exercise that is not part of normal training program
Bloating	Guilt about eating
Swollen salivary glands	Claims of feeling fat at normal weight despite reassurance from others
Amenorrhea	Preoccupation with food
Carotinemia—yellowish palms or soles of feet	Avoidance of eating in public and denial of hunger
Sores or callouses on knuckles or back of hand from inducing vomiting	Hoarding food
Hypoglycemia—low blood sugar	Disappearing after meals
Muscle cramps	Frequent weighing
Stomach complaints	Binge eating
Headaches, dizziness, or weakness from electrolyte disturbances	Evidence of self-induced vomiting
Numbness and tingling in limbs due to electrolyte disturbances	Use of drugs such as diet pills, laxatives, or diuretics to control weight
Stress fractures	

Adapted from Garner and Rosen, 1991.

eating. Bulimics often hide food and disappear after eating (so they can purge the food just eaten). Whenever possible, fitness educators should observe the eating patterns of students and athletes, looking for abnormalities. There are also standardized self-report inventories to diagnose eating disorders, but these should only be administered and interpreted by trained professionals (e.g., a licensed psychologist).

As a coach, teacher, athletic trainer, or exercise leader, if you identify someone who demonstrates symptoms, you'll need to solicit help from a specialist familiar with eating disorders. Some people exhibit some of these signs without having a disorder. Others are afflicted, and it would be a serious mistake to think the problem will correct itself.

If you or a colleague suspects an eating disorder, the person who has the best rapport with the individual should schedule a private meeting to discuss his or her concerns (Garner & Rosen, 1991). The emphasis here should be on feelings, rather than directly focusing on eating behaviors. Be supportive in such instances and keep all information confidential. Make a referral then to a specific clinic or person, rather than giving a vague recommendation such as "You should seek some help." If an athlete is still hesitant, suggest that he or she see the referral person simply for an assessment to determine if there is

■ APPLICATION ■

Preventing Eating Disorders in Athletes and Exercisers

Although it is important for professionals to be able to recognize and effectively deal with eating disorders among participants in sport and exercise settings, an even greater contribution would be to help prevent or at least reduce the probability of these disorders' occurrence in the first place. Here are some suggestions for being proactive in reducing eating disorders in athletes and exercisers.

- *Promote proper nutritional practices.* Research indicates that many sport participants have limited information or incorrect views on proper sport nutrition. Many individuals turn to coaches, trainers, and peers for nutritional advice, and these exercisers and athletic personnel should therefore become educated about good nutrition and methods of weight control (*Coaches' Guide to Nutrition and Weight Control* [Eisenman, Johnson, & Benson, 1990] is one good source of nutritional information).

- *Focus on fitness, not body weight.* We must move the focus away from obsessing about weight to fitness itself. There is no ideal body composition or weight for an athlete or exerciser. At any rate, appropriate weight and body composition fluctuate greatly, depending on the type of sport, body build, metabolic rate, and natural variations in a person's body composition. Rather, an ideal *range* might better be targeted, with input from professionals such as nutritionists and exercise physiologists.

- *Be sensitive to weight issues.* Athletic personnel should be made aware of the issues athletes contend with regarding weight control and diet, and they should act with sensitivity in these areas. Coaches and fitness leaders often exert powerful influence on individuals, and they should exercise care when making remarks about weight control. Practices such as repeated weigh-ins, associating weight loss with enhanced performance, setting arbitrary weight goals, and making unfeeling remarks must be avoided at all costs.

- *Promote healthy management of weight.* As the incidence of and focus on disordered eating practices in sport and exercise have increased in recent years, so too has the availability of educational material. For example, the NCAA produced an informative set of three videos along with supportive educational material on eating disorders in sport (National Collegiate Athletic Association, 1989). Sport and exercise science professionals need to keep up with the latest information regarding weight loss and eating disorders. In this way they not only can pass this information along to sport and exercise participants but also help inform their teaching and coaching.

a problem. Several dos and don'ts regarding eating disorders are presented in Table 20.2. (For comprehensive treatment of the many issues and variables of this complex subject, see Thompson and Sherman's *Helping Athletes With Eating Disorders,* 1993.)

Substance Abuse

It is no secret that performance-enhancing drugs have been used by world-class athletes and Olympians for decades, or that some athletes will do almost anything to gain a competitive advantage. What is surprising is that despite the dire warnings of the negative psychological and physiological effects of steroids and other performance-enhancing drugs, their use appears on the upswing. Even the threat of death is evidently not a deterrent as long as victory is guaranteed. Consider the results from a 1995 poll of 198 sprinters, swimmers, power lifters, and other athletes, most of them U.S. Olympians or aspiring Olympians, who were given the following scenarios:

> *You are offered a banned performance-enhancing substance with two guarantees: (a) you will not be caught, and (b) you will win. Would you take the substance?*

> *You are offered a banned performance-enhancing substance that comes with two guarantees:*

(a) you will not be caught, and (b) you will win every competition you enter for the next five years and then die from the side effects of the substance. Would you take the substance?

In answering the first question, 195 athletes said yes; three said no—a stunning 98%. Even more shocking, in answering the second question, 120 of the athletes still said yes (approximately 60%) and 75 said no.

Fortunately, not all drugs are bad or even out of place in sport or physical activity settings. Drugs are useful tools in sports medicine. Imagine undergoing surgery without pain-killing drugs or treating a serious infection without antibiotics. Some drugs can offset intense pain and enhance healing. So drugs per se are not the problem as long as the drugs being used are legal, are prescribed by appropriate medical personnel, and are not one of the banned substances in the world of competitive sport. In essence, it's the misuse of drugs and the use of illegal and harmful drugs that are the real problems in sport and exercise environments. And abuse occurs both with performance-enhancing drugs, such as steroids, and so-called recreational or social drugs, such as cocaine and marijuana.

People abuse drugs for different reasons but with the same negative consequences. Substance abuse can lead to long-term, sometimes fatal, health and psychological problems, including addiction. The *Diagnostic and Statistical Manual of Mental Disorders* (American Psychiatric Association, 1994) lists

Table 20.2
Dealing With Eating Disorders: Dos and Don'ts

Dos	Dont's
Get help and advice from a specialist.	Ask the athlete to leave team or curtail participation, unless so instructed by a specialist.
Be supportive and empathetic.	
Express concern about general feelings, not specifically about weight.	Recommend weight loss or gain.
	Hold team weigh-ins.
Make referrals to a specific person and, when possible, make appointments for them.	Single out or treat the individual unlike other participants.
Emphasize the importance of long-term good nutrition.	Talk about the problem with nonprofessionals who are not directly involved.
Provide information about eating disorders.	Demand the problem be stopped immediately.
	Make insensitive remarks or tease individuals regarding their weight.

Adapted from Garner and Rosen, 1991.

© Terry Wild Studio

the following criteria as indicating psychoactive substance abuse:

A. A maladaptive pattern of psychoactive substance use indicated by at least one of the following:

1. Continued use despite knowledge of having a persistent or recurring social, occupational, psychological, or physical problem that is caused or exacerbated by use of the psychoactive substance.

2. Recurrent use in situations in which the use is physically hazardous (e.g., driving while intoxicated).

B. Some symptoms of the disturbance have persisted for at least one month, or have occurred repeatedly over a longer period of time.

Any psychoactive substance including alcohol, marijuana, cocaine, amphetamines, and hallucinogens can be included in this diagnostic criteria. Identifying

Drug addiction is a state in which both discontinuing or continuous use of a drug creates an overwhelming desire, need, and craving for more of the substance.

signs and symptoms of substance use and abuse will be discussed later in the chapter.

An in-depth examination of how substance abuse affects athletes is beyond our scope here. For more detailed information, we recommend several excellent books on the subject (Asken, 1988; Stainback, 1997; Tricker & Cook, 1990; Voy & Deeter, 1991). For our purposes here we'll concentrate on four issues: (a) prevalence of substance abuse; (b) why athletes and exercisers take and abuse drugs; (c) major drug categories and their effects; and (d) the fitness or sport professional's role in preventing and detecting substance abuse.

Prevalence of Substance Abuse in Sports

Similar to the reporting of eating disorders, it is inherently difficult to get an accurate picture of substance use and abuse due to its sensitive and personal nature. Thus, once again, you should view this data with caution. To begin with, there is much anecdotal evidence regarding substance use and abuse. For example, Tommy Chaikin, football player for the University of South Carolina, provided a poignant report on drug use in *Sports Illustrated* (1988). Chaikin's report gives significant insight into the numerous social and psychological pressures that foster drug use in sport (in this case anabolic steroids), including the encouragement of coaches and the pressures to succeed. From his abuse of steroids he developed chronic aggression, depression, testicular shrinkage, hair loss, insomnia, poor vision, chronic anxiety, hypertension, a heart murmur, and benign tumors—and almost died.

As alluded to by Chaikin, coaches often are knowingly involved implicitly or explicitly in their athletes' use of drugs. For example, after having his gold medal taken away, sprinter Ben Johnson asserted that his coach knowingly gave him a banned substance. "Charlie Francis was my coach. . . . If Charlie gave me something to take, I took it (*Time*, June 26, 1989, p. 57). Then there is a list of high profile professional athletes who have admitted to or been caught using illegal drugs or have abused alcohol, such as Dwight Gooden, John Daly, Darryl Strawberry, Dexter Manley, Steve Howe, Chris Mullen, and Roy Tarpley. In some cases, their careers have been terminated and they have served prison sentences for repeated drug use and violations of league policy.

In other cases, athletes who use performance-enhancing substances face less implicit consequences. Mark McGwire, under incredible pressure to beat Roger Maris's home run record, used steroids that were legal in baseball, although the long-term effects of such usage are not really known.

Looking at the scientific evidence, most of the studies have focused on alcohol and steroid use, sometimes with a good deal of variability among studies. One study found that 55% of high school athletes reported using alcohol in the past year (Green, Burke, Nix, Lambrecht, & Mason, 1996), whereas another (Carr, Kennedy, & Dimick, 1990) found 92% of high school athletes reported such alcohol use. In college samples, alcohol intake was consistent across studies, with reported uses being 88% (College of Human Medicine, 1985) and 87%

(Evans, Weinberg, & Jackson, 1992). Most studies show use of alcohol by male athletes to be higher than by nonathletes, whereas they find no significant differences between female athletes and nonathletes in drinking alcohol.

Regarding the use of performance-enhancing drugs, especially anabolic steroids, several large-scale studies conducted in the United States, Canada, Australia, and Europe showed in general that only a small percentage (usually less than 5%) of athletes and high school or college students reported using performance-enhancing drugs (see Anshel, 1997). Interestingly, many of the nonathletes (mostly males) took steroids to become more muscular—not to increase performance but rather to increase self-esteem and peer approval. However, the numbers of athletes reporting steroid use dramatically increases when elite Olympic level athletes are surveyed, their usage rates sometimes approaching 50%. In addition, when athletes are asked about the use of performance-enhancing drugs by their teammates, estimates again rise to between 40% and 60%. This is obviously an area where usage estimates must be viewed with extreme caution.

Still, the use of illegal drugs is minimal compared with the widespread use of legal drugs, such as alcohol and tobacco, the two most abused drugs in America. And sustained use of these substances has been linked to a host of negative health effects (see Table 20.3).

Why Athletes and Exercisers Take Drugs

Athletes and exercisers do not start out abusing drugs. Rather, they take them for what they perceive to be good reasons. Although the reasons for using performance-enhancing drugs might differ from recreational ones, we will group them together under three general categories: (a) physical, (b) psychological, and (c) social (see Anshel, 1993; 1997 for extensive reviews of the causes of drug use).

Physical Reasons

The most common physical reason for taking drugs is to enhance performance. Athletes take drugs to improve performance with the expectation that they might increase their strength, endurance, alertness, and aggression, or decrease their fatigue, reaction time, and anxiety. Winning is paramount and doing anything to improve performance is critical. However, performance-enhancing drugs have clearly documented health risks. In addition, taking drugs

Table 20.3

Negative Health Effects Associated With Prolonged Use of Alcohol and Tobacco

Substance	Negative health effect
Alcohol	Gastrointestinal diseases (e.g., ulcers) Liver damage Cardiovascular disease Cancers Brain damage Accidents, murders, and suicides
Nicotine	Lung, mouth, larynx, and esophagus cancers Emphysema Heart disease and irregularities
Smokeless tobacco (snuff)	Mouth cancer Gum damage

Adapted from Bump, 1988.

to enhance performance is clearly cheating. Those who take drugs and win must realize that winning is not a result solely of their action but is in part a result of cheating. If caught, they will be subjected to considerable public scorn. Even if they are not caught, they'll always know the victory was not their own.

Rehabilitation from injury is another physical reason why athletes take drugs. They will sometimes take drugs without a prescription from a doctor, trying to attenuate pain or to cope psychologically with the physical discomfort of the injury. Fear of losing a starting position is a reason athletes often give: They want to rush back from an injury and sometimes think drugs can speed that recovery process.

Many exercisers take drugs (especially steroids) simply to look better and be more attractive to the opposite sex. These individuals are not necessarily interested in performing better; rather they are concerned with simply having their bodies look good, strong, and firm.

Athletes take drugs, especially, amphetamines and diuretics, to control appetite and reduce fluid weight. These can reduce weight quickly, allowing athletes to compete in a lower weight classification (as noted earlier). Finally, athletes also take drugs to help them "psych up" and increase energy, perceived as especially important in such contact sports as football and hockey. Some exercisers also consider that taking diuretics to keep slim and trim is much easier than following a strict dietary regimen.

Psychological Reasons

By far the most common rationale for using recreational drugs among athletes is psychological or emotional. These drugs seem to offer a convenient escape from unpleasant emotions in the course of dealing with competitive experiences. Stress and anxiety are inherent in sport competition, and these pressures can be attenuated through the use of certain drugs. In addition, some individuals find that balancing academic pursuits, training schedules, and personal relationships provides extra stress. They sometimes use drugs to help deal with these pressures both on and off the field.

Still other athletes and exercisers use drugs to build self-confidence. Self-doubts about one's ability often haunt participants, and certain drugs can help make them feel better about their abilities and feel more competitive. Aggressive behavior, often seen as a side effect of taking steroids, can also give individuals a sense of invulnerability, which can temporarily enhance their self-confidence. Related to low self-confidence is a fear of failure, which is tied to an athlete's strong affiliation between sport success and self-esteem. Friends, parents, and coaches often set expectations of success that are too high, and then athletes might view drugs as a resource to help combat this source of stress and protect their self-esteem. Fitness and sport professionals therefore have an important role to play in enhancing participants' self-esteem. By doing so, they can provide a barrier to substance abuse. Fortunately, sport and physical activity themselves appear to be excellent vehicles for improving self-esteem.

Social Reasons

Perhaps there is no greater cause of drug use than social pressure. Pressure from peers and the need to gain group acceptance are especially apparent among adolescents who want to fit in. They may drink, smoke, or take performance-enhancing drugs not so much because they want to, but to be accepted by their peers. Sometimes adolescents become addicted before realizing that true friends like people for who they are, not for going along with the crowd. This is especially problematic for males who seem to be more prone to "macho behavior" in the desire to fit in with the group. Thus, it is important for teachers, coaches, and athletic trainers to repeatedly communicate the importance of being oneself and not giving in to pressure from so-called friends.

Athletes have become highly visible on television and through other media, and many youngsters use these professional, Olympic, and college athletes as role models. Therefore, the development of appropriate as well as inappropriate behaviors in young athletes is often derived from watching and reading about their sport heroes. For some youngsters making enormous amounts of money (e.g., long-term contracts worth more than $100 million) and becoming a national celebrity have become part of the culture to which they aspire. This combination seemingly provides easy access to drugs. Unfortunately, perceptions that these highly skilled athletes ingest drugs and the mind-set that "it doesn't hurt them so much so it won't hurt me" provide an attractive rationale for aspiring young athletes to take drugs (Anshel, 1997). In essence, drug use seems implicitly sanctioned to young athletes using professionals as a role model. This modeling effect is particularly influential during adolescence, when many youngsters are exploring their identities and often experimenting with drugs. To counter this, parents, coaches, teachers, and other professionals should provide alternative models for youngsters, with the focus on personal responsibility.

Major Drug Categories and Their Effects

In the sport and exercise realm drugs are classified by their purpose: (a) performance-enhancing drugs and (b) recreational, social, or street drugs. Performance-enhancing drugs include anabolic steroids, beta-blockers, and stimulants used by athletes or exercisers to increase strength, calm nerves, or block pain. Table 20.4 lists six general categories of performance-enhancing drugs, their potential performance-enhancing effects, and psychological and medical side effects associated with their use.

> *Reasons athletes and exercisers take drugs include*
> * *peer pressure,*
> * *thrill-seeking and curiosity,*
> * *the need to achieve success, and*
> * *wanting to increase self-esteem.*

Recreational drugs (also known as street drugs) are substances that people seek out and use for personal pleasure. They may be trying to escape pressures, fit in with friends who use drugs, or find thrills and excitement that seem to escape them in everyday life. Table 20.5 lists three common recreational drugs—alcohol, cocaine, and marijuana—and their side effects. Tobacco is another widely used recreational drug associated with negative health effects. Most people know the negative effects of cigarettes and cigars, but smokeless tobacco should not be forgotten, as its use has recently increased in teenage athletic populations. Snuff and chewing tobacco are associated with lip, gum, and other oral cancers.

Preventing Substance Abuse

Because substance abuse is a clinical matter, sport and fitness personnel lacking additional training are unlikely to be involved in drug-treatment programs. However, we can play major roles in drug prevention. These are some suggestions for helping prevent or at least reduce the probability of drug use:

1. Provide a supportive environment that addresses the reasons individuals take drugs. Work toward empowering participants through increased self-esteem and self-confidence, because people who feel good about themselves are less likely to take drugs. Keep winning in perspective and reduce the pressure to win at all costs. The coach who allows performance outcome to supersede the concern for the player's health and welfare is as dishonest and unethical in performing his or her job as is the athlete taking the drugs. Along these lines, simply telling athletes not to take drugs but then ignoring symptoms of substance abuse is also inappropriate and unethical. The stories of Tommy Chaikin and Ben Johnson are prime examples of coaches implicitly and explicitly supporting the use of performance-enhancing drugs. Drug use and abuse are unfortunately growing, and sport and fit-

Table 20.4
Major Categories of Performance-Enhancing Drugs in Sport

Drug category	Definition/use	Performance-enhancing effect	Side effects
Stimulants	Various types of drugs that increase alertness, reduce fatigue, and may increase competitiveness and hostility	Reduced fatigue, increased alertness, endurance, and aggression	Anxiety, insomnia, increased heart rate and blood pressure, dehydration, stroke, heart irregularities, psychological problems, death
Narcotic analgesics	Various types of drugs that kill pain through psychological stimulation	Reduced pain	Constricted pupil size, dry mouth, heaviness of limbs, skin itchiness, suppression of hunger, constipation, inability to concentrate, drowsiness, fear and anxiety, physical and psychological dependence
Anabolic steroids	Derivatives of the male hormone testosterone	Increased strength and endurance, improved mental attitude, faster training and recovery rates	Increased risk of liver disease and premature heart disease, increased aggression, loss of coordination, a variety of gender-related effects (e.g., infertility in males and development of male sex characteristics in females)
Beta-blockers	Drugs used to lower blood pressure, decrease heart rate, and block stimulatory responses	Steadied nerves in sports such as shooting	Excessively slowed heart rate, heart failure, low blood pressure, light-headedness, depression, insomnia, weakness, nausea, vomiting, cramps, diarrhea, bronchial spasm, tingling, numbness
Diuretics	Used to help eliminate fluids from the tissues (increase secretion of urine)	Temporary weight loss	Increased cholesterol levels, stomach distress, dizziness, blood disorders, muscle spasms, weakness, impaired cardiovascular functioning, decreased aerobic endurance
Peptide hormones and analogues (e.g., human growth hormone)	Chemically produced drugs designed to be chemically similar to or have similar effects as already existing drugs	Increased strength and endurance and muscle growth	Increased growth of organs, heart disease, thyroid disease, menstrual disorders, decreased sexual drive, shortened life span

Adapted from Bump, 1988.

ness professionals must become involved in drug prevention and education efforts.

2. Educate participants about the effects of drug use. The key here is to be informative and accurate regarding both the negative and positive (performance-enhancing) effects of various drugs. Using examples of well-known athletes can be effective, such as the example of Green Bay quarterback Brett Farve: Addicted to pain-killing drugs,

he had to undergo therapy at a treatment center to deal with the problem. You might also convey this information through involving peer athlete leaders and using role-playing and group-facilitation techniques.

3. Inform participants of legal sanctions against drug use. Coaches can discuss such examples as former Miami Dolphin football star Mercury Morris, imprisoned for involvement with drugs;

■ MORE INFORMATION ■

Coaches and Substance Abuse

With so much news coverage of athletes and substance abuse, we sometimes forget that some coaches also have alcohol problems. For example, police made public the drunken rampage that Gary Moeller, Michigan football coach, embarked on inside and outside of a restaurant. The accounts depicted a 54-year-old man out of control, smashing drink glasses on his table, singing loudly, and attempting to dance with other women after his wife left the restaurant. He suffered from alcohol poisoning, was incoherent, abusive, and relentlessly vulgar. When police arrived, Moeller punched an officer before being arrested and charged with disorderly conduct and assault and battery (these actions forced him to resign the next day).

Dennis Erickson, coach of the Seattle Seahawks, was ordered to enter an alcohol rehabilitation program after being arrested for driving while intoxicated and having a blood alcohol–induced car accident that left one of his players, Mike Frier, paralyzed. His drinking problems had surfaced earlier and were known from his coaching at the University of Miami. Unfortunately, problems among coaches demonstrating a lack of self-control, such as excessive drinking and even spousal abuse, have been occurring (or are at least being reported) with alarming frequency in recent years. Perhaps the high-stress associated with coaching is contributing to these out-of-control episodes (see chapter 23). Coaches, like their players, aren't icons but only imperfect humans.

Table 20.5

Common Recreational Drugs and Their Side Effects

Drug	Side effects	
Alcohol	Mood swings Euphoria False confidence Slowed reaction time Distorted depth perception Difficulty staying alert Reduced strength Reduced speed	Emotional outbursts Lost inhibitions Muscular weakness Decreased reaction time Dizziness Liver damage Reduced power Reduced endurance
Marijuana	Drowsiness Decreased hand-eye coordination Increased blood pressure Distorted vision Decreased physical performance	Decreased alertness Increased heart rate Memory loss Slowed reaction time Decreased mental performance
Cocaine	Physical and psychological addiction Increased strength Dizziness Rapid blood pressure fluctuations Anxiety	Death from circulatory problems Violent mood swings Decreased reaction time Vomiting Distorted depth perception Hallucination

Adapted from Bump, 1988.

basketball player Roy Tarpley, suspended from professional basketball because of repeated drug use; and Canadian sprint star Ben Johnson, suspended for 2 years and his Olympic gold medal revoked for using performance-enhancing drugs.

4. Set a good example. Actions speak louder than words, so coaches and exercise leaders should moni-

Snuff and chewing tobacco are associated with lip, gum, and other oral cancers; nevertheless, the use of smokeless tobacco is on the rise in some populations.

■

Only specifically trained professionals work in drug-treatment programs. However, sport and fitness personnel play a major role in drug prevention and detection.

tor their own actions and not smoke, chew tobacco, or drink excessively. This in itself sends a powerful message against the use of drugs. Professionals are not immune to drug abuse. If a coach has personal concerns, he or she should get help.

Detecting Substance Abuse

Substance use and abuse is detected by formal procedures (e.g., drug testing) and informal procedures (e.g., observation and listening). Properly conducted drug testing is very expensive. Here we'll focus on the less formal but nonetheless effective methods of observing and listening.

There are several signs and symptoms that characterize people who are substance abusers:

- Changes in behavior (lack of motivation, tardiness, absenteeism)
- Changes in peer group
- Major changes in personality
- Major changes in athletic or academic performance
- Apathetic or listless behaviors
- Impaired judgment
- Poor coordination
- Poor hygiene and grooming
- Profuse sweating
- Muscular twitches or tremors

If you observe these symptoms in athletes and exercisers, it does not necessarily mean they are substance users or abusers; these symptoms can also reflect other emotional problems. Thus, a fitness professional who observes particular symptoms

Hard-core substance abusers are notorious for lying and denying their substance abuse.

should first talk to the concerned party to validate his or her suspicions. Hard-core substance abusers are notorious for lying and denying the problem, however. So, if doubts remain after the initial talk with the individual, confidential advice should be solicited from a substance-abuse specialist. When you deal with an individual who has substance-abuse problems, follow a referral process similar to the one described earlier for eating disorders.

Listening is a simple—and excellent—way to obtain information about substance use and abuse. We are not suggesting that sport and fitness professionals eavesdrop on students, athletes, or clients. But if you hear drug use being discussed, you should address the issue in a nonaccusatory manner (e.g., "I didn't recognize the voices, but I heard someone talking about steroids in the locker room the other day. Let me tell you a few things about performance-enhancing drugs, in case anyone has misinformation about them and their effects. . . ."). If individuals tell you that they are using drugs, respect their confidentiality but solicit professional help.

Setting up policies and procedures to detect substance use and abuse under the umbrella of a formal drug-education program has also proved to be effective. For example, the NCAA Drug Education Committee has developed a set of minimum guidelines for policy consideration by its member institutions (Carr & Murphy, 1995), and these might be successful for athletes at other levels as well. This model provides drug education for athletes and athletic officials, treatment support, and training sessions for coaches, athletic trainers, and team physicians to help detect and handle drug- and alcohol-related problems.

Compulsive Gambling: An Odds-On Favorite for Trouble

The focus of this chapter has thus far been on two high-visibility problems prevalent in today's sport

427

and exercise environments. However, we now turn to a problem that, despite its long history in competitive sport, is only now getting the public's and media's attention: compulsive gambling. Bookies have been taking and placing bets for a long time (legally and illegally) in and on sports. The Black Sox baseball scandal in the 1920s was one of the first large-scale, documented scandals in which players were betting on their own games and sometimes performing poorly to ensure that the proper bets were "covered." Basketball scandals received publicity in the 1950s and early 1960s, when 37 basketball players from 22 schools were documented to have participated in "point shaving" and illegal betting. The point shaving done by collegiate basketball players from the City University of New York (CUNY) especially shook the sporting world. Back then, the players didn't really see anything wrong with winning by 6 points instead of 12. They weren't being asked to lose the game but to control the point spread.

More recently, gambling in and on sports has received increased visibility in high-profile cases involving, for example, quarterback Art Schlicter (detailed at the outset of the chapter), Pete Rose (banned from the Hall of Fame for betting on baseball), and Boston College, Northwestern, and Tulane University basketball and football players betting on their games. In addition, University of Maine baseball and football players, University of Rhode Island football players, and University of Arkansas athletes in four sports were found to have bet on games. Even Michael Jordan has been known to wager large amounts of money (usually on his golf game—not on basketball). But the high-profile cases are evidently only the "tip of the iceberg," and gambling on sporting events is evidently widespread.

Prevalence of Sports Gambling

Sports betting, illegal in almost all locales, is thriving across the country. The FBI estimates that gambling on sports accounts for 50% of the $28 billion bet each year in the United States. Estimates from the NCAA Director of Enforcement suggest that $2.5 to $3 billion was bet illegally on the men's NCAA Final Four in each of the past few years. This illegal gambling is often fostered by the fact that most daily newspapers offer betting odds and lines for upcoming events. Readers also see advertisements from popular Las Vegas bookmakers of-

fering a "free" tip on the game. People who have interest in gambling can simply choose from a growing number of World Wide Web sites around the world. With this easy access to gambling, experts on compulsive gambling agree that college students are especially vulnerable. According to national statistics, about 1.5% of the population are compulsive gamblers and another 4% are problem gamblers (not addicted but overindulging in gambling). It is estimated that 6% to 8% of college students are compulsive gamblers, those believed to be so addicted as to be out of control. This is more than in any other demographic group.

The fact that these gambling figures are estimated to be significantly higher for college students than others in the populace in part led *Sports Illustrated* in 1995 to run a three-part series detailing the vast gambling activity on campuses throughout the country. Extensive student bookmaking operations were documented, and the report revealed how easy it is for students to bet with a bookie, who is usually a fellow college student consumed with wagering and in over his head. For example, a University of Nevada-Las Vegas student stole a total of $89,000 from eight Las Vegas banks, and a University of Texas student stole more than $12,000 from a bank, both of them trying to pay off gambling debts. The students received prison sentences of about 10 years.

But gambling doesn't start in college, and experts agree that teenage gambling by high school students is "incredibly extensive." For example, police arrested four men for running a sports-betting and loan-sharking operation in New Jersey where at least 50 high school students were clients. The problem in investigating these types of cases is that parents tend to have one of three reactions: (a) They are afraid to say anything because they think organized crime is involved, (b) they think they can handle it themselves at home, or, the most common response, (c) they say "Thank God, it's not drugs." In essence, they just don't think it's a serious problem, and they are often wrong in this assessment (*Sports Illustrated,* 1995).

Signs of Compulsive Gambling

Compulsive gamblers exhibit certain characteristics such as boastfulness, arrogance, unbounded optimism, and extreme competitiveness while often being quite intelligent. But picking a compulsive gambler out of a crowd, experts say, is next to impossible. Since gambling is something lots of people do, it falls into the realm of alcohol consumption—it's not noticed until there are negative consequences, such as in the case of Art Schlicter. One expert notes, "Sports gambling on campus is a dirty little secret of college life in America, and it's rampant and thriving." (*Sports Illustrated,* 1995). There-

fore, as professionals, we must be cognizant of this problem and not put our collective heads in the sand. Referrals to such programs as Gamblers Anonymous or the National Council on Problem Gambling are appropriate if you identify a compulsive gambling problem.

■ CLOSE-UP ■

Gambler's Anonymous 20 Questions

Gambler's Anonymous has 20 questions that it asks new members. Compulsive gamblers usually answer "yes" to at least 7 of the 20 questions.

1. Do you lose time from work due to gambling?
2. Does gambling make your home life unhappy?
3. Does gambling affect your reputation?
4. Do you ever feel remorse after gambling?
5. Do you ever gamble to get money with which to pay debts or to otherwise solve financial difficulties?
6. Does gambling cause a decrease in your ambition or efficiency?
7. After losing, do you feel you must return as soon as possible to win back your losses?
8. After a win, do you have a strong urge to return and win more?
9. Do you often gamble until your last dollar is gone?
10. Do you ever borrow to finance your gambling?
11. Do you ever sell anything to finance gambling?
12. Are you reluctant to use "gambling money" for normal expenditures?
13. Does gambling make you careless about the welfare of your family?
14. Do you ever gamble longer than you planned?
15. Do you ever gamble to escape worry or trouble?
16. Do you ever commit, or consider committing, an illegal act to finance your gambling?
17. Does gambling cause you to have difficulty sleeping?
18. Do arguments, disappointments, or frustrations create within you an urge to gamble?
19. Do you have an urge to celebrate good fortune by a few hours of gambling?
20. Do you ever consider self-destruction as a result of your gambling?

Note. This information is available at the Web site maintained by the Gamblers Anonymous International Service office, P.O. Box 17173, Los Angeles, CA 90017, but this particular version above came from the North American Training Institute, a division of Minnesota Council on Compulsive Gambling, Inc., 314 West Superior Street, Suite 702, Duluth, Minnesota 55802, phone: 218-722-1503, fax: 218-722-0346. The Web page is copyrighted. Gambler's Anonymous is credited as the creator of the list, though this version is not the one that they use.

429

SUMMARY

1 *Define and discuss the prevalence of eating disorders in sport.*

Anorexia nervosa and bulimia are the two most common eating disorders. Both these eating disorders are defined in the *Diagnostic and Statistical Manual of Mental Disorders*. Although a variety of symptoms are associated with each of these disorders, anorexia nervosa is characterized by an intense sense of gaining weight and a distorted body image, whereas bulimia is characterized by recurrent episodes of binge eating and regular, self-induced vomiting. Athletes (particularly athletes in sports where weight is a concern, such as wrestling, gymnastics, and track) appear to have higher rates of eating-related problems than does the general population.

2 *Identify predisposing factors for developing eating disorders.*

There are many factors that predispose individuals for developing an eating disorder, some being more biologic and genetic, and others being more environmental (e.g., weight restrictions and standards) or sociological (coach and peer pressure).

3 *Describe how to recognize disordered eating.*

The signs and symptoms of bulimia and anorexia nervosa are both physical (e.g., weight too low, bloating, swollen salivary glands) and psychological or behavioral (excessive dieting, binge eating, preoccupation with food). We must help individuals get appropriate specialized assistance. A referral system should be set up confidentially and professionally to help individuals deal with eating-related problems.

4 *Define and discuss the prevalence of substance abuse in sport.*

Substance abuse is one of the most severe problems facing our society today. It is typically related to the continued and recurrent use of psychoactive substances in situations that are either physically hazardous or in which one's personal or professional life suffers. Although it is difficult to get exact figures regarding the use of certain drugs, we do know that many athletes and exercisers take both performance-enhancing drugs and recreational drugs, and both types of drugs have dangerous side effects.

5 *Explain why some athletes and exercisers take drugs.*

Athletes and exercisers usually take drugs for either physical (e.g., to enhance performance), psychological (e.g., to relieve stress), or social (e.g., to satisfy peer pressure) reasons.

6 *Discuss how to detect and prevent substance abuse.*

Substance use and abuse is detected by both formal procedures, such as drug testing, and informal procedures, such as observation and listening. Because drug testing is expensive and often difficult to implement, we must be able to recognize the signs and symptoms of substance use and abuse. Sport and exercise professionals can help prevent substance abuse by setting a good example, educating participants about the effects of substance use and abuse, and most importantly, providing a supportive environment that addresses the reasons individuals take drugs.

7 *Discuss the problem of compulsive sports gambling.*

Gambling in and on sports has a long history, although it appears to be on the increase in recent years. National statistics estimate that 6% of college students are compulsive gamblers, and extensive bookmaking can be found on many college campuses. Gambling is often not thought of as a serious problem, but, in fact, like drugs and alcohol it can be an addiction. Compulsive gamblers are usually boastful, arrogant, have unbounded optimism, and are extremely competitive.

KEY TERMS

anorexia nervosa
bulimia
substance abuse

substance use
performance-enhancing drugs
recreational drugs

REVIEW QUESTIONS

1. Define, compare, and contrast anorexia nervosa and bulimia.

2. How do you recognize individuals with eating disorders? (Describe signs and symptoms.) What is the approximate incidence of eating disorders and eating problems with athletes?

3. Discuss three predisposing factors that might increase the likelihood of an eating disorder occurring?

4. If you suspect someone has an eating disorder, how would you approach him or her with your concern? What should and should not be done?

5. Define substance abuse. What do the data indicate regarding the use of drugs in athletics?

6. Discuss the physical, psychological, and social reasons athletes take drugs.

7. Identify the major categories of performance-enhancing and recreational drugs and their reported side effects.

8. What are four strategies sport and exercise professionals can use to prevent and detect substance abuse?

9. Identify the relation between substance abuse and feelings of self-worth and competence.

10. What signs and symptoms help identify drug abusers?

11. Discuss and provide examples of the increase in gambling in high schools and colleges.

CRITICAL THINKING QUESTIONS

1. You are hired as a consultant for a collegiate athletic department. Your main job is to devise a program that will reduce the drug and alcohol use by athletes on the campus. Discuss in detail what type of program you would implement, showing how it relates to the reasons for substance use.

2. You are coaching a women's gymnastics team at the high school level. You know that eating disorders tend to be high with this population. How would you structure your practices and competitions to minimize the possibility of eating disorders occurring with your athletes? What would you do if you found out that one of your athletes had an eating disorder?

© Photo: Action Images

Burnout and Overtraining

After reading this chapter you should be able to

1 define overtraining, staleness, and burnout;

2 discuss different models of burnout;

3 describe the causes of overtraining and burnout;

4 identify the symptoms of overtraining and burnout;

5 explain the research evidence of burnout in sport; and

6 describe the treatment and prevention of burnout.

The pressure to win and train year-round with vigor and intensity has increased dramatically in recent years, due in large part to the tremendous financial rewards, publicity, and status achieved by successful coaches and athletes. There used to be separate seasons and off-seasons for different sports, whereas now one season tends to run into the next leaving little time for an extended rest. Even in the "off-season" athletes lift weights and do other physical fitness activities to keep in shape and get bigger and stronger for the upcoming season. In addition to the blurring of the seasons and off-season, specialized training camps or academies have recently been developed in many individual sports (e.g., tennis, ice skating), where youngsters attend school and train (usually away from parents) with the hope of later obtaining a college scholarship, professional career, or Olympic medal. The theory is that more training is better, you have to start training early, and you then must train year-round if you are to compete at a high level.

But the price for this unrelenting focus on training and winning can be overtraining and subsequent burnout. And it is not only competitive athletes and coaches who overdo it and burn out. Exercisers, in their quest to feel and look better, sometimes go too far, overtrain, and burn out. Support personnel, too, such as officials and athletic trainers get caught up in the pressures to win, which can lead to increased stress and potential burnout. A couple of quotes describe the pressures that can lead to burnout.

> *Often in the middle of a game I'd think to myself, What am I doing here? These guys are going to eat me alive. The frustrations, abuse, and hassles sort of wear on you.*
>
> **—High school basketball and football official**

> *It's a long, long grind. It's either preseason practice, the season itself, postseason weight training, or recruiting. The demands to win can also be very stressful. When we were successful, there was pressure and high expectations to stay successful. When we were losing, there was pressure to start winning real soon. This schedule and pressure can wear you down and make you just want to leave everything behind for awhile.*
>
> **—College football coach**

So overtraining and burnout have become significant problems in the world of sport, short-circuiting many promising careers. Therefore, it is important for coaches, exercise leaders, and other administra-

tive personnel to better understand the symptoms and causes of burnout and learn strategies to help reduce the possibility of burnout from occurring in the first place. Let's start by defining what we mean by overtraining and burnout.

Defining Overtraining, Staleness, and Burnout

Some confusion still exists among common definitions for the related terms *overtraining, burnout,* and *staleness.* We'll present a set of definitions that represent our viewpoint, although we recognize that not all sport and exercise psychologists would define these terms exactly the same way.

Overtraining

Periodized training is the deliberate strategy of exposing athletes to high-volume and high-intensity training loads that are followed by a lower training load, known as the *rest* or *taper* stage (McCann, 1995). The goal in periodized training is to condition athletes so that their performance peaks at a specific date or in a particular time frame (usually before major competitions or championships). Coaches purposefully overload and taper athletes. Thus, the scientific and artistic challenge for athletes and coaches is to slowly increase the training load so that optimal adaptations accrue and negative side effects, such as injury and staleness, do not (O'Connor, 1997).

Unlike overloading and tapering, which result in increases in performance, overtraining refers to a short cycle of training (lasting a few days to a few weeks) during which athletes expose themselves to excessive training loads that are near or at maximal capacity. In this state, coaches and athletes unwittingly impose too much overload on the athlete without providing enough tapering or rest. This definition of overtraining has three important features: (a) Overtraining involves a series of acute bouts in a process; (b) overtraining consists of a significant increase in the training stimulus, compared with recent training history; and (c) overtraining involves exercise of a high frequency (often more than one session per day) that is near or at maximal capacity (O'Connor, 1997). In essence, overtraining is an abnormal

> *Overtraining is an abnormal extension of the training process culminating in staleness.*

454

> *One athlete's overtraining might be another athlete's optimal training regimen.*

> *A stale athlete has difficulty maintaining standard training regimens and can no longer achieve previous performance results.*

extension of the training process culminating in a state of staleness (Morgan, O'Connor, Sparling, & Pate, 1987).

The difference between overtraining and periodized training depends largely on individual differences and capabilities. That is, what is seen as overtraining (detrimental) for one athlete can be seen as positive or optimal training for another. For example, Mark Spitz, who broke seven world records in swimming and won seven gold medals at the 1972 Olympics, never trained more than 10,000 yards a day. On the other hand, Vladimir Salnikov, a Soviet Olympic swimming champion, trained at 2-week schedules called "attack mesocycles," which involved swimming up to 20,000 meters (21,880 yards) a day. His distances would be excessive for many elite swimmers, but they apparently facilitated Salnikov's performance (Raglin, 1993).

This substantial variability in the exercises prescribed for athletes must be considered, and it should be recognized that the most talented performers are not necessarily the ones with the greatest capacity to endure periods of overtraining. Furthermore, it has been demonstrated that athletes of similar capacity respond differently to standard training regimens: Some resist the negative effects of intensive training, whereas others are quite vulnerable. Thus, a particular training schedule may improve the performance of one athlete, be insufficient for another, and be downright damaging for a third.

Staleness

The American Medical Association (1966) has defined the term staleness as "a physiological state of overtraining which manifests as deteriorated athletic readiness" (p. 126). Thus, staleness is seen as the end result or outcome of overtraining when the athlete has difficulty maintaining standard training regimens and can no longer achieve previous performance results. The truly stale athlete has a significant reduction in performance (e.g., 5% or greater) for an extended period of time (e.g., 2 weeks or longer) that occurs during or following a period of overtraining and fails to improve in response to short-term reductions in training (O'Connor, 1997). The principal behavioral sign of staleness is impaired performance, whereas the principal psychological symptoms are mood disturbance and increases in perceptual effort during exercise. For example, it has been reported that about 80% of stale athletes are clinically depressed. The relationship between overtraining and staleness is depicted in Figure 21.1, showing that overtraining can be viewed as a stimulus, and staleness as a response (Morgan et al., 1987).

Burnout

Burnout has received more attention than overtraining or staleness, in many anecdotal reports as well as research investigations focusing on burnout (e.g., Dale & Weinberg, 1990; Gould, Tuffey, Udry, & Loehr, 1996a, b; Vealey, Udry, Zimmerman, & Soliday, 1992). A complex concept, burnout is an exhaustive psychophysiological response exhibited as a result of frequent, sometimes extreme, and generally ineffective efforts to meet excessive training and competitive demands. In essence, burnout involves a psychological, emotional, and sometimes physical withdrawal from a formerly enjoyable activity in response to excessive stress or dissatisfaction over time (Smith, 1986). The following are characteristics of burnout:

- Exhaustion, both physical and emotional, in the form of lost concern, energy, interest, and trust.
- Depersonalization, seen as being impersonal and unfeeling. This negative response to others is in large part due to mental and physical exhaustion.
- Feelings of low personal accomplishment, low self-esteem, failure, and depression. This is often visible in low job productivity or a decreased performance level.

Unlike other phases of the training stress syndrome, once a person experiences burnout, withdrawal from the stress environment is often inevitable. In sport, burnout differs from simply dropping out because it involves such characteristics as psychological and emotional exhaustion, negative responses to others, low self-esteem, and depression. There are many reasons why athletes drop out of sport participation, and burnout is just one of them. In fact,

© Photophile

Figure 21.1 *Relationship of overtraining and staleness.*

it appears that few athletes and coaches completely drop out of sport due solely to burnout, although they often exhibit many of the characteristics of burnout. For example, despite feeling burned out, athletes often remain in their sport due to such things as financial rewards (e.g., scholarships), and parental or coach pressures and expectations. In essence, individuals typically discontinue sport involvement only when the costs outweigh benefits relative to alternative activities. Athletes and coaches who discontinue sport involvement due to the high cost of excessive long-term stress are typically viewed as being burned-out.

Frequency of Overtraining, Staleness, and Burnout

Although there have been no large-scale, systematic studies of the epidemiology of overtraining, staleness, and burnout, what we know from research suggests that these are not trivial problems. For example, a survey of college varsity athletes from the Atlantic Coast Conference regarding their experiences dealing with training stress revealed that 66% of them felt they had experienced overtraining (with the average being two experiences during their collegiate careers); almost 50% indicated that it was a bad experience. In addition, 72% of the athletes reported some staleness during their sport seasons, and 47% reported feeling burned-out at some point during their collegiate career (Silva, 1990). In an interview study (Cohn, 1990) of 10 high school golfers, all said they had burned out of golf at some time during their careers, resulting in 5 to 14 days of discontinued participation. Other research found that 60% of female and 64% of male elite distance runners have had at least one episode of staleness in their running

436

careers, whereas staleness was reported in 30% of sub-elite highly trained distance runners (Morgan, O'Connor, Ellickson, & Bradley, 1988; Morgan, O'Connor, Sparling, & Pate, 1987). Although more common in elite athletes, staleness is not confined to elite athletes, as has been commonly assumed.

Some interesting research by Raglin and Morgan (1989) found that of swimmers who developed staleness during their freshman year, 91% became stale in one or more subsequent seasons. Yet only 30% of the swimmers who did not become stale as freshmen later developed the disorder in a subsequent season. Apparently, once staleness is experienced, subsequent bouts become more probable.

Models of Burnout

Three sport-specific models of burnout have been developed to help explain the burnout phenomenon. Each of the models has some interesting and useful information concerning the different factors affecting burnout, as well as individuals' responses to burnout. All three have received some scientific support

and should be considered when attempting to understand the complex process of burnout.

Cognitive-Affective Stress Model

Smith (1986) developed a four-stage, stress-based model of burnout in sport (see Figure 21.2). In Smith's model, burnout is a process involving physiological, psychological, and behavioral components that progress in predictable stages. In turn, each of these components is influenced by level of motivation and personality.

In the first stage, termed situational demands, high demands are placed on the athlete, such as high volumes of physical practice or excessive pressure to win. Typically, when the demands of a situation outweigh potential resources, stress occurs, which over time can lead to burnout. In the second stage, which Smith labels cognitive appraisal, individuals interpret and appraise the situation. Some individuals will view the situation as more threatening than others will. For example, one football coach whose team loses three games in a row might get uptight and fear that he will lose his job, whereas another coach in the same situation might see the

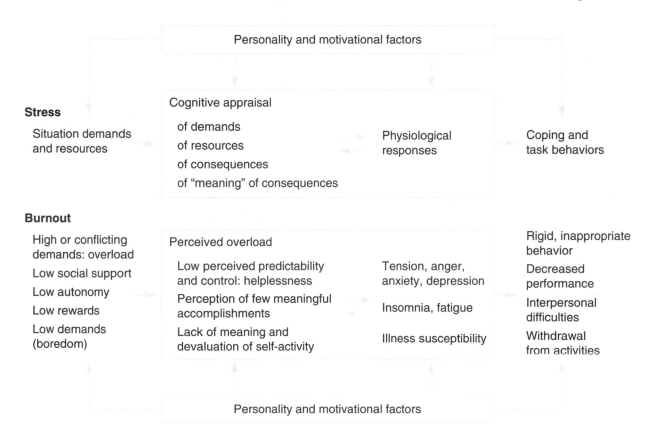

Figure 21.2 Smith's cognitive-affective model of athletic burnout.
Adapted from Smith, 1986.

> *Cognitive appraisal: Nothing is either good or bad, but thinking makes it so. People differ in how they respond to prolonged stress in sport and exercise settings.*

losing streak as a challenge and an opportunity to show that the team can come back from adversity. In the third stage, physiological responses, if you appraise a situation as harmful or threatening, then over time, as your perception becomes chronic, stress can produce physiological changes, such as increases in tension, irritability, and fatigue. Typically, victims of athletic burnout feel emotionally depleted and, having little positive emotion, develop a susceptibility to illness and lethargy. In the fourth stage, behavioral responses, the physiological response leads to some type of coping and task behaviors, such as decreased performance, interpersonal difficulties, and eventual withdrawal from the activity. Finally, Smith argues that reaction to stress in sport is moderated by personality and motivation, and an individual's unique personality and intrinsic motivation often determine whether the person will burn out or cope.

Negative-Training Stress Response Model

Silva's model (1990) to explain burnout focuses more on responses to physical training, although it recognizes the importance of psychological factors. Specifically, he suggests that physical training stresses the athlete physically and psychologically and can have both positive and negative effects. Positive adaptation is a desirable outcome of training, such as overloading the body by doing lots of sprint work in order to become faster. Too much training, however, can result in negative adaptation. This negative adaptation is hypothesized to lead to negative training responses, such as overtraining and staleness, which eventually will result in burnout.

Unidimensional Identity Development and External Control Model

The models by Smith (1986) and Silva (1990) focused primarily on stress, whereas Coakley's (1992) model is more sociological in nature. Although Coakley agrees that stress is involved in burnout, he argues that it is simply a symptom. He believes the real cause of burnout, especially in young athletes,

is related to the social organization of high-performance sport and its effects on identity and control issues in young athletes. In particular, Coakley contends that burnout occurs because the structure of highly competitive sport does not allow youngsters to develop a normal identity: They don't get to spend enough time with their peers outside of the sporting environment. Thus, young athletes focus on and identify almost exclusively with success in sport, and when they experience an injury or lack of success, the associated stress can ultimately lead to burnout.

Coakley also contends that the social worlds of competitive young athletes are organized in such a way that their control and decision making is inhibited. In essence, coaches and parents make most of the decisions and exert wide-ranging control in most organized competitive youth sport settings, leaving young athletes powerless to control events and make decisions about the nature of their experiences and direction of their own development. Once again, this leads to stress and potentially burnout.

The three models, as well as research and practical articles on burnout, have identified the factors related to burnout that you can view in Table 21.1. We have organized these under Smith's (1986) cognitive-affective stress framework, which is inclusive enough to represent the broad range of factors related to burnout. A recent study examining 10 case studies of burned-out junior tennis players also used Smith's model (Gould, Tuffey, Udry, & Loehr, 1997). This does not imply that Silva's and Coakley's models are not useful, only that their components can fit into the Smith model.

Factors Leading to Athlete Burnout

We will now discuss specific factors that lead to or cause burnout. First we will consider some anecdotal reports before turning to the research evidence.

Anecdotal Reports

Anecdotal evidence is plentiful regarding why some athletes burn out at a relatively young age. Some players start as early as 5 years old and others are pressured to turn pro when they are barely teenagers. Tennis phenomenon Jennifer Capriati turned pro at age 13 and, due to a clothing contract, was a millionaire before she even hit a ball as a professional. Her early fame and fortune might be partly to blame for her dropping out of tennis and experimenting with

Table 21.1
Factors Related to Athlete Burnout

Situational demands	Cognitive appraisal of the situation	Physiological/Psychological responses	Behavioral responses	Personality and motivational factors
High conflicting demands	Perceived overload	Decreased motivation	Physical withdrawal	High trait anxiety
Lack of control/powerlessness; dependency	Few meaningful accomplishments	Fatigue	Emotional withdrawal	Low self-esteem and low perceived competence
High expectations by self and others	Lack of meaning and devaluation of activity	Decreased concentration	Psychological withdrawal	Competitive orientations: fear of failure, fear of poor evaluation
Low social support	Lack of enjoyment	Weight gain or loss	Decreased performance	Unidimensional self-concept
Excessive demands on time	Chronic stress	Illness or injury susceptibility	Giving up during play, tanking	High need to please others
Limited social relationships	Learned helplessness	Moodiness and impatience	Rigid, inappropriate behavior	Low assertiveness
Parental involvement: restrictive, inconsistent feedback, negative feedback	Decreased life satisfaction	Poor sleep	Interpersonal difficulties	Self-critical
Coach involvement: inconsistent feedback, negative feedback	Identity crisis	Anger; irritability	Lowered school performance	Perfectionism
Injuries	Stifled; trapped	Muscle soreness		Low perceived control
Training loads: repetitive, high volume, number of competitions		Boredom		Low frustration

Adapted from Gould et al., 1996.

Athletes are starting to train at younger ages, which can negatively affect their home and family life.

Training in many sports is virtually year-round, and the intensity of training loads makes it almost impossible to compete successfully in more than one sport.

drugs. She has attempted a comeback in the past few years but has, to date, not regained the form she had in her youth. The names of Vince Cartier, Curtis Beck, and Eric Hulst (all elite junior runners) are probably less familiar, but these athletes were national champions as teenagers, only to become burned-out and discontinue their participation in competitive sport a few years after setting national records or winning junior division titles. In these highly competitive environments, young athletes practice 25 to 30 hours a week, with little time off for vacation.

Besides so early a start and the pressures and expectations placed on young athletes, training in most sports now involves year-round workouts, with off-seasons becoming ever shorter. In fact, in sports such as tennis, gymnastics, and swimming there really is no off-season. Specialized training camps or academies have been developed for ice skating, tennis,

golf, and gymnastics where young athletes live, attend school, and train. This extended time away from home can put great strains on youngsters, who typically cannot maintain a normal home and family life. It is no wonder, given these excessive psychological and physical demands, that some athletes burn out.

Research Evidence

Although a wide variety of factors have been hypothesized to lead to burnout, until recently there was little empirical data to substantiate these contentions. A recent series of studies on competitive youth tennis players (Gould et al., 1996a, b; 1997) has helped supply this needed evidence. Specifically, the studies revealed that an interaction of personal and

440

situational factors cause burnout, including these categories:

■ *Physical concerns.* These include injury, overtraining, feeling tired all the time, and lack of physical development, as well as erratic performance, losing, and getting beat by people you used to beat.

■ *Logistical concerns.* These include the travel grind as well as the demands on time that tennis players felt could dominate their lives, leaving them little or no time with friends and at school.

■ *Social or interpersonal concerns.* These include dissatisfaction with social life, negative parental influences (e.g., being "suffocated" by dad or mom), and competing with a sibling for a parent's attention. Other dissatisfactions were identified within the tennis world, such as a negative team atmosphere, cheating by competitors, and unhelpful coaches.

■ *Psychological concerns.* By far the most frequently noted factor, accounting for more than 50% of the reasons given for burnout, these include unfulfilled or inappropriate expectations, such as an overemphasis on rankings, a realization that a professional career was unlikely, and feeling a lack of improvement or talent. The lack of enjoyment was another theme, characterized by coach and parental pressure to practice and win, pressure to win or maintain scholarships, self-pressure to win and play well, and being uncertain of parental support. Motivational concerns included wanting to try other sport and nonsport activities, as well as simply being "sick" of tennis and lacking motivation.

In summary, Gould et al. (1996b) suggest that there are two different "strains" of burnout. The dominant strain is social-psychological in nature, further divided into athlete perfectionism and situational pressure substrains. Specifically, some young athletes are such perfectionists that it eventually predisposes or puts them at risk for burnout (even in situations that are not considered unusually demanding by most tennis professionals). In other cases athletes are placed in situations where tremendous psychological pressure is generated by others, particularly parents. Stress results from having expectations to win in an effort to please others and feel worthy. A "physically driven" strain of burnout also surfaces, but much less frequently. In these cases athletes cannot meet the demands for physical training placed on them, which results in considerable physical and psychological stress and then burnout.

Individual Differences

Although we have discussed the most common factors related to burnout, it is important to realize that burnout is also a unique personal experience. People attempting to help athletes cope with feelings of burnout must recognize and appreciate these variations. Figure 21.3 provides what Gould and his colleagues

■ RESEARCH ■

Is Athlete Burnout More Than Just Stress?

Although most researchers have conceptualized burnout to be closely related to stress, another viewpoint explains burnout within the context of sport commitment. Specifically, athletes can be committed to sport because they want to participate, because they feel they have to participate, or both. But athletes may also feel entrapped by sport when they do not really want to participate in it but feel they must maintain their involvement because their self-identity is in it, they lack attractive alternatives to sport, or they have invested too much time and energy in sport to stop participating.

Using this approach, Raedeke (1998) studied more than 200 competitive swimmers. He showed that some swimmers who were no longer attracted to swimming—feeling little enjoyment, few benefits, but high costs—still felt they had to participate due to social pressure from others and their perceived lack of control over the situation. These swimmers were most likely to experience burnout and a decreased commitment to swimming. Coaches and parents can learn from this to (a) ensure that athletes enjoy their participation and that it remains fun, (b) encourage and support the athletes but not pressure them, and (c) make sure the athletes are involved or have input into the decision making regarding practice and competition.

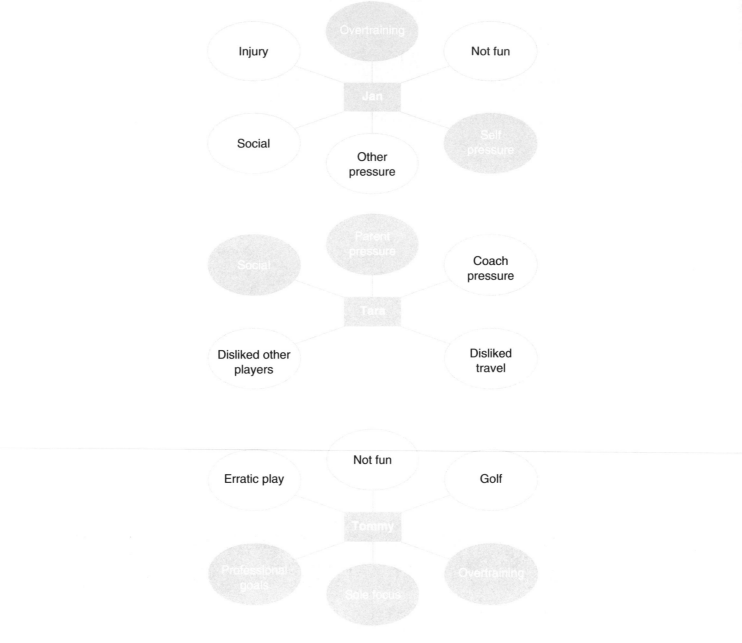

Figure 21.3 *Motivational map of burnout in junior tennis players. Shaded circles signify the most salient motives.*

(1997) call a "motivational map" depicting the varying reasons three athletes gave for discontinuing or curtailing their involvement in tennis. As you inspect this figure, you can see that the players did not burn out for only one reason; rather, there were multiple causes of burnout. For example, the three players shared such reasons as overtraining, not having fun, experiencing social concerns and pressure from others. Other reasons were specific to a particular athlete (e.g., injury, erratic play, and disliking travel).

Symptoms of Overtraining and Burnout

Overtraining and burnout are physical and psychological in nature. Some common symptoms of *overtraining* include physical fatigue, mental exhaustion, grouchiness, depression, apathy, and sleep disturbances. Symptoms of *burnout* include a loss of interest, no desire to play, physical and mental exhaustion, lack of caring, depression, and increased anxiety. Research summarizing the characteristics of over-

Table 21.2

Signs and Symptoms of Overtraining and Burnout

Overtraining	Burnout
Apathy	Low motivation or energy
Lethargy	Concentration problems
Sleep disturbance	Loss of desire to play
Weight loss	Lack of caring
Elevated resting heart rate	Sleep disturbance
Muscle pain or soreness	Physical and mental exhaustion
Mood changes	Lowered self-esteem
Elevated resting blood pressure	Negative affect
Gastrointestinal disturbances	Mood changes
Retarded recovery from exertion	Substance abuse
Appetite loss	Changes in values and beliefs
	Emotional isolation
	Increased anxiety
	Highs and low

Adapted from Hackney, Perlman, and Nowacki, 1990

training and burnout (Gould et al., 1996b; Hackney, Perlman, & Nowacki, 1990) is presented in Table 21.2.

Overtraining and Mood States

Overtraining is assumed to affect athletic performance and mental health; a few researchers have asked how. For example, Morgan and his colleagues at the University of Wisconsin have investigated the relation between overtraining and psychological mood states. To measure mood, they administered the Profile of Mood States (POMS; McNair, Lorr, & Droppleman, 1971) to 400 competitive swimmers during different parts of the training and competitive season. The POMS measures six transitory emotional states (tension, depression, anger, vigor, fatigue, and confusion). After analyzing the data from studies done over a 10-year period, they (Morgan et al., 1987) concluded that mood-state disturbances increase as the training stimulus increases (in a dose-responsive manner). The heavier the training (in this case, the swimming distance each week), the greater the mood disturbance. This mood disturbance included increased depression, anger, and fatigue and decreased vigor. Conversely, reductions in training load are associated with improvements in mood (Raglin, Eksten, & Garl, 1995; Raglin, Stager, Koceja, & Harms, 1996).

The psychological mood profile of successful athletes also differed from that of unsuccessful athletes.

Athletes experience increased mood disturbance under especially heavy training workloads, especially over time. The heavier the workload, the greater the mood disturbance.

Successful athletes exhibit high levels of vigor and low levels of negative mood states, an optimal combination. Overtrained athletes show an inverted iceberg profile, with negative states pronounced.

Specifically, top-level athletic performers had what Morgan has called an iceberg profile (see chapter 2). The iceberg profile shows that, in comparison with the population average, more successful athletes tend to score higher on vigor and lower on anxiety, depression, fatigue, and confusion (see Figure 21.4). Interestingly enough, when athletes are overtrained and become stale due to the increased training demands, they display an inverted iceberg profile. That is, the negative states of depression, anxiety, fatigue, confusion, and tension become elevated, whereas vigor is decreased. There was a stepwise increase in the swimmers' mood disturbances that coincided directly with increases in swimming training. And

443

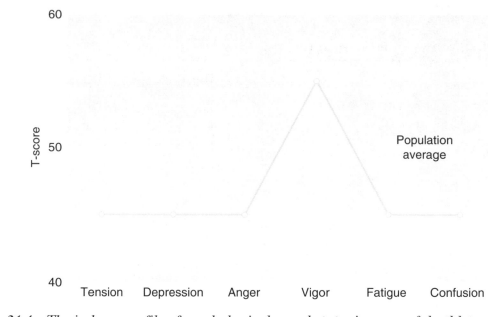

Figure 21.4 *The iceberg profile of psychological mood states in successful athletes.*

subsequent decreases in the training regimen (i.e., tapering off) were associated with improvements in mood state.

Overtraining and Performance

One well-controlled study investigated the effects of increased training loads on mood states and performance for Olympic judoists (Murphy, Fleck, Dudley, & Callister, 1990). For 4 weeks the conditioning training volume was increased, and then for 2 weeks sport-specific training volume was increased. The increased conditioning training volume did not result in negative mood state increases, whereas the increased sport-specific training volume did increase anger and anxiety levels (although there were no signs of clinical distress, such as depression or irrational thinking). However, both the conditioning and sport-specific training sessions showed decreases in the physical-performance measures of strength and anaerobic endurance. This study shows that overtrained and stale athletes are at risk of developing mood disturbances, which can result in decreased performance levels and dropout. Sport and exercise professionals should therefore carefully monitor how much training athletes require: The old strategy "More is better" may backfire in the long run.

Measuring Burnout

Probably the best way to study burnout would be to find people who have left sport because they felt burned out and compare them to athletes who are currently participating in sport and exercise (as was done by Gould et al., 1996b). But it is difficult to locate these people, and many burned-out players remain in sport for reasons such as money, prestige, or pressure from a coach or parent. So researchers have also developed a paper-and-pencil method to measure burnout.

The most widely used and accepted instrument is the Maslach Burnout Inventory (Maslach & Jackson, 1981), which measures both the perceived frequency and intensity of the feelings of burnout. Their inventory measures three components of burnout:

- Emotional exhaustion—feelings of emotional overextension and exhaustion.

- Depersonalization—an unfeeling and impersonal response to other people in one's environment. These are detached feelings toward people and a sense of just going through the motions.

- Personal accomplishment—the feeling of competence and successful achievement in one's work with people. Low feelings of achievement often result in perceived lack of ability to control situations.

Maslach's Burnout Inventory has been used with professionals in a variety of potentially stressful occupations, including nurses, lawyers, social workers, physicians, psychologists, police officers, counselors, and probation officers. It has been especially

> *The Maslach Burnout Inventory is a reliable instrument to measure burnout, and has been adapted and modified for use in sport and exercise settings.*

Burnout in Sport Professionals

We now turn to some of the major findings regarding burnout in competitive sports. Studies have examined burnout not only in athletes but also in athletic trainers, officials, and coaches.

useful in studying teachers, whose work environment typically includes long hours, excessive expenditure of mental and emotional energy, and high expectations from principals and parents. Coaches and athletes face similar stressors in competitive sport: long hours of practice, great physical and mental energy expenditure, and performance pressures on game days. However, only recently has empirical research focused on burnout in competitive sport, spurred by Smith's model of athletic burnout. Some of this research has adapted Maslach's Burnout Inventory to sport (Weinberg & Richardson, 1990) or developed sport-specific burnout scales (Eades, 1991). However, from the point of view of scale reliability and validity, additional development would be useful.

Burnout in Athletic Trainers

Few people are aware of the long hours that trainers put in before and after games and during practice. Trainers at the high school or college level are often responsible for several teams, working in the training room or on the field most of the day. Coaches pressure them to prepare athletes for game day, which

> *Trainers with Type A personalities are more likely to burn out than their Type B counterparts.*

© Mike Morris/Unicorn Stock Photos

> *Role conflict and role ambiguity are related to burnout in both trainers and sport officials.*

> *It has yet to be established whether male coaches or female coaches experience higher levels of burnout.*

adds stress. Gieck, Brown, and Shank (1982) were the first to study how burnout affects athletic trainers, and they demonstrated that trainers indeed experience great job stress. Many trainers reported that being at the beck and call of several teams made it difficult to devote enough quality time to individuals. Trainers with Type A personalities (i.e., excessive anxiety about time urgency) were especially prone to burnout.

Some trainers feel when their several roles become blurred (i.e., *role ambiguity*), they are more likely to feel burned out (Capel, 1986). Conversely, athletic trainers who feel more in control of their situations (i.e., *internal locus of control*) experience less burnout than colleagues with little sense of control (i.e., *external locus of control*). For example, trainers often play the role of counselor and friend, which can conflict with their official role.

Burnout in Officials

Officials also face great stress, and they receive few compensations for it other than the satisfaction of a job well done. This leads to high turnover rates and a shortage of officials. Evidently the fear of failure is the strongest predictor of burnout with sport officials (Taylor, Daniel, Leith, & Burke, 1990). Using the Maslach Burnout Inventory, officials report that making bad calls is a major stressor related to perceived burnout and that players, coaches, and spectators are more likely to evaluate them negatively than positively (Anshel & Weinberg, 1995b). Like athletic trainers, officials who feel role conflicts also have higher levels of perceived burnout.

Burnout in Coaches

Coaches are prime candidates for burnout and the box on p. 447 highlights some anecdotal reports of coaches regarding their perceived high levels of stress and burnout. The wide variety of stressors they report includes the pressure to win, administrative and parental interference or indifference, disciplinary problems, multiple roles to fulfill, extensive travel commitments, and intense personal involvement. Let's look at some of the research examining the specific factors related to burnout in coaches.

Gender Differences

More and more female coaches are feeling the pressure that their male counterparts have felt for years. In fact, most studies (Caccese & Mayerberg, 1984; Kelley, 1994; Kelley & Gill, 1993; Vealey et al., 1992) have found that females have higher levels of perceived burnout than males do, although some studies report higher levels of burnout in males (e.g., Dale & Weinberg, 1990). It has been suggested that the increased levels of stress and burnout perceived by female coaches can be explained by their being expected to not only take on additional responsibilities related to coaching but also the time to be more nurturing of their athletes. Athletic administrators may need to reexamine the differential demands placed on female, compared with male, coaches and possibly make some changes to ensure that roles and responsibilities are equitable.

Age and Experience Differences

Studies have found that younger and less-experienced coaches have higher levels of perceived burnout than do older coaches (Dale & Weinberg, 1990; Kelley & Gill, 1993; Taylor et al., 1990). Of course, coaches who feel extremely high levels of stress and burnout have probably already quit coaching. Thus, the older coaches who remain likely have good coping skills for stressors in their environment. Researchers thus face the problem that those coaches who have truly burned out (i.e., are out of the profession) are unavailable for study.

Coaching Style

Dale and Weinberg (1990) investigated high school and college coaches and found that those with a consideration style of leadership (caring and people-oriented) had higher levels of perceived burnout than coaches who were more goal-oriented and authoritarian (an initiating-structure leadership style). It may well be that coaches who develop closer personal ties with their athletes suffer greater burnout because they care more. This is not to say that coaches should care less—rather, they should be aware that this style requires

■ MORE INFORMATION ■

Stress and Burnout in Coaches

The stresses and strains of coaching (especially in college and professional sports) have increasingly led to coaches experiencing burnout, or at least taking "time-outs" to cope with the pressures they feel. Some examples include Digger Phelps at Notre Dame, Ricky Byrdsong at Northwestern, Tim Grugrich at the University of Nevada at Las Vegas, Mike Krzyzewski at Duke, Phil Jackson of the Chicago Bulls, and Dick Vermeil of the Philadelphia Eagles. Some of the reasons for this increased stress and burnout are captured by the following quotes:

© Nathaniel S. Butler/NBA Photos

I don't want this to sound like I'm comparing what I do to war, because I'm not. But this job is a little like it was for the guys over in Vietnam. If you're not careful, it can really turn you into somebody else, somebody you don't want to be.

—*Rudy Tomjanovich, coach of the Houston Rockets (LeUnes & Nation, 1996, p. 497)*

I think in a lot of ways sometimes you have to compromise—compromise your coaching values and your coaching philosophy—just to accommodate people and make things work. And that's the toughest thing about it, the tendency of this job to change you and your losing control of it.

—*Pat Riley, coach of the Miami Heat (LeUnes & Nation, 1996, p. 497)*

Why the recent wave of burned-out coaches? Sports gives them tremendous responsibilities but, ultimately, little control. Coaches can only coach; they can't actually run the plays. But if their team loses, they still get fired.

—*"Bureau Report," Time Magazine*

Young coaches appear to have higher levels of perceived burnout than older coaches, partly because some older coaches have already burned out of the profession.

Coaches who are more caring and people-oriented appear more vulnerable to perceived burnout than goal-oriented, authoritarian coaches.

a lot of energy, emotion, and time, which can take a toll long-term.

Social Support

Coaches who report higher levels of satisfaction with social support also experience lower levels of perceived stress and burnout (Kelley, 1994; Kelley & Gill, 1993). Some coaches need reminders to seek out satisfying social support during their times of high

stress and to become more aware of the importance of social support in their personal and professional lives.

Burnout in Fitness Instructors, Administrators, and Physical Education Teachers

There is no reason to believe that fitness instructors, administrators, and physical educators are less susceptible to stress and burnout than other sport and exercise professionals. In fact, research in nonsport settings with teachers and other individuals in the helping professions has found elevated levels of burnout. After all, these professionals are often asked to do more with less, help others, and cope with hectic schedules. Although fitness instructors, administrators, and physical educators have not been studied extensively by sport psychologists, they also should also take steps to prevent burnout.

Treating and Preventing Burnout

The goal in studying overtraining, staleness, and burnout is to learn how to develop programs and strategies that help sport personnel either prevent these conditions or at least treat them effectively. We offer the following suggestions.

Set Short-Term Goals for Competition and Practice

Setting short-term goals with incentives for reaching them not only provides feedback that the athlete is on the right course but also enhances long-term motivation. Meeting short-term goals is a success, which can enhance self-concept. Toward the end of the season it is particularly important to include fun goals. Most of an athlete's time is taken up in practice, rather than competition, so incorporate fun goals there. For example, if a team has been working really hard, its coach could say the practice goal is to simply have fun. She might let a soccer team play basketball or relax the game so that "everything goes" (no rules). These activities provide a break and reduce monotony. Similarly, exercisers trying to maintain a regular program of physical activity need short-term goals to keep them motivated and provide them with feedback concerning their progress to meeting their long-term goals.

■ MORE INFORMATION ■

Reducing Burnout in Young Tennis Players

In interviewing burned-out tennis players, Gould et al. (1996b) asked what advice they would give parents, coaches, and other players to help prevent burnout. Some of their suggestions include the following:

Advice for Other Players

- Play for your own reasons.
- Balance tennis and other things.
- Try to make it fun.
- Take time off and relax.

Advice for Parents

- Recognize what is an optimal amount of "pushing."
- Give support, show empathy, and reduce the importance of outcome.
- Involve players in decision making.
- Lessen involvement.

Advice for Coaches

- Have two-way communication with players.
- Cultivate personal involvement with players.
- Utilize player input.
- Understand players' feelings.

Communicate

When professionals constructively analyze and communicate their feelings to others, burnout is less likely and less severe if it does occur. Coaches, athletes, officials, trainers, and physical education teachers can be encouraged to express their feelings of frustration, anxiety, and disappointment and to seek out social support from colleagues and friends. In fact, social support networks should be developed so they can be tapped when necessary. Self-awareness and preparation early-on might prevent burnout later.

Take Relaxation (Time-Out) Breaks

It is essential for mental and physical well-being to take some time off from jobs and other stresses. The business world has vacations, holidays, and weekends away from work. But in the competitive sport and the fitness industry many people work almost year-round under continuous pressure. The myth that more is better is still afloat when it comes to practice and workouts. Time off is seen as falling behind your opposition. Yet the weekly grind of practice and competitions produces mental and physical fatigue. In truth, cutting back on training loads and intensities as a burnout treatment or prevention is associated with increases in positive mental health. The key here is to develop balance in your life.

Learn Self-Regulation Skills

Developing psychological skills such as relaxation, imagery, goal setting, and positive self-talk can ward off much of the stress that leads to burnout. For example, setting realistic goals can help manage time for balancing professional and personal lives. People who overtrain in sport or exercise usually do so at the expense of their family and personal lives. By setting realistic goals, you have time for both your sport and exercise and other responsibilities, helping you avoid the burnout syndrome.

Keep a Positive Outlook

It is easy for officials, for example, to let news commentary and criticism from coaches, spectators, and players get them down. Even when they officiate a great game, the losing coach may be upset and then blame them. The antidote for officials is to focus on what they do well. A positive focus means working on the things you can control to get better—and not dwelling on unwarranted criticism. One way to accomplish this is to seek people who provide social support (for example, other colleagues) to help you keep a positive outlook.

Manage Postcompetition Emotions

Although many coaches and athletes know to control pregame anxiety and tension, few consider what happens after competition. The final buzzer does not necessarily stop the intense psychological feelings aroused by the competition. Emotions often intensify and erupt into postgame quarrels, fights, drinking binges, and other destructive behaviors. On the other hand, some athletes become depressed, despondent, and withdrawn after losing or performing poorly. Henschen (1998) suggests some ways for coaches to handle postcompetition stress in athletes:

1. Provide a supportive atmosphere immediately after the contest.
2. Concentrate on your players' emotions, not your own.

■ CLOSE-UP ■

Time-Out

An Olympic athlete used to live and train in southern California, where the weather is typically good year-round. In that sunny, warm environment she said she always felt guilty for missing a practice or taking a day off, but with her year-round training regimen she found herself getting injured often and feeling stressed and somewhat burned out. She moved to the middle of the country, where the weather was more variable—often extremely hot in the summer and extremely cold in the winter. When the weather was very bad, she either took the day off or shortened her workout. To her surprise, the days off did not hurt her performance; instead her performance actually improved because she avoided injury and started to regain her enthusiasm. This led her to schedule relaxation or "off" days into her training.

3. Try to be with your team after a contest (not on the radio or TV).

4. Provide an unemotional, realistic assessment of each athlete's performance.

5. Talk to all team members, even those who did not play.

6. Once athletes have dressed, have a group activity for the team (e.g., postgame meal, swimming, bowling, movie).

7. Keep athletes away from well-meaning but demanding peers and parents.

8. Do not allow team members to gloat over success or be depressed over a loss.

9. Begin preparation for the next opponent at the very next practice.

Stay in Good Physical Condition

Your body and mind have a reciprocal relationship: Each affects the other. Chronic stress usually takes a toll on your body, so it's critical that you take good care of yourself through diet and exercise. Eating improperly, gaining weight, or losing too much weight only contributes to low self-esteem and self-worth, feeding into the burnout syndrome. When you feel particular stress, make a special attempt to stay in good physical condition to help your mental state stay strong.

SUMMARY

1 *Define overtraining, staleness, and burnout.*

Overtraining is the abnormal extension of the training process with loads too intense for athletes to adapt to. Staleness is the end result of overtraining, a state in which athletes have difficulty maintaining their standard training regimens and performance results. Burnout is another, more exhaustive psychophysiological response of withdrawal from excessive training and competitive demands.

2 *Discuss different models of burnout.*

Three sport-specific models of burnout have been developed to help explain the burnout phenomenon. The cognitive-affective model is probably the most developed and presents a four-stage process of burnout involving situational demands, cognitive appraisal of the situation, physiological responses, and coping behaviors. The negative-training stress response model focuses more attention on responses to physical training, although psychological factors are also seen as important. The unidimensional identity development and external control model is more sociological in nature, viewing stress as a symptom of social and societal factors.

3 *Describe the causes of overtraining and burnout.*

The causes of burnout and overtraining fall into four general categories: These include physical concerns (e.g., injury, a high frequency and intensity of training), logistical concerns (e.g., travel grind, time demands), social-interpersonal concerns (e.g., dissatisfaction with social life, negative parental influences), and psychological concerns (e.g., inappropriate expectations, lack of enjoyment).

4 *Identify the symptoms of overtraining and burnout.*

Some common symptoms of overtraining include apathy, mood changes, muscle pain, and appetite loss. Some common symptoms of burnout include a lack of caring, emotional isolation, and increased anxiety.

5 *Explain the research evidence of burnout in sport.*

Although the interest in burnout originally focused on athletes, recent research has examined burnout in other sport professionals such as coaches, officials, and athletic trainers. In general, these different people share much in terms of the causes of burnout and their reactions to it.

6 *Describe the treatment and prevention of burnout.*

Several strategies have been developed to help prevent or reduce the probability of burnout in sport and exercise settings. These include setting short-term goals for practices and competitions, taking relaxation breaks, keeping a positive outlook, and learning self regulation skills.

KEY TERMS

periodized training	situational demands
overtraining	cognitive appraisal
staleness	physiological responses
burnout	behavioral responses

REVIEW QUESTIONS

1. Discuss research regarding the frequency of overtraining, staleness, and burnout in athletes.
2. Define the terms *overtraining*, *staleness*, and *burnout*, pointing out similarities and differences.
3. Based on research by Gould and his colleagues, discuss five causes of burnout in athletes, including the importance of individual differences.
4. Use Morgan's "iceberg profile" to discuss the relation between psychological mood and performance.
5. Describe Raedeke's approach to burnout using sport commitment.
6. What are the four stages of burnout? Describe each in detail.
7. Discuss the findings of research on burnout among trainers and officials.
8. Discuss the impact of gender, age, experience, and social support on the susceptibility and reactions to burnout that coaches experience.
9. Describe three different antidotes, or treatments, for burnout and overtraining in sport.

CRITICAL THINKING QUESTIONS

1. Three models of burnout in sport were presented: the cognitive-affective stress model, the negative-training stress model, and the unidimensional identity development and external control model. Describe the similarities and differences among these models. Based on these models, what are three things you would do if you were a coach to prevent burnout in your athletes?
2. Gould and his colleagues conducted in-depth interviews with young tennis players who had left the game early because they felt burned out. Based on the findings from that study, discuss five pieces of advice that you might give coaches, parents, and athletes for avoiding burnout.

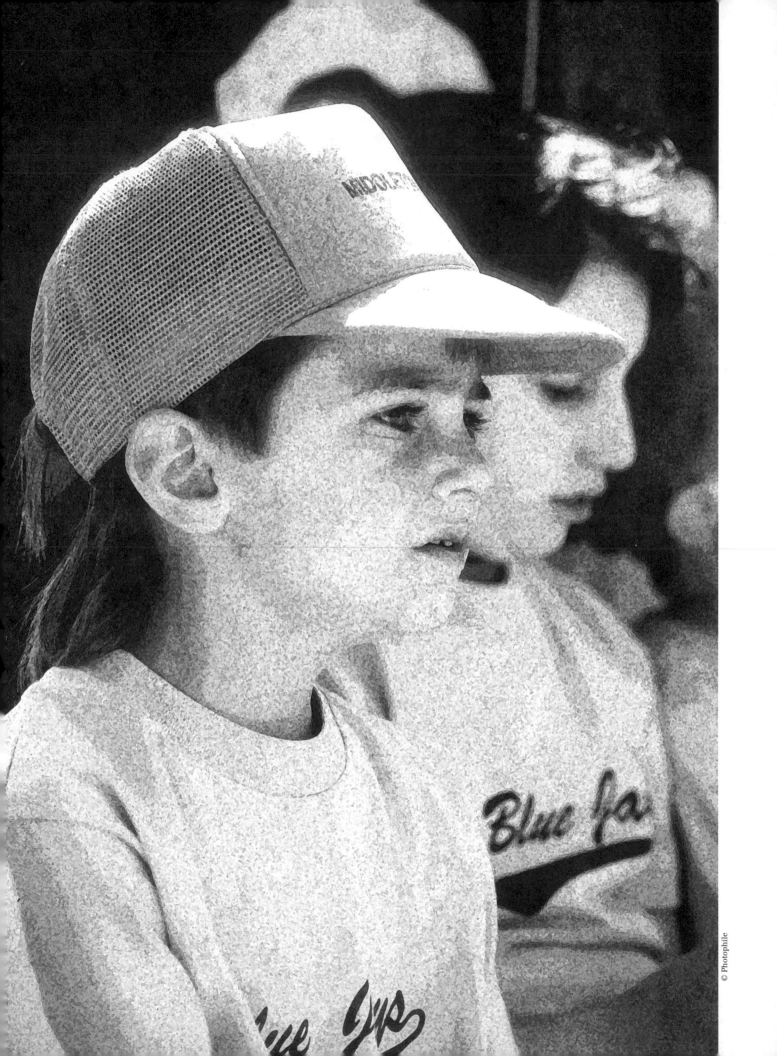

Part VII

Facilitating Psychological Growth and Development

As we have learned, sport and exercise psychology focuses on helping people enhance performance through the use of mental skills. But this represents only part of the field. Sport psychology also deals with how psychological development and well-being occur as consequences of participation in sport and physical activity. The chapters in this part concern three main topics of psychological development and well-being important to both society and sport and exercise psychology.

Chapter 22 examines children's psychological development through sport participation, looking at such important issues as the levels of stress youngsters experience, developing their self-esteem, and effective coaching practices for helping kids. Chapter 23 focuses on the important topic of aggression in sport. Unfortunately, a growing number of incidents have occurred recently, in which athletes have lost control of their emotions both on and off the playing field and displayed a variety of aggressive and abusive behaviors. In this chapter you'll read about the causes underlying aggression, spectator aggression, and some recommendations that might lessen unwanted aggression. In chapter 24 we discuss issues of moral development and sportspersonship in sport and physical activity contexts. Besides the development of moral behavior and the factors associated with moral development, we describe new programs in physical education targeted at enhancing moral development.

© Human Kinetics

Children's Psychological Development Through Sport

After reading this chapter you should be able to

1 discuss the importance of studying the psychology of the young athlete,

2 explain the major reasons children participate in and drop out of sport,

3 discuss the importance of peer relationships in youth sports,

4 describe stress and burnout effects in young athletes,

5 identify and explain how to apply effective coaching practices with youngsters, and

6 discuss the role of parental involvement in youth sports.

As many as 45 million children participate in sport in the United States What motivates them? Is competitive sport too stressful for them? Why do so many youngsters drop out of sport after the age of 12? Is there something wrong with how they're being coached? These are among the important questions we'll try to answer in this chapter.

It is ironic that most people think of sport psychology as applying principally to elite athletes. In fact, youngsters comprise the greatest population of sport participants, and since the mid-1970s a small but highly committed number of sport psychologists have devoted their careers to examining the important psychological issues in children's sport participation. Their work has major implications for creating safe and psychologically healthy sport programs for children.

Why a Psychology of the Young Athlete?

In the United States alone, an estimated 45 million children under the age of 18 years are involved in school and extracurricular physical activity programs, ranging from youth basketball and baseball to cross-country skiing and rodeo (Ewing, Seefeldt, & Brown, 1996; Seefeldt, Ewing, & Walk, 1993). Some of sport psychology's most important contributions, therefore, are potentially to children's sport.

Many children are intensely involved in organized sports. On average, they participate in their specific sport 11 hours weekly for an 18-week season (Gould & Martens, 1979). Sport is one of the few areas in children's lives in which they can participate intensively in an activity that has meaningful consequences for themselves, their peers and family, and the community alike (Coleman, 1974).

For most children sport participation peaks near the age of 12 years (State of Michigan, 1976). And we know from research in developmental psychology, this age and the time leading up to it are critical times for children, having important consequences on their self-esteem and social development. Thus, the youth sport experience can have important life-

Some of the most important implications of sport psychology are in the children's sports arena. For most children, sport participation peaks around the age of 12 years.

long effects on the personality and psychological development of children.

Contrary to popular belief, participation in organized sport is not automatically beneficial for the child (Martens, 1978). Character development, leadership, sportspersonship, and achievement orientations do not magically occur through mere participation. These benefits usually follow competent, adult supervision from leaders who understand children and know how to structure programs that provide positive learning experiences. An important first step to becoming a qualified youth sport leader is understanding the psychology of young athletes.

Why Children Participate in Sports

Some 8,000 youths (49% male, 51% female) involved in sponsored sports throughout the United States, both in school and after school, were asked to rank in importance a number of possible reasons for their participating (Ewing & Seefeldt, 1989). Boys and girls in both school and nonschool athletic programs had similar responses (see Table 22.1), and their comments were consistent with previous research into the motivation for participation (Gould & Horn, 1984). Most children participate in sport to have fun. Other reasons most of them cite are to do something they are good at, improve their skills, get exercise and become fit, be with their friends and make new friends, and compete.

Why Children Discontinue Participation in Sports

Children's sport participation peaks between the ages of 10 and 13 years and then consistently declines to the age of 18, when a relatively small percentage of youths remain involved in organized sport (Ewing & Seefeldt, 1989; State of Michigan, 1976). Moreover, dropout rates for organized youth sport programs average 35% in any given year (Gould & Petlichkoff, 1988). So, of every 10 children who begin a sport season, 3 to 4 of them will drop out by the start of the next season.

An in-depth study of 50 swimming dropouts, ranging in age from 10 to 18 years, found that "other things to do" and "a change in interest" were the major reasons the vast majority of children gave for discontinued involvement (Gould, Feltz, Horn, & Weiss, 1982). Other reasons the sample rated as im-

For every 10 children who begin a sports season, 3 to 4 quit before the season ends.

Children with low perceptions of their athletic abilities drop out of or do not participate in sport, whereas children with high perceptions of their competence participate and persist.

portant (but less important than other interests and change of interests) were "not as good as I wanted to be," "not enough fun," "wanted to play another sport," "didn't like the pressure," "boredom," "didn't like the coach," "training was too hard," and "not exciting enough." So most young swimmers who quit did so because of interest in other activities. However, as many as 28% of the swimmers cited negative factors—such as excessive pressure, dislike of the coach, failure, a lack of fun, and an overemphasis on winning—as being important influences on their decision to withdraw.

Perceived Competence

The reasons youths give for participation and dropping out are their surface-level responses, not the deeper, underlying motives some sport psychologists have sought (see Figure 22.1). For example, children who discontinue often have low perceived com-

petence, focus on outcome goals, and experience considerable stress.

Maureen Weiss, a leading researcher in this area, concluded that youth sport participants differ from nonparticipants and those who drop out in their level of perceived competence (Weiss & Chaumeton, 1992). That is, children with low perceptions of their abilities to learn and perform sport skills do not participate (or they drop out), whereas children who persist have higher levels of perceived competence.

From this information, you can infer that one crucial task of youth sport leaders and coaches is to discover ways to enhance children's self-perceived ability. One way to do this is to teach children to evaluate their performances by their own standards of improvement rather than by competitive outcomes (winning or losing).

Table 22.1

Motives for Participation in Youth Sports

Reasons for participating in nonschool sports

BOYS	GIRLS
1. To have fun	1. To have fun
2. To do something I'm good at	2. To stay in shape
3. To improve my skills	3. To get exercise
4. For the excitement of competition	4. To improve my skills
5. To stay in shape	5. To do something I'm good at
6. For the challenge of competition	6. To learn new skills
7. To get exercise	7. For the excitement of competition
8. To learn new skills	8. To play as part of a team
9. To play as part of a team	9. To make new friends
10. To go to a higher level of competition	10. For the challenge of competition

Reasons for participating in school sports

BOYS	GIRLS
1. To have fun	1. To have fun
2. To improve my skills	2. To stay in shape
3. For the excitement of competition	3. To get exercise
4. To do something I'm good at	4. To improve my skills
5. To stay in shape	5. To do something I'm good at
6. For the challenge of competition	6. To be part of a team
7. To be part of a team	7. For the excitement of competition
8. To win	8. To learn new skills
9. To go to a higher level of competition	9. For team spirit
10. To get exercise	10. For the challenge of competition

Adapted from Ewing and Seefeldt, 1989.

Sport-Specific and Sport-General Dropouts

Youth sport leaders usually want to know if children are withdrawing from their programs and entering other sports (sport-specific dropouts) or withdrawing from sport participation altogether (sport-general dropouts). For example, in the swimming study cited earlier, 68% of the youngsters who discontinued competitive swimming were active in other sports (Gould et al., 1982). Similarly, in a study of former competitive gymnasts, 95% were participating in another sport or were still in gymnastics, but at a less intense level (Klint & Weiss, 1986). Thus, we need to distinguish between sport-specific drop-

Learn whether children are withdrawing from a particular sport or program or from sport participation altogether.

outs or sport transfers and those children who discontinue involvement in all of sport (Gould & Petlichkoff, 1988).

Youth Sport Participation: Implications for Practice

The research on why children participate or withdraw from sports leads to a number of general conclusions:

458

Why children participate	Why children withdraw
• Learn new skills • Fun • Affiliation • Thrills and excitement • Exercise and fitness • Competitive challenge/winning	• Failure to learn new skills • Lack of fun • Lack of affiliation • Lack of thrills and excitement • Lack of exercise and fitness • No challenge/failure

Underlying psychological motive for participation or withdrawal
• Perceived competence
• Goal orientations
• Stress response

Figure 22.1 *A motivational model of youth sport participation and withdrawal.*
Adapted from Gould and Petlichkoff, 1988.

■ Most of the motivations children have for participating in sport (i.e., having fun, learning new skills, doing something one is good at, being with friends, making new friends, fitness, exercise, and to experience success) are intrinsic in nature. Winning clearly is neither the only nor the most common reason for participation.

■ Most young athletes have multiple reasons for participation, not a single motive.

■ Although most children withdraw because of interest in other activities, a significant minority discontinue for negative reasons such as a lack of fun, too much pressure, or disliking the coach.

■ Underlying the descriptive reasons for sport withdrawal (e.g., no fun) is the child's need to feel worthy and competent. When young athletes feel worthy and competent about the activity, they tend to participate. If they don't feel confident about performing the skills, they tend to withdraw.

Think about the interactional model of motivation—how a person interacts with a situation (see chapter 3). If you understand the reasons children participate in sport, you can enhance their motivation by structuring environments that better meet their needs. Study Table 22.2, which shows strategies a coach can use to structure the environment for skill development, fun, affiliation, excitement, success, and fitness.

By emphasizing individual goal setting, where children compare their athletic performances to their own standards (self-referenced standards), you will

> *Teach young athletes to view success as exceeding their own goals, not merely as winning contests.*

help them not focus sole attention on the outcomes of competitions (Martens, Christina, Harvey, & Sharkey, 1981), and they will more likely feel competent. When self-evaluation depends on winning and losing, 50% of young athletes can lose and develop low self-worth, making them less likely to continue sport participation.

Youth sport leaders can keep—and analyze—participation statistics and conduct "exit interviews" with children who drop out. In this way they can track how many children begin, continue, and complete seasons and, if they discontinue, whether they chose to participate in another sport or to discontinue involvement in sport altogether. They can ask whether young athletes discontinued because of conflicts with other interests (something adult leaders may not have control over) or because of poor coaching, competitive pressure, or a lack of fun (which adult leaders can better control).

For example, a high school football coach was concerned about the low number of players coming out for his squad. He examined previous participation records at all levels of play and saw that many youngsters had participated in elementary and middle school programs but few had participated in the ninth grade. The coach spoke with some of the

Table 22.2

Strategies for Structuring Sport Situations to Meet the Needs of Young Athletes

Need	Coaching strategy
Learn and improve new skills	Implement effective instructional practices (e.g., effective demonstrations; contingent feedback) Foster a positive approach to instruction, emphasizing what the child does correctly Know the technical and strategic aspects of the sport
To have fun	Form realistic expectations to avoid negative coaching results and frustration Keep practices active—avoid lines and standing around Joke and kid around freely with the children
Affiliation	Provide time for children to make friends Schedule social events (e.g., pizza party) outside practice Incorporate periods of free time before and during practices
Excitement	Do not overemphasize time spent on drills; incorporate variety into practices Incorporate change-of-pace activities (e.g., water polo for swimmers) into practices Focus on short, crisp practices
Exercise and fitness	Teach young athletes how to monitor their own fitness Organize planned, purposeful practices specifically designed to enhance fitness
Competitive challenge and winning	Allow children to compete Help children define winning as not only beating others but as achieving one's own goals and standards

players who had discontinued during middle school and discovered that some very negative coaching had occurred at the seventh- and eighth-grade levels. He discussed with these coaches the advantages of a positive approach to coaching (explained later in this chapter) and found in subsequent years that more players were coming out for his high school team.

Petlichkoff (1996) suggests that when children discontinue sport involvement, a coach should ask the following questions:

■ Has the child developed an interest in another sport or activity?

■ Does the child's withdrawal appear to be permanent or temporary?

■ Did the child have a part or choice in the decision to withdraw or was she cut from a team or injured?

■ What effect does the withdrawal have on the child's well-being?

Based on the responses to these questions, the coach can determine whether the child's withdrawal is appropriate (a child selects soccer participation

Rigorously analyze why young athletes withdraw from sport.

over basketball) or inappropriate (a child discontinues all sport and physical activity participation because of low perceived competence). We should be particularly concerned when children permanently withdraw, have no choice in the decision, or when the withdrawal has negative effects on their well-being.

Role of Friends in Youth Sport

Affiliation is a major **motive** children have for sports participation. Thus, children enjoy sport because of the opportunities it provides to be with friends and make new friends. While affiliation is certainly important in its own right, sport psychology researchers have discovered that friends and the peer group have other important effects and consequences on young athletes.

Peer Relationships and Children's Psychological Development

Developmental psychologists have long known that friends and peers play a major role in the psychological development of children. Peer relations are related to a child's acceptance, self-esteem, and motivation. So it is natural that sport psychology researchers have turned their attention to this important area.

Leading developmental sport psychologist Maureen Weiss and her colleagues have studied friendship and peer relationships in sport. For example, they conducted in-depth interviews with 38 sport participants, 8 to 16 years of age, to learn how children view the component of friendship in sport (Weiss, Smith, & Theeboom, 1996). They identified both positive and negative dimensions in this facet of sport participation. These were some positive dimensions they heard about:

- Companionship (spending time or "hanging out" together)

- Pleasant play association (enjoying being around one's friend)

- Enhancement of self-esteem (friends saying things or taking actions that boost one's self-esteem)

- Help and guidance (providing assistance relative to learning sport skills as well as general assistance in other domains, such as school)

- Prosocial behavior (saying and doing things that conform to social convention, such as sharing and not saying negative things)

- Intimacy (mutual feelings of close, personal bonds)

- Loyalty (a sense of commitment to one another)

- Things in common (shared interests)

- Attractive personal qualities (positive characteristics such as personality or physical features)

- Emotional support (expressions and feelings of concern for one another)

- Absence of conflicts (some friends do not argue, fight, or disagree)

- Conflict resolution (other friends are able to resolve conflicts)

© Caroline Woodham

Fewer negative dimensions of friendship were identified by the young athletes, but those they commented on included the following:

- Conflict (verbal insults, arguments, and disagreements)
- Unattractive personal qualities (undesirable behavioral or personality characteristics, such as being self-centered)
- Betrayal (disloyalty or insensitivity on the part of a friend)
- Inaccessibility (lack of opportunity to interact with one another)

Girls were more apt than boys to identify emotional support as positive features of friendship in sport. The older children among these subjects saw intimacy as more important, whereas children under 13 years mentioned prosocial behavior and loyalty more often. Respondents older than 10 years also cited attractive personal qualities more frequently.

In a follow-up study, Smith (1997) studied peer relationships and physical activity participation in 207 female and 211 male middle school children. Children who perceived more positive relationships with peers in physical activity also reported more positive feelings toward physical activity and their physical self-worth. Hence, peer relations had a great deal to do with the child's motivation for physical activity, which suggests that promoting positive peer relationships can enhance participation in physical activity.

Friendship in Sport: Implications for Practice

The initial research on peer relationships and friendship has a number of implications for practice (Weiss et al., 1996). First, time should be provided for children to be with their friends and for making new friends. The old adage that all work and no play makes Jack (or Jill) a dull boy (or girl) has a ring of truth.

Second, coaches and parents should encourage positive peer reinforcement in an effort to enhance self-esteem among youngsters participating in physical activity. Positive statements to teammates should be reinforced, whereas derogatory remarks, teasing, and negative comments should not be tolerated. Children must be taught to respect others and refrain from verbal aggression. In chapter 23, we will discuss a number of techniques for doing this.

Third, the importance of teamwork and the pursuit of group goals should be emphasized. Techniques to foster group cohesion (see chapter 8) and goal setting (see chapter 15) should be frequently employed in the youth sport setting.

Stress and Burnout in Children's Competitive Sport

Stress and burnout are among the most controversial concerns in children's competitive sport. Critics argue that competitive sport places excessive levels of stress on youngsters, who often burn out from it. Proponents contend that young athletes do not experience excessive competition and that competition teaches children coping strategies, which transfer to other aspects of their lives.

Are Young Athletes Under Too Much Stress?

Levels of stress in young athletes have been assessed by using state anxiety measures that were administered in competitive game situations (where stress is predicted to be maximal). Most young athletes do not experience excessive levels of state anxiety in competition. For example, 13- and 14-year-old wrestlers took the Competitive State Anxiety Inventory for Children just before competition (see Figure 22.2, showing the distribution of anxiety scores of the 112 wrestlers). Their prematch state-anxiety level averaged 18.9 out of a possible 30. Only 9% of the wrestlers had scores in the upper 25% of the scale, which could be considered extremely high. Thus, 91% of the wrestlers did not experience excessive stress (Gould, Eklund, Petlichkoff, Peterson, & Bump, 1991).

Simon and Martens (1979) measured state anxiety levels of boys, ages 9 to 14, in both practice and socially evaluative settings. State anxiety levels in this study were compared among participants in band music (both soloists with the band and band ensemble members), academic tests, competitive physical education classes, and in competitive baseball, basketball, tackle football, gymnastics, ice hockey, swimming, and wrestling. Levels exhibited in sport competition were not significantly greater than those

State anxiety levels in children during sport competitions are not usually significantly higher than those during other childhood evaluative activities.

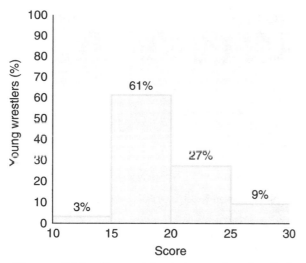

Figure 22.2 *Prematch state anxiety levels in youth wrestlers as measured with the Competitive State Anxiety Inventory for Children.*

in the other activities tested. State anxiety was elevated more in competition than in practices, but this change was not dramatic. In fact, band soloists reported the greatest state anxiety levels (M = 21.5 out of 30).

These studies didn't answer the question of whether there might be long-term stress effects apparent in the children's trait anxiety levels. So later investigators examined sport participation's influence on children's trait anxiety (i.e., their predisposition to perceive competition as threatening and respond with heightened nervousness). From this research, it appears that young athletes have at most only slightly elevated trait anxiety levels. Moreover, in half the studies no differences were found (see Gould, 1993, for a detailed review).

Factors Associated With Heightened State Anxiety in Young Athletes

Although most children who participate in sport do not experience excessive state or trait anxiety levels, stress can be a problem for certain children in specific situations. And although this may be true of only 1 of 10 children who participate in the United States, among 45 million young participants that could mean 4.5 million children with heightened stress. For this reason, sport psychologists also examine what personal and situational factors are associated with heightened state anxiety by administering various background and personality measures away from the competitive setting (e.g., trait anxiety, self-esteem, team and individual performance expectancies, ratings of parental pressure to participate), as well as

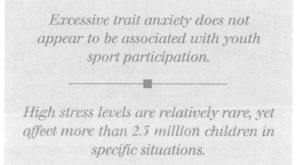

Excessive trait anxiety does not appear to be associated with youth sport participation.

High stress levels are relatively rare, yet affect more than 2.5 million children in specific situations.

state anxiety assessments in practice, immediately before competition, and immediately after it. Links are then made between heightened levels of state anxiety and factors related to these changes (see Scanlan, 1986 for a detailed review).

Using the findings from these studies researchers have developed a profile of the young athlete at risk for experiencing unhealthy levels of competitive state anxiety (see the box on p. 464). A thorough knowledge of these characteristics will help you detect a child at risk.

Most of the research has studied youngsters under 14 years of age, usually in local competitions. However, some studies have looked at elite junior athletes of high school age. For instance, elite, high school distance runners experienced stress in performing up to their ability, improving on their last performance, participating in championship meets, not performing well, and not being mentally ready (Feltz & Albrecht, 1986). Elite junior wrestlers cited similar stressors (Gould, Horn, & Spreemann, 1983). Thus, elite junior competitors seem primarily stressed by a fear of failure and feelings of inadequacy.

Situational Sources of Stress

Situations, too, can increase stress, particularly these types of factors:

- Defeat—children experience more state anxiety after losing than after winning.
- Event importance—the more importance placed on a contest, the more state anxiety experienced by the participants.
- Sport type—children in individual sports experience more state anxiety than children in team sports.

Consequently, youth sport leaders must understand both the personalities of children at risk of having high levels of competitive stress and the situations most likely to produce heightened state anxiety. We cannot help children deal with excessive

■ MORE INFORMATION ■

Characteristics of Children at Risk for Heightened Competitive State Anxiety

- High trait anxiety
- Low self-esteem
- Low performance expectancies relative to the team
- Low self-performance expectations
- Frequent worries about failure
- Frequent worries about adult expectations and social evaluation by others
- Less perceived fun
- Less satisfaction with their performance, regardless of winning or losing
- Perceiving it is important to their parents that they participate in sport
- Outcome goal orientation and low perceived ability

Stress in elite junior competitors is caused by a fear of failure and feelings of inadequacy.

Burnout is a special case of sport withdrawal in which a young athlete discontinues sport involvement in response to chronic stress.

stress until we identify the particular stresses that specific situations elicit in them.

Stress-Induced Burnout

We discussed burnout at length in the previous chapter, including its implications for children. Here we'll only elaborate on earlier points, focusing on burnout as a stress-induced phenomenon in young athletes.

Burnout, which is a growing concern with children's competitive sport, is thought to occur when children lose interest as a result of specializing in a specific sport at a very early age and practicing for long hours, under intense pressure for several years. Children as young as age 4 begin participating in sports like gymnastics, swimming, and tennis, some of them attaining world-class levels by their early teens. When careers end early or performance declines prematurely, burnout is suspected. We can understand burnout as a special case of sport withdrawal when a young athlete discontinues or curtails sport involvement in response to chronic or long-term stress (Smith, 1986). A previously enjoyable activity is no longer pleasurable because of the stress it causes. Children withdraw from sport, of course, for reasons other than burnout.

As mentioned in chapter 21, Coakley (1992) found that adolescents who burned out of sport typically had one-dimensional self-definitions, seeing themselves only as athletes and not in other possible roles, such as students, musicians, or school-activity leaders. Also, young athletes who burned out had seriously restricted control of their own destinies, both in and out of sport. Their parents and coaches made the important decisions regarding their sporting lives, with little or no input from them. As you learned in the section on feedback and reinforcement in chapter 6, someone else controlling a person's destiny almost always results in decreased intrinsic motivation.

Some prominent factors associated with burnout have been reported (see the box on p. 465; Gould, 1993), resulting also in increased state anxiety. Unlike the usual state anxiety experienced before a contest, however, for a child en route to burnout the stress does not abate but instead builds constantly. Thus, burnout is best viewed as the end result of long-term stress.

Dealing With Stressed Children: Implications for Practice

Once children with stress, or at high risk of experiencing stress, have been identified, what can adult leaders do to help them learn to cope? Adults should make concerted efforts, first, to help children develop confidence by creating a positive environment and a constructive attitude toward mistakes. Stress can be

■ MORE INFORMATION ■

Factors Associated With Burnout in Young Athletes

- Very high self- and other-imposed expectations
- Win-at-all-costs attitude
- Parental pressure
- Long repetitive practices with little variety
- Inconsistent coaching practices
- Overuse injuries from excessive practice
- Excessive time demands
- High travel demands
- Love from others displayed on the basis of winning and losing
- Perfectionism

alleviated by reducing social evaluation and the importance of winning (e.g., no more "win one for the gipper" pep talks). Adult anxiety-reduction techniques (progressive muscle relaxation, breath control, mental training, autogenic training, systematic desensitization, biofeedback, and cognitive-affective stress-management strategies) can be adapted for use with children. For instance, Terry Orlick (1992) has adapted progressive muscle relaxation for children by creating a "spaghetti toes" exercise (see box on p. 466). Orlick and McCaffrey (1991) also have these suggestions for modifying arousal regulation and stress-management strategies for children:

■ Use concrete and physical strategies (e.g., a little "stress bag" for children to put their worries in).

■ Use fun strategies (e.g., have children release muscle tension by making their bellies turn to Jell-o).

■ Use simple strategies (e.g., imagine changing TV channels to change one's mind focus).

■ Vary approaches to the same exercise.

■ Individualize approaches to the children's interests.

■ Remain positive and optimistic.

■ Use role models (e.g., tell them Michael Jordan uses positive self-talk).

General directions (e.g., "Just relax" or "You can do it") are not enough to help children manage stress. You'll need to develop strategies to make the directions fun and relevant to the children.

Effective Coaching Practices for Young Athletes

You may have heard about or seen Little League coaches who emulate big-time college or professional coaches to try to achieve success and impress people. For example, former Vice President Dan Quayle once boasted that he modeled his coaching of his 12-year-old son's basketball team after Indiana University basketball coach Bobby Knight. But is Knight's style (especially his use of punishment, severe criticism, and emotional outbursts) appropriate to use with 12-year-olds? Probably not. Coaching practices designed for adult elite athletes are often inappropriate for developing young athletes. Sport psychologists have found many coaching practices that are more effective with youngsters.

What Research Says About Coaching Children

The classic research about coaching children was conducted at the University of Washington by Ron Smith, Frank Smoll, and their colleagues. They examined the relation between coaching behaviors (e.g., reinforcement, mistake-contingent technical instruction) and self-esteem in young baseball players and whether coaches could learn effective coaching practices (Smith, Smoll, & Curtis, 1979). Their study had

Children have special coaching needs, much different from the needs of adults.

465

■ APPLICATION ■

Orlick's Spaghetti Toes Relaxation Exercise

There are lots of games you can play with your body. We'll start with one called Spaghetti Toes. I wonder how good you are at talking to your toes. I'll bet you're pretty good. Let's find out.

Tell the toes on one of your feet to wiggle. Are they wiggling? On just one foot? Good! Now tell these toes to stop wiggling. Tell the toes on your other foot to wiggle. Tell them to wiggle real slow . . . and faster . . . and real slow again . . . slower . . . stop! Did your toes listen to you? Good.

If you talk to different parts of your body, as you just did with your toes, your body will listen to you . . . especially if you talk to them a lot. I'm going to show you how you can be the boss of your body by talking to it.

First, I want to tell you something about spaghetti. I like spaghetti. I bet you do, too. But did you ever see spaghetti before it's cooked? It's kind of cold and hard and stiff, and it's easy to break. When it's cooked, it's warm and soft and kinda' lies down and curls up on your plate.

I want to see if you can talk to your toes to get them to go soft and warm and sleepy like cooked spaghetti lying on your plate. You might have to talk to them quite a bit to make them know what you want them to do, but I know they can do it.

Wiggle your toes on one foot. Now tell these toes to stop wiggling. Tell them to go soft and sleepy like warm spaghetti lying on your plate. Now wiggle the toes on your other foot. Stop wiggling. Turn those toes into soft spaghetti. Good.

Now wiggle one leg. Stop wiggling. Tell the leg to go soft and sleepy like warm spaghetti. Now wiggle the other leg. Stop. Tell it to go soft and sleepy. Wiggle your behind. Let it go soft and sleepy.

Wiggle your fingers on one hand. Tell your fingers to stop wiggling. See if you can make those fingers feel warm and soft and sleepy like spaghetti lying on your plate. Now wiggle your fingers on your other hand. Slowly. Stop. Make those fingers feel warm. Tell them to go soft and sleepy.

Now wiggle one arm. Stop. Tell your arm to go soft and sleepy. Now wiggle the other arm and tell it to go soft and sleepy. Good.

Try to let your whole you go soft and warm and sleepy, like soft spaghetti lying on your plate. [Pause] That's really good. Your body is listening well. Let your body stay like spaghetti and just listen to me. I want to tell you about when spaghetti toes can help you.

When you are worried or scared of something, or when something hurts, your toes and your hands and muscles get kinda' hard and stiff—like hard spaghetti before it's cooked. If you are worried, scared, or something hurts you, you feel a lot better and it doesn't hurt so much if your hands and toes and muscles are like warm, soft spaghetti lying on a plate. If you practice doing your spaghetti toes, you'll get really good at it. Then you can tell your hands and toes and muscles to help you by going warm and soft and sleepy, even if you are scared or something hurts.

Before you go, let's try talking to your mouth. Wiggle your mouth. Let it go soft and sleepy. Wiggle your tongue. Let it go soft and sleepy. Wiggle your eyebrows. Let them go soft and sleepy. Let your whole you go warm and soft and sleepy. Let your whole you feel good. (Orlick, 1982a, p. 325)

two phases. In the first phase, 52 male youth-baseball coaches were observed while coaching and assessed using a specially developed instrument, the Coaching Behavior Assessment System (CBAS). The researchers also interviewed 542 players about their Little League baseball experiences and found that coaches who gave technical instruction were rated more positively than those who gave general communication and encouragement. The coaches who used more reinforcement and mistake-contingent technical instruction (gave instruction after errors) were also highly rated—and these results held even when the team's win-loss records were considered. Positive reinforcement and mistake-contingent

© Photophile

encouragement (encouraging a player after a mistake) positively affected postseason self-esteem measures, liking of teammates, and liking of baseball.

Unfortunately, the first phase did not show that the coaching behaviors actually caused changes in the athletes' perceptions, only that these factors were correlated. In a second phase investigators assigned 32 baseball coaches to either a control condition—in which they coached as they had always done—or to an experimental coaching education program in which they received training based on results of the first phase. The experimental group received guidelines on desirable coaching behaviors, saw these behaviors modeled, and were monitored until they increased the frequency of their encouraging remarks by 25%. The control group did not receive any special training (their coaching, however, was not excessively negative).

As you might expect, the experimental group coached differently from the control group: They were more encouraging, gave more reinforcement, and were less punitive. The players in the experimental group rated their coaches as better teachers, liked their teammates more, liked their coaches more,

and showed greater positive changes in self-esteem than did the control group players.

These findings clearly identify coaching behaviors associated with positive psychological development in children. Moreover, the research shows that coaches can learn these positive behaviors.

Other studies have found that remarks from coaches must be not only positive but also sincere to be effective (Horn, 1985); giving information frequently after good performances and encouragement combined with information after poorer performances is associated with effectiveness, competence, and enjoyment (Black & Weiss, 1992); and learning a positive approach to coaching results in lower (5%, compared to 26% with untrained coaches) player-dropout rates (Barnett, Smoll, & Smith, 1992).

A coach's technical instruction, reinforcement, and mistake-contingent encouragement correlate with a player's self-esteem, motivation, and positive attitudes.

467

Coaching Young Athletes: Implications for Practice

Some ready observations for practical work follow from these studies. The following 11 coaching guidelines are drawn from Smoll and Smith (1980) and Weiss (1991).

1. Catch kids doing things right and give them plenty of praise and encouragement. Praise young children frequently. Add such rewards as a pat on the back and a friendly smile. The best way to give encouragement is to focus on what youngsters do correctly rather than on the errors they make.

2. Give praise sincerely. Praise and encouragement are ineffective unless they are sincere. Telling a young athlete she did a good job when she knows she did not conveys that you are trying only to make her feel better. Insincerity destroys your credibility as a leader or coach. Recognize poor performance in a nonpunitive, specific way (put your arm around the child and say, "It can be really tough out there"), but also offer some encouragement ("Stick with it; it will come").

3. Develop realistic expectations. Realistic expectations appropriate to the child's age and ability level make it much easier for a coach to offer sincere praise. You can't expect of an 11-year-old what you might of a 16-year-old.

4. Reward effort as much as outcome. It's easy to be positive when everything is going well. Unfortunately, things don't always go well—teams lose and sometimes perform poorly. However, if a youngster gives 100% effort, what more can you ask? Reward efforts of young athletes as much as—or even more than—game outcomes.

5. Focus on teaching and practicing skills. All the positive coaching techniques in the world will do little good unless youngsters see improvement in their physical skills. Design practice sessions that maximize participation and include plenty of activity and drill variety. Keep instructions short and simple. Give plenty of demonstrations from multiple angles. Maximize equipment and facility use.

6. Modify skills and activities. One of our goals is for children to experience performance successes. Modifying activities so they are developmentally appropriate is an excellent way to ensure success. For example, make sure baskets are lowered, batting tees used, and field distances modified. "Match the activity to the child, not the child to the activity" (Weiss, 1991, p. 347). Use appropriate skill progressions.

7. Modify rules to maximize action and participation. Rules can also be modified to ensure success and enhance motivation. You might modify the traditional baseball or softball rules so that coaches pitch to their own teams, which greatly increases the probability of hits. In basketball, instruct referees to call only the most obvious fouls until the child becomes more skilled. Children can rotate positions to give everyone a chance to be in the action. Modify rules to increase scoring and action. This will keep scores close and games exciting.

8. Reward correct technique, not just outcome. A common mistake in coaching youngsters is to reward the outcome of a skill (e.g., getting a base hit in baseball or softball), even when the process of skill execution is done incorrectly (poor swing). In the long run, this isn't helpful: Proper form is usually needed to achieve desirable outcomes consistently. Encourage and reward correct technique regardless of outcome.

9. Use a positive "sandwich" approach when you correct errors. How can you give frequent praise when young athletes are learning and making many mistakes? One way is to use the positive sandwich approach, as discussed in chapter 10. When a child makes a mistake, first mention something she did correctly ("Good try, you didn't give up on the dive"). This will help reduce her frustration in making the error. Second, provide information to correct the error made (e.g., "Tuck earlier and tighter"). Then end positively with an encouraging remark ("Stick with it—it's a tough dive, but you'll get it").

10. Create an environment that reduces the fear of trying new skills. Mistakes are a natural part of the learning process, what UCLA basketball coach John Wooden called the "building blocks of success." Provide an encouraging atmosphere where ridicule is not tolerated.

11. Be enthusiastic! Children respond well to positive, stimulating environments. Breed enthusiasm in the pool, the gym, or on the playing field. As Maureen Weiss says, enthusiasm is contagious! Smile, interact, and listen.

Role of Parents

In recent years considerable attention has been placed on better understanding and identifying the role that parents play in youth sports and physical activity participation. Much of this increased interest has been stirred by accounts in the popular press of the

© Terry Wild Studio

negative side effects that children's participation in sports can cause. For example, Joan Ryan's (1995) best-selling book *Little Girls in Pretty Boxes* presented heartbreaking stories of young girls whose dreams of becoming Olympic gymnasts and figure skaters were shattered by unhealthy and abusive training environments, often fueled by overly involved, pushy parents. And parental concerns are not limited to elite youth sports: Accounts of overzealous "Little League" parents pushing their children on the playing field or in the gym are all too common in every community.

Parenting Research in Youth Sports

Responding to these concerns sport psychologists have begun to examine the role of parents in children's sport. Krane, Greenleaf, and Snow (1997), for example, conducted a case study of a former elite youth gymnast. They found that this athlete participated in an overly competitive ego goal-oriented environment (e.g., an environment created by

coaches and parents who emphasized winning, perfect performance, and performing with [despite] pain), which led to an overreliance on social comparison, a need to demonstrate her superiority, and an emphasis on external rewards and feedback. It also resulted in unhealthy behaviors, such as practicing when seriously injured, disordered eating, overtraining, and refusing to listen to medical advice.

On a more positive note, Brustad (1993) studied male and female youth basketball participants and their parents, and found that parental enjoyment of physical activity was related to their encouraging their children's involvement in it and, in turn, that the encouragement influenced the child's perceived competence and actual participation. In a study of adolescent, elite soccer players, VanYperen (1995) found that parental support buffered the youngsters who might otherwise have suffered adverse stress-related effects after their below-average soccer performances. And in yet a third study, Duda and Hom (1993) demonstrated that children's goal orientations were significantly related to those adopted by their

Sport Parent Responsibilities and Code of Conduct

Sport Parent Responsibilities

1. Encourage your children to play sports, but don't pressure them. Let your child choose to play—and quit—if she or he wants.

2. Understand what your child wants from sport and provide a supportive atmosphere for achieving those goals.

3. Set limits on your child's participation in sport. You need to determine when your child is physically and emotionally ready to play and to ensure that the conditions for playing are safe.

4. Make sure the coach is qualified to guide your child through the sport experience.

5. Keep winning in perspective, and help your child do the same.

6. Help your child set realistic performance goals.

7. Help your child understand the valuable lessons sports can teach.

8. Help your child meet his or her responsibilities to the team and the coach.

9. Discipline your child appropriately when necessary.

10. Turn your child over to the coach at practices and games—don't meddle or coach from the stands.

11. Supply the coach with information regarding any allergies or special health conditions your child has. Make sure your child takes any necessary medications to games and practices.

© Jean Higgins/Unicorn Stock Photos

Sport Parent Code of Conduct

1. Remain in the spectator area during games.
2. Don't advise the coach on how to coach.
3. Don't make derogatory comments to coaches, officials, or parents of either team.
4. Don't try to coach your child during the contest.
5. Don't drink alcohol at contests or come to a contest having drunk too much.
6. Cheer for your child's team.
7. Show interest, enthusiasm, and support for your child.
8. Be in control of your emotions.
9. Help when asked by coaches or officials.
10. Thank coaches, officials, and other volunteers who conduct the event.

Source: American Sport Education Program (1994)

parents. These studies all show ways in which the motivational climate provided by the parents influenced (positively or negatively) the child's motivation.

One final example of parental influence appears in an interview study of youth sport coaches. Strean (1995) identified instances of parents both interfering with and facilitating children's involvement in a sport program. Negative interference included parents' coaching their child from the sidelines in ways that contradicted what the child was told by their official coach, encouraging their children to fight, or saying vicious things to opposing players. Facilitating actions included parents' positively affecting the motivation of their children and disciplining their child for misbehaving in practices.

Researchers, then, have found that parents can play a highly positive and or a highly negative role in the youth sport experience. The challenge for people involved in youth sport is to identify the precise ways parents can positively affect the experience for youngsters and to encourage parents to employ these practices. Simultaneously, we must identify negative actions and facilitate efforts to eliminate them.

Educating Parents

Although negative parental behaviors will never be completely eliminated from youth sport, much can be accomplished by educating parents and improving the lines of communication among parents, coaches, and league organizers. The American Sport Education Program (1994), for instance, has developed a sport parent program that offers excellent suggestions concerning parental responsibilities and practices (see the box on p. 470). Additionally, parent orientation meetings should be held at the start of the season to inform and discuss such things as the coach's qualifications; program philosophy; the roles played by coach, parent, and athlete; sportspersonship; and team rules. Having an assistant coach or parent as a liaison is also an excellent way to maintain good lines of communication (Strean, 1995).

Understanding the Tricky Business of Parental Support

Finally, as professionals we must appreciate how difficult the job of successful sport parenting really is. It is easy to blame parents for inappropriate actions and problems in our programs. Unfortunately, however, when children are born they do not come with a sport involvement instruction manual, and most parents have had scant training in sport parenting. Moreover, as the child grows and develops, the role of the sport parent changes. For instance, research has shown that prior to age 10, youngsters feel much greater effect from parental feedback than when they are older, whereas after age 10 peer feedback becomes much more important to them (Horn & Weiss, 1991).

An excellent example of the tricky business of parental support comes from the youth-sport burnout research discussed in chapter 21. Junior tennis players who had burned out from tennis indicated there was an optimal amount of parental push they needed. That is, these young athletes indicated that at times they needed their parents to "push" them—for example, getting them out of bed to practice when they were being lazy. However, they also mentioned that such pushing was only appropriate up to a point, and that parents who became overly involved in tennis created a great deal of stress and contributed to burnout.

A critical role for the exercise and sport science professional, then, is to educate and inform parents about how they can help make their child's sport experience optimal.

SUMMARY

1 *Discuss the importance of studying the psychology of the young athlete.*

Applying strategies from sport psychology is vital in youth sport settings because children are at such critical points in their developmental cycles. Qualified adult leadership is crucial to assure a beneficial experience. Moreover, the youth sport experience can have important lifelong effects on the personality and psychological development of children.

2 *Explain the major reasons children participate in and drop out of sport.*

Children cite many reasons for sport participation, including having fun, skill improvement, and being with friends. They also have various reasons for dropping out of sport, including new or additional interests in other activities. Underlying these motives is the young athlete's need to feel worthy and competent. Children who perceive themselves as competent seek out participation and stay involved in sport, whereas children who see themselves as failing often drop out. Adult leaders can facilitate children's participation in sport activity and deter withdrawal in these ways: structuring the environment to encourage the young athletes' motivation, enhancing self-worth by focusing on individual performance goals and downplaying social-comparison or outcome goals, tracking participation and dropout statistics, and conducting exit interviews to determine why youngsters discontinue program involvement.

3 *Discuss the importance of peer relationships in youth sports.*

Peer relationships in youth sport affect a child's sense of acceptance, level of motivation, and self-esteem. Adult leaders should provide time for children to be with friends and make new friends, encourage positive peer reinforcement, emphasize teamwork and the pursuit of group goals, and teach children to respect others and refrain from verbal aggression.

4 *Describe stress and burnout effects in young athletes.*

Most young athletes do not experience excessive levels of competitive stress in sport, but a significant minority do. High trait anxiety, low self-esteem, low self-performance expectations, frequent worry about evaluation, less fun and satisfaction, and parental pressure combine to put children at risk for excessive state anxiety. Losing a competition, attaching great importance to an event, and individual events are situational factors that add to stress. Stress-induced burnout is a specialized withdrawal in which a young athlete discontinues or curtails involvement in response to long-term stress. Knowing potential causes of burnout helps adults teach children to cope with stress. Arousal-management techniques can be adapted for use with children.

5 *Identify and explain how to apply effective coaching practices with youngsters.*

Research findings in sport psychology have clearly shown that certain coaching behaviors are associated with positive psychological development in children. Effective coaching behaviors include having realistic expectations; using techniques that provide youngsters with positive, encouraging, and sincere feedback; rewarding effort and correct technique as much as outcomes; modifying skill requirements and rules; and employing a positive approach to error correction. Following the 11 guidelines in this chapter can create a good sport environment for children.

6 *Discuss the role of parental involvement in youth sports.*

Parents play a particularly important role in the youth sport experience. Parental attitudes and behaviors have major effects, both positive and negative, on young athletes' sport involvement, motivation, self-esteem, and mental health. Educating parents and maintaining open lines of coach-parent communication are important ways to ensure beneficial parental influence in children's sport. Successful parenting for youth sport can be difficult but is worthwhile.

KEY TERMS

perceived competence
sport-specific dropouts

sport-general dropouts
affiliation motive

REVIEW QUESTIONS

1. Why is it important for people who work with young athletes to know sport psychology?

2. What reasons do children cite for sport participation and withdrawal? How does a child's level of perceived athletic competence relate to participation and withdrawal?

3. Distinguish between sport-specific and sport-general withdrawal. Why is this distinction important?

4. What are the positive and negative components of peer relationships in young athletes? Why are these important?

5. Are young athletes placed under too much stress in sport? What children in what situations are at risk of experiencing the highest levels of stress?

6. What is burnout? What causes young athletes to burn out of sport?

7. What can be done to help young athletes cope with stress? What strategies can be employed?

8. What were the major findings of the research that Smith, Smoll, and their colleagues conducted?

9. Identify and describe 11 practical coaching guidelines from research into youth-sport coaching effectiveness.

10. Describe how parents influence the youth sports experience.

CRITICAL THINKING QUESTIONS

1. You are working as a youth sport director of a YMCA that sponsors numerous sport programs. Based on what you learned in this chapter, what policies and programs would you initiate to ensure positive psychological experiences for the children involved?

2. You are the coach of a middle school basketball program. Identify and outline what topics would be important to discuss in a parent-orientation meeting for a team of 10- to 12-year-old young athletes.

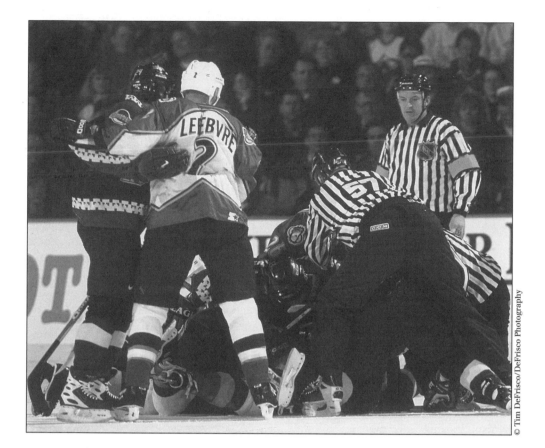

© Tim DeFrisco/DeFrisco Photography

Aggression in Sport

After reading this chapter you should be able to

1 define what is meant by aggression,
2 identify the causes of aggression,
3 explain the aggression-performance relation, and
4 derive implications from research for helping control aggression.

Aggression in sport has become all too common. In a much publicized case, Latrell Sprewell, Golden State Warrior NBA star, was fired and suspended from the league for a year after he attacked and threatened to kill his coach P.J. Carlesimo. Professional boxer Mike Tyson became frustrated in the ring and responded by biting off part of his opponent's ear. Unfortunately, incidents like the Sprewell and Tyson affairs are the well-publicized and extreme examples of aggressive behavior that takes place throughout the sport world. We see it in the bleachers, on the benches, and most commonly on the fields or courts of sport arenas: bench-clearing brawls, brushback pitches and retaliatory beanings, and ice hockey fights. Fan behavior at professional soccer matches has become so violent that a decision resulted to dig moats and construct electric fences. Still other examples of unbridled aggression are citywide rioting to "celebrate" championship wins, stalkers preying on star athletes, weapons uncovered at high school football games, an Australian sport psychologist held hostage at gunpoint by a disgruntled athlete, and a frenzied fan attacking a popular tennis star during a break between games. Even Little League coaches settle altercations with their fists, and one father murdered a coach in a dispute over his son's playing time.

The world was shocked in 1998 to learn of the Jonesboro, Arkansas, case in which two boys, aged 11 and 14, pulled a fire alarm, waited outside the school, and then systematically killed a teacher and a number of their classmates as they exited the school building. We have all witnessed the increased violence in our schools. Fist fighting by itself is bad enough, but ever more children are bringing knives and guns to school—and using them to deal with conflicts that may arise. This has given rise to school administrators' hiring security guards and using metal detectors, and it has created climates of fear for both students and teachers alike. Security guards and metal detectors, though necessary, are not enough. Children must be taught the skills of nonviolent conflict resolution.

Sport has the potential to be a vehicle to control or curb violence. Midnight inner-city basketball games have become popular because they are thought to keep gang members off the street; many people see boxing, wrestling, and, to a lesser extent, football as socially acceptable channels for aggression. Others see these very sports as primarily aggressive.

Given these examples it is clear that aggression is a major concern for those involved in sport. Before we can begin to examine these issues, however, we must understand what aggression is or is not.

What Is Aggression?

The term **aggression** is used in several ways in sport and exercise. We speak of "good" aggression (e.g., going after a loose ball in volleyball or lowering your shoulder in a drive toward the basket) and "bad" aggression (e.g., taking a cheap shot in soccer or committing a flagrant foul in basketball). The term seems to draw automatic associations and produce positive or negative value judgments and emotional responses (Gill, 1986). However, most aggressive behavior in sport and physical activity settings appears not to be inherently desirable or undesirable but to depend on interpretation. Two people watching a particular hard but clean check in ice hockey might disagree whether the hit was good or bad aggression. Actually, aggression is easier to talk about if you avoid the good-bad dichotomy and instead view it neutrally—as a behavior you want to understand (Gill, 1986).

Criteria for Aggression

Psychologists define aggression as "any form of behavior directed toward the goal of harming or injuring another living being who is motivated to avoid such treatment" (Baron & Richardson, 1994, p. 7).

In examining this and similar definitions, four criteria of aggression emerge (Gill, 1986):

- It is a behavior.
- It involves harm or injury.
- It is directed toward a living organism.
- It involves intent.

Aggression is physical or verbal behavior: It is not an attitude or emotion. Aggression involves harm or injury, which may be either physical or psychological (e.g., we would all agree that hitting someone with a baseball bat is an aggressive act, but so too is purposely embarrassing someone or saying something hurtful). Aggression is directed toward another living thing. Punching someone is certainly aggressive, as is slapping a cat who scratches your new chair. But throwing your helmet in disgust after striking out in softball, although in bad taste, is not aggressive. Finally, aggression is intentional. Accidental harm, even unintentionally shooting someone, is not aggressive when harm was not intended.

Aggression is defined as any behavior directed toward intentionally harming or injuring another living being.

■ CLOSE-UP ■

Aggressive or Nonaggressive?

Using Gill's four criteria, circle A or N to indicate whether you consider the behavior in each of these situations to be aggressive (A) or nonaggressive (N).

A   N   1. A football safety delivers an extremely vicious but legal hit to a wide receiver and later indicates he wanted to punish the receiver and make him think twice about coming across the middle again.

A   N   2. A football safety delivers an extremely vicious and illegal hit to a wide receiver.

A   N   3. A basketball coach breaks a chair in protesting a disputed call.

A   N   4. Marcia, a field hockey midfielder, uses her stick to purposely hit her opponent in the shin in retaliation for her opponent's doing the same thing to her.

A   N   5. A race car driver kills a fellow competitor by running into the competitor's stalled car coming out of a turn.

A   N   6. Trying to make a field goal kicker on the opposing team worry and think about the negative ramifications of a game-winning field goal, Coach Sullivan calls a time-out.

A   N   7. Barry knows that John is sensitive and self-conscious about his ability to putt under pressure, so he tells John that Coach Hall said if he does not putt better he will be replaced in the lineup. Coach Hall never said this.

A   N   8. Jane beans Fran with a fastball that got away from her.

Answers

1. Aggressive. (Although the hit was legal, the intent was to inflict harm.)
2. Nonaggressive. (There was no intent to inflict harm.)
3. Nonaggressive. (The action was not directed at another living being.)
4. Aggressive. (Although the athlete felt she was hit first, her intent was to inflict harm.)
5. Nonaggressive. (Although the other driver was killed, there was no intent to do harm.)
6. Aggressive. (Although many would consider this a tactically smart move, the intent was to inflict psychological harm in the form of fear and anxiety to another.)
7. Aggressive. (As in Question 6, the intent was to inflict psychological harm.)
8. Nonaggressive. (Although harm resulted, there was no intent to harm.)

So, when sport psychologists discuss aggression in general they are referring to what many people would call "bad" aggression. But not all "bad" aggression would be aggressive according to the sport psychology definition.

What many people call examples of good aggression in sport (e.g., charging the net in tennis) are labeled *assertive* behaviors in sport psychology (Husman & Silva, 1984)—that is, playing within the rules with high intensity and emotion but without intention to do harm.

Now that you're getting comfortable with this new way of thinking about aggression, try the test in the box above to check your understanding of the criteria marking aggression.

Hostile and Instrumental Aggression

Psychologists distinguish two types of aggression (Husman & Silva, 1984): hostile, or reactive,

477

aggression, and instrumental aggression. With **hostile aggression** the primary goal is to inflict injury or psychological harm on someone else. **Instrumental aggression**, on the other hand, occurs in the quest of some nonaggressive goal. For instance, when a boxer lands a solid blow to an opponent's head, injury or harm is usually inflicted. However, usually such an action is an example of instrumental aggression—the boxer's primary goal is to win the bout, and by inflicting harm to his opponent (scoring points or by knocking him out) he can do that. If a boxer pinned his opponent to the ropes and purposely tried to punish him with blows to the head and body while consciously trying not to end the match, this would qualify as hostile (reactive) aggression.

Most aggression in sport is instrumental, such as

■ a wrestler's squeezing an opponent's ribs to create discomfort and turn him over,

> *In hostile aggression the primary goal is to inflict injury or psychological harm to another, whereas instrumental aggression occurs in the quest of some nonaggressive goal.*

■ a cornerback's delivering a particularly hard hit to a receiver to deter him from running a pass route across the middle of the field, or

■ a basketball coach's calling a time-out when an opposing player is on the foul line, trying to cause psychological discomfort (heightened state anxiety) and poor performance.

Of course, hostile and instrumental aggression both involve the intent to injure and harm. Although most sporting aggression is instrumental, that does not make it acceptable. Professionals in

478

> *Professionals in sport and exercise science must have well-thought-out philosophies distinguishing between acceptable and unacceptable instrumental aggression.*

sport and exercise science must have a philosophy that is well thought-out as to what is acceptable assertive behavior and unacceptable instrumental aggressive behavior. Let's now turn to causes of aggression: Understanding the causes might help us reduce the possibility of aggression's occurrence.

Causes of Aggression

Why are some children more aggressive than others? What causes some athletes to lose control? Are aggressive individuals born, or are they a product of their environment? Psychologists have advanced four important theories regarding causes of aggression: (a)

> *There is little support for the instinct theory of aggression or its tangential notion of catharsis.*

instinct theory; (b) frustration-aggression theory; (c) social learning theory; and (d) revised frustration-aggression theory. We'll next discuss each of these theories.

Instinct Theory

According to the **instinct theory** (Gill, 1986), people have an innate instinct to be aggressive that builds up until it must inevitably be expressed. This instinct can either be expressed directly by attacking another living being or displaced through **catharsis**, in which aggression is released or "blown off" through socially acceptable means such as sport. Thus, for an instinct theorist, sport and exercise play an extremely important function in society in that they allow people to channel their aggressive instincts in socially acceptable ways.

© The Picture Desk

> *The frustration-aggression theory, which maintains that frustration always causes aggression, is generally dismissed today.*
>
> ———■———
>
> *There's little evidence that frustrated athletes lower their levels of aggression by participating in contact sports.*

> *The social learning theory, which explains aggression as behavior learned through observing others and then having similar behavior reinforced, has considerable scientific support.*

Unfortunately, no biologically innate aggressive instinct has ever been identified and no support has been found for the notion of catharsis. So we cannot cite the instinct theory in claiming that physical education and sport programs provide a socially acceptable means of channeling natural aggressive urges.

Frustration-Aggression Theory

The frustration-aggression theory, sometimes called the drive theory, states simply that aggression is the direct result of a frustration that occurs because of goal blockage or failure (Dollard, Doob, Miller, Mowrer, & Sears, 1939). The hypothesis at first made intuitive sense to psychologists because most aggressive acts are committed when people are frustrated. For example, when a soccer player feels she has been illegally held by her opponent, she becomes frustrated and takes a swing at the defender. However, this view has little support today because of its insistence that frustration must always cause aggression. Research and experience repeatedly show that people often cope with their frustration or express it in nonaggressive ways.

Frustration-aggression theorists counter that aggressive responses that occur are not always obvious: They may get channeled through socially acceptable outlets such as competitive contact sports. Thus, like instinct theorists, frustration-aggression proponents view catharsis as playing a major role. As we've mentioned, little evidence exists of catharsis in sport. Consequently, there's also little evidence that frustrated, aggressive participants in contact sports lower their aggression levels through participation (Gill, 1986). In fact, in some instances they become more aggressive (Arms, Russell, & Sandilands, 1979). Despite its shortcomings, the frustration-aggression hypothesis has contributed a valuable awareness of frustration's role in the aggression process.

Social Learning Theory

Social learning theory explains aggression as behavior people learn through observing others who model particular behaviors, followed by receiving reinforcement for exhibiting similar actions. Psychologist Albert Bandura (1973) found that children who watched adult models commit violent acts (beat up bobo dolls) repeated those acts more than children not exposed to such aggressive models. These modeling effects were especially powerful when the children were reinforced for copying the actions of the adult models.

Sport psychologists and sport sociologists have studied ice hockey because of the pervasiveness of illegal aggressive actions, such as fighting, in the sport. Smith (1988) found that the violence prevalent in the professional game is modeled by young amateur players. In fact, aggression is valued in ice hockey, and players quickly learn that being aggressive is a way to gain personal recognition. Many coaches, parents, and teammates accept and reinforce these aggressive acts. Young hockey players watch their heroes on television modeling aggressive behavior and later they receive reinforcement for exhibiting similar behavior.

Social learning research in sport shows that most athletes are not taught to be blatantly violent. However, aggression can and does occur in every sport. A figure skater, for example, may attempt to psych out an opponent and make upsetting remarks, such as "I heard that the judges said a costume like that is illegal this year." This is a subtler example of aggression, but the intent still is to harm another. Most parents and coaches do not condone unprovoked attacks on others, yet aggression is often sanctioned in response to another's aggressive act. For example, a young basketball player is instructed not to violate rules and hit others, but in a particularly rough game with shoving and elbowing under the boards, he or she is taught to retaliate in kind.

■ CASE STUDY ■

Bad Billy

Seven-year-old Billy, a goalie with the midget hockey league's Buffalo Bombers, gets entangled with teammates and opponents in a skirmish around his net. Billy is hit and dazed but uncertain by whom or what. Angry, he retaliates by punching the nearest opponent in the nose. The referee throws Billy out of the game. Billy's coach tells him he shouldn't throw a punch because the team needs him and he is of no help sitting on the bench. However, Billy later overhears his coach boast to an assistant, "What a scrapper and competitor that Billy is," which makes Billy feel good.

At home, Billy's dad seems proud of Billy's performance. He tells Billy never to start a fight and just hit anybody out there on the ice, but he's got to be a man and defend himself: "Hockey is a dog-eat-dog game, and you can't let anybody push you around out there—after all, you don't see the NHL goalies take any guff."

Lately, Billy has become a goalie his opponents fear—anybody in the crease is liable to get extra rough treatment from him. Billy now watches the pros to learn how to be rough and tough without getting kicked out of the game! (Adapted from Martens, 1982a)

Social learning theory has considerable scientific support (Bandura, 1977b; Thirer, 1993). It emphasizes the important role that significant others have on the development or control of aggression, since modeling and reinforcement are the key ways people learn aggressive behavior.

Revised Frustration-Aggression Theory

A **revised frustration-aggression theory** combines elements of the original frustration-aggression hypothesis with social learning theory. This widely held view holds that although frustration does not always lead to aggression, it increases the likelihood of aggression by increasing arousal and anger (Berkowitz, 1965, 1969, 1993; Baron & Richardson, 1994). However, increased arousal and anger only result in aggression when socially learned cues signal the appropriateness of aggression in the particular situation. If the socially learned cues signal that aggression is inappropriate, it will not result.

Figure 23.1 depicts the aggression process, based on Berkowitz's model. First, the individual becomes frustrated in some way, perhaps by losing the game or playing poorly. Then increased arousal, usually in the form of anger or pain, results from the frustration. Aggression will not automatically result, and increased arousal and anger lead to aggression only if the individual has learned that it is appropriate to be aggressive in such a situation. Thus, a football safety who is frustrated after being badly beaten on a deep pass pattern for a touchdown might lash out at his opponent if his coaches have previously toler-

The revised frustration-aggression theory is currently one of the most popular theories of aggression.

ated this behavior. The strengths of the revised frustration-aggression theory are that it combines the best elements of the original frustration-aggression and the social learning theories and uses an interactional model (the individual's level of arousal-anger within the context of socially learned environmental cues) to explain behavior.

Aggression in Sport: Special Considerations

Not only have sport psychologists tested theories of aggression in the sport setting, but they have also examined other important issues. These are three of the other important issues: spectators and aggression, game reasoning and aggression, and athletic performance and aggression. Each of these will now be discussed.

Spectators and Aggression

Competitive sport differs from many activities in that it is usually conducted in the presence of fans and spectators. Fans at games and matches are not usually passive observers—they actively identify with their teams. Their involvement is usually well-mannered and supportive, but instances of fan violence

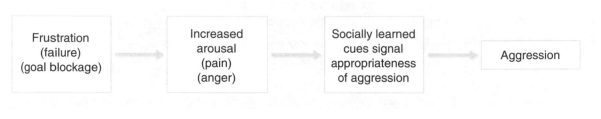

Figure 23.1   Components of the revised frustration-aggression theory.

appear to be on the rise. In response to concerns about fan violence, sport psychologists have studied spectator aggression.

Psychologists first tested the catharsis theory to determine whether fans become more or less aggressive after watching sport events. In general, they found that observing a sporting event does not lower the level of the spectator's aggression. Moreover, watching some violent contact sports actually increases a spectator's readiness to be aggressive (Isoahola & Hatfield, 1986). However, aggression usually does not occur without other environmental or game-related factors. For instance, studies of hockey spectators have found that fan aggression is more likely with younger, disadvantaged male spectators in crowded conditions and under the influence of alcohol (Cavanaugh & Silva, 1980; Russell & Arms, 1995). Rivalries are also associated with fan violence. Smith (1983) also found small-scale aggressive acts on the field (e.g., a brief shoving match between players or a heated argument over a call) to be associated with subsequent spectator aggression.

Sport managers and administrators should be apprised of these findings to help them decrease the probability of violence (e.g., by eliminating sales of alcohol and enforcing strict seating capacities that minimize crowd density). Obviously, coaches and players should maintain emotional control on the field to ensure they are not triggers for fan aggression.

Game Reasoning and Aggression

An alarming research finding is that many athletes view some aggressive acts as inappropriate in general but appropriate in the sport environment (Bredemeier & Shields, 1984, 1986). For example, fighting is deemed appropriate in certain sport situations (e.g., if a pitcher intentionally beans you), whereas no form of fighting would be tolerated in the school band. This double standard is called **game reasoning** (or *bracketed morality*).

Unfortunately, people are learning and believing it is okay to be more aggressive in sport than in other life contexts. This presents a problem. First, aggres-

sion carries the risk of injury and harm. Also, sport can and should serve to teach children how to behave appropriately inside and outside of sport. Allowing (or applauding) aggressive behavior in sport sends the wrong message to children. Sport professionals must specifically define appropriate behavior and make clear that any form of aggression not sanctioned in society is also inappropriate in sport.

Interestingly, upon banning Latrell Sprewell, NBA Commissioner David Stern said, "A sports league does not have to accept or condone behavior that would not be tolerated in any other segment of society" (Mihoces, 1997), clearly showing that bracketed morality would not be tolerated. Fan reaction supported Stern's and the league's action, hopefully signaling a change in a previously accepting attitude for bracketed morality in sport.

Athletic Performance and Aggression

Some coaches and athletes feel that aggressiveness enhances athletic performance, either at the team or individual level. For instance, basketball player Kermit Washington said that being mean helped keep him from being pushed around on the court. Football safety Jack Tatum said his team had a greater likelihood of succeeding if he punished his opponent on every play (Papanek, 1977). Certainly, the relation between aggression and performance is complex, and there have been many cases where aggressive acts have "paid off" regarding outcome. Consider, for example, the strategy of having a lower-skilled player commit aggressive acts against a higher-skilled opponent to distract the superior player or draw him into a fight.

Some sport psychologists agree that aggression facilitates performance outcome (Widmeyer, 1984), whereas others feel it does not (Gill, 1986). The research is difficult to interpret because clear distinctions have not been drawn between aggression and assertive behavior. Silva (1980) argues that aggression would not facilitate performance because it elevates a person's arousal level and shifts attention

> *Sport and exercise science professionals must decide if they value enhanced performance at the cost of increased aggression or if they are concerned more about how sports affects its participants.*

to nonperformance issues (e.g., hurting the opponent).

In the end, the relation of aggression to performance may be of secondary importance. More central issues are whether you value performance at any cost, your concern about sport participants, and ensuring that aggression does not pay—but that those acting aggressively do (Widmeyer, 1984).

Implications for Practice

Let's now consolidate what we know of aggression and discuss how we might develop strategies to control aggression in sport and physical activity settings. First, we'll examine situations where aggression is most likely to occur. Next, we'll discuss strategies for modifying aggressive actions and teaching appropriate behavior.

Understanding When Aggression Is Most Likely to Occur

Expect certain situations to provoke aggressive behavior. Aggression is likely when athletes are frustrated. Participants typically feel frustrated when they are losing, perceive unfair officiating, are embarrassed, are physically in pain, or are playing below their capabilities. Teachers and coaches, therefore, should be particularly sensitive to detecting and controlling aggression in these frustrating situations.

Modifying Aggressive Reactions

Unfortunately, we cannot always control these situations. But we can observe participants more closely and remove them from the situation at the first signs of aggression. Or, better yet, we can teach athletes skills to control their emotions and their reactions to frustration. For example, an ice hockey player who often became frustrated during games, responded aggressively, and spent increasingly more time in the

© Anthony Neste Photography

483

> *Stress-management training can help students and athletes deal with frustrating situations.*

> *Sport and exercise professionals have a moral responsibility to clearly distinguish between assertive behavior and aggression with the intent to harm.*

penalty box was able to learn stress-management skills (Silva, 1982). Through training, the player reduced his aggressive responses and remained in the game instead of in the box.

An overemphasis on winning is at the root of much frustration. Trying to win isn't wrong, but winning should not be emphasized to the point that aggression results after a loss. Such frustration is a sign that winning needs to be put into perspective.

Sport and exercise science professionals have a moral responsibility to distinguish between aggres-

sion with the intent to harm and assertive behavior. We must delineate aggression from intensity and assertiveness (good aggression) and instruct participants accordingly.

Teaching Appropriate Behavior

Once you have been determined what constitutes aggression and what is appropriate, intense, or assertive play, you can use social learning strategies

■ CASE STUDY ■

Good or Bad Aggression

Tom Martinez is the new head football coach at Aurora High School. He takes over a program with a losing tradition and a reputation for overly aggressive players who commit flagrant fouls and take cheap shots. A former major college player himself, Tom knows it takes intensity to be successful, but he is committed to his philosophy that cheap shots and playing to physically hurt opponents are inappropriate. He feels the first step toward remedying the situation at Aurora is to differentiate for the players what are appropriate and inappropriate aggressions. He remembers how confusing and frustrating it was for him when one coach rewarded him for aggressive play and others reprimanded him for the same actions.

Tom meets with his coaching staff, and they all agree to be consistent in distinguishing between assertive play and aggression. They adopt the guidelines below, explain them to the team, and consistently reward the demonstration of good, clean intense play while immediately punishing aggression.

Aurora High School Guidelines

Appropriate Actions

> Hard hits within the rules and within the field of play
> Helping opponents off the turf after hard hits
> Acknowledging good plays by the opponents

Inappropriate Actions

> Out-of-bounds tackles and hits
> Legal acts aimed at physically punishing opponents (e.g., forearm shivers to the head of receivers)
> Head hunting (tackles aimed at the head) or blind-side blocks aimed at the knees
> Pushing and shoving opponents after the whistle has blown
> Intimidating remarks (e.g., "If you think that was a hard shot, wait for the next one")
> Off-the-field trash talk about hurting or getting opponents

(modeling and reinforcement; see chapter 6) to teach participants these behaviors. You should explain to players why particular behaviors are appropriate and inappropriate. (This topic will be discussed in more detail in chapter 24.)

In addition to learning appropriate behavior, physical activity participants should know how to resolve conflicts and disputes in nonviolent fashions. A middle school in Maryland instituted a program to provide this training, which improved the school climate (Miller, 1993). Its peer conflict-resolution program began by identifying students with good leadership and communication skills to serve as peer mediators in resolving conflicts among other students. These peer leaders were then taught to implement the following steps in nonviolent conflict resolution.

1. Agree to meet: Have disputants agree to meet with the student mediator (but not sit next to one another at the meeting).

2. Record the facts: Each disputant is given an opportunity to tell his or her account of the event. The student mediator listens, but does not take sides.

3. Express feelings: Each disputant expresses his or her feelings regarding the event, and the mediator repeats what is said to ensure clarity of meaning.

4. Aim to resolve: The desirable consequences of resolving the conflict are expressed by each disputant. The mediator emphasizes areas of agreement relative to the benefits of resolving the conflict.

5. Outline necessary changes: The disputants list what they each could do to resolve the conflict.

6. Develop an action plan: A plan of action is developed and each disputant signs it, indicating his or her commitment to the action plan and to resolving the conflict cooperatively.

7. Follow up on the plan: After a short time, the disputants are asked if the problem still exists.

Although this example is not the only conflict-resolution model and would not necessarily work in all settings, it clearly demonstrates the value and importance of teaching children how to resolve conflicts nonviolently. Given increasing levels of violence in society, it is unlikely that school violence

© Photo: Action Images

will abate on its own. Physical educators and coaches must teach children nonviolent techniques to resolve disputes.

Controlling Spectator Aggression

Not only can we work with athletes to control aggression, we can also use strategies with spectators.

Here are some general strategies for controlling spectator aggression:

1. Develop strict alcohol-control policies or ban alcohol for spectators at athletic competitions.

2. Penalize spectators (e.g., kick them out) immediately for aggressive acts. Stop

■ MORE INFORMATION ■

Aggression and Violence in Sport

The International Society of Sport Psychology has adopted the following stand on aggression and violence in sport:

Recommendation 1: Management should make fundamental pentalty revisions so that rule-violating behavior results in punishments that have greater punitive value than potential reinforcement.

Recommendation 2: Management must ensure proper coaching of teams, particularly at junior levels, which emphasizes a fair-play code of conduct among participants.

Recommendation 3: Management should ban the use of alcoholic beverages at sporting events.

Recommendation 4: Management must make sure facilities are adequate regarding catering and spacing needs and the provision of modern amenities.

© Human Kinetics

Recommendation 5: The media must place in proper perspective the isolated incidents of aggression that occur in sport, rather than making them "highlights."

Recommendation 6: The media should promote a campaign to decrease violence and hostile aggression in sport, which should also involve the participation and commitment of athletes, coaches, management, officials, and spectators.

Recommendation 7: Coaches, managers, athletes, media, officials, and authority figures (i.e., police) should take part in workshops on aggression and violence to ensure they understand the topic of aggression, why it occurs, the cost of aggressive acts, and how aggressive behavior can be controlled.

Recommendation 8: Coaches, managers, officials, and the media should encourage athletes to engage in prosocial behavior and punish those who perform acts of hostility.

Recommendation 9: Athletes should take part in programs aimed at helping them reduce behavioral tendencies toward aggression. The tightening of rules, imposing of harsher penalties, and changing of reinforcement patterns are only parts of the answer to inhibiting aggression in sport. Ultimately, the athlete must assume responsibility.

Source: Tenenbaum, Stewart, Singer, & Duda, 1997

aggression as soon as it starts and inform other spectators it will not be tolerated.

3. When you are hiring officials, request people whom you know won't tolerate aggression on the field.

4. Inform coaches that aggressive displays on their part will not be tolerated.

5. Work with the media to convey the importance of not glorifying aggressive acts in sports coverage.

The International Society of Sport Psychology has developed a position statement of aggression in sport (see the box on p. 486). It includes recommendations for all personnel involved in sport: managers, coaches, media representatives, and athletes.

SUMMARY

1 *Define what is meant by aggression.*

Aggression is behavior directed toward the goal of harming or injuring another living being. For an act to be considered aggression it must meet four criteria: It must be an actual behavior, involve harm or injury, be directed toward another living thing, and involve intent. Aggression is distinct from assertive behavior in sport.

2 *Identify the causes of aggression.*

These four theories explain why aggression occurs: the instinct, frustration-aggression, social learning, and revised frustration-aggression theories. Little support has been found for the instinct theory or the original frustration-aggression hypothesis; nor is there support for the notion that catharsis (releasing pent-up aggression through socially acceptable sport and physical activity) abates aggression. Strong support has been found for the revised frustration-aggression and social learning theories. Frustration predisposes individuals to aggressiveness, and aggression occurs if it has been learned to be an appropriate reaction to frustration. Modeling and reinforcement can be powerful determinants of aggressive behavior. Spectators also use aggression, and they as well as sport participants sometimes condone behaviors that would not be considered appropriate in society (game reasoning).

3 *Explain the aggression-performance relation.*

Some sport psychologists have found inconsistent results in examining the aggression-performance relationship. That is, aggression facilitates athletic performance in some cases but not in others. In the end, the relation of aggression to performance may be less important than whether coaches value performance at any cost or are more concerned with whether participants learn that aggression is not appropriate or useful.

4 *Derive implications from research for helping control aggression.*

Some research findings yield important implications for guiding practice. These include recognizing when aggression is most likely to occur, teaching athletes how to handle these situations, teaching appropriate behaviors, and modifying inappropriate aggressive actions.

KEY TERMS

aggression
hostile aggression
instrumental aggression
instinct theory
catharsis

frustration-aggression theory
social learning theory
revised frustration-aggression theory
game reasoning

REVIEW QUESTIONS

1. What is aggression? How does it differ from assertive behavior?
2. Describe the four criteria for considering an act aggression.
3. What are four theories of aggression? Describe the major contentions of each. Which have the strongest support and why?
4. What is catharsis? What implications does it have for guiding practice?
5. What factors are associated with spectator aggression?
6. What is sport-specific game reasoning, or bracketed morality? What are its implications for professionals?
7. Explain the relation between athlete aggression and performance.
8. In what situations is aggression most likely to occur?

CRITICAL THINKING QUESTIONS

1. You have learned that aggression can involve both physical and psychological harm to others. Although it is fairly easy to come up with examples of physical aggression in sport and physical activity settings, psychological aggression may be subtler and harder to identify. Identify forms of psychological aggression that you have experienced or witnessed in sport and physical activity settings.
2. You have been named commissioner of the National Hockey League. Because of increasing concerns over fighting and aggressive play, the government has threatened to intervene in the league's administration unless the situation improves within a year. Discuss what you will do to curb fighting and aggression.

Character Development and Sportspersonship

After reading this chapter you should be able to

1 define what character development and sportspersonship are,

2 explain how character and sportspersonship develop,

3 identify the important link between moral reasoning and moral behavior,

4 discuss how character and sportspersonship can be influenced, and

5 describe the effects of winning on character development and sportspersonship.

For years we have heard that sport and physical activity build character and develop moral values. There are dozens of shining examples: As an undergraduate, Wake Forest football player Chip Reeves began a Santa's helper program to provide gifts to the needy at Christmas. Professional golfer Patty Sheenan sponsors a home for troubled teens. Olympic marathon champion Kip Keino has adopted and raised more than 100 orphan children in his native Kenya (Deford, 1987).

Yet some of the most popular role models in recent years have been the "bad boys" of sports—John McEnroe in tennis, Jack Tatum (nicknamed the assassin) in football, and Charles Barkley in basketball, whose antics include spitting on fans he doesn't like. And the coverage of the 1994 Winter Olympics was swamped with news that associates of figure skater Tonya Harding had attacked her rival Nancy Kerrigan. In the face of such occurrences, can we really say that sport participation builds character? If so, do sport and exercise science professionals play a role in character development? Let's first try to define what we mean by character and sportspersonship.

Defining Character and Sportspersonship

Defining character and sportspersonship is difficult. We all generally know what they mean, but we seldom define them precisely (Martens, 1982a) or agree exactly on their meaning. Tennis great Chris Evert, for example, says that sportspersonship is acting in a classy, dignified way (Ross, 1992). Basketball great David Robinson defines sportspersonship as playing with all your heart and intensity, yet still showing respect for your opponents (Ross, 1992). These are two very different definitions. And what exactly is acting respectfully or in a classy and dignified manner? A golfer might say it means you don't talk to your opponent during play, but a baseball player might think it's fine to talk to the opposing pitcher. Similarly, sliding hard into second base to break up a double play is expected and not inappropriate in college baseball, yet most of us would discourage it in T-ball with 6- and 7-year-olds.

There is no universally accepted definition of sportspersonship.

Shields and Bredemeier (1995), in their book *Character Development and Physical Activity,* indicate that although character and sportspersonship are difficult to define, they fall within the general area of morality in the context of sport. That is, they deal with our beliefs, judgments, and actions as to what is right and ethical and what is wrong and unethical in sport. Specifically, Shields and Bredemeier contend that morality in sport comprises three related concepts, namely, fair play, sportspersonship, and character.

Fair Play

Fair play is necessary if all participants are to have an equitable chance to pursue victory in competitive sport. Fair play requires that all contestants understand and adhere not only to the formal rules of the game but also to the spirit of cooperation and unwritten rules of play necessary to ensure a contest is fair (Shields & Bredemeier, 1995). For example, a youth football program designed to maximize participation of all the children may require that each player take part in each quarter of the contest. However, one coach may violate the spirit of the rule by having substitutes enter the game for only one play per quarter or to just bring in plays—and then leave before the play is actually executed. It is essential that parents, coaches, and officials espouse the virtue of fair play early, often, and throughout their athletic careers.

Sportspersonship

Sportspersonship is the second component of morality in sport. Shields and Bredemeier (1995, p. 194) contend that sportspersonship "involves an intense striving to succeed, tempered by commitment to the play spirit such that ethical standards will take precedence over strategic gain when the two conflict." In other words, you adhere to fair play even when it may mean losing. For example, U.S. Open tennis champion Patrick Rafter demonstrated good sportspersonship when he informed an official that a line call was incorrect—even though doing so meant he lost the match.

Whereas Shields and Bredemeier defined sportspersonship based on their conceptual understanding of the literature, Canadian sport psychologist Robert Vallerand and his colleagues (Vallerand, Deshaies, Cuerrier, Briere, & Pelletier, 1996; Vallerand, Briere, Blanchard, & Provencher, 1997) conducted an extensive study to understand how athletes themselves define the term. In particular, their 1996 study sur-

© Photophile

veyed 1,056 French-Canadian athletes between the ages of 10 and 18 years who represented seven different sports. Using pilot research with a similar population of athletes, the researchers constructed a sportspersonship survey and administered it to the athletes. Factor analysis (a statistical technique that groups liked response patterns in data) was used, which revealed that sportspersonship consists of these five factors:

1. Full commitment toward participation (showing up and working hard during all practices and games; acknowledging one's mistakes and trying to improve)

2. Respect and concern for rules and officials (even when the official appears incompetent)

3. Respect and concern for social conventions (shaking hands after the contest, recognizing the good performance of one's opponent, being a good loser)

4. Respect and concern for the opponent (lending one's equipment to the opponent, agreeing to play even if the opponent is late, and refusing to take advantage of injured opponents)

5. Avoiding poor attitudes toward participation (avoiding a win-at-all-costs approach; not showing temper after a mistake; not only competing for individual trophies and prizes)

Hence, their research suggests that sportspersonship is defined by athletes as "concern and respect for the rules and officials, social conventions, the opponent, as well as one's full commitment to one's sport, and the relative absence of a negative approach toward sport participation" (Vallerand et al., 1997, p. 198).

Although these attempts to define sportspersonship are helping to guide research in the area, from a practical perspective Martens (1982a) concluded that there is no one universally accepted definition of sportspersonship. Rather, sportspersonlike behaviors must be specifically identified: They are tied to the type of sport, level of play, and age of the participant. So although there is no universal definition of the term, it is still important that we each identify sportspersonship and try to develop situation-specific definitions of it as we work professionally in sport, physical education, and exercise settings.

Character

Character, the third concept in morality, refers to an array of characteristics (usually connoting a positive moral overtone—we all want participants to develop good character in sport) that can be developed in sport. Those who espouse the character-developing benefits of sport contend that participants learn to overcome obstacles, cooperate with teammates, develop self-control, and persist in the face of defeat (Ewing, Seefeldt, & Brown, 1996). Shields and Bredemeier (1995) view character as an overarching concept that integrates fair play and sportspersonship with two other important virtues, compassion and integrity. Hence, character in sport comprises four interrelated virtues: compassion, fairness, sportspersonship, and integrity.

Although fair play and sportspersonship have already been defined, compassion and integrity have not. Compassion is related to empathy and is the ability to take on and appreciate the feelings of others. Hence, when we have compassion, we feel for our competitors and seek to understand their feelings and perspectives. Integrity is the ability to maintain one's morality and fairness coupled with the belief that one can (and will) fulfill one's moral intentions. In essence, it is an athlete's or a coach's moral self-efficacy: It is the belief she or he will do the right thing when faced with a moral dilemma.

In summary, when we discuss character in sport we are referring to knowing the rules and standards of behavior expected of participants (sportspersonship), adhering to the rules and the spirit of the rules while competing (fairness), being able to be compassionate and take on the feelings of others, and having integrity or being confident that one knows what is right and will exhibit behaviors in line with what is right, even when alternative choices make doing so difficult.

Approaches to Developing Character and Sportspersonship

Although people have differing views about how character and sportspersonlike attitudes and behaviors develop, three particular approaches are most accepted today: social learning, structural-developmental, and social-psychological.

Social Learning Approach

Aggression and character development are linked in many ways, and similar theories explain both. The social learning approach to character development, best summarized in the work of Albert Bandura (1977b), views specific sportspersonlike attitudes and behaviors as learned through modeling or observational learning, reinforcement, and social comparison (see Figure 24.1).

For example, by observing other children being praised for reporting false sit-up scores to the instructor, Zoe learns in physical education class that it is acceptable to cheat on a fitness test. Wanting praise and attention from the teacher, she copies or models the behavior of the other students that she compares herself to and begins to report more sit-ups than she really did. The physical educator notes the reported improvement in the number of sit-ups executed and praises her. Thus, Zoe learns from observing the other children and through her own experience that if she lies about the number of sit-ups, she receives reinforcement.

Conversely, a selfish child may learn to share and be more caring by observing classmates receive attention and praise for helping. And, over time, when the child models these helping actions and is praised,

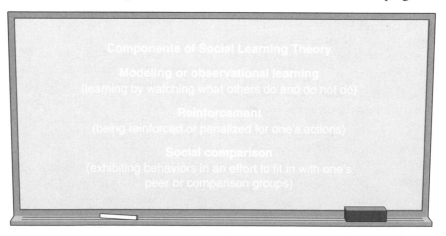

Figure 24.1 Components of social learning theory.

the prosocial behavior is reinforced. Thus, both sportspersonlike and unsportspersonlike attitudes and behavior are affected by the social learning process.

In one study of social learning theory, fifth-grade boys who acted unsportspersonlike (e.g., swore) received instruction about their inappropriate behaviors, saw the appropriate behaviors modeled, and took part in a reinforcement system (points leading to desired prizes could be earned for exhibiting sportspersonlike be-haviors). Over time, the reinforcement system was effective, although more so in eliminating undesirable behaviors than in getting the boys to exhibit sportsperson like or desirable behaviors (Geibenk & McKenzie, 1985).

Former tennis great Bjorn Borg was known for his excellent sportspersonlike behavior, but he hadn't always behaved that way. When he was 12, Borg threw his racquet in disgust, exhibiting a temper tantrum on the court. Such actions were quickly curtailed because his mother would not tolerate them. Borg had his racquet taken away for 6 months and was not allowed to play.

Structural-Developmental Approach

Instead of focusing on modeling, reinforcement, and social comparison, the structural-developmental approach focuses on how psychological growth and developmental changes in a child interact with environmental experiences to shape moral reasoning (Weiss & Bredemeier, 1991). Moreover, sport psychologists have derived specific definitions of moral development, moral reasoning, and moral behavior. Note that when we use the term *moral*, we do not mean to imply religious values.

Moral reasoning is defined as the decision process in which the rightness or wrongness of a course of action is determined. Thus, moral reasoning focuses on how one decides if some course of action (e.g., a coach violating NCAA rules by paying to fly a player home to see her dying mother) is right or wrong.

In contrast, moral development is the process of experience and growth through which a person develops the capacity to reason morally. For example, in planning a system-wide physical education curriculum, a district coordinator would want to understand what experiences and cognitive developmental changes are most likely to enhance the children's abilities to determine the rightness or wrongness of an action. Lastly, moral behavior is actually carrying out an act that is deemed right or wrong.

- *Moral reasoning is the decision process through which one determines the rightness or wrongness of a course of action.*
- *Moral development is the process of experience and growth through which a person develops the capacity to morally reason.*
- *Moral behavior is the execution of an act that is deemed right or wrong.*

Moral reasoning and behavior depend on an individual's level of cognitive development.

So, moral reasoning results from individual experiences, as well as the psychological growth and development of the child, and is thought to guide moral behavior. Moreover, moral reasoning is seen as a series of general ethical principles that underlie situationally specific acts of sportspersonship.

Structural developmentalists contend that the ability to reason morally depends on a person's level of cognitive or mental development (e.g., a child's ability to think in concrete or abstract terms). Thus, if a 4-year-old boy, able to think in only very concrete terms, is inadvertently pushed in line at preschool, he responds by hitting the child who was pushed into him. This child is not able to judge intent, and he knows only that the other child hit him. However, given the process of normal growth and cognitive development, an 11-year-old child who is inadvertently pushed in line will not necessarily push back, because he can already judge intent and realizes the other child didn't bump him on purpose. Thus, structural developmentalists view moral reasoning and behavior as dependent, in large part, on cognitive development.

Developmental psychologists have identified sequential stages of moral development in children. Figure 24.2 depicts the five levels, or stages, of moral development first identified by Norma Haan (Haan, Aeerts, & Cooper, 1985) and later explained in more practical sport psychological terms by Maureen Weiss (1987; Weiss & Bredemeier, 1991). As a child matures, she progresses in moral reasoning from Level 1 through Level 5. Not everyone reaches Level 5, however, and we don't always use the highest level of moral thinking that we're capable of. In fact, we may use several different levels at once.

Level 1 reasoning is at the external control stage: the "It's okay as long as I don't get caught" stage. At this level a child's determination of what is right or wrong is based on self-interest and, in particular, the outcome of her actions. Thus, Kim would decide whether kicking an opponent in soccer (illegally playing the person, not the ball) is right or wrong depending on whether she got away with it. If she did get away with it, she would think it was an acceptable course of action. But if she were penalized for it, she would view playing the person as inappropriate behavior.

Level 2 still focuses on maximizing self-interests, but the child now doesn't see only the action's

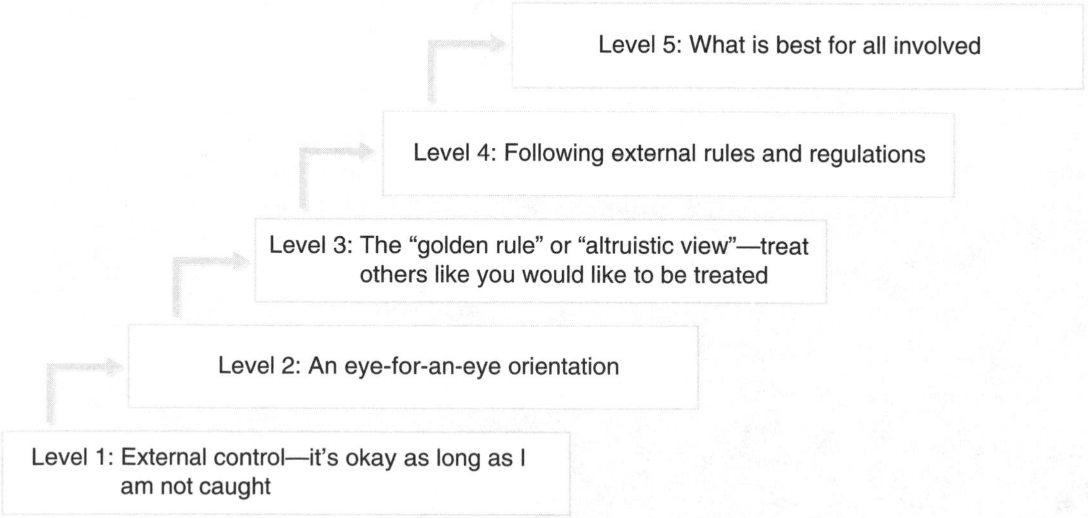

Level 5: What is best for all involved

Level 4: Following external rules and regulations

Level 3: The "golden rule" or "altruistic view"—treat others like you would like to be treated

Level 2: An eye-for-an-eye orientation

Level 1: External control—it's okay as long as I am not caught

Figure 24.2 *Levels of moral reasoning.*
Adapted from Seefeldt, 1987.

outcome. Instead, this is an "eye-for-an-eye" stage, where the individual can compromise and make tradeoffs to maximize self-interest. For instance, Kim decides that it is acceptable to illegally kick another player because Lee has been doing just that to her for most of the first half. Or an elite track-and-field athlete takes illegal performance enhancing drugs, defending the action on the premise that "everybody does it."

Level 3 is to treat others as you would like to be treated. Unlike the first two levels, self-interest is not the sole focus here. The person adopts a helping or altruistic view. Kim now would view illegally kicking another player as inappropriate because she would not want to be treated that way.

Level 4 of moral reasoning focuses on following external rules. The person has learned that not all people can be trusted to do the right thing and recognizes that official rules were developed for the common good. At this stage, for instance, Kim views illegally kicking an opponent as inappropriate because it is against the rules, and one must play by the rules because they are designed to promote everyone's self-interest.

Moral reasoning at Level 5 focuses on what is best for everyone involved, whether or not it is in accordance with official rules and regulations. This reasoning is considered the most mature because the individual seeks to maximize the interests of the group through mutual agreements or "moral balances." Thus, Kim reasons that it is inappropriate to kick another player not only because it is against the rules but also because it violates the fundamental rights of both parties—the right to play in a safe and healthy environment.

In summary, with moral development, reasoning progresses from decisions based on self-centered interests to a concern with mutual interests of all the people involved. This development depends on the person's ability to think abstractly.

Social-Psychological Approach

Vallerand and his colleagues (1996, 1997) offer a third approach to studying morality in physical ac-

tivity. Specifically, they suggest taking a more broadly viewed, social-psychological approach. That is, in looking at morality and character you would consider the *personal elements* in the structural-developmental approach (e.g., the individual's level of moral development) *plus* a wide range of *social factors* (e.g., type of sport, competitive level of athletes, pressure from the coach) that go beyond the reinforcement, modeling, and social-comparison elements of the social learning approach. An important feature of this view is the notion that social agents (e.g., parents and coaches) label or define sportspersonship. So Vallerand's team proposes taking a more complex, person-by-situation perspective that considers a variety of both personal and situational factors in determining sportspersonship.

Cultural attitudes, values, and norms of the particular individuals and groups, as well as the stages of moral reasoning, are all considered to understand how to enhance character development and sportspersonship. Consequently, it seems best to take advantage of what has been learned through both the social learning and structural-developmental approaches and to adopt the social-psychological approach.

Moral Reasoning and Moral Behavior

A consistent relation exists between aggression and people with less-mature moral reasoning: People whose moral reasoning is less mature behave more aggressively (Bredemeier & Shields, 1987). Not surprisingly, the link between moral reasoning and behavior is not perfect. Nor would you expect it to be—all of us, at one time or another, have known that something was probably wrong, but gone ahead and done it anyway.

One reason the link between moral reasoning and behavior is not absolute is that several steps must take place to translate moral reasoning into moral action. Miller, Bredemeier, and Shields (1997) have identified four moral-action stages to the moral

Character development progresses from basing one's decisions about the rightness or wrongness of actions on self-centered interests to being concerned with the mutual interests of all involved.

Although aggression is linked with immature moral reasoning, the connection between reasoning and behavior is not perfectly understood.

495

reasoning-behavior link, basing their work on Rest (1984). These are

1. interpreting the situation as one that involves some sort of moral judgment,
2. deciding on the best course of moral action,
3. making a choice to morally act, and
4. implementing a moral response.

For instance, Brian the captain of the tennis team, must judge whether his opponent's serve at match point is in or out (Brian feels that it is in). If he says it is out, he and his team win the sectional tournament. If he says it is in, he and his team may lose.

Following the four moral-action stages, Brian must first interpret the situation, seeing it as involving a moral choice. His compassion and his ability to see the perspective of others are critical here. Brian remembers how he felt when an opponent cheated on line calls against him.

If Brian interprets the situation as involving a moral choice, he must then weigh various competing moral choices (make the correct call, lie, or say he couldn't tell whether the serve was in or out). That is, he must use his moral reasoning to define a moral course of action.

Brian then engages in a process to decide whether to give priority to moral values or self-gain. Will he do the honest thing by making the correct call and potentially losing the match? Will he say the ball was out, and receive the rewards associated with the victory? He may be influenced in this stage by such factors as his coach's leadership style and the team's norms as to what is right and wrong.

Finally, Brian must marshal the physical and psychological resources to translate his moral decision into action. For example, Brain must be confident that he will be able to deal with what his teammates might say if he makes the correct call and loses the match. His integrity would be important here. Only after working through these stages will Brian act.

Knowing how individuals morally reason and translate the reasoning into action is important not only for understanding people we work with but also for guiding our practical interventions. Miller, Bredemeier, and Shields (1997), for instance, designed a sociomoral educational program for at-risk physical education students based on these moral-action processes or stages. They identified specific psychological objectives related to those processes and then designed and developed intervention strategies, such as cooperative learning, to achieve the various psychological goals and influence the moral-action processes (see Table 24.1).

Do Sport and Physical Education Enhance Character Development?

Most of us like to believe that participation in physical activity programs automatically builds character, enhances moral reasoning, and teaches sportspersonship, but we have little evidence supporting the belief that it builds character (Hodge, 1989). Participation in sport and physical education settings does not automatically produce better or worse people. Character is not caught—but taught—in sport and physical activity settings. And teaching moral reasoning and sportspersonship involves the systematic use of certain strategies.

Let's look at an example of such a strategy. Fifth-grade physical education students were divided into experimental and control groups for one field study (Romance, Weiss, & Bockoven, 1986). All the children participated in an 8-week program, playing the

> *Character is not caught but taught in sport, exercise, and physical activity settings.*

Table 24.1
Moral Action Processes, Sociomoral Education Goals, and Program Intervention Strategies

	Stage 1	Stage 2	Stage 3	Stage 4
Moral action process:	Perception/ Interpretation	Judgment/ Deciding	Choice	Implementation
Program goal:	Empathy	Moral reasoning	Task orientation	Self-responsibility
Intervention:	Cooperative learning	Moral community	Mastery climate	Power transfer

Reprinted from Miller, Bredemeier, and Shields, 1997.

same activity games for identical lengths of time. However, the experimental group was also exposed to specific game-related moral-reasoning strategies. For instance, teams of two students were asked to compete in basketball, with the first team to reach 10 points winning. After the activity, a discussion was held during which each student explained how they determined who would shoot and whether that was fair. The control group children did not participate in such activities.

The children in the experimental group demonstrated significantly greater gains in their moral reasoning, both in sport and in everyday life situations. Evidently, with a well-designed strategy, moral reasoning can be taught through physical education. That changes did not occur in the control group of children suggests that participation in physical education alone, however, does not enhance moral reasoning.

Youth Sport as a Deterrent to Negative Behavior

It is not only physical educators who claim that participation enhances character development and positive behaviors. Sport administrators, coaches, and community leaders also often claim that taking part in sport keeps youth off the street, out of trouble, and out of gangs. This has led sport psychologists and sociologists to study two specific questions: Does sport participation deter delinquency? And does participation in sport decrease gang violence?

Sport Participation and Delinquency

Research has supported the claim that participants in organized sport are less likely than nonparticipants to engage in delinquent behavior (Seefeldt & Ewing, 1997; Shields & Bredemeier, 1995). Moreover, the negative relationship between sport participation and delinquency seems especially strong for youth in poorer neighborhoods and athletes in minor sports. What is not clear, however, is why this relationship exists.

We'll look at four possible explanations for why sport participants are less likely to engage in delinquent behavior: differential association, social bonding, labeling, and the economic strain.

Explaining the negative relation between sport participation and delinquency by a differential association proposes that athletes have less frequent, shorter, and less intense interactions with delinquent others. In other words, participation in sport keeps kids off the streets and out of trouble.

The social bonding view contends that kids who participate in sport develop attachments with significant others who represent dominant, prosocial values. A young athlete identifies with his or her coach and team, and in so doing learns such values as teamwork, hard work, and achievement.

The labeling hypothesis takes a different tack, contending that sport participation does not facilitate youth values. Rather, because many people in society value sport, being labeled an "athlete" often leads to getting special treatment. That is, because of their athletic status, some youngsters receive preferential treatment and get away with more delinquent behaviors than their nonathletic counterparts. At the same time, other youngsters get labeled as "delinquents," and then fall into a self-fulfilling prophecy of escalating trouble, meanwhile getting no breaks in the legal system.

Finally, the economic strain explanation for the sport-delinquency relationship holds that delinquency occurs because many youth are impoverished but still desire the high standard of living they see others enjoying. Sport participation, however, allows impoverished youngsters to gain prestige and status and, in turn, reduces the strain between their dreams of a better life and beliefs about attainable goals.

Although these explanations may help us better understand why sport participation is associated with decreases in delinquency, they do not give us definitive conclusions (Shields & Bredemeier, 1995). Most likely the sport participation–delinquency relationship is best explained by some combination of these views, and in any case, it requires further research.

Sport Participation and Gang Behavior

Gangs and the negative behaviors associated with them (e.g., crime, fights, murder) are of critical concern in North American society. Gang behavior has infiltrated many suburban and rural communities as well as many inner-city neighborhoods.

Sport participation is proposed as an alternative to gang behavior for several reasons (Seefeldt & Ewing, 1997). First, some of the reasons that youth join gangs are alienation from family and peers, low self-esteem, and a lack of positive role models. Second, kids maintain their gang membership because the gang fills their needs in some way. That is, the gang provides an identity for its members and serves many functions that a family might.

It has been suggested, on the other hand, that sport participation can serve as an important substitute for gang membership. Specifically, sport participation can fill the gap for underserved youth (e.g., children who are economically deprived or have little or no parent supervision) by facilitating increased self-esteem, providing an important source of identity, lending social support, and giving participants positive role models. In fact, it has been recommended that selling sport participation as an alternative to gang activity has become an important recruitment strategy for youth sport leaders (Ewing, Seefeldt, & Brown, 1996).

Finally, it is essential to recognize that sport will only serve as an alternative to negative behavior if programs are properly run, organized, and implemented. Sport does nothing by itself. As repeatedly emphasized in this book, quality experiences in sport give rise to psychological benefits.

In no place is this principle better demonstrated than in Trulson's study (1986) of delinquent teenagers, boys matched in background and important personality characteristics (e.g., aggression) and assigned to one of three groups that met three times a week for one hour. One group participated in a modern Tae Kwon Do program emphasizing fighting and self-defense techniques. The second group took part in traditional Tae Kwon Do, which emphasized philosophical reflection, meditation, and physical practice. The third group served as a control and played football and basketball.

After six months members of the modern "fighting" Tae Kwon Do group were less well-adjusted and scored higher on delinquency and aggression measures than when the study began! Members of the "traditional" Tae Kwon Do group, however, exhibited below-normal aggression and demonstrated less anxiety, more social skills, and enhanced self-esteem. Children in the control football and basketball group showed little change in personality or delinquency, but improved in self-esteem and social skills. What is most important about these findings is that they reveal that sport participation alone was not enough to positively influence negative behaviors—the program had to blend social and psychological teachings with the physical activities.

Strategies for Enhancing Character Development

The social learning, structural-developmental, and social-psychological approaches have facilitated our understanding of sportspersonship and enhanced character development. Nine strategies have been derived from these approaches. We'll discuss each of these strategies to learn how it can enhance character development.

> *If sportspersonship is not specifically defined, people do not know what constitutes acceptable and unacceptable behavior.*

Define Sportspersonship in Your Program

As you learned, there is no one universal definition of sportspersonship. And without a specific definition, people in your program will not know what you mean by appropriate and acceptable behavior or inappropriate and unacceptable behavior. You can develop a personal definition of the term, however. Table 24.2 contains an example of such a written code for a children's sports program, specifically identifying sportspersonlike and unsportspersonlike behaviors.

Reinforce and Encourage Sportspersonlike Behaviors

It is important to reinforce and encourage those behaviors and attitudes that you define in your program as good sportspersonship. Conversely, penalize and discourage inappropriate behaviors. Consistency in reinforcing and penalizing these behaviors and actions is essential. Follow the behavior modification guidelines in chapter 6.

Model Appropriate Behaviors

Many people look up to professionals in our field, identifying with them and modeling their actions. Because actions speak louder than words, it is important that exercise and sport professionals provide a good model of sportspersonship. Easier said than done, you say? Indeed, professionals may make mistakes (e.g., lose control and be charged with a technical foul for arguing with the officials). When they lose control, they should admit their error and apologize to the players or students.

Some coaches with strict sportspersonlike guidelines for their players believe it is their job to argue with officials and stick up for their team. Their efforts may be well-intended, but coaches should realize that by demonstrating poor sportspersonship they send mixed messages that undermine their efforts to enhance sportspersonship.

Explain Why Behaviors Are Appropriate Behaviors

Only when people have internalized a guiding moral principle for determining right or wrong can we expect them to consistently behave well in different situations. Thus, it is important to include an accom-

498

Table 24.2

A Written Code of Sportspersonship for a Youth Sport Program

Areas of concern	Sportspersonlike behaviors	Unsportspersonlike behaviors
Behavior toward officials	• Questioning officials in the appropriate manner (e.g., lodging an official protest; having only designated individuals, such as a captain, address officials)	• Arguing with officials • Swearing at officials
Behavior toward opponents	• Treating all opponents with respect and dignity at all times	• Arguing with opponents • Making sarcastic remarks about opponents • Making aggressive actions toward opponents
Behavior toward teammates	• Giving only constructive criticism and positive encouragement	• Making negative comments or sarcastic remarks • Swearing at or arguing with teammates
Behavior toward spectators	• Making only positive comments to spectators	• Arguing with spectators • Making negative remarks and swearing at spectators
Rule acceptance and infractions	• Obeying all league rules	• Taking advantage of loopholes in rules (e.g., every child must play, so coach tells unskilled players to be sick on day of important game)

Adapted from Gould, 1981.

Fitness and sport professionals must be models of sportspersonship.

■

Explain your rationales frequently for the rightness or wrongness of actions.

---

panying rationale for the various components of your sportspersonship code. Rationales provide explanations based on the key elements underlying the levels of moral reasoning: that is, altruism, impartial rules, and moral balances based on mutually determined agreements (Weiss, 1987). Most important, rationales should be regularly conveyed to participants. For example, if several youngsters are excluding a less-skilled classmate in a physical education game, you need to ensure that the less-skilled child is included and also to emphasize the reason behind the decision (e.g., "It is important to treat others as you want them to treat you instead of just doing what you want").

It should also be emphasized how important intention is in actions. The ability to judge intent starts developing at about the age of seven or eight (Martens, 1982a). With children about 10 years old, you can already emphasize **role taking** (i.e., seeing oneself in someone else's role). Then you can add higher levels of empathy—the ability of two people to take each other's perspectives into account when deciding how to act (Newman & Newman, 1991). Many coaches like to have players officiate practice scrimmages of their teammates. The players can then better understand the rules of the game and see things from an official's perspective. By adding a brief postscrimmage discussion, this role taking can serve as a valuable tool for helping players learn to empathize.

Discuss Moral Dilemmas and Choices

For effective moral education to occur, participants should engage in self-dialogue and group discussions about choices and moral dilemmas. A **moral dilemma** requires participants to decide what is morally correct or incorrect (see the box on p. 501). Rule violations, when and why injured participants should play, and who should play are other excellent topics for discussion (Bredemeier & Shields, 1987). Discuss various gray areas of right and wrong that

499

© Human Kinetics

may or may not be against the rules (e.g., is it okay to intentionally say something upsetting to an opponent at the start of a contest? [Weiss, 1987)]).

Build Moral Dilemmas and Choices Into Practices

Some dilemmas you might pose to young athletes during practice include the following (Weiss, 1987, p. 148):

- Not putting out enough of the "best" equipment for all athletes.

- Devising a drill with unequal opportunities for practice; for example, one person is always on defense.

- Devising a drill in which players might be tempted to hurt with words (laughing, yelling), such as having someone demonstrate weak skills or having unfair relay teams.

- Devising a drill that provides possible opportunities for rough play—for example, the hamburger rebound drill, in which two individuals block out one person simultaneously and go for the ball.

After the players try to solve the dilemmas, follow up with discussion about the underlying moral reasoning.

These strategies for enhancing character development and sportspersonship require time, planning, and effort. For optimal effect, they should be repeated consistently across time, not just once or twice at the start of the season or when a child is causing a problem.

Teach Cooperative Learning Strategies

Earlier in this book (chapter 5) competition and cooperation were defined and discussed. Although both competition and cooperation are necessary for the development of optimal achievement motivation, we explained that children in Western society are much more often exposed to competition than cooperation. For this reason we emphasized that physical activity participants should be taught cooperative learning strategies. Researchers into moral development also have shown that the ability to learn how to cooperate is critical to character development (Miller et al., 1997). Doing so might involve the use of superordinate goals in games (e.g., make the most possible

■ CLOSE-UP ■

When to Shoot Toward an Opponent's Injured Leg

Rodd and Kevin are two evenly matched 150-pound wrestlers involved in a close match. Rodd injures his left knee, takes an injury time-out for treatment, and then returns to the mat. He is in obvious pain with greatly constrained movement and cannot place weight on his injured leg. Imagine that you are Kevin and respond to the following questions:

© Human Kinetics

Should you execute moves to the side of the injured leg because it will be easier to score points?

Once you are in contact with your injured opponent, should you put extra pressure on his injured leg to cause him pain and allow you to turn him to his back and pin him?

Should you avoid executing moves toward his injured leg unless the match is close in score?

Should you avoid executing moves toward his injured leg entirely and try to beat him at his best?

---

passes in three minutes), contrasted to competitive goals (e.g., score more points than your opponents) or focusing on cooperative games.

Create a Task-Oriented Motivational Climate

A task-oriented motivational climate focuses on having participants adopt task, rather than ego, goals (see chapter 3) so they can judge their ability by their own performance, rather than through socially compared improvements. It is easier to teach sportspersonship and develop character when social comparison and competition are de-emphasized and individual improvement and learning are instead emphasized (Miller et al., 1997). However, this does not mean that character cannot be developed in a competitive climate— only that there are major benefits to initiating the efforts toward character development in a task-oriented motivational climate. Once participants have developed good character, competition might indeed provide good tests of what values they have developed.

Transfer Power From Leaders to Participants

Character development is best fostered in environments that progressively transfer power from leaders to participants. Hellison and Templin (1991), for example, have developed a physical education curriculum designed to help students grow in their sense of personal and social responsibility. This realistically based program first focuses on children who are acting irresponsibly, helping them regain their self-control by removing them from class so that they do not disrupt others. Self-control is then developed, followed by later steps toward involvement, self-direction, and caring (see Table 24.3).

Guiding Practice in Character Development

To guide your practice, you should consider several philosophically oriented issues which cover a broad

501

Table 24.3

Hellison's Levels of Responsibility

Level	Description
0—Irresponsibility	This level describes students who are unmotivated and whose behavior is disruptive. The goal of the physical educator is to help them get their behavior under control (thereby advancing them to Level 1) or to remove them from the setting so they do not interefere with others' rights.
1—Self-control	Students at this level may not participate in the day's activities, but they control their behavior enough to not need to be removed from the setting. The goal of the physical educator is to help these students become involved in the activities (thereby advancing them to Level 2) or, minimally, to learn to respect the rights and feelings of others enough that their behaviors and attitudes do not intefere with teaching and learning.
2—Involvement	Students at Level 2 participate in the physical education activities. Involvement may take many forms, from going through the motions to setting and pursuing objectives. The goal of the physical educator is to encourage students to take increasing responsibility for their own development and definitions of success. For example, students may come to define success as an effort, improvement, goal setting, achievement of a norm or standard, or being socially responsible as a player or leader.
3—Self-direction	This level describes students who can work effectively and independently on self-improvement in areas of personally identified need or aspiration. The goal of the physical educator is to enable them to acquire the skills needed to work independently and set realistic goals. A relevant knowledge base is also critical, and students should be gradually confronted with broader philosophical issues that connect with their self-defined objectives: "Who do I want to be? Why do I want to . . . ?"
4—Caring	Up to this point, the only necessary regard for others is a respect for their fundamental rights. At Level 4, students move beyond the focus on self and are motivated by an other-regarding, prosocial orientation. The goal of the physical educator is to provide opportunities to cooperate, give support, show concern, help others, and the like.

Reprinted from Shields and Bredemeier, 1995.

range. They include the physical educator's and coach's roles in moral development. In addition, you should look at the role of winning, how the moral behavior you teach can be transferred beyond the playing field, and recognizing the imperfect nature of character development.

The Educator's Role in Character Development

Some people believe teachers and coaches have no business teaching morals and values to youth. Character and morals are the domain of parents and the church, they argue, not the school, especially not the public schools. We certainly agree

that it is not sound practice to mix religious values into the public school curriculum. However, avoiding character education in basic values like honesty, empathy, and methods of solving disputes is a grave mistake. And we contend that physical educators, coaches, and exercise leaders do influence many values, intentionally or not. As Shields and Bredemeier (1995, p. 3) state, "Despite the problems associated with competitive sport, sport is replete with opportunities to encounter, learn, transform, and enact moral values." For example, coaches recommend whether to argue with officials, physical educators take positions on teaching competitive or cooperative games, and athletic

Physical educators, coaches, and exercise leaders are in positions to positively influence character behavior and development.

trainers recommend when to play an injured athlete. Such decisions often affect the participants' attitudes, and so it is important to have developed a philosophical stance on these issues. It is much better to recognize the moral values you're fostering and discouraging than to affect someone else's values haphazardly.

Reducing Youth Risk by Fostering Resiliency

Despite the strategies that physical educators and coaches can use to teach character and sportspersonship to children and youth, it must be recognized that many children live in environments that place them at risk for negative behavioral development (e.g., drug addiction, teenage pregnancy, and gang activity). Moreover, it is unlikely that physical activity specialists can eliminate such major risk factors as poverty, an absence of parental involvement in someone's life, abuse, and undesirable role models. Nevertheless, Martinek and Hellison (1997), two physical educators who have spent countless hours working with underserved youth, contend that developing psychological resiliency is one of the most important life skills that we can foster in these children.

Resiliency is the ability to rebound and bounce back successfully after exposure to severe risk or distress; in essence, it is righting oneself in conditions where one is thwarted (Martinek & Hellison, 1997). Moreover, educators and social scientists have studied resilient youth and found they possess three primary attributes: social competence, autonomy, and optimism or hope.

Social competence

Social competence is the ability to interact socially with others and in so doing create strong networks of social support. Having flexibility and empathy are seen as critical to the development of this important attribute. Especially important is learning how to negotiate, confront, and handle challenges from others (e.g., learning non-

violent peer conflict-resolution skills; see chapter 23).

Autonomy

Resilient youth also have a clear sense of who they are, feel they can exert control over their environments, and feel they can act independently. In essence, they feel a sense of autonomy, that they can function as individuals on their own—in an autonomous fashion.

Optimism and Hope

In chapter 3 we discussed learned helplessness, where an individual feels that despite his or her putting forth effort, little change will take place. Resilient youth are characterized by their being at the other end of the spectrum: They have not learned helplessness. Rather, they have a sense of optimism and hope and feel their efforts will be rewarded.

Martinek and Hellison (1997) contend that one of the best ways to enhance resiliency in underserved youth is through the development of physical activity programs. Moreover, they have outlined specific strategies for doing so (see the box on p. 504).

The Double-Sided Role of Winning

Winning plays a dual role in character development (Martens, 1982a). On the one hand, an emphasis on winning pressures some individuals to cheat, break rules, and behave in ways they would consider inappropriate off the field. On the other hand, when a player resists the temptations to cheat or commit other immoral acts—despite a high value having been placed on winning—integrity develops and moral lessons become more meaningful. Winning itself is neutral to moral development. The key is finding the right emphasis to place on winning.

Transferring Values to Nonsport Environments

It is a myth that the lessons and values learned in the gym or pool or on the athletic field transfer au-

If your goal is to teach values through sport and physical activities, learn to discuss how these values transfer to nonsport environments.

Strategies for Developing Resiliency in Youth

- Focus on the athlete's strengths rather than the weaknesses. Build his or her self-confidence.
- Don't focus only on the sport or physical activity. Focus on the whole child and her emotional, social, economic, and educational needs.
- Be sensitive to the youngster's individuality, as well as his cultural differences. Get to know him as a person.
- Encourage independence and control over one's life by providing the athlete with input about the program and leadership responsibilities.
- Incorporate a strong set of values and clear expectations into the program. Make sure the athlete knows what you expect and value.
- Help youth see possible future occupations for themselves.
- Provide a physically and psychologically safe environment.
- Keep program numbers small and emphasize long-term involvement.
- Provide leadership that makes the program work despite obstacles.
- Make sure the program links with the community and neighborhood.
- Provide quality contact with adult models who care and offer support.

Adapted from Martinek & Hellison, 1997, pp. 42-43.

---

tomatically to other environments. For such a transfer to occur, the lesson must be drawn out or extended (Danish, Nellen, & Owens, 1996; Danish & Nellen, 1997; Danish, Petitpas, & Hale, 1992). If you want to teach values through sport and physical activity, you must discuss how the values transfer to the nonsport environment. For instance, a coach who wants to teach young athletes an attitude of cooperation to carry over to nonsport situations can discuss how and when teamwork works well in other contexts (e.g., working on a school project). In fact, this is one advantage of a structural-developmental approach. Social learning principles, which enhance specific sportspersonlike attitudes and behaviors, tend to be highly situation-specific. That is, teaching a child to be honest in gym class will not transfer to math class. However, if you can help raise someone's underlying moral reasoning, his or her behavior tends to be affected across a variety of situations.

Having Realistic Expectations

Unfortunately, enhancing sportspersonship and developing character through sport and physical activity are imperfect processes (Martens, 1982a). We cannot reach all individuals at all times. More likely, we'll experience some tremendous successes along with other dismal failures. Recognizing the imperfect nature of character development and having realistic expectations enables us to remain optimistic, despite experiencing some setbacks.

SUMMARY

1 *Define what character development and sportspersonship are.*

Character development and sportspersonship concern morality in sport and physical activity; that is, they are our views and actions about what is right or ethical and what is wrong or unethical in sport and physical activity settings. Character comprises four interrelated virtues: compassion, fairness, sportspersonship, and integrity. These virtues are also closely related to moral development, moral reasoning, and moral behavior.

2 *Explain how character and sportspersonship develop.*

There are three views as to how character and sportspersonship develop in athletes. The social learning approach emphasizes modeling, reinforcement, and social comparison. The structural-developmental approach contends that moral reasoning is related to a person's level of cognitive development. The analysis of five levels in moral reasoning reflects a progression from judging an action's rightness or wrongness according to self-centered interests to having a concern with the mutual interests of all involved. Third, the social-psychological approach combines the first two approaches and suggests that a complex perspective of person-by-situation determines character development and sportspersonship.

3 *Identify the important link between moral reasoning and moral behavior.*

One's moral reasoning and moral behavior are linked by a moral-action process that includes four stages: interpreting the situation as one that involves some sort of moral judgment, deciding on the best course of action, making a choice to act morally, and implementing a moral response. Although a consistent relationship exists between moral reasoning and moral behavior, the relationship is not perfect.

4 *Discuss how character and sportspersonship can be influenced.*

Research shows that physical education and youth sports participation can deter negative behaviors such as delinquency and gang violence and enhance positive character development. For this positive development to occur requires using well-thought-out, designed, and implemented strategies for character development. Nine strategies for developing character and sportspersonhip were delineated, based on the social learning, structural-developmental, and social-psychological approaches. These were to define what you consider sportspersonship in precise terms; reinforce and encourage sportspersonlike behaviors and penalize and discourage unsportspersonlike behaviors; model appropriate behaviors; convey rationales, emphasizing why actions are appropriate or inappropriate, the intent of actions, role taking, compassion, and empathy; discuss moral dilemmas; build moral dilemmas and choices into practice and class contexts; teach cooperative learning strategies; engineer task-oriented, motivational climates; and transfer power from leaders to participants.

5 *Describe the effects of winning on character development and sportspersonship.*

Some philosophically oriented issues to consider in facilitating character development are the educator's role in character development, the double-sided role of winning, transferring values to nonsport environments, and maintaining realistic expectations of the character-development process. Physical activity specialists also play an important role in fostering resiliency in underserved youth.

KEY TERMS

fair play
sportspersonship
character
compassion
integrity
moral reasoning
moral development
moral behavior
differential association

social bonding
labeling hypothesis
economic strain
role taking
moral dilemma
resiliency
social competence
autonomy
optimism and hope

REVIEW QUESTIONS

1. Define character and its components.

2. What is the social learning approach to sportspersonship and character development? Name the three major means through which social learning takes place.

3. Describe the structural-developmental approach to moral reasoning and development.

4. What is the social psychological approach to character and sportspersonship?

5. What are Haan's five stages of moral reasoning? Why are these important?

6. What is the relationship between athletic participation and delinquency or gang behaviors?

7. Describe the relation between moral reasoning and moral behavior. What implication does this have for guiding practice?

8. Explain each of the following strategies for enhancing character development and sportspersonship:

   ■ Defining sportspersonship in your particular context
   ■ Reinforcing and encouraging sportspersonlike behaviors; penalizing and discouraging nonsportspersonlike behaviors
   ■ Explaining your thinking about appropriate behaviors
   ■ Discussing moral dilemmas
   ■ Building moral dilemmas and choices into practices and classes
   ■ Teaching cooperative learning strategies
   ■ Engineering a task-oriented motivational climate
   ■ Transferring power from leaders to participants

9. How can winning both enhance and deter the development of sportspersonship and moral reasoning?

10. Why is it important to teach character development for transfer?

CRITICAL THINKING QUESTIONS

1. What should be the role of the physical educator in enhancing character development and teaching sportspersonship?

2. Design a moral dilemma for the following situations:

   ■ Physical education class
   ■ Youth-sport team practice
   ■ Varsity high school contest

Finish

You should now have a good grasp of strategies that can be used to foster psychological change and development. This knowledge will help you choose the most appropriate ways to achieve the objectives of your psychological skills program. However, unless you put this knowledge into practice, it will be of little use.

As a professional in sport and exercise science you will be responsible for implementing what you have learned. You now know that a knowledge of sport and exercise psychology can have tremendous payoffs when applied in professional practice settings. So adopt the active approach to professional practice that we discussed in the beginning of this text; implement the ideas conveyed here and consistently evaluate your strategies in light of your professional experience. Be aware of current research. Use the gym, pool, and athletic field as your laboratory to continue your growth and professional development. Don't make the mistake of simply taking your final exam, finishing the course, and then never again thinking about the material. Refer to the text when you are faced with practical problems. Use what you have learned and apply and try to improve upon it. Take it from us, seeing someone achieve his or her goals through developing psychological skills is one of the most rewarding professional experiences you can have.

References

Abell, R. (1975). Confessions of a compulsive. *Runner's World, 10,* 30-31.

Abernathy, B. (1991). Visual search strategies and decision making in sport. *International Journal of Sport Psychology, 22,* 189-210.

Abernathy, B. (1993). Attention. In R.N. Singer, M. Murphey, & K. Tennant (Eds.), *Handbook of research on sport psychology* (pp. 127-170). New York: Macmillan.

Ahsen, A. (1984). The triple code model for imagery and psychophysiology. *Journal of Mental Imagery, 8,* 15-42.

Ajzen, I., & Fishbein, M. (1980). *Understanding attitudes and predicting social behavior.* Englewood Cliffs, NJ: Prentice Hall.

Ajzen, I., & Madden, T.J. (1986). Prediction of goal-directed behavior: Attitudes, intentions, and perceived behavioral control. *Journal of Experimental Social Psychology, 22,* 453-474.

Albrecht, R.R., & Feltz, D.L. (1987). Generality and specificity of attention related to competitive anxiety and sport performance. *Journal of Sport Psychology, 9,* 241-248.

Allison, M.G., & Ayllon, T. (1980). Behavioral coaching in the development of skills in football, gymnastics, and tennis. *Journal of Applied Behavior Analysis, 13,* 297-314.

American Medical Association. (1966). *Standard nomenclature of athletic injuries.* Chicago, IL: American Medical Association.

American Psychiatric Association. (1994). *Diagnostic and statistical manual of mental disorders* (4th ed.). Washington, DC: American Psychiatric Association.

American Psychological Association. (1985). *Standards for educational and psychological testing.* Washington, DC: American Psychological Association.

American Psychological Association. (1992). Ethical principles for psychologists and the code of conduct. *American Psychologist, 47,* 1597-1611.

American Sport Education Program. (1994). *Sport parent.* Champaign, IL: Human Kinetics.

Ames, C. (1987). The enhancement of student motivation. In D.A. Kleiber & M. Maehr (Eds.), *Advances in motivation and achievement* (pp. 123-148). Greenwich, CT: JAI Press.

Ames, C. (1992). Achievement goals, motivational climates, and motivational processes. In G.C. Roberts (Ed.), *Motivation in sport and exercise* (pp. 161-176). Champaign, IL: Human Kinetics.

Amorose, T., Horn, T., & Miller, V. (1994). Intrinsic motivation in collegiate athletes: Relationships with athletes' scholarship status and coaching behaviors. *Journal of Sport and Exercise Psychology, 16,* S26.

Andersen, M.B., & Williams, J.M. (1988). A model of stress and athletic injury: Prediction and prevention. *Journal of Sport and Exercise Psychology, 10,* 294-306.

Anshel, M. (1990). *Sport psychology: From theory to practice.* Scottsdale, AZ: Gorsuch Scarisbrick.

Anshel, M.H. (1993). Psychology of drug use. In R. Singer, K. Tennant, & M. Murphey (Eds.), *Sport psychology* (pp. 851-876). New York: Macmillan.

Anshel, M.H. (1994). *Sport psychology: From theory to practice.* Scottsdale, AZ: Gorsuch Scarisbrick.

Anshel, M.H. (1997). Drug use in sport: Causes and cures. In J. Williams (Ed.), *Applied sport psychology: Personal growth to peak performance.* Mountain View, CA: Mayfield.

Anshel, M.H., Brown, J.M., & Brown, D.F. (1993). Effectiveness of a program for coping with acute stress on motor performance, affect, and muscular tension. *Australian Journal of Science and Medicine in Sport, 25,* 7-16.

Anshel, M.H., & Weinberg, R.S. (1995a). Coping with acute stress among American and Australian basketball referees. *Journal of Sport Behavior, 19,* 180-203.

Anshel, M.H., & Weinberg, R.S. (1995b). Sources of acute stress in American and Australian basketball referees. *Journal of Applied Sport Psychology, 7,* 11-22.

Apitzsch, E. (1995). Psychodynamic theory of personality and sport performance. In S.J.H. Biddle (Ed.), *European perspectives on exercise and sport psychology* (pp. 111-127). Champaign, IL: Human Kinetics.

Arms, R.L., Russell, G.W., & Sandilands, M.L. (1979). Effects of viewing aggressive sports on the hostility of spectators. *Social Psychology Quarterly, 42,* 275-279.

Asch, S. (1956). Studies of independence and conformity: A minority of one against a unanimous majority. *Psychological Monographs, 70,* (9, Whole No. 416).

Ashe, A. (1981). *Off the court.* New York: New American Library.

Asken, M.J. (1988). *Dying to win: The athletes' guide to safe and unsafe drugs in sports.* Washington, DC: Acropolis Books.

Asken, M.J. (1991). The challenge of the physically challenged: Delivering sport psychology services to physically disabled athletes. *The Sport Psychologist, 5,* 370.

Atkinson, J.W. (1974). The mainstream of achievement-oriented activity. In J.W. Atkinson & J.O. Raynor (Eds.), *Motivation and achievement* (pp. 13-41). New York: Halstead.

Auweele, Y.V., Cuyper, B.D., Van Mele, V., & Rzewnicki, R. (1993). Elite performance and personality: From description and prediction to diagnosis and intervention. In R.N. Singer, M. Murphey, & L.K. Tennant (Eds.), *Handbook of research on sport psychology* (pp. 257-289). New York: Macmillan.

Bahrke, M.S., & Morgan, W.P. (1978). Anxiety reduction following exercise and meditation. *Cognitive Therapy and Research, 2,* 323-334.

Bandura, A. (1965). Vicarious processes: A special case of no-trial learning. In L. Berkowitz (Ed.), *Advances in experimental social psychology* (Vol. 2). New York: Academic Press.

Bandura, A. (1973). *Aggression: A social learning analysis.* Englewood Cliffs, NJ: Prentice Hall.

Bandura, A. (Ed.). (1974). *Psychological modeling: Conflicting theories.* New York: Lieberton.

Bandura, A. (1977a). Self-efficacy: Toward a unifying theory of behavioral change. *Psychological Review, 84,* 191-215.

Bandura, A. (1977b). *Social learning theory.* Englewood Cliffs, NJ: Prentice Hall.

Bandura, A. (1986). *Social foundations of thought and actions: A social cognitive theory.* Englewood Cliffs, NJ: Prentice Hall.

Barnett, N.P., Smoll, F.L., & Smith, R.E. (1992). Effects of enhancing coach-athlete relationships on youth sport attrition. *The Sport Psychologist, 6,* 111-127.

Baron, R.A., & Richardson, D.R. (1994). *Human aggression.* New York: Plenum.

Barrow, J. (1977). The variables of leadership: A review and conceptual framework. *Academy of Management Review, 2,* 231-251.

Bass, B.M. (1962). *The orientation inventory.* Palo Alto, CA: Consulting Psychologists Press.

Baumeister, R.F., & Steinhilber, A. (1984). Paradoxical effects of supportive audiences on performance under pressure: The home field disadvantage in sports championships. *Journal of Personality and Social Psychology, 43,* 85-93.

Becker, M.H., & Maiman, L.A. (1975). Sociobehavioral determinants of compliance with health care and medical care recommendations. *Medical Care, 13,* 10-24.

Bell, K. (1980). *The nuts and bolts of psychology for swimmers.* Austin, TX: Keel.

Bell, K. (1982). *Winning isn't normal.* Austin, TX: Keel.

Benson, H. & Proctor, W. (1984). *Beyond the relaxation response.* New York: Berkley.

Benyo, R. (1990). *The exercise fix.* Champaign, IL: Human Kinetics.

Berger, B.G. (1996). Psychological benefits of an active lifestyle: What we know and what we need to know. *Quest, 48,* 330-353.

Berkowitz, L. (1965). The concept of aggressive drive: Some additional considerations. In L. Berkowitz (Ed.), *Advances in experimental social psychology* (Vol. 2, pp. 301-329). New York: Academic Press.

Berkowitz, L. (1969). *Roots of aggression.* New York: Atherton Press.

Berkowitz, L. (1993). *Aggression: Its causes, consequences and control.* Philadelphia: Temple University Press.

Bernstein, F. (1973, March 16). *The New Yorker*, pp. 87-88.

Betts, G.H. (1909). *The distributions and functions of mental imagery.* New York: Teacher's College, Columbia University.

Biddle, S. (1993). Attribution research and sport psychology. In R.N. Singer, M. Murphey, & L.K. Tennant (Eds.), *Handbook of research on sport psychology* (pp. 437-464). New York: Macmillan.

Biddle, S. (1995). Exercise and psychosocial health. *Research Quarterly for Exercise & Sport, 66,* 292-297.

Black, J. (1979). The brain according to Mandell. *Runner, 1* (7): 78-80, 82, 84, 87.

Black, S.J., & Weiss, M.R. (1992). The relationship among perceived coaching behaviors, perceptions of ability, and motivation in competitive age-group swimmers. *Journal of Sport and Exercise Psychology, 14,* 309-325.

Blair, S. (1995). Exercise prescription for health. *Quest, 47,* 338-353.

Blake, R., & Moulton, J. (1969). *Building a dynamic corporation through grid organization development.* Reading, MA: Addison-Wesley.

Blumenthal, J.A., Emery, C.F., Walsh, M.A., Cox, D.K., Kuh, C.M., Williams, R.B., & Williams, R.S. (1988). Exercise training in healthy type A middle-aged men: Effects on behavioral and cardiovascular responses. *Psychosomatic Medicine, 50,* 418-433.

Botterill, C. (1983). Goal setting for athletes with examples from hockey. In G.L. Martin & D. Hrycaiko (Eds.), *Behavior modification and coaching: Principles, procedures, and research.* Springfield, IL: Charles C. Thomas.

Botterill, C. (1990). Sport psychology and professional hockey. *The Sport Psychologist, 4,* 369-377.

Bouffard, M., & Crocker, P.R.E. (1992). Coping by individuals with physical disabilities with perceived challenge in physical activity: Are people consistent? *Research Quarterly for Exercise and Sport, 63,* 410-417.

Bowers, K.S. (1973). Situationism in psychology: An analysis and a critique. *Psychological Review, 80,* 307-336.

Bradley, B. (1986). *Life on the run.* New York: Bantam.

Brawley, L. (1990). Group cohesion: Status, problems, and future directions. *International Journal of Sport Psychology, 21,* 355-379.

Brawley, L., Carron, A., & Widmeyer, W. (1987). Assessing the cohesion of teams: Validity of the Group Environment Questionnaire. *Journal of Sport Psychology, 9,* 275-294.

Brawley, L., Carron, A., & Widmeyer, W. (1988). Exploring the relationship between cohesion and group resistance to disruption. *Journal of Sport and Exercise Psychology, 10,* 199-213.

Brawley, L., Carron, A., & Widmeyer, W. (1993). The influence of the group and its cohesiveness on perception of group goal-related variables. *Journal of Sport and Exercise Psychology, 15,* 245-266.

Bredemeier, B., & Shields, D. (1986). Athletic aggression: An issue of contextual morality. *Sociology of Sport Journal, 3,* 15-28.

Bredemeier, B.J., & Shields, D. (1984). Divergence in moral reasoning about sport and everyday life. *Sociology of Sport Journal, 1,* 234-257.

Bredemeier, B.J., & Shields, D. (1987). Moral growth through physical activity: A structural developmental approach. In D. Gould & M.R. Weiss (Eds.), *Advances in pediatric sport sciences: Behavioral issues* (Vol. 2, pp. 143-165). Champaign, IL: Human Kinetics.

Brewer, B. W. (1994). Review and critique of models of psychological adjustment to athletic injury. *Journal of Applied Sport Psychology, 6,* 87-100.

Brewer, B.W., & Petrie, T.A. (1996). Psychopathology in sport and exercise psychology. In J.L. Van Raalte & B.W. Brewer (Eds.), *Exploring sport and exercise psychology* (pp. 258-274). Washington, DC: American Psychological Association.

Brownell, K., Stunkard, A., & Albaum, J. (1980). Evaluation and modification of exercise patterns in the natural environment. *American Journal of Psychiatry, 137,* 1540-1545.

Brownell, K.D., & Rodin, J. (1992). Prevalence of eating disorders in athletes. In K.D. Brownell, J. Rodin, & J.H. Wilmore (Eds.), *Eating, body weight, and performance* (pp. 128-145). Malvern, PA: Lea & Febiger.

Brustad, R.J. (1993). Who will go out and play? Parental and psychological influences on children's attraction to physical activity. *Pediatric Exercise Science, 5,* 210-223.

Buffone, G. (1984). Exercise as a therapeutic adjunct. In J.M. Silva & R.S. Weinberg (Eds.), *Psychological foundations in sport and exercise* (pp. 445-451). Champaign, IL: Human Kinetics.

Bump, L.A. (1988). Drugs and sport performance. In R. Martens (Ed.), *Successful coaching* (pp. 135-147). Champaign, IL: Human Kinetics.

Burke, K.L. (1997). Communication in sports: Research and practice. *Journal of Interdisciplinary Research in Physical Education, 2,* 39-52.

Burton, D. (1984). Evaluation of goal-setting training on selected cognitions and performance of collegiate swimmers. (Doctoral dissertation, University of Illinois, 1983). *Dissertation Abstracts International, 45,* 116A.

Burton, D. (1989a). The impact of goal specificity and task complexity on basketball skill development. *The Sport Psychologist, 3,* 34-47.

Burton, D. (1989b). Winning isn't everything: Examining the impact of performance goals on collegiate swimmers' cognitions and performance. *The Sport Psychologist, 3,* 105-132.

Butler, R.J., & Hardy, L. (1992). The performance profile: Theory and application. *The Sport Psychologist, 6,* 253-264.

Caccese, T.M., & Mayerberg, C.K. (1984). Gender differences in perceived burnout of college coaches. *Journal of Sport Psychology, 6,* 279-288.

Cameron, J., & Pierce, W.D. (1994). Reinforcement, reward and intrinsic motivation: A meta-analysis. *Review of Educational Research, 64,* 363-423.

Canadian Fitness and Lifestyle Research Institute. (1996). *Progress in prevention.*

Capel, S.A. (1986). Psychological and organizational factors related to burnout in athletic trainers. *Research Quarterly for Exercise & Sport, 57,* 321-328.

Carpenter, W.B. (1894). Principles of mental physiology. New York: Appleton.

Carr, C.M., Kennedy, S.R., & Dimick, K.M. (1990). Alcohol use and abuse among high school athletes: A comparison of alcohol use and intoxication in male and female high school athletes and non-athletes. *Journal of Alcohol and Drug Education, 36,* 39-45.

Carr, C.M., & Murphy, S.M. (1995). Alcohol and drugs in sport. In S.M. Murphy (Ed.), *Psychological interventions in sport* (pp. 283-306). Champaign, IL: Human Kinetics.

Carron, A., & Chelladurai, P. (1982). *Cohesiveness, coach-athlete compatibility, participation orientation and their relationship to relative performance and satisfaction.* Paper presented at the meeting of the North American Society for Sport Psychology and Physical Activity, College Park, MD.

Carron, A., Widmeyer, W., & Brawley, L. (1985). The development of an instrument to assess cohesion in sport teams: The Group Environment Questionnaire. *Journal of Sport Psychology, 7,* 244-267.

Carron, A.V. (1982). Cohesiveness in sport groups: Interpretations and considerations. *Journal of Sport Psychology, 4,* 123-138.

Carron, A.V. (1984). Cohesion in sport teams. In J.M. Silva and R.S. Weinberg (Eds.), *Psychological foundations of sport* (pp. 340-351). Champaign, IL: Human Kinetics.

Carron, A.V., & Ball, J.R. (1977). Cause effect characteristics of cohesiveness and participation motivation in intercollegiate ice hockey. *International Review of Sport Sociology, 12,* 49-60.

Carron, A.V., & Dennis, P. (1998). The sport team as an effective group. In J. Williams (Ed.), *Applied sport psychology: Personal growth to peak performance* (pp. 127-141). Champaign, IL: Human Kinetics.

Carron, A.V., & Spink, K.S. (1993). Team building in an exercise setting. *The Sport Psychologist, 7,* 8-18.

Carron, A.V., & Spink, K.S. (1995). The group, size-cohesion relationship in minimal groups. *Small Group Research, 26,* 86-105.

Carron, A.V., Spink, K.S., & Prapavessis, H. (1997). Team building and cohesiveness in the sport and exercise setting: Use of indirect interventions. *Journal of Applied Sport Psychology, 9,* 61-72.

Cartwright, D., & Zander, A. (1968). *Group dynamics: Research and theory* (3rd ed.). New York: Harper & Row.

Cattell, R.B. (1965). *The scientific analysis of personality.* Baltimore: Penguin.

Cavanaugh, B.M., & Silva, J.M. (1980). Spectator perceptions of fan misbehavior: An additudinal inquiry. In C.H. Nadeau, W.R. Halliwell, K.M. Newell, & G.C. Roberts (Eds.), *Psychology of motor behavior and sport.* Champaign, IL: Human Kinetics.

Chan, C. (1986). Addicted to exercise. In *Encyclopedia Britannica Medical and Health Annual* (pp. 429-432).

Chan, C., & Grossman, H. (1988). Psychological effects of running loss on consistent runners. *Perceptual and Motor Skills, 66,* 875-883.

Chase, M., Lirgg, C., & Feltz, D. (1997). Do coaches' efficacy expectations for their teams predict team performance? *The Sport Psychologist, 11,* 8-23.

Chelladurai, P. (1978). A contingency model of leadership in athletics. Unpublished doctoral dissertation, Department of Management Sciences, University of Waterloo, Canada.

Chelladurai, P. (1990). Leadership in sports: A review. *International Journal of Sport Psychology, 21,* 328-354.

Chelladurai, P. (1993). Leadership. In R. Singer, M. Murphey, & L. Tennant (Eds.), *Handbook of research on sport psychology.* New York: Macmillan.

Chelladurai, P., & Arnott, M. (1985). Decision styles in coaching: Preferences of basketball players. *Research Quarterly for Exercise and Sport, 56,* 15-24.

Chelladurai, P., & Haggerty, T.R. (1978). A normative model of decision styles in coaching. *Athletic Administrator, 13,* 6-9.

Chelladurai, P., Haggerty, T.R, & Baxter, P.R. (1989). Decision style choices of university basketball coaches and players. *Journal of Sport and Exercise Psychology, 11,* 201-215.

Chelladurai, P., Imamura, H., Yamaguchi, Y., Oinuma, Y., & Miyauchi, T. (1988). Sport leadership in a crossnational setting: The case of Japanese and Canadian university athletes. *Journal of Sport & Exercise Psychology, 10,* 374-389.

Chelladurai, P., Malloy, D., Imamura, H., & Yamaguchi, Y. (1987). A cross-cultural study of preferred leadership in sports. *Canadian Journal of Sport Sciences, 12,* 106-110.

Chelladurai, P., & Saleh, S.D. (1978). Preferred leadership in sports. *Canadian Journal of Applied Sport Sciences, 3,* 85-92.

Chodzko-Zajko, W.J., & Moore, K.A. (1994). Physical fitness and cognitive functioning in aging. *Exercise and Sport Science Reviews, 22,* 195-220.

Cierpinski, W. (1980). *Track and Field News, 27.*

Clark, R.A., & Sachs, M.L. (1991). Challenges and opportunities in psychological skills training in deaf athletes. *The Sport Psychologist, 5,* 392.

Coakley, J. (1992). Burnout among adolescent athletes: A personal failure or social problem? *Sociology of Sport Journal, 9,* 271-285.

Coakley, J. (1994). *Sport in society: Issues and controversies* (4th ed). St. Louis: Times Mirror/Mosby College.

Coakley, J. (1997). *Sport in society: Issues and controversies* (5th ed). St. Louis: Times Mirror/Mosby College.

Cohn, P. (1990). An exploratory study on sources of stress and acute athlete burnout in youth golf. *The Sport Psychologist, 4,* 95-106.

Cohn, P.J., Rotella, R.J., & Lloyd, J.W. (1990). Effects of a cognitive-behavioral intervention on the preshot routine and performance in golf. *The Sport Psychologist, 4,* 33-47.

Coleman, J.S. (1974). *Youth: Transition to adulthood.* Chicago: University of Chicago Press.

College of Human Medicine, Michigan State University. (1985, June). *The substance use and abuse habits of college student-athletes.* Report presented to NCAA Drug Education Committee, Michigan State University.

Comrey, A., & Deskin, G. (1954). Group manual dexterity in women. *Journal of Applied Psychology, 38,* 178.

Connelly, D., & Rotella, R.J. (1991). The social psychology of assertiveness communication: Issues in teaching assertiveness skills to athletes. *The Sport Psychologist, 5,* 73-87.

Conrad, P. (1987). Who comes to work-site wellness programs? A preliminary review. *Journal of Occupational Medicine, 29,* 317-320.

513

Cote, J., Salmela, J.H., & Russell, S. (1995). The knowledge of high-performance gymnastic coaches: Competition and training considerations. *The Sport Psychologist, 9,* 76-95.

Cox, R.H. (1998). *Sport psychology: Concepts and applications* (4th ed.). Boston: WCB/McGraw-Hill.

Cox, R.H., Qui, Y., & Liu, Z. (1993). Overview of sport psychology. In R.N. Singer, M. Murphey, & L.K. Tennant (Eds.). *Handbook of research on sport psychology* (pp. 3-31). New York: Macmillan.

Crace, R.K., & Brown, D. (1996). *Life Values Inventory.* Chapel Hill, NC: Life Values Resources.

Crace, R.K., & Hardy, C.J. (1997). Individual values and the team building process. *Journal of Applied Sport Psychology, 9,* 41-60.

Crawford, S., & Eklund, R.C. (1994). Social physique anxiety, reasons for exercise, and attitudes toward exercise settings. *Journal of Sport & Exercise Psychology, 16,* 70-82.

Crews, D. (1993). Self-regulation strategies in sport and exercise. In R. Singer, M. Murphey, & L.K. Tennant (Eds.), *Handbook of research in sport psychology* (pp. 557-568). New York: Macmillan.

Crocker, P.R.E. (1992). Managing stress by competitive athletes: Ways of coping. *International Journal of Sport Psychology, 23,* 161-175.

Crocker, P.R.E., Alderman, R., Murray, F., & Smith, R. (1988). Cognitive-affective stress-management training with high performance youth volleyball players: Effects on affect, cognition, and performance. *Journal of Sport and Exercise Psychology, 10,* 448-460.

Csikszentmihalyi, M. (1975). *Beyond boredom and anxiety.* San Francisco: Jossey-Bass.

Csikszentmihalyi, M. (1990). *Flow: The psychology of optimal experience.* New York: Harper & Row.

Dale, J., & Weinberg, R.S. (1990). Burnout in sport: A review and critique. *Journal of Applied Sport Psychology, 2,* 67-83.

Daniels, F.S., & Landers, D.M. (1981). Biofeedback and shooting performance: A test of disregulation and systems theory. *Journal of Sport Psychology, 4,* 271-282.

Danish, S.J., & Nellen, V.C. (1997). New roles for sport psychologists: Teaching life skills through sport at-risk youth. *Quest, 49*(1), 100-113.

Danish, S.J., Nellen, V.C., & Owens, S.S. (1996). Teaching life skills through sport: Community-based programs for adolescents. In J.L. Van Raalte and B. Brewer (Eds.), *Exploring sport and exercise psychology* (pp. 205-225). New York: American Psychological Association.

Danish, S.J., Owens, S.S., Green, S.L., & Brunelle, J.P. (1997). Building bridges for disengagement: The transition process for individual and teams. *Journal of Applied Sport Psychology, 9,* 154-167.

Danish, S.J., Petitpas, A.S., & Hale, B.D. (1992). A developmental-educational intervention model of sport psychology. *The Sport Psychologist, 6,* 403-415.

Dawe, S.W.L., & Carron, A.V. (1990, October). *Interrelationships among role acceptance, role clarity, task cohesion, and social cohesion.* Paper presented at the meeting of the Canadian Society for Psychomotor Learning and Sport Psychology. Windsor, Ontario.

Dawson, P.P. (1985). *Fundamentals of organizational behavior: An experiential approach.* Englewood Cliffs, NJ: Prentice Hall.

Deaux, K. (1985). Sex and gender. *Annual Review of Psychology, 36,* 49-81.

deCharms, R. (1968). *Personal causation.* New York: Academic Press.

Deci, E.L. (1971). Effects of externally mediated rewards on intrinsic motivation. *Journal of Personality and Social Psychology, 18,* 105-115.

Deci, E.L. (1972). The effects of contingent and noncontingent rewards and controls on intrinsic motivation. *Organizational Behavior and Human Performance, 8,* 217-229.

Deci, E.L. (1975). *Intrinsic motivation.* New York: Plenum Press.

Deci, E.L., & Ryan, R.M. (1985). *Intrinsic motivation and self-determination in human behavior.* New York: Plenum Press.

Deford, P. (1987). A little lower than angels. *Sports Illustrated, 71*(12), 12-31.

DeMille, R. (1973). *Put your mother on the ceiling: Children's imagination games.* New York: Viking Press.

Deutsch, M. (1949). An experimental study of the effects of cooperation and competition upon group process. *Human Relations, 2,* 199-231.

Deutsch, M. (1982). Interdependence and psychological orientation. In V.J. Derlega and J. Grzelak (Eds.), *Cooperation and helping behavior.* New York: Academic Press.

DeVore, S., & DeVore, G. (1981). *Sybervision: Muscle memory programming for every sport.* Chicago: Chicago Review Press.

Dishman, R.K. (1981). Biologic influences on exercise adherence. *Research Quarterly for Exercise and Sport, 52,* 143-159.

Dishman, R.K. (Ed.). (1988). *Exercise adherence: Its impact on public health.* Champaign, IL: Human Kinetics.

Dishman, R.K. (1994). *Advances in exercise adherence.* Champaign, IL: Human Kinetics.

Dishman, R.K., & Buckworth, J. (1996). Increasing physical activity: A quantitative synthesis. *Medicine and Science in Sport and Exercise, 28,* 706-719.

Dishman, R.K., & Buckworth, J. (1997). Adherence to physical activity. In W.P. Morgan (Ed.), *Physical activity and mental health* (pp. 63-80). Washington DC: Taylor & Francis.

Dishman, R.K., & Buckworth, J. (1998). Exercise psychology. In J. Williams (Ed.), *Applied sport psychology: Personal growth to peak performance* (pp. 445-462). Champaign, IL: Human Kinetics.

Dishman, R.K., & Sallis, J.F. (1994). Determinants and interventions for physical activity and exercise. In C. Bouchard, R. Sheppard, & T. Stephens (Eds.), *Physical Activity, Fitness, and Health: International Proceedings and Consensus Statement* (pp. 214-238). Champaign, IL: Human Kinetics.

Dollard, J., Doob, J., Miller, N., Mowrer, O., & Sears, R. (1939). *Frustration and aggression.* New Haven, CT: Yale University Press.

Donahue, J.A., Gillis, J.H., & King, H. (1980). Behavior modification in sport and physical education: A review. *Journal of Sport Psychology, 2,* 311-328.

Donnelly, P., Carron, A.V., & Chelladurai, P. (1978). *Group cohesion and sport* (Sociology of Sport Monograph Series). Ottawa, Ontario: Canadian Association for Health, Physical Education and Recreation.

Duda, J.L. (1993). Goals: A social-cognitive approach to the study of achievement motivation in sport. In R.N. Singer, M. Murphey, & L.K. Tennant (Eds.), *Handbook of research on sport psychology* (pp. 421-436). New York: Macmillan.

Duda, J.L., & Hom, H.L. (1993). Interdependence between the perceived and self-reported goal orientations of young athletes and their parents. *Pediatric Exercise Sciences, 5,* 234-241.

Dweck, C.S. (1975). The role of expectations and attributions in the alleviation of learned helplessness. *Journal of Personality and Social Psychology, 31,* 674-685.

Dweck, C.S. (1980). Learned helplessness in sport. In C.M. Nadeau, W.R. Halliwell, K.M. Newell, & G.C. Roberts (Eds.), *Psychology of motor behavior and sport—1979* (pp. 1-11). Champaign, IL: Human Kinetics.

Dweck, C.S. (1986). Motivational processes affecting learning. *American Psychologist, 41,* 1040-1048.

Eades, A. (1991). An investigation of burnout in intercollegiate athletes: The development of the Eades Athlete Burnout Inventory. Paper presented at the North American Society for the Psychology of Sport and Physical Activity National Conference, Asilomar, CA.

Eisenberger, R., & Cameron, J. (1996). Detrimental effects of reward: Myth or reality? *American Psychologist, 51,* 1153-1166.

Eisenman, P.A., Johnson, S.C., & Benson, J.E. (1990). *Coaches' guide to nutrition and weight control* (2nd ed.). Champaign, IL: Human Kinetics.

Eklund, R.C., Kelley, B., & Wilson, P. (1997). The social physique anxiety scale: Men, women, and the effects of modifying item 2. *Journal of Sport & Exercise Psychology, 19,* 188-196.

Ellis, A. (1962). *Reason and emotion in psychotherapy.* New York: Lyle Stuart.

Epstein, L.H., Wing, R.R., Thompson, J.K., & Griffiths, M. (1980). Attendance and fitness in aerobics exercise: The effects of contract and lottery procedures. *Behavior Modification, 4,* 465-479.

Epstein, M.L. (1980). The relationship of mental imagery and mental rehearsal in performance of a motor task. *Journal of Sport Psychology, 2,* 211-220.

Erling, J., & Oldridge, N.B. (1985). Effect of a spousal support program on compliance with cardiac rehabilitation. *Medicine and Science in Sport and Exercise, 17,* 284.

Essing, W. (1970). Team line-up and team achievement in European football. In G.S. Kenyan (Ed.), *Contemporary psychology of sport* (pp. 349-354). Chicago: Athletic Institute.

Etnier, J.L., Salazar, W., Landers, D.M., Petruzzello, S.J., Han, M., & Nowell, P. (1997). The influence of physical fitness and exercise upon cognitive functioning: A meta-analysis. *Journal of Sport and Exercise Psychology, 19,* 249-277.

Etzel, E. (1979). Validation of a conceptual model characterizing attention among international rifle shooters. *Journal of Sport Psychology, 1,* 281-290.

Evans, L., & Hardy, L. (1995). Sport injury and grief responses: A review. *Journal of Sport and Exercise Psychology, 17,* 227-245.

Evans, M., Weinberg, R.S., & Jackson, A.W. (1992). Psychological factors related to drug use in college athletes. *The Sport Psychologist, 6,* 24-41.

Ewing, M.E., & Seefeldt, V. (1989). *Participation and attrition patterns in American agency-sponsored and interscholastic sports: An executive summary.* Final Report. Sporting Goods Manufacturer's Association, North Palm Beach, FL.

Ewing, M.E., Seefeldt, V.D., & Brown, T.P. (1996). *Role of organized sport in the education and health of American children and youth.* Background Report on the Role of Sports in Youth Development. New York: Carnegie Corporation of New York.

Eysenck, H.J., & Eysenck, S.B.G. (1968). *Eysenck Personality Inventory Manual.* London: University of London Press.

Feltz, D.L. (1984a). Self-efficacy as a cognitive mediator of athletic performance. In W.F. Straub & J.M. Williams (Eds.), *Cognitive sport psychology* (pp. 191-198). Lansing, NY: Sport Science Associates.

Feltz, D.L. (1984b). The psychology of sport injuries. In P.E. Vinger & E.F. Hoerner (Eds.), *Sport injuries: The unthwarted epidemic* (2nd ed., pp. 336-344). Boston: John Wright, PSG.

Feltz, D.L., & Albrecht, R.R. (1986). Psychological implications of competitive running. In M.R. Weiss & D. Gould (Eds.), *Sports for children and youth* (pp. 225-230). Champaign, IL: Human Kinetics.

Feltz, D.L., & Landers, D.M. (1983). The effects of mental practice on motor skill learning and performance: A meta-analysis. *Journal of Sport Psychology, 5,* 25-57.

Festinger, L. (1954). A theory of social comparison processes. *Human Relations, 7,* 117-140.

Festinger, L., Schacter, S., & Back, K. (1950). *Social pressures in informed groups: A study of a housing project.* New York: Harare.

Fiedler, F. (1967). *A theory of leadership effectiveness.* New York: McGraw-Hill.

Fisher, A.C., & Zwart, E.F. (1982). Psychological analysis of athletes' anxiety responses. *Journal of Sport Psychology, 4,* 139-158.

Folkins, C.H., & Sime, W.E. (1981). Physical fitness training and mental health. *American Psychologist, 36,* 373-389.

Fox, K.R. (1997). *The physical self: From motivation to well being.* Champaign, IL: Human Kinetics.

Francis, D., & Young, D. (1979). *Improving work groups: A practical manual for team building.* San Diego: University Associates.

Gardner, D.F., Shields, D.L., Bredemeier, B.J., Bostrom, A. (1996). The relationship between perceived coaching behaviors and team cohesion among baseball and softball players. *The Sport Psychologist, 10,* 367-381.

Garfield, C.A., & Bennett, H.Z. (1984). *Peak performance: Mental training techniques of the world's greatest athletes.* Los Angeles, CA: Warner.

Garland, D.L., & Barry, J.R. (1990). Personality and leader behaviors in collegiate football: A multidimensional approach to performance. *Journal of Research in Personality, 24,* 355-370.

Garland, H. (1985). A cognitive mediation theory of task goals and human performance. *Motivation and Emotion, 9,* 345-367.

Garner, D.M., & Rosen, L.W. (1991). Eating disorders among athletes: Research and recommendations. *Journal of Applied Sport Science Research, 5*(2), 100-107.

Gauron, E. (1984). *Mental training for peak performance.* Lansing, NY: Sport Science Associates.

Geibenk, M.P., & McKenzie, T.C. (1985). Teaching sportsmanship in physical education and recreation: An analysis of intervention and generalization efforts. *Journal of Teaching Physical Education, 4,* 167-177.

Gentry, W.D., & Kosaba, S.C. (1979). Social and psychological resources mediating stress illness relationships in humans. In R.B. Haynes, D.W. Taylor, & D. Sackett (Eds.), *Compliance in health care* (pp. 87-116). Baltimore: Johns Hopkins University Press.

Gieck, J., Brown, R.S., & Shank, R.H. (1982, August). The burnout syndrome among athletic trainers. *Athletic Training,* 36-41.

Gill, D.L. (1979). The prediction of group motor performance from individual member abilities. *Journal of Motor Behavior, 11,* 113-122.

Gill, D.L. (1986). *Psychological dynamics of sport.* Champaign, IL: Human Kinetics.

Gill, D.L. (1988). Gender differences in competitive orientation and sport participation. *International Journal of Sport Psychology, 19,* 145-159.

Gill, D.L., & Deeter, T.E. (1988). Development of the Sport Orientation Questionnaire. *Research Quarterly for Exercise and Sport, 59,* 191-202.

Gillovich, T., Vallone, R., & Tversky, A. (1985). The hot hand in basketball: On the misperceptions of random sequences. *Cognitive Psychology, 17,* 295-314.

Girdano, D.A., Everly, G.S, & Dusek, D.E. (1990). *Controlling stress and tension: A holistic approach* (3rd ed.). Englewood Cliffs, NJ: Prentice Hall.

Glasser, W. (1976). *Positive addiction.* New York: Harper & Row.

Goffi, C. (1984). *Tournament tough.* London: Ebury Press.

Goldsmith, P.A., & Williams, J.M. (1992). Perceived stressors for football and volleyball officials from three rating levels. *Journal of Sport Behavior, 15,* 106-118.

Gordon, S., Milios, D., & Grove, R.J. (1991). Psychological aspects of recovery process from sport injury: The perspective of sport physiotherapists. *The Australian Journal of Science and Medicine in Sport, 23*(2), 53-60.

Gould, D. (1993). Intensive sport participation and the prepubescent athlete: Competitive stress and burnout. In B.R. Cahill & A.J. Pearl (Eds.), *Intensive participation in children's sports* (pp. 19-38). Champaign, IL: Human Kinetics.

Gould, D. (1998). Goal setting for peak performance. In J. Williams (Ed.), *Applied sport psychology: Personal growth to peak performance* (2nd ed., pp. 182-196). Mountain View, CA: Mayfield.

Gould, D., & Eklund, R. (1991). The application of sport psychology for performance optimizations. *The Journal of Sport Science, 1,* 10-21.

Gould, D., Eklund, R., & Jackson, S. (1992a). Coping strategies used by more versus less successful Olympic wrestlers. *Research Quarterly for Exercise and Sport, 64,* 83-93.

Gould, D., Eklund, R.C., & Jackson, S. (1992b). 1988 U.S. Olympic wrestling excellence: I. Mental preparation, precompetitive cognition, and affect. *The Sport Psychologist, 6,* 358-382.

Gould, D., Eklund, R.C., & Jackson, S. (1992c). 1988 U.S. Olympic wrestling excellence: II. Thoughts and affect occurring during competition. *The Sport Psychologist, 6,* 383-402.

Gould, D., Eklund, R., & Jackson, S. (1993). Coping strategies used by U.S. Olympic wrestlers. *Research Quarterly for Exercise and Sport, 64,* 83-93.

Gould, D., Eklund, R., Petlichkoff, L., Peterson, K., & Bump, L. (1991). Psychological predictors of state anxiety and performance in age-group wrestlers. *Pediatric Exercise Science, 3,* 198-208.

Gould, D., Feltz, D., Horn, T., & Weiss, M. (1982). Reasons for attrition in competitive youth swimming. *Journal of Sport Behavior, 5,* 155-165.

Gould, D., Finch, L. & Jackson, S. (1993). Coping strategies used by national figure skating champions. *Research Quarterly for Exercise and Sport, 64,* 453-468.

Gould, D., Giannini, J., Krane, V., & Hodge, K. (1990). Educational needs of elite U.S. national team, Pan American, and Olympic coaches. *Journal of Teaching Physical Education, 9,* 332-344.

Gould, D., Greenleaf, C., & Krane, V. (in press). The arousal-athletic performance relationship: Current status and future directions. In T. Horn (Ed.), *Advances in sport psychology* (2nd ed.). Champaign, IL: Human Kinetics.

Gould, D., Hodge, K., Peterson, K., & Giannini, J. (1989). An exploratory examination of strategies used by elite coaches to enhance self-efficacy in athletes. *Journal of Sport and Exercise Psychology, 11,* 128-140.

Gould, D., & Horn, T. (1984). Participation motivation in young athletes. In J.M. Silva & R.S. Weinberg (Eds.), *Psychological foundations of sport* (pp. 359-370). Champaign, IL: Human Kinetics.

Gould, D., Horn, T., & Spreemann, J. (1983). Sources of stress in junior elite wrestlers. *Journal of Sport Psychology, 5,* 159-171.

Gould, D., Horn, T., & Spreemann, J. (1984). Competitive anxiety in junior elite wrestlers. *Journal of Sport Psychology, 5,* 58-71.

Gould, D., Jackson, S., & Finch, L. (1993). Life at the top: The experience of U.S. national champion figure skaters. *The Sport Psychologist, 7,* 354-374.

Gould, D., & Martens, R. (1979). Attitudes of volunteer coaches toward significant youth sport issues. *Research Quarterly, 50*(3), 369-380.

Gould, D., Medbery, R., Damarjian, N., & Lauer, L. (1998a). A survey assessment of mental skills training knowledge, opinions, and practices of a national sample of junior tennis coaches. Manuscript submitted for publication.

Gould, D., Medbery, R., Damarjian, N., & Lauer, L. (1998b). An examination of mental skills training in junior tennis coaches. Manuscript submitted for publication.

Gould, D., & Petlichkoff, L. (1988). Participation motivation and attrition in young athletes. In F. Smoll, R. Magill, & M. Ash (Eds.), *Children in sport* (3rd ed., pp. 161-178). Champaign, IL: Human Kinetics.

Gould, D., Tammen, V., Murphy, S., & May, J. (1991). An evaluation of U.S. Olympic sport psychology consultant effectiveness. *The Sport Psychologist, 5,* 111-127.

Gould, D., & Tuffey, S. (1996). Zones of optimal functioning research: A review and critique. *Anxiety, Stress, and Coping, 9,* 53-68.

Gould, D., Tuffey, S., Udry, E., & Loehr, J. (1996a). Burnout in com-

petitive junior tennis players: I. A quantitative psychological assessment. *The Sport Psychologist, 10,* 322-340.

Gould, D., Tuffey, S., Udry, E., & Loehr, J. (1996b). Burnout in competitive junior tennis players: II. Qualitative content analysis and case studies. *The Sport Psychologist, 10,* 341-366.

Gould, D., Tuffey, S., Udry, E., & Loehr, J. (1997). Burnout in competitive junior tennis players: III. Individual differences in the burnout experience. *The Sport Psychologist, 11,* 257-276.

Gould, D., & Udry, E. (1994a). Psychological skills for enhancing performance: Arousal regulation strategies. *Medicine and Science in Sports & Exercise, 26*(4), 478-485.

Gould, D., & Udry, E. (1994b). The psychology of knee injuries and injury rehabilitation. In L.Y. Griffin, (Ed.), *Rehabilitation of the injured knee* (pp. 86-98). St. Louis: Mosby.

Gould, D., Udry, E., Bridges, D., & Beck, L. (1996). Helping skiers come back from season-ending injuries. *American Ski Coach, 18,* 10-12.

Gould, D., Udry, E., Bridges, D., & Beck, L. (1997a). Psychological strategies for helping elite athletes cope with season-ending injuries. *Athletic Therapy Today, 2,* 50-53.

Gould, D., Udry, E., Bridges, D., & Beck, L. (1997b). Stress sources encountered when rehabilitating from season-ending ski injuries. *The Sport Psychologist, 11,* 361-378.

Gould, D., & Weiss, M. (1981). The effects of model similarity and model talk on self-efficacy and muscular endurance. *Journal of Sport Psychology, 3,* 17-29.

Gould, D., Weiss, M., & Weinberg, R. (1981b). The effects of model similarity and model task on self-efficacy and muscular endurance. *Journal of Sport Psychology, 3,* 17-29.

Gowan, G.R., Botterill, C.B., & Blimkie, C.J.R. (1979). Bridging the gap between sport science and sport practice. In P. Klavora & J.V. Daniel (Eds.), *Coach, athlete and the sport psychologist* (pp. 3-9). Ottawa, Canada: Coaching Association of Canada.

Green, E.K., Burke, K.L., Nix, C.L., Lambrecht, K.W., & Mason, D.C. (1996). Psychological factors associated with alcohol use by high school athletes. *Journal of Sport Behavior, 18,* 195-208.

Greenspan, M.J., & Feltz, D.F. (1989). Psychological interventions with athletes in competitive situations: A review. *The Sport Psychologist, 3,* 219-236.

Griest, J.H., Klein, M.H., Eischens, R.R., & Faris, J.T. (1978). Running out of depression. *The Physician and Sportsmedicine, 6,* 49-56.

Griffin, J., & Harris. (1996). Coaches' attitudes, knowledge, experiences, and recommendations regarding weight control. *The Sport Psychologist, 10,* 180-194.

Griffith, C.R. (1926). *Psychology of coaching.* New York: Scribners.

Griffith, C.R. (1928). *Psychology of athletics.* New York: Scribners.

Grimsley, W. (1982, June 28). "Lack of respect": Biggest problem facing pro tennis. *Vancouver Sun,* p. C3.

Gruber, J.J. (1986). Physical activity and self-esteem development in children: A meta-analysis. *American Academy of Physical Education Papers, 19,* 30-48.

Gruber, J.J., & Gray, G.R. (1982). Responses to forces influencing cohesion as a function of player status and level of male varsity basketball competition. *Research Quarterly for Exercise and Sport, 53,* 27-36.

Haan, N., Aerts, E., & Cooper, B. (1985). *On moral grounds.* New York: University Press.

Hackney, A.C., Perlman, S.N., & Nowacki, J.M. (1990). Psychological profiles of overtrained and stale athletes: A review. *Journal of Applied Sport Psychology, 2,* 21-33.

Hale, B.D. (1982). The effects of internal and external imagery on muscular and ocular concomitants. *Journal of Sport Psychology, 4,* 379-387.

516

Hall, C. R., Mack, D., Pavio, A., & Hausenblas, H.A. (1997). Imagery use by athletes: Development of the Sport Imagery Questionnaire. *International Journal of Sport Psychology, 28,* 1-17.

Halliburton, S., & Sanford, S. (1989, July 31). Making weight becomes torture for UT swimmers. *Austin American Statesman,* D1, D7.

Halliwell, W. (1990). Providing sport psychology consulting services to a professional sport organization. *The Sport Psychologist, 4,* 369-377.

Hanin, Y.L. (1980). A study of anxiety in sports. In W.F. Straub (Ed.), *Sport psychology: An analysis of athlete behavior* (pp. 236-249), Ithaca, NY: Mouvement.

Hanin, Y.L. (1986). State and trait anxiety research on sports in the USSR. In C.D. Spielberger & R. Diaz-Guerreo (Eds.), *Cross-cultural anxiety* (Vol. 3, pp. 45-64), Washington, DC: Hemisphere.

Hanin, Y.L. (1997). Emotions and athletic performance: Individual zones of optimal functioning. *European Yearbook of Sport Psychology, 1,* 29-72.

Hanrahan, S., & Gallois, C. (1993). In R.Singer, K. Tennant, & M. Murphey (Eds.), *Handbook on sport psychology* (pp. 623-646). New York: Macmillan.

Hanson, T.W., & Gould, D. (1988). Factors affecting the ability of coaches to estimate their athletes' trait and state anxiety levels. *The Sport Psychologist, 2,* 298-313.

Hardy, C.J., & Crace, R.K. (1990). Dealing with injury. *Sport Psychology Training Bulletin, 1*(6), 1-8.

Hardy, C.J., & Crace, R.K. (1991). Social support within sport. *Sport Psychology Training Bulletin, 3*(1), 1-8.

Hardy, C.J., & Crace, R.K. (1997). Foundations of team building: Introduction to the team-building primer. *Journal of Applied Sport Psychology, 9,* 1-10.

Hardy, C.J., & Latane, B. (1988). Social loafing in cheerleaders: Effects of team membership and competition. *Journal of Sport and Exercise Psychology, 10,* 109-114.

Hardy, L. (1990). A catastrophe model of performance in sport. In J.G. Jones & L. Hardy (Eds.), *Stress and performance in sport* (pp. 81-106). Chichester, England: Wiley.

Hardy, L. (1996). Testing the predictions of the Cusp catastrophe model of anxiety and performance. *The Sport Psychologist, 10,* 140-156.

Hardy, L., Jones, G., & Gould, D. (1996). *Understanding psychological preparation for sport: Theory and practice for elite performers.* Chichester, England: John Wiley and Sons.

Harris, D.V., & Harris, B.L. (1984). The athlete's guide to sports psychology: Mental skills for physical people. New York: Leisure Press.

Harris, D.V., & Robinson, W.J. (1986). The effects of skill level on EMG activity during internal and external imagery. *Journal of Sport Psychology, 8,* 105-111.

Hart, E., Leary, M.R., & Rejeski, W.J. (1989). The measurement of social physique anxiety. *Journal of Sport & Exercise Psychology, 11,* 94-104.

Harter, S. (1988). Causes, correlates, and functional role of global self-worth: A life-span perspective. In J. Kolligan & R. Sternberg (Eds.), *Perceptions of competence and incompetence across the life-span.* New Haven, CT: Yale University Press.

Heider, F. (1958). *The psychology of interpersonal relations.* New York: Wiley & Sons.

Hellison, D., & Templin, T. (1991). *A reflective approach to teaching physical education.* Champaign, IL: Human Kinetics.

Hellstedt, J.C. (1987). Sport psychology at a ski academy: Teaching mental skills to young athletes. *The Sport Psychologist, 1,* 56-68.

Hemery, D. (1986). *Sporting excellence: A study of sport's highest achievers.* Champaign, IL: Human Kinetics.

Hemery, D. (1991). *Sporting excellence: What makes a champion* (2nd ed). Wiley: New York.

Henschen, K. (1998). Athletic staleness and burnout: Diagnosis, prevention and treatment. In J. Williams (Ed.), *Sport psychology: Personal growth to peak performance* (pp. 398-408). Palo Alto,

CA: Mayfield.

Hird, J.S., Landers, D.M., Thomas, J. R., & Horan, J. J. (1991). Physical practice is superior to mental practice in enhancing cognitive and motor task performance. *Journal of Sport and Exercise Psychology, 8,* 281-293.

Hobson, M.L., & Rejeski, W.J. (1993). Does the dose of acute exercise mediate psychophysiological responses to mental stress? *Journal of Sport and Exercise Psychology, 15,* 77-87.

Hodge, K.P. (1989). Character-building in sport: Fact or fiction? *New Zealand Journal of Sports Medicine, 17*(2), 23-25.

Hollander, E.P. (1967). Principles and methods of social psychology. New York: Holt, Rinehart, & Winston.

Horn, T.S. (1985). Coaches' feedback and children's perception of their physical competence. *Journal of Educational Psychology, 77,* 174-186.

Horn, T.S. (1986). The self-fulfilling prophecy theory: When coaches' expectations become reality. In J. Williams (Ed.), *Applied sport psychology: Personal growth to physical performance* (pp. 59-74). Mountain View, CA: Mayfield.

Horn, T.S. (1987). The influence of teacher-coach behavior on the psychological development of children. In D. Gould & M.R. Weiss (Eds.), *Advances in pediatric sport sciences*: Vol. 2. Behavioral issues (pp. 121-142). Champaign, IL: Human Kinetics.

Horn, T.S. (1993). Leadership effectiveness in the sport domain. In T.S. Horn (Ed.), *Advances in sport psychology* (pp. 151-200). Champaign, IL: Human Kinetics.

Horn, T.S., & Weiss, M.R. (1991). A developmental analysis of children's self-ability judgements in the physical domain. *Pediatric Exercise Science, 3,* 310-326.

Horn, T.S., Lox, C., & Labrador, P. (1998). The self-fulfilling prophecy theory: When coaches' expectations become reality. In J.M. Williams (Ed.), *Sport psychology: Peak performance to personal growth* (pp. 74-91). Palo Alto, CA: Mayfield.

Hoyt, M.F., & Janis, I.L. (1975). Increasing adherence to a stressful decision via a motivational balance-sheet procedure: A field experiment. *Journal of Personality and Social Psychology, 35,* 833-839.

Huddleston, S., Doody, S.G., & Ruder, M.K. (1985). The effect of prior knowledge of the social loafing phenomenon on performance in a group. *International Journal of Sport Psychology, 16,* 176-182.

Hume, K.M., Martin, G.L., Gonzalez, P., Cracklen, C., & Genthon, S. (1985). A self-monitoring feedback package for improving freestyle figure skating practice behaviors. *Journal of Sport Psychology, 7,* 333-345.

Husman, B.F., & Silva, J.M. (1984). Aggression in sport: Definitional and theoretical considerations. In J.M. Silva & R.S. Weinberg (Eds.), *Psychological foundations of sport* (pp. 246-260). Champaign, IL: Human Kinetics.

Ievleva, L., & Orlick, T. (1991). Mental links to enhanced healing. *The Sport Psychologist, 5*(1), 25-40.

Ingham, A.G., Levinger, G., Graves, J., & Peckham, V. (1974). The Ringelmann effect: Studies of group size and group performance. *Journal of Experimental Social Psychology, 10,* 371-384.

Ismail, A. II, & Young, R.J. (1973). The effect of chronic exercise on the personality of middle-aged men by univariate and multivariate approaches. *Journal of Human Ergology, 2,* 47-57.

Isoahola, S.E., & Hatfield, B. (1986). *Psychology of sports: A social psychological approach.* Dubuque, IA: William C. Brown.

Issac, A., Marks, D., & Russell, D. (1986). An instrument for assessing imagery of movement: The vividness of movement imagery questionnaire. *Journal of Mental Imagery, 10,* 23-30.

Jackson, S. (1992). Athletes in flow: A qualitative investigation of flow states in elite figure skaters. *Journal of Applied Sport Psychology, 4,* 161-180.

Jackson, S. (1995).Factors influencing the occurrence of flow state in elite athletes. *Journal of Applied Sport Psychology, 7,* 138-166.

517

Jacobson, E. (1931). Electrical measurements of neuromuscular states during mental activities. *American Journal of Physiology, 96,* 115-121.

Jacobson, E. (1938). *Progressive relaxation.* Chicago: University of Chicago Press.

James, W. (1890). *Principles of psychology.* New York: Holt, Rinehart, & Winston.

Johnson, D.W., & Johnson, F.P. (1987). *Joining together: Group therapy and group skills* (3rd ed.). Englewood Cliffs, NJ: Prentice Hall.

Johnson, D.W., & Johnson, R.T. (1985). Motivational processes in cooperative, competitive, and individualistic learning situations. In C. Ames & R. Ames (Eds.), *Research on motivation in education* (vol. 2, pp. 249-286). Orlando, FL: Academic Press.

Jones, G. (1993). The role of performance profiling in cognitive behavioral interventions in sport. *The Sport Psychologist, 7,* 160-172.

Jones, G. (1995). More than just a game: Research developments and issues in competitive anxiety in sport. *British Journal of Psychology, 86,* 449-478.

Jones, G., Hanton, S., & Swain, A. (1994). Intensity and interpretation of anxiety symptoms in elite and non-elite sports performers. *Personality and Individual Differences, 17*(5), 657-663.

Jones, G., & Hardy, L. (1989). Stress and cognitive functioning in sport. *Journal of Sport Sciences, 7,* 41-63.

Jones, G., & Hardy, L. (1990). Stress in sport: Experiences of some elite performers. In G. Jones & L. Hardy (Eds.), *Stress and performance in sport* (pp. 247-277). Chichester, Wiley.

Jones, G., & Swain, A. (1992). Intensity and direction as dimensions of competitive state anxiety and relationships with competitiveness. *Perceptual and Motor Skills, 74,* 467-472.

Jones, G., & Swain, A. (1995). Predisposition to experience debilitative and facilitative anxiety in elite and nonelite performers. *The Sport Psychologist, 9,* 201-211.

Jones, G., Swain, A., & Hardy, L. (1993). Intensity and direction dimensions of competitive state anxiety and relationships with performance. *Journal of Sports Sciences, 11,* 525-532.

Jones, K. (1994, November). Foreman is again the man. *The Irish Times.*

Jones, M.B. (1974). Regressing group on individual effectiveness. *Organizational Behavior and Human Performance, 11,* 426-451.

Jordan, M. (1994). *I can't accept not trying.* New York: Harper Collins.

Kelley, B.C. (1994). A model of stress and burnout in collegiate coaches: Effects of gender and time of season. *Research Quarterly for Exercise and Sport, 65,* 48-58.

Kelley, B.C., & Gill, D.L. (1993). An examination of personal/situational variables, stress appraisal, and burnout in collegiate teacher-coaches. *Research Quarterly for Exercise and Sport, 64,* 94-102.

Kelley, H.H., & Stahelski, A.J. (1970). Social interaction basis of cooperators' and competitors' beliefs about others. *Journal of Personality and Social Psychology, 36,* 385-418.

Kerlinger, F.N. (1973). *Foundations of behavioral research* (2nd ed.). New York: Holt, Rinehart, & Winston.

Kerr, G., & Goss, J. (1996). The effects of a stress management program on injuries and stress levels. *Journal of Applied Sport Psychology, 8,* 109-117.

Kerr, G., & Leith, L. (1993). Stress management and athletic performance. *The Sport Psychologist, 7,* 221-231.

Kerr, J.H. (1985). The experience of arousal: A new basis for studying arousal effects in sport. *Journal of Sport Sciences, 3,* 169-179.

Kerr, J.H. (1997). *Motivation and emotion in sport: Reversal theory.* East Sussex, United Kingdom: Psychology Press Ltd.

Kimiecik, J., & Gould, D. (1987). Coaching psychology: The case of James "Doc" Counsilman. *The Sport Psychologist, 1,* 350-358.

King, A.C. (1994). Clinical and community interventions to promote and support physical activity participation. In R.K. Dishman (Ed.). *Advances in exercise adherence.* Champaign, IL: Human Kinetics.

King, A.C., Blair, S.N., & Bild, D. (1992). Determinants of physical activity and interventions in adults. *Medicine and Science in Sport and Exercise* (Suppl. 24), S221-S236.

King, A.C., & Frederiksen, L.W. (1984). Low-cost strategies for increasing exercise behavior: Relapse preparation training and social support. *Behavior Modification, 8,* 3-21.

Kingston, K.M., & Hardy, L. (1997). Effects of different types of goals on processes that support performance. *The Sport Psychologist, 11,* 277-293.

Kioumourtzoglou, E., Tzetzis, G., Derri, V., & Mihalopoulou, M. (1997). Psychological skills of elite athletes in different ball games. *Journal of Human Movement Studies, 32,* 79-93.

Kirschenbaum, D. (1998). *Mind matters: Seven steps to smarter sport performance.* Carmel, IN: Cooper.

Kirschenbaum, D.S., Ordman, A.M., Tomarken, A.J., & Holtzbauer, R. (1982). Effects of differential self-monitoring and level of mastery on sports performance: Brain power bowling. *Cognitive Therapy and Research, 6,* 335-342.

Klint, K.A., & Weiss, M.R. (1986). Dropping in and dropping out: Participation motives of current and former youth gymnasts. *Canadian Journal of Applied Sport Sciences, 11,* 106-114.

Kohn, A. (1986). *No contest: The case against competition.* Boston: Houghton Mifflin.

Komaki, J., & Barnett, F. (1977). A behavioral approach to coaching football: Improving the play execution of the offensive backfield on a youth football team. *Journal of Applied Behavioral Analysis, 10,* 657-664.

Koop, S., & Martin, G.L. (1983). Evaluation of a coaching strategy to reduce swimming stroke errors with beginning age-group swimmers. *Journal of Applied Behavior Analysis, 16,* 447-460.

Kosaba, S.C., Maddi, S.R., Puccetti, M.C., & Zola, M.A. (1985). Effectiveness of hardiness, exercise, and social support as resources against illness. *Journal of Psychosomatic Illness, 29,* 525-533.

Kramer, J., & Shaap, D. (1968). *Instant replay: The Green Bay diary of Jerry Kramer.* New York: Signet.

Krane, V., Greenleaf, C.A., & Snow, J. (1997). Reaching for gold and the price of glory: A motivational case study of an elite gymnast. *The Sport Psychologist, 11,* 53-71.

Kraus, J.F., & Conroy, C. (1984). Mortality and morbidity from injuries in sports and recreation. *Annual Review of Public Health, 5,* 163-192.

Kroll, W., & Lewis, G. (1970). America's first sport psychologist. *Quest, 13,* 1-4.

Kubler-Ross, E. (1969). *On death and dying.* London: Macmillan.

Kyllo, L. B., & Landers, D. M. (1995). Goal setting in sport and exercise: A research synthesis to resolve the controversy. *Journal of Sport and Exercise Psychology, 17,* 117-137.

Lacey, J.I. (1967). Somatic response patterning and stress: Some revision of activation theory. In M.H. Appley & R. Trumbell (Eds.), *Psychological stress: Issues in research* (pp. 170-179). New York: Appleton-Century-Crofts.

Landers, D.M. (1985). Psychophysiological assessment and biofeedback: Applications for athletes in closed-skilled sports. In J.H. Sandweiss & S.L. Wolf (Eds.), *Biofeedback and sports science* (pp. 63-105). New York: Plenum Press.

Landers, D.M. (1994). Performance, stress, and health: Overall reaction. *Quest, 46,* 123-135.

Landers, D.M., & Boutcher, S.H. (1998). Arousal-performance relationships. In J.M. Williams (Ed.), *Applied sport psychology: Per-*

sonal growth to peak performance (pp. 197-218). Palo Alto, CA: Mayfield.

Landers, D.M., Boutcher, S., & Wang, M.Q. (1986). A psychobiological study of archery performance. *Research Quarterly for Exercise and Sport, 57,* 236-244.

Landers, D.M., Han M., Salazar, W., Petruzello, S.J., Kubitz, K.A., & Gannon, T.L. (1994). Effects of learning on electroencephalographic and electrocardiographic patterns of novice archers. *International Journal of Sport Psychology, 25,* 313-330.

Landers, D.M., & Lueschen, G. (1974). Team performance outcome and cohesiveness of competitive coaching groups. *International Review of Sport Sociology, 2,* 57-69.

Landers, D.M., Wang, M.Q., & Courtet, P. (1985). Peripheral narrowing among experienced and inexperienced rifle shooters under low- and high-stress conditions. *Research Quarterly, 56,* 122-130.

Landers, D.M., Wilkinson, M.O., Hatfield, B.D., & Barber, H. (1982). Causality and the cohesion-performance relationship. *Journal of Sport Psychology, 4,* 170-183.

Lang, P.J. (1977). Imagery in therapy: An information-processing analysis of fear. *Behavior Therapy, 8,* 862-886.

Lang, P.J. (1979). A bio-informational theory of emotional imagery. *Psychophysiology, 17,* 495-512.

Larson, G.A., Starkey, C., & Zaichkowsky, L.D. (1996). Psychological aspects of athletic injuries as perceived by athletic trainers. *The Sport Psychologist, 10,* 37-47.

Lasco, R.A., Curry, R.H., Dickson, V.J., Powers, J., Menes, S., & Merritt, R.K. (1989). Participation rates, weight loss, and blood pressure changes among obese women in a nutrition-exercise program. *Public Health Reports, 104,* 640-646.

Latane, B., Williams, K.D., & Harkins, S.G. (1979). Many hands make light the work: The causes and consequences of social loafing. *Journal of Personality and Social Psychology, 37,* 823-832.

Layden, T. (1995, April 3). Better education. *Sports Illustrated,* 70-90.

Lazarus, R.S. (1966). *Psychological stress and the coping process.* New York: McGraw-Hill.

Lazarus, R.S. (1982). Thoughts on the relation between emotion and cognition. *American Psychologist, 37,* 1019-1024.

Lazarus, R.S., & Folkman, S. (1984). *Stress, appraisal and coping.* New York: Springer-Verlag.

Legwold, C. (1987). Incentives for fitness programs. *Fitness in Business, 2,* 131-133.

Leith, L.M., & Taylor, A.H. (1992). Behavior modification and exercise adherence: A literature review. *Journal of Sport Behavior, 15,* 60-74.

Lenk, H. (1969). Top performance despite internal conflict: An antithesis to a functional proposition. In J.W. Loy & G.S. Kenyan (Eds.), *Sport, culture and society: A reader on the sociology of sport* (pp. 224-235). New York: Macmillan.

Lepper, M.R., & Greene, D. (1975). Turning play into work: Effects of adult surveillance and extrinsic rewards on children's intrinsic motivation. *Journal of Personality and Social Psychology, 31,* 479-486.

Lepper, M.R., Greene, D., & Nisbett, R.E. (1973). Undermining children's intrinsic interest with extrinsic rewards: A test of the overjustification hypothesis. *Journal of Personality and Social Psychology, 28,* 129-137.

LeUnes, A., & Nation, J. (1996). *Sport psychology* (2nd ed.). Chicago: Nelson-Hall.

Lieber, J. (1991). Deep scars. *Sports Illustrated, 75*(5), 36-44.

Lilliefors, J. (1978). *The running mind.* Mountain View, CA: World Publications.

Lirgg, C.D., & Feltz, D.L. (1991). Teacher versus peer models revisited: Effects on motor performance. *Research Quarterly for Exercise and Sport, 62,* 217-224.

Lirgg, C.D., & Feltz, D.L. (1994). Relationship of individual and collective efficacy to team performance. *Journal of Sport and Exercise Psychology, 16* (suppl., S17).

Locke, E.A., & Latham, G.P. (1985). The application of goal setting to sports. *Journal of Sport Psychology, 7,* 205-222.

Locke, E.A., & Latham, G.P. (1990). *A theory of goal setting and task performance.* Englewood Cliffs, NJ: Prentice Hall.

Locke, E.A., Shaw, K.N., Saari, L.M., & Latham, G.P. (1981). Goal setting and task performance. *Psychological Bulletin, 90,* 125-152.

Lombard, D.N., Lombard, T.N., & Winett, R.A. (1995). Walking to meet health guidelines: The effect of prompting frequency and prompt structure. *Health Psychology, 14,* 164-179.

Long, B.C. (1984). Aerobic conditioning and stress inoculations: A comparison of stress management intervention. *Cognitive Therapy and Research, 8,* 517-542.

Long, B.C., & Haney, C.J. (1988). Coping strategies for working women: Aerobic exercise and relaxation interventions. *Behavior Therapy, 19,* 75-83.

Long, B.C., & Stavel, R.V. (1995). Effects of exercise training on anxiety: A meta-analysis. *Journal of Applied Sport Psychology, 7,* 167-189.

Lowe, R. (1971). *Stress, arousal, and task performance of Little League baseball players.* Unpublished doctoral dissertation. University of Illinois, Urbana.

Lox, C.L., McAuley, E., & Tucker, R.S. (1995). Exercise as an intervention for enhancing subjective well-being in an HIV-1 population. *Journal of Sport and Exercise Psychology, 17,* 345-362.

Loy, J.W. (1970). *Where the action is: A consideration of centrality in sport situations.* Paper presented at the meeting of the Second Canadian Psychomotor Learning and Sport Psychology Symposium, Windsor, Ontario.

Madden, C. (1995). Ways of coping. In T. Morris & J. Summers (Eds.), *Sport psychology: Theory, applications and issues* (pp. 288-310). Brisbane, Australia: John Wiley.

Madsen, M.C., & Shapira, A. (1970). Cooperative and competitive behavior of urban Afro-American, Anglo-American, Mexican-American and Mexican village children. *Developmental Psychology, 3,* 16-20.

Madsen, M.C., & Shapira, A. (1977, August). Cooperation and challenge in four cultures. *Journal of Social Psychology, 102*(2), 189-195.

Maehr, M., & Nicholls, J. (1980). Culture and achievement motivation: A second look. In N. Warren (Ed.), *Studies in cross-cultural psychology:* Vol. 2 (pp. 53-75). New York: Academic Press.

Mahoney, M.J., & Avener, M. (1977). Psychology of the elite athlete: An exploratory study. *Cognitive Therapy and Research, 1,* 135-141.

Mahoney, M.J., Gabriel, T.J., & Perkins, T.S. (1987). Psychological skills and exceptional athletic performance. *The Sport Psychologist, 1,* 181-199.

Mallett, C., & Hanrahan, S. (1997). Race modeling: An effective cognitive strategy for the 100 m sprinter. *The Sport Psychologist, 11,* 72-85.

Marcus, B.H., Banspach, S.W., Lefebvre, R.C., Rossi, J.S., Carleton, R.A., & Abrams, D.A. (1992). Using the change model to increase the adoption of physical activity among community participants. *American Journal of Health Promotion, 6,* 424-429.

Marcus, B.H., Buck, B.C., Pinto, B.M., & Clark, M.M. (1996). Exercise initiation, adoption, and maintenance. In B. Brewer & J.W. Raglte (Eds.), *Exploring sport and exercise in psychology* (p. 123-158). Washington, DC: American Psychological Association.

Marcus, B.H., Pinto, B.M., Simkin, L.R., Audrain, J.E., & Taylor, E.R. (1994). Application of theoretical models to exercise behavior among employed women. *American Journal of Health Promotion, 9,* 49-55.

Marcus, B.H., Rossi, J.S., Selby, V.C., Niaura, R.S., & Abrams, D.B. (1992). The stages and processes of exercise adoption and maintenance in a worksite sample. *Health Psychology, 11,* 386-395.

Marks, D.F. (1977). Imagery and consciousness: A theoretical review from an individual differences perspective. *Journal of Mental Imagery, 2,* 275-290.

Marsh, H.W. (1997). The measurement of physical self-concept: A construct validation approach. In K. R. Fox (Ed.), *The physical self: From motivation to well being* (pp. 27-58). Champaign, IL: Human Kinetics.

Marsh, H.W., & Redmayne, R.S. (1994). A multidimensional physical self-concept and its relations to multiple components of physical fitness. *Journal of Sport & Exercise Psychology, 16,* 43-55.

Marsh, H. W., & Sonstroem, R.J. (1995). Importance ratings and specific components of physical self-concept: Relevance to predicting global components of self-concept and exercise. *Journal of Sport and Exercise Psychology, 17,* 84-104.

Martens, R. (1975). The paradigmatic crisis in American sport personology. *Sportwissenschaft, 5,* 9-24.

Martens, R. (1976). *Competitiveness in sport.* Paper presented at the International Congress of Physical Activity Sciences, Quebec, Canada.

Martens, R. (1977). *Sport competition anxiety test.* Champaign, IL: Human Kinetics.

Martens, R. (1978). *Joy and sadness in children's sports.* Champaign, IL: Human Kinetics.

Martens, R. (1982a). Kids sports: A den of iniquity or land of promise. In R.A. Magill, M.J. Ash, & F.L. Smoll (Eds.), *Children in sport* (2nd ed., pp. 204-218). Champaign, IL: Human Kinetics.

Martens, R. (1982b). *Imagery in sport.* Paper presented at the Medical and Scientific Aspects of Elitism in Sport Conference, Brisbane, Australia.

Martens, R. (1986). Youth sports in the USA. In M.R. Weiss & D. Gould (Eds.), *Sport for children and youths* (pp. 27-33). Champaign, IL: Human Kinetics.

Martens, R. (1987). Science, knowledge and sport psychology. *Sport Psychologist, 1,* 29-55.

Martens, R. (1990). *Coaches guide to sport psychology.* Champaign, IL: Human Kinetics.

Martens, R., Burton, D., Vealey, R.S., Bump, L.A., & Smith, D. (1982, June). Cognitive and somatic dimensions of competitive anxiety (CSAI-2). Paper presented at NASPSPA Conference, University of Maryland, College Park.

Martens, R., Christina, R.W., Harvey, J.S., & Sharkey, B.J. (1981). *Coaching young athletes.* Champaign, IL: Human Kinetics.

Martens, R., Landers, D., & Loy, J. (1972). *Sports cohesiveness questionnaire.* Washington, DC: AAHPERD.

Martens, R., Vealey, R.S., & Burton, D. (Eds.). (1990). *Competitive anxiety in sport.* Champaign, IL: Human Kinetics.

Martin, F., & Lumsden, J. (1987). Coaching: An effective behavioral approach. St. Louis: Times Mirror/Mosby.

Martin, G.L., & Hyrcaiko, D. (1983). *Behavior modification and coaching: Principles, procedures, and research.* Springfield, IL: Charles C. Thomas.

Martin, G.L., & Pear, J.J. (1992). *Behavior modification: What it is and how to do it* (4th ed.). Englewood Cliffs, NJ: Prentice Hall.

Martin, J., Dubbert, P.M., Katell, A.D., Thompson, J.K., Raczynski, J.R., Lake, M., Smith, P.O., Webster, J.S., Sikora, T., & Cohen, R.E. (1984). The behavioral control of exercise in sedentary adults: Studies 1 through 6. *Journal of Consulting and Clinical Psychology, 52,* 795-811.

Martinek, T., & Hellison, D.R. (1997). Fostering resiliency in underserved youth through physical activity. *Quest, 49*(1), 34-49.

Martinek, T., & Johnson, S. (1979). Teacher expectations: Effects on dyadic interactions and self-concept in elementary age children. *Research Quarterly, 50,* 60-70.

Martinsen, E. (1993). Therapeutic implications of exercise for clinically anxious and depressed patients: Exercise and psychological well-being. *International Journal of Sport Psychology, 24,* 185-199.

Martinsen, E., & Stephens, T. (1994). Exercise and mental health in clinical and free-living populations. In R.K. Dishman (Ed.), *Advances in exercise adherence* (pp. 55-72), Champaign, IL: Human Kinetics.

Maslach, C., & Jackson, S.E. (1981). The measurement of experienced burnout. *Journal of Occupational Behavior, 2,* 99-113.

Maynard, I.W., & Cotton, C.J. (1993). An investigation of two stress management techniques in a field setting. *The Sport Psychologist, 7,* 375-387.

Maynard, I.W., Hemmings, B., & Warwick-Evans, L. (1995). The effects of a somatic intervention strategy on competitive state anxiety and performance in semiprofessional soccer players. *The Sport Psychologist, 9,* 51-64.

Maynard, I.W., Smith, M.J., & Warwick-Evans, L. (1995). The effects of a cognitive intervention strategy on competitive state anxiety and performance in semiprofessional soccer players. *Journal of Sport and Exercise Psychology, 17,* 428-446.

McAuley, E. (1985). Modeling and self-efficacy: A test of Bandura's model. *Journal of Sport Psychology, 7,* 283-295.

McAuley, E. (1992). The role of efficacy cognitions in the prediction of exercise behavior of middle-aged adults. *Journal of Behavioral Medicine, 15,* 65-88.

McAuley, E. (1993a). Self-efficacy and the maintenance of exercise participation in older adults. *Journal of Behavioral Medicine, 16,* 103-113.

McAuley, E. (1993b). Self-referent thought in sport and physical activity. In T.S. Horn (Ed.), *Advances in sport psychology* (pp. 101-118). Champaign, IL: Human Kinetics.

McAuley, E., Poag, K., & Gleason, A. (1990). Attrition from exercise programs: Attributional and affective perspectives. *Journal of Social Behavior and Personality, 5,* 591-602.

McAuley, E., & Tammen, V.V. (1989). The effects of subjective and objective competitive outcomes on intrinsic motivation. *Journal of Sport & Exercise Psychology, 11,* 84-93.

McCallum, J. (1991, Nov. 11). For whom the Bull toils. *Sports Illustrated, 75,* 106-118.

McCann, S. (1995). Overtraining and burnout. In S. Murphy (Ed.), *Psychological interventions in sport* (pp. 347-368) . Champaign, IL: Human Kinetics.

McClelland, D. (1961). *The achieving society.* New York: Free Press.

McClements, J. (1982). Goal setting and planning for mental preparations. In L. Wankel & R.B. Wilberg (Eds.), *Psychology of sport and motor behavior: Research and practice.* Proceedings of the Annual Conference of the Canadian Society for Psychomotor Learning and Sport Psychology, Edmonton, Canada: University of Alberta.

McCullagh, P., & Noble, J.M. (1996). Educational training in sport and exercise psychology. In J. L. Van Raalte & B.W. Brewer (Eds.), *Exploring sport and exercise psychology* (pp. 377-394). Washington, DC: American Psychological Association.

McCullagh, P., Weiss, M.R., & Ross, D. (1989). Modeling considerations in motor skill acquisition and performance: An integrated approach. In K. Pandolf (Ed.), *Exercise and Sport Science Reviews:*Vol. 17 (pp. 475-513). Baltimore: Williams & Wilkins.

McDonald, D.G., & Hodgdon, J.A. (1991*). Psychological effects of aerobic fitness training.* New York: Springer-Verlag.

McGrath, J.E. (1962). The influence of positive interpersonal relations on adjustment and effectiveness in rifle teams. *Journal of Abnormal and Social Psychology, 65,* 365-375.

McGrath, J.E. (1970). Major methodological issues. In J.E. McGrath (Ed.), *Social and psychological factors in stress* (pp. 19-49). New York: Holt, Rinehart, & Winston.

McKenzie, T.L., & Rushall, B.S. (1974). Effects of self-recording on attendance and performance in a competitive swimming training environment. *Journal of Applied Behavior Analysis, 7,* 199-206.

McNair, D., Lorr, M., & Droppleman, L. (1971). *Profile of Mood States manual.* San Diego, CA: Educational and Testing Service.

Mechikoff, R.A., & Kozar, B. (1983). *Sport psychology: The coach's perspective.* Springfield, IL: Charles C. Thomas

Meichenbaum, D. (1977). *Cognitive-behavior modification: An integrative approach.* New York: Plenum Press.

Meichenbaum, D. (1985). *Stress inoculation training.* New York: Pergamon Press.

Mento, A.J., Steel, R.P., & Karren, R.J. (1987). A meta-analytic study of the effects of goal-setting on task performance: 1966-1984. *Organizational Behavior and Human Decision Processes, 39,* 52-83.

Meyers, A. (1995). Ethical principles of AAASP. *AAASP Newsletter, 10,* 15 and 21.

Mihoces, E. (1997, December 5). Player-coach battle stirs debate. *USA Today,* C1-2.

Miller, R.W. (1993). In search of peace: Peer conflict resolution. *Schools in the Middle, Spring,* 11-13.

Miller, S., & Weinberg, R. (1991). Perceptions of psychological momentum and their relationship to performance. *The Sport Psychologist, 5,* 211-222.

Miller, S.C., Bredemeier, B.J.L., & Shields, D.L.L. (1997). Sociomoral education through physical education with at-risk children. *Quest, 49,* 114-129.

Ming, S., & Martin, G.L. (1996). Single-subject evaluation of a self-talk package for improving figure skating performance. *The Sport Psychologist, 10,* 227-238.

Moore, W.E., & Stevenson, J.R. (1994). Training for trust in sport skills. *The Sport Psychologist, 8,* 1-12.

Moran, A. (1996). *The psychology of concentration in sport performance: A cognitive approach.* East Sussex, England: Psychology Press.

Morgan, W.P. (1979a). Negative addiction in runners. *Physician and Sportsmedicine, 7*(2):56-63, 67-70.

Morgan, W.P. (1979b). Prediction of performance in athletics. In P. Klavora & J.V. Daniel (Eds.), *Coach, athlete, and the sport psychologist* (pp. 173-186). Champaign, IL: Human Kinetics.

Morgan, W.P. (1980). The trait psychology controversy. *Research Quarterly for Exercise and Sport, 51,* 50-76.

Morgan, W.P. (1987). Reduction of state anxiety following acute physical activity. In W.P. Morgan & S.E. Goldston (Eds.), *Exercise and mental health* (pp. 105-109). Washington, DC: Hemisphere.

Morgan, W.P. (1994). Physical activity, fitness, and depression. In C. Bouchard, R.J. Sheppard, & T. Stephens (Eds.), *Physical activity, fitness, and health* (pp. 851-867). Champaign, IL: Human Kinetics.

Morgan, W.P., Brown, D.R., Raglin, J.S., O'Connor, P.J., & Ellickson, K.A. (1987). Psychological monitoring of overtraining and staleness. *British Journal of Sport Medicine, 21,* 107-114.

Morgan, W.P., & Goldston, S.E. (1987). *Exercise and mental health.* Washington, DC: Hemisphere.

Morgan, W.P., O'Connor, P.J., Ellickson, K.A., & Bradley, P.W. (1988). Personality structure, mood states, and performance in elite distance runners. *International Journal of Sport Psychology, 19,* 247-269.

Morgan, W.P., O'Connor, P.J., Sparling, P.B., & Pate, R.R. (1987). Psychologic characterization of the elite female distance runner. *International Journal of Sports Medicine, 8,* 124-131.

Morgan, W.P., Roberts, J.A., Brand, F.R., & Feinerman, A.D. (1970). Psychological effect of chronic physical activity. *Medicine and Science in Sports, 2,* 213-217.

Moritz, S.E., Hall, C.R., Martin, K.A., & Vadocz, E. (1996). What are confident athletes imaging? An examination of image content. *The Sport Psychologist, 10,* 171-179.

Moses, J., Steptoe, A., Mathews, A., & Edwards, S. (1989). The effects of exercise training on mental well-being in the normal population: A controlled trial. *Psychosomatic Research, 33,* 47-61.

Mullen, B., & Cooper, C. (1994). The relation between group cohesiveness and performance: An integration. *Psychological Bulletin, 115,* 210-227.

Mumford, P., & Hall, C.R. (1985). The effects of internal and external imagery on performing figures in figure skating. *Canadian Journal of Applied Sport Science, 10,* 171-177.

Murphy, S. (1990). Models of imagery in sport psychology: A review. *Journal of Mental Imagery, 14,* 153-172.

Murphy, S. (1994). Imagery interventions in sport. *Medicine and Science in Sport and Exercise, 26,* 486-494.

Murphy, S. (1996). *The achievement zone.* New York: G.P. Putnam's Sons.

Murphy, S.M. (Ed.). (1995). *Sport psychology interventions.* Champaign, IL: Human Kinetics.

Murphy, S., & Jowdy, D. (1992). Imagery and mental practice. In T. Horn (Ed.), *Advances in sport psychology,* Champaign, IL: Human Kinetics.

Murphy, S., Jowdy, D., & Durtschi, S. (1990). *Report on the U.S. Olympic Committee survey on imagery use in sport.* Colorado Springs, CO: U.S. Olympic Training Center.

Murphy, S.M., Fleck, S.J., Dudley, G., & Callister, R. (1990). Psychological and performance concomitants of increased volume training in athletes. *Journal of Applied Sport Psychology, 2,* 34-50.

Murray, H.A. (1938). *Explorations in personality.* New York: Oxford University Press.

Mutrie, N., & Biddle, S.J.H. (1995). The effects of exercise on mental health of nonclinical populations. In S.J.H. Biddle (Ed.), *European perspectives in exercise and sport psychology* (pp. 50-70). Champaign, IL: Human Kinetics.

National Collegiate Athletic Association (1989). *Nutrition and eating disorders in collegiate athletics* (videotape). Kansas City, MO: National Collegiate Athletic Association.

Nelson, L.R., & Furst, M.L. (1972). An objective study of the effects of expectation on competitive performance. *Journal of Psychology, 81,* 69-72.

Ness, R.G., & Patton, R.W. (1979). The effects of beliefs on maximum weight-lifting performance. *Cognitive Therapy and Research, 3,* 205-211.

Newman, B.M., & Newman, P.R. (1991). *Development through life: A psychological approach.* Pacific Grove, CA: Brooks/Cole.

Newsom, M.M. (Ed.). (1989). *Drug free: The goals of the U.S. Olympic Committee.* Colorado Springs, CO: U.S. Olympic Committee.

Nicholls, J. (1984). Concepts of ability and achievement motivation. In R. Ames & C. Ames (Eds.), *Research on motivation in education: Student motivation:* Vol. 1 (pp. 39-73). New York: Academic Press.

Nicklaus, J. (1976). *Play better golf.* New York: King Features.

Nideffer, R. (1976). Test of attentional and interpersonal style. *Journal of Personality and Social Psychology, 34,* 394-404.

Nideffer, R. (1981). *The ethics and practice of applied sport psychology.* Ithaca, NY: Mouvement.

Nideffer, R.M. (1976). *The inner athlete.* New York: Crowell.

Nideffer, R.M. (1983). The injured athlete: Psychological factors in treatment. *Orthopedic Clinics of North America, 14,* 373-385.

Nideffer, R.M. (1985). *Athlete's guide to mental training.* Champaign, IL: Human Kinetics.

Nixon, H.L. (1977). "Cohesiveness" and team success: A theoretical reformulation. *Review of Sport and Leisure, 2,* 36-57.

521

North, T.C., McCullagh, P., & Tran, Z.V. (1990). Effects of exercise on depression. *Exercise and Sport Science Reviews, 18,* 379-415.

Ntoumanis, N., & Biddle, S.J.H. (1997). A review of psychological climate in physical activity settings with specific reference to motivation. *Journal of Sport Sciences,*

O'Brien, M. (1995). *Who's got the ball: And other nagging questions about team life.* San Francisco: Jossey-Bass Publishers.

O'Brien, R.M., & Simek, T.C. (1983). A comparison of behavioral and traditional methods for teaching golf. In G.L. Martin & D. Hrycaiko (Eds.), *Behavior modification and coaching: Principles, procedures and research.* Springfield, IL: Charles C. Thomas.

O'Connor, P.J. (1997). Overtraining and staleness. In W.P. Morgan (Ed.), *Physical activity and mental health* (pp. 145-160). Bristol, PA: Taylor & Francis.

O'Connor, P.J., & Youngstedt, S.D. (1995). Influence of exercise on human sleep. In Holloszy, J.O. (Ed.), *Exercise and sport sciences review* (pp. 105-134). Baltimore: Williams & Wilkins.

Ogilvie, B.C., & Tutko, T.A. (1966). *Problem athletes and how to handle them.* London: Palham Books.

Ogilvie, B.C., & Tutko, T.A. (1970). Self-perceptions as compared with measured personality of selected male physical educators. In G.S. Kenyon (Ed.), *Contemporary psychology of sport* (pp. 73-78). Chicago: The Athletic Institute.

Oldridge, N.B., Donner, A.P., Buck, C.W., Jones, N.L., Andrew, G.M., Parker, J.O., Cunningham, D.A., Kavanagh, T., Rechnitzer, P.A., & Sutton, J.R. (1983). Predictors of dropouts from cardiac exercise rehabilitation: Ontario exercise-heart collaborative study. *American Journal of Cardiology, 51,* 70-74.

Oldridge, N.B., & Jones, N.L. (1983). Improving patient compliance in cardiac rehabilitation: Effects of written agreement and self-monitoring. *Journal of Cardiac Rehabilitation, 3,* 257-262.

Orlick, T. (1978). *The cooperative sports and games book.* New York: Pantheon.

Orlick, T. (1986). *Psyching for sport: Mental training for athletes.* Champaign, IL: Human Kinetics.

Orlick, T. (1990). *In pursuit of excellence: How to win in sport and life through mental training* (2nd ed.). Champaign, IL: Human Kinetics.

Orlick, T. (1992). *Freeing children from stress: Focusing and stress control activities for children.* ITA Publications, P.O. Box 1599, Willits, CA.

Orlick, T., & McCaffrey, N. (1991). Mental training with children for sport and life. *The Sport Psychologist, 5,* 322-334.

Orlick, T., McNally, J., & O'Hara, T. (1978). Cooperative games: Systematic analysis and cooperative impact. In F. Smoll & R.E. Smith (Eds.), *Psychological perspectives in youth sports.* New York: Hemisphere.

Orlick, T., & Partington, J. (1988). Mental links to excellence. *The Sport Psychologist, 2,* 105-130.

Ost, L.G. (1988). Applied relaxation: Description of an effective coping technique. *Scandinavian Journal of Behavior Therapy, 17,* 83-96.

Papanek, J. (1977, October 31). The enforcers. *Sports Illustrated,* 43-49.

Parcells, B., & Coplon, J. (1995). *Finding a way to win: The principles of leadership, teamwork, and motivation,* New York: Doubleday Dell Publishing Group.

Partington, J., & Orlick, T. (1987a). The sport psychology consultant: Olympic coaches' views. *The Sport Psychologist, 1,* 95-102.

Partington, J., & Orlick, T. (1987b). The sport psychology consultant evaluation form. *The Sport Psychologist, 1,* 309-317.

Pavio, A. (1985). Cognitive and motivational functions of imagery in human performance. *Canadian Journal of Applied Sport Sciences, 10,* 22-28.

Pease, D.G., & Kozub, S. (1994). Perceived coaching behaviors and team cohesion in high school girls basketball teams. *Journal of Sport and Exercise Psychology: NASPSPA Abstracts, 16,* S93.

Perry, C., & Morris, T. (1995). Mental imagery in sport. In T. Morris & J. Summers (Eds.), *Sport psychology: Theory, applications and issues.* Brisbane: John Wiley.

Petitpas, A., & Danish, S. (1995). Caring for injured athletes. In S. Murphy (Ed.), *Sport psychology interventions* (pp. 255-281). Champaign, IL: Human Kinetics.

Petlichkoff, L.M. (1996). The drop-out dilemma in youth sports. In O. Bar-Or (Ed.), *The child and adolescent athlete* (pp. 418-430). Cambridge, MA: Blackwell Science.

Petruzzello, S., Landers, D.M., Hatfield, B., Kibitz, K., & Salazar, W. (1991). A meta-analysis on the anxiety-reducing effects of acute and chronic exercise: Outcomes and mechanisms. *Sports Medicine, 11,* 143-182.

Piaget, J. (1936). *The moral judgment of the child.* New York: Harcourt & Brace.

Poag-DuCharme, K.A., & Brawley, L.R. (1994). Perceptions of the behavioral influence of goals: A mediational relationship to exercise. *Journal of Applied Sport Psychology, 6,* 32-50.

Pollock, M.L., Foster, C., Salisbury, R., & Smith, R. (1982). Effects of a YMCA starter fitness program. *Physician and Sportsmedicine, 10,* 89-100.

Prapavessis, H., Carron, A.V., & Spink, K.S. (1997). Team building in sport groups. *International Journal of Sport Psychology, 27,* 269-285.

President's Council on Physical Fitness and Sport. (1996) "What you need to know about the Surgeon General's Report on Physical activity and Health." *Physical Activity and Fitness Research, 2,* 1-8.

Prochaska, J.O., DiClemente, C.C., & Norcross, J.C. (1992). In search of how people change. *American Psychologist, 47,* 1102-1114.

Prochaska, J.O., Velicer, W.F., Rossi, J.S., Goldstein, M.G., Marcus, B.H., Rakowski, W., Fiore, C., Harlow, L.L., Redding, C.A., Rosenbloom, D., & Rossi, S.R. (1994). Stages of change and decisional balance for twelve problem behaviors. *Health Psychology, 13,* 39-46.

Raedeke, T. (1998). Is athlete burnout more than just stress? A sport commitment perspective. *Journal of Sport and Exercise Psychology, 20,* 4, 396-417.

Raglin, J.S. (1993). Overtraining and staleness: Psychometric monitoring of endurance athletes. In R. Singer, M. Murphey, & K. Tennent (Eds.), *Handbook of research on sport psychology* (pp. 840-850). New York: Macmillan.

Raglin, J.S., Eksten, F., & Garl, T. (1995). Mood state responses to a pre-season conditioning program in male collegiate basketball players. *International Journal of Sport Psychology, 26,* 214-225.

Raglin, J.S., & Morgan, W.P. (1987). Influence of exercise and "distraction therapy" on state anxiety and blood pressure. *Medicine and Science in Sport and Exercise, 19,* 456-463.

Raglin, J.S., & Morgan, W.P. (1989). Development of a scale to measure training-induced distress. *Medicine and Science in Sport and Exercise, 21* (suppl.), 60.

Raglin, J.S., Stager, J.M., Koceja, D.M., & Harms, C.A. (1996). Changes in mood state, neuromuscular function, and performance during a season of training in female collegiate swimmers. *Medicine and Science in Sport and Exercise, 28,* 372-377.

Ransom, K., & Weinberg, R.S. (1985). Effect of situation criticality on performance of elite male and female tennis players. *Journal of Sport Behavior, 8,* 144-148.

Rees, C.R., & Segal, M.W. (1984). Role differentiation in groups: The relationship between instrumental and expressive leadership. *Small Group Behavior, 15,* 109-123.

Rejeski, W.J., & Brawley, L.R. (1988). Defining the boundaries of sport psychology. *The Sport Psychologist, 2,* 231-242.

Renger, R. (1993). A review of the profile of mood states (POMS) in the prediction of athletic success. *Journal of Applied Sport Psychology, 5,* 78-84.

Rest, J.R. (1984). The major components of morality. In W. Kurines & J. Gewirtz (Eds.), *Morality, moral behavior, and moral development* (pp. 356-429). New York: Wiley.

Richardson, A. (1967a). Mental practice: A review and discussion (Part 1). *Research Quarterly, 38,* 95-107.

Richardson, A. (1967b). Mental practice. A review and discussion (Part 2). *Research Quarterly, 38,* 263-273.

Riley, P. (1993). *The winner within: A life plan for team players.* New York: G.P. Putnam's Sons.

Ripol, W. (1993). The psychology of the swimming taper. *Contemporary Psychology on Performance Enhancement, 2,* 22-64.

Roberts, G. (1993). Motivation in sport. Understanding and enhancing the motivation and achievement of children. In R.N. Singer, M. Murphey, & K.L. Tennant (Eds.), *Handbook of research on sport psychology* (pp. 405-420). New York: Macmillan.

Roche, P. (1995, August). Second gold medal for Smith. *The Irish Times.*

Rodgers, W., Hall, C.R., & Buckholtz, E. (1991). The effect of an imagery training program on imagery ability, imagery use, and figure skating performance. *Journal of Applied Sport Psychology, 3,* 109-125.

Romance, T.J., Weiss, M.R., & Bockoven, J. (1986). A program to promote moral development through elementary school physical education. *Journal of Teaching Physical Education, 5,* 126-136.

Rooney, E.M. (1993). Exercise for older patients: Why it's worth your effort. *Geriatrics, 48,* 68-77.

Rosenfeld, L., & Wilder, L. (1990). Communication fundamentals: Active listening. *Sport Psychology Training Bulletin, 1*(5), 1-8.

Rosenfeld, L.B., & Richman, J.M. (1997) Developing effective social support: Team building and the social support process. *The Sport Psychologist, 9,* 133-153.

Rosenthal, R., & Jacobson, L. (1968). *Pygmalion in the classroom: Teacher expectations and pupils' intellectual development.* New York: Holt, Rinehart, & Winston.

Ross, M.S. (1992, Summer). Good sports report. *Fantastic Flyer,* 16-17.

Rotella, R.J., & Heyman, S.R. (1986). Stress, injury and the psychological rehabilitation of athletes. In J.M. Williams (Ed.), *Applied sport psychology: Personal growth to peak performance* (pp. 343-364). Palo Alto, CA: Mayfield.

Rowley, A.J., Landers, D.M., Kyllo, L.B., & Etnier, J.L. (1995). Does the iceberg profile discriminate between successful and less successful athletes? A meta-analysis. *Journal of Sport and Exercise Psychology, 17,* 185-199.

Ruder, M.K., & Gill, D.L. (1982). Immediate effects of win-loss on perceptions of cohesion in intramural and intercollegiate volleyball teams. *Journal of Sport Psychology, 4,* 227-234.

Ruffer, W.A. (1976a). Personality traits of athletes. *The Physical Educator, 33*(1), 50-55.

Ruffer, W.A. (1976b). Personality traits of athletes. *The Physical Educator, 33*(4), 211-214.

Rushall, B., & Siedentop, D. (1972). *The development and control of behavior in sport and physical education.* Philadelphia: Lea & Febiger.

Rushall, B.S. (1983). Coaching styles: A preliminary investigation. In G.L. Martin and D. Hrycaiko (Eds.), *Behavior modification and coaching: Principles, procedures, and research* (pp. 299-320). Springfield, IL: Charles C. Thomas.

Rushall, B.S., Hall, M., & Rushall, A. (1988). Effects of three types of thought content instructions on skiing performance. *The Sport Psychologist, 2,* 283-297.

Russell, G.W., & Arms, R.L. (1995). False consensus effect, physical aggression, anger, and a willingness to escalate a disturbance. *Aggressive Behavior, 21,* 381-386.

Ryan, E.D. (1977). Attribution, intrinsic motivation, and athletics. In L.I. Gedvilas & M.E. Kneer (Eds.), *Proceedings of the NAPECW/NCPEAM National Conference* (pp. 346-353). Chicago: Office of Publications Services, University of Illinois at Chicago Circle.

Ryan, E.D. (1980). Attribution, intrinsic motivation, and athletics: A replication and extension. In C.H. Nadeau, W.R. Halliwell, K.M. Newell, & G.C. Roberts (Eds.), *Psychology of motor behavior and sport—1979* (pp. 19-26). Champaign, IL: Human Kinetics.

Ryan, J. (1995). *Little girls in pretty boxes: The making and breaking of elite gymnasts and figure skaters.* New York: Doubleday.

Sachs, M.L. (1978). Selected psychological considerations in running. Invited presentation at a running clinic. Tallahassee, FL.

Sachs, M.L. (1980). On the trail of the runner's high—a descriptive and experimental investigation of characteristics of an elusive phenomenon. Unpublished doctoral dissertation, Florida State University.

Sachs, M.L. (1981). Running addiction. In M.H. Sacks & M.L. Sachs (Eds.), *Psychology of running* (pp. 116-121). Champaign, IL: Human Kinetics.

Sachs, M.L. (1984). The runner's high. In M.L. Sachs & G.W. Buffone (Eds.), *Running as therapy: An integrated approach* (pp. 273-287). Lincoln: University of Nebraska Press.

Sachs, M.L., & Pargman, D. (1984). Running addiction. In M.L. Sachs & G.W. Buffone (Eds.), *Running as therapy: An integrated approach* (pp. 231-253). Lincoln: University of Nebraska Press.

Sackett, R.S. (1934). The influences of symbolic rehearsal upon the retention of a maze habit. *Journal of General Psychology, 13,* 113-128.

Sage, G. (1977). *Introduction to motor behavior: A neuropsychological approach* (2nd ed.). Reading, MA: Addison-Wesley.

Sage, G. (1978). Humanistic psychology and coaching. In W.F. Straub (Ed.), *Sport psychology: An analysis of athlete behavior* (pp. 215-228). Ithaca, NY: Mouvement.

Sallis, J.F., Haskell, W.L., Fortmann, S.P., Vranizan, K.M., Taylor, C.B., & Solomon, D.S. (1986). Predictors of adoption and maintenance of physical activity in a community sample. *Preventive Medicine, 15,* 331-341.

Sallis, J.F., Howell, M.F., Hofstetter, C.R., Elder, J.P., Hackley, M., Caspersen, C.J., & Powell, K.E. (1990). Distance between homes and exercise facilities related to frequency of exercise among San Diego residents. *Public Health Reports, 105,* 179-180.

Salmela, J.H. (1992). *The world sport psychology source book* (2nd ed.). Champaign, IL: Human Kinetics.

Sarason, I.G. (1975). Test anxiety and the self-disclosing coping model. *Journal of Consulting and Clinical Psychology, 43,* 148-153.

Sathre, S., Olson, R.W., & Whitney, C.I. (1973). *Let's talk.* Glenview, IL: Scott, Foresman.

Savelsbergh, G.P., Whiting, H.T.A., & Pijpers, J.R. (1992). The control of catching. In J.J. Summers (Ed.), *Approaches to the study of motor control and learning* (pp. 313-342). Amsterdam: North-Holland.

Scanlan, T.K. (1986). Competitive stress in children. In M.R. Weiss & D. Gould (Eds.), *Sport for children and youths* (pp. 113-118). Champaign, IL: Human Kinetics.

Scanlan, T.K. (1988). Social evaluation and the competition process: A developmental perspective. In F.L. Smoll, R.A. Magill, & M.J. Ash (Eds.), *Children in sport* (3rd ed., pp. 135-148). Champaign, IL: Human Kinetics.

Scanlan, T.K., Stein, G.L., & Ravizza, K. (1991). An in-depth study of former elite figure skaters—Part 3. Sources of stress. *Journal of Sport Exercise Psychology, 13*(2), 103-120.

Schachter, S. (1966). The interaction of cognitive and physiological determinants of emotional state. In C. Spielberger (Ed.), *Anxiety and behavior.* New York: Academic Press.

Scherf, J., & Franklin, B. (1987). Exercise compliance: A data documentation system. *Journal of Physical Education, Recreation, and Dance, 58,* 26-28.

Schmidt, R.A. (1982). *Motor control and learning: A behavioral emphasis.* Champaign, IL: Human Kinetics.

Schomer, H. (1986). Mental strategies and the perception of effort of marathon runners. *International Journal of Sport Psychology, 17,* 41-59.

Schultz, J., & Luthe, W. (1969). *Autogenic methods* (Vol. 1). New York: Grune and Stratton.

Schurr, K.T., Ashley, M.A., & Joy, K.L. (1977). A multivariate analysis of male athlete characteristics: Sport type and success. *Multivariate Experimental Clinical Research, 3,* 53-68.

Seabourne, T., Weinberg, R.S., Jackson, A., & Suinn, R.M. (1985). Effect of individualized, nonindividualized, and package intervention strategies on karate performance. *Journal of Sport Psychology, 7,* 40-50.

Seefeldt, V., Ewing, M., & Walk, S. (1993). *Overview of youth sports programs in the United States.* Unpublished manuscript commissioned by the Carnegie Council on Adolescent Development.

Seefeldt, V.D., & Ewing, M.E. (1997). Youth sports in America. *President's Council on Physical Fitness and Sports Research Digest, 2*(11), 1-11.

Seeman, J.C. (1978). *Changes in state anxiety following vigorous exercise.* Unpublished master's thesis, University of Arizona, Phoenix.

Sheehan, G. (1979). Negative addiction: A runner's perspective. *Physician and Sportsmedicine, 7*(6), 49.

Sheppard, R. (1996). Habitual physical activity and quality of life. *Quest, 48,* 354-365.

Sherif, M., & Sherif, C.W. (1969). *Social psychology.* New York: Harper & Row.

Shields, D.L.L., & Bredemeier, B.J.L. (1995). *Character development and physical activity.* Champaign, IL: Human Kinetics.

Shumaker, S.A., & Brownell, A. (1984). Toward a theory of social support: Closing conceptual gaps. *Journal of Social Issues, 40,* 11-36.

Siedentop, D. (1980). The management of practice behavior. In W.F. Straub (Ed.), *Sport psychology: An analysis of athletic behavior* (2nd ed.). Ithaca, NY: Mouvement.

Silva, J.M. (1980). Understanding aggressive behavior and its effects upon athletic performance. In W.F. Straub (Ed.), *Sport psychology: An analysis of athlete behavior* (2nd ed.). Ithaca, NY: Mouvement.

Silva, J.M. (1982). Competitive sport environments: Performance enhancement through cognitive intervention. *Behavior Modification, 6,* 443-463.

Silva, J.M. (1984). Factors related to the acquisition and exhibition of aggressive sport behavior. In J.M. Silva & R.S. Weinberg (Eds.), *Psychological foundations of sport* (pp. 261-273). Champaign, IL: Human Kinetics.

Silva, J.M. (1990). An analysis of the training stress syndrome in competitive athletics. *Journal of Applied Sport Psychology, 2,* 5-20.

Silva, J.M., & Applebaum, M.I. (1989). Association and dissociation patterns of United States Olympic marathon trial contestants. *Cognitive Therapy and Research, 13,* 185-192.

Simek, T.C., O'Brien, R.M., & Figlerski, L.B. (1994). Contracting and chaining to improve the performance of a college golf team: Improvement and deterioration. *Perceptual and Motor Skills, 78,* 1099-1105.

Simon, J., & Martens, R. (1979). Children's anxiety in sport and nonsport evaluative activities. *Journal of Sport Psychology, 1*(1), 160-169.

Simonton, O.C., Matthews-Simonton, S., & Creighton, J.L. (1978). *Getting well again.* New York: Bantam.

Skinner, B.F. (1968). *The technology of teaching.* New York: Appleton-Century-Crofts.

Smith, A. (1997). *Peer relationships in physical activity participation in early adolescence.* Unpublished doctoral dissertation, University of Oregon, Eugene.

Smith, H.W. (1994). *The 10 natural laws of successful time and life management: Proven strategies for increased productivity and inner peace.* New York: Warner.

Smith, M.D. (1983). *Violence and sport.* Toronto: Butterworths.

Smith, M.D. (1988). Interpersonal sources of violence in hockey: The influence of parents, coaches, and teammates. In F.L. Smoll, R.A. Magill, & M.J. Ash (Eds.), *Children in sport* (3rd ed., pp. 301-313). Champaign, IL: Human Kinetics.

Smith, R.A., & Biddle, S.J.H. (1995). Psychological factors in the promotion of physical activity. In S. Biddle (Ed.), *European perspectives on exercise and sport psychology.* Champaign, IL: Human Kinetics.

Smith, R.E. (1980). A cognitive-affective approach to stress management training for athletes. In C.H. Nadeau, W.R. Halliwell, K.M. Newell, & G.C. Roberts (Eds.), *Psychology of motor behavior and sport* (pp. 54-72). Champaign, IL: Human Kinetics.

Smith, R.E. (1984). Theoretical and treatment approaches to anxiety reduction. In J. Silva and R. Weinberg (Eds.), *Psychological foundations in sport and exercise* (pp. 157-170). Champaign, IL: Human Kinetics.

Smith, R.E. (1986). Toward a cognitive-affective model of athletic burnout. *Journal of Sport Psychology, 8,* 36-50.

Smith, R.E. (1989). Applied sport psychology in the age of accountability. *Journal of Applied Sport Psychology, 1,* 166-180.

Smith, R.E. (1993). A positive approach to enhancing sport performance: Principles of positive reinforcement and performance feedback. In J. Williams (Ed.), *Applied sport psychology: Personal growth to peak performance* (pp. 25-35). Palo Alto, CA: Mayfield.

Smith, R.E., & Christensen, D.S. (1995). Psychological skills as predictors of performance and survival in professional baseball. *Journal of Sport & Exercise Psychology, 17,* 399-415.

Smith, R.E., & Johnson, J. (1990). An organizational empowerment approach to consultation in professional baseball. *The Sport Psychologist, 4,* 347-357.

Smith, R.E., Schutz, R.W., Smoll, F.L., & Ptacek, J.T. (1995). Development and validation of a multidimensional measure of sport-specific psychological skills: The Athletic Coping Skills Inventory-28. *Journal of Sport and Exercise Psychology, 17,* 379-398.

Smith, R.E., & Smoll, F.L. (1990). Athletic performance anxiety. In H. Leitenberg (Ed.), *Handbook of Social and Evaluation Anxiety* (pp. 417-454). New York: Plenum Press.

Smith, R.E., & Smoll, F.L. (1996). *Way to go, coach: A scientifically-proven approach to coaching effectiveness.* Portola Valley, CA: Warde Publishers.

Smith, R.E., & Smoll, F.L. (1997). Coach-mediated team building in youth sports. *Journal of Applied Sport Psychology, 9,* 114-132.

Smith, R.E., Smoll, F.L., & Curtis, B. (1979). Coach effectiveness training: A cognitive-behavioral approach to enhancing relationship skills in youth sport coaches. *Journal of Sport Psychology, 1,* 59-75.

Smith, R.E., Smoll, F.L., & Hunt, E. (1977). A system for the behavioral assessment of athletic coaches. *Research Quarterly, 48,* 401-407.

Smith, R.E., Smoll, F.L., & Ptacek, J.T. (1990). Conjunctive moderator variables in vulnerability and resiliency research: Life stress, social support and coping skills, and adolescent sport injuries. *Journal of Personality and Social Psychology, 58*(2), 360-369.

Smith, R.E., Smoll, F.L., & Schutz, R.W. (1990). Measurement and correlates of sport-specific cognitive and somatic trait anxiety: The Sport Anxiety Scale. *Anxiety Research, 2,* 263-280.

Smith, R.E., Zane, N.W.S., Smoll, F.L., & Coppel, D.B. (1983). Behavioral assessment in youth sports: Coaching behaviors and children's attitudes. *Medicine and Science in Sports and Exercise, 15,* 208-214.

Smoll, F.L., & Smith, R.E. (1979). *Improving relationship skills in youth sport coaches.* East Lansing, MI: Michigan Institute for the Study of Youth Sports.

Smoll, F.L., & Smith, R.E. (1980). Psychologically oriented coach training programs: Design, implementation, and assessment. In C.H. Nadeau, W.R. Halliwell, K.M. Newell, & G.C. Roberts (Eds.), *Psychology of motor behavior and sport—1979.* Champaign, IL: Human Kinetics.

Smoll, F.L., & Smith, R.E. (1996). *Coaches who never lose: A 30-minute primer for coaching effectiveness.* Portola Valley, CA: Warde Publishers.

Smoll, F.L., Smith, R.E., Curtis, B., & Hunt, E. (1978). Toward a mediational model of coach-player relationships. *Research Quarterly, 49,* 528-541,

Solomon, G., Striegel, D. Eliot, J., Heon, S., & Maas, J. (1996). The self-fulfilling prophecy in college basketball: Implications for effective coaching. *Journal of Applied Sport Psychology, 8,* 44-59.

Solso, R.L. (1995). *Cognitive psychology* (4th ed.). Boston: Allyn & Bacon.

Sonstroem, R.J. (1984). Exercise and self-esteem. In R.L. Terjung (Ed.), *Exercise and sport science reviews* (pp. 123-155). Toronto: Collare.

Sonstroem, R.J. (1997a). Physical activity and self-esteem. In W.P. Morgan (Ed.), *Physical activity and mental health* (pp. 127-143). Washington, DC: Hemisphere.

Sonstroem, R.J. (1997b). The physical self-system: A mediator of exercise and self-esteem. In K.R. Fox (Ed.), *The physical self: From motivation to well being* (pp. 3-26). Champaign, IL: Human Kinetics.

Sonstroem, R.J., Harlow, L.L., & Josephs, L. (1994). Exercise and self-esteem: Validity of model expansion and exercise association. *Journal of Sport & Exercise Psychology, 16,* 29-42.

Sonstroem, R.J., & Morgan, W.P. (1989). Exercise and self-esteem: Rationale and model. *Medicine and Science in Sport and Exercise, 21,* 329-337.

Sorrentino, R.M., & Sheppard, B.H. (1978). Effects of affiliation-related motives on swimmers in individual versus group competition: A field experiment. *Journal of Personality and Social Psychology, 36*(7), 704-714.

Spence, J.T., & Spence, K.W. (1966). The motivational components of manifest anxiety: Drive and drive stimuli. In C.D. Spielberger (Ed.), *Anxiety and behavior.* New York: Academic Press.

Spielberger, C.D. (1966). Theory and research on anxiety. In C.D. Spielberger (Ed.), *Anxiety and behavior* (pp. 3-22). New York: Academic Press.

Spielberger, C.D., Gorsuch, R.L., & Lushene, R.F. (1970). *Manual for the state-trait anxiety inventory.* Palo Alto, CA: Consulting Psychologists Press.

Spink, K.S., & Carron, A.V. (1992). Group cohesion and adhesion in exercise classes. *Journal of Sport and Exercise Psychology, 14,* 78-86.

Spink, K.S., & Carron, A.V. (1993). The effects of team building on the adherence patterns of female exercise participants. *Journal of Sport and Exercise Psychology, 15,* 50-62.

Spino, M. (1971). Running as a spiritual experience. In J. Scott (Ed.), *The athletic revolution* (p. 222). New York: Free Press.

Stainback, R.D. (1997). *Alcohol and sport.* Champaign, IL: Human Kinetics.

State of Michigan (1976). *Joint legislative study on youth sports programs. Phase 2.* East Lansing, MI: State of Michigan.

Steiner, I.D. (1972). *Group process and productivity.* New York: Academic Press.

Stephens, T. (1988). Physical activity and mental health in the United States and Canada: Evidence from four population surveys. *Preventive Medicine, 17,* 35-47.

Stogdill, R.M. (1948). Personal factors associated with leadership: Survey of literature. *Journal of Psychology, 25,* 35-71.

Strean, W.B. (1995). Youth sport contexts: Coaches' perceptions and implications for intervention. *Journal of Applied Sport Psychology, 7,* 23-37.

Suinn, R.M. (1972). Behavior rehearsal training for ski racers. *Behavior Therapy, 3,* 519.

Suinn, R.M. (1976, July). Body thinking: Psychology for Olympic champs. *Psychology Today,* pp. 38-43.

Suinn, R.M. (1993). Imagery. In R. Singer, M. Murphey, & K. Tennant (Eds.), *Handbook of research in sport psychology* (pp. 492-510). New York: Macmillan.

Summers, J.J., & Ford, S. (1995). Attention in sport. In T. Morris & J. Summers (Eds.), *Sport psychology: Theory, applications, and issues* (pp. 63-89). Chichester: John Wiley.

Swoap, R.A., & Murphy, S.M. (1995). Eating disorders and weight management in athletics. In S. Murphy (Ed.), *Psychological interventions in sport* (pp. 307-329). Champaign, IL: Human Kinetics.

Syer, J. (1986). *Team spirit.* London: Simon & Schuster.

Tarshis, B. (1977). *Tennis and the mind.* New York: Tennis Magazine.

Tatum, J., & Kushner, B. (1980). *They call me assassin.* New York: Avon.

Taylor, A.H., Daniel, J.V., Leith, L., & Burke, R.J. (1990). Perceived stress, psychological burnout and paths to turnover intentions among sport officials. *Journal of Applied Sport Psychology, 2,* 84-97.

Taylor, J. (1995). A conceptual model for integrating athletes' needs and sport demands in the development of competitive mental preparation strategies. *The Sport Psychologist, 9,* 339-357.

Tenenbaum, G., & Bar-Eli, M. (1995). Personality and intellectual capabilities in sport psychology. In D.H. Saklofski & M. Zeidner (Eds.), *International handbook of personality and intelligence: Perspectives on individual differences* (pp. 687-710). New York: Plenum Press.

Tenenbaum, G., Stewart, E., Singer, R.N., & Duda, J. (1997). Aggression and violence in sport: An ISSP position stand. *ISSP Newsletter, 1,* 14-17.

Tennant, C., Mihailidou, A., Scott, A., Smith, R., Kellow, J., Jones, M., Hunyor, S., Lorang, M., & Hoschel, R. (1994). Psychological symptom profiles in patients with chest pain. *Journal of Psychosomatic Medicine, 38,* 365-371.

Terry, P. (1995). The efficacy of mood state profiling with elite performers: A review and synthesis. *The Sport Psychologist, 9,* 309-324.

Tharp, R.G., & Gallimore, R. (1976, January). What a coach can teach a teacher. *Psychology Today, 9,* 74-78.

Thayer, R.E., Newman, R., & McClain, T.M. (1994). Self-regulation of mood: Strategies for changing a bad mood, raising energy, and reducing tension. *Journal of Personality and Social Behavior, 67,* 910-925.

Theodorakis, Y., Beneca, A., Goudas, M., Panagiotis, A., & Malliou, P. (1997). *The effect of self-talk on injury rehabilitation.* Paper presented at the Association for Advancement of Applied Sport Psychology, San Diego, CA.

Theodorakis, Y., Malliou, P., Papaioannou, A., Beneca, A., & Filactakidou, A. (1996). The effect of personal goals, self-efficacy, and self-satisfaction on injury rehabilitation. *Journal of Sport Rehabilitation, 5,* 214-233.

Thirer, J. (1993). Aggression. In R.N. Singer, M. Murphey, L.K. Tennant (Eds.), *Handbook of research on sport psychology* (pp. 365-378). New York: Macmillan.

Thomas, J.R., Landers, D.M., Salazar, W.J., & Etnier, J. (1994). Exercise and cognitive functioning. In C.Bouchard, R.J. Sheppard, & T. Stephens (Eds.), *Physical activity, fitness, and health* (pp. 521-529). Champaign, IL: Human Kinetics.

Thompson, C.E., & Wankel, L.M. (1980). The effects of perceived choice upon frequency of exercise behavior. *Journal of Applied Social Psychology, 19,* 436-443.

Thompson, R.A. (1987). Management of the athlete with an eating disorder: Implications for the sport management team. *The Sport Psychologist, 1,* 114-126.

Thompson, R.A., & Sherman, R. (1993). *Helping athletes with eating disorders.* Champaign, IL: Human Kinetics.

525

Tippett, S.R., & Voight, M.L. (1994). *Functional progressions for sport rehabilitation.* Champaign, IL: Human Kinetics.

Titley, R.W. (1976, September). The loneliness of a long-distance kicker. *The Athletic Journal, 57,* 74-80.

Tomporowski, P.D., & Ellis, N.R. (1986). Effects of exercise on cognitive process: A review. *Psychological Bulletin, 99,* 338-346.

Travis, C.A., & Sachs, M.L. (1991). Applied sport psychology and persons with mental retardation. *The Sport Psychologist, 5,* 382.

Treasure, D.C., & Roberts, G.C. (1995). *The motivational climate matters: Children's cognitive and affective responses in physical education.* Manuscript submitted for publication.

Tricker, R., & Cook, D.L. (1990). (Eds.), *Athletes at risk: Drugs and sport.* Dubuque, IA: Wm. C. Brown.

Triplett, N. (1898). The dynamogenic factors in pacemaking and competition. *American Journal of Psychology, 9,* 507-553.

Trulson, M.E. (1986). Martial arts training: A novel cure for juvenile delinquency. *Human Relations, 39,* 1131-1140.

Tuckman, B.W. (1965). Developmental sequence in small groups. *Psychological Bulletin, 63,* 384-399.

Udry, E., Gould, D., Bridges, D., & Beck, L. (1997). Down but not out: Athlete responses to season-ending ski injuries. *Journal of Sport and Exercise Psychology, 3,* 229-248.

U.S. Centers for Disease Control and Prevention. (1993). Prevalence of sedentary lifestyle-behavioral risk factor surveillance system. United States, 1991. *Morbidity and Mortality Weekly Report, 42,* 576-579.

U.S. Department of Health and Human Services. (1991). *Healthy people 2000: National health promotion and disease prevention objectives.* Washington, DC: Public Health Service, DHHS publication no. (PHS) 91-50212.

U.S. Department of Health and Human Services. (1996). *Physical activity and health: A report of the Surgeon General.* Washington, DC: U.S. Department of Health and Human Services, Centers for Disease Control and Prevention, National Center for Chronic Disease Prevention and Health Promotion.

U.S. Department of Health and Human Services, Public Health Service, & Centers for Disease Control and Prevention. (1997). Guidelines for school and community programs to promote lifelong physical activity among young people. *Morbidity and Mortality Weekly Report, 46,* 1-37.

Vadocz, E.A., Hall, C.R., & Moritz, S.E. (1997). The relationship between competitive anxiety and imagery use. *Journal of Applied Sport Psychology, 9,* 241-253.

Vallerand, R.J. (1983). Effect of differential amounts of positive verbal feedback on the intrinsic motivation of male hockey players. *Journal of Sport Psychology, 5,* 100-107.

Vallerand, R.J., Briere, N.M., Blanchard, C., & Provencher, P. (1997). Development and validation of the multidimensional sportspersonship orientation scale. *Journal of Sport & Exercise Psychology, 19,* 197-206.

Vallerand, R.J., Deci, E., & Ryan, R.M. (1987). Intrinsic motivation in sport. In K. B. Pandolff (Ed.), *Exercise and sport science reviews* (pp. 389-425). New York: Macmillan.

Vallerand, R.J., Deshaies, P., Cuerrier, J.P., Briere, N., & Pelletier, L.C. (1996). Towards a multidimensional definition of sportsmanship. *Journal of Applied Sport Psychology, 8,* 89-101.

Vallerand, R.J., Gauvin, L.I., & Halliwell, W.R. (1986a). Effects of zero-sum competition on children's intrinsic motivation and perceived competence. *Journal of Social Psychology, 126,* 465-472.

Vallerand, R.J., Gauvin, L.I., & Halliwell, W.R. (1986b). Negative effects of competition on children's intrinsic motivation. *Journal of Social Psychology, 126,* 649-657.

Vallerand, R.J., & Reid, G. (1984). On the causal effects of perceived competence on intrinsic motivation: A test of cognitive evaluation theory. *Journal of Sport Psychology, 6,* 94-102.

Van Raalte, J.L., Brewer, B.W., Rivera, P.M., & Petitpas, A.J. (1994). The relationship between self-talk and performance of competitive junior tennis players. (Suppl.) *NASPSPA Conference Abstracts, 16,* S118 (abstract).

Van Schoyck, S.R., & Grasha, A.F. (1981). Attentional style variations and athletic ability: The advantages of a sports-specific test. *Journal of Sport Psychology, 3,* 149-165.

VanYperen, N.W. (1995). Interpersonal stress, performance level, and parental support: A longitudinal study among highly skilled young soccer players. *The Sport Psychologist, 9,* 225-241.

Vealey, R. (1986). Conceptualization of sport-confidence and competitive orientation: Preliminary investigation and instrument development. *Journal of Sport Psychology, 8,* 221-246.

Vealey, R. (1988). Future directions in psychological skills training. *The Sport Psychologist, 2,* 318-336.

Vealey, R. (1989). Sport personality: A paradigmatic and methodological analysis. *Journal of Sport and Exercise Psychology, 11,* 216-235.

Vealey, R. (1992). Personality in sport: A comprehensive view. In T. Horn (Ed.), *Advances in sport psychology* (pp. 23-59). Champaign, IL: Human Kinetics.

Vealey, R., & Greenleaf, C. (1998). Imagery training for performance enhancement and personal development. In J. M. Williams (Ed.), *Applied sport psychology: Personal growth to peak performance,* 3rd ed., (pp. 237-269). Mountain View, CA: Mayfield.

Vealey, R., Udry, E., Zimmerman, V., & Soliday, J. (1992). Interpersonal and situational predictors of coaching burnout. *Journal of Sport and Exercise Psychology, 14,* 40-58.

Vealey, R. & Walter, S. (1993). Imagery training for performance enhancement and personal development. In J. Williams (Ed.), *Applied sport psychology. Personal growth to physical performance,* 2nd ed., (pp. 200-224). Mountain View, CA: Mayfield.

Veroff, J. (1969). Social comparison and the development of achievement motivation. In C.P. Smith (Ed.), *Achievement-related motives in children* (pp. 46-101). New York: Russell Sage Foundation.

Voy, R., & Deeter, K.D. (1991). *Drugs, sport and politics.* Champaign, IL: Human Kinetics.

Wankel, L.M. (1980). Involvement in vigorous physical activity: Considerations for enhancing self-motivation. In R.R. Danielson & K.F. Danielson (Eds.), *Fitness motivation: Proceedings of the Geneva Park workshop* (pp. 18-32). Toronto: Ontario Research Council on Leisure.

Wankel, L.M. (1984). Decision-making and social support structures for increasing exercise adherence. *Journal of Cardiac Rehabilitation, 4,* 124-128.

Waters, B. (1981). Defining the runner's personality. *Runner's World, 33,* 48-51.

Weinberg, R.S. (1981). The relationship between mental preparation strategies and motor performance: A review and critique. *Quest, 42,* 195-213.

Weinberg, R.S. (1988). *The mental advantage: Developing your psychological skills in tennis.* Champaign, IL: Human Kinetics.

Weinberg, R.S. (1992). Goal setting and motor performance: A review and critique. In G.C. Roberts (Ed.), *Motivation in sport and exercise* (pp. 177-197). Champaign, IL: Human Kinetics.

Weinberg, R.S., Burke, K., & Jackson, A. (1997). Coaches' and players' perceptions of goal setting in junior tennis: An exploratory investigation. *The Sport Psychologist, 11,* 426-439.

Weinberg, R.S., Burton, D., Yukelson, D., Weigand, D. (1993). Goal setting in competitive sport: An exploratory investigation of practices of collegiate athletes. *The Sport Psychologist, 7,* 275-289.

Weinberg, R.S., & Comar, W. (1994). The effectiveness of psychological interventions in competitive sport. *Sports Medicine, 18,* 406-418.

Weinberg, R.S., Gould, D., & Jackson, A. (1979). Expectancies and performance: An empirical test of Bandura's self-efficacy theory. *Journal of Sport Psychology, 1,* 320-331.

Weinberg, R.S., Grove, R., & Jackson, A. (1992). Strategies for building self-efficacy in tennis players: A comparative analysis of American and Australian coaches. *The Sport Psychologist, 6,* 3-13.

Weinberg, R.S., & Hunt, V.V. (1976). The interrelationships between anxiety, motor performance, and electromyography. *Journal of Motor Behavior, 8*(3), 219-224.

Weinberg, R.S., & Jackson, A. (1979). Competition of extrinsic rewards: Effect on intrinsic motivation and attribution. *Research Quarterly, 50,* 494-502.

Weinberg, R.S., & Ragan, J. (1979). Effects of competition, success/failure, and sex on intrinsic motivation. *Research Quarterly, 50,* 503 510.

Weinberg, R.S., & Richardson, P.A. (1990). *Psychology of officiating.* Champaign, IL: Human Kinetics.

Weinberg, R.S., Seabourne, T.G., & Jackson, A. (1981). Effects of visuo-motor behavior rehearsal, relaxation, and imagery on karate performance. *Journal of Sport Psychology, 3,* 228-238.

Weinberg, R.S., Yukelson, D., & Jackson, A. (1980). Effect of public versus private efficacy expectations on competitive performance. *Journal of Sport Psychology, 2,* 340-349.

Weiner, B. (1985). An attribution theory of achievement motivation and emotion. *Psychological Review, 92,* 548-573.

Weiner, B. (1986). *An attribution theory of motivation and emotion.* New York: Springer-Verlag.

Weiss, M.R. (1987). Teaching sportsmanship and values. In V. Seefeldt (Ed.), *Handbook for youth sports coaches* (pp. 137-151). Reston, VA: AAHPERD.

Weiss, M.R. (1991). Psychological skill development in children and adolescents. *The Sport Psychologist, 5,* 335-354.

Weiss, M.R. (1993). Psychological effects of intensive sport participation on children and youth: Self-esteem and motivation. In B.R. Cahill & A.J. Pearl (Eds.), *Intensive participation in children's sports* (pp. 39-69). Champaign, IL: Human Kinetics.

Weiss, M.R., & Bredemeier, B.J. (1991). Moral development in sport. In K.B. Pandolf & J.O. Holloszy (Eds.), *Exercise and Sport Science Reviews, 18,* 331-378.

Weiss, M.R., & Chaumeton, N. (1992). Motivational orientations in sport. In T.S. Horn (Ed.), *Advances in sport psychology* (pp. 61-99). Champaign, IL: Human Kinetics.

Weiss, M.R., & Friedrichs, W.D. (1986). The influence of leader behaviors, coach attributes, and institutional variables on performance and satisfaction of collegiate basketball teams. *Journal of Sport Psychology, 8,* 332-346.

Weiss, M.R., Smith, A.L., & Theeboom, M. (1996). "That's what friends are for": Children's and teenagers' perceptions of peer relationships in the sport domain. *Journal of Sport and Exercise Psychology, 18,* 347-379.

Westre, K.R., & Weiss, M.R. (1991). The relationship between perceived coaching behaviors and group cohesion in high school football teams. *The Sport Psychologist, 5,* 41-54.

Weyerer, S. (1992). Physical inactivity and depression in the community: Evidence from the Upper Batavia Field Study. *International Journal of Sports Medicine, 13,* 492-496.

Whitehead, J.R., & Corbin C.B. (1991). Youth fitness testing: The effect of percentile-based evaluation feedback on intrinsic motivation. *Research Quarterly for Exercise and Sport, 62,* 225-231.

Whyte, W.F. (1943). *Street corner society. The social structure of an Italian slum.* Chicago: University of Chicago Press.

Widmeyer, W.N. (1984). Aggression-performance relationships in sport. In J.M. Silva & R.S. Weinberg (Eds.), *Psychological foundations of sport* (pp. 274-286). Champaign, IL: Human Kinetics.

Widmeyer, W.N., Brawley, L.R., & Carron, A.V. (1985). *The measurement of cohesion in sport teams: The group environment questionnaire.* London, Ontario, Canada: Sports Dynamics.

Widmeyer, W.N., Brawley, L.R., & Carron, A.V. (1990). Group size in sport. *Journal of Sport and Exercise Psychology, 12,* 177-190.

Widmeyer, W.N., Carron, A.V., & Brawley, L.R. (1993). Group cohesion in sport and exercise. In R. Singer, M. Murphey, and K. Tennant (Eds.), *Handbook of research in sport psychology* (pp. 672-692). New York: Macmillan.

Widmeyer, W. N., & Ducharme, K. (1997). Team building through team goal setting. *Journal of Applied Sport Psychology, 9,* 61-72.

Widmeyer, W.N., & Martens, R. (1978). When cohesion predicts performance outcome in sport. *Research Quarterly, 49,* 372-380.

Widmeyer, W.N., & McGuire, E.J. (1993). Reducing injury in ice hockey by reducing player aggression. In C.R. Castalki, B.J. Bishop, & E.F. Horner (Eds.), *Safety in ice hockey: Section Vol. ASTM STP 1212* (pp. 109-120). Philadephia: American Society for Testing Materials.

Widmeyer, W.N., Silva, J.M., & Hardy, C. (1992, October). *The nature of group cohesion in sport teams: A phenomenological approach.* Paper presented at the annual meeting of the Association for the Advancement of Applied Sport Psychology, Colorado Springs, CO.

Widmeyer, W.N., & Williams, J. (1991). Predicting cohesion in coaching teams. *Small Group Research, 22,* 548-557.

Wiese, D.M., & Weiss, M.R. (1987). Psychological rehabilitation and physical injury: Implications for the sports-medicine team. *The Sport Psychologist, 1*(4), 318-330.

Wiese, D.M., Weiss, M.R., & Yukelson, D.P. (1991). Sport psychology in the training room: A survey of athletic trainers. *The Sport Psychologist, 5*(1), 15-24.

Wiggins, D.K. (1984). The history of sport psychology in North America. In J.M. Silva & R.S. Weinberg (Eds.), *Psychological foundations of sport* (pp. 9-22). Champaign, IL: Human Kinetics.

Wilkinson, M.O., Landers, D.M., & Daniels, F.S. (1981). Breathing patterns and their influence on rifle shooting. *American Marksman, 6,* 8-9.

Williams, J.M. (1980). Personality characteristics of the successful female athlete. In W.F. Straub (Ed.), *Sport psychology: An analysis of athlete behavior.* Ithaca, NY: Mouvement.

Williams, J.M., & Andersen, M.B. (1998). Psychosocial antecedents of sport and injury: Review and critique of the stress and injury model. *Journal of Sport and Exercise Psychology, 10,* 5-25.

Williams, J.M., & Hacker, C.M. (1982). Causal relationships among cohesion, satisfaction, and performance in women's intercollegiate field hockey teams. *Journal of Sport Psychology, 4,* 324-337.

Williams, J.M., & Harris, D.V. (1998). Relaxation and energizing techniques for regulation of arousal. In J. M. Williams (Ed.), *Applied sport psychology: Personal growth to peak performance.* (3rd ed., pp. 219-236). Mountain View, CA: Mayfield.

Williams, J.M., & Krane, V. (1998). Psychological characteristics of peak performance. In J. M. Williams (Ed.), *Applied sport psychology: Personal growth to peak performance.* (3rd ed., pp. 158-170). Mountain View, CA: Mayfield.

Williams, J.M., Tonyman, P., & Andersen, M.B. (1991). The effects of stressors and coping resources on anxiety and peripheral narrowing. *Journal of Applied Sport Psychology, 3,* 126-141.

Williams, K., Harkins, S., & Latane, B. (1981). Identifiability and social loafing: Two cheering experiments. *Journal of Personality and Social Psychology, 40,* 303-311.

Willis, J.D., & Campbell, L.F. (1992). *Exercise psychology.* Champaign, IL: Human Kinetics.

Wilmore, J.H. (1992). Body weight standards and athletic performance. In K.D. Brownell, J. Rodin, & J.H. Wilmore (Eds.), *Eating, body weight, and performance* (pp. 315-333). Malvern, PA. Lea & Febiger.

Wold, B., & Anderssen, N. (1992). Health promotion aspects of family and peer influences on sport participation. *International Journal of Sport Psychology, 23,* 343-359.

Wolko, K.I., Hrycaiko, D.W., & Martin, G.L. (1993). A comparison of two self-management packages to standard coaching for improving performance of gymnasts. *Behavior Modification, 17,* 209-223.

Wong, E.H., & Bridges, L.J. (1995). A model of motivational orientation for youth sport: Some preliminary work. *Adolescence, 30,* 437-452.

Wooten, I. L. (1997). Positively winning. *The University of Virginia Alumni News, LXXXVI,* 26-27.

Wrisberg, C.A., & Pein, R.L. (1992).The preshot interval and free throw accuracy: An exploratory investigation. *The Sport Psychologist, 6,* 14-23.

Youngstedt, S.D. (1997). Does exercise truly enhance sleep? *The Physician and Sportsmedicine, 25,* 72-82.

Youngstedt, S.D., O'Connor, R.J., & Dishman, R.K. (1997). The effects of acute exercise on sleep: A quantitative synthesis. *Sleep, 20,* 203-214.

Yukelson, D. (1993). Communicating effectively. In J. Williams (Ed.), *Applied sport psychology: Personal growth to peak performance* (pp. 122-136). Mountain View, CA: Mayfield.

Yukelson, D. (1997). Principles of effective team building interventions in sport: A direct services approach at Penn State University. *Journal of Applied Sport Psychology, 9,* 73-96.

Yukelson, D. (1998). Communicating effectively. In J. Williams (Ed.), *Sport psychology: Peak performance to personal growth* (3rd ed., pp. 142-157). Mountain View, CA: Mayfield.

Yukelson, D., Weinberg, R., & Jackson, A. (1984). A multidimensional group cohesion instrument for intercollegiate basketball teams. *Journal of Sport Psychology, 6,* 103-117.

Zaichkowsky, L.D., & Fuchs, C.Z. (1988). Biofeedback applications in exercise and athletic performance. In K.B. Pandolf (Ed.), *Exercise and sport science reviews* (pp. 381-421). New York: Macmillan.

Zaichkowsky, L.D., & Fuchs, C.Z. (1989). Biofeedback-assisted self-regulation for stress management in sports. In D. Hackfort & C.D. Spielberger (Eds.), *Anxiety in sports: An international perspective* (pp. 235-245). New York: Hemisphere.

Zaichkowsky, L.D., & Takenaka, K. (1993). Optimizing arousal level. In R. Singer, M. Murphey, & L.K. Tennant (Eds.), *Handbook of research in sport psychology* (pp. 511-527). New York: Macmillan.

Zajonc, R.B. (1965). Social facilitation. *Science, 149,* 269-274.

Zander, A. (1982). *Making groups effective.* San Francisco: Jossey-Bass.

Ziegler, S.G. (1987). Effects of stimulus cuing on the acquisition of ground strokes by beginning tennis players. *Journal of Applied Behavior Analysis, 20,* 405-411.

Index

About the Authors

Robert S. Weinberg is a professor in the Department of Physical Education, Health, and Sport Studies at Miami University in Ohio. Before coming to Miami University, Weinberg was a professor in the Department of Kinesiology at the University of North Texas from 1978 to 1992, including Regents Professor from 1988 to 1992. He was also voted one of the top 10 sport psychology specialists in North America by his peers.

In addition to teaching undergraduate sport psychology for more than 20 years, Weinberg has written extensively on topics related to sport psychology. He has published more than 125 journal articles and presented more than 250 scholarly papers at sport psychology conferences.

He has served as president of both the North American Society for the Psychology of Sport and Physical Activity and the Association for the Advancement of Applied Sport Psychology. He also has served on the editorial board of the *Journal of Sport and Exercise Psychology* and *The Sport Psychologist*. Currently he is editor of the *Journal of Applied Sport Psychology.* He is a certified consultant and a member of the United States Olympic Committee Sport Psychology Registry.

Dr. Weinberg earned his PhD in sport psychology from the University of California, Los Angeles, in 1977. He lives in Oxford, Ohio, and his children, Kira and Josh, live in Oxford and Dallas, respectively. In his free time Dr. Weinberg enjoys tennis, basketball, and traveling.

Daniel Gould is a professor in the Department of Exercise and Sport Science at the University of North Carolina, Greensboro. He has taught sport psychology for more than 20 years. An active researcher, Dan has published more than 100 articles on sport psychology. He was also the founding coeditor of *The Sport Psychologist*.

Dan has been voted one of the top 10 sport psychology specialists in North America and was the first Australian sport psychology scholar. In 1994, he received the university's coveted Alumni-Teaching Excellence Award, an all-campus teaching honor.

Gould is the former president of the Association for the Advancement of Applied Sport Psychology (1988-89) and the American Alliance for Health, Physical Education, Recreation and Dance Sport Psychology Academy (1986). In addition to teaching undergraduate sport psychology, Dr. Gould is extensively involved in coaching education from youth sports to Olympic competition. He also uses his psychology skills as a consultant for Olympic and world-class athletes and worked with U.S. athletes at the Nagano Olympic Games.

Daniel, his wife, Deb, and his two sons, Kevin and Brian, live in Greensboro, NC. In his leisure time, Dr. Gould enjoys swimming, fitness activities, and spending time with his children.